# Bernard Schmitt's Quantum Macroeconomic Analysis

The aim of Bernard Schmitt's analysis of the monetary economy of production was twofold: to introduce and to explain the logical character of the macroeconomic laws governing our economies; and to explain the origin of the pathologies that follow if these laws are not complied with. Schmitt's main original contributions concern the theories of value, profit, and capital, as well as his explanation of inflation, unemployment, and international payments, unified as quantum macroeconomic analysis. This book expounds on the key principles of quantum macroeconomic analysis as he conceived and developed them.

Schmitt's starting point was the analysis of bank money and the way it is associated with produced output. His macroeconomics was not founded on microeconomics nor derived from the aggregation of microeconomic variables. Schmitt's theory does not rely on mathematics and modelling either; instead, it is based on logical laws derived from the nature of money and monetary payments. Part I of this book deals with the quantum macroeconomic analysis of capitalism and its pathologies developed by Schmitt and provides the elements necessary to understand its 'structural' mechanism. Parts II and III deal with the principles of two reforms that enable the passage from capitalism to post-capitalism and from the present non-system of international payments to an orderly system.

This book provides essential reading for all those interested in heterodox approaches to macroeconomics, monetary economics, banking, international economics, and the history of economic thought.

**Alvaro Cencini** is Emeritus Professor of Economics, University of Lugano (USI), Switzerland.

## Routledge Frontiers of Political Economy

**Corporations, Accounting, Securities Laws, and the Extinction of Capitalism**
*Wm. Dennis Huber*

**Moral Discourse in the History of Economic Thought**
*Laurent Dobuzinskis*

**Economics and Art Theory**
*Edited by Stratos Myrogiannis and Constantinos Repapis*

**Capitalism and Agrarian Change**
Production and Reproduction in Indonesia
*Muchtar Habibi*

**Capitalist Agriculture and the Global Bee Crisis**
*Rebecca Ellis*

**China, Trust and Digital Supply Chains**
Dynamics of a Zero Trust World
*Warwick Powell*

**Macroeconomic Modelling, Economic Policy and Methodology**
Economics at the Edge
*Edited by Mikael Randrup Byrialsen, Hamid Raza and Finn Olesen*

***Economics, Anthropology and the Origin of Money as a Bargaining Counter***
*Patrick Spread*

***Bernard Schmitt's Quantum Macroeconomic Analysis***
*Alvaro Cencini*

***Blockchain and the Commons***
*Vangelis Papadimitropoulos*

**Globalization and the Decline of American Power**
*Cyrus Bina*

For more information about this series, please visit: www.routledge.com/Routledge-Frontiers-of-Political-Economy/book-series/SE0345

# Bernard Schmitt's Quantum Macroeconomic Analysis

Alvaro Cencini

Routledge
Taylor & Francis Group
LONDON AND NEW YORK

First published 2023
by Routledge
4 Park Square, Milton Park, Abingdon, Oxon OX14 4RN

and by Routledge
605 Third Avenue, New York, NY 10158

*Routledge is an imprint of the Taylor & Francis Group, an informa business*



*British Library Cataloguing-in-Publication Data*
A catalogue record for this book is available from the British Library

*Library of Congress Cataloging-in-Publication Data*
Names: Cencini, Alvaro, author.
Title: Bernard Schmitt's quantum macroeconomic analysis / Alvaro Cencini.
Description: 1 Edition. | New York, NY : Routledge, 2023. | Series: Routledge frontiers of political economy | Includes bibliographical references and index.
Identifiers: LCCN 2022021325 (print) | LCCN 2022021326 (ebook) | ISBN 9781138576018 (hardback) | ISBN 9781032366654 (paperback) | ISBN 9781351271325 (ebook)
Subjects: LCSH: Schmitt, Bernard. | Macroeconomics. | Money. | Quantum logic.
Classification: LCC HB172.5 .C416 2023 (print) | LCC HB172.5 (ebook) | DDC 339--dc23/eng/20220502
LC record available at https://lccn.loc.gov/2022021325
LC ebook record available at https://lccn.loc.gov/2022021326

ISBN: 978-1-138-57601-8 (hbk)
ISBN: 978-1-032-36665-4 (pbk)
ISBN: 978-1-351-27132-5 (ebk)

DOI: 10.4324/9781351271325

Typeset in Bembo
by Deanta Global Publishing Services, Chennai, India

# Contents

# Figures

# Tables

# Acknowledgements

This book would have never been written had I not had the opportunity to work closely with Bernard Schmitt for more than forty years. I am indebted to him both as a *maître à penser* and as a friend.

Bernard's eldest daughter, Isabelle, helped me to recollect the main events of his family life. She revised the biographical note, written in the form of a foreword to the volume. Schmitt's nephew, Valentin Lab, helped me recover all the files still available on his computers. Guy Devillebichot, an old friend and colleague of Bernard's, together with Edouard Maciejewski and José Cerqueira filled some remaining gaps in my knowledge of Bernard's professional life. I thank them heartily.

The first drafts of the manuscript have greatly benefited from the linguistic revision and the comments of Helga Wild and Niklas Damiris. Andrea Carrera generously plotted all the tables and figures. Simona Cain, a friend and former colleague at USI, has proved once again to be the guardian angel of English style as well as an attentive reader, whose suggestions have contributed in improving the final draft. I am grateful to all of them for their help and their affectionate support.

Many friends and colleagues from the Universities of Fribourg, Dijon, and Lugano have encouraged and supported me intellectually during the years of extensive work in preparing the book. I am thankful to them as well as to all the other economists and non-economists who appreciate our common effort to make Bernard Schmitt's analysis better known.

Finally, I thank the *Banca Stato del Canton Ticino* for their financial support of my project.

# Foreword: A biographical note on Bernard Schmitt

## From birth to professorship (1929–1970)

### *From Alsace to Burgundy*

Bernard Schmitt, son of Marguerite Schneider and Marcel Schmitt, both residents of the tormented region of Alsace, was born in Colmar on 6 November 1929. A month later his mother died, leaving him to spend the first seven years of his life with his father and his sister Simone, two years older than him. In 1936, Bernard's father remarried. His second wife was Emma Pitoizet from the Burgundy region. The family settled in Colmar. The first years of their life together were not easy for the two siblings and their stepmother, but as time went by, an intellectual rapport developed between Bernard and Emma. Manon Schmitt-Lab, the first child of the new marriage, describes the evolution:

> Bernard is more vulnerable [than his sister], of a less practical attitude. In 1936 he is seven: good-looking, terribly strong-willed, and stubborn. Beginnings are hard. The atmosphere is tense, Emmy is the intruder. The second wife. He rebels. She tenses up. But little by little, through living under the same roof, and quite naturally, a tacit, mutual understanding on intellectual matters develops between them, a shared enjoyment of juggling ideas, a knack for manipulating abstractions, which will firmly bind them together.
>
> (Lab 2015: 55, m.t.)

The caring presence of his father and the birth of Manon (1937), Bruno (1938), and Claudie (1940) contributed greatly to consolidating the new family, which was soon to be confronted with the dark years of the German annexation of Alsace. In this period, Bernard spoke Alsatian for the most part, but also French and German. In 1940, during the German occupation, he and his father left Colmar and moved to Mannheim. They both returned to Alsace in 1941 and re-joined their family in Turckheim, where they had moved to in Summer 1940. In this small town near Colmar Emma gave birth to her third baby girl, Christel (January 1942) and they all lived there until the end of WW2. During the years of the Nazi occupation of France and Alsace, Bernard and his sister were forced to attend a German school so that, in 1945, he became more fluent in German than he was in French. Only later, during his academic studies at the University of Nancy, was French to become his 'intimate' language.

From 1945 to 1948, Bernard and his sister were sent to Dijon, where he attended the Lycée Carnot as a boarder. He obtained his Advanced-level General Certificate of Education, majoring in mathematics (*Bac Mathématiques*), with excellent grades in both philosophy and mathematics. In a small village, Segrois, less than ten minutes' drive from Nuits-Saint-Georges, lived the father of Bernard's stepmother. Bernard later settled there with his wife Denise; there and in Dijon, they raised their three daughters, Isabelle, Anne-Claire, and Marielle.

### *Academic studies and family losses*

After his *baccalauréat*, Bernard entered the Faculty of Law of the University of Nancy, where he graduated in 1952. In the meantime, Bernard's and Simone's stepmother gave birth to her last son, Dominique, in 1950. After graduating, Bernard decided to pursue further academic studies and started working on a PhD thesis at the University of Strasbourg, under the supervision of Professor Goetz-Girey. During this period, he spent a year at Trinity College, Cambridge (1953–1954) as a research student working under the supervision of Dennis Robertson and Richard Kahn, his official supervisors, as well as Piero Sraffa, Maurice Dobb, and Joan Robinson. His stay in Cambridge was extended for a further three years. During this time, he shared a flat with his friend Derick (Frederick Hemming) McClintock, a criminologist, and went regularly back to France.

While a research student at Cambridge, he clashed with Joan Robinson, who did not like his questioning of her interpretation of Keynes's thought, and with Sraffa, who did not accept his critical appraisal of Marx. Sraffa went as far as to ask Robinson, who was administratively in charge, to write to Professor James in France recommending that Bernard be excluded from his PhD programme. Professor James did not give in to Sraffa's request and instead showed Robinson's letter to Bernard. It is to Schmitt's credit that, despite what had happened in 1954, some years later he agreed to translate a book by Joan Robinson into French.

1957 was a dreadful year for Bernard, who was confronted first with the death of his father Marcel from a stroke, and three months later by that of his sister Simone in an accident. Bernard coped with these terrible events as best as he could and helped his stepmother to deal with the ensuing legal and administrative fallouts.

His doctoral thesis was well advanced, and he submitted it the following year in Paris-Panthéon as a *Thèse d'Etat*. The members of the examining commission were Robert Goetz-Girey, supervisor, Pierre Dieterlen, research director at the CNRS (Centre national de la recherche scientifique), Alain Barrère, and

Jean Weiller. Professor Dieterlen was also to become Schmitt's 'parrain' (godfather) at the CNRS, of which Bernard became a member in 1959. His thesis was published two years later by Sirey, Paris, under the title *La formation du pouvoir d'achat*. It is a dense and thought-provoking volume in which Schmitt introduced the founding elements of his ground-breaking analysis of monetary macroeconomics; it also contains many of the intuitions he later developed, and which are analyzed in the present book.

### *Marriage*

1960 was a crucial year in Bernard's life, not only for the publication of his first book, but most importantly because he married Denise Fauvet on 28 May, in Paris. Born in Nancy on 19 April 1933, Denise was a brilliant scholar herself, who graduated in classic literature (*Lettres classiques*), French, Latin, and Greek, at one of France's 'grand écoles', the Ecole Normale Supérieure, Sèvres. After graduation, she started teaching classical literature at the Lycée Camille Sée in Colmar. Among her first students was Claudie Schmitt, who liked her very much and invited her home. It was during one of her frequent visits during the school year 1957–58 that Denise met Bernard.

Their intellectual understanding and affinity would bind them together for the rest of their lives. Their relationship was strongly shaped by Bernard's tireless research in economics. Yet, though he was often physically absent or lost in thought, they were true soulmates. He shared all his worries and his excitements with her; when away from home he called her every day, and she never stopped encouraging him. They addressed each other using the formal '*vous*' instead of the common, familiar '*tu*', which is only in appearance a sign of distance: in reality it created complicity between them that was much stronger than the artificiality of a '*tu*'.

The burden of handling the family's daily life rested on her. She looked after their three daughters and after the house and taught classical literature first at the Lycée Marcel Pardé and then at the Lycée Carnot, in Dijon, until 1972. Then, from 1972 to 1986, she taught Latin at the University of Dijon. Her French was outstanding, and Bernard called on her regularly for advice. His own French was extremely good and rigorous, but he often looked for her approval and enjoyed listening to her literary comments. She was also a good cook, and I still remember with pleasure our meals under a big, old walnut-tree in their garden in Segrois and her delicious apple pie '*renversée*' (*Tarte Tatin*). He called her 'Fauvette', a nickname that plays on her maiden name, Fauvet, and its resemblance to the name of a lovely songbird living in the bushes.

Bernard never tired of repeating that without his Fauvette he would never have been able to achieve what he had. She provided him with the balance and strength, not to say the time and the quiet, he needed to develop his thoughts and work out his quantum macroeconomic analysis.

A year after their marriage, on 25 April 1961, Denise gave birth to their first daughter, Isabelle, nowadays an English teacher. In the same year, the CNRS awarded him the bronze medal for his research achievements. He started teaching as Professor of macroeconomics at the University of Dijon, but he maintained the status of a CNRS researcher. A second daughter, Anne-Claire, entered the world on 19 January 1964. A year later, the University of Fribourg, Switzerland, offered him a tenure-track position. He started in 1965 as a lecturer in economics, became '*Professeur extraordinaire*' a year later, and in 1970 he was promoted to full professorship.

### *Early teaching years*

Bernard Schmitt was an engaging, brilliant teacher; his students were fascinated by his enthusiasm as well as by the depth and logical rigour of his analysis. His teaching was thought-provoking; he guided his students into the intellectual adventure of scientific discovery through a process that often took the form of dialectical progression. He started with a well-established theory, explained it accurately and logically, and convinced his students of its correctness. Then he told them that the apparently correct theory is in reality wrong and proved why it is so. Finally, he re-examined the entire problem from an alternative viewpoint and provided its correct analysis. Even students who got lost in Schmitt's rigorous analysis recognized his uncompromising passion for logic and his constant research of the root causes of macroeconomic events.

When I started my undergraduate studies in Fribourg in 1968, Schmitt was teaching monetary macroeconomics to students in years 3 and 4 of the undergraduate programme, but his courses had already become a topic of discussion even among freshmen, so much so that some decided to attend them well before their third year. University education is first of all about teaching critical reasoning, teaching students how to develop their analytical skills in order to obtain a better understanding of the world. Bernard was a master in this. His students learned how to use logic to explain the hidden nature of economic events and to unmask the mistakes of mainstream economics.

Like any great researcher, Bernard did not hesitate to introduce his students to the latest findings of his analysis. The classroom became a laboratory, where old and new ideas were thrown together, dissected, and placed under the microscope. Logical argumentation was the only instrument – the only tools he needed were blackboard and chalk. He never used slides, nor did he read from a text: he stood in front of his students, walked around, drew some figures and diagrams on the blackboard, and spoke freely about the topic of the day without a scrap of a note – and all the time he followed a rigorous, logical thread. He invited his students to capture his presentation only in outline or not at all, because later he would provide them with a written, fully developed text.

In each term he analyzed different topics or, when he came back to the same problem, he analyzed it from a different angle or in a totally different way. He never taught the same thing in the same way, which is emblematic of how his investigation developed, and which also explains the great number of manuscripts distributed to his students in Dijon and Fribourg during his teaching years.

Fully devoted to his research, Schmitt endeavoured to convey his enthusiasm to his students and did so without sparing himself. But he was irritated by lack of attention; if he caught a student chatting to another or yawning, his first thought was that the student was uninterested or bored; and if so, he invited them to leave the room. While he was very sympathetic in other areas, when it came to logical rigour, he was uncompromising; extremely demanding with himself, he applied the same standard to his fellow economists and students.

## *Weltanschaung*

He treated people around him with great respect and sympathy, irrespective of their cultural background or their social status. He admired any form of intelligence, from the practical one of the Portuguese bricklayers who built his and Fauvette's Burgundy tower in Segrois to the analytical one of Józef Bochenski, a Polish Dominican Professor of philosophy at the University of Fribourg. Indeed, his interest in philosophy dated back to his college years and never faded. Starting with the Greeks, he read all the great authors and enjoyed discussing their ideas with his wife as well as with his closest collaborators. He liked Spinoza, St Augustin, and Wittgenstein; he was impressed by Kant's considerations on quanta and read with interest Heidegger, Bergson, and Sartre, among others. In many ways, his approach to economics was philosophical: he investigated the very foundations of crucial concepts such as economic value and prices and looked for their root causes.

Socio-political and economic events interested him, and he kept up to date by listening regularly to BBC radio on a very good portable radio-set he carried around with him. He also enjoyed taking pictures and owned several very good cameras – his favourite was a Leica. In his early twenties and thirties, he used to develop and print his photos himself. I still remember installing for him a sophisticated darkroom for the printing of colour photos with the help of Claude Gnos, one of his PhD students in Dijon and a faithful collaborator ever since, who shared his passion for photography and bikes.

Classical music was another interest of his. He kept reading about the best high-end music apparatus and owned a top-quality one, on which he played his favourite recordings. He liked the Classics and the French composers but enjoyed also listening to Wagner, Verdi, Puccini, and Rossini. In his teens he used to play the piano; his sister Simone was a good piano player, and so was his father, while his stepsister Manon still devotes part of her time to piano playing. Like his father, who was a passionate connoisseur, he particularly enjoyed listening to opera.

Intrigued by his analysis, several of his young students decided to pursue PhD studies and undertake an academic career first as research and teaching assistants, then as lecturers and readers. At the time, I was working as Schmitt's research and teaching assistant at the University of Fribourg, and I often went to see Bernard in Segrois and became acquainted with his family and with the group of researchers working on his theory at the University of Dijon.

Even though most of his followers had a Marxian background, one would be mistaken to believe that their interest in Schmitt's analysis was politically driven. He himself never was a member of any political party and never took a stance in favour of any of them. Yet, this did not prevent him from following with great concern the events of the day and speaking out about his opinions. His existential stance was to have an open mind and deep empathy for the victims of injustice or violence. His engagement was thereby political in the broad sense of the term: he aimed at providing society with an economic 'structure' free from capitalist pathologies, thus supplying the 'neutral' framework on which a more human an equitable system can be built.

He believed in the power of thought, in the capacity of humankind to improve its understanding of itself and of the cultural and natural world and their interdependence. He was well aware of the evil surrounding us all, of the destructive and wild instincts we are so often confronted with. In his view, this was due mainly to ignorance in all its manifestations and was convinced that, by exercising intellectual and spiritual wisdom, we can contribute to building a better future.

As Xavier Bradley recalls, during a lecture at the University of Dijon in 1977, Schmitt severely criticised Michel Debré, prime minister in General De Gaulle's government, for his plea in favour of the gold standard, which pleased Bernard's left-wing students. Yet, Bernard's arguments were scientific, and a few weeks later these same students were presented with a devastating critique of Jacques Attali (a left-wing economist) with an argument as rigorous and objective as the one against Debré.

Bernard was not a religious person in the traditional sense. He did not believe in any religion, even though he formally remained a member of the Catholic church. However, he strongly believed in the spiritual dimension of mankind. He rejected the idea that our earthly death is the final act of our existence and suggested the possibility, derived from his analysis of time, that each moment of our earthly life is for ever inscribed, recorded in time. Be that as it may, Bernard Schmitt's faith in the spiritual component of our existence grew out of an existential crisis in which he was confronted with the dismal, unacceptable prospect of considering death as a point of no return, a dead end. I remember discussing this with him in July 2007 while walking in nature – as he liked to do – after working on his concept of quantum time and the need to apply to economics a more advanced logic than the binary one.

There was a scientific source to Bernard's spirituality, which rests on the idea that time must be conceived as a radiation, as an emission. As is the case for light, time too might have a speed; its speed would be greater than that of light. We should therefore speak of the creation of time and of a time frame where it is possible to go beyond the speed of light but not that of time. Time, too, would have corpuscular and wavelike aspects. The corpuscular aspect would be the material or dimensional one (the space–time dimension), whereas the wavelike aspect would be the immaterial or spiritual one. Time would thus be an emanation of the spirit that materializes in the real world.

### *Research, teaching, and family: a difficult balance*

In 1966 Presses Universitaires de France (PUF) published Bernard's second book, *Monnaie, salaires et profits*. The book is an expansion of his 1960 volume; it explores the fundamental distinction between *nominal* and *real* money and is one of Schmitt's milestones in national macroeconomic analysis.

In 1969, Guy Devillebichot, a well-known French economist, wrote an enthusiastic review of the book in the *Revue d'économie politique*. Devillebichot, who would write another review article on Bernard's analysis in the same journal ten years later, can undoubtedly be considered one of Bernard Schmitt's best friends and supporters. Henri Guitton was another major supporter of Schmitt's analysis. One of the most influential French economists, in 1984 he wrote a long preface to Bernard's masterly book on inflation, unemployment, and capital malformations. I must not forget to mention Jean Claude Eicher, together with Devillebichot and Guitton, a professor of economics at the University of Dijon, member of the *Commission d'agrégation* that examined Schmitt in Paris and a true friend of Bernard and his family, as well as Pietro Balestra, Professor of econometrics at the Universities of Fribourg and Dijon, whose friendship and support never wavered until his premature death in 2005. Gérard Destanne de Bernis was also among Bernard's close academic acquaintances, together with Professors Jean Valarché, Maurice Villet, Gerhard Aschinger, and several others, who will I hope forgive me for not mentioning them.

On 31 March 1968, two years after the publication of his pathbreaking book, Bernard and Denise celebrated the birth of their third daughter, Marielle. By now Isabelle was about seven years old and Anne-Claire four; the family lived in a rented flat in Dijon and in their nice country house set in a vast park in Segrois, where Fauvette tended a vegetable garden and flowerbeds and where Bernard, with my help first and then with that of Wulf Rohland – a German economist who wrote his PhD thesis under Bernard's supervision and who later translated Schmitt's book *Théorie unitaire* into German – planted numerous fruit-bearing trees. To work in isolation, Bernard had a small cottage near the house transformed into a study, where, between 1961 and 1975, he wrote six books and three articles.

Although he was quite interested in people, he preferred to work alone. This did not mean that he avoided confrontation; on the contrary, he submitted his analysis to the scrutiny of his students and assistants and looked forward to the criticism of his fellow economists. In fact, he was the most uncompromising and rigorous critic of his own theories and the first to notice their shortcomings, if any.

He worked relentlessly; his analysis became more general and encompassed the fields of national and international macroeconomics, but this was not without consequences for the rest of the family. His wife and his daughters were very important to him and at the centre of his affective concerns; yet he was too absorbed in his work to devote them the time and attention they needed. He knew it, but this did not help him find a way to make up for his absence. Reality made it harder to find a balance: he lectured weekly in Dijon and Fribourg and had to travel back and forth by car, crossing the French and Swiss Jura; she taught in Dijon; he needed to work at Segrois; she had to look after their daughters mainly in Dijon; he was invited to talk in various universities and travelled across the UK to promote his English book on macroeconomics; they could not enlist the help of their own parents, and so their daughters did not get the opportunity to be looked after by their grandparents.

## 1970–1984: intense and dramatic years

### *The drama*

The period from 1970 to 1984 began with a major drama in Denise's and Bernard's life. In June 1972, a careless driver ran into Fauvette's car; the collision was violent and its consequences severe: Fauvette and Anne-Claire were badly injured, the mother spent a long period in hospital and the (second-born) girl suffered brain damage, which affected her mobility and intellectual capacities for the rest of her life. Isabelle and Marielle were only superficially injured, but the shock was devastating; the eldest, then 11 years old, still remembers clearly the blood all around her and her despair while attempting to help her mother and sister. Marielle was only four years old, but it is easy to imagine how deeply the incident must have affected her too.

Bernard was powerless and did what he could to cope with the situation at best. As time went by, the wounds healed a bit, but their consequences remained. To forget them was impossible: Anne-Claire was the helpless victim and a constant reminder of the dramatic accident. Her condition improved greatly thanks to her own efforts and the loving support of Denise. Bernard worked hard to stimulate her by setting physical objectives. For example, they cycled together all the way from Dijon to Lourdes twice, and once he walked with her from Clermont Ferrand to Lourdes in an attempt to improve her physical performance and encourage her to go on fighting against adversity. Yet, despite some relevant, positive progress, family life would never recover the relative harmony it had known before June 1972.

### *From 1972 to 1984*

After the life-changing experience of that car crash, Bernard worked harder than ever on his earlier insights with the explicit intent to build a unified theory explaining the monetary working of economics, nationally and internationally. In 1973 he was awarded a silver medal by the CNRS for his research work, the highest award in any single discipline. In 1977 he sat his *agrégation* in Paris. Until then, his professorship at the University of Dijon had been on secondment from the CNRS. From 1977 until his retirement, his status remained that of a full professor, and his appointment was officially endorsed by the *Commission d'agrégation d'Etat*. Nothing changed substantially apart from the certainty that he would go on teaching in Dijon until his retirement.

At the time, he was already surrounded by a group of students working on their PhDs under his supervision, both in Dijon and in Fribourg. Some of them were to form the hard 'core' of his followers. Among them was Jean-Jacques Friboulet, who later was appointed to a professorship at the University of Fribourg but then abandoned his research in quantum macroeconomics; Jean-Luc Bailly, who has consistently investigated Schmitt's concept of production; Claude Gnos, whose attempts to disseminate Schmitt's analysis among Keynesians and post-Keynesians deserves a special mention; and Xavier Bradley, who is still teaching Schmitt's analysis at the University of Burgundy (the former University of Dijon). In Fribourg, Schmitt's first research and teaching assistant, Gianluigi Socchi, stopped working as a researcher after his PhD thesis; and it was only in the Nineties that the circle of staunch scholars of this unique French economist was joined by Sergio Rossi, now full professor at the same University and whose intense activity contributes to the circulation of Schmitt's analysis among the post-Keynesians, and Nadia Piffaretti, economist at the World Bank and still true to Bernard's teachings.

But there are many more former PhD students of Schmitt. Some of them have not pursued an academic career for different reasons; other have turned their back on Schmitt's theory, either because they deemed it too difficult and demanding or because they thought it likely to hamper their professional career. Swimming against the tide is never easy and seldom rewarding. Of those who decided not to remain in the academic world, some have played an important role in Bernard's life both because of their friendship and of their external support for his research. I shall mention them as the opportunity arises in the context of this biographical note.

Between 1972 and 1984, Schmitt developed his analysis of the main topics of national macroeconomics: value, price, profit, capital accumulation, inflation, and unemployment; as well as of international macroeconomics: duplication, interest payment, exchange rate fluctuations, the international system of payments, and its reform. He analyzed the problem of European monetary unification and advocated a *new* 'theory of the circuit' (monetary circular flow analysis).

His teaching and research activities were very intense. With the intent to isolate himself as much as possible and in order to split his weekly trip to Fribourg into two parts he bought a small studio in Métabief, a village in the French Jura near the border with Switzerland. He drove a Citroen 2 CV and was not afraid of long distances. In May 1977, he drove all the way from Fribourg to Poland, accompanied by me, his teaching and research assistant in Fribourg at the time, and by Jean-Jacques Friboulet, his teaching and research assistant in Dijon. It was a long journey; we travelled through East Germany and reached first Poznan, then Lodz. There, Bernard gave two lectures that sparked great interest in the audience, because he introduced his own analysis through that of Michal Kalecki. He was often invited to speak, mainly in French universities, and for a while taught a course at the European University of Nancy, where he met Taïeb Chtioui, a young Tunisian economist who became a faithful follower of his theory.

In January 1978, he travelled from Dijon to Salerno, this time by plane and train, to be the best man at my wedding to Ginevra Mauro. Two years later he came to visit us in London, where Ginevra and I were spending the first five years of our marriage. At my suggestion, Professor George Akerlof invited Bernard to give a lecture in the seminar on money he was directing at the LSE. Victoria Chick and Meghnad Desai attended the seminar. The reaction to Bernard's presentation was positive, and the ensuing formal and informal discussions promising. However, as was to become the norm in future years, projects and promises were not followed up, and the meeting at the LSE remained a pleasant but inconsequential memory. This did not prevent Bernard from increasing his efforts to get at the core of capitalism by investigating the fundamental laws of monetary macroeconomics.

### *1984: a hallmark in Schmitt's scientific production*

This all-important period of his research activity led Bernard to the publication, in 1984, of one of his masterpieces, *Inflation, chômage et malformations du capital*. Published by Routledge in 2021 in English translation, this volume is the manifesto of *quantum* macroeconomic analysis. It opens the way to a new conception of economic production and its relationship with time. The ensuing theory of *emissions* is a new paradigm in economics, drawing a line of demarcation between the traditional Newtonian conception, shared by Neoclassical and Keynesian economists alike, and a new quantum approach based on the concepts of creation, destruction, instantaneity, and time quanta.

A few years earlier, just before starting to work on the book, Bernard had considered the possibility of writing it with Henri Guitton, who wholeheartedly supported Bernard's analysis and admired his scientific rigour. Gradually, Guitton withdrew from this project and decided to limit his contribution to a long foreword, leaving Bernard to write the book alone.

But 1984 is also the year of a major publication devoted to monetary sovereignty and international payments. Less well known than the volume on quantum analysis, *La France souveraine de sa monnaie* is no less important. It deals with the problem of countries' external debt in a revolutionary way, which became the hallmark of Schmitt's analysis of international payments and provided the element for a one-country solution, set to remain substantially the same all through his investigation. Several other pieces would be added later to the mosaic of Bernard's analysis of 1984, yet his main insights are all there in his 1984 volume, which no doubt takes pride of place in his scientific production.

In 1984, Treccani, a renowned Italian publisher, commissioned Bernard to write a substantial introduction to the Italian edition of Ricardo's monetary writings. Bernard accepted the request, which had been mediated by Marcello Corti, one of his PhD students in Fribourg, who translated Bernard's introduction to Ricardo in Italian and became a good friend of Bernard and his family. The brilliant investigation into the nature of Ricardo's analysis of money throws new light on the Anglo-Portuguese economist's insights, thereby helping the reader to grasp all the originality of an author who Bernard considered the most logically rigorous in the field of economics.

This same year, Schmitt was invited to a two-day meeting organized by Professor Augusto Graziani at the University of Naples; the invitation included research assistants and readers working with him in Dijon at the time, and myself. The topic of discussion was circular flow analysis. Graziani was the perfect host. He welcomed us as guests of honour and invited us to a party at his own house, where we had the pleasure to meet his family. This was to be the first of numerous subsequent meetings Bernard and I were to enjoy with the famous Italian economist over the years.

At the end of those two days, Bernard and I rented a car and drove from Naples to Salerno to visit my parents-in-law and to enjoy the Amalfi Coast. It was the ideal setting to discuss quantum time, Bernard's main concern at the time, taking walks on the seashore and admiring the seascape. Reasoning, following a line of thought, while immersed in nature was what Bernard liked best, as many of those who worked with him know well. The journey to Naples and Salerno was also an opportunity to eat good fish, his favourite dish, and to smoke cigars. Together with a good glass of wine (he was a connoisseur of Burgundy, and his wine cellar in Segrois was well-stocked) these are the main good vices he indulged in.

### *The years of international activity (1984–2005)*

The year 1984 was a milestone in Schmitt's research activity also because it marked the end of the period of his major publications. From 1984 onwards, all his manuscripts except one would remain unpublished. This was so partly because he did not want to spend time searching for a publisher and on the drudgery that accompanies the process of publication; and partly because he was constantly looking for new ways of giving the best possible form to his ideas. This does not mean that he was writing less. On the contrary, his texts were numerous and well thought out; many were distributed to his students, and some were planned and worked out as fully self-contained manuscripts practically ready for publication. Yet, his research drive was so relentless and demanding that he no longer felt the need to publish his texts.

He saw himself as an instrument chosen to achieve an end – convey the idea of quantum macroeconomics – acting as a kind of intermediary at the service of this revolutionary new idea, a duty he would be ready to discharge when called upon. His working hours were not regular; he would write down his analytical considerations whenever an intuition presented itself, day or night, and worked on it until he succeeded in grasping it entirely. This did not prevent him from accepting invitations to write papers for economic reviews, as contributions to edited volumes or in the series of working papers of the RMELab (Research Laboratory in Monetary Economics), of which he was the co-director (with me) and which is part of the Centre for Banking Studies in Lugano.

### *Washington DC, Mexico City, and Denise's lymphoma*

In Summer 1984, Bernard visited Edouard Maciejewski, one of his former students in Dijon, who was working at the IMF and was to become Assistant Director. Bernard and Denise spent a week as Edouard's guests in Washington, and he met up with a historian of the IMF. It was his first attempt to establish contact with this institution. His second attempt took place two and a half years later, when he went back to Washington, alone, and again stayed at Edouard's and met Edouard's director at the IMF. The meeting was informal, courteous, and pleasant but unproductive from a scientific viewpoint. In August 1984, Bernard was invited to an international meeting on political economy taking place in Rio de Janeiro, where he presented a paper that was later inserted as an Annex in his 1984 pamphlet *Les pays au régime du FMI*.

A more interesting meeting took place in Autumn 1990, when Bernard was invited to the World Bank by Yves Tencalla, Swiss Executive Director at the World Bank, an acquaintance of mine, who was kind enough to organize a conference with the economists of the World Bank and to put me up for a week while Bernard was once more the guest of Edouard. The conference was well attended but, although Bernard's speech captivated the audience's interest, sadly there was no follow-up.

In 2000, Bernard returned to Washington to meet some of the members of the African department of the IMF, in particular Pedro Morais, the Angolan Executive Director for Austral Africa at the IMF, and Roberto Cippà, a former student of Bernard's in Fribourg and then Executive Director for Switzerland at the IMF. At the last moment, Cippà was unable to attend and asked the Polish member of the Bureau of the Swiss administration to stand in for him. The meeting went wrong, Bernard and the Pole quarrelled, and there was no follow-on. Edouard Maciejewski was also present at the meeting, together with José Cerqueira, an Angolan PhD student of Bernard in Dijon, who would play an important role in the following years as regards Bernard's activity.

There was one last attempt with the Swiss administration and the African department at the IMF in 2004. Schmitt was accompanied by José, but neither Edouard nor Morais could attend the meeting. This time everything went well, and Bernard's speech about the double payment of interest on countries' external debt was well received. However, the novelty of Bernard's approach and its intrinsic difficulty were such that, back to their daily engagements, the economists attending his lectures did not find the time to work on his suggestions, and his message gradually faded out of their memories.

Washington DC was not the only destination of his trips outside Europe. In 1985 he visited me in Mexico City, where I was spending two months teaching an advanced seminar to the academic staff of the Economics Department, Universitad Autónoma Metropolitana. He spent ten days with me and José, who had joined us, working on the presentation for a conference and on an article on the debt issue for a Mexico City daily.

The two following years were marred by medical problems. His wife Denise was diagnosed with a malignant lymphoma, which required an operation; she underwent surgery in 1987. Fortunately, the procedure was successful, and she was able to get back to normal life, once more showing her exceptional strength and resilience.

### *Angola*

The year after Denise's surgery saw the start of Bernard's mission to Angola. Thanks to José, the Angolan Department of Finance asked Bernard to work on Angola's external debt and to elaborate a reform that avoided the pathological payment of interest on this same debt. Bernard asked me to join him in the project and in 1988 we flew together to Luanda to meet with José and the officials in charge of the Ministry of Finance and of the Angolan Central Bank.

The week in Luanda was very fruitful, and we were officially mandated to work on a joint project with a group of government experts. Because of a series of problems mainly due to political instability, the project took much longer than initially planned. After the visit of an Angolan delegation to Fribourg, during which we submitted and explained our results, Bernard flew again to Luanda, where he submitted his final report in 1996. Unfortunately, the report remained without follow-up: the financial gain Angola would have derived from the implementation of Bernard's reform would have been substantial but still not as high as the one the corrupt government of the country could derive from the royalties on petrol and from the huge gap between the official exchange rate and the parallel exchange rate of the kwanza and the US dollar.

Despite the lack of encouraging signals from the government, José did not give up the hope of finding enough support from one of the subsequent ministers of finance to implement Schmitt's plan of reform.

Our last attempt took place in 2005, when Bernard and I flew to Luanda one final time. After a week of pointless meetings, we returned to Europe having learned the lesson that next time we would have to target a more democratic country than Angola. However, it would be wrong to think that working for the Angolan government had been a waste of time. Quite the opposite: the experience with Angola prompted Bernard to work harder and step-up his work on the analysis of pathological external debt servicing, on the formation of countries' external debts and the development of a single-country reform.

### *1998 and 1999: two milestones*

While devoting a substantial part of his time and efforts after 1984 to developing and presenting his analysis on international payments, Bernard also pursued his investigation of national macroeconomics and the fundamental critique of general equilibrium analysis. Thus, in 1988 he published a paper on the nature of money. In the same year the two of us were invited to a conference on *The Future of the International Monetary System* held at Glendon College, Toronto, where Bernard presented a paper entitled *External Debt – Eternal Debt* and where we met Professor Lorie Tarshis and his former student, Omar Hamouda.

In 1995 Bernard distributed to his students a manuscript on the topic of external debt, and in 1996 he wrote two contributions, one on unemployment and the other on money prices, published in two books edited, respectively, by M. Baranzini and A. Cencini, and by G. Deleplace and E.J. Nell. From 4 to 6 September 1998, Schmitt attended a Conference on the *Wealth of Nations and Economic Theory* held at Monte Verità, Ascona (CH), organized by Mauro Baranzini and myself. Luigi Pasinetti was among the leading contributors, and Bernard took the opportunity to devote his speech to a critical analysis of Pasinetti's input-output analysis and pure labour theory of value. A few years earlier, Luigi Pasinetti had invited Bernard to give a lecture in his seminar at the Catholic University of Milan, and the discussion that followed had shown that the main difference in their analyses lies in the role money plays in one or the other: almost absent in Pasinetti's theory, for Schmitt, money is the key concept.

1998 and 1999 were the two years in which Bernard produced a significant part of his most relevant contributions to both national and international macroeconomics. In particular, his new analysis in terms of prices of unemployment was written in 1998 together with two important, unpublished papers on relative prices; whereas in 1999, while he added two more relevant texts to his critical analysis of the neoclassical paradigm, he started writing extensively on the payment of interest on external debts. It was only after 2000 that Schmitt's analysis was to focus mainly on the problems of international payments. He still worked on his critique of relative prices, but most of his writing concerned the problem of external debt servicing and that of the very formation of countries' sovereign debt.

On 6 November 1999 Bernard was seventy years old. Marcello Corti organized a dinner in Fribourg to celebrate Bernard's birthday. He was in good health. He suffered from type-B diabetes, but he kept it at bay by riding his bike whenever he could. Biking was his favourite sport, and he would not give it up until his stroke in 2010. In his youth, he had also done a lot of skiing. At seventy, he was still physically fit and as intellectually productive as ever. Some years earlier he had retired from the University of Dijon; he was now coming to the end of his academic career in Fribourg. But official retirement from his teaching commitments did not slow down his research activity; on the contrary, it gave him more time to devote to his analysis and his international engagements.

### *2004: World Bank and IMF*

The last and most important attempt to present and test the theory with the experts of the World Bank and the IMF took place in June 2004. It is thanks to the open-mindedness of the Swiss Executive director at the WB, Pietro Veglio, that I was able to organize visits for Bernard to the two institutions. A former student of Bernard at Fribourg, Veglio arranged a series of meetings with various experts of the WB and the IMF that were to take place over a whole week, as well as a luncheon with François Bourguignon, the chief economist of the WB at the time, and his staff. José was also present at the meetings.

Bernard's presentations were well received, and the ensuing discussions were lively, but not aggressive, which was a state of mind that Bernard could not bear, as it never failed to trigger vehement reactions. The experts were genuinely interested; they did their best to understand the originality of Schmitt's message and to accommodate it within the traditional vision of economic theory they were accustomed to. They did so critically but constructively. None of their criticism came as a surprise, and Bernard was never at a loss for a response.

At the end of the week, we flew back, Bernard and I to Europe and José to Angola, with the clear sense that, even though the theory had easily survived the judgement of the WB and the IMF experts, we would have to wait longer and work harder before his breakthrough could be implemented.

### *From 2005 to 2014*

From 2005 until his stroke in 2010 Bernard worked mainly on the problem of external debt servicing. In 2006, he spent a month in Lugano as an invited professor at USI (Università della Svizzera italiana). He held a series of advanced lectures to the PhD students in economics, elaborated on his analysis with me, whenever possible while walking by the lake in the outskirts of Lugano, talked with some of my colleagues, particularly with Mauro Baranzini, who considers him, together with Luigi Pasinetti, as one of his masters and whose support for our research never wavered along the years, and enjoyed the company of his wife Denise who joined him in Lugano. During his stay at USI, he kept working on his theory and produced two texts known as 'Lugano papers' on Brazil's external debt burden.

### *Brazil*

In 2007, once more thanks to José's intervention, we flew to Brasilia for the first meeting organized by a friend of José, Raimundo Lima, with a foundation working for the Brazilian government, Aiporé, which was supposed to help us present Bernard's analysis and plan of reform to people closely connected with President Lula and, subsequently, with experts of Brazil's Central Bank. The two meetings with the director of the Foundation and his chief collaborator led to the signing of a contract between the foundation on one side and Bernard, José and me on the other side.

The meeting with the Brazilian Central Bank's experts was less smooth; they were somewhat sceptical of Bernard's analysis and of the great financial gain that would be generated by the implementation of his reform. However, they were not against investigating the matter further and left us with the promise to read the paper that Bernard was willing to carefully draft over the following weeks.

In time it became evident that these promises would not be kept: the open letter Schmitt addressed to President Lula was never handed to him; neither was the letter promoting Bernard's reform with the Brazilian government. Bernard, for his part, never sent another paper to the experts at the Brazilian Central Bank. Instead, he went on working hard to find a new and simpler way to explain the pathological duplication of external debt servicing, as he was firmly convinced that the burden of proof rested with him and that it was his duty to go on looking for a version capable of convincing even the most unreceptive readers.

Two years later, February 2009, the three of us embarked on another expedition to Brazil. José's friend Raimundo told us that he had organized a meeting with the Governor of the State of Bahia, Jacques Wagner, whom we were supposed to meet in Salvador de Bahia two days later. In the afternoon of the following day, we met the Finance Secretary of the State of Bahia, Arno Augustin. During this long meeting, Schmitt explained the nature of the problem faced by Brazil, presented his plan for reform, and emphasized the gains that Brazil would derive from its implementation. At the end of the meeting, the Secretary assured us of his support, specifying that he would speak to the Governor before our meeting scheduled for the day after. He told us that he feared the hostility of the Central Bank, but he was not pessimistic.

The next day we waited for the Governor's secretary to call us with a time for our meeting with Governor Wagner: the call never came. Disappointed and angry, we decided to cut short our stay in Bahia and fly back to Europe, which we did the next day. Raimundo asked the Finance Secretary for an explanation and was told that, after his briefing, the Governor felt that Schmitt's project was too good to be true and that he was not prepared to take the risk involved in granting it political support.

Once again, Bernard was left facing the response of people unable to get their heads around the fact that indebted countries end up paying twice the amount required to service their external debt, whereas a simple reform would correct that, making sure that interest payment is carried out only once and the difference is claimed as their own, legitimate gain. Economists continue to find Schmitt's analysis too difficult and are unwilling to make the effort to understand it, while politicians are not enlightened enough to foresee the great advantages that his reform would provide to their country.

Bernard did not react negatively. He was unshakeable in his belief that, if a theory is correct, sooner or later it will be recognized as such and adopted by the scientific community. As the history of scientific thought shows, this has always been the case, even though some theories have been known to take a relatively long time to be accepted. The speed at which a new paradigm is accepted depends on the general scientific background of the moment. If times are not yet ripe to accept a revolutionary theory, little can be done to accelerate its acceptance. Yet, with his love for scientific research Bernard was not one to sit on the fence. He saw the failure to convince the Brazilians as a sign that his analysis had to be further explained by adding new, more convincing proofs and be extended to encompass the formation of countries' sovereign debts.

### *Schmitt's last years*

On 6 November 2009, Bernard turned eighty. I organized a one-day seminar at USI to mark the occasion. Bernard drove to Lugano accompanied by his colleague and friend Guy Devillebichot and by Christopher Chabin, one of his former students in Dijon. The seminar was attended, among others, by Mauro Baranzini, José Cerqueira, Jean-Jacques Friboulet, Sergio Rossi, and several research assistants and students. Bernard talked passionately about economics for three hours in the morning and two more hours in the afternoon and had still enough energy to liven up the dinner party organized in his honour in a restaurant on the outskirts of Lugano.

Schmitt's last years of intense research were devoted to explaining the fact that countries, considered as sets of their residents, carry an external debt, their sovereign debt, even though their residents pay for the totality of their imports, commercial and financial, net imports included. It was a daunting task, which increased Bernard's interest and spurred him to fully exploit the potentialities of quantum logic. Freed from any administrative and teaching burden, he devoted almost all this time to research. He wrote to me about his discoveries, his doubts, his new approaches, almost daily, and we spoke on the phone at least once a week.

In 2010 we decided to meet for three days at Edouard's country house in Clomot, where, together with Edouard and Pierlauro Lopez, my research and teaching assistant at USI at the time, we would work on the official data concerning countries' external debts. On 30 September, I drove from Lugano to Dijon with Pierlauro and took Bernard on board to join Edouard in Clomot. Bernard looked fit and in good spirits. The previous day, while cycling on the outskirts of Dijon he had a mechanical problem with his bike and was forced to walk a long distance to find help. Yet, he did not seem to be suffering any repercussions and was ready to work with us with his usual enthusiasm.

After supper we planned the activity for the next three days and went to sleep in the three bedrooms Edouard had prepared for us on the first floor of his house. For breakfast we were all supposed to meet in the spacious kitchen on the ground floor of Edouard's house, but Bernard did not show up. Surprised by this unusual event, since Bernard used to get up early in the morning, we went up to his bedroom to inquire about his health. He was awake and perfectly conscious. He told us that he felt a little dizzy when he got up from his bed but that he was not ill and would simply rest for a while. He was perfectly lucid and reasoned as well as ever. He ate his lunch with appetite and agreed to see a doctor in the nearby village of Pouilly. Walking down the stairs to the ground floor, and then from the car park to the doctor's study, he was noticeably unsteady on his feet, but the young doctor who visited him did not find anything wrong with him. He gave him a drug that should have improved his balance and recommended rest.

Back at Edouard's place we worked a few hours, had supper, and retired to bed for the night. In the morning, we heard a noise coming from Bernard's bedroom; Edouard was the first to find Bernard at the foot of his bed tapping on the floor to attract our attention. Edouard telephoned Bernard's eldest daughter Isabelle, who told him to send for a doctor she knew. As soon as the doctor saw Bernard, he phoned an ambulance. Bernard was taken to the general hospital of Dijon. A severe stroke was diagnosed.

Denise, with whom we had been in contact from day one and who had warned us that Bernard would never accept to be taken to the hospital unless very seriously ill, was already waiting for her husband at the hospital. There was nothing we could do except wait for the doctors' response. Most likely, Bernard had suffered several brain strokes, and the last had caused the most serious damage.

After a few days in the hospital, where his condition stabilized, Bernard was transferred to a rehabilitation facility. His intellectual capacities had not been affected; he spoke, read, and reasoned well, but he could not walk because one side of his body was partially paralyzed. Fully determined to fight through adversity, Bernard tried to speed up his recovery by exercising with the aid of a walking frame. He was indeed making substantial progress, but, unfortunately, one day he lost his balance while attempting to leave his room. He fell badly and hurt his head. Nothing was broken, but for a few days he was confused, which made us doubt his capacity for recovery and worry about a possible effect on his mind.

Yet, once more Bernard showed great strength and resilience, which helped him to emerge from the 'dark tunnel' and begin the journey to recovery. He was transferred to another clinic, in Darois, near Dijon. Denise had been at his side all the time, even though her own physical condition was deteriorating; she went to see him daily and spent most of her time with him. Before he was again able to write with his computer, he dictated to her; she then transcribed on her computer the notes she had taken by hand and sent them to me.

Throughout his illness he was visited by many of his collaborators and by former students. In particular, I remember seeing Edouard Maciejewski, Jean Tramuset, and Christopher Chabin more than once while staying with him. Bernard very much appreciated and was touched by their affection. All his close collaborators and friends visited, and all were impressed by his intellectual lucidity and his undiminished enthusiasm for economic analysis, as well as by his interest in science and society. If there are some I do not mention by name, it is only because I cannot remember them all.

Thanks to his perseverance, Bernard recovered part of his mobility and started working again on a text about the problem of countries' sovereign debt. He typed it up on his computer, and we resumed our daily exchanges by e-mail. He had not lost an iota of his intellectual capacities, as the text published posthumously on SSRN testifies. In the meantime, he never stopped exercising physically and planned to go back to Segrois, where his half-brothers Bruno and Dominique had undertaken to restructure the ground floor of his Burgundy tower to adjust it to his new needs.

His wife was not in favour of this solution. Segrois is about forty minutes' drive from Dijon, where she had to stay because of her medical condition, and she could not drive back and forth to look after him. Ignoring Fauvette's advice, he settled in Segrois. He hoped to recover significantly and was looked after by two nurses, who visited twice daily and by a physiotherapist.

He worked as much as he could to finish his paper, since he was increasingly worried about how little time he had left. This concern became a certainty when his beloved wife Fauvette was hospitalized and died, without seeing him one last time, on 3 September 2013. From then on, knowing that he would join her soon, Bernard redoubled his efforts to complete his analysis, which he managed to do just a few days before his conditions worsened. He was taken by ambulance to Dijon, where he died on 26 March 2014.

# Introduction

It is widely believed, nowadays, that economics is a science whose main concepts are fully established and need to be further developed only for statistical purposes. No deeper investigation into the nature of these concepts seems necessary in a discipline where mathematical models rule the roost. From such a standpoint there seems to be no room for fundamental insights since the integration of Keynes's contribution into the framework of general equilibrium analysis. However, a minority of economists refuse to share this view and contest the axioms of mainstream economics. Systematically marginalized, their chance of being taken seriously is extremely low as long as they are not prepared to accept the supremacy of equilibrium analysis – whether in its traditional, neoclassical version or in its Keynesian formulation – and limit their contribution to some marginal improvements of the established paradigm. Yet, the world never stops providing evidence – through the disorderly working of our economic systems – of the limits of economic analysis as currently practised.

Financial crises are a frequent, worrisome occurrence in today's economies; nobody has ever come up with a satisfactory answer to unemployment, in its various forms; the sovereign debt crisis increasingly weighs on deficit countries; poverty is rising throughout the world. Is it not too facile and callous to treat these problems as unavoidable side-effects of a process of economic growth that will eventually benefit everyone? The same question can be asked of those for whom this situation is the result of the unpredictable, irrational behaviour of economic agents and/or of unexpected external events altering the conditions under which the economy operates. Economies were already in serious trouble *before* WW2 as well as *before* the current coronavirus pandemic, and economic agents' behaviours are no more irrational and unpredictable than they have been in the past.

Instead of asking themselves whether something might be profoundly wrong with their presuppositions, mainstream economists keep developing new mathematical models in a hopeless attempt to mirror reality. In so doing they find themselves facing a dilemma:

DOI: 10.4324/9781351271325-1

1) Should they try to build a model that meets the needs of an increasingly complex real world, which would be mathematically too complex to deliver sensible solutions, or
2) Should they build a series of simplified models delivering a mathematical solution while remaining indifferent to reality

As neither alternative is satisfying, mainstream economists ought to have re-examined their entire approach: specifically, a thorough review of the role of mathematics would seem to be in order, as well as a critical evaluation of their assumption that economics is an axiomatic science. What these economists are still far from acknowledging is that their sophisticated models rest on rather poor conceptual foundations. The sole law they constantly refer to is that of the balancing of supply and demand, and as for their scientific rendering of the economic world, it does not go beyond emulating the simplest of Newton's laws in classical mechanics: the interaction between forces in the search for equilibrium.

The crucial role played by money is underestimated, and money itself is identified as a positive asset, a mistake the Classics understood and avoided, but which is symptomatic of the conceptual superficiality of mainstream economics.

It is also important to note here that mainstream economics has been influenced by the increasingly widespread pragmatism characteristic of the Anglo-Saxon approach to science after WW2. In that spirit, Keynes's most profound intuitions were interpreted according to the principles of general equilibrium analysis (GEA), and their originality was almost completely lost. Even Walras's concept of the *numéraire* was confined to the marginal role of a commodity-standard and not investigated further.

Attempts have been made to overcome this pragmatism and the dominance of mathematical modelling, and two of these must be mentioned: the post-Keynesians' and Bernard Schmitt's. The first comprises the works of many important authors, sometimes very different from each other both conceptually and methodologically, but with a common denominator, namely a deep dissatisfaction with GEA and the desire to overcome its microeconomic foundations by deploying Keynes's insights. The second is the work of the French economist to whose analysis this book is devoted.

If I do not identify Schmitt with post-Keynesian economists, it is not because he does not share their dissatisfaction with GEA or because he rejects Keynes' intuitions but because his analysis goes much further than theirs and encompasses Keynes's achievements while overcoming their flaws. As Keynes himself claims in the preface of his *General Theory*, the 'difficulty lies not in the new ideas, but in escaping from the old ones, which ramify, for those brought up as most of us have been, into every corner of our minds' (Keynes 1936/1946: viii). Unlike Keynes, Schmitt was not indoctrinated by the 'dominant ideas' of mainstream economics and so was able to grasp the revolutionary implications of Keynes's intuitions and build, on their basis, his own macroeconomic analysis.

It is only to the extent that Schmitt was inspired by Keynes's 'fundamental equations' that he could be considered a post-Keynesian economist. However, his analysis went much further than that of Keynes and clashed in places with the claims of the Cambridge economist. This is why it would be reductive and mistaken to assimilate Schmitt to the post-Keynesian school of thought.

## Schmitt's contribution

This book is about Bernard Schmitt's quantum macroeconomic analysis. Its aim is to provide a thorough overview of the development of his approach, from his first investigation into the nature of money to his last inquiry into the nature of countries' sovereign debts.

The presentation of his analysis follows a chronological *and* conceptual order, with the latter prevailing over the former. The reader must be aware that the developments ascribed to a certain chronological period can often be traced back to previous periods and can also be observed again as constitutive parts of the analysis of later periods. When it became necessary to give a more articulated picture of a given argument, I did not hesitate to disclose in advance the results obtained by Schmitt in later writings.

Logical consistency is the predominant principle for Schmitt. His methodology is simply that of applying logic, both inductive and deductive, to economic reality in order to discern its principles and derive its concepts. Induction must be understood in its Aristotelian meaning, as a process leading to the discovery of what is not deducible from axioms and assumptions. Schmitt's use of logic is extremely rigorous and relentless but always connected to reality and never in the service of building models abstracted from it. For him, economics is not a branch of mathematics, and models represent a vain attempt to mirror a reality that exists only in the imaginary universe of mainstream economists.

Schmitt was passionate about logic, as any of his readers is bound to feel. His passion moved him to constantly search for the root causes of economic events. Sometimes the reader might get the impression that his analysis is too abstract and might find it difficult to link it to factual evidence. Yet, this is only a first impression; within Schmitt abstraction is never a goal but a necessary means to understand the actual economy.

The aim of scientific investigation is to explain the real world, and Schmitt's quantum macroeconomic analysis is no exception. Economic reality must be interpreted, and it can be done through an analytical lens. For the analysis to be rigorous, economists must not be afraid of abstraction, on the condition that the world always is the point of departure and of arrival. Schmitt develops his research along these lines with uncompromising rigour. His style is precise and often concise, which might be off-putting on the first impact. The difficulties experienced by the reader are inherent to the subject matter itself; Schmitt explicates them, but fully understanding them remains a hard task.

Schmitt's search for the best scientific explanation is constant, always accompanied by the need to dig deeper. As a result, even his clearest texts are rich in intellectual challenges for the reader. Schmitt's capacity for hard work was prodigious; when focused on a specific topic, he kept at it almost day and night, writing down the results of his investigations on an ongoing basis. He then would move to another topic to do the same, though that would not stop him from revisiting the crucial steps of his analysis to test them further.

## *The choice of texts*

His published and unpublished texts run in the hundreds. Extremely clear and didactic texts distributed to his students at the University of Fribourg, Switzerland, and the University of Dijon, France, alternate with very dense and arduous ones. From the beginning of his research until the end of the 1980s, most of his books were published by French and Swiss presses. A radical change occurred in the late 1980s: from then to his death in 2014, he no longer published one single book. Only some of his papers were published, mostly as contributions to collective volumes and a few in peer-reviewed journals. Partly the reason is that he lost interest in academic publishing, but mainly it was that he became too absorbed in his research and wanted to devote most of his time to it. The numerous manuscripts of this period include full-length books that could easily be revised and published. Most of his texts were distributed solely to his students or to a handful of people interested in pursuing his approach.

For this volume I have made detailed use of only *some* of Schmitt's published and unpublished manuscripts. The choice has not always been easy, and I have reluctantly resisted the impulse to quote other texts. My aim has been to provide an exegesis as faithful and complete as possible of Schmitt's analysis. Some of the unpublished manuscripts in my possession are untitled and undated. I have tried to order them chronologically to the best of my knowledge and given them indicative titles. Most manuscripts are in French, and I have provided my own translation of relevant excerpts from them. (Note that 'm.t.' after these quotations means 'my translation'.)

The volume follows the evolution of Schmitt's analysis, emphasizing its most relevant passages and presenting Schmitt's main arguments in support of his results. A critique levelled at Schmitt and his collaborators is that they exacerbate the need to prove everything and to provide many versions of proofs, sometimes only slightly differing from one another. It is true that the constant search for new logical proofs makes it arduous to summarize Schmitt's contribution and might sometimes discourage the reader. Yet, it is also certain that any new analysis must provide more than a single proof of its truth if it aims to supersede the orthodox vision of mainstream economics. The abundance of proofs provided by Schmitt, and reproduced in this volume, must be seen as a valuable intellectual patrimony that, hopefully, will be the object of investigation for future generations of researchers.

### *About Schmitt's terminology*

A few remarks concerning Schmitt's terminology are in order. The first and most general remark is that none of his definitions is purely nominal and that none has the status of an axiom. In Schmitt's analysis, and this must be true of any scientific analysis, the definition of a concept is never given *a priori* but is always the result of a logical investigation. This explains why Schmitt's understanding of widely used concepts such as money, profit, interest, capital, inflation, and external debt differs from that taken for granted by mainstream economists.

Even though the terms used by Schmitt and by traditional economists are often the same, their meaning is sometimes quite different. This might create some additional difficulties for the reader accustomed to the old definitions. The best way of dealing with these problems is to avoid considering any economic concept as a given but to start from a clean slate and let the mind follow logic free from preconceptions.

Attention should be paid to the use of the word '*real*'. In everyday language, 'real' is used as a synonym of 'existent', 'actual', 'genuine', 'true' and is opposed to 'unreal', 'imaginary', 'false'. In economics, authors use 'real' in relation to money and income to distinguish what can effectively be purchased by a particular income or by national income in general, from the numerical or nominal expression of these incomes. Schmitt does the same and applies it also to goods. Thus, the expression 'real goods', which might sound redundant, indicates physical goods as opposed to goods conceived in their monetary or nominal form. 'Real goods' are not merely goods that really exist, but the physical goods that result from the process of production and define the 'content' of money-income, the object of the purchasing power of money. Likewise, 'real capital' is capital in its physical form, and so are 'real interest', 'real profits', and so on: they are the physical goods constituting the content of their monetary form.

Schmitt's analysis is essentially macroeconomic. It concerns the economic system as a whole and investigates the impact of economic events on the *set* of economic agents. The word '*set*' recurs regularly in Schmitt's texts; it must be understood in its mathematical meaning, namely as a collection of elements (agents, objects, numbers, and so on) considered as an entity in its own right, which cannot be reduced to the mere *sum* of its elements. First introduced in mathematics, the concept of set finds a significant application in economics, whereby macroeconomics is defined as the analysis of the economic transactions that, whether carried out by a single agent or by any number of agents, modifies the situation of the set of economic agents and, consequently, of the whole economy.

The present criterion of distinguishing microeconomics from macroeconomics based on the number of agents involved in each transaction is both superficial and wrong. *It is not the number of agents involved that matters, but the nature of their economic activity*. Hence, the production of a single worker is macroeconomic because it increases the income available in the whole economy. The loan granted by income holders to consumers, on the other hand, defines a microeconomic event even if it is carried out by a great number of agents, because it merely re-distributes a given income without either increasing or decreasing it. The concept of set is also useful when the analysis concerns all the elements of a given class taken as a whole as, for example, the set of workers, of households, of firms, of banks, and so on. In particular, it finds a fruitful application in international economics, where a country considered as a whole is identified with the set of its residents.

### *Quantum macroeconomics*

Other terms and phrases proper to Schmitt's terminology are worth noting: 'quantum macroeconomics' and the use of terms such as 'emission', 'corpuscular', 'wave-like' and 'quantum time'. Although they are taken from physics, these concepts find a new field of application in economics, where their meaning is specific to this discipline. An emission of money, for example, is an instantaneous creation-destruction of an immaterial flow and not of a particle or a wave as in quantum physics. Another example is the concept of quantum. In physics it refers to an indivisible discrete amount or 'chunk' of energy like Einstein's photon, or to a charge in a spread-out field as in quantum field theory; in Schmitt's macroeconomics it relates to time.

It is important to emphasize that Schmitt's quantum macroeconomic approach to economics is not a transposition of quantum mechanics principles into the field of economics. Schmitt's analysis developed independently from physics, and the fact that economics and physics seem to converge on a new perception of reality must be seen as a sign of the natural evolution of science and not as an attempt to construe economics by borrowing from physics.

Specific to Schmitt's research is the use of a modern form of logic that goes beyond the traditional binary form. The main difference between his and the binary form of logic is that the former rejects the generalized application of the principle of the *excluded middle* (*tertium non datur*). Already found wanting by some philosophers and mathematicians, binary logic is also ill-suited to explain the complexity of economic phenomena such as production, profit, amortization, stagflation, etc.

Distinct from the fundamental principle of non-contradiction, the law of the excluded middle restricts the analysis so much that it can no longer account, for example, for amortization being at the same time a reproduction and a new production, or prices being simultaneously identical to and greater than values. Schmitt succeeds in accounting for these conundrums without falling into contradiction thanks to the use of a logic that may soon replace the old binary form in every scientific field.

## The structure of the volume

The book is subdivided into three parts, each corresponding to a period of Schmitt's activity characterized by its main contributions to specific areas of investigation. The chronological distinction is somehow arbitrary and far from clear-cut since Schmitt's research extends over a period of more than sixty years without interruption, and the main topics of his investigation were always at the centre of his interest. It is nonetheless possible to pinpoint three main phases in the conceptual development of his analysis, which I designate as his greatest intuitions, his further in-depth discoveries, and his final years of ground-breaking analysis.

The last sections of 13 out of the 14 chapters of Part I and Part II are devoted to a critical comparison of Schmitt's analysis with that of other economists, both orthodox and heterodox. This comparison will help contextualize Schmitt's intellectual achievements and show what unites and what separates his analysis from that of other prominent economists, in general, and of Keynesian and post-Keynesian economists, in particular.

### *Part I*

Part I deals with Schmitt's first discoveries in the field of national economics and international economics and spans the period from 1959 to 1987. During these years of intense research, Schmitt investigates all the main topics of macroeconomics, writing and then publishing some of his masterpieces. This first part is made up of nine chapters, six concerned with national economics and three with international economics.

#### *Chapter 1*

Chapter 1 deals with the central element of Schmitt's analysis: bank money. By referring to several of his publications and unpublished manuscript, it is shown that Schmitt elaborates his notion of bank money far more rigorously than the great majority of his fellow economists. The starting point of his analysis is double-entry bookkeeping and the crucial role played by the number zero. The simultaneous entering of positive and negative numbers into banks' balance sheets demonstrates that money as such cannot be issued either as a net asset or as a net liability. Far from surprisingly, this means that banks cannot create a positive asset in isolation from the rest of the economy.

Chapter 1 shows that money is issued by banks as an *asset-liability*, which is a *mere numerical form*, and explains how this purely numerical 'container' can acquire positive purchasing power. Already investigated by the Classics, the transition from nominal money (a valueless, numerical form) to 'real' money (endowed with a positive value or purchasing power) requires the intervention of production. It is through the remuneration of the factors of production that money and output are so closely 'associated' that they define the two aspects of one and the same reality. Schmitt's analysis confirms the Classics' idea that it is through human labour that money acquires positive purchasing power, as well as Walras's intuition that economic value is not a dimension but rather a mere numerical relationship.

### *Chapter 2*

The formation of money's purchasing power is investigated further in Chapter 2, with arguments mainly derived from Schmitt's second published volume: *Monnaie, salaires et profit* (1966). It is in his 1966 book that Schmitt claims that, from a macroeconomic viewpoint, the factors of production must always be traced back to a single one, namely human labour, and therefore wages are the only macroeconomic cost of production. Definitively demonstrated in 1984, this claim rests on the fact that the payment of wages is the only transaction by which an output can become the object of a bank deposit. Yet, if wages are the only macroeconomic income formed by production, how can we explain the existence of other incomes, in particular profit? Schmitt's answer is in line with Keynes's *General Theory*, that is, with the inclusion of profit into national income: profit is derived from wages and so are interest, dividends, and rents.

Chapter 2 refers to Schmitt's effort to provide the building blocks of a theory of national money and production, and an explanation of how profit is part of wages. A highly controversial topic in economics, the theory of profit becomes a cornerstone of Schmitt's early analysis of capitalism. Starting from the role played by bank money and the way money is associated with produced output, Schmitt is able to show that the formation of profit is perfectly consistent with the identity of national income and nominal wages. His 1966 analysis is placed in a historical frame, shown as the first step towards a quantum theory of profit, subsequently presented in his 1984 book on inflation, unemployment, and capital malformations.

While developing his own theory, Schmitt analyzed in depth the theories advocated by his predecessors and his contemporaries, highlighting both their positive contributions and their shortcomings. His critical assessment of Keynesian and Marxian economics was mostly elaborated in the first three decades of his research, whereas his critical investigation of general equilibrium analysis lasted almost until his death.

### *Chapter 3*

Chapter 3 deals with Schmitt's critical appraisal of Walras's general equilibrium analysis, Keynes's income analysis, Marx's theory of value and surplus-value, and Sraffa's attempt at determining relative prices through the methods of production.

In this chapter, I consider Schmitt's first attempts to show that neither Walras nor Patinkin or the quantity theorists succeed in integrating money into the theoretical framework of GEA. The dichotomy between real world and monetary world, on which GEA rests, does not allow for the transformation of relative into monetary prices.

Walras's failure to integrate money into his system of equations is not corrected by the advocates of the quantity theory of money: it remains trapped in the logical impossibility to transform an identity, Fisher's equation of exchange in its various forms, into a condition of equilibrium. Patinkin's real-balance effect does not succeed in overcoming Walras's impasse either, because the adjustment of the supply of, and demand for, real goods through which individuals equilibrate their real balances cannot determine at the same time the value of money, i.e. its purchasing power, and the prices of goods. Patinkin's mistake is the same as that of the quantity theorists: it consists in deriving the purchasing power of money from the general price level, whereas it should be clear that the adjustment determining the price of goods leaves the value of money unaltered.

In order to discover the reasons underlying the logical indeterminacy of relative prices, Schmitt follows Walras in his initial analysis of the direct exchange between two goods, stresses the crucial importance of what is known as Walras's law, and questions its logical status. His answer is that Walras's law is nothing more than a tautology without explanatory power.

Contrary to what Walras and his followers believe, the law supposed to equalize the number of variables and of GEA's independent equations is an identity only when exchanges occur. Before exchange, in the phase of adjustment that is supposed to lead to the determination of relative prices, Walras's law does not apply, which means that the number of independent equations cannot be reduced. The ensuing over-determinacy of Walras's system of equations has an unavoidable, distressing consequence: the logical indeterminacy of Walras's relative prices.

The second part of Chapter 3 is devoted to part of Schmitt's critical appraisal of Keynesian economics, in particular of some of the main macroeconomic topics analyzed by Keynesian economists: the attempt to determine national income starting from a system of equations derived from Keynes's identities, as well as the world-famous theory of the income multiplier and its relationship with the principle of effective demand.

The multiplier theory is probably the one that most contributed to Keynes's renown, though not one of his original contributions, and despite its metaphysical flavour. It is taught by Keynesian economists (new-Keynesians and post-Keynesians included) to this day and came under attack by Schmitt in his 1971 volume on the macroeconomic analysis of income.

As shown in Chapter 3, the kernel of his critical analysis lies in the role played by saving and hoarding, respectively. The nature of bank deposits and the necessary compliance with the principles of double-entry bookkeeping establish beyond doubt that hoarding is always, and necessarily, equal to zero. Consequently, if indeed, as the multiplier theory assumes, consumption reproduces income, the process of multiplication that follows an exogeneous increase in income will go on endlessly. Schmitt's proposed alternative is clear: instead of being at the origin of new income, consumption, i.e. the final purchase of produced output, leads to the destruction of the income spent by consumers.

The third part is concerned with Schmitt's critique and synthesis of Marx's economic thought, with reference to his theory of value and surplus-value.

Even though Schmitt's favourite classical author was undoubtedly Ricardo, his interest in Marx was not secondary, as testified by his deep knowledge of *Das Kapital*. Schmitt's published and unpublished texts on Marxian economics deserve our attention, not only because they throw new light on the logical shortcomings of Marx's analysis but also because they contribute to a better understanding of Schmitt's own theory. In two volumes published by Castella, the founding blocks of Marx' theory of capital are critically analyzed with the twofold intent of emphasizing the positive aspects of Marx's analysis of value, while pointing out its weaknesses.

Already present in the works of Smith and Ricardo, the labour theory of value is a pivotal element of classical political economy, which finds in Marx its most accomplished version. Even though quantum macroeconomics confirms the claim that labour is alone at the origin of economic value, the classical attempt to measure value in terms of working time is doomed to failure. The very heterogeneity of labour does not allow the use of labour time as a standard of value.

What is new in Schmitt's analysis is the explanation of why it is logically impossible to measure economic value, time included, with a dimensional rod. By extension, Marx's theory of surplus-value is then dismissed on logical grounds, because *no fundamental distinction can be drawn between labour and labour power*. Marx's attempt to explain profit in terms of surplus-value fails for this very reason and because it cannot explain the monetary realization of surplus-value.

The last part of Chapter 3 is devoted to Schmitt's critique of Sraffa's attempt to provide a successful alternative to Walras's system of relative price determination. Sraffa seeks to determine the ratio of exchange between real goods through a system of equations relating to their methods of production. Starting from the idea that commodities are produced by means of commodities, he assumes that production takes place through consumption in a scheme that he describes as a self-replacing state. He also distinguishes the case in which production occurs without a surplus from that in which a surplus is formed and distributed in proportion to the capital invested in each industry.

Schmitt considers the two cases and shows that the prices Sraffa believes to be determined by his equations are the very definition of his assumptions. The ratio of exchange between the commodities produced in the two industries Sraffa refers to is implicit in the choice of the self-replacing state and of the absence of a surplus or of its distribution in proportion to the advances of each industry.

Schmitt also shows that, in the case of a positive surplus, Sraffa's equations are inconsistent with the assumption that a surplus is formed in each industry, unless the commodities produced by them, iron and wheat, are considered interchangeable, as if iron were merely a kind of wheat and vice versa.

The physical heterogeneity of real goods should have prevented Sraffa from writing his equations, whereas he adds up iron and wheat as if they were different quantities of one and the same object.

Like Walras's, Sraffa's failure to determine relative prices through exchange is due to the lack of the common numerical standard necessary to transform physically heterogeneous objects into economic products. Exchange being a bipolar transaction, none of the goods exchanged can be defined as the standard of the other without at the same time defining the latter as the standard of the former. Heterogeneous before exchange, Sraffa's commodities are bound to remain distinct and heterogeneous even during or after their exchange, which is further proof of the logical impossibility of determining relative prices in his theoretical framework.

Chapter 3 ends with a short note on Schmitt's critique of Pasinetti's input–output analysis and his pure labour theory of value.

### *Chapter 4*

Chapter 4 deals with the all-important question of the relationship between production and time. In his 1984 volume on *Inflation, Unemployment and Capital Malformations* Schmitt advocates a new notion of time and shows that production is not a function of continuous or discontinuous time, but an *instantaneous event* that defines a positive and indivisible portion of time: a quantum of time. His quantum macroeconomic analysis marks a crucial point in the history of economic thought.

Conceived as an instantaneous event quantizing time, production becomes the object of economics as a *sui generis* scientific inquiry. Schmitt is thus able to transform economics into a scientific practice rather than aping it or distorting it – which is what happens when one views scientific description and explanation as synonymous with mathematical representation – and to specify the logical laws on which it rests. The analysis of production remains central, because it is through production that *money is transformed into income* and output becomes its object. As an economic event, production coincides with a payment that gives a numerical form to physical output.

Since Einstein we have become aware that time – still a mysterious concept – is a component of a new dimension, space-time, and that its measure requires light as a constant. However, the experientially important 'arrow of time' remains unexplained, since physical laws are timeless; or so it has seemed till recently. Schmitt's view of time is not at odds with how we ordinarily experience it. It provides a complementary vision of time. Quantum time derives directly from the specific nature of economic production and its relationship with the period of transformation of matter or energy required to obtain any physical output.

Economic production is instantaneous, because it is nothing other than the 'moment' at which physical output is given a numerical form through the payment of wages. The result of economic production is the transformation of physical output into a sum of money. This does not mean that the process of production is irrelevant or that physical output does not matter. Indeed, the payment of wages refers necessarily *to a finite time period*, corresponding to that of the physical transformation of matter or energy, which is precisely the definition of quantum time: *the result of the (instantaneous) emission of a finite period of time.*

The originality of Schmitt's thought and his efforts to free economics from its subservience to mathematics and physics derive from his intuition that Keynes's equation between global supply, $Y$, and global demand, $C + I$, is an identity. To maintain that production and consumption are the two opposite phases of a sole emission, and that each production creates the income necessary and sufficient for the final purchase of its output, one must show that investment, too, defines a final transformation of income. Indeed, it is through investment that income is transformed into fixed capital.

### *Chapter 5*

Chapter 5 is devoted to the analysis of the way fixed capital is formed. At least since the works of Ricardo, it has been understood that *capital is closely related to time*. What still remained unclear was the passage from capital-time – as Schmitt calls it – to fixed capital. Following Keynes's claim that capital is what enables us to build a bridge between present and future, Schmitt shows that capital could not exist in the absence of banks and their financial intermediation. It thus appears that capital is formed through the investment of savings.

The distinction between capital-time and fixed capital is due to the fact that the former belongs to a reversible process through which saved-up income is transformed into capital, whereas the latter derives from the irreversible or definitive transformation of income into capital. In both cases, saved-up income is invested, but in the first case saving can be recovered and spent for the final purchase of the output stocked by firms, while in the second case saving is forever fixed in the instrumental goods, whose production it finances.

The study of fixed capital formation in capitalist economies is crucial for the understanding of the pathologies that affect them. Schmitt develops it along two lines of thought, one in his 1984 volume and the other in an unpublished manuscript of 1998. Consistent with the chronological order I follow in this scientific biography, only the first of these two analyses is presented in Chapter 5.

### *Chapter 6*

Chapter 6 completes the investigation of the main elements of a capitalist economy of production. The use of fixed capital makes it necessary to account for its maintenance and its replacement. Amortization grants the maintenance and replacement of fixed capital and, as such, it coincides with the production of amortization-goods. Hence a question arises: is amortization a reproduction, or does it define a new production comparable to that of new investment-goods? Schmitt's quantum macroeconomic analysis shows that amortization is both a reproduction and a new production.

Far from being self-contradictory, Schmitt's analysis is an example of the fact that the logic of economics goes beyond the principle of the excluded middle. Schmitt is thus able to show that, in the present capitalist system, the production of amortization-goods adds to the production of consumption- and investment-goods.

The analysis developed in Chapter 6 concerns the genesis and nature of inflation and unemployment.

Too often identified with a generalized rise in prices and quantified through the use of a consumption price index, inflation is in reality a pathology leading to a decrease in the purchasing power of money. It is an anomaly affecting the relationship between money and output in such a way that a given output becomes the real content of an increased number of monetary units.

To explain inflation is to show that a numerical difference can exist between global demand, D, and global supply, Y, without contradicting the fact that D and Y are the terms of an identity. Schmitt shows that what might seem an impossible claim is, on the contrary, the only possible way to arrive at a correct understanding of how money units can lose part of their purchasing power in a context where production is the only macroeconomic source of income.

As for unemployment, what Schmitt investigates is *pathological* unemployment – Keynes's involuntary unemployment. Once again, what is under scrutiny is the macroeconomic working of our capitalist economies and its compliance with the principles governing money, income, capital, and their interrelations.

The search for the cause of unemployment is arduous, and Chapter 6 analyzes how Schmitt deals with the problem in his 1984 volume on capital. There he shows that pathological unemployment is the unavoidable consequence of a process of capital accumulation, whose by-product is the increasing fall in what Wicksell called the *natural rate of interest*, the ratio between total profit and accumulated capital. When this rate drops below the market rate of interest, the production of new fixed capital-goods must be reduced. Indeed, at this point the system reaches a critical level of accumulated capital and is forced to reduce its rate of growth. This is so because capital must be remunerated and, when the natural rate of interest falls below the market rate, the profits firms can make are no longer sufficient to guarantee the payment of interest.

The second section of Part I is concerned with Schmitt's contributions to the field of international economics during his first intense period of research activity.

As a matter of fact, Schmitt's interest in international economics goes back even further, to the late sixties, and is the consistent generalization of his intuitions concerning the nature of bank money. From that time on, he worked painstakingly on both national and international economics, developing a unified theory of money.

The second section of Part I of Schmitt's scientific biography is devoted to his main achievements in the field of international payments and rests on his published and unpublished manuscripts dated between 1960 and 1988.

## *Chapter 7*

Chapter 7 shows how Schmitt's conception of money can be applied to international transactions and how he managed to work out a common theoretical framework encompassing both national and international economics.

International economics differs from national economics in that the former is not directly at the origin of any production. Yet, this has no impact on the way money is issued by banks and relies on the logically incoherent view of treating money as a positive asset. In an international framework, it is particularly clear that no national currency can be considered as if it was real good. Issued by banks as a spontaneous acknowledgement of debt, outside its national border, a national currency defines an IOU of the whole banking system. It is plain, therefore, that national currencies not only have no redeeming power, but they cannot be themselves the object of any international payment.

Chapter 7 is based mainly on one of Schmitt's most successful books: *Théorie unitaire de la monnaie, nationale et internationale* (1975). Translated into German, Portuguese and Italian, this book marks the start of a period of renewed interest in the old theory of the circuit as well as in its modern formulation. A number of heterodox economists were to follow Schmitt's example and contribute to the diffusion of circuit theory. Yet, their analyses differ substantially from that of Schmitt regarding the logical distinction between money and income. Furthermore, none of them saw the relevance of applying circuit theory to the field of international economics.

Chapter 7 also shows that today's international transactions are a cause of inflation. Schmitt explains why this is so in *Les pays au régime du FMI*, published in 1984 by Castella. He tackles the case in which a country's imports are balanced by its exports as well as the case in which a country's exports are net and shows that the pathology derives in both cases from the fact that, contrary to its nature, money is considered a real good.

In the first case, this leads to the monetization of the foreign currencies paid by foreign importers. It is this additional creation of domestic money that pathologically increases the number of domestic money units initially associated with current output.

In the second case, inflation is due to a process of duplication, whereby the net importing country pays for its net imports by transferring to the creditor countries a mere IOU. Since the totality of foreign currency remains deposited with foreign banks, creditors are paid in what Rueff calls a duplicate, a simulacrum that pathologically increases the financial capital available in the net exporting country.

Another topic analyzed in Chapter 7 is that of currency exchange rates. Most economists consider the rate of exchange as the relative price of currencies, because of the mistaken identification of money with an asset. Emulating what Walras did in the case of real goods and services, they think it is possible to determine the equilibrium rate of exchange between currencies by adjusting their supply and demand on the forex.

Dismissing this view of the exchange rate, Schmitt maintains that if the erratic fluctuation of exchange rates is indeed due to the speculative purchase and sale of currencies on the forex, the cause must be the erroneous treatment of money as a net asset. If currencies were considered for what they actually are, the present regime of relative exchange rates would be replaced by a new regime of *absolute exchange rates*, compatible with the use of money as a *means* rather than an object of exchange.

### *Chapter 8*

Chapter 8 argues that a positive analysis must lead to a normative result and provides the principles that facilitate *the transition from disorder to order*. Schmitt's inquiry into the nature of international payments and of their systems (or non-systems) leads indeed to a plan for an international monetary reform. Chapter 8 deals with the reform he first put forward in 1973 and with the influence of Keynes's Plan for the Establishment of an International Clearing Union (ICU) presented at Bretton Woods in 1944.

Keynes's Plan contained two original proposals, none of which was correctly understood by the scientific community of the time:

1) The institution of a supranational bank (the ICU); and
2) The emission of an international currency, the bancor, distinct from any national money.

According to Keynes, the emission of the new currency should have been based on the principles of banking, that is to say, on the necessary equality between credit and debit. The bancor would have conveyed all the payments among countries, and a mechanism based on multilateral clearing would have guaranteed a perfect match between monetary and real payments. Unfortunately, Keynes's Plan was not sufficiently elaborated and clear-cut, so it was not implemented.

Schmitt's own plan supplies what is still missing in Keynes's and puts forward the logical principles and the practical arrangements that would make it possible to transform the present non-system of international payments into a truly orderly system. In his 1973 book *New Proposals for World Monetary Reform*, Schmitt sets out a regulatory framework for a reform, which he would develop further in his 1977 book *L'or, le dollar et la monnaie supranationale*, and to which he will return on several occasions during his long-lasting involvement with the problems of world monetary disorders and their solutions.

### *Chapter 9*

As Chapter 9 points out, Schmitt published three volumes about the problem of European monetary unification between 1975 and 1988. The debate on the advantages and disadvantages of adopting a European currency was derailed by the confrontation between advocates and adversaries of an eminently political project that soon took over. Anyone who dared point out the existence of critical difficulties, likely to hamper the project, was accused of Euro-scepticism, a euphemism that really meant that any critique was seen as a stance against the EU.

Schmitt's texts attempt to keep the debate within a strictly economic context, to analyze the European project from a scientific and macroeconomic viewpoint rather than from a political one. More specifically, Schmitt seeks to understand which countries adopting the European money would suffer. His approach rests on the nature of money, income, and capital as well as on the role played by national monetary systems vis-à-vis the free movements of capital. Indeed, monetary sovereignty is a 'safety belt' against the loss of domestic capital. Even when invested abroad, domestic capitals remain deposited within the banking system of the country in which they originate. Apparently contrary to common sense, this state of affairs is imposed by double-entry bookkeeping, and understanding it is crucial for a correct evaluation of the pros and cons of monetary unification.

Does this mean that European countries were, and still are, confronted with two equally negative alternatives? Namely, either give up monetary sovereignty and accept the increase in economic divergences between them or to maintain their monetary sovereignty and accept the erratic fluctuation of exchange rates between their domestic currencies. No, it does not. As shown in Chapter 9, Schmitt developed the principles of a reform that would allow European countries to remain monetarily sovereign – at least until economic convergence is attained – and at the same time guarantee the automatic and costless stability of their national currencies.

## ***Part II***

Part II covers a period of roughly ten years of Schmitt's activity, 1987 to 1998, and is characterized by an increased effort towards a more in-depth analysis of national economics as well as criticism of general equilibrium analysis, GEA. Those were very prolific years in terms of manuscripts. As most of them have remained unpublished, Schmitt's substantial improvements to his analyses are much harder to show. A choice must be made if we want to preserve the specificity of Schmitt's message.

### *Chapter 10*

Schmitt was always fascinated by the problem of international payments and their pathological implications, and he devoted a substantial part of his research to it. In particular, from 1987 to 1995, he worked relentlessly on one of his main discoveries: the double charge of external debt servicing.

Chapter 10 deals with this difficult topic. Starting from the observation that *cross-border payments affect both countries and their residents*, it shows that the servicing of countries' external debt is characterized by an asymmetry that prevents compensation of the payments affecting indebted countries themselves. In the present non-system of international payments, two payments are necessary to fulfil a country's obligation to service its external debt: a payment by the indebted country's residents, carried out in domestic currency, and a payment, in foreign currency, by the country itself.

Since external debt servicing defines an *unrequited transfer*, it implies a unilateral transfer of foreign currency forcing indebted countries *to purchase the vehicular means of payment, which today's system of international payments fails to provide for free*. Schmitt provides several arguments supporting his claim and tackles the problem from different angles in search of the clearest way to demonstrate why the charge of external debt servicing is twice as high as it should be.

Chapter 10 presents some of these arguments and introduces the first elements of a reform that will find its final and complete formulation only later (see Chapter 18). Although the analysis developed by Schmitt from 1987 to 1995 is self-contained and includes all the necessary elements to prove the *double cost of external debt servicing*, Schmitt was not entirely satisfied with it; he went on delving into the problem until he reached the heart of it and was able to fully demonstrate what he called the '*interest theorem*' (see Chapter 15).

### *Chapter 11*

Chapter 11 considers the problem of capital and interest, first analyzed by Schmitt in his 1984 book on inflation, unemployment, and capital malformations, in income or value terms.

From 1993 to 1998 Schmitt went back to this subject in a series of lectures delivered at the University of Fribourg, Switzerland, which were collected in the form of mimeo transcripts. They contain a number of highly relevant observations concerning *the nature of interest and its relationship with national income as well as with capital*. These observations deserve being presented in this volume because they are relevant in and of themselves, and because they pave the way for a new analysis of (involuntary) unemployment developed by Schmitt in 1998.

Is interest a macroeconomic income? Is it additional to wages? What is the rationale for the existence of positive interest? These are some of the questions dealt with in Chapter 11 and answered by Schmitt in his all-important manuscripts.

### *Chapter 12*

Chapter 12 explains that unemployment is, beyond doubt, one of the most worrying consequences of the crisis that is still besetting our economies. At the same time, it has turned out to be one of the most difficult subjects for economic analysis, with economists still far from able to provide a satisfactory explanation of its origin, let alone how to overcome it.

Schmitt's 1998 analysis provides a new explanation of this pathology, based on 'sectors' rather than on 'periods' (as he had done in his 1984 book). The main idea is that, because of a substantial inconsistency between the present structure of national payments and the nature of money, income, and capital, *production takes place in three different sectors*, which owe their existence to the macroeconomic lending of bank deposits formed following the investment of profit.

Logically, once invested, profit defines the irreversible transformation of income into fixed capital. If our systems of payments were in line with this requirement, banks would never be able to lend any income transformed into fixed capital on the financial market. Since this is not the case, a pathology arises whose unavoidable consequence is a process of capital over-accumulation, which in turn leads to a reduction in the rate of profit and, finally, to a decrease in current production and an increase in unemployment.

Chapter 12 deals with Schmitt's analysis of unemployment as developed in his 1998 unpublished manuscript *Le chômage et son éradication* and shows how it can be reconciled with the one advocated in his book *Inflation, Unemployment and Capital Malformations*.

### *Chapter 13*

Chapter 13 relates to Schmitt's critique of the neoclassical attempt at determining relative prices, which dates back to 1960 and was further developed in the early1990s. Relative prices are the topic that stimulated Schmitt's theoretical interest in mainstream economics. This is not surprising, because the entire GEA is founded on the possibility of determining prices through exchange. According to Walras's psychological–mathematical approach, prices are determined simultaneously by a system of independent equations of supply and demand. If it were indeed possible to determine prices in this way, the neoclassical theory would be irreproachable, and the use of mathematically sophisticated models could thus justify itself as the correct and rigorous methodology to study economic phenomena. On the other hand, if it can be shown that *relative prices are logically indeterminate*, the neoclassical analysis would have to be abandoned once and for all.

In his extensive critical investigation, Schmitt analyzes relative prices from various points of view, and provides several proofs of their logical indeterminacy. Starting from the logical status of Walras's law, he goes on to show that the system of equations providing the rationale behind general equilibrium analysis is over-determined. The problem itself is conceptually arduous, hence the difficulty one experiences in following Schmitt's critical analysis. Yet, its relevance is commensurate with its difficulty, which explains why Schmitt pursued his analysis almost until the end of his life (see Chapter 17).

*Chapter 14*

Chapter 14 explains how implementing Schmitt's domestic reform of 1984 would promote the transition from the present capitalist regime to a new economic regime dubbed by the French economist as 'post-capitalism'. The suffix 'post' refers to the need to abandon the present version of capitalism once and for all, rather than to attempt to build an economic system without capital.

A post-capitalist regime will still be marked by the existence of fixed capital as well as by a process of capital accumulation. Yet, contrary to what happens today, the accumulation of fixed capital would no longer give rise to inflation and unemployment. The mechanism leading to the fall in the rate of profit would be replaced by one in which the accumulation of fixed capital would not take place at the expense of households.

Contrary to what happens in the present regime, where part of current output is appropriated by what Schmitt calls 'depersonalized firms' or 'pathological capital', in a post-capitalist regime the totality of output – fixed capital-goods included – would be owned by the undifferentiated set of households and their representatives (the State, 'personalized firms', and other institutions acting on behalf of the economy's individual agents). Chapter 14 presents the main aspects of post-capitalism as advocated by Schmitt in his 1998 manuscript on the causes of unemployment and the way to eradicate it.

***Part III***

Part III of the volume considers the last 15 years of Schmitt's scientific activity, which, apart from the elaboration of his final criticism of general equilibrium analysis, were devoted to the completion of his investigation on net interests, which he had launched in the 1990s, and to the discovery of the pathological nature of countries' sovereign debt. Together with his quantum macroeconomic analysis of national economies, Schmitt's investigation of countries' external debt is another significant result of his research.

Unlike what often happens to researchers as time goes by, the intensity and quality of Schmitt's insights did not diminish. He completed one of his signature pieces, the paper on countries' sovereign debt published posthumously by SSRN, a few days before his death, and his final criticism of relative prices, together with his most pregnant texts on the 'interest theorem' were elaborated in 2010. Part III deals with his last, seminal contributions to economic analysis during the last and tormented period of his personal and professional life.

*Chapter 15*

Chapter 15 rests on the fact that, starting from the early eighties, Schmitt devoted a great part of his research to the study of the interest payments on countries' external debts. His long-lasting investigation of this subject brought him to the discovery of what he called *the interest theorem*. Even though he made this breakthrough as early as in 1984 with his small book *Les pays au regime du FMI*, Schmitt devoted more than two decades of his life to working out the clearest way to present it. The great difficulty of this fascinating problem lies in its apparent absurd claim that *each indebted country must pay twice the interest on its debt*, which sounds odd and highly unlikely.

Within a national economy, no indebted agent is subjected to paying twice the interests on their debt. Why should things differ substantially when we move from the national to the international framework? The answer is simple: a proper system of payments exists nationally, whereas this is not yet the case for payments between countries (economists speak of the non-system of international payments).

It is the absence of a true system of international payments that forces net indebted countries to cover the cost of both paying creditors their due and obtaining the foreign currency necessary to 'vehiculate' or convey the payment. What is hard to prove is that the payments of interest in real terms and in foreign currency are indeed separate and cumulative and multiply by two the total cost to the indebted country. Schmitt does it by investigating the various aspects of the problem and thus revealing how deep-rooted it is.

The first part of Chapter 15 follows his line of arguments and provides an overview of the long development that brought Schmitt to formulate his 'interest theorem' in 2005.

The second part of Chapter 15 is concerned with the most relevant versions of Schmitt's analyses of the double cost of interest payments after 2005, and with his last efforts to convince experts and politicians of their centrality.

The impressive number of unpublished manuscripts, mimeo courses, and official reports Schmitt wrote about the problem of interest from 1990 to 2010 testifies to its importance and complexity, as well as to the intensity of the effort to make it known to academics and politicians. During his numerous visits to Angola, Mexico, Brazil, and Washington, he presented his analysis to government officials, central bankers, and IMF and World Bank experts. These meetings testify both the interest aroused by Schmitt's 'interest theorem' and the effort required to convince experts and politicians of the need for a substantial reform of the present (non) system of international payments.

Chapter 15 shows Schmitt's renewed attempt to arrive at the simplest and clearest presentation of the pathology affecting the payment of countries' interests on debt. As a matter of fact, he provides more than one such presentation, each of which has its own specificity and its own pros and cons.

The intrinsic difficulty of the subject cannot be evaded, and the advantage of investigating it from different angles is that of offering a variety of arguments converging on a single conclusion. On the other hand, a list of too many alternative analyses is likely to confuse the reader, which is why a selection is made and presented in Chapter 15.

### *Chapter 16*

Chapter 16 sets out to present a seminal paper published in 2012 as Chapter 1 of a book promoting monetary macroeconomics (Gnos and Rossi, 2012), where Schmitt argues that *relative prices are plagued by a mathematical error.* This is how he provides the final proof of the 'inanity' of the neoclassical framework of mainstream economics: he demonstrates that general equilibrium analysis is undermined by the fact that one price out of two goes missing because of the inverse relationship defined by relative prices.

To be clear, the mathematical error is not a fault of mathematics, per se, but is due to the incorrect application of mathematics to the neoclassical scheme of relative prices determination.

Given the inverse relationship existing between relative prices, the multiplication of one of them is simultaneously the division of the other by the same coefficient, for any variation in the price of one good in terms of another defines the inverse variation of the price of the latter in terms of the former. This makes it impossible to determine relative prices through a process of groping (Walras's tâtonnement) because in the comparison between all the possible prices of one good and all the possible prices of the other, one relative price in two is 'lost'. Chapter 16 deals with this crucial argument and provides a historical account of its genesis.

### *Chapter 17*

Chapter 17 explains how Schmitt analyzed the problem of the *formation of countries' external debt* after his investigation of the pathological payment of interests on these debts.

Starting from the accepted notion of a sovereign debt crisis, he makes it clear from the outset that a country's sovereign debt must *not* be identified with its public debt. In an orderly economic environment, countries should not carry any external debt on top of that carried by their public and private sectors. Indeed, sovereign debts should not exist at all: the only justifiable external debts are those incurred by countries' residents (the State included). Unfortunately, this is not the case at present.

As shown by Schmitt in his 2012 and 2014 writings, the payment of a country's net global imports, commercial and financial, inevitably leads to a duplication of its cost and ends up forming an external debt, which affects the country as a whole. In his one hundred-page long paper of 2014, he gives several proofs of the *pathological nature of countries' sovereign debt*, most of which are based on the discovery that net indebted countries have to obtain foreign loans in order to pay the rest of the world for their net global imports.

By pointing out that the true object of this loan is part of the indebted country's *future output* and not, as generally thought, an amount of foreign currency, Schmitt is able to show that net imports have to be paid twice, once in real terms and once in money terms. Since the two payments are added together, net importing countries are forced to incur two foreign debts, one of which is entirely pathological and results in the formation of their sovereign debt.

*Chapter 18*

Chapter 18 refers to the *one-country solution* advocated by Schmitt in his 2014 text, a solution that each single country can implement, irrespective of what the other countries do and without affecting any of them. This solution, which would protect the country that implements it from the devastating consequences of the present non-system of international payments, is Schmitt's last contribution to macroeconomic normative analysis. It presents the series of logical and practical steps that would enable any country to pay for its net global imports, commercial and financial, without running up an external debt.

Today, net importing countries pay twice for their net global imports. The reform would reduce the payment to one, and thus avoid the loss of domestic income suffered on top of that of an equivalent amount of the country's future output. This solution requires the institution of a sovereign Bureau charged to carry out all the external payments of the country and to which all the payments of the rest-of-the-world, R, would be addressed. Yet, this alone is not enough. Nothing would radically change, if the Bureau did not lend to R an amount of foreign currency equivalent to the amount of the country's net global imports.

Chapter 18 explains the rationale behind this loan as well as the benefit that the net importing country (its Bureau) would derive from the *internalization of the external payments carried out by the country's residents*. It also shows that no creditor country would suffer from the reduction in the payment carried out by debtor countries, because today's second payment only goes to feed the international financial bubble.

By avoiding the duplication of the payment made by indebted countries, the reform would create the conditions for a substantial increase in their economic development and, by the same token, for an increase in their external exchanges, thus benefiting creditor countries too. Schmitt's one-country solution is one of the most important outcomes of his legacy, and its implementation would mark the transition from a non-system to an authentic system of international payments.

*Conclusion*

A brief conclusion summarizes the specificity and the main results of Schmitt's analysis and places it in the history of economic thought.

# Part I

# 1959–1987: The years of Schmitt's greatest insights

The aim of Schmitt's macroeconomic analysis of what Keynes identified as a monetary economy of production is twofold:

1) To introduce and explain the logical character of the macroeconomic laws governing our economies.
2) To explain the origin of the pathologies caused by these laws not being complied with.

His starting point was the analysis of bank money and the way bank money is associated with produced output. His approach is macroeconomic, but it is macroeconomics not founded on microeconomics, nor derived from the aggregation of microeconomic variables. In this respect, Schmitt is the heir to the Classics and Keynes, and his analysis stands in stark contrast with general equilibrium analysis.

Schmitt published most of his books and enunciated all his main discoveries concerning the analysis of both national and international economics during the first thirty years of his research. In the first six chapters of Part I, we examine Schmitt's greatest insights into the analysis of money, income, and capital as well as his critical assessment of mainstream and Marxian economics. Emphasis is placed on his discovery of quantum time and on his quantum analysis of money's circular flow, production, and capital accumulation. The analysis developed in these initial chapters leads to Schmitt's new diagnosis of inflation and unemployment and to his reform proposals for an orderly system of national payments.

The last three chapters of Part I deal with Schmitt's 1959–1987 crucial insights into the problem of international payments. His ground-breaking analysis, which led him to a new proposal for a world monetary reform, is the logical result of his quantum macroeconomic approach applied to cross-border transactions and their monetary settlement. Part I ends with a chapter devoted to Schmitt's original contribution to the debate sparked by the European project of monetary unification.

DOI: 10.4324/9781351271325-2

# A

# From money to capital

# 1 The discovery of the true nature of money and the origin of its purchasing power

Schmitt's macroeconomic analysis is built on the concept of money as a numerical standard and its relationship with production. As he often acknowledged, his crucial intuition owes much to his reading of Keynes's works on the monetary theory of production, in particular to Keynes's definition of national income, its formation, and its expenditure.

In this chapter, we shall investigate Schmitt's analysis of money and of money's purchasing power, emphasizing the logical distinction between money and income, the role of banks as monetary and financial intermediaries, the *absolute* exchange linking monetary creation and production, and the necessary coupling of production and consumption. To this end, I will refer predominantly to Schmitt's first two published books: *La formation du pouvoir d'achat* (1960) and *Monnaie, salaires et profits* (1966), and to his papers 'L'équilibre de la monnaie' (1959) and 'Le problème de l'intégration de la monnaie' (1971). Since Schmitt never stopped developing his analysis of money, I shall sometimes refer also to later texts, which help clarify his initial insights and facilitate their understanding. In particular, I will refer to Schmitt's unpublished manuscripts *Cours de théorie monétaire* (1995–96) and *Le chômage et son éradication* (1998).

## Schmitt's starting point: Keynes's equations

It was while reading Keynes's two main books, *The Treatise on Money* (1930) and *The General Theory* (1936), that Schmitt had his first great intuition about the nature of money and its relationship with produced output.

Analyzing national income in his *Treatise*, Keynes spells out his intention to reject the traditional approach of the quantity theory of money and replace it with a new one, which emphasizes the role played by money in the formation and the expenditure of income.

> I propose therefore to break away from the traditional method of setting out from the total quantity of money irrespective of the purposes on which it is employed, and to start instead – for reasons that will become clear as we proceed – with the flow of the community's earnings or money-income, and with its twofold division: (1) into the parts which have been

DOI: 10.4324/9781351271325-4

> *earned* by the production of consumption-goods and of investment-goods respectively, and (2) into the parts which are *expended* on consumption-goods and on savings respectively.
>
> (Keynes 1930/1971: 121)

Using a modern symbolic formulation, the ensuing 'fundamental' equations may be written as follows:

$$Y = C' + I' \tag{1.1}$$

$$Y = C + (Y - C) = C + S, \tag{1.2}$$

where $Y$ stands for money-income, $C'$ for the amount earned in the production of consumption-goods, $I'$ for the income earned in the production of investment-goods, and $C$ and $S$ for the income spent on the purchase of consumption-goods and on savings, respectively.

Six years later, in *The General Theory*, Keynes reiterates his macroeconomic approach and proposes the following 'general' equations:

'Income = value of output = consumption + investment
Saving = income – consumption' (Keynes 1936/1946: 63)

As stressed by Schmitt (1960), if these two equations were written as follows:

$$Y = C + I \tag{1.3}$$

$$Y = C + (Y - C) = C + S, \tag{1.4}$$

they would lead straightaway to the conclusion that saving, $S = Y - C$, is always and necessarily equal to investment. The identity between $S$ and $I$ would then merely derive from the definitions chosen from the start, where saving and investment are both defined as the complementary parts of $C$ in the measure of national income.

To be clear, Keynes's general equations as defined in Chapter V of his *General Theory* are less well-defined and innovative than his fundamental equations in *The Treatise*. Taken literally, they establish the identity between saving and investment as the mechanic consequence of the definitions of income and saving. It is only in the light of what Keynes asserted six years earlier that it is possible to appreciate the originality of his message.

In *The Treatise* (1930) Keynes draws a clear distinction between flows leading to the formation of national income and flows implying its expenditure.

> Let E be the total money-income or earnings of the community in a unit of time, and I' the part of it which has been earned by the production of investment-goods, so that I' measures the cost of production of new investment and E – I' the cost of production of the current output of consumption-goods.
>
> (ibid.: 121)

Whereas Equations (1.3) and (1.4) have no heuristic value, Equations (1.1) and (1.2) are genuine propositions and open the way to an unprecedented analysis of money and income. As Schmitt (1960) claims, it is only by distinguishing income formed in the production of consumption- and investment-goods, from income spent in the purchase of consumption- and investment- or saving-goods, that Keynes's general equations acquire a heuristic value.

The relevant equations are the following:

$$Y_1 = C' + I' \tag{1.5}$$

$$S = Y_2 - C \tag{1.6}$$

It is by keeping logically separate the transactions leading to the formation of income from those defining its final expenditure, and by showing that $Y_1$ and $Y_2$ are necessarily equal, that Keynes's analysis provides the building blocks of a new macroeconomic theory of income.

It must be noted that, in his 1960 book, Schmitt adopts the symbols corresponding to the definitions used by Keynes in *The General Theory*, so that Equation (1.1) takes the form of

$$Y = C + I, \tag{1.7}$$

where $C$ and $I$ are, respectively, the income formed in the production of consumption- and investment-goods, that is, what we have denoted as $C' + I'$ in (1), following Keynes's choice of symbols in *The Treatise*.

This change in symbols has no consequences on the analysis, but it may create confusion. To avoid any such risk, it is opportune to specify that, in this chapter, I shall adopt the symbols used by Schmitt in his 1960 book and represent them by $C + I$ the formation of income and by $C' + I'$ its final expenditure as they occur in the production and the final purchase of consumption- and investment-goods. Later on, I will switch back to the symbols chosen by Keynes in his 1930 book, following Schmitt's chosen practice from 1971 onward.

Schmitt is the first author to have fully sensed the great implications of Keynes's fundamental equations as well as those of his general equations and of the inclusion of profit into the definition of national income. Starting from Keynes's equations, in his first published book, *La formation du pouvoir d'achat* (1960), Schmitt shows that the formation of national income passes through what he calls the 'investment of money', a transaction through which money is 'invested' or 'vested' with a positive purchasing power over produced output.

Schmitt's objective is to show that the term 'investment', besides the specific meaning it acquires when related to the production and purchase of investment-goods, may be used to denote a more general concept to do with the relationship between money and the production of consumption- and investment-goods. This is where the investigation of the true nature of money enters the picture and where the question of how money is created needs an answer.

## The nature of bank money and the formation of the purchasing power of money

### *Material money*

An inquiry into the nature of money could start from the times when *material* money was used as a unit of account and means of payment. Indeed, an analysis of material money would show that each transaction implying money as a unit of account is a monetized exchange even when money is identified with a precious metal, say gold, or with any other specific material. It is only if transactions were to occur directly between real goods and real money (as, for example, a quantity of gold) that exchanges would be reduced to barter.

In a text distributed to his students in Fribourg in the seventies, Schmitt showed that in a system where payments are carried out by means of a material money acting also as a unit of account, money is both 'real' and 'nominal'. Its circulation defines at the same time a circular flow of nominal or 'vehicular' money and a unilateral displacement of real money from purchasers to sellers.

Payments are monetized exchanges, and exchanges imply the circular flow of a sum of units of account, which each economic agent involved in the transaction instantaneously obtains and loses. This means that when a purchaser, P, pays a seller, S, in a material money, S obtains a sum of real money (gold) through the vehicular flow of a nominal money that instantaneously flows back to its point of departure. It is true that P gives a sum of real money in exchange for a sum of real goods. Yet, it is only if these two sums are valued through a numerical standard and if vehicular money carries it out that the result is a monetized transaction between P and S. It thus appears that the material money (gold) used as a means of payment carries a double functionality by acting both as a vehicle and as a final good, in conformity with the distinction between (nominal) money and its gold content.

Analysis of material money is made pointlessly complicated by the constant need to distinguish between, for example, gold as money from gold as its real content. It is therefore more rewarding to concentrate instead on the analysis of bank money, which is the generalized form taken by money worldwide: its analysis provides the elements for a thorough investigation into the pathologies of our monetary systems.

## *Bank money*

What one must investigate first is how banks issue money. It is obvious that *money must have been created* before any exchange can take place. Banks create money by spontaneously incurring a debt to a client. To do so, banks rely on double-entry bookkeeping and on their faculty to spontaneously enter into their accounts a debt to the economy.

Let us call F the client that is credited and B the bank (representative of the set of banks – commercial and central – making up the banking system of any given country) that incurs the debt to F. Resulting from B entering a debt to F, bank money 'is a claim on banks [B], a personal credit' (Schmitt 1966a: 181, my translation (m.t.)) obtained by F. Now, F does not obtain as a net asset the personal debit of the bank; F does not own it. This is so because the bank *lends* to F its acknowledgement of debt, so that F incurs an equivalent debt to B. The bank lends its personal debt to F and at the same time acquires a credit on F, which leads Schmitt to the conclusion that money is essentially an asset-liability: what F borrows is due by it to the bank. 'The object created by banks is of a double nature: it is simultaneously positive and negative for the same amount. By definition, money is an asset and a liability, in other words an asset-liability' (Schmitt 1975a: 13, m.t.).

Having established that 'money is an acknowledgement of debt that has its initial source in the bank' (Schmitt 1971b: 220, m.t.) and that it is obtained by the real economy both as an asset and a liability, one must now explain the object of the bank's debt.

Let us first establish what the object of the bank's acknowledgement of debt *is not*.

Schmitt's 1984 distinction between ordinary and quantum credit is of help here. If banks created money through ordinary credit, the object of their debt would be a real good or asset. Indeed, a bank can lend only what is deposited with it. In its ordinary sense, a credit implies the previous existence of some real assets financially deposited with banks. Hence, when a bank lends part of its deposits, it acts as an intermediary between lenders, owners of financial deposits, and borrowers. 'To the extent that the bank lends part of its deposits, it transfers an already existing money and acts as a financial intermediary' (Schmitt 1966a: 161, m.t.).

In other words, ordinary credit is the transfer of a sum of income saved up by its initial holders and every such sum pre-exists its transfer, mediated by banks, from lenders to borrowers. This means that

1) 'The expression "creation of credit" is a contradiction in terms' (Schmitt 1995–96: 11, m.t.); and that

2) The object of ordinary credit is a sum of real goods, real content of the income deposited by lenders.

On the other hand, the creation of (nominal) money results from what Schmitt calls a quantum credit, that is, from a credit that banks grant to the public and whose object is the banks' acknowledgement of debt itself.

As it shall become clear in Chapters 4 and 5, the term 'quantum' denotes the fact that Schmitt's monetary macroeconomics is founded on the concept of emissions: instantaneous events characterized by the unity of creation and destruction and defining a finite and indivisible period of time, a *quantum of* time. It thus follows that nobody owns (nominal) money: neither the economy because money is merely lent to the economy, which must pay it back, nor the bank because by flowing back money is destroyed.

### *The creation of bank money*

At this point, it seems that the creation of bank money is to no avail, because the beneficiary of the creation would merely obtain an acknowledgement of debt of the bank both as the object of its credit and of its equivalent and simultaneous debit. Schmitt, who shows that the object of the debt spontaneously incurred by banks is a flow of payments, brilliantly avoids this discouraging conclusion. 'The true object of economic agents' credit on banks [...] is to obtain a flow and not a stock' (Schmitt 1998a: 4–5, m.t.). Hence 'money units "only" enable creditors to obtain that the issuing banks (commercial or central) carry out payments in their stead' (ibid.: 5, m.t.). The flow nature of money is a consequence of the way it is issued by banks and of the logical impossibility for banks as well as for any other institution to create a net asset.

Given that the creation of money defines, at the same time, a credit and a debit of the same amount for the issuing bank and for its client, it brings together in one and the same objective transaction a positive and a negative entry. Every issuing bank recovers instantaneously the money it creates.

What most economists have failed to observe is that double-entry bookkeeping requires the simultaneous credit and debit of each agent involved. They have thus ended up attributing the creditor and the debtor positions to two distinct agents, which would make the bank a net creditor and its client a net debtor.

The two positions, positive and negative, are verified both for the issuing bank *and* for its client. It is because the emission of money implies the credit-debit of F *and* the debit-credit of B for $x$ money units that it is a *creation-destruction* and not a net creation of money. From which it immediately follows that money cannot be deposited in time and that it cannot pertain to the category of stocks. A monetary emission being an instantaneous creation-destruction, no bank money can be stocked by the economy, which establishes beyond doubt that money's nature is that of a flow.

What banks can issue to the benefit of the economy is only a sum of units of account, of pure and valueless numbers. To this extent, money can be defined as a numerical form or as a numerical vehicle, a means of payment gratuitously provided by banks. Indeed, 'we speak of *creation* only when the operation is free of cost; on the contrary, we speak of *production* and of its result (the product) when the operation and thus its result are *costly*' (Schmitt 1995–96: 23, m.t.).

What banks create is merely the monetary form of transactions, that is, the nominal money required to convey payments between economic agents. What banks *cannot* create is the *object*, that is, the real money (income) required for payments to be redeeming. The intervention of banks as monetary intermediaries is therefore mandatory to provide the units of account required to give products their numerical expression and to provide the numerical means or vehicle required to convey payments between economic agents.

### *Money as a flow*

As a *numerical form*, money is an asset-liability lent by banks to the productive economy; as a *numerical vehicle*, money is a flow conveying payments from purchasers to sellers. When a bank lends its spontaneous acknowledgement of debt to a client, F, it agrees to carry out a payment on its behalf. What the bank agrees to lend to its client is only the *numerical means of payment* necessary to convey the payment and not its real content or object. '[T]he bank creates the payment and not its object, which means that it creates only the monetary form of the transaction considered; the *object* of the transaction is not created by the bank' (ibid.: 23, m.t.).

To create a payment is to provide a monetary flow, a vehicular money that in no way can be transformed into a stock. This is to say that (nominal) money is issued any time a payment occurs and is destroyed immediately after the payment has taken place. In a moment we will see that payments cannot be reduced to their monetary component and that when we consider their real component, stocks make their appearance and must be accounted for. For now, let us repeat that 'the object of money is a flow and not a stock [and that] nobody can transform a flow into a stock' (Schmitt 1998a: 5, m.t.).

Let us go back to the instant when a bank agrees to carry out a payment of say $x$ money units (m.u.) on behalf of its client F. When such an agreement is signed, B says to F that it is prepared to pay $x$ to its economic partners and F accepts to become a debtor to B up to the amount of the payment. The agreement is made before the payment occurs and is technically defined as the opening of a line of credit. Its bookkeeping representation is as follows (Table 1.1).

*Table 1.1* Opening of a credit line

| *Bank* | | | |
|---|---|---|---|
| *Assets* | | *Liabilities* | |
| Client F | m.u. x | Client F | m.u. x |

Even though the result of this double entry is zero, and no money unit has yet been created, Table 1.1 is useful to introduce the idea that the flow of money implies the contemporaneous credit-debit of each agent involved in a payment. It is true that the result of entry (1) is zero, yet it obtains by simultaneously crediting and debiting F for $x$ money units. This helps to understand that money is a flow precisely because in every transaction (payment) each of the two agents earns and spends it: each agent is at the same time credited and debited for the same amount of money.

Another interesting piece of information that we can derive from Table 1.1 is that, since double-entry bookkeeping is based on the *necessary equality* between credits and debits (assets and liabilities), by lending its own acknowledgement of debt, the bank enters a negative deposit on the liabilities side of its balance sheet and an equivalent positive deposit on the assets side. Through the opening of a line of credit, B simultaneously credits (positive deposit) and debits (negative deposit) F. How can the creation of money become nevertheless positive? This is what Schmitt explains in his analysis of money's purchasing power.

### *The purchasing power of money*

Defined as an asset-liability, money is nothing more than a numerical form deprived of any possible value. 'Let us say it from the outset: every sum of money is a collection of pure numbers' (Schmitt 1995–96: 37, m.t.). Its finality is to monetize the economy, to allow for real goods – physically heterogeneous – to acquire a numerical expression that makes them homogeneous. By issuing money, banks act as monetary intermediaries and provide the real economy with positive and negative numbers defining positive and negative bank deposits. How is it then that a valueless numerical form can acquire a positive purchasing power?

Schmitt deals with this question in his PhD thesis and in all his subsequent texts of the sixties and early seventies. Significantly enough, the title of his first published book is *La formation du pouvoir d'achat* (1960). In this important book, rich in ground-breaking intuitions that he developed along the years, Schmitt identifies the formation of money's purchasing power with what he calls 'the investment of money', making it immediately clear that the process through which money acquires a purchasing power is to be found in its relationship with real production.

As previously observed, one must understand the term 'investment' in its broadest meaning, that is, as referring to the whole of production. The investment of money is its 'association' with the production of consumption- and investment-goods, every specific production being subsumed in these two broad categories. Schmitt's objective is to show that (national) income results from the investment of money.

In contrast with the widespread opinion that money is created already endowed with a positive purchasing power so that the investment of money is identified with the expenditure of a pre-existing income, Schmitt starts his analysis from the observation that money is a valueless collection of numbers. 'Money, a collection of pure units of account, is thus deprived of purchasing power. This is the point of departure' (Schmitt 1960: 64, m.t.).

The problem he tackles is that of finding a monetary transaction granting the transformation of (nominal) money into income (real money). It is here that Schmitt refers to Keynes's fundamental equations and identifies, in the payment of the factors producing consumption- and investment-goods, the transaction defining the investment of money.

The identity between $C + I$ and $C' + I'$ is that between the income earned in the production of consumption- and investment-goods, on the one hand, and the income spent in the final purchase of consumption- and investment-goods on the other hand. Hence, income is first formed in the market for productive services and then spent on the commodity and financial markets.

> The monetary income of society is *spent* for the purchase of consumption-goods (C') and for the purchase of instrumental goods (I'). Income cannot be *formed* by these very purchases. We see only one category of expenditures that can engender it: the remuneration of the factors of production.
>
> (ibid.: 57, m.t.)

Schmitt first develops this idea in a paper entitled 'L'équilibre de la monnaie' (1959). There, he shows that money is substantially transformed when it is paid out to the factors of production. Schmitt puts forward three arguments that are worth recalling here, for they emphasize the passage from money as a pure unit of account (nominal money) to money 'invested' with a positive purchasing power (real money) by relating to the transformation of money into a new monetary possession. Indeed, when firms are lent money, they do not *own* it, but *owe* it to their banks. Formed as the object of a line of credit, money does not belong to firms.

The payment of the factors of production is radically different: workers become the owners of the monetary units they obtain in exchange for their productive services. As Schmitt observes, firms have to pay back their initial debit to banks, which they do by selling the produced output. The purchase of output entails the expenditure and simultaneous destruction of the income formed as the monetary possession of producers, which shows that the money paid to the factors of production is indeed formed as a positive purchasing power over current output.

In Schmitt's own words:

> a) Entrepreneurs do not lose the possession of distributed money, because they do not own it [...]. On the other hand, factors acquire the possession of distributed money. It follows that the distribution of [$x$] units of money to factors defines a net formation of [$x$] units of monetary possession within the body of society.

> b) Since distributed money must be paid back, the acquisition of goods is subsequent to their production. For goods to be acquired by society, it is necessary that the monetary possession disappears.
> c) The sacrifice of the new monetary possession suffices to the social acquisition of produced goods. From there it finally appears that *money distributed* to factors of production is invested with the power to purchase the new goods.
>
> (Schmitt 1959: 943, m.t.)

If we go back to our example, the payment for the production factors (W), carried out by bank B on behalf of its client F, would be entered in B's balance sheet as follows (Table 1.2).

The identity of client F is now revealed: the payment being that of the costs of production, F is a firm. As a result, W is the owner of a positive bank deposit whose object is a sum of produced goods that are financially deposited with B as real content of the negative deposit owned by F. We are thus confronted with two distinct bank monies. A *nominal* money, which banks simultaneously create and destroy, and a *real* money are formed through the monetization of produced output.

Nominal money has no *monetary* object, yet, through production, bank money acquires a *real* object. '[F]actors' remunerations *transform* money: they take it as a simple "personal" credit on banks and enrich it into a real credit, [...] *into the power to purchase newly produced goods*' (Schmitt 1966b: 97–8, m.t.). Even though the money issued in the monetization of output is immediately destroyed, an income (real money) takes its place. This new income defines W's credit and is matched by F's debit, where produced output is stocked.

While nominal money has no purchasing power, real money (income) has some, which derives from the association between nominal money and output as determined by the payment of its costs of production. 'This transformation of pure availability into possession, of money into monetary income, of personal credit into real credit is the whole problem of integration. Initially a circulatory means, money is formed into purchasing power' (Schmitt 1966a: 236, m.t.)

## *The formation of money's purchasing power*

As claimed by Schmitt (1998a), 'given that its nature is that of a flow, money can neither displace itself, nor any real good' (15, m.t.). This is to say that

*Table 1.2* Payment of production costs

| *Bank* | | | |
|---|---|---|---|
| *Assets* | | *Liabilities* | |
| Firm | m.u. x | Workers | m.u. x |

money acquires a real object through the payment related to production and that it is thanks to money that produced output is not directly appropriated by consumers but is formed as the real content or object of the income deposited with the issuing bank. 'Money creation meets this need: *it gives current production its nominal support*' (Schmitt 1966a: 169, m.t.).

What remains to be explained is the specific nature of the payment whereby (nominal) money turns into income (real money).

To say that this payment is that of the factors of production and that it corresponds to the payment of the costs of production of current output, is too generic because nothing is said about the specificity of these factors and costs. The analysis becomes more focused when it distinguishes between micro- and macroeconomic costs of production and it is made clear that the possible source of the purchasing power of money is the payment of the macroeconomic costs of production. Inter-industrial transactions imply the pre-existence of income and cannot be at its origin.

Having established that only macroeconomic costs matter when the formation of (national) income is at stake, the analysis must go further and determine what these macroeconomic costs are.

It is in his second published book, *Monnaie, salaires et profits* (1966a), and in a paper published by the *Revue d'économie politique* (1966b) that Schmitt provides the first proofs that labour is the only macroeconomic cost of production and the only source of income. In his 1966 book, Schmitt's demonstration develops following the method of progressive exclusion. He starts by showing that land cannot be considered a macroeconomic factor because it is not a necessary and sufficient condition of production. Land, in its broadest sense,

> is a necessary condition of every production (even in industries); but this condition being fulfilled, as it is, "from the beginning of each period", it is the foundation from which the work of man will develop, like weight is a condition of movement. In short, land is not a sufficient condition; and labour, logically subsequent, is a necessary and sufficient condition.
>
> (Schmitt 1966a: 280, m.t.)

Capital-goods, on the other hand, do not generate any new income. At most, they can maintain their value, but this is possible only through amortization, that is, through a new production of capital-goods that replaces the old one.

As we shall see in Chapter 6, the value lost by capital-goods is in a certain sense 'transferred' to newly produced output, but this simply means that capital-goods give up the value they receive: in no case are they the source of a new value. '[C]apital has no capacity to perpetuate itself, the illusion coming from the fact that the factors reproducing capital are accounted for in the same way as those producing with the aid of a given capital' (ibid.: 280, m.t.).

Finally, the 'entrepreneurship' factor is discarded because firms cannot 'project a monetary possession in their own assets' (ibid.: 280, m.t.). Firms can obtain an income (profit) by deriving it from a pre-existent income; they can never become the owners of a positive bank deposit created *ex nihilo*. Under no circumstances can firms benefit from a payment carried out by banks out of nothing.

Thus, it follows that *human labour* is the sole macroeconomic factor of production and that the *payment of wages* is the only transaction whose result is a net income for society as a whole, i.e. a macroeconomic income. Being at the origin of a net income, labour is also the source of economic value (a mere numerical relationship between money and produced output) and, as such, it cannot identify with any real good whatsoever. Together with the fact that workers are paid via the emission of purely nominal money, this means that the payment of wages cannot be identified with the purchase of labour or, in other words, that wages are not the counterpart of labour or of its product. 'In no case are wages the counterpart of labour: wages are simply the very definition, in a numerical form, of workers' product' (Schmitt 1995–96: 78, m.t.).

### *Human labour as the source of the purchasing power of money*

Schmitt was able to provide further proofs of labour being the sole macroeconomic factor of production, the most profound being based on the nature of money and on the possibility for a payment to imply the financial deposit of produced output in the banking system. A payment giving rise to new income is a payment implying the substitution of a real production for money, which means that 'money creation is but the mirror image of real production' (Schmitt 1998a: 18, m.t.).

It is the payment of wages that, by enabling produced output to become the real content of a bank deposit, makes this substitution possible. Indeed, the payment of wages is the only transaction creating a monetary deposit whose object is a real product financially deposited with banks.

At the very moment wages are paid, they are deposited, and the object of the deposit is the product of workers, which they receive in the form of money. The *absolute exchange* between the product of workers and this same product in the form of money establishes the logical identity between monetary and real wages.

An absolute exchange is an exchange between physical goods and money units, whereby the physical output is *changed* or transformed into a sum of money. It is not an exchange between two terms, each having its own value, but between a real and a monetary term, where money is a mere sum of numerical units of account.

In other words, 'emission of money and production of goods are one and the same action implying a monetary or numerical face and one real face' (Schmitt 1995–96: 52, m.t.). The payment of wages is the only payment granting the absolute exchange between real products and money, which is why human labour is the sole macroeconomic factor of production.

Let us reproduce here the proof provided by the French economist in the *Annex* of his unpublished typescript of 1998.

- Real production is positive only if a creation of money (temporarily) takes its place.
- Only the "factors" of a positive production are true factors of production.
- Only economic agents that can be paid in money units can therefore be factors of production.
- Labour can be paid in this way, but capital cannot; it is formally impossible to substitute a creation of money for the (assumed) production of capital.

(Schmitt 1998b: 13, m.t.)

The crucial idea here is that money is the only numerical form of products and that the macroeconomic transaction on which our monetary economic systems are founded is the substitution of a creation of money for a real production.

Monetary units must replace produced output, which is their real object or content, and it is through the payment of the factors of production that this substitution occurs. Now, the only payments individuals can benefit from, and which define a creation of money, is the payment of wages to workers. 'Only *individuals* can obtain a sum of money' (ibid.: 12, m.t.); neither land nor capital can be paid through money creation. It is true that rent and interest are paid to individuals, i.e. the owners of land and/or capital, yet these payments require the pre-existence of an income: none of them can be carried out through money creation.

> It would be illogical to claim that a substitution can occur between income and real productions; only sums of money – and not sums of monetary income – can replace real products; every income is the *result* of the substitution of a real production by a monetary creation.
>
> (ibid.: 13, m.t. and emphasis)

It is worth noting that, as was so often the case with him, Schmitt had already announced this proof in 1966. On page 280 of *Monnaie, salaires et profits* he writes that, indeed, 'labour is the only factor of production; any criticism would rest on the wrong understanding of today's money, which intervenes daily between real production and its appropriation' (m.t.).

### *Money and exchange*

The payment of wages is the only transaction through which real output is given a monetary form. Through it 'labour obtains the whole output *in monetary form*; because, distributed to wage-earners, money is enriched [...] of the power to purchase current production' (ibid.: 281, m.t.).

Schmitt confirms the centrality of production and of the payment of wages when he dismisses the possibility of relative exchange to create money. In a hypothetical economy of exchange without production, no money could be created. 'From the moment an economy is "monetized", it is its production that is so [monetized]; from the moment an economy does not involve any production or does not monetize any of its productions, it is necessarily deprived of any money' (Schmitt 1995–96: 43, m.t.).

As shown by Schmitt (1998a), it is double-entry bookkeeping that provides proof that no money creation can occur in an economy based on relative exchanges. Indeed, when a bank carries out a payment in favour of its client C on behalf of client A, it must immediately obtain compensation for it. Double entry requires it. The bank carries out the payment by issuing its own acknowledgement of debt and thus incurs a debt that an equivalent credit must instantaneously match. 'It is therefore necessary that the object of the payment be deposited with the bank at the very moment the bank carries out the payment' (Schmitt 1998a: 13, m.t.).

If the economy were an economy of relative exchanges, the payment of C would transfer to C the real asset previously owned by A. Yet, it would be impossible for the real object of the payment to be simultaneously transferred to C and deposited with the bank.

In Schmitt's own words: 'it is impossible for the term of a relative exchange to exists twice at the same instant, a first time with one of the traders and a second time with the bank taking over the monetary payment of this term' (ibid.: 13, m.t.). The only possible solution rests on the payment of wages and on the substitution that it entails between real output and money.

Production and money creation are so closely linked that, in absolute exchange, one takes the place of the other, which is what substantially distinguishes macro- from microeconomics. Now, it is through the payment of wages that physical output is deposited with the bank and earned by workers in a monetary form. Wage-earners obtain their product not in kind but as the real object of their money-income. In conformity with double-entry bookkeeping, the product is simultaneously present in a negative deposit of the bank and as the real content of wages. '[W]age payments are actions that transform, convert or change real productions into creation of money units' (Schmitt 1998a: 18, m.t.).

Real production and monetary creation are the two terms of an absolute exchange, which is an exchange between two identical terms. Schmitt's concept of absolute exchange derives logically from his analysis of money's purchasing power and can be found *in nuce* (in a nutshell) in *Monnaie, salaires et profits*: 'the money distributed to the factors of production is suddenly transformed into purchasing power; it has newly produced output in its power' (Schmitt 1966a: 255, m.t.). Indeed, money acquires its purchasing power when it is transformed into income through the payment of wages.

Given that income is nothing other than the 'product-in-the-money', that is, money enriched with real content, it logically follows that the payment of wages brings forth the transformation or the change of physical output into a sum of money.

> *The exchange of a given product against itself is* [...] *a piece of information of the greatest scientific interest since this absolute exchange is defined as a monetary exchange.* The proposition on which the entire body of macroeconomics is founded is thereby the following: *in each period every country exchanges its total product against a sum of purely numerical money.*
>
> (Schmitt 1995–96: 37, m.t.)

It is because money is essentially made up of numbers and because production associates current output with numbers that absolute exchange is the cornerstone of macroeconomics. As we have already pointed out, when banks carry out the payment of wages on behalf of firms, physical output becomes the real content of firms' negative deposit and the object of wage-earners' positive deposit.

## Banks' monetary and financial intermediation

The substitution of monetary creation to real production requires the intermediation of banks and firms.

> In a regime of paid work, workers are confronted with two distinct intermediaries, namely, the firm where they carry out their activity and their country's banking system. By exerting their function "hand in hand", firm and bank substitute a creation of money for workers' real production.
>
> (Schmitt 1998a: 18, m.t.)

On the other hand, banks' intermediation is of two different kinds: monetary and financial.

### *Monetary intermediation*

When they monetize the economy by issuing their acknowledgement of debt and by paying wages on behalf of firms, banks act as monetary intermediaries. The nature of money being that of a flow, banks issue it, use it, and recover it all at once as a numerical means of payment.

When bank B pays wage-earners W on behalf of firm F, F and W are simultaneously credited and debited in nominal money and, through the circular flow of money, firm F is debited, and workers are credited in real money.

The existence of the instantaneous circulation of money is difficult to grasp, in particular because entries in banks' books concern the result of money flows and not the flows themselves. Table 1.2 does not show the flows involved in the payment of wages. If we were to introduce, explicitly, the entries relative to these flows, we would have to enter them similarly to what Schmitt did in

*Table 1.3* Stocks and flows concerning the payment of wages

| *Bank* | | | |
|---|---|---|---|
| *Assets* | | *Liabilities* | |
| Firm, stock | m.u. x | Firm, flow (1) | m.u. x |
| Firm, flow (2) | m.u. x | Workers, flow (3) | m.u. x |
| Firm, flow (4) | m.u. x | Workers, bank deposits | m.u. x |

a paper he wrote for his students in the early seventies and entitled *Monnaie matérielle et monnaie bancaire; flux monétaires et stocks de monnaie* (Table 1.3).

Flow (1) shows that when bank B pays workers W on behalf of firm F, it both credits and debits F in (nominal) money. The credit of F stands for the spontaneous acknowledgement of debt incurred by B and lent to F, while its debit describes the fact that F takes advantage of its line of credit and, as a consequence, spends – in the payment of W – the money lent to it by B.

Credited, flow (1), and debited, flow (2), of a sum of nominal money equal to *x*, the firm incurs a debt of *x* units of real money, a stock, to the bank. That is, '*flows* (1) and (2) generate a deficit in the bank creating money, a net liability that is balanced by a *stock*' (Schmitt 1973b: 16, m.t.).

On the other hand, workers are credited in money following the payment of wages flow (3) and are also immediately debited (flow (4)): money flows back to the bank and workers obtain a net credit in real money, that is, wage-earners become the owners of a bank deposit whose real object is the physical output stocked with the firm. 'It is not at all difficult to grasp the exact meaning of the debit of [W] at instant t: this debit simply means that [W] acquires, at instant t, a positive deposit with the bank' (Schmitt 1995–96: 19, m.t.).

The circular flow of (nominal) money leaves behind it a negative and a positive bank deposit. The negative deposit accommodates financially the product physically stocked with the firm, while the positive deposit defines the purchasing power owned by workers. Wage-earners own current output in money, a result that is made possible by the monetary intermediation of B and which implies the simultaneous creation of a negative deposit for F and a positive deposit for W.

> It seems difficult, at first, to advocate the formation of *negative* deposits, a concept that is new. However, this concept is imposed by logical analysis. Since it is established that a positive deposit is formed to the benefit of income holders, it inevitably follows, as an effect of a symmetry that is self-evident, that a negative deposit of the same value is formed for [F].
>
> (ibid.: 38, m.t.)

The transaction that monetizes production is a payment defining a creation of money, and the creation of money implies its simultaneous presence in the worlds of positive and negative numbers. 'The flow "in creation" is not "conservative"; it is mutant: being nourished by a money equal to zero, at one extremity it creates a negative money, and at the other, it projects a positive money' (Schmitt 1966a: 235, m.t.). It thus appears that the flow nature of money is the direct result of the fact that it is issued by banks in conformity with the principles of double-entry bookkeeping.

### *Financial intermediation*

In *La formation du pouvoir d'achat* (1960), Schmitt had already understood that the role played by money is not that of an intermediary or a medium of exchange, but that of separating production, the formation of income, from consumption, the final expenditure of income.

> *The remuneration of producers ensures the co-formation of products and of monetary power (money's purchasing power). Money is not merely an intermediary in the process of exchange; it goes much deeper, intervening between the production of goods and their acquisition.*
>
> (Schmitt 1960: 147, m.t.)

Banks are thus called to act not only as monetary intermediaries, but also as *financial intermediaries*. Besides issuing money, they receive as a deposit the income formed by the monetization of production and lend it out to their clients. The best-known form of financial intermediation is the loan of saved-up income. What often remains somehow hidden is the financial intermediation that banks assure automatically at the instant wages are paid and income forms.

What happens to the income deposited in the form of wages?

Once more, the right answer is provided by double-entry bookkeeping. Indeed, if firms were to spend their own deposit on the payment of wages, this payment would not give rise to a negative deposit of F. What characterizes the payment of wages made by banks (see Table 1.2) is the formation of a negative deposit for F, which is entered on the assets side of banks' balance sheets. What makes possible the formation of such a negative deposit is the expenditure by firms of the positive deposit of wage-earners. Therefore, the negative deposit of firms is the mirror image of the positive deposit of workers. This means that banks lend to firms the positive deposit of wage-earners, which 'feeds' firms' payment of wages.

As soon as income is formed, it is deposited with the banking system and becomes the object of financial intermediation. Banks immediately and automatically lend to firms the income earned by workers and entered on the liabilities side of B's balance sheet. Before the payment of wages, no income is available in the system. Wages can nevertheless be paid, because this payment does not require the availability of any pre-existing income.

As soon as wages are paid to wage-earners, a positive deposit is formed, and banks append a financial intermediation to their monetary one. The traditional claim that banks finance production is therefore correct only to the extent that it refers to the payment of wages, and that the funding has its source in the income formed by the payment itself. This is to say that wage-earners are at the origin of the income lent to firms, whose initial investment is financed by wage-earners and not by banks, which are mere financial intermediaries.

The coexistence of a monetary and a financial intermediation is the mark of monetary transactions. In particular, in the payment of wages, monetary intermediation defines a circular flow, from and to B, triggering the formation of real money, an income deposited with B, which feeds a financial intermediation. For the time being, let us consider what happens when income is spent for the final purchase of produced output and, secondly, let us consider the logical relationship between production and consumption established by the intervention of money as the flow of payments.

## Money and the logical relationship between production and consumption

In his 1959 paper, Schmitt writes that

> goods are not acquired by society merely through their physical production. In order to switch from production to acquisition of goods, society must take on an additional cost: it must sacrifice its additional monetary possessions. *Products do not acquire products, the purchasing power of money does it, and undoes itself in this exercise.*
>
> (Schmitt 1959: 947, m.t.)

This idea is summed up in *La formation du pouvoir d'achat*, where Schmitt claims, referring to Keynes's fundamental equations, that the expenditure of income in the final purchase of consumption- and investment-goods entails its destruction.

> [T]he money spent for the purchase of consumption-goods is at once dis-invested of its purchasing power: C' is disappearance, elimination of the monetary income of society. [...] As the purchase of consumption-goods, the purchases of investment-goods erase the power of money.
>
> (Schmitt 1960: 67, m.t.)

While production gives rise to a negative deposit of firms and to a positive deposit of workers, the final purchase of produced output entails a debit of workers and a credit of firms: both negative and positive deposits reduce to zero.

Let us substitute workers with income holders, IH, that is, let us consider the situation once the initial income formed through the payment of wages has been partly redistributed among a variety of economic agents. Such a transfer is

*Table 1.4* Redistribution of income from workers to income holders

| *Bank* | | | |
|---|---|---|---|
| *Assets* | | *Liabilities* | |
| Firms | m.u. x | Workers | m.u. x |
| Workers | m.u. x | Income holders | m.u. x |
| Firms | m.u. x | Income holders | m.u. x |

*Table 1.5* Final expenditure of income

| *Bank* | | | |
|---|---|---|---|
| *Assets* | | *Liabilities* | |
| (1) Firms | m.u. x | Income holders | m.u. x |
| (2) Income holders | m.u. x | Firms | m.u. x |
| | 0 | | 0 |

a microeconomic operation that does not alter the amount of income available in the economy (Table 1.4).

The final expenditure of *x* units of income by IH is entered, as in entry (2) of Table 1.5, and the immediate compensation between the debit and credit of income holders and the credit and debit of firms reduces to zero the end balance of both income holders and firms.

This shows that two half-emissions make up the emission of income, a negative half-emission following necessarily every positive half-emission.

What is true of money is also necessarily true of income. Money does not survive its creation and is destroyed as soon as it is spent, that is, any time banks carry out a payment on behalf of their clients. Income also is destroyed when it is spent on the final purchase of real goods, the difference being that while money is created and destroyed simultaneously, income is created by production, say at time $t_0$, and is destroyed only later, say at $t_1$, when it is spent by income holders and their monetary possession is replaced by a real possession.

> Money is not invested with its purchasing power forever; time comes when society changes its monetary income into a real income. This conversion, which defines the loss of monetary income, takes place through the social purchase of produced goods. This can be explained without a major effort. Only money newly acquired by society is invested with a [purchasing] power. Now, by purchasing produced goods, society sacrifices its new monetary possession.
>
> (Schmitt 1959: 944, m.t.)

Let us call consumption the final purchase of produced output, whether it is made up of consumption-goods only or of consumption- and investment-goods.

Production at $t_0$ coincides with the payment of wages and defines the first emission of nominal money, resulting in the formation of a real money (income) initially owned by wage-earners. Consumption, at $t_1$, defines another emission (creation-destruction) of nominal money and entails the final destruction of the real money spent by income holders.

The first and the second emission of money are logically complementary, the first being necessarily followed by the second. This is so because, even though both emissions define the simultaneous creation and destruction of nominal money, the first is a positive creation of real money and the second is required to complete its emission.

In the real world, there is no room for lasting net creations; an equivalent event of opposite sign, a destruction, must complete every creation. This is precisely what happens here. The first emission of money is a creation-destruction defining the monetization of production. The second emission of money is another creation-destruction (again of nominal money) defining the demonetization of production. 'The outflow [first emission of money] leads money to its transformation into income. The inflow [second emission of money] is the opposite movement when monetary income is finally lost through its transformation into real products' (Schmitt 1966a: 226, m.t.).

In *Monnaie, salaires et profits*, the necessary complementarity of production and consumption, that is, of the formation and the destruction of real money, is explained in terms of the negative deposit formed when banks pay wage-earners on behalf of firms. This deposit defines the debt of firms, and one can visualize it as a 'hole', which will be filled up only when produced output is purchased by income holders and income converted into real goods.

Schmitt shows that the filling of the hole is a necessary and sufficient condition for the emission of income to be completed.

First, it is necessary because firms must pay back banks. 'Seen from the viewpoint of firms, the monetary remuneration of factors is the beginning of a circle to be completed. Between outflow and inflow, formation and expenditure of income, unity is truly circular' (Schmitt 1966a: 255, m.t.).

Second, it is a sufficient condition, because if the hole disappears, circulation ends, and no income remains. It thus follows that

> [n]ew goods are produced and acquired in the social setting only on condition that the monetary 'hole' disappears. And there is only one way to fill that 'hollow': monetary holdings are dropped into it and are voided for everyone to see.
>
> (ibid.: 255, m.t.)

In conclusion, money acquires a positive purchasing power when it is associated with current output, and produced output is '*definitively acquired in the social space only through the final expenditure, the cancellation of distributed income*' (ibid.: 255, m.t.). As already claimed by Schmitt in 1960, 'born out of production, [money's purchasing] power is cancelled through consumption. [...] The instantaneous effect of every social purchase is the abolition of purchasing power' (Schmitt 1960: 148–49, m.t.).

## Schmitt's theory of bank money compared with orthodox and heterodox analyses

Schmitt himself evaluates the main contributions of classical and neoclassical economists to the analysis of money and exposes their logical shortcomings. He has a predilection for Ricardo, whose logical rigour he admires. However, he rejects the Anglo-Portuguese economist's analysis of money and of its purchasing power, because money identified with a commodity runs into the problem that its value as a means of payment usually differs from its value as a commodity.

While it is true that Ricardo's search for an invariable standard of value was doomed to failure, because he was looking for a commodity whose production was to always imply the same proportion of variable and fixed capital, it is also true that, for Ricardo and the Classics, 'money circulating in a society, whatever its abundance, has always the power to purchase only the products already produced' (ibid.: 127, m.t.).

The duality of money as such and money as a commodity is what makes the Classics' analysis obsolete and what led Walras to replace the concept of absolute value with that of relative prices. This passage signalled that progress had been made in that it did away with the identification of value with a dimensional quality of goods (such as embodied labour) and introduced the idea of value being a relationship between real goods and numbers.

Walras's concept of *numéraire*, however, would have been truly innovative if Walras himself had not ended up switching from the *numéraire* as such (a mere numerical form) to the *numéraire* as a commodity chosen from the set of produced goods.

Walras's failure to see that it is through the mediation of a money-*numéraire* that produced output can find its numerical expression led to the development of general equilibrium analysis, a theoretical framework that leaves no room for money and admits only direct exchange between real goods.

Fisher's attempt to introduce money into the neoclassical setting and determine the purchasing power of money through its famous equation, $MV = PT$, leads nowhere for at least two reasons.

First, the equation $MV = PT$ is nothing more than a tautology, a mere definition of prices that cannot be used to determine any of its terms.

> Fisher's equation, which indicates the equality of price with its definition, that is, with itself, is satisfied whatever the state of the world, real and monetary, were it to be in equilibrium, in disequilibrium or in an impenetrable eternal chaos.
>
> (Schmitt 1959: 924, m.t.)

Second, the equation is believed to explain money's purchasing power, which is defined as the inverse of the general price level, through the adjustment of its two terms. In other words, Fisher's analysis claims that money's purchasing power can be derived from exchange, which is at odds with Fisher's own claim that 'the price level is not determined by individual prices, but [...], on the contrary, any individual price presupposes a price level' (Fisher 1925: 180).

If the price level precedes the determination of individual prices, how can it derive from exchange, that is, from the transaction that is assumed to determine individual prices? In reality, as shown by Schmitt (1960), exchange cannot be the place where money's purchasing power is exercised *and at the same time* formed.

> Money exchanges against goods, because it has the power to do so. Unquestionable proposition. Money derives its power from exchange. Absurd proposition. The same act cannot both exert and create purchasing power. The power is used in exchange; thus, it is formed separately. [...] Purchase is a manifestation of the monetary power: its exercise, its use, its application, *its expenditure*. [Purchasing] Power cannot come out of purchase, because [purchasing] power is the condition of purchase.
>
> (Schmitt 1960: 134–35, m.t.)

And what can we say about modern heterodox economics? More specifically, is post-Keynesian macroeconomic analysis of money in line with Schmitt's?

To answer this question, let us refer to the work of Graziani, one of the most influential post-Keynesian economists who investigated the monetary circuit, and who knew Schmitt personally and was acquainted with his work. After each meeting between the two economists and between Graziani and myself, it became clearer that the main controversial point concerned the distinction between money and income. According to the Italian economist, banks finance production, and the payment of wages is the expenditure of a positive amount of (real) money issued by them. 'Through the credit obtained from banks, firms are capable to start the productive process, by purchasing labour and means of production' (Graziani 1988: xx, m.t.).

No distinction is drawn between nominal and real money, and the circuit of money is likened to a flow of income, which is not so far away from the neoclassical idea of a stock set in motion. So much so that Graziani and, in general, the great majority of post-Keynesian economists, maintain that the circuit of money is inscribed in chronological time and that money flows back to its point of emission more or less rapidly.

Consumer behaviour, like the behaviour of firms and banks is an element influencing the circulation of money and determining whether it takes place in an equilibrated way or not (see Graziani 1988). This is another point of divergence between post-Keynesian analysis and Schmitt's analysis: according to the latter money is a flow so that its circulation can only be instantaneous irrespective of economic agents' behaviour, whereas, according to the former, behaviour matters and the circulation of money takes time. In this respect, Schmitt's analysis of money is entirely macroeconomic, while microeconomic considerations continue to heavily influence post-Keynesian positions.

The distinction between nominal and real money is not straightforward, one of the reasons being the level of abstraction needed to grasp the a-dimensional, purely nominal nature of bank money. The instantaneous flow of money is another concept that requires the capacity to capture intellectually what our senses cannot physically discern, though it exists in reality. Double-entry bookkeeping comes to our rescue here: it provides a representation of the marks left by money's instantaneous circulation every time it is used as a means of (or a numerical vehicle for) payments.

It is encouraging to observe that Graziani – an open-minded economist truly interested in research and ready to discuss and, if convinced, follow new ideas – considered Schmitt's distinction between money and income with the greatest attention and told me, when we last met in Lugano, that he believed to have finally understood and accepted it.

# 2 The building blocks of a theory of national money

## From *Monnaie salaires et profits* (1966) to *Théorie unitaire de la monnaie, nationale et internationale* (1975)

Another important step in Schmitt's analysis of money is his investigation of the role played by the payment of wages within a theory of money's circular flow. Based on the logical implications of Keynes's fundamental identities, Schmitt's analysis of the relationship between income creation and income destruction (and of the monetary circular flows it implies) leads to a macroeconomic definition of national income unrelated to the idea of aggregation advocated by mainstream economists. The identification of national income with nominal wages derives from the very nature of money and its connection with produced output. Schmitt's theory of the monetary circuit provides the logical foundations for this identification while, at the same time, accounting for the formation of profit. This chapter pieces together Schmitt's original analysis of monetary circular flow. It is based, essentially, on his books *Monnaie, salaires et profits* (1966) and *Théorie unitaire de la monnaie, nationale et internationale* (1975), as well as on a manuscript distributed to his students in the early 1970s, which I have entitled *Théorie du circuit* and dated 1972, and on a paper co-authored with Spartaco Greppi and published in 1996.

### The logical relationship between wages and national income

The asset-liability nature of bank money and the centrality of human labour are the key elements of Schmitt's monetary macroeconomics, one of their main implications being that national income is determined by the totality of direct and indirect wages paid out in each economic system. Far from being too restrictive, this definition is sufficiently broad to encompass any productive activity measured in money units. Independent workers of any kind can indeed be considered as part of the broad category of wage-earners since the purchase of their output defines a twofold operation: a final purchase and an implicit payment of labour.

Whether workers sell their labour services or their products, a monetization occurs that assimilates their activity with that of wage-earners. When workers are wage-earners, their product 'fills up' the negative deposit of firms, which it will 'leave' the moment income holders pay for its final purchase. When workers' production coincides with the sale of its result, the

DOI: 10.4324/9781351271325-5

product is instantaneously moved in and out from a negative deposit. It is as if workers who sell their productive services directly to consumers were also a firm.

To identify national income with the total amount of nominal wages is tantamount to confirming Keynes's claim that wage-units are the only proper unit of measure in economics. The search for a satisfactory standard goes back to the early days of economic analysis, but it was Keynes who first seriously questioned the old-fashioned conceptions based on the choice of a dimensional unit. The discovery of the wage-unit rests on two fundamental principles of Keynes's analysis: the key role played by human labour, and the identity between national income and the macroeconomic cost of producing consumption- and investment-goods.

To be sure, Keynes's search for the correct unit of measure in economics is not straightforward and his concept of wage-unit is still unclear. As Harcourt and Riach (1997) pointed out, he seems to hesitate between the choice of the labour-unit as *numéraire* and that of the wage-unit as a fully accomplished standard. The decisive step toward a modern definition of the true *numéraire* requires the final rejection of any idea of the economic standard as a 'substance' or a 'dimension'. Keynes was not far from this, as is confirmed by his decision to retain the wage-unit and not the labour-unit, as the proper economic unit of measure.

It is Schmitt's analysis of money that provides the definitive arguments in favour of Keynes's wage-unit. No solution will be found as long as an economic unit of measure is searched for within a theoretical framework where prices are assumed to be determined through the direct exchange of already existing goods. And the reason is that money units are goods and 'a good can neither measure itself, nor measure another good' (Schmitt 1998a: 61, m.t.). The only way out is 'to start not from already existing goods, but from the creation of goods' (ibid.: 61, m.t.). In order to make physically heterogeneous goods homogeneous it is necessary to give them a common or measurable form, and this is precisely what happens when physical objects are transformed into or created as economic products. Economic products are created through the payment of wages and are given a numerical form that makes them homogeneous.

Numbers, though not a unit of measure, are a necessary component of any unit of measure. Likewise, money is necessary to express wages numerically and thus 'counts' or expresses numerically produced goods and services. Yet, money in itself is not and cannot be the economic unit of measure, because products can be expressed in money units only if they are given a numerical form, which can be done only through the payment of wages. The unit of measure is determined by the same transaction that gives physical output the numerical form of money. This means that the unit of measure is *both* a unit of money *and* a product. 'It would be mistaken to judge that the unit of measure is a product; it is not so simple, because it is a product seized within money' (ibid.: 66, m.t.).

The logical identity of form and content leads to the logical identity of product and wages and, consequently, of national income and nominal wages. It is through the payment of wages that money acquires real content and is transformed into income. It thus follows that wages are the totality of income created by production. At the same time, the payment of wages transforms the physical output into economic goods, which implies that the totality of produced output is necessarily made up of wage-goods. But, if the totality of production consists of wage-goods and the totality of income is measured in wages, how can we explain the existence of profit-goods and non-wage income?

### *The first step toward a theory of profit*

In *Monnaie, salaires et profits* (1966), Schmitt provides the first elements of a theory of profit that he would not complete until the 1980s. He begins by observing that neither the Classics nor the neo-Classics provide a satisfactory explanation of the way profits are formed and spent.

The Classics consider profit and wages as complementary parts of national income, while claiming that labour is the sole source of value. This means that 'national income is a *global* datum, resulting from the totality of spent labour (Schmitt 1966a: 284, m.t.). Income is formed as a whole by labour and is only subsequently subdivided into wages and profit: this is the foundation of Smith's and Ricardo's analysis. As for Marx's attempt, its difference resides in that, in his view, the totality of labour is made up of two complementary parts: the labour necessary for the reproduction of workers' labour power and that spent on the production of surplus-value. Be that as it may, both analyses are confronted with an insurmountable obstacle: the law of exchange between equivalents, which imposes the necessary equality of prices and values.

If profits must derive from labour, and if labour is given as a whole, their formation must take place through a transfer operated in the commodity market. Yet, such a transfer is possible only if the produced output can be sold at a price higher than its value, which contradicts the law of exchange.

> Smith and Ricardo faced a great difficulty, which continues to puzzle us today. If price is identical to value, selling can only be the exact repetition of products formation, the market being unable to operate the slightest redistribution of the product between its initial and its final holders.
>
> (Schmitt 1979: 5.12, m.t.)

If profits, as Marx claimed, emerge in the production process derived from surplus-labour, then the law of exchange is a fatal obstacle to the monetary realization of surplus-value. Real goods obtained cost-free by firms cannot be sold on the commodity market, because the only income available in the economy is that earned by workers and corresponds to the value of their wage-goods.

Whether we choose the explanation provided by Smith and Ricardo or we prefer Marx's theory of surplus-value, we are still troubled by the impossibility of reconciling their analyses with the logical constraint imposed by the law of exchange. In the absence of a monetary theory of production, and because they identified value with a substance, the Classics could in no way introduce a degree of freedom between prices and values while respecting their necessary equality.

General equilibrium analysis, GEA, fares worse. In the neoclassical theoretical framework, there is no room for profit, because for Walras and his followers the market for goods was indistinguishable from the market for productive services. 'The unity between the two markets (services and products) denotes the economy of exchange and the intrinsic incapacity of the model to extend to the economy of production' (Schmitt 1966a: 285, m.t.). Every monetary transaction in the general equilibrium system is a purchase; the remuneration of productive services pertains therefore to the category of purchases, as is the case for the sale of goods on the commodity market. This implies that 'firms are intermediaries and transfer what they obtain' (ibid.: 285, m.t.) so that profits 'are null by definition' (ibid.: 285, m.t.).

What Schmitt is looking for is a theory of profit consistent with the fact that labour is the sole macroeconomic factor of production and that, as a necessary consequence, wages are the sole source of national income. The identity between nominal wages, *W*, and national income, *Y*, indicates that profit can derive only from the final expenditure of households: 'only the final purchases carried out by *households* are a source of profit; final purchases by firms are mere conversions of already existing profits' (Schmitt 1996d: 34, m.t.).

### *Profit and wages*

Schmitt takes over Keynes's intuition that profit is included in wages. To a first approximation, profit is thus an income derived from wages: a *substitution* income. 'To the extent of their profit, entrepreneurs take the place of productive factors in the possession of distributed money' (Schmitt 1960: 83, m.t.). It is in the goods market that profit is formed. By selling produced output at a mark-up, firms are able to derive part of the wages initially paid to wage-earners. This transfer of purchasing power from households to firms can be explained by introducing a distinction between what Schmitt calls '*social expenditures*' and '*individual expenditures*'.

Social expenditures are determined by the economic value of purchased goods and imply the destruction of the equivalent amount of income spent on their purchase. Individual expenditures define the total amount spent by income holders in their purchase of produced output and can include a transfer of income to the benefit of firms, because the amount spent on individual purchases can exceed the cost of production of the goods sold by firms. Hence, for example, if 100 units of money-income are paid for goods whose production costs are 100 wage-units, individual expenditures coincide with social expenditures, and no profit is formed. If the same goods, whose social price is 100 wage-units, were sold at an individual price of 200 wage-units, the individual expenditure of 100 income units by income holders would define a social expenditure of 50 wage-units only and a transfer of 50 wage-units to firms. 'Social expenditures are to individual expenditures what social price is to individual price. The arithmetical complement of this ratio defines the rate at which other agents, notably entrepreneurs, replace productive factors in the possession of distributed money' (Schmitt 1959: 945, m.t.).

The message conveyed by Schmitt in his early publications centres on the analysis of money and its integration with real goods. It is the formation of money's purchasing power that is now foregrounded. Unsurprisingly, therefore, his initial analysis of profit emphasizes the fact that wages being the only income created by production, profits can only be formed as substitution income. '*Profits are positive incomes because they are incomes of substitution*' (Schmitt 1966a: 288, m.t.). Schmitt distinguishes between three categories of expenditures: those that create, those that destroy, and those that transfer income. The payment of wages pertains to the first category and is the source of money's purchasing power. Social expenditure belongs to the second category and defines the complementarity aspect of the emission of wages. Profit pertains to the third category; it comes from the difference between individual and social prices.

Wages, both direct and indirect, define the totality of national income, yet profit can be positive. To achieve this, all you need to know is that '*firms succeed in selling their products at prices higher than distributed wages*' (ibid.: 288, m.t.). When the expenditure of income holders covers the cost of production of purchased goods, the income spent is destroyed: the positive bank deposit of income holders matches the negative bank deposit of firms, and they reciprocally cancel out. If the income spent is greater than the cost of production (measured in wage-units), the difference goes to firms and takes the form of profit.

Income is formed in the labour market *and is formed as a whole*, no distinction being possible between wage and non-wage income. As Schmitt claimed, 'in terms of flows, net incomes are all wages' (Schmitt 1996b: 56, m.t.). The transformation of wages into profit concerns the *stock* aspect of income. This means that the totality of national income is formed in a transaction (a flow) only: the payment of wages so that profit is not an income of production. Yet the stock of income generated by production can be subdivided into (real) wages and profit. Hence, profit is formed through a repartitioning of wages. 'Production generates wages only; repartition is the operation by which withdrawals are operated on wages in favour of profit' (ibid.: 56, m.t.).

Finally, while national income, $Y$, is defined by the totality of (nominal) wages, $W$,

$$Y \equiv W, \tag{2.1}$$

once formed, it can be redistributed between wages and profit

$$Y \equiv \text{real wages} + \text{real profit}. \tag{2.2}$$

Both equations, (2.1) and (2.2), are correct and perfectly consistent with one another, because (2.1) refers to the formation of national income, whereas (2.2) concerns its subsequent subdivision. (2.1) describes an expenditure, a flow, while (2.2) describes a stock situation resulting from the substitution of firms for households as income holders.

## Schmitt's first explanation of profit is incomplete

As pointed out by Schmitt himself, the explanation of profit based on the process of circulation is problematic. There is a snare in the claim that profit is formed through the sale of produced output at a price inclusive of profit: the law of exchange establishing the necessary equality between price and value. An insurmountable obstacle, as long as money is treated as a commodity, because a commodity-money can only be used in exchanges between equivalent terms. At first sight, moving from the old-fashioned and wrong conception of money as a substance to that of money as a mere numerical form does not seem to be enough to overcome this obstacle. Indeed, it would be incongruous to state that a unit of money can have both a purchasing power determined by its value and a purchasing power determined by its price.

One might as well claim that value and price are two distinct units of measure, a claim that would be fatal to the theory and would leave profit totally unexplained. 'The value of money (its content) having been determined, it can only be strictly the same in the market for the factors of production and in the market for products' (ibid.: 53, m.t.). A rigorous and accomplished theory of profit must be able to show that firms' income can indeed be derived from wages, a *conditio sine qua non*, without contradicting the logical identity of values and prices. To this extent, the analysis developed by Schmitt in the first decade of his research activity remains incomplete.

Once again, another argument provided by Schmitt helps to clarify what is missing in theory confined to the explanation of profit formation in the circulating process. If we were to limit our analysis to the market for products claiming that profit is both formed and spent in the purchase of produced output, we would deprive ourselves of the possibility of explaining the very existence of profit-goods. Indeed, if firms were to derive their profit from the expenditure of wages and were to spend it on purchasing part of current output, they would merely obtain an amount of wage-goods. The reason for this is that the real content of money is entirely made up of wage-goods, and that goods do not change their economic definition no matter who purchases them in the product market.

> Whatever the identity of buyers, households or firms, it is logically impossible that through the expenditure of their income they obtain objects other than the goods 'housed' by money: [...] profit-goods would definitively be wage-goods if they were obtained through payments made directly in the market for produced goods
>
> (ibid.: 58, m.t.)

Any theory leading to this conclusion would be contradictory. It would indeed be a flagrant contradiction to pretend that firms own profit-goods while endorsing an analysis in which firms purchase them in the product market, where only wage-goods are purchased.

The fact is that a sound theory of profit must explain both its formation and its expenditure consistently with the law of exchanges and with the necessity that profit be spent on the purchase of profit-goods. Any theory that fails to provide a satisfactory answer for how profit is formed and spent is unfit for purpose. But how can we explain the formation of profit without contradicting the need to respect the identity of values and prices? And how and where is profit to be spent if this transaction is to define the purchase of profit-goods? It was in the late 1970s and early 1980s that Schmitt provided a detailed answer to these questions (see Chapter 4). In the meantime, I shall devote the remainder of this Chapter to another central topic investigated by Schmitt in the 1970s: circular flow analysis.

## Circular flow analysis or the theory of the circuit

Although the idea of a circular flow is already embedded in Schmitt's early works on money, the first explicit references to it are to be found in his 1966 book *Monnaie, salaires et profits*.

Schmitt's analysis of bank money led him to define it as an asset-liability, a numerical form issued by banks and lent to the economy. This is to say that money is owned neither by firms, which have to pay it back to banks, nor by wage-earners, who deposit it as soon as they are credited and become the owners of a financial claim. 'Money will be paid back after circulation, the object due being the object borrowed itself seized at the other end of the "circle"' (Schmitt 1966a: 232, m.t.). At this stage, the circulation of money is still seen as functional to the creation – its association with produced output – and destruction – the final purchase of produced output – of its purchasing power. The circular flow of nominal money is not yet investigated in any detail. Yet, the idea of money being 'vehicular' (ibid.: 258, m.t.) indicates that Schmitt was already contemplating it.

This is also what happens with regard to the circuit of income. Schmitt's early considerations about the circular flow of income concern the necessary purchase of produced output by income holders. In order to pay back the initial loan granted by banks, firms have to sell their product, a transaction that, when final, implies the destruction of the income created by production. The first *raison d'être* of the circular flow of income is the necessity to match the outgoing flow of money from banks with an equivalent incoming monetary flow. '*Nominal income holders can "consume" it in only one way: for the purchase of produced goods, ensuring by the same token the flow back of distributed money*' (ibid.: 244, m.t.). It thus appears that the circular flows of money and income are closely intertwined, the former being the necessary condition for the existence of the latter.

Several problems are left unsolved by Schmitt's first hints at circular flow analysis. Is the circuit of money a condition of equilibrium or a logical necessity? Can money flow more or less rapidly, and does its circulation take time? Does income's circular flow occupy a positive interval of chronological time? What is the logical relationship between production – income creation – and consumption – income destruction? All these questions are crucial and find a satisfactory answer in Schmitt's subsequent investigation of the flows of money and income as developed in several published and unpublished texts of the following two decades.

## *The circular flow of vehicular money*

In his manuscript *Théorie du circuit* (1972c), Schmitt develops a thorough analysis of the circular flow of nominal money in an economy of *exchange*. Let us follow him.

Transactions between economic agents selling and purchasing goods are conveyed by a vehicular money issued by banks as their spontaneous acknowledgement of debt and lent to the first economic agent of the chain, A. Agent A will have to pay back to the issuing bank the vehicular money obtained from it.

What must be analyzed is the chain of purchases and sales between any number of economic agents, from A to B, from B to C, and so on, until we are back to A, Figure 2.1.

This is how Schmitt clarifies the logical condition for the existence of a monetary circular flow: 'the equality of purchases and sales for each element, including A, the point of injection of the money derived from the issuing banks' (Schmitt 1972c: 6, m.t.). It is worth noting that, because of the immaterial nature of bank money, one cannot assume the existence of a hypothetical circuit in which money would flow. No such circuit exists in reality: it is money itself that, through its circular flow, defines the monetary circuit. A monetary circuit in which money did not flow is a contradiction in terms. In

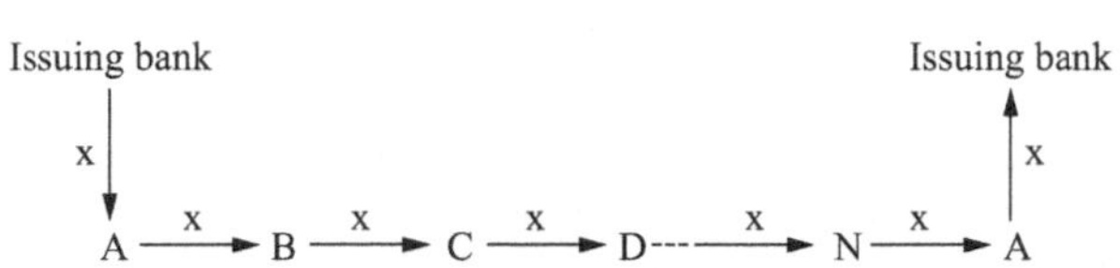


*Figure 2.1* Circular flow of vehicular money.

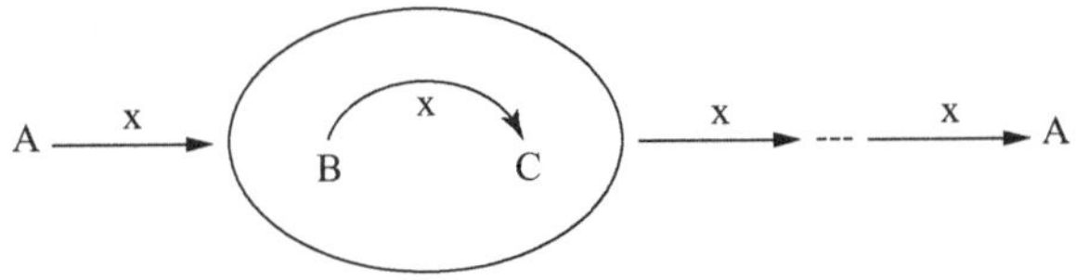


*Figure 2.2* Agent A's composite circular flow. Source: Schmitt 1972c: 7.

the case of vehicular money in an economy of exchange, this implies that 'only money that is spent can exist within the circuit' (ibid.: 7, m.t.).

The equality between each element's sales and purchases is a logical necessity and not a condition of equilibrium. It is 'the very definition of the circular flow that requires that each element of the circuit be identically a purchaser and a seller' (ibid. 8, m.t.). That said, how could we reconcile this logical requirement with the indisputable possibility for any economic agent to save part of what they earn from their sales? The answer provided by Schmitt is straightforward: if any economic agent, say B, saves part or the totality of their earnings, they are not an element of the circuit but are included in what Schmitt calls a 'composite' element. Indeed, what B saves is lent, usually through the financial intermediation of banks, to some other agent, say C, who will spend it in their stead. The circuit would look like Figure 2.2.

It is therefore confirmed that the equality between sales and purchases of every element, simple or composite, is a building block of monetary circular flow analysis.

### *Time and the circular flow of money*

Another characteristic of the circuit of vehicular money is its *logical instantaneity*. Once again, this result derives from the nature of bank money. If money did not flow immediately back to its point of injection, the elements of its circuit, or at least one of them, would not verify the necessary equality of their sales and purchases. If this were the case, if any element were to be a seller without being immediately a purchaser, a net sale would occur, in open contrast with the asset-liability nature of bank money. Yet, money as such is not a net asset and cannot finance any net purchase. In order to respect the asset-liability definition of money, each element of its circuit *must be simultaneously* a seller and a purchaser, which clearly implies the logical instantaneity of money's circular flow. 'Now, the very existence of the nominal circuit requires the expenditure of any element – simple or composite – to be identical with its receipt' (ibid.: 10, m.t.).

The determination of the time-dimension of money's circular flow provides a good example of Schmitt's methodology, which essentially consists in applying logic to one's object of inquiry and following up the consequences as rigorously as possible to the very end. Schmitt could have claimed that, once issued by banks and used as a vehicular means of payment in a chain of purchases, money flows back to its point of departure only after a finite period of time and on the condition that every agent involved in the process spends it in full or lends the totality of their savings to other agents who spend it in their stead. This makes sense as it describes our everyday experience. Yet, it is inconsistent with the correct definition of bank money.

Schmitt's belief in logic is too strong for him to give it up in favour of the easier, orthodox view. If logical analysis establishes that money can be issued only as an asset-liability, the theory has to be consistent with it. If this means going against traditional thinking and common sense, so be it. Money cannot change its nature to please economists or to make their efforts easier.

The instantaneity of monetary circular flows is a logical consequence of money being an asset-liability – so is the identity of each element's sales and purchases. Despite their apparent oddity, these results are compelling, and the economist must endeavour to understand their meaning and show that they conform to reality; this is Schmitt's approach to macroeconomics. The priority of logic is incontrovertible, because logic is the only means we have to establish the validity of economic concepts in the field of macroeconomics. In the case we are examining, logic guides Schmitt to the pure theory of monetary circular flows and to the conclusion that money flows necessarily back, instantaneously and fully, to its issuing bank whatever the behaviour of the economic agents using it to convey their payments. Being governed by logic, this conclusion is stronger than any other and cannot be disproved by facts. On the contrary, this conclusion helps us understand facts beyond their appearance.

## *The circular flow of money and exchange*

Monetary circular flow analysis (MCFA) is founded on the function played by money in exchange. As Schmitt claimed in a paper on the aspects of MCFA in German economic literature and co-authored with Greppi (1996), '[a]s a unit of account (number) and a unit of payment (flow), money is present in all exchanges which are of any interest, in theory and in practice' (p. 343). Indeed, money plays a pivotal role both because it enables the transformation of physical goods into numbers and because it makes their subsequent generalized exchange possible.

What we must remember here is that money acts as a *mere intermediary*, the terms of every exchange being always made up of real goods. Money itself is never a term of any exchange, and this is so because of the very nature of bank money, an asset-liability whose use necessarily entails the simultaneous credit and debit of each economic agent involved in a transaction. Hence, in conformity with the principle of double-entry bookkeeping, the purchase of A from B defines, at the same time, the credit-debit of A and the credit-debit of B.

What many economists have not yet understood is that the principle of double-entry bookkeeping must be verified for each single agent and not simply for the sum of the agents involved in a given transaction. In our example, to claim that A's debit is matched by B's credit is a platitude, a tautological statement that deprives double-entry of any heuristic value. In reality, if the discovery of double-entry has indeed been the starting point of a true revolution in economics, both from a theoretical and a practical viewpoint, it is because it makes it possible to issue money as a spontaneous acknowledgement of debt and use it as a *means* of payment. Thus, A pays B by means of *x* money units, which does not mean that *x* money units are the object of A's payment, but that, thanks to the vehicular use of *x* money units, A can convey to B the real payment of its purchases. In other words, to pay for its purchases of B's real goods, A must convey to B another, equivalent amount of real goods, money being only an intermediary between the real goods exchanged between A and B.

Schmitt states it again and again: money would be a term of exchange in the sale (purchase) of a real good only if it were itself an asset. This not being the case, the credit-debit nature of money forces us to conclude that money is but an intermediary and that it is only through a simultaneous sale that a purchase can be financed. The necessary circular flow of money follows. 'Being an asset-liability, money can only be used in its own flow. [...] assets-liabilities can only be intermediaries in real exchanges: they can be used only in a circular way' (Schmitt 1975a: 41, m.t.).

In an economy of exchange, purchases of real goods can be financed only through equivalent sales of real goods. The role of money is to convey payments that are not financed by money but by equivalent sales. Each element of a monetary circular flow is precisely a seller (purchaser) and a purchaser (seller) because it can derive its purchasing power only from the sale of produced output. In this theoretical framework '[t]he purchasing power of money is not original, but purely borrowed. [...] it is inconceivable that an individual be a purchaser of products without being simultaneously the seller of equivalent products' (Schmitt 1972c: 47, m.t.). This is so even if the seller, say B, were to save part or the totality of the money it receives from the purchaser. Two different, albeit related, arguments lead to this result.

The first implies the introduction of the financial market and rests on the fact that saved-up money is immediately transformed into a bank deposit. Hence, when B saves, it spends its money-income on the purchase of equivalent claims on bank deposits. This amounts to a purchase of financial assets, and since financial assets are real goods 'by destination', it appears that even in this particular case the exchange, mediated by money, takes place between real goods or products.

The second argument is that what is saved by an agent, B, is lent to another, say C, which spends it in their stead. Taken together, saver and borrower finance their purchases of real goods through the sale of real goods of the same value.

Schmitt concludes his analysis by observing that, even in an economy of pure exchange, the identity between each element's sales and purchases takes the most rigorous form of identity between *each agent's* sales and purchases.

Through its saving, B gives C the opportunity to purchase products of an equivalent value. What really matters is the fact that it is the income of B that finances the purchases of C, and since B obtains its income only through the sale of its products, we can legitimately infer that B matches its sales of real goods with equivalent purchases of real goods in the form of financial assets.

> Every sale by any individual is identically and simultaneously a purchase of the same subject. If the seller does not purchase anything – because he has chosen to save – everything happens as if he purchased the product chosen by his borrower in order to lend it to him.
>
> (ibid.: 49, m.t.)

As astonishing as it might appear at first sight, Schmitt's conclusion of his analysis of the monetary circular flow in an economy of exchange is that 'each element of the vehicular circuit is its own purchaser' (ibid.: 30, m.t.). The nature of money is what explains the identity between each agent's sales and purchases, and this identity is what allows Schmitt to conclude that, as far as money is concerned, each agent is their own purchaser or seller. In real terms, every agent sells their own product and purchases the product of some other agent. This is what Schmitt calls the 'external' aspect of the exchange. The 'internal' aspect refers to money only: 'monetary exchange is "internal": vehicular money being a mere intermediary in real exchanges, every element of the circular flow is its own purchaser or identically its own seller' (ibid.: 30, m.t.).

## The circular flow of nominal money and income in an economy of production

It is with the investigation of an economy of production that a monetary circular flow analysis acquires all its significance. Monetary creation is a meaningful event only when it is related to production, and the formation of income can only be explained as the result of the association between money and current output. Money and income are closely interconnected and so are their circuits. Schmitt's analysis of money and income circular flows rests on his explanation of the way money is issued by banks and transformed into income by production and is deeply rooted in Keynes's fundamental equations establishing the equivalence between production ($C+I$) and consumption ($C'+I'$). In this logical identity, Schmitt identifies the foundation of MCFA: 'the equivalence between the formation and the expenditure of macroeconomic income is nothing but the affirmation of the circuit in all its perfection' (Gnos and Schmitt 1989: 154, m.t.).

### *From the circular flow of money to that of income*

*Théorie unitaire de la monnaie, nationale et internationale* (1975) is Schmitt's the most successful book. Translated into German, Italian, and Portuguese, it lays the foundations for modern MCFA. In this book Schmitt starts from the definition of money as an asset-liability and shows that it is the origin of what he calls the four fundamental laws of monetary economies. The first law establishes the purely numerical 'dimension' of value in economics. Economic value is in no way a physical dimension. As claimed by Walras (1874/1954), value is a mere relationship, yet, contrary to what the founding father of GEA claimed, the measure of value is expressed only in numerical terms and not in terms of a real good chosen as *numéraire*. 'Money [...] does not give the dimension of the economic value of goods. All money does is *number* real goods, *count* them' (Schmitt 1975a: 15, m.t.).

The second law is of a particular relevance for MCFA, because it states that 'every purchase is necessarily financed by a sale, money being only an intermediary in the transaction' (ibid.: 19, m.t.). As we already know, this law derives directly from the fact that money 'can only flow in a circuit: the asset-liability flows necessarily back to its point of "injection"' (ibid.: 19, m.t.). The law of the logical identity between sales and purchases derives also from the discovery that every production creates a supply and an equivalent demand, which is why Schmitt calls it Say's law. 'Say's law demands that every purchaser be simultaneously a seller' (ibid.: 19, m.t.), which is what is implied in Say's claim that supply creates its own demand. Keynes conveys the same idea when he claims that the payment of wages for the production of consumption- and investment-goods ($C' + I'$) is always and necessarily equal to the demand exerted by income holders ($C + I$). It is because macroeconomic supply and demand are instantaneously co-determined through one and the same transaction that sales and purchases of produced output are the terms of an identity, and that money can never *finance* any transaction.

According to Schmitt's third law, money's competence is further limited by the logical impossibility for any purchaser to pay using their own acknowledgement of debt. Establishing the need to keep the issuer and the users of money separate, this law is almost self-evident. Indeed, it should be clear to everyone that nobody can pay by getting indebted. A payment is such if it enables the payer to free himself from the debt entailed by his net purchase. To give one's own IOU in exchange for real goods is to incur a debt to the seller of those real goods, to promise a payment that will be settled at a future date.

If an economic system was to allow purchasers to 'pay' with their own acknowledgement of debt, sellers would not really be paid, and the entire system would rest on a series of non-payments. In reality, this is not what happens: a 'distance' logically separates banks, the issuers of money, from the set of purchasers. Money is an IOU, it is true, yet it is not the IOU of any purchaser, which is why payments carried out through the vehicular use of bank money have a redemption function.

What is true of the set of purchasers is also true of banks when they have to pay each other on behalf of their clients. No commercial bank can pay another by crediting it directly, because this would amount to sending it a mere IOU with no real object. 'The rule according to which nobody pays by means of his own debt requires the indebted bank to send something different from its own debt to the creditor bank, because, in the banking system, banks' debts are not proper money' (ibid.: 21, m.t.). The problem of inter-bank payments is well-known to bankers, who have addressed and solved it through the creation of a system of settlement based on the use of central bank money. Central banks operate as monetary (and financial) intermediaries between banks in the same way as commercial banks act with respect to their clients and, in doing so, they act as 'catalyst' facilitating the transformation of private or commercial bank monies into undifferentiated units of national currencies.

Finally, Schmitt's fourth law refers to international economics, and I will come back to it in Part II of this volume.

### *The role of firms*

Having established the logical background of MCFA, Schmitt sets out to show that firms are the necessary point of 'injection' and 'rejection' of money. Issued by banks, money is lent to firms and, because the identity between sales and purchases holds true for firms, economic transactions are consistent with the circular flow of money and income. Indeed, the payment of wages carried out by banks on behalf of firms creates the totality of macroeconomic income; and through their sale of produced output, firms cannot obtain more than what they spend in their payment of labour's productive activity. 'Firms are an element of the circuit, because if they purchase products [payment of wages] for an amount of money equal to $x$, it is logically necessary for them to simultaneously sell products for $x$ units of money' (ibid.: 50, m.t.). This holds true whether income holders are willing to spend the entirety of their income or not and does not in the least hamper the formation of profit.

As we already know, one only needs to consider the intermediation occurring in the financial market to prove that what is saved by some is lent to and spent by others, firms included. Even though firms are a simple element of money and income circular flows, nothing prevents them from being also part of a composite element. This is the case when they benefit from a loan or a profit. In the former case, firms borrow from income holders the amount of income required to cover the cost of production of unsold goods; in the latter they derive their own income from that spent by households. The distinction between simple and composite elements of income circular flow is determined by the distinction between income creation (and destruction) and income transfer. Wages, the sole source of macroeconomic income, are paid and finally spent by a simple element, whereas 'every other income is transferred within a composite element' (ibid.: 54, m.t.).

Two circular flows are involved in Schmitt's analysis.

The first is the circular flow of nominal or vehicular money. Its *raison d'être* lies in the very nature of money, and its time-dimension is the instant because payments do not take time, and money, as a means of payment, does not survive any of them. An instant is enough for banks to carry out a payment, which occurs at the very moment the purchaser is debited and the seller credited. A circular flow of money takes place in every payment, whether it relates to the formation of income, to its distribution, or to its final expenditure. Every payment is in itself a perfect circular flow, each money unit intervening as the means through which each payment is carried out. Banks recover instantaneously the money they pay out, each real purchase being financed by an equivalent sale.

The second circular flow is that of income. Formed through production, income is destroyed in the final purchase of produced output. Production and consumption are the two interdependent phases of the circular flow of income. Their simultaneity is perfectly consistent with the necessary instantaneity of such flow, yet it is not self-evident and calls for further investigations. Hoarding is one of the apparent obstacles. At a superficial glance, it seems obvious that if part of the income formed by production was hoarded instead of being saved and explicitly or implicitly invested in the financial market, income circulation would be correspondingly reduced. This would indeed be the case if hoarding was an option, if economic agents could withdraw income from banks and hide it somewhere, so that it would no longer be available for the financing of global demand. Yet, the nature of bank deposits is such that nobody can modify their amount except by increasing it through a new production or decreasing it through consumption.

### *Hoarding and the circular flow of income*

This is not to say that their owners cannot hide banknotes. They obviously can, but their doing so does not in the least reduce the amount of bank deposits or, as a consequence, of global demand. As a matter of fact, banknotes are but claims on bank deposits or deposit certificates. There is a perfect correspondence between banknotes and bank deposits: for any banknote held by income holders, there is a bank deposit precisely because bank deposits are the very object of the debt of banks to the holders of banknotes. 'The banknote is merely the certificate of the debit and not the debit itself. It follows that commercial banks can give up the certificate without losing the certified deposit' (Schmitt 1972c: 77, m.t.). Finally, as Schmitt claims, '[i]t also follows that not a single fraction of savings – whether made up of scriptural money or banknotes – can degenerate into hoarding' (ibid.: 77–8, m.t.).

Hoarding being always and necessarily equal to zero, the totality of income formed in a given period, say $p_0$, will sooner or later be spent for the final purchase of the product of $p_0$. The circular flow of income takes place between the moment of its creation and that of its final destruction. Analysis shows that production, the *creation* of income, and consumption, its *destruction*, are equivalent and complementary, the totality of produced output being necessarily purchased by income holders.

Is this enough to establish that, although these two payments, *income creation* and *income destruction*, occur at different instants in continuous time, the circular flow they define is eventually timeless? In other words, although indisputably 'relative to a given physical output, "income-forming" (IF) and "income-destroying" (ID) payments are *successive events in chronological time*' (Schmitt and Greppi 1996: 361), is it nevertheless possible to maintain that they 'constitute a timeless identity' (ibid.: 361)? Schmitt and Greppi show this to be the case, because income creation and income destruction 'relate to the same physical output' (ibid.: 361).

### *Time and the circular flow of income*

The relationship between income creation and destruction is that of an identity, and identities are timeless. Whatever the interval of time separating the two transactions, no difference can ever be found between the income created by the production of a given period and that spent for its final purchase. This is why production and consumption are the two terms of a logical identity, a necessary condition for the circular flow of income to exist. 'Circular flow analysis links production and consumption flows so strongly to one another that no production could possibly take place unless simultaneously defined as an equal consumption. To produce means to "produce-consume". Production and consumption are the two sides of the same "coin"; if one side is nil so is the other' (ibid.: 351).

Another way to prove the timeless nature of the circular flow of income is by referring to the relationship between the formation of income and its immediate expenditure by wage-earners. Here, we do not consider income's final expenditure or destruction as it occurs when physical output is definitively demonetized and appropriated by consumers, but its initial expenditure for the purchase of produced output. What matters here is what happens when wages are paid out to wage-earners.

On the one hand, the payment of wages defines a monetary payment, which implies the instantaneous creation-destruction of a sum of money units, that is, a monetary circular flow.

On the other hand, the income obtained by wage-earners takes immediately the form of a bank deposit. In other words, wage-earners spend their income at once on the financial purchase of their own output. Through this implicit expenditure, wage-earners obtain their product in the form of financial obligations; they acquire a net credit from banks, whose object is the commercial goods they have produced.

> In a monetary economy, factors of production instantly *purchase their own output* – not in *kind* but in *money* – at the very moment when they receive their money wages. [...] money wages are therefore *spent* – in *money*, not in *kind* – as soon as they are *received*.
>
> (ibid.: 360)

To say that wage-earners deposit their income with banks is to say that they spend their income for the purchase of financial claims. By doing so, they enable banks to lend their income to firms, which immediately invest it in the formation of a stock. Income formed at the moment wages are paid is thus spent by wage-earners for the purchase of financial claims on bank deposits, lent by banks, and invested by firms. Even though the initial expenditure of income occurring at the very instant income is formed does not entail its final destruction, it establishes the 'necessary equality of income received and income spent' (ibid.: 360). The necessary equality of sales and purchases is therefore verified also in the case of income. It is because the necessary equality between wage-earners' sales and purchases remains valid from the very moment wages are paid that MCFA applies both to nominal money and income.

### *The inclusion of profit in the circular flow of income*

As we have seen, firms are the key element of money and income's circular flows. The identity between firms' sales and purchases is the necessary and sufficient condition for the existence of these circular flows. Since the income earned by workers is instantaneously spent by them, albeit 'unknowingly', on the financial market and immediately lent to firms, it is correct to say that the payment of wages is financed by wage-earners. It is wage-earners' income that is invested by firms, and it is through this investment that produced output is initially purchased by firms and constituted as a stock of wage-goods.

While it remains true that products are purchased by wage-earners *financially*, it is also correct to say that firms purchase them through the payment of wages and transform them into a stock of goods to be sold on the commodity market. This means that produced output is at the same time owned by wage-earners *in income terms* and at the disposal of firms in the form of stock. Wage-earners own it as the object of their bank deposits but can obtain it in kind only through its purchase in the market for products. Firms do not own it, because their stock of goods derives from the investment of a *borrowed* income, yet they can decide when, how, and at which price to sell it to income holders.

Consistently with the principles of MCFA, firms' purchase of produced output is necessarily equal to their sale of it in the market for goods. Indeed, wages are the only original income created by production, and they also define the amount spent in the final purchase of produced goods. Yet, the identity of firms' purchases and sales of current output does not prevent the formation of positive profit.

As Keynes tacitly maintained and Schmitt explicitly and definitively proved, profit is derived from wages. The mechanism consists in selling consumption-goods at a mark-up, and the result is a transfer of income from its initial owners to firms whose profit is therefore a substitution income. The formation of profit is perfectly consistent with the identity of firms' sales and purchases and is no obstacle to the circular flow of income. In *Théorie unitaire* (1975), Schmitt explains it by showing that, insofar as firms make a positive profit, they are also part of a composite element of income's circular flow. The representation of a circular flow of income in the case of a positive profit is the same as in Figure 2.2, where income-earners lend part of their income to firms. 'The difference between these loans and the formation of profit lies simply in the reversible character of loans as opposed to the irreversible character of profit' (Schmitt 1975a: 52, m.t.).

The difficulty of reconciling the necessary equality of firms' sales and purchases with the explanation of profit does not lie with the need to account for its formation within the logical framework of MCFA. Income transfers are easily explained. What is less straightforward is the explanation of how profit is spent. In his 1975 book, Schmitt does not get to the bottom of the question and limits his analysis to the observation that profit is spent by firms on firms: the purchases of the composite element of which firms are part encompass the purchases of wage-earners and those of firms. Albeit still incomplete, Schmitt's analysis of profit is consistent with his theory of money and money's circular flows, and in Chapter 4, we will see that this consistency remains unaltered when the analysis of profit is fully elaborated.

### *The law of the circuit is compatible with the presence of inflation and deflation*

Having established that each bank's outflows are necessarily matched by its inflows, Schmitt points out that the necessary equality of firms' sales and purchases applies also in a situation of monetary disequilibrium. Indeed, Say's law requires that there be close equivalence between the economic value of firms' sales and purchases, but not between their numerical expressions. In other words, the identity of values might be accompanied by a numerical difference.

Identities are much stronger than conditions of equilibrium. Once logically established, an identity cannot be jeopardized by anything, not even by the numerical imbalance of its two terms. Nobody can deny that if a numerical difference was to be found between F's sales and purchases, this would define a pathological disequilibrium, but it would not justify doubting their identity. Quite the opposite: it is because F's sales and purchases are identical that their numerical difference acquires a precise meaning and enables us to define disequilibria such as inflation and deflation.

As an example, let us reproduce Schmitt's figure of a circular flow compatible with an inflationary disequilibrium due to what Keynes (1930/1971) called a widow's cruse, in Figure 2.3.

The reasons behind the formation of an inflationary profit are investigated in Chapters 6 and 8. For the time being, let us concentrate on the meaning of the identity, imposed by the law of the circuit, between $x$ and $x+y$. What the identity of F's sales and purchases tells us is that the value of F's purchases, as defined by the payment of the macroeconomic costs of production, is necessarily equal to the value of F's sales. Hence, the identity

$$x \equiv x + y$$

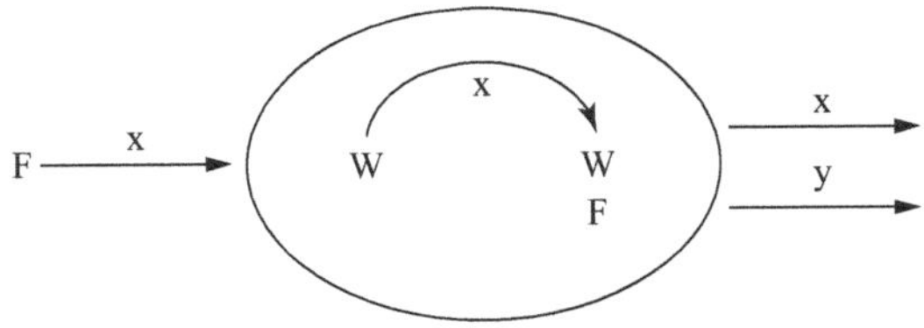


*Figure 2.3* An example of inflationary circular flow. Source: elaboration from Schmitt 1975a: 64.

represents the case where, although equal in value, F's purchases are numerically less than its sales. $x$ is the number of money units paid as wages, and $x+y$ is the number of money units obtained by F in the sale of produced output.

The necessary equality between the value of $x$ and $x+y$ money units has only one possible meaning: the inflationary increase of money units from $x$ to $x+y$ reduces the value of each monetary unit. Initially conveyed by $x$ money units, the value created by production is distributed over a higher number of money units, so that each money unit obtained by F has a lesser economic value than each money unit spent by F. '[I]nitially established between the physical product of [labour] and x units of money, the logical correspondence resulting from integration relates by now [$x+y$] money units to the same physical product' (Schmitt 1975a: 68, m.t.).

The case of deflation is just the opposite: the same economic value being conveyed by a decreasing number of money units, deflation defines a decrease in value of each money unit. All in all, 'every positive or negative difference between $x$ and [$x+y$] causes a disequilibrium because it is necessarily reabsorbed by a variation in the economic value of the money units' (ibid.: 67, m.t.).

In an orderly system, no numerical difference would be possible between F's purchases and sales, whose identity would be respected both in value terms and numerically. As Schmitt (1975a) claimed '[t]he equality of the *economic* values of each element's purchases and sales is *logical*, while the equalities of the *arithmetic* values of purchases and sales is a *condition of equilibrium*' (ibid.: 74, m.t.). Today's rule of the daily equality of each bank's monetary outflows and inflows is not enough to guarantee the numerical equilibrium required to avoid inflation and deflation. A reform is required, and, in his 1975 book, Schmitt calls for the banks to distinguish between a monetary and a financial department, in such a way that the daily destruction of all the money created on each client would be guaranteed.

As will become clearer in Chapter 6, this twofold distinction is not sufficient to prevent the formation of inflation and deflation when the economic system includes capital growth and amortization. Schmitt's 1975 analysis is mainly concerned with money and income's circular flows and does not investigate capital. To the extent that monetary disequilibria can be imputed to the behaviour of banks and firms, the reform advocated in *Théorie unitaire* is fit for purpose and provides the founding elements of the broader reform of 1984.

## Schmitt's profit and monetary circular flow analysis as compared to those of his contemporaries

Orthodox or heterodox economists have not investigated the problem of profit in any original way in the last several decades. To a great extent this may be due to the widespread belief that everything has already been explained simply by referring to the possibility for firms to sell their output at a mark-up. The question asked by Keynes, whether profit must be included or not in national income, no longer arouses any theoretical interest, and it is generally believed that the complementarity of wages and profits is all that matters.

To be fair, this latest claim refers mostly to Keynesian economists at large, and does not apply to GEA. Indeed, in a Walrasian theoretical setting there is logically no room for profit, that is, for an income obtained by firms at zero cost. The economy is essentially taken to be an economy of exchange, and money is subordinated to the determination of relative prices through direct exchange between real goods. Production itself is analyzed as an exchange between products and productive services, which leads to the identification of profit with interest. Yet, in GEA, interest is the cost of capital, and can therefore not be considered a net gain. If, as assumed by GEA, capital is a productive factor and if the remuneration of productive services is a purchase, no distinction is drawn between the market for products and that for productive services; production is reduced to a relative exchange, and profit proper is necessarily nil.

Keynesian economists, on the other hand, have mostly analyzed the impact of profit on economic equilibrium according to the propensity to save, first out of wages and then out of profit itself. To be in line with Keynes's thought, Keynesian and post-Keynesian analyses should explain the complementarity of profit and wages consistently with the fact that labour is the sole macroeconomic factor of production, so that profit cannot be considered a direct result of production.

The challenge faced by Keynesianism at large is to show that wages and profit can be complementary even though wages are the only macroeconomic income generated by production. It is fair to say that so far neither Keynesian, new-, or post-Keynesian economists have satisfactorily met this challenge. For example, no explanation has yet been found for how profit formation and expenditure comply with the logical principle of the necessary equality of values and prices. If the theory of profit did not go beyond the selling at a mark-up, it would lead to a double and irreducible measure of production, in value and in price, and would have to be abandoned.

As for monetary circular flow analysis, Schmitt's version differs substantially from that of other famous theoreticians of the circuit such as Parguez and Graziani. In Chapter 1, we already mentioned the fact that Schmitt's logical distinction between money and income has vanished in the work of his contemporaries. By conflating money and income, the authors miss the crucial point of the necessary equality between sales and purchases of each element of the circuit and, in particular, of firms. Consequently, they do not hesitate to claim that monetary outflows – firms' expenditures – may be different from monetary inflows – firms' sales – and that money flows more or less rapidly according to economic agents' behaviours. What they seem unable to see is that an interrupted circular flow is no circular flow at all; that the identity of firms' sales and purchases is a logical requirement for a monetary circular flow to exist. Having missed the founding principle of MCFA, they are also not aware of the logical instantaneity of any circular flow.

Had Keynesian economists properly appreciated the originality of Keynes's message as conveyed by his fundamental equations, they would have understood that production and consumption are the two faces of a single reality, and that it is precisely because of the close relationship between these two events that monetary circular flows exist. Keynes himself was not fully aware of all the implications of his fundamental equations. It is also certain that he did not sense that his equations provided a final proof of the validity of Say's law, which Keynes rejected on the grounds that it does not account for the existence of unemployment. As a matter of fact, Keynes's critique misses its target, because Say's law, like Keynes's fundamental equations, establishes a logical relationship that holds true whether the economic system is at equilibrium or not. The analysis of disequilibrium is logically subsequent and can achieve its goal thanks to, and not in opposition to, Say's law and Keynes's fundamental equations.

# 3 Schmitt's critical analysis of neoclassical, Keynesian, Marxian, and Sraffian economics from 1959 to 1988

Part of Schmitt's research is devoted to a critical appraisal of the most relevant theories since the time of the Physiocrats. Of particular importance are his investigations of general equilibrium analysis (GEA), Marx's economic theory, Keynesian economics, and Sraffa's attempt at determining relative prices through inter-industrial relations. His interest in the works of these authors goes back to the years of his doctoral studies and lasted almost to his last days. He was most fascinated by the problem of the logical indeterminacy of relative prices and irked by that of the Keynesian multiplier. What mattered to him was the search for those concepts that can help build a flawless economic theory deeply embedded in the real world. His critical analysis is always oriented towards this aim and is foundational to the development of his quantum macroeconomic theory.

The main references are to his books *Monnaie, salaires et profits* (1966), *L'analyse macroéconomique des revenus* (1971); *Macroeconomic theory: A fundamental revision* (1972); *La pensée de Karl Marx. Critique et synthèse*, Vol. I *La valeur* (1976), Vol. II *La plus-value* (1977) (both co-authored with me). I refer as well to three unpublished papers: one was presented at the 'Grand séminaire' of the University of Dijon (1986–87); another was presented at a Conference held at Monte Verità, Ascona, Switzerland from the 4th to 6th of September 1998; and the last, which I have labelled *Prix relatifs* and dated 1987, was lecture material intended for students at the Universities of Fribourg and Dijon.

## Schmitt's first critical assessment of general equilibrium analysis (GEA)

### *The logical indeterminacy of money*

Schmitt's starting point is the neoclassical dichotomy between relative prices, determined by direct exchange and expressed in real terms, and absolute prices, expressed in monetary terms. In GEA, exchanges between real goods come first: supply and demand, which are supposed to determine prices, are themselves of a 'real' nature. Money plays no role in the determination of relative prices, which are strictly dependent on the real sector only. 'Commodities are

DOI: 10.4324/9781351271325-6

confronted with commodities, and the prices to be determined are "relative", expressed in kind' (Schmitt 1966a: 31, m.t.). If, in GEA, money is considered neutral, it is precisely because it does not participate in the determination of relative prices; it 'adds nothing to the real sector' (ibid.: 32, m.t.).

Let us consider the impact of the neoclassical dichotomy on the economy as a whole by taking into account both exchange, as it occurs on the products' market, and production. According to Walras (1874/1954), money does not alter equilibrium prices, which are supposed to guarantee the equality between the payment of productive services and the final sale of produced goods. This enables Schmitt to propose an alternative definition of the neoclassical dichotomy, which he identifies with the claim that '*the remuneration of productive services is a purchase*' (ibid.: 34, m.t.).

Firms pay or remunerate productive services. By so doing, they indirectly purchase the product of these services, and Schmitt shows that in this respect firms are mere intermediaries. Indeed, they either purchase produced goods from productive services and sell them to consumers – in which case they purchase on behalf of consumers – or fail to sell them to consumers – in which case they have to cover their costs of production. In both cases, consumers own the totality of produced output. Productive services and consumers are therefore the only two relevant categories, firms playing no active role except when they are themselves considered as a factor of production.

The determining forces are 'the supply of productive services and the demand for produced goods' (ibid.: 35–6, m.t.). Firms being not actively involved in the process of price determination, money itself is nothing more than a passive intermediary between productive services and products.

> Money is a shrewd middleman that gives all that he gets and gets all that he gives, without taking part either in production or in consumption. As a consequence, monetary prices have no substance; whatever the variation of absolute prices, the "true" prices, real prices remain unaffected.
>
> (ibid.: 36, m.t.)

Thus expressed, the neoclassical dichotomy rests on the centrality of the payment of productive factors and the need, if money is to be determined by the system, to find a way to reconcile relative and absolute prices.

A kernel of GEA is Walras's law, which essentially states that, real goods being exchanged for real goods, the sum of supplied goods is necessarily equal to the sum of demanded goods. In a two-goods economy, this means that the demand for one good is always equal to the supply of the other and vice versa. Extended to an economy made up of *n* goods plus a commodity-money, Walras's law establishes that the supply of money defines the demand for goods and the demand for money the supply of goods. This amounts to saying that the equation equalizing the demand for and the supply of money is included in the equations equalizing the demand for and the supply of real goods and can therefore always be discarded. In other words, Walras's law is the founding principle of the neoclassical dichotomy and of the priority attributed to relative prices over absolute or monetary prices.

In such a theoretical framework, is it still possible to avoid the logical indeterminacy of money? This is the question asked by Schmitt in *Monnaie, salaires et profits*. Looking for a counter-intuitive, positive answer, he observes first that money would be bound to remain logically undetermined if the neoclassical dichotomy were identified with the homogeneity postulate. As it is well known, according to this postulate any possible variation of monetary prices has no effect at all on relative prices. Demand and supply functions of the real sector are unaffected by variations in the absolute level of monetary prices in a world where only subjective preferences matter. It follows that, to open the door to a possible reconciliation between GEA and the need to overcome money's indeterminacy, it is necessary to reject the homogeneity postulate while retaining Walras's law and the neoclassical dichotomy.

### *Fisher's equation*

A famous attempt to integrate money into GEA is that of Fisher and of the advocates of the quantity theory of money. Fisher's equation, $MV=PT$, establishes a relationship between the product of the quantity of money, $M$, and its velocity of circulation, $V$, on one side, and the product of the transactions occurring in the market for goods, $T$, and the prices of the goods sold (purchased), $P$. Thus expressed, the quantitative equation merely states that prices at which goods are effectively sold (purchased) on the market are equal to $MV/T$, and its heuristic status is not far from tautological.

It is true that Fisher distinguishes between price and price level, and that he believes that his equation is far more than a tautology, because it is supposed to establish the causes determining price levels. Yet, whether Fisher's equation is referred to 'effective' prices or to the price level, it remains true that '[i]n both cases there is nothing more than a definition, and the equation $P=MV/T$ carries only one meaning: *it defines prices*' (Schmitt 1959: 923, m.t.). The unavoidable consequence of this inference is that Fisher's equation is an identity, a necessary equality that, as such, cannot be considered as a condition of equilibrium (ibid.: 923). That being the case, it appears that, despite Fisher's efforts, GEA fails to integrate money.

As observed by Schmitt (1959, 1960, 1971a, 1972a), Fisher's equation can refer to either flows or stocks. Considered as the equation of exchanges, it concerns the flows of expenditure as they occur in the goods market, and it is a tautology pure and simple. Considered as the instrument for determining the price level, it relates the stock of money to the stock of goods and amounts to a proposition that has to be tested to establish whether it is admissible or not. It is in this second case that Fisher's equation deserves our attention. Indeed, Fisher himself observes that 'the price level is not determined by individual prices, but [...], on the contrary, any individual price presupposes a price level' (Fisher 1925: 180).

In other words, the determination of money's purchasing power – the obverse of the price level – is the first, necessary step towards monetary exchanges: 'no monetary exchange can take place unless money has a positive purchasing power' (Schmitt 1960: 134, m.t.). Does this simply mean that money can exchange for real goods because it has the power to purchase them, or is there more to it? Fisher's ambition goes far beyond the mere statement of a tautology. What he would like to show is not only that money exerts its purchasing power in the market for goods, but also that money *derives* its purchasing power from exchange.

Unfortunately, Fisher's analysis misses its target, because a single transaction – exchange – 'cannot at the same time exert and create purchasing power. The power is used in the exchange; it is therefore formed separately' (ibid.: 134, m.t.). According to Fisher and GEA, real goods derive their (relative) value from exchange and so does the commodity chosen as money. Money has a positive purchasing power because it exchanges for real goods and not the other way around. Schmitt's conclusion is unequivocal: '[b]y deriving purchasing power from the equivalence, Fisher does not enunciate a truism; he makes an abominable mistake. The equation of exchange does not encompass the cause of money's purchasing power' (ibid.: 135, m.t.). Being a tautological definition, Fisher's equation 'is satisfied whatever the state of the world, real and monetary, be it in equilibrium, disequilibrium or in an impenetrable eternal chaos' (Schmitt 1959: 924, m.t.).

Does the quantity theory of money (QTM) succeed in overcoming Fisher's impasse? At first sight a positive answer seems possible, because it is no longer claimed that the purchasing power of money is derived from exchange, but, less ambitiously, that the quantity of money (a stock) influences the price level. In its simplest form, the QTM states that, once determined, purchasing power distributes over a quantity of money units: varying the quantity has repercussions for the purchasing power of every single unit. The global purchasing power of money is a given, while the purchasing power of the money unit varies according to the variation of the total stock of money. The main shortcoming of the QTM is clear: it leaves the *formation* of money's purchasing power totally unexplained. Moreover, it takes it for granted that an increase in money units leaves unaltered the total amount of purchasing power, thus excluding a priori – without the shadow of a proof – that newly issued money can acquire an entirely new purchasing power.

### *Patinkin's real-balance effect*

Neither Walras's law, nor Fisher's equation and the QTM provide an explanation of the economic determination of money. Does Patinkin's real-balance effect succeed in the attempt to safeguard the essential message of GEA as epitomized by Walras's law, while explaining how real and monetary sectors can reciprocally integrate? Schmitt's analysis shows that it does not.

To avoid Walras's failure to integrate money into GEA, Patinkin suggests an approach based on 'the utility of *holding* money, not with that of *spending* it' (Patinkin 1965: 79). Patinkin's idea is that money, though undetermined when GEA refers to flows (expenditures), can become determined when the analysis turns to the effects of a variation in the stock of money held by economic agents as cash reserves. What matters is the variation in real balances caused by a change in the money supply, whose origin is external and independent of relative prices.

The real-balance effect implies previous knowledge of money's purchasing power, that is, of the general price level. Yet, according to Patinkin, the adjustment of individuals' cash holdings has an impact on the demand for, and supply of goods and may engender a variation in prices and, consequently, in the purchasing power of money. The core of GEA remains unaltered: equilibrium prices are assumed to be determined through direct exchange. However, money can play a role in that it may induce a change in prices through the real-balance effect.

Schmitt's first critical remark is that individuals adjust their real balances through a variation in their demand for, and supply of real goods. Indeed, if real-money reserves 'are insufficient, individuals are ready to sell real goods to increase their cash holdings. If reserves appear excessive, people prepare to get rid of the surplus in purchases of real goods' (Schmitt 1972a: 170). This means that we are back to a flow analysis, where the determining factors are the sales and purchases of real goods. This conclusion remains valid even when the variation in real balances refers to a wealth effect including financial and physical assets in individuals' portfolio (see Patinkin 1965). '[F]inally, the utility of holding money is identified with the utility of spending or earning it, or, in short, with the utility of buying and selling real goods' (Schmitt 1972a: 171). Patinkin's attempt fails, because his real-balance effect is entirely absorbed in a variation in the flow of expenditures and therefore cannot account for the determination of the value of money.

If a variation in money supply causes an adjustment of economic agents' supply and demand to maintain the same proportion in their real-money balances, this can only lead to the determination of new money prices and not, additionally, to that of the value of money. Patinkin believes that the value of goods and that of money can be determined simultaneously by a singular kind of adjustment, i.e. the equalization of the demand for and supply of real goods (commercial and financial). Schmitt rightly observes that 'such an integration is schizophrenic' (ibid.: 174), because 'when only *one* adjustment factor is available, it cannot possibly yield *two* determinations' (ibid.: 174).

In Patinkin's model, prices are initially considered as given and what is studied is their variation as engendered by a change in money supply. What is wrong with it is not the assumption that such a change can affect equilibrium prices by, but the claim that a variation in the monetary prices of goods entails a new determination of the purchasing power of money. 'The error lies in deriving the purchasing power of money from the general price level' (ibid.: 172), it elides the fact that '[*w*]*hen supply and demand of real goods are newly adjusted, the purchasing power of money remains exactly equal to what it was before these adjustments*' (ibid.: 175).

Schmitt's critical arguments against Patinkin's attempted solution are numerous, particularly in *Monnaie, salaires et profit* (1966). Let us just say a few words about the argument emphasizing the fact that *the purchasing power of money cannot form through its expenditure.* In Patinkin's analysis, the value of money is given from the outset as a necessary pre-requisite to reason in terms of real-money balances. Hence, what he endeavours to explain is not the initial determination of the purchasing power, but its new level of equilibrium as influenced by the real-balance effect. This leads Schmitt to claim that one is thereafter confronted with only two possible alternatives: either

1) The purchasing power of money is a price, or
2) It calls for a proper explanation (Schmitt 1966a: 85).

In the first case, the value of money defines (and is defined by) the 'equilibrium value of supply and demand' (ibid.: 85, m.t.). Equilibrium is set at the intersection of the supply and demand functions and depends on individual behaviour. This makes it logically inconsistent to assume that the purchasing power of money is given from the outset. 'Yet, unless we reason in a barter situation, from the opening of the market it is *necessary to start from a positive monetary power*' (ibid.: 86, m.t.). The conclusion is inescapable: 'the purchasing power of money is not an ordinary price' (ibid.: 86, m.t.), and therefore cannot be derived from the general price level.

Finally, however formally possible 'to suppose the existence of prices to construct the functions of supply and demand [... while] *deducing* the final price from the intersections of their curves' (ibid.: 87, m.t.), it is illogical to assume that purchasing power is 'at the same time an initial datum and a variable' (ibid.: 87, m.t.). Yet, this is precisely what Patinkin does, who assumes the prior existence of the purchasing power of money – a necessary condition for the very existence of real balances – and simultaneously claims that this same purchasing power derives from the determination of prices.

## The logical indeterminacy of relative prices

### *Schmitt's 1986–87 paper*

At the beginning, the paper establishes that GEA requires goods to be expressed in pure numbers, that is, in numbers whose dimension is purely numerical. This is so because physically heterogeneous goods can be compared only if they are made homogeneous through their transformation into dimensionless numbers. If goods were expressed in a number of different physical units, they would remain heterogeneous and no relationship could be established between them, no matter whether they are exchanged or not.

*First proof*

The homogeneity of goods 'can derive only from the determination of relative prices on the condition that these prices be expressed in pure numbers' (Schmitt 1986–87: 4, m.t.). In his 1986–87 paper Schmitt provides three proofs that relative prices are in reality logically undeterminable within GEA. The first proof consists in showing that the equations of supply and demand exclude the determination of the numerical value of exchanged goods.

Following Schmitt, let us consider an economy where only two goods, *a* and *b* are exchanged. To measure *a*'s and *b*'s supply and demand we must ascertain that the numerical value of the quantity of *a* exchanged on the market is equal to the numerical value of the quantity of *b*. This is certainly true when exchange takes place and one good is taken as the *numéraire*. Yet, to conclude that relative prices can indeed be determined by GEA it must be shown that supply and demand can be measured even *before* exchange, in a phase of reciprocal adjustment that alone can account for a true process of determination.

Two equations are available to determine $x$, the numerical value of the quantity exchanged of good *a*, and $y$, the numerical value of the quantity exchanged of good *b*:

$$\text{Supply of } a = \text{Demand for } a \quad (3.1)$$
$$\text{Supply of } b = \text{Demand for } b \quad (3.2)$$

The number of independent equations being equal to the number of variables, the system is apparently determinate and capable of determining $x$ and $y$. As shown by Schmitt (1986–87), however, advocates of GEA take over Walras's concept of relative exchange and claim that, even during the phase of adjustment, the supply of *a* is always necessarily equal to the demand for *b*, and the supply of *b* is always equal to the demand for *a*. Known as Walras's law, these identities derive from the belief that exchange takes place directly between real goods and that, to demand one (or more) good(s) it is necessary to offer another good (or other goods), and vice versa. As a consequence, the number of independent equations is reduced by one, because 'in order to write (and solve) the equations it is necessary to be at equilibrium' (ibid.: 6, m.t.).

The key consideration here is that to establish the numerical equality of $x$ and $y$ it is necessary to introduce *a* and *b* into the same numerical 'space', in other words, to make them homogeneous. '[N]o exchange can even be conceived disregarding the mathematical or numerical equality of the value of its terms' (ibid.: 7, m.t.). In GEA this numerical equality is given only at equilibrium, when exchanges actually take place. However, at equilibrium Walras's law applies, which reduces the number of independent equations and leaves the system undetermined.

*Second proof*

Schmitt's second proof develops along the same lines as the first, the only substantial difference being that, this time, the variables are the numerical prices of *a* and *b*. Neoclassical authors believe that in this case the reduction in independent equations is accompanied by a reduction in the number of variables, which would make the system perfectly determined. This result would become possible by choosing *a* or *b* as a *numéraire*, and by assuming that the price of the *numéraire*-good is constant and equal to one. Now, GEA's advocates forget that it is not enough to assume that the price of the *numéraire* is equal to unity, because '*there remains to be determined the physical quantity of the good to which the number one is associated*' (ibid.: 9, m.t.).

Even assuming that the number one hypothetically expresses the price of one unit of the *numéraire*

> we still do not know what the price of the quantity of the *numéraire*-good effectively exchanged will be, because this price is equal to *x*, where *x* is the unknown quantity of the good *a* [the *numéraire*] mobilized in the exchange.
>
> (ibid.: 9, m.t.)

As in Schmitt's first proof, the number of variables is equal to two, the numerical price of *a* and that of *b*, whereas Walras's law reduces the number of equations by one: the system is logically indeterminate. '[W]hen n = 2, the variables are also equal to number 2 so that the solution is *undetermined*; we are confronted with a single equation involving two independent variables' (ibid.: 9, m.t.).

### *Third proof*

The third proof considers the case in which prices are announced by the auctioneer and establishes that, even in this case, the system propounded by GEA cannot determine equilibrium prices. Suppose that a price of *a* in terms of *b* is proposed to the market by the auctioneer. One must verify if GEA accepts the existence of an excess demand for one of the two goods compared to the other. 'But if this measure is impossible, or if the excess demand is identical to zero whatever the price proposed, we would have to conclude that the theory is meaningless' (ibid.: 9, m.t.). This is indeed the result Schmitt's critical analysis delivers, by showing that the excess demand of each good is necessarily equal to zero.

When the price 'cried out' by the auctioneer is not that of equilibrium, it is apparently possible to verify the existence of a positive excess demand of one agent equal to the excess supply of the other. This implies that 'to determine excess demand, positive for one good and negative for the other, it is necessary to consider simultaneously the plans of the two agents' (ibid.: 10, m.t.). Taken separately, each agent equalizes their demand and their supply. Taken together, in their interaction, the demand of A is greater or lesser than that of B and, apparently, excess demand is possible during the search for equilibrium. Now, Schmitt shows that this is not so, because when considering the interaction of A and B's subjective plans, the excess demand for each good is formally nil.

The reason for the failure of GEA to account for a phase of reciprocal adjustment, is once again the assumption that the sum of demanded goods is always equal to the sum of supplied goods, that is that Walras's law holds good even before exchange. In our example, if A's demand for $b$ is equal to $x$, the implementation of Walras's law implies that A's supply of $a$ is also equal to $x$. Likewise, B's demand for $a$ being of $y$ units, its supply of $b$ is equal to $y$. The consequence for A is that its demand, measured initially by $x$, is now measured by $y$, and that B's demand for $a$ – initially measured by $y$ – is now measured by $x$.

> We verify that the incidence of the demand and supply of B on A's plan is *equal and of opposite sign*: the excess demand of good $a$, as it results from the interaction of agents' plans, is therefore identically equal to zero.
>
> (ibid.: 12, m.t.)

Suppose $x$ to be greater than $y$. A must realize the equality of the supply of and the demand for $a$, while B must realize the equality of its supply of and demand for $b$. The conditions of equilibrium making up for the system of independent equations are

$$\text{Demand of A} = \text{Supply of A} \tag{3.1}$$
$$\text{Demand of B} = \text{Supply of B} \tag{3.2}$$

Consider now the effects of the demand and supply of B on the relation of equilibrium of A. The impact of the supply of B on A's plan is to generate an excess demand equal to $x - y$, because it reduces to $y$ the value of A's demand, thus creating a gap between the equilibrium value of the demand A would like to be exerted on $a$ and the demand exerted by B (through its supply of $b$). At the same time, the impact of B's demand on A's plan is to cause an excess supply of $a$ also equal to $x - y$, because it decreases to $y$ the amount of A's supply that is matched by B's demand. As observed by Schmitt (1986–87), this result is general, so that 'the interaction of subjective plans invariably ends up defining an excess demand of a good if and only if it simultaneously defines an equal excess supply *of the same good*' (ibid.: 12, m.t.). The necessary nullity of any excess demand deprives GEA of any mechanism of adjustment accounting for the determination of relative prices, which remain totally unexplained.

### *Schmitt's 1987 paper*

In this paper, Schmitt shows that, although it would be absurd to claim that each economic agent's commercial purchases are always necessarily equal to their commercial sales, GEA cannot avoid assuming, albeit implicitly and unconsciously, that goods are always exchanged in compliance with the numerical equality of their measure. This is verified by what Schmitt calls the hidden assumption of GEA: 'commercial goods are entered into the set of real numbers as constant, "numerical masses"' (Schmitt 1987f: 3, m.t.). More specifically, he sets up to show that at equilibrium goods exchange in accordance with their numerical masses, so that each agent obtains and spends the same amount in each market session.

Schmitt analyzes the only three conceivable cases and shows that, whether goods exchange directly for one another, expressed in the *numéraire*, or exchange through the intermediation of money, GEA rests on the assumption that goods have a numerical mass.

In the first case, the constancy of goods' numerical mass is an implicit assumption of relative price determination. Given two commodities, *a* and *b*, the price of *a* in terms of *b* and conversely, of *b* in terms of *a*, is determined by letting *a* and *b* vary from zero to infinity until an agreement is found between A and B, and the two commodities are effectively exchanged for one another. Hence, agents are confronted with a price system for each quantity of their respective commodity, which means that they are 'confronted with an *infinity* of *price systems*' (ibid.: 7, m.t.). This leads Schmitt to observe that while 'an *equilibrium price* can be found in a given *price system* [...], in an *infinity of price systems*, "the" *equilibrium price* remains undetermined' (ibid.: 7, m.t.).

The advocates of GEA wrongly believe, in the case of two commodities, that the relationship between two quantities varying from zero to infinity can be replaced with a relationship between a fixed quantity of one commodity and an infinitely variable quantity of the other. The reason for their mistake resides in the neoclassical attempt to transform economics into a branch of mathematics. If commodities could be reduced to numbers, the relationship variable quantity of *b* / fixed quantity of *a* would allow us to relate all the possible variations of *a* to all the possible variations of *b* while keeping the denominator fixed. Indeed, in mathematics 'every variation of the denominator is superfluous because it takes us back, up to a scale factor, to a value already given relatively to the fixed denominator' (ibid.: 8, m.t.). Unfortunately for GEA, economics cannot be reduced to mathematics. In particular, it is not possible to maintain that physical quantities of heterogeneous goods are a-dimensional numbers.

Two conclusions derive from Schmitt's critical analysis.

(1) GEA 'is illogical because it takes physically heterogeneous goods to be dimensionless numbers' (ibid.: 8, m.t.).
(2) GEA takes it as a hidden assumption that 'goods have a "numerical mass" as objective as the physical mass of physical bodies' (ibid.: 8, m.t.).

The constancy of each commodity's numerical mass means that the ratio of exchange between physical goods is predetermined and the adjustment of supply and demand cannot modify it. In the example of two goods, both *a* and *b* are implicitly given a numerical mass before being exchanged, so that the determination of their equilibrium price is reduced to that of the absolute quantities of each good that economic agents agree to exchange. Hence, the hidden assumption of GEA amounts to imposing relative prices to the market. GEA is stuck between the devil and the deep blue sea: either it does not assume physical goods to be numbers axiomatically, in which case relative prices are logically undetermined, or it endorses the numerical mass axiom, in which case relative prices are predetermined by a *deus-ex-machina* and exchanged quantities are the only variable of the system.

The preceding conclusion remains essentially the same when a commodity is chosen as a *numéraire* and is arbitrarily identified with a dimensionless number. Indeed, to determine the equilibrium price of our two goods it is not enough to make one of them, say *a*, vary from zero to infinity as opposed to the other expressed by a pure number, say 1. The equilibrium price of *b* is as little known as that of *a*, and to assume, for example, that 10 units of *a* are equal to the number 1 'does not provide any information about the quantity of the good-*numéraire* that will finally be the object of an effective exchange' (ibid.: 11, m.t.). It is therefore mistaken to assume that, expressed in a *numéraire*, the price of *b* is constant during the search for equilibrium. Like in the previous case, GEA is incapable of determining relative prices – both *a* and *b* must vary from zero to infinity – unless goods are given a numerical mass, which would mean claiming that prices are predetermined, a statement in open contradiction with the objective of GEA.

Analyzing the third case, in which money is introduced in GEA as a mere intermediary, Schmitt observes that money can indeed be a *numéraire*, a dimensionless number as opposed to a real good, only if 'every agent spends the sum of money that he earns and earns the sum of money that he spends, precisely and instantaneously' (ibid.: 42, m.t.). It is only if this condition is fulfilled that the monetary price of one good can be maintained constant vis-à-vis the variation of the monetary prices of any other good, and an equilibrium price can be determined. In other words, it is only if money is never held as a good that relative prices can be expressed in money units and thus avoid indeterminacy.

To conclude, I want to make it clear that Schmitt does

> absolutely not pretend that goods are effectively endowed with *numerical masses*; but if they are not, GEA is without object. If we claim that the very idea of a numerical mass of goods is *absurd*, then we might as well call GEA *absurd* too.
>
> (ibid.: 16, m.t.)

Schmitt's critical investigation of GEA and, in particular of the neoclassical theory of relative prices, brings to the fore the logical inconsistency of an approach heavily based on the use of mathematics. In their attempt to transform economics into a branch of mathematics, the advocates of GEA make two serious mistakes. First, they assume as an axiom that goods, physically heterogeneous, can be 'any real number' (Debreu 1959: 30). Second, they believe that, thanks to mathematics, the infinite price systems economic agents are confronted with before exchange can be reduced to a single price system. The first assumption is clearly metaphysical, the second misses the point that 'the prejudicial question of the determination of one and *only one price system* pertains to "ordinary" logic (à la Wittgenstein) and not to mathematical logic (à la Whitehead)' (ibid.: 17, m.t.).

## The shortcomings of Keynesian analysis

### *The problem of income determination*

The starting point of Schmitt's critical assessment of the Keynesian theory of income determination is Keynes's fundamental identity between $Y$, total supply, and $C+I$, total demand. As is well-known, Keynesian economists maintain that Keynes's identity holds good only at equilibrium for a level of national income determined through the adjustment of aggregate supply and demand.

In the simplest model of income determination, equilibrium would result from the solution of two independent equations:

$$Y = C + I \tag{3.3}$$

$$C = a + c \cdot Y \tag{3.4}$$

Where it is assumed that consumption is a function of income, investment is a constant, and $a$, the necessary consumption, and $c$, the propensity to consume, are given, numerical coefficients. The system apparently consists of two independent equations and seems therefore apt to determine its two variables, $Y$ and $C$. This would indeed be the case if $Y = C+I$ could be considered as a conditional equality, if 'Y were to stand for one concept and C+I for another' (Schmitt 1972a: 34). Yet, Keynes's equality between $Y$ and $C+I$ stems from a definition and pertains to the category of identities, which means that $Y$ and $C+I$ are two faces of the same coin, they 'designate the same thing' (ibid.: 34).

Keynesian economists recognize this as a matter of fact and endeavour to reconcile it with what they believe to be the need to consider Keynes's identity as a condition of equilibrium. 'If Keynes had stopped with this identity, we would be left with an indeterminable system' (Samuelson 1966: 1198). Ignoring the open contradiction inherent in the fact of considering $Y = C+I$ as an identity and a conditional equality at the same time, they postulate that $Y$ is equal to $C+I$ by definition *and* that $Y$ is equal to $C+I$ only for the equilibrium value of national income.

The reason for the Keynesian attempt to transform a definition into a condition of equilibrium lies in the influence exerted by GEA and in the belief that, like relative prices, national income would be determined through the reciprocal adjustment of supply and demand. Following Hicks's neoclassical interpretation of Keynes's *General Theory*, most Keynesian economists have elaborated their models along the lines advocated by Walras. The search for equilibrium has replaced Keynes's conceptual definitions, and the use of mathematics has been adopted as the privileged methodology for economic investigation.

Yet, 'as far as the analysis of national income determination is concerned, the mathematical instrument is inoperative. Mathematically, the identity $Y \equiv C + I$ has the same meaning as $Y \equiv Y$' (Schmitt 1971a: 358, m.t.). Schmitt's argument is clear:

1) Keynes's equation is an identity, because $C + I$ defines $Y$, and the amount of available income, $Y$, defines total demand, $C + I$.
2) 'No equation *in any field* can be defined simultaneously as an identity and a condition of equilibrium' (Schmitt 1972a: 35).

The analogy between relative prices and national income determination breaks down, because there cannot be instants in time where $Y$ is different from $C + I$. Income is generated by production, and production takes time. There is no such thing as an instantaneous product: 'no amount of national income can ever be produced instantaneously' (ibid.: 23). A finite period of continuous time is necessary for an economic production to be positive.

Following Schmitt, let us distinguish between instants $i_1$, when income is actually determined, and infinite instants $i_2$ separating two successive instants $i_1$. Keynes's equation could be considered as a conditional equality if its two terms were distinct and numerically different during the span of time separating one production from another, that is, at instants $i_2$. Two arguments show that this can never be the case.

The first is based on the fact that no instant $i_2$ can be detected in the analysis of income determination. Every production brings about and defines an income that refers to the period of time during which the productive activity takes place. As soon as income is formed, it defines simultaneously a supply – the product – and an equal demand, whose scientific measure is given by the amount of available income. The identity thus formed extends to the entire period of production, so that no instants $i_2$ exist where total demand could differ from total supply.

> The theory of income does not differentiate two families of instants, for income, unlike prices, cannot be determined instantaneously. [...] At any point, whatever the instantaneous level of national income, the measure of income is zero. For income must have a time dimension. [...] The theory of income does not differentiate the two families of instants $i_1$ and $i_2$.
>
> (ibid. 35–6)

The second argument is closely connected to the first and concerns the distinction between virtual and realized magnitudes and the idea that, even though, as realized quantities, $Y$ and $C+I$ are necessarily equal, they can differ and reciprocally adjust in virtual time. Once production has occurred no adjustment is possible, but before any given income is actually produced it seems possible to assume that virtual, desired, supply is free to adjust to virtual or desired demand. This is to forget that a virtual income is only an imaginary magnitude, and that virtual or imaginary forces cannot have any positive impact and can therefore not be the source of any real equilibrating process. '*To virtual prices correspond real factors of supply and demand. To virtual income corresponds a total demand which is as virtual as income itself*' (ibid. 66). If total supply is merely virtual, so is total demand because imaginary income can only feed imaginary demand: 'related to virtual income, forces of demand for consumption- and investment-goods are themselves virtual' (Schmitt 1971a: 357, m.t.).

Once more, the purported analogy between relative prices and income determination turns out to be logically unfounded and misleading. Whereas in the theory of relative prices one may assume that, before exchange, economic agents exert real demand even though prices are still undetermined, before income is produced demand and supply remain virtual, they actually are inexistent. On the other hand, after production has taken place, demand and supply are given together, and there is no room for any adjustment between $Y$ and $C+I$. 'Once demand is realized, income is already determined, since no adjustment is possible between two identical terms' (Schmitt 1972a: 68).

### *The principle of effective demand*

Despite the fact that no adjustment is possible between total supply and total demand, it is nevertheless correct to claim that virtual demand determines realized income. This is not to say that virtual demand and virtual income confront each other as two distinct forces whose equilibrium determines realized income. There is no market on which virtual demand and supply adjust each other according to a mechanism like the one posited in relative prices theory. However, if the adjustment is meant to describe what happens before firms decide to produce a given income, then clearly virtual demand plays a central role.

> The determining factor in national income, pure Demand, is virtual. Realized Demand does not determine National Income. Once demand is realized, income is already determined, since no adjustment is possible between two identical terms. Virtual Income is brought into equilibrium with virtual, expected Demand. In Income theory, the determinant factor is virtual.
>
> (ibid.: 68)

The adjustment of virtual income to virtual demand Schmitt refers to is nothing other than Keynes's principle of *effective demand*, which states that '[v]irtual

Demand raises Supply to its own level, which is not necessarily the level of full employment' (ibid.: 121).

According to Keynes

> the volume of employment is given by the point of intersection between the aggregate demand function and the aggregate supply function; for it is at this point that the entrepreneurs' expectation of profits will be maximised. The value of D at this point of the aggregate demand function, where it is intersected by the aggregate supply function, will be called *the effective demand.*
>
> (Keynes 1936/1946: 25)

What one must understand is that the aggregate demand function Keynes refers to is the virtual demand as expected by entrepreneurs, who are keen to set production at a level where the equilibrium between costs and receipts is compatible with the maximization of profit. 'The equality of virtual income and virtual demand is conditional: it drives firms to effectively distribute the amount of the imaginary equilibrium income' (Schmitt 1971a: 13, m.t.).

Schmitt's reading of Keynes is highly original, in stark contrast to the interpretations of Keynesian economists. He uncompromisingly rejects the attempt to retain Keynes's equation $Y = C + I$ as a condition of equilibrium and shows that Keynes's theory is revolutionary only if Keynes's fundamental equations are considered as *identities*. He also identifies, in the principle of effective demand, Keynes's specific contribution to the theory of income determination. '[Keynes's] innovation will survive in the history of thought: the discovery of the virtual factors of supply and demand' (Schmitt 1972a: 115).

The relevance of Keynes's discovery is even greater if, with Schmitt, we observe that 'effective demand is *simultaneously* a flux and a reflux' (Schmitt 1971a: 345, m.t.). Firms' decision to produce is taken when their expected sales match their estimated costs, that is, when virtual demand for consumption- and investment-goods matches virtual income. At the point of intersection, the flow of firms' planned expenditures is identical to the flow of their expected receipts. It is at this point that effective demand is defined, which is itself specified by the coincidence of the two virtual flows. 'Hence, regarding effective demand exactly interpreted, Keynes has no precursor; for the first time in the history of economic thought, we find an analysis in terms of imaginary flux-reflux' (ibid.: 345, m.t.).

### *The multiplier and the multiplicand*

Schmitt's critique of Keynes's income multiplier is highly articulated and confirms Schmitt's appreciation of the relevance of Keynes's urge to escape from old ideas 'which ramify [...] into every corner of our minds' (Keynes 1936/1946: viii). Almost all of Schmitt's 365-page long book *L'analyse macroéconomique des revenus* (1971) is devoted to

1) A critical analysis of the multiplier and the proof that 'national income is newly created in each period: *it does not form a chain in time*' (Schmitt 1971a: 5, m.t.), and to
2) The positive analysis of the multiplicand.

I will now briefly address these two topics.

According to the theory of the multiplier, successive incomes are functionally correlated, any given income being the source of a series of induced incomes. The relationship between the totality of incomes (initial + induced) and the first income of the chain is called the multiplier or the coefficient of multiplication, $k$. In equation

$$\Delta Y = k \cdot \Delta A \tag{3.5}$$

$k$ is the multiplier, $\Delta A$ the multiplicand, and $\Delta Y$ the total income generated by the process. Schmitt starts his analysis by distinguishing the area of virtual quantities from that of realized magnitudes and by showing that in both areas $k$ is necessarily equal to 1. If firms' foreseen purchases of their output are $A^\star$, 'the equilibrium of virtual income is

$$Y_0{}^* = k^* \cdot A^*, \tag{3.6}$$

where $k^\star$ is logically equal to 1. Income, which will be produced by firms, is equal to expected purchases' (Schmitt 1972a: 126). We reach the same result if we consider an increase in virtual demand $\Delta A^\star$. Faced with an expected demand equal to $A^\star + \Delta A^\star$, firms will adjust their plans and bring virtual supply to the level of virtual demand: $k^\star$ is again logically equal to 1.

In the field of realized quantities, Schmitt's proof runs as follows.

1. The traditional theory of the multiplier rests on two assumptions: a) expenditures of a given income generate new income; b) hoarding reduces available income. Analysis must establish whether these assumptions stand up to logical scrutiny.
2. Hoarding is necessarily nil. In conformity with the asset-liability nature of money, income forms as a bank deposit, and bank deposits cannot be hoarded. Income can be saved, of course, but savings do not decrease the amount of income available in a banking system. On the contrary, savings are lent and feed borrowers' expenditures: 'no fraction of income can be hoarded. An unspent income is a theoretical monster, for all income is defined by consumption and investment expenditures' (ibid.: 129).
3. The logical impossibility to hoard bank deposits entails the necessary expenditure of the totality of available income: $Y = C + I$. Given that 'no fraction of distributed income can be held and saved as a macroeconomic

hoarding, the income formed is necessarily spent' (Schmitt 1971a: 335, m.t.).

4. If one considers the hypothesis that expenditures recreate income, the only value of *k* consistent with the logical impossibility to reduce the amount of bank deposits through hoarding is *infinity*. Indeed, the totality of income formed being necessarily spent by income-earners and/or by borrowers (firms included), if expenditures reproduced income, there would be no end to the process of multiplication.
5. Confronted with the choice between an infinite chain of income induced from income, $k=\infty$, and a coefficient of induction necessarily equal to 1, the researcher has to conclude that expenditure leads to the destruction of income and not to its reproduction: 'incomes are spent and not reproduced by purchases' (Schmitt 1972a: 137).

In his analysis of Keynes's multiplier, Schmitt goes beyond mere critique and ends up showing that 'the multiplier theory offers to analysis a category of expenditures previously unknown, injections or the multiplicand' (ibid.: 137). Emphasis switches from an unrealistic process where income is supposed to derive from income to the event that brings about the initial income of the hypothetical chain. Where does the initial income, the multiplicand, come from? This is the key question that the theory of the multiplier brings to the fore.

Once shown that an income's expenditure does not reproduce it, what has to be determined is the expenditure that creates income. '*[T]he multiplicand is an injection of income, an income whose source is not an income*' (Schmitt 1971a: 99, m.t.). It is Keynes himself who provides the answer:

> E, the total money income or earnings of the community in a unit of time [is equal to] I', the part of it which has been earned by the production of investment goods, so that I' measures the cost of production of new investment and E – I' [C'] the cost of production of the current output of consumption goods.
>
> (Keynes 1930/1971: 121)

I conclude with two passages excerpted from Schmitt.

> The theory of the multiplier ends up [...] as a *causal law*. Measured by final purchases, income is formed through the remuneration of the production factors. Derived from the multiplier, the causal identity of (C + I) and (C' + I') is a fundamental law.
>
> (Schmitt 1972a: 87–8, m.t.)

'Equation

$Y$ = multiplicand

states the causal law upon which all macroeconomics is based' (Schmitt 1971a: 138).

## The critical appraisal of Marx's analysis of value and profit

Schmitt's interest in Marx's economic analysis dates to the 1960s and finds its peak with the publications of two books, co-authored with me: *La pensée de Karl Marx, critique et synthèse*. Vol. I *La valeur*, Vol. II *La plus-value*. Let us consider the two topics of value and profit in succession.

### *The critical appraisal of Marx's theory of value*

As is well-known, Marx initiated his economic analysis by tackling the problem of the physical heterogeneity of goods and by claiming, as previously done by Smith and Ricardo, that human labour is the common denominator that makes goods commensurable. Only by expressing the exchange value of goods in a common unit of measure can commodities be made homogeneous, and an economic system be worked out. In Marx's theory, '*goods can be exchanged on the products market, and it is possible to speak of their exchange value only if they are first measured*' (Cencini and Schmitt 1976: 17, m.t.). Labour is identified as the source of value and the unit of measure. In this respect, it is essential to observe that Marx is adamant: being the source of value, labour itself has no value. Labour measures commodities, but labour does not measure itself. Labour and commodities are two distinct concepts, the former is the unit through which the latter is measured, and it would be a big mistake to mix them up.

Exchange values are determined by labour alone, which is the sole factor of production. Fixed capital goods increase the physical productivity of labour and are a major cause of increase in the production of use values. Yet, exchange values are unaffected: they do not depend on the quantity of physical goods produced but on the labour socially necessary to produce them. It is relevant to observe that in Marx we find two conceptions of value and two ways of measuring it. The first, and by far the less fruitful, identifies value with a substance resulting from the materialization of labour-time. The second and more modern conception considers value as a relation between commodities and the abstract labour socially required to produce them.

Marx distinguishes also between concrete labour, the source of use values, and abstract, undifferentiated social labour determining values in exchange. The transformation of the different kinds of skilled and unskilled labour into abstract labour-time is a well-known obstacle marring Marx's analysis. The search for a common denominator between different kinds of labour is doomed to failure if labour is measured in time-units. To claim that '[a] commodity may be the outcome of the most complicated labour, but through its *value* it is posited as equal to the product of simple labour, hence it represents only a specific quantity of simple labour' (Marx 1867/1976: 135) is tantamount to claiming that complex labour is reduced to simple labour by goods' own values. The circularity of such a claim is clear: 'the reduction of a kind of labour to another depends on the measure of goods, which can be determined only once the reduction has occurred' (Cencini and Schmitt 1976: 101, m.t.). The only way out is to measure labour in (numerical) wages, a solution Marx glimpsed but did not follow up, and which would have substantially modified his labour theory of value.

Another important feature of Marx's theory of value is the law of exchange between equivalents. Exchange between goods takes place only once they have been produced, and in conformity with their respective values. '*First heterogeneous products must be made commensurable, then they can be exchanged at parity*' (ibid. 43, m.t.). It is through the mediation of money that exchanges occur; yet money does in no way alter Marx's law of exchange. This is so because money is identified with the *general equivalent*, a commodity chosen from the set of goods and whose value is determined like that of any other commodity.

The choice of a commodity-money and the claim that on the labour market firms purchase workers' labour-power – that is, a commodity sold by workers at its precise value measured in labour-time – led Marx to the most rigorous formulation of the law of exchange. Every exchange occurring on the labour or the product market must comply with the identity between value and price, no degree of freedom being conceivable between them. Unfortunately, this causes a major difficulty that leads to a logical inconsistency fatal to Marx's theory of value.

Let us consider the impact of capital on the measure of value. Circulating capital does not cause any problem, for 'it is nothing other than a material element that, once transformed by labour, is again present in the final product' (ibid.: 54, m.t.). The presence of circulating capital does not alter the measure of output, which is determined by the totality of labour spent on its production, circulating capital included. '*Since stocks represent nothing other than commodities sold through the intermediation of final output, it is totally logical that their measure be included in that of selling output*' (ibid.: 57, m.t.). No difference between value and price can be detected because the stocks of goods entering the production process as circulating capital raise both the value of final output and its selling price.

Things are radically different when we consider the impact of fixed capital on value and prices. Consistent with Marx's theory of value, instrumental capital does not increase the value of products, because it is not a macroeconomic factor of production. Labour alone creates value, which is measured by the quantity of social labour spent on producing final output. It is true that Marx claims that part of the value of fixed capital transfers to the final product. However, it is also certain that this transfer occurs only to the extent that labour preserves the value of fixed capital.

> The worker does not perform two pieces of work simultaneously, one in order to add value to the cotton, the other in order to preserve the value

> of the means of production [...]. But by the very act of adding new value, he preserves their former values.
>
> (Marx 1867/1976: 307)

To say that fixed capital transfers part of its value to the new product only insofar as labour reconstitutes the value of fixed capital is equivalent to saying that 'living' labour generates and measures the totality of value. Since fixed capital is not part of the final product, its measure does not add to that of the labour entirely supplied by workers, which includes the labour required to restore the initial value of instrumental goods.

Using Marx's symbols, we would say that the final measure of current output is

$$v + s,$$

where $v$ represents the value of variable capital (the labour required to produce circulating capital and workers' labour-power) and $s$ stands for the surplus-value. Now, a major difficulty arises when amortization of fixed capital has to be accounted for financially. It is clear, indeed, that the price at which final output has to be sold must be equal to

$$v + s + c,$$

where $c$ indicates the part lost by fixed capital to be reinstated. It is only by selling the product at a price of $v+s+c$ that firms can amortize monetarily their fixed capital.

Yet, this inevitably leads to a disparity between value and price, which stands for an open contradiction in Marx's theory. Values are defined in the sphere of production, prices in that of circulation. Values are determined by the equivalence between goods and social labour, prices by that between goods and money. These 'two equivalences enter into contradiction *from the moment money is considered as a commodity*' (Cencini and Schmitt 1976: 94–5, m.t.). If money is a commodity, it can only exchange with products according to their respective values. As value and prices can in no way differ, the amortization of fixed capital remains unexplained, and Marx's theory is severely affected.

### *The critique of Marx's theory of profit*

Confronted with the need to respect the law of exchange between equivalents, Marx starts his analysis by observing that profit cannot form in the sphere of circulation. He then notes that the same result would apply to the sphere of production if firms' payment of wages defined their purchase of labour. To avoid the dismal conclusion that the labour theory of value cannot explain profit, Marx introduces a distinction between labour and labour-power and identifies the latter as the commodity purchased by firms on the labour market.

Profit, which Marx calls surplus-value, derives from the labour-power's capacity to create a greater value than is needed for its reproduction. If 'the value of labour-power, and the value which that labour-power valorizes [verwertet] in the labour-process, are two entirely different magnitudes' (Marx 1867/1976: 300), which is always the case in a capitalist economy, a positive surplus-value appears in the sphere of production.

The difficulty facing Marx's theory of surplus-value concerns the monetary realization of the goods obtained by firms as surplus-value. The only income available is workers' wages, and the expenditure of wages ensures the monetary realization of wage-goods only. Marx's question 'where does the money come from which it [surplus-value] is turned into?' (Marx 1885/1978: 404) is doomed to remain unanswered if its theoretical framework is that of the identity between prices and values and of the identification of money with a commodity.

> The formation of a surplus is insufficient, if it is not accompanied by its monetary realization. In other words, formation and realization represent two half-circles whose unity defines the circulation of surplus-value. It follows that a profit formed and not realized is a profit that has never existed.
>
> (Cencini and Schmitt 1977: 57, m.t.)

This is an inescapable conclusion, and we will prove it starting from Marx's own attempt to avoid it by resorting to the advance of profit.

What must be clear from the outset is that it is not enough to assume that monetary profit is advanced to explain its formation. On the contrary, it is only by explaining its formation that profit can be given in advance. Moreover, this method can be adopted only if and when the reconstitution of advances has been explained. 'Every advance must be reconstituted, in conformity with the law of reproduction' (ibid.: 84, m.t.). Spent in advance, profit must not be spent a second time once firms have recovered it.

As claimed by Marx, it is a

> law that, in the normal course of reproduction (whether simple or on an expanded scale), the money advanced to circulation by the capitalist-producer must return to its starting-point (it being immaterial here whether the money belongs to him or is borrowed).
>
> (Marx 1885/1978: 533)

In the case of simple reproduction, monetary capital advanced to firms and spent on the payment of wages flows back through the expenditure of workers. In this respect, it is important to note that Marx strongly maintains that capitalist firms never lose variable capital. '*Since this variable capital always remains in one form or the other in the hands of the capitalist, it can in no way be said to be converted into revenue for anyone*' (ibid.: 523).

This point is central, because it shows that firms do not transfer any value to workers, whose wages do not come out of a transformation of variable capital but are created by labour. It also shows that one must understand the advance of variable capital as an advance of money enabling, through the payment of wages, the value produced by labour to be given a monetary form. 'Up to *v*, output can receive its money-form, because the payment of wages implies the confrontation of two persons' (Cencini and Schmitt 1977: 101, m.t.): entrepreneurs and workers. The inflow defined by the expenditure of wages then matches the outflow of money defined by the payment of workers, and the money advanced as a variable capital can be recovered.

When surplus-value enters the process, things change radically: 'as far as *s* is concerned, it is formally impossible for the product to receive its money-form, because the transaction involved would be defined between the capitalist and himself' (ibid.: 101, m.t.). The reason of this impossibility is that Marx's surplus-value has no monetary cost of production: it is obtained by firms at zero cost. Hence, while the outflow of wages is matched by the inflow of their expenditure, profit is spent on a unidirectional transaction, which hampers the reconstitution of the monetary profit advanced to firms. The conclusion is unavoidable: the logical impossibility to realize monetarily Marx's surplus-value is confirmed, and his entire theory of profit must be reformulated.

## Critical analysis of Sraffa's attempt at determining relative prices

In his dense little volume entitled *Production of Commodities by Means of Commodities*, Sraffa (1960) maintains that the prices of products can be derived from their methods of production. He starts his analysis by considering two industries producing iron and wheat respectively. In Sraffa's simplest case, in which surpluses are zero in both industries, the necessity to reproduce, at the end of the process, the situation present at the beginning in each industry (*self-replacing state*) seems enough to determine the equilibrium rate of exchange between iron and wheat. 'There is a unique set of exchange-values which if adopted by the market restores the original distribution of the products and makes it possible for the process to be repeated; such values spring directly from the methods of production' (Sraffa 1960: 3).

Before the two goods are exchanged in order to reproduce the *status quo ante*, they are heterogeneous: they do not 'pertain to the same "space of measurement"' (Cencini and Schmitt 1976: 116, m.t.). Does their 'exchange of production' make them homogeneous? Sraffa does not claim so. Indeed, it is only if production involved transformation that the quantity of iron and wheat exchanged at the end of the production process would be equivalent. If we reject the 'alchemist' idea of production-transformation, it appears that, heterogeneous before exchange, iron and wheat remain so even during or after their exchange. It is certain, in fact, that direct exchange does not provide for the objects exchanged to be measured by a common standard.

The reason for this logical impossibility is simply the fact that direct exchange is a *bipolar* transaction. '*The transformation of iron into the standard of wheat defines identically the transformation of wheat into the standard of iron. It is therefore formally impossible to end up with a single standard*' (ibid.: 119, m.t.). Since every exchange is a two-way transaction, the definition of one good as the standard of the other necessarily implies the definition of the latter as standard of the former. These two standards would be reduced to one only if they were commensurable, that is, if iron and wheat were homogeneous, which they are not.

Sraffa does not claim anywhere that exchange can introduce the homogeneity of physically heterogeneous goods, but he believes it possible to determine their relative prices by determining their methods of production. Does he succeed where Walras failed? Can the equilibrium rate of exchange derive from a system of equations defining the production of commodities by means of commodities? Sraffa's reply to the latter question is yes. Taking over the Physiocrats concept of *productive consumption*, he believes that production is an exchange capable of determining the equilibrium prices left undetermined in Walras's general equilibrium system. To do so, he assumes that iron and wheat are exchanged according to a rate of exchange for a system in a self-replacing state.

However, as Schmitt observes, Sraffa's self-replacing state cannot be considered as a condition *imposed* by the system because, if it were, this would imply that the system could never reckon with any surplus of production. Its logical status can only be that of an assumption introduced to simplify the analysis. The annoying fact is that the self-replacing state and zero production surpluses are jointly introduced by Sraffa as simplifying assumptions. Taken together, the two 'assumptions' deprive Sraffa's system of any heuristic value: instead of facilitating the determination of the ratio of exchange between iron and wheat, they merely define it. 'Given the two assumptions, nothing follows from it. Prices are not the consequence of the assumptions but their very definition' (ibid.: 126, m.t.).

Sraffa could write his equations only if iron and wheat admitted of a common standard. The bipolar nature of exchange forbids that the two products share a single, common standard and makes it logically impossible to write down any equation relating one good to the other. Sraffa's initial system seems to work only because he assumes a situation of self-replacing state without production surplus. In reality, in this particular case the ratio of exchange between iron and wheat proposed by Sraffa satisfies his 'equations' only because it is defined by them. 'Finally, Sraffa has no standard, no equivalences, and no equations. Hence, his two assumptions – the (temporary) absence of surplus and the self-replacing state – define prices directly, while apparently providing the conditions for their determination' (ibid.: 127, m.t.).

Things do not change substantially when we move on to the analysis of production with a surplus. This time Sraffa's assumptions are that the system of production be able to start all over again at the end of each period (self-replacing state) and that the surplus be distributed proportionally to the advances in each industry. '[T]he surplus (a profit) must be distributed in proportion to the means of production (or capital) advanced in each industry' (Sraffa 1960: 6), which implies that the rate of profit must be uniform for all industries.

As in the previous case, the prices Sraffa believes to be determined simultaneously with the rate of profit by his system of equations are in reality fully pre-determined by his initial assumptions. Prices and rate of profit are merely defined by Sraffa's equations and not determined by them.

Schmitt's critique goes further. Let us consider only two of the arguments he puts forward. The first concerns Sraffa's hidden assumption that the two commodities of his example, iron and wheat, are merely two different kinds of the *same commodity*. Sraffa builds his analysis on the explicit assumptions that:

1) Consumption is a production: productive consumption;
2) The system is in a self-replacing state;
3) Profit is proportional to advances.

In his numerical example, the methods of production are described in Table 3.1.

Transformed by Sraffa into equations, they are supposed to determine a rate of exchange of 15 quarter of wheat for 1 ton of iron and a rate of profit of 25% in each industry. How is this possible given that the totality of iron produced by the second industry, 20 tons, is used up in the production of iron and wheat? As Schmitt observes, it is contradictory to claim that the production of iron is entirely consumed and that it gives rise to a surplus. Yet, Sraffa is convinced that his example respects both these opposite requirements without falling into contradiction. He claims in fact that the wheat surplus is enough to guarantee each industry a surplus of 25% in wheat.

The problem remains. No surplus in iron is formed, and yet Sraffa maintains that the industry producing iron achieves a surplus. He also maintains that the surplus obtained by the industry producing wheat is equal to 25%, which should lead to a total production of wheat equal to 560 qr. and not to the 575 qr. calculated by Sraffa. Everything comes out right, if it is assumed that the industry producing iron achieves a surplus in wheat, which amounts to assuming 'that *wheat is a kind of iron*' (Cencini and Schmitt 1976: 131, m.t.), and which shows 'the deep meaning of [Sraffa's] equations' (ibid.; 131, m.t.).

Schmitt's final argument is that of the '*indeterminacy of prices when commodities remain heterogeneous*' (ibid.: 132, m.t.). The question asked here is not whether or not exchange can make the goods exchanged homogeneous, which it cannot because it is a bipolar transaction, but whether prices can

*Table 3.1* Sraffa's methods of production

| | |
|---|---|
| 280 qr. wheat + 12 t. iron ⟶ | 575 qr. Wheat |
| 120 qr. wheat + 8 t. iron ⟶ | 20 t. iron |

Source: Sraffa 1960: 7

be determined through an operation that leaves commodities heterogeneous. Schmitt's answer is straightforward no, because if commodities remain heterogeneous, prices themselves, as pure relations of exchange, are bound to remain heterogeneous. 'The conclusion is very clear: if commodities are definitely heterogeneous, prices cannot be determined, because the determination of prices supposes their commensurability, which entails their homogeneity' (ibid.: 132, m.t.).

Sraffa's failure to determine equilibrium prices through the methods of production confirms the logical impossibility to determine relative prices through direct exchange of real goods, whether analyzed within Walras's model of GEA, Sraffa's system of production of commodities by means of commodities or within any other conceivable scheme deprived of a common numerical standard.

## The critique of Pasinetti's theory of value

Let me conclude this chapter by observing that Schmitt's critique to Sraffa's model applies equally well to Pasinetti's input–output model. Even though Pasinetti avoids Sraffa's mistake of adding iron to wheat and pigs by proposing an input-output scheme in which only different quantities of the same commodity are added to one another, the ratio of exchange he derives from it is pre-determined by his assumption: the self-replacing state, which Pasinetti calls *stationary state*. However, Schmitt's critique concerns another aspect of Pasinetti's analysis: the introduction of a surplus distributed to the 'final sector', that is, of a surplus consumed by workers whose services contribute to the production of iron, wheat, and turkeys (Sraffa's pigs).

The central point here is the definition of labour, delivered by the final sector. If labour is considered as a commodity – an assumption implicit in the way Pasinetti (1975) calculates the rates of exchange in his analysis of Sraffa's methods of production – a difficulty arises concerning the very existence of a physical surplus. If production is investigated from a purely physical viewpoint, it is immediately clear that output can be identical only to input.

Assuming that it can be calculated, the sum of physical input (that is, of all the components entering a process of production, including those provided by nature like rain, sun, soil fertility and so on) can but be equal to the sum of physical output. Lavoisier's law and Einstein's equivalence of mass and energy leave no room for a miraculous physical surplus. Moreover, if labour is considered as a commodity, Pasinetti's analysis does not substantially differ from the neoclassical one, which is exactly the opposite of what the Italian economist is aiming for.

Pasinetti's objective is to work out a *pure labour theory* where labour plays the role of the sole source of value: '[l]abour is, therefore, the only factor of production' (Pasinetti 1993: 16). If labour is the sole factor of production and the standard of value, the price of goods must be expressed in labour quantities, which requires labour to be homogeneous.

Pasinetti refers to Sraffa and assumes that labour has somehow already been made homogeneous, without explaining how. The only hint he gives concerns the use of wages. However, in Pasinetti's theoretical framework wages are expressed in terms of the final goods distributed to households; they are not money wages. This implies that labour measures not only the price of real goods and services but also the price of labour itself, that is, of wages.

Pasinetti is thus trapped between the two terms of an alternative, neither of which is satisfactory.

1) The claim that labour is made homogeneous by wages, in which case goods themselves are made homogeneous by wages so that, contrary to what Pasinetti endeavours to establish, 'wages and not labour are the sole measure of the value of products' (Schmitt 1998e: 13, m.t.).
2) The claim that labour measures the value of products and that wages are themselves measured by labour, in which case labour is bound to remain heterogeneous since wages can no longer be used to make it homogeneous.

Pasinetti's attempt at building a pure labour theory of value fails because it rests on the neoclassical assumption that prices can be determined through direct exchange. To move from a model of pure exchange based on individual preferences to a pure labour model based on production techniques and structural change is not enough. What needs to be done is to work out a *monetary* labour theory of value, in which money is integrated from the outset: either money 'is present from the beginning, which leads to the measure of the value of products by money wages, or it is too late to do anything' (ibid.: 13, m.t.).

# 4 1979–1984: The discovery of quantum time

The late 1970s and early 1980s were momentous years in Schmitt's macroeconomic analysis coinciding as they did with his discovery of a revolutionary concept that may be useful to other sciences but does not derive from any of them: quantum time. The concept of quantum time is the logical outcome of Schmitt's analysis of money and its integration or association with production. It was developed together with his theory of emissions and is at the centre of two manuscripts. One of these, entitled *Le temps quantique* (1979), remains unpublished, while the second, *Inflation, chômage et malformations du capital*, was published in 1984 by Economica (Paris) and Castella (Albeuve, CH), the English translation of which was published in 2021 by Routledge (London and New York). The present chapter relies essentially on these two texts, more precisely on the parts in them that deal with the relationship between production, expenditures, and time within a macroeconomic analysis centred on the theory of emissions.

Let me make clear from the outset that Schmitt's quantum macroeconomic approach is not at all derived from quantum physics. The reader should not be misled by the use of terms such as 'quantum', 'wavelike', and 'corpuscular'. Even though the meanings evoked by these terms are similar to those used in physics, in economics, for the first time in the history of science, they refer to time. Macroeconomics is an autonomous science, and Schmitt has never stopped providing new arguments against any attempt to transform economics into a branch of mathematics or physics. Quantum physics is no exception, even though it is interesting to note the existence of 'striking parallels' (Schmitt 1986a: 126) between quantum macroeconomics and quantum physics.

## Production and time

Is production a process of transformation? Or is it a creation with a positive cost? From a purely physical viewpoint, it cannot be denied that production is a transformation of matter or energy so that its result, its output, is neither greater nor lesser than its input. If every input is – as it must be – accounted for, no difference can be found between what enters the process

DOI: 10.4324/9781351271325-7

of transformation and what comes out of it in physical terms. In conformity with the laws of physics, a process of transformation cannot generate a net product.

Things change radically with the economic analysis of production, when we take into consideration the original role played by the work of man and its impact on value. What we are referring to here is obviously not a hypothetical economic dimension like those discussed in physics. Man cannot create matter or energy out of nothing; hence neither matter or energy can account for economic value, and the same conclusion necessarily also applies to the product which the economic object value refers to.

Economic analysis of production is the analysis of how man's activity can create a net product. Schmitt's starting point is a critical investigation of the mainstream assumption that production is a function of time. If this were indeed the case, the analysis of production would require the use of mathematics, more precisely, of differential equations, when production is considered as a function of continuous time, and of finite difference equations when it is taken to be a function of discontinuous time. In the first case, continuous analysis applies, while the second calls for period analysis. Whether we choose continuous or discontinuous analysis, the result is the same and, if confirmed by experimental observation, it would establish once and for all the superiority of the mathematical approach to economics advocated by so many orthodox economists.

Let us consider the simplest of cases and assume that production is a continuous function of time whose value is constant in period, $p_0$. According to this assumption, the product of $p_0$ is determined by multiplying the productive activity by the time during which this activity is exercised (Figure 4.1).

This representation treats production as a mechanical process whose result is greater the longer the activity lasts. It implies that human labour produces like a machine and is not the critical macroeconomic factor of production. Capital would appear to be much more productive than human labour, and the product would be equal to production, the productive activity, multiplied by a positive period of time, $\Delta t$:

$$\text{product} = \text{production} \cdot \Delta t \tag{4.1}$$

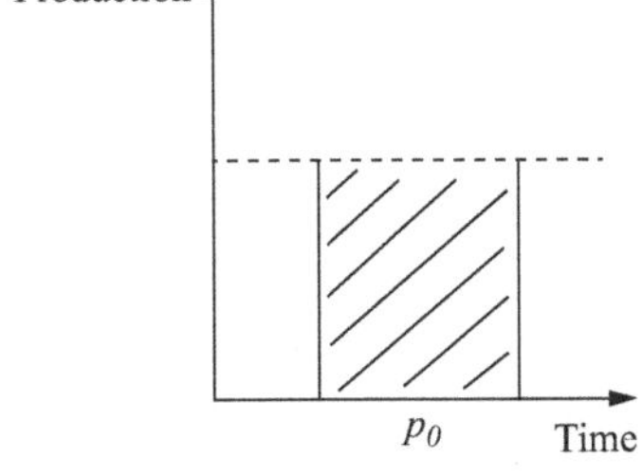


*Figure 4.1* Product as a result of production taken as a constant function of continuous time.

The appeal of the analogy between classical mechanics and the orthodox analysis of production is self-evident. In the same way as the distance covered by a physical body moving at a constant speed during $x$ units of time is equal to

$$\text{space} = \text{velocity} \cdot x, \tag{4.2}$$

output would be determined by the implementation of production in a finite time period. In other words, according to this view 'production is a flow because it develops over time: the product is positive only if the time during which the productive action is performed is itself positive' (Schmitt 1979: 1.3, m.t.).

Does the supposed analogy stand up to rigorous investigation? Schmitt shows that this is not the case. His first observation sets the stage for his argument: the space travelled by a moving body varies according to the length of time during which it moves, but the division of time does not entail any reduction in its velocity.

> Extending in time, displacements are divided by the division of time. However, the division of displacements by time, displacements/time [velocity], is obviously not divided when time is divided, because numerator and denominator are simultaneously divided. This is why the velocity of the moving body does not tend towards zero when the time of application of this velocity tends towards zero.
>
> (ibid.: 1.3, m.t.)

Within any length of time interval, the speed of a moving body remains the same when the body is moving at a constant speed. Hence, its velocity of displacement is positive at each instant in time, while the space it covers instantaneously is nil. A positive period is necessary for the moving body to cover a positive distance, yet its instantaneous velocity is positive.

Things are substantially different in economics, where production can only be known starting from its result. If the product could be measured in physical units, no obstacle would hinder the determination of production and its velocity. 'But the reciprocal is equally true: observation establishes the heterogeneity of physical products; the production of physical goods is a void concept. So defined, production has no content. We infer from this that the notion of velocity of production is absurd' (ibid.: 2.1, m.t.). The fact is that if, like the velocity of a moving body, production were positive in any instant of time, its result would be infinite in any finite interval of time.

In classical mechanics, the product of an instantaneous velocity and a finite period of time is a finite displacement, whereas in economics an instantaneous production is necessarily equal to zero. Indeed, it is the product that measures production, and no positive product can result from an instantaneous production. '[T]he product of any period is equal to the production of this period, whereas in mechanics the displacement of a moving body is not equal to its speed during the interval of time under consideration' (Schmitt 2021: 7).

### *Production and quantum time*

Although production is not a function of continuous or discontinuous time, production of any finite period is undoubtedly positive and equal to the product of this period. The equation

$$\text{product} = \text{production} \cdot \Delta t \tag{4.1}$$

is correct if and only if $\Delta t = 1$, which means that production is given as a whole and, as such, refers to a finite period also given as a whole.

Before analyzing the implications of the fact that production is an instantaneous event defining an indivisible interval of time, let us summarize how Schmitt (1984a/2021) explains why the economic analysis of production differs substantially from what is claimed by Newton's mechanics. By examining the so-called paradoxes of the Greek philosopher Zeno of Elea, Schmitt observes that if the arrow reaches its target, it is because space pre-exists the displacement of the arrow. Once shot, the arrow moves into a space that is not created by its movement. The same is obviously true for Achilles chasing the tortoise or for any other physical moving body.

Physical displacement takes place in a predetermined space; this is why Zeno's paradoxes do not hold in the real world. Or do they? Schmitt shows that the paradoxes do not lose strength because, while it undoubtedly moves in space, 'the moving body is *immobile through time*' (ibid.: 13). Zeno's arrow is chrono-stationary, and space is not created by its displacement. Being motionless in time, the arrow cannot create anything, let alone the space it moves into, which exists independently of its displacement. In economics, the product is not pre-determined; unlike space, it does not exist before production occurs: 'the product does not exist before production, its only source' (ibid.: 13). If, like the arrow, production was simply occurring in time, it would be chrono-stationary and '*would create a strictly zero space or product*' (ibid.: 13). This would imply that production itself would remain entirely unexplained, a zero-product entailing necessarily a zero production.

Is production identifiable with a movement that creates its own space, the product, or is it a movement taking place in a pre-determined space? Schmitt's answer is clear: since the product does not pre-exist production, it must be an instantaneous creation, an instantaneous action defining a quantum of time. The product, the 'space' created by production, '*is nothing else than a quantum of time and its measure is that of the quantized time*' (ibid. 14). Let me explain this in more detail.

As we have seen, in Equation (4.1) $\Delta t$ is necessarily equal to the number one, $\Delta t = 1$. This is so because product and production are given *uno actu*: the result of the action is the very measure of the action itself. $\Delta t$, the period production refers to, is therefore given as a whole and consists of a finite and indivisible interval of time: a quantum of time. 'If Δt cannot be reduced to a quantity of time smaller than a finite quantity, no matter how small, Δt is defined in quantum time' (Schmitt 1979: 1.8, m.t.). To claim that production *creates* a quantum of time is to claim that production is an emission of time, an instantaneous event whose result is a finite portion of time.

> Although production is an action extended through time, it is linked to the product by a relation of equivalence, which is *independent of time*. It follows that the mathematical product of production and time is a "*quantum integral*", production time being the integer 1, or a whole multiple of this number.
>
> (Schmitt 1986a: 127)

Bear in mind that production cannot imply the creation of matter or energy but only that of a dimensionless *form*. 'We can say that to produce means to cast matter (or energy) into a preconceived utility-form' (Guitton 2021: 392). The process of transformation of matter takes time, a finite portion of continuous time, but it is only when this process ends that matter acquires a new utility-form. It is at this precise instant that economic production takes place, and the product emerges as its instantaneous outcome.

The utility-form is first conceived by man and exists only as a project. Through a physical transformation, matter (energy) is gradually moulded into the imaginary utility-form. All these changes occur in continuous time, they prepare or anticipate production, which has not taken place yet. Before the process of transformation is completed, the product is still virtual or imaginary and so is production. When the last physical impulse is given, the product is literally issued as a whole; together with production, it goes from the realm of virtual to that of realized magnitudes. '[P]roduction being nothing more than the completion of a project, that is the sudden meeting, after a more or less long preparation, of matter and its imaginary form' (Schmitt 2021: 40).

### *Production as a quantum of action*

Let us suppose that the physical process of transformation starts at time $t_0$ and is completed a week later, at time $t_1$. Matter and energy acquire their new utility-form at $t_1$, the instant at which production occurs and the product is created. What must be shown is that production is at the same time an instantaneous event and a flow in time. If production were instantaneous and timeless, its result could only be nil. Mere observation tells us that this is not the case, a fact that is explained by the double nature of production, an event that is both wavelike and corpuscular. At $t_1$ the interval of time $t_0 - t_1$ is covered by production from $t_1$ to $t_0$ and back, from $t_0$ to $t_1$, in a wavelike movement defining the emission of a quantum of time. '[P]roduction, as a quantum of action […] is a flux-reflux. Production is an action that flows back instantly to instant [$t_0$]

where it was started, to go back to instant [$t_1$] when it is positively completed' (ibid.: 292).

The quantum of time emitted at $t_1$ is the result of the wavelike aspect of production and the definition of the product. Unlike what is suggested by mainstream economics, *production is a displacement in time not in space*: the time-dimension of this event is precisely defined by the wave that quantizes an interval of continuous time. Through its instantaneous circular flow, production defines an action, a wavelike movement, whose result is the moulding of matter into a new utility-form. The corpuscular aspect of production consists precisely in the identification of the product with the result of the introduction of matter into a utility-form. As a quantum of time, the product is not matter, though 'the result of production does have a close link with matter. In this regard, one might speak of the corpuscular nature of production and product' (ibid.: 293).

A fundamental implication of the quantum nature of economic production is that, being an emission, it entails the instantaneous creation and destruction of the product. '[T]he wavelike nature of production has the logical consequence of strictly limiting the duration of the product's existence: it comes about at the instant of the completion of production and it disappears *at the same instant*' (ibid.: 292). At $t_1$, matter is cast in a new utility-form and is immediately expelled from it to be made available as value-in-use. Neither production, nor its result persists in time; they have no inertia. The utility-form is not dimensional; it is not something that would be added to matter or energy by production. It is an expression of man's creative imagination, a virtual mould that disappears as soon as the project is completed. Matter (or energy) comes out of production as a new value-in-use but does not carry or incorporate any new dimensional form. The easiest way to understand the instantaneity of production as a creation-destruction is to refer to its wavelike nature.

Because it is an instantaneous *circular* flow, production cannot have a positive duration in time. Its wavelike movement defines the positive and negative aspects of an emission, hence, necessarily, the emission of the product is both a creation and a destruction. Being an emission,

> production is a creation-destruction; that is to say that quantized time, i.e. the product, does not, by a single instant, survive production, which, in all certainty, is instantaneous. *Any product (in goods and services) evaporates at the very instant it comes about.*
>
> (ibid.: 38)

Schmitt's quantum macroeconomic analysis of production leads to the astonishing conclusion that production and consumption are simultaneous. Every production is wavelike and defines the creation and destruction of the product, so that production is immediately accompanied by consumption. '[A]ny *positive* production defines immediately an equal *positive* consumption. The object of economic analysis is not production followed by consumption but one single reality with two sides, production-consumption' (ibid.: 294).

If readers find it difficult to understand the far-reaching implications of Schmitt's analysis, it is because they wrongly conflate economic and physical consumption. Two mistakes must be avoided when entering the realm of economic analysis:

1) The product and its measure must not be identified with any of its physical characteristics, and
2) Its economic destruction must be kept distinct from its physical disappearance.

This requires a clear understanding of the nature of economic production as an instantaneous event whose result does not survive its creation. The physical object resulting from the process of physical transformation is obviously not destroyed at the very instant its 'production' is completed; neither does its use-value disappear.

The economic concept of consumption is subtler and inexorably dependent on that of production. Correctly understood, production is a creation, a concept that, metaphysics apart, cannot apply to matter or energy. It is only if the productive activity of man is seen as the realization of a project consisting in moulding matter into a utility-form that production may be defined as a creation. An instant is enough to issue the product as the unity of matter with its utility-form. Immediately after the process of transformation is achieved, the economic product gives way to a new value-in-use, which can be physically consumed according to its material characteristics.

What remains to be explained is whether and how the necessary unity of production and consumption may be reconciled with the possibility for consumption to take place at a later moment in chronological or continuous time. The analysis developed so far does not seem to imply such a possibility. Before showing that this is not the case and that quantum analysis succeeds in reconciling the unity production-consumption with the distinction of these two events in continuous time, let us briefly investigate Schmitt's extension of quantum macroeconomic analysis to expenditure.

## Expenditure and time

The analysis of the logical relationship between monetary expenditure and time is analogous to that concerning the relationship between production and time. The mainstream assumption that the sum spent is obtained by multiplying the action of spending by the time during which this action is carried out, is clearly nonsense, because expenditure is measured by the whole sum spent and vice versa. 'It is wrong [to believe] that the application of an expenditure must extend in time for its result to be positive; in reality, expenditure, an instantaneous action, has a result that is itself instantaneous' (Schmitt 1979: 1.4, m.t.).

In the equation

$$\text{sum spent} = \text{expenditure} \cdot \Delta t \tag{4.3}$$

$\Delta t$ can only be equal to 1, which means that the time-dimension of expenditure is nothing other than the number 1. As in the case of production, it is undeniable that the expenditure defines a time interval greater than zero, even though it is instantaneous, that is, it does not move in time. The reconciliation between the instantaneity of monetary expenditure and the fact that it is a flow is made possible by the concept of quantum time.

Schmitt (1979) proposes a proof *ad absurdum* of the existence of quantum time. It goes as follows. Let us suppose that the sum spent, $E$, obtains by multiplying the expenditure $E^x$, by $\Delta t$. The necessary equality of expenditure and sum spent leads us to the following equalities

$$E^x = E = E^x \cdot \Delta t = E \cdot \Delta t \tag{4.4}$$

If $\Delta t$ tends towards zero, $E \cdot \Delta t$ tends also towards zero. Yet, it remains true that, even if $\Delta t = 0$, $E \cdot \Delta t$ is equal to $E^x$:

$$E \cdot \Delta t = E \cdot 0 = 0 = E^x, \tag{4.5}$$

where $E^x$ is positive. The same absurdity would be reached if we reduced $\Delta t$ to zero and pretended to derive the sum spent from $E^x \cdot \Delta t$, while recognizing that the expenditure is always equal to the sum spent. In this case we would have:

$$E^x \cdot \Delta t = E^x \cdot 0 = 0 = E, \tag{4.6}$$

where $E$ is the sum spent at a given point in time. As Schmitt claims, '[t]he absurdity derives from the fact that we make $\Delta t$ tend towards zero. To avoid contradiction, we must fund the analysis on quantum time, $\Delta t$ being a finite and indivisible time' (Schmitt 1979: 1.9, m.t.). Schmitt interestingly observes that each positive sum spent can be infinitely subdivided but cannot be divided by continuous or discontinuous time. 'In other words, when expenditure is concerned, time is the set of natural numbers and not the set of real numbers' (ibid.: 1.9, m.t.).

In the same unpublished manuscript, Schmitt provides a suggestive example of how one can intuitively conceive quantum time. He asks the reader to think of the case of a blow of force 10 given every day with a hammer. The problem is: is it possible to spread the blow of the hammer over time? In other words, is it possible to give *n* blows over a period of time 'in such a way that no interval of finite time separates two successive blows? If the problem could be solved, the hammer would rest on the nail and, motionless, it would apply a continuously nil force. The force 10 can only be obtained by the application of a *finite* number of hammer blows of *finite* force' (ibid.: 1.10, m.t.). By analogy, only a finite expenditure referring to a finite time period can give a positive result. The period defined by expenditure is necessarily given as a whole and is equal to the number 1.

In the years preceding the publication of *Inflation, chômage et malformations du capital*, Schmitt's analysis of the relationship between expenditure and time was already on the right track, and it was clearly established that it is only through the concept of quantum time that the flow nature of monetary expenditure can be reconciled with its instantaneity. '[F]rom experience we know that expenditure has a time-dimension, and reasoning tells us that the time-dimension of monetary expenditure is given in an emission and is, as a matter of fact, a quantum of time' (ibid.: 2.5, m.t.).

The simplest way to understand how it is that expenditure quantizes time is to investigate its relationship with production. What has to be shown is that 'production and expenditure are not movements in any [given] space since the *product-space* and the *number-space* are created by these events' (Schmitt 2021: 28). This is to say that production and expenditure are 'exclusively movements through time: the time dimension of these events is precisely defined by the wave that quantizes an interval of the continuum, by going through it in an instant, going and coming back at one go' (ibid.: 28). By showing that every production [is] an expenditure and every expenditure [...] a production (ibid.: 28), Schmitt can prove that these two operations are the two aspects of a single event, which is why they quantize the same period of time. '*Any production and (identically) any expenditure is an emission, creation-destruction of the same object, the product and the spent sum*' (ibid.: 29).

## The theory of emissions

### *Production and money*

In *La formation du pouvoir d'achat*, Schmitt had already clearly established that '*the primordial effect of production is enrichment in money, not in real value*' (Schmitt 1960: 150, m.t.). This is so because money is the numerical form necessary to transform physical output into a measurable economic product. The link between production and money is so close that initially the product takes the form of a sum of money, and it is only through production that a monetary creation can occur. Without money, physical output would be a heap of heterogeneous objects, and national output would be a void concept. Physical production would not be impossible, of course, but it could not be expressed numerically, and no economic system could be conceived in the absence of an invariable unit of measure. The logical indeterminacy of relative prices confirms it. Indeed, through his analysis of the formation of money's purchasing power, Schmitt (1960, 1966a) shows that the emission of money and the production of goods are the two aspects, monetary and real, of a single event resulting in physical goods being integrated into a numerical form.

The orthodox attempt to introduce money through its relative exchange with produced output fails for the twofold reason that money is not a real asset and that direct exchange between real assets cannot transform any of them into a dimensionless *numéraire*. What Schmitt shows is that a relationship between money and real output can be established only through an *absolute exchange* taking place between two *actions*, the creation of money and the production of goods. The only possible exchange between money and real goods is that through which the production of goods is exchanged with or, literally, changed into a production of money. It is through the payment of wages that this absolute exchange occurs, and it is this payment that is first analyzed by Schmitt in his theory of emissions in order to establish its logical relationship with time.

### *The emission of wages*

Money is positively created only through its conflation with production, and the first expenditure creating this association is the payment of wages. The analysis of the emission of wages starts from the payment carried out by banks on behalf of firms and to the benefit of workers. From this analysis (see Chapter 2), we can easily infer that the emission of wages is at the same time the emission of the product. Workers create the product and receive it in the form of money. 'The exchange of the two emissions gives to the debt of producing firms a perfectly defined object, the physical product of workers' (Schmitt 1979: 2.11, m.t.).

The payment of wages is an instantaneous operation with a positive dimension in quantum time. 'The positive quantum deposit of wage-earners is the *economic* definition of the physical product filling up the negative quantum deposit of firms' (ibid.: 2.16, m.t.). Nominally issued by banks, money is therefore created by workers, whose activity is wavelike and corpuscular at the same time: 'the product of workers is the body of money' (ibid.: 2.17, m.t.). In other words, the emission of wages is positive only insofar as it is associated with the 'real emission' of workers, which implies that the payment of wages is at the same time a monetary and a real emission.

> [I]ncome is defined as the exchange between two simultaneous emissions, a monetary one and a real one. Without this exchange the monetary emission would be empty and production non-existent, since purely physical goods are a collection of heterogeneous objects rather than a product.
>
> (Schmitt and Cencini 1982: 139)

'Paid in money, workers do not exchange their product but their production, the activity – not its result. The exchange of production means its transformation: instead of producing physical goods, workers produce francs' (Schmitt 1979: 2.17, m.t.). Taken literally, this means that money is created by production and not by banks. It is true, of course, that money is issued by banks as their spontaneous IOUs, yet this emission would lead nowhere if it were not associated with production. If money were issued as a net asset, it would exchange against real goods. As this cannot logically and factually be the case, that is, as money can only be issued as an asset-liability, the determining exchange is that between money and production.

It is production that eventually creates money because the sum of wages is 'the definition of national product and not its counter-value; francs do not circulate in the economy crossing paths with physical products, as it were, because francs and products are one and the same object' (ibid.: 2.17, m.t.).

Production creates money, and the set of workers is the only source of economic production, which implies that in the market for productive services the payment of wages is the only monetary expenditure. In economic terms, the product is the result of the work of man, which is the only macroeconomic factor of production. Through the payment of wages, workers exchange their activity, its result, against the emission of a sum of money. Physical output, a quantum of time, fills up the negative quantum deposit of firms, and the positive quantum deposit of workers defines the net economic product of the period. It is because workers are the source of a real emission that, thanks to the payment of wages, a monetary emission occurs, and the result of production is a positive creation of a net sum of money.

Through the association of the units of nominal money issued by banks and the physical output resulting from the activity of workers, the economic product is emitted as a sum of wages. Since neither land nor capital nor any other 'factor' is at the origin of a monetary emission, '*they cannot transfer to their owners the quantum deposits they are incapable of forming themselves*' (ibid.: 3.9, m.t.). It thus follows that the payment of wages is the sole monetary emission defined by and defining production.

### *Production as an expenditure*

In his 1984 book, Schmitt takes his previous analysis of monetary emissions a little further and reiterates the fact that production and expenditure are the two complementary aspects of a single emission. He starts his reasoning by claiming once more that money is not emitted by banks, because the only source of money's purchasing power is the work of man: '*human labour only is an emission*' (Schmitt 2021: 31). He then sets to work to show that '*every (monetary) payment is an emission of wages*' (ibid.: 31). Let me summarize his main arguments.

The first payment one must consider is that of wages. Through the payment of wages, money is associated to current output and the product is identified with a sum of money. It is through this absolute exchange that workers obtain their physical product in the form of money: '*workers do not obtain money distinct from the product but as the nominal form of their product*' (ibid.: 34). If the work of man did not define a real emission and if money were not created through the payment of wages, banks' acknowledgement of debt would have no real object.

> At the moment the bank promise finds its object in the (new) product, it is replaced by money proper. The mutation of promises into money is the result of labour, it is not at all the consequence of the bank emission.
> (ibid.: 47)

As issued by banks, (nominal) money is a numerical form whose content is issued by production. In the payment of wages, form and content are given in one single stroke, a result that confirms the logical priority of the emission of labour over that of banks. '*Wages are not the result of a money expenditure: they are the product of a labour expenditure*' (ibid.: 42).

Wages result from the real emission of workers, which means that the 'money issued by banks is only the faithful image of the money created in the economy, outside of banks' (ibid.: 44). It means also that real and monetary emissions form a unity, a conclusion that must be confronted with the fact that the payment of wages defines only a half real emission. From a monetary viewpoint, the payment of wages is a complete emission, a creation-destruction of the money issued by banks.

Money does not survive its circulation: it flows instantaneously back to its point of departure, where it is immediately destroyed. What workers obtain is not an empty sum of money units, but the product itself in the form of money. The product, result of workers' real emission, is given a monetary form, which is bound to disappear at the very instant wages are paid to workers. Yet, the immediate destruction of money does not imply that of the product, whose final consumption can take place at a later moment in continuous time. In other words, when wages are paid out to workers, an income is formed that will be definitively spent only later.

The intervention of money allows separating production from consumption in chronological time, even though production and consumption are and remain the two instantaneous moments of one and a single emission. In the same way, income has a positive existence in continuous time, even though it must obey the law of emissions, which requires its instantaneous destruction. How can these two, apparently contradictory requirements apply at the same time? How is it possible for income to have a positive existence in time and simultaneously be immediately destroyed? Likewise, how to reconcile the chronological separation of production and consumption with their necessary coincidence? The answer is provided by quantum time, and by its coexistence with continuous time.

Schmitt observes first that the payment of wages can indeed correspond to the real emission of workers only if the income it forms is deposited in time. 'The payment of wages can be associated to the real emission only *if the credited amount is net among workers' assets*' (ibid.: 50). Wage-earners are free to spend their income as and when they prefer, and they are bound to remain creditors of theirs banks if they do not spend it. Yet, this is only half of the story, since the payment of wages is necessarily matched by their final expenditure. Despite occurring at separate moments in time, these two events coincide in quantum time, because they refer, positively and negatively, to the same production.

In the same way as production is an instantaneous event referring to a finite and indivisible interval of time, consumption identifies itself with the (instantaneous) final expenditure of wages and, quite logically, refers to the same quantum of time. Analogously, formed in the payment of wages, income is finally spent and destroyed in consumption. This clearly means that, referring to the same product, the formation and destruction of income coincide in quantum time.

As claimed by Schmitt, 'the payment of wages *breaks the real emission into two half-emissions*' (ibid.: 51), one corresponding to the formation of income (production) and the other to its final expenditure (consumption). The two real half-emissions are separate in continuous time, but they are superposed in quantum time where, by defining the same, indivisible period, they form the joint parts of a sole emission. 'Thus, the two true statements are both preserved; the expenditure of income is *at first posterior*; however, *it takes effect retroactively*, so that, in the last analysis, it is immediate' (ibid.: 51–2).

Having argued that consumption is an emission (or re-emission) of wages, Schmitt (1984a/2021) goes on to show that even expenditures relating to non-wage incomes pertain to the broad category of emissions as that of wages. In particular, he analyzes the logical relationship between wages and profit.

## The quantum analysis of profit

The emission of money coincides initially with the payment of wages, and so it is correct to say that money is issued by the work of man, which is the only macroeconomic cost of production. It follows that wages define the totality of national income, and that the existence of non-wage incomes can be explained only by deriving them from wages.

We have already seen (Chapter 2) how Schmitt (1966a) explains the formation of profit without infringing on the identity of wages and national income. The reader will remember that Schmitt's initial analysis of profit is incomplete because it does not provide the full explanation of how profit is formed and spent consistently with the law that establishes the necessary equality of prices and values. His analysis of monetary and real emissions fills the gap. What it shows is that equations

$$Y = W + \pi \tag{4.7}$$

and

$$Y = W, \tag{4.8}$$

where $\pi$ stands for profit, $Y$ for income, and $W$ for wages, are not opposed to one another. Indeed, as claimed by Schmitt (1984a/2021: 63), while Equation (4.8) defines the *formation* of income, Equation (4.7) defines its *expenditure* or its destruction. Let us follow Schmitt's arguments.

### *Profit, value, and prices*

The first step consists in establishing that there is no contradiction in claiming that

1) Wages (direct and indirect) are the totality of national income and that
2) Wages are not the only form of income.

According to the definition of profit as transfer income, profit is derived from wages; it is formed in the market for products through the sale of output at a mark-up. Even though they are obtained through a redistribution of wages, profits are not wages, which proves that propositions (1) and (2) are finally consistent with one another. However, this analysis does not explain the expenditure of profit and still rests on a difference between prices and values that cannot find any logical justification. Indeed, on the one hand, economic goods can be produced as homogeneous real goods only in the form of money and, on the other, no amount of money could ever be created if the emission of bank money were not related to the productive activity of workers.

From the moment of its creation, money is identified with the product and the product with money. 'The observation of facts teaches us the joint birth, in the same operation – the exchange of monetary and real emissions – of money and product, definitions of the same object' (Schmitt 1979: 5.11, m.t.). This implies that no difference can subsist between values and prices unless we are prepared to maintain that a unit of money could be greater or smaller than itself. 'Value is the "association" of money and product as defined within production; price is the "association" of money and product as defined in the sale of production' (ibid.: 5.12, m.t.).

The necessary identity of production and consumption, the two joint and complementary phases of one and the same emission, is the substantial reason for the identity of values and prices. '[T]he final purchase of any product implies an exchange between equal amounts of positive and negative quantum deposits' (Schmitt and Cencini 1982: 141). At this point of the analysis, we are apparently stuck at an impasse. Either we reject the theory of emissions and go back to square one, in which case both values and prices are doomed to remain undeterminable, or we embrace the theory of the emission and give up all hope of explaining the formation of non-wage incomes.

If the identity of prices and values were to hold at each instant of continuous time, it would be impossible to explain the formation of profit through the sale of produced goods and services at a mark-up. Profit is an income obtained by firms at zero cost. This means that, if values and prices are always necessarily equal, firms cannot derive any gain from the sale of produced output, whereas, if prices are greater than values, part of firms' output is bound to remain unsold, the value of the national product being forcefully greater than the sum of available income. This latest conclusion derives from the fact that, in the market for products, gross profits 'have a purchasing power defined in prices and not in value' (Schmitt 1979: 5.13, m.t.). Even if a positive profit could be derived from the sale of part of firms' output, its amount would not be enough to finance the purchase of the remaining output, which would also be sold at a mark-up in the market for products.

To get out of this impasse we need to show that prices can be greater than values and at the same time identical to them. It is the theory of emissions that guides Schmitt to the solution of this apparent contradiction. In his view, profit can indeed be formed in the market for products while respecting the equivalence of money and product as established by the payment of wages. Essentially, the purchase of national output defines an exchange of positive and negative money, the physical output contained in the negative quantum deposit of firms being cast out of its monetary form by the expenditure of an equivalent positive quantum deposit of income holders. This means that, even if wage-goods are sold at a price greater than their cost of production – which must be the case if a profit is formed through the expenditure of wages – transactions take place in conformity with the identity of values and prices.

Quantum macroeconomic analysis provides the only possible way to reconcile these two opposite requirements: *the payment of wages includes the expenditure of profit to the same extent that the expenditure of wages includes the formation of profit*. Production, the payment of wages, and consumption, the expenditure of wages, are identical operations but of different sign. The latter is the second emission of wages and their unity is the unavoidable consequence of the fact that the two emissions of wages taken together define one and the same real emission whereby output is issued as a quantum of time.

As Schmitt observes,

> [t]he mistake behind the positive difference between price and value is due to the dichotomy of markets or, more simply, to the implicit assumption that the market for products can be considered on its own, separately, as if the two markets did not form a sole reality.
>
> (ibid.: 5.15, m.t.)

As a matter of fact, labour and commodity markets are closely interconnected, the purchase in the latter being equal to the purchase in the former. When the two markets are considered together, it appears that when a positive profit is formed in the commodity market a positive expenditure (of profit) takes place in the labour market. '[A] positive profit implies an expenditure of money within the payment of wages: the nominal payment of wages by *F* is simultaneously a final expenditure of profit' (Schmitt and Cencini 1982: 142).

Let us go over Schmitt's numerical example. If wages are equal to 100 money units and if, through their expenditure, wage-earners obtain only 80% of their production (because wage-goods are sold at a price of 125 money units), this means that '*the totality of wages purchases the totality of output*' (Schmitt 1979: 5.16, m.t.). This is so because the income transferred to firms in the market for products is instantaneously spent in the labour market. The expenditure of 100 units of income by wage-earners defines the purchase of 100 money units of product, 80 to the benefit of wage-earners and 20 to the benefit of firms. It is true that wage-goods are sold at a microeconomic price of 125 money units; yet, correctly defined, the price is made up of the sum of money effectively spent in the market for products, 100 money units in Schmitt's numerical example.

### *Retroactivity*

It is because the expenditures occurring in the two markets are substantially the two faces of the same coin that the expenditures taking place in the commodity market modify, retroactively, those occurring in the labour market. The concept of retroactivity is difficult to master and has proved highly controversial in several scientific fields. Physicists, for example, are aware of the problem posed by the reversibility of the physical laws of classical dynamics and, to some extent, of Einstein's theory of relativity, whose validity does not depend upon the direction of time, and the irreversibility of the arrow of time, whose flow is unidirectional. In economics, retroactivity is far less difficult to conceive because it does not concern matter or energy. What is at stake is not the possibility of human beings to go back in time, but that of verifying retroactively the effects of an expenditure occurring at a given instant of time.

The quantum definition of production helps us understand Schmitt's argument. Production is the first part of the real emission of produced output. Through the payment of wages, the product is emitted in the form of money. The payment of wages is an (instantaneous) expenditure whose time-dimension is the quantum of time that defines the product of workers.

Consumption is the second and complementary part of the real emission of produced output. While it takes place at a moment of continuous time, $t_1$, subsequent to that of the payment of wages, $t_0$, consumption is also an instantaneous event quantizing time. Now, the finite interval of time quantized by consumption corresponds to the product purchased and, since the product purchased at $t_1$ is the same produced at $t_0$, it necessarily follows that both production and consumption define the same quantum of time.

The time-dimension of production being the same as that of consumption, it appears that the expenditure in the labour market coincides with that in the commodity market even though they take place at different instants of continuous time. Retroactivity is a corollary of the identity of production and consumption, two half-emissions whose unity defines the real emission proper to the world of economics.

Since the expenditure of wages coincides with the payment of wages in quantum time, it modifies that payment to the extent that it includes the formation of positive profits. In Schmitt's numerical example, if the expenditure of 100 units of money-wages goes to form 20 units of profit, its subdivision into the purchase of 80 money units of wage-goods and the formation of 20 money units of profit entails the immediate and retroactive subdivision of the payment of wages into a formation of 80 money units of real wages and an expenditure of profit of 20 money units. At $t_0$, the amount that will be later spent on the final purchase of wage-goods and the amount that will be earned by firms as profit are not yet known. It is only at $t_1$ that we will know if and to what extent profits are formed in the market for products. If the expenditure of wages gives rise to the formation of a positive profit at $t_1$, we immediately know that, at $t_0$, an expenditure of profit was included in the payment of wages. What happens at $t_1$ helps us reinterpret what happens at $t_0$. If 'wages in physical goods are of a value smaller than the sum of wages spent, the difference defines a positive expenditure in the market for products that "slid" into the payment of wages' (ibid.: 5.23, m.t.).

The inclusion of the expenditure of profit within the payment of wages defines what Schmitt (1979, 1984a) calls a 'nested expenditure' (*dépense gigogne*) and what explains the formation-expenditure of profit without contravening the law of the necessary equality of values and prices.

What happens in the real world is that 'the market for products has a degree of freedom compared to the market for productive services' (ibid.: 5.24, m.t.), so that prices may differ from values in continuous time while being identical to values in quantum time. The reader must get this point right: quantum time is not a figment of Schmitt's imagination, a concept created *ad hoc* to make ends meet. Quantum time is directly derived from the analysis of the very nature of economic production and is as real as production itself. Likewise, the identity of values and prices is not a falsifiable assumption introduced to support a particular economic analysis.

It is because every exchange defines the equivalence of its two terms that the product cannot be sold for a sum of money greater or smaller than that defining its value. In Schmitt's words, no produced good 'can be "expelled" or taken out of the numerical form of money in which it is contained unless by an expenditure strictly equal to its cost of production' (Schmitt 1996d: 3, m.t.). At the same time, it is also certain that if values and prices never differed from one another, no profit could ever be formed in the economy, because no redistribution of income between wage-earners and firms could occur in the market for products.

The solution advocated by Schmitt is perfectly consistent with the need to comply with the law of exchange and to allow for a degree of freedom of prices with respect to values. Let us present his argument by distinguishing the synthetic from the analytic proof of the identity price-value.

### *Synthetic proof of the identity price-value*

Formation and expenditure of wages are two half-emissions quantizing the same period of time, which means that they coincide in quantum time. Even though it occurs at a different moment in chronological time, the expenditure of wages takes place retroactively at the same instant of production, that is, of the payment of wages: 'incomes have only an instantaneous life' (Schmitt 1984a/2021: 67). Given that the flow of the expenditure of wages coincides with that of their payment, any partitioning of one of them entails necessarily the same partitioning of the other. In particular, 'if a part of wages is transferred in the products market, an equal part of wages is transferred in the producing services market' (ibid.: 68). If prices were not identical to values eventually, the two flows would be the object of two different distributions between wages and profit, which is logically impeded by the necessary coincidence of the two flows.

Following Schmitt (1984a/2021), let us measure in $x$ money units the amount of wages paid to workers at $t_0$, and in $y$ money units the amount of wages transformed into profit. Up to $y$ money units, the payment of wages defines an expenditure of profit, which means that the real wages obtained by workers are equal to $x - y$ money units. 'In simple terms, we shall say that the $x$ units of money obtained by workers (in direct and indirect wages) contain $(x - y)$ units of wages' (ibid.: 69). It is true that the amount of wages actually paid at $t_0$ is equal to $x$ units of nominal money. Yet, $y$ out of these $x$ money units are transferred to firms and spent by them to pay wages. Once labour and commodity markets are taken together, as they must, we observe that 'workers receive $(x - y)$ units of money positively and $y$ units both positively and negatively: in the end, monetary wages are of $(x - y)$ units only' (ibid.: 69).

The formation of profit is included in the expenditure of wages, which necessarily implies, because of the identity of production and consumption, that the expenditure of profit is included in the payment of wages. If a profit is formed when wages are spent, this allows us to infer that the payment of wages was inclusive of an expenditure of profit. The presence of a positive profit within the payment of wages means that production consists of wage- and profit-goods from the start.

Chronologically, the distinction of wages and profit is determined at $t_1$ and depends on the possibility for prices to be greater than values. Yet, as soon as profit is formed, the quantum coincidence of production and consumption allows for the retroactive adjustment for the formation of profits over that of wages. Since the expenditure of profit takes place, retroactively, within the payment of wages, its inclusion reduces the amount of income obtained by workers, whose expenditure in the market for products must be reinterpreted accordingly. '[T]he formation of any difference between price and value cancels out in the logical reinterpretation of the emission of wages: the positive difference between wage-goods' price and cost confirms, measure for measure, the production of non-wage goods' (ibid.: 72).

### *Analytic proof of the identity price-value*

Production identifies itself with the emission of wages, and the emission of wages defines the identity of their formation and their expenditure. It necessarily follows that each firm is at the origin of a monetary circular flow defining the payment and the expenditure of a given sum of money. Even though income holders are free to spend their income as they please, after the compensation for generalized exchange it appears that a circuit forms for each single firm: each firm issues its own money and recovers it through the sale of its output. 'The outcome is a surprising but indubitable piece of information: the profit of any firm is part of the income produced by this same firm' (ibid.: 74).

The rationale for this apparently unrealistic claim is the fact that '*every firm sells its product only to its own workers*' (ibid.: 74). At first sight, this seems to be merely another unrealistic claim replacing the former. In reality, the necessary correspondence of the production and sale of each firm's output to its own workers is perfectly consistent with the freedom of workers to purchase whatever and wherever they want. The principle of generalized exchange is not opposed to the fact that the income formed by a given production of a given firm is necessarily spent on the purchase of this same production.

Logical laws are much stronger than individual behaviour and apply independently of it. The wavelike nature of production leaves no room for doubt: the real emission of a product entails the necessary equivalence and quantum simultaneity of its production and its consumption. The emission of wages of any single firm defines simultaneously their formation and their expenditure, so that the formation of the profit of any given firm, F, 'is a special case of the emission of wages by that firm' (ibid.: 75). Workers of F are at the origin of the entirety of F's production, of wage-goods as well as profit-goods. The partitioning between these two kinds of goods is determined by the formation of profit: the creation-destruction of profit is a movement included in the destruction-creation of wages.

If F realizes a positive profit in the sale of its output, this means that its workers produce part of the firm's output in the form of profit-goods. The difference between price and value of the wage-goods sold by F in the market for products is therefore the cost of production or the value of profit-goods. '*The price of wage goods is higher than their value only because it includes the price of non-wage goods*' (ibid.: 76).

### *Profit and wages in a theory of emissions*

Wages are the definition of national output. Profit is part of national output. Yet, profit is not a wage. This is the conundrum monetary macroeconomics is confronted with. And this shows once again that economics requires the use of a more developed kind of logic than binary logic if it is to prove that profits are included into wages but are not wages.

Together with Schmitt (1984a/2021), let us distinguish between *W*, the sum of nominal wages paid to wage-earners, and *W*', the part of wages spent in the final purchase of consumption-goods. We observe that wages *W* are greater than *W*' so that the difference defines a transfer of income from wage-earners to firms and the formation of a profit equal to *W* – *W*'.

If our analysis stopped here, we would have to conclude that profit reduces wages, because of the difference introduced between price and value of consumption-goods. This would lead to the annoying result that profits are wages, whereas it is obvious that profits do not belong to the category of wages. A correct analysis of profit shows us that profit is positive and is not a wage, even though the totality of national income is defined by wages alone. In other words, it must be shown that *W* and *W*' are logically identical and that, at the same time, *W* can be greater than *W*', which is also to say that prices and values are always necessarily equal and that they can nevertheless differ from one another.

The solution to this apparent contradiction is found in the theory of emissions and can be properly understood only by giving up the principle of the excluded middle. 'The principle of the excluded middle is broken [… because] the expenditure and the formation of wages include the formation and the expenditure of profits' (ibid.: 82). Schmitt's conclusion is clear: '[*t*]*he circuit of profits* (their formation-expenditure) *is therefore embedded in the circuit of wages*, of which it is a nested category' (ibid.: 82–3).

Schmitt's figure (ibid.: 83), accurately reproduced here (Figure 4.2) shows very clearly that the formation of profit, *a*', is included in the expenditure of wages, represented by half-circle *b*, while the expenditure of profit, *b*', is included in the formation of wages, half-circle *a*.

'The circular flow of profits (*a*', *b*') is indeed included in the circuit wages (*a*, *b*), even though it is defined solely by the flows of creation and destruction of wages' (ibid.: 83).

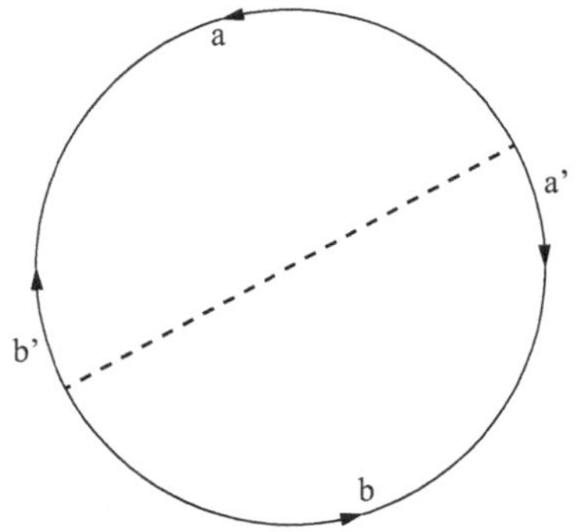


*Figure 4.2* Inclusion of the circuit of profits in the circuit of wages. Source: Schmitt 2021: 83

## A brief comparison with orthodox economics

Schmitt's quantum macroeconomic analysis of production is original and cannot be traced back to the work of other economists. None of them has considered production as an event whose time-dimension is a quantum of time, and none of them has ever thought of identifying the payment of wages as part of an emission implying the coincidence of production and consumption. Most economists still confuse economics with physics and are lured into believing that production can be considered a function of continuous or discontinuous time. They are totally unaware of the instantaneous nature of economic production and far from understanding that its result is a finite and indivisible period of time.

The same applies to the analysis of monetary expenditures, which are also generally considered continuous or discontinuous functions of time. Neither neoclassical nor Keynesian economists are aware that no functional relationship exists between successive expenditures, that every expenditure relates to a given production, and that every production defines the creation-destruction of a specific income. Schmitt's quantum macroeconomic approach leads to a theory of emissions: the payment of wages and their final expenditure are joint events corresponding to the production-consumption pair, which defines the real emission specific to economics. As sophisticated and complex as they may be from a mathematical viewpoint, mainstream economic theories are conceptually very poor, and none of them provides a satisfactory explanation of the nature of economic production and consumption. Nor does any of them explain how an instantaneous event (production or expenditure) can possibly generate a positive result.

Concerning the analysis of profit, it is fair to say that, despite Keynes's ground-breaking intuition that wages include profit, neither Keynesians nor post-Keynesians have been able to propose a theory explaining both the formation and expenditure of profit while respecting the necessary equality of values and prices. The possibility for a given expenditure to be included into another expenditure 'as a sword into its sheath' (Schmitt 1996d: 46, m.t.) is totally alien to their analysis – and so is the idea that the expenditure of profit is the purchase of a production. The expenditure of profit is assimilated to a purchase in the market for products, a view that prevents distinguishing profit from wages. What these economists miss is the inclusion of the expenditure of profit in the payment of wages, which is 'a composite payment, because it is defined by a purchase in the market for products *contained* in an equivalent purchase in the market for productive services' (ibid.: 61, m.t.).

# 5 Quantum economics and capital

Income is formed by production as the-product-in-the-money, and is spent and destroyed in consumption, its final expenditure. Between the instant of production, $t_0$, and that of consumption, $t_1$, income is saved. Does this mean that in the interval $t_0 - t_1$ income subsists as such or that the passing of time necessarily transforms it into capital? Most economists would go for the second answer, aware of the close relationship between capital and time. Yet, they would also add that the transformation of income into capital is not as automatic as the word 'necessary' implies. Indeed, they would argue that only if saved-up income is invested financially by its savers is it transformed into capital.

Schmitt's quantum economic analysis is stricter and provides evidence that the formation of macroeconomic capital is independent of economic agents' behaviour. In this chapter I will essentially refer to his 1984 book *Inflation, chômage et malformations du capital* (English version of 2021) and to the complementary manuscripts *Théorie macroéconomique* (1993–94) and *Cours de théorie monétaire* (1996), which were distributed to Schmitt's students at the University of Fribourg.

## Ordinary versus quantum credit

Is the introduction of a financial market a necessary and sufficient condition for the formation of positive capital? The answer varies according to whether we are looking for the formation of a positive, net capital or we are merely interested in explaining the formation of a microeconomic capital. It is only in the latter case that the answer would be affirmative because the income saved by its owner and lent to another economic agent would define a positive capital for the saver. It is clear, however, that this transaction would not give rise to any positive macroeconomic capital. As far as the economy as a whole is concerned 'the loan is a zero-sum operation, the financial capital of the lender is exactly compensated by the negative financial capital formed in the borrower's assets' (Schmitt 2021: 85). No net capital results from the mere introduction of a financial market.

Things change radically when banks' financial intermediation is related to their monetary intermediation, more precisely, to the payment of wages.

DOI: 10.4324/9781351271325-8

An *ordinary credit* is a transaction where positive (real) money is transferred from one economic agent to another. On the other hand, the nature of the monetary emission corresponding to the payment of wages is such that

1) The money paid to workers is created in the payment itself, and that
2) Creation is accompanied by a simultaneous and equivalent destruction.

This means that, as far as its monetary aspect is concerned, the payment of wages defines a *quantum credit* as opposed to an ordinary credit. As Schmitt claims, 'quantum credit creates two equal monies face to face, one positive and the other negative [whereas o]rdinary credit transmits the positive money (created in quantum credits)' (ibid.: 87). The positive money Schmitt refers to is the income formed because of the payment of wages, and the transfer of income from lender to borrower is what occurs in the financial market. Though clearly distinct, monetary and financial intermediations are therefore closely connected; quantum credit gives rise to ordinary credit, that is, to the immediate loan of the income resulting from production.

### Monetary and financial loans

The necessary and immediate loan of newly formed wages results from both factual and conceptual considerations. Let us begin with the latter. The emission of money imposes its instantaneous creation and destruction. A mere instant is enough to carry out the payment of wages and for physical output to acquire a numerical form.

Once measured – through its association with money – physical output abandons its monetary form and subsists as a use-value. Since income is the product-in-the-money, the destruction of money also implies the destruction of income. In Schmitt's own words,

> income is matter (or energy) taken at the precise instant of its 'moulding' completed in the utility-form. It would therefore be vain to try to follow income in the passing of time; no income flows with time since all incomes meet the continuum only in the space of an instant.
>
> (ibid.: 318)

Yet, it would be a mistake to claim that income is subject to a final expenditure that destroys it at the very instant it is formed. Production and consumption are the two sides of one real emission, whose duality is verified in quantum time, whereas in continuous time they are distinct events separated by a positive time-interval. The destruction of income happening at the moment of the payment of wages is therefore not final and takes place through its saving and immediate lending.

Evidence of the disappearance of income through banks' financial intermediation is provided by double-entry bookkeeping. The principle of double-entry is the necessary coupling of credit and debit for each single economic agent: it establishes the logical identity of each economic agent's sales and purchases. In the payment of wages, both firms and workers are at the same time debited and credited (firms) and credited-debited (workers). If money were transferred as a net asset from firms to workers, the former would only be debited and the latter credited. Given that the payment of wages does not imply the expenditure of pre-existing money, its emission entails a creation-destruction both on firms and workers. 'Money is not an object that would be debited on one side and credited on the other; *it is, on the contrary, nothing other than the identity of a simultaneous debit and credit for one and the* <u>*same*</u> *agent*' (Schmitt 1996d: 17, m.t.).

It is a fact that, when banks credit them with positive money, workers spend it instantaneously in the purchase of equivalent bank deposits. Indeed, wage-income is formed immediately as bank deposits: the money paid to workers is spent at once and flows instantaneously back to banks. The duality of debits and credits defines a monetary circular flow and implies the immediate destruction of income: 'an income can only be created by an operation that destroys it in its monetary form' (ibid.: 18, m.t.).

Once again it must be stressed that the destruction of income, which occurs at the moment wages are paid to workers, is not final and must not be confused with the final destruction occurring at the moment of consumption. The 'initial' destruction of income occurs when it is loaned in the financial market. The income earned by workers is immediately lent to firms, and so the banks' initial monetary loan to firms is transformed into a financial one: 'the bank transforms a monetary "loan" into a financial loan' (Schmitt 1979: 6.19, m.t.). In the same way and at the same instant as workers lose their positive money – destroyed in its circular flow – firms lose their negative deposit, which is immediately replaced by a financial debt to the bank. Formed in the emission of wages through a quantum credit, income is the object of an ordinary credit as it is lent to firms.

### *Quantum credit and capital*

Ordinary credit is part of banks' financial intermediation, but, unless it results from the transformation of a quantum credit, it does not produce net capital. The transfer of an already existing income from A to B is a zero-sum transaction for the economy as a whole. A positive net capital is created only when the income saved and lent is the income formed in the payment of wages. It is only in this case, in fact, that an equivalent borrowing does not neutralize the loan granted by banks to firms. This is so because the loan finances the purchase of produced output by firms; it is an investment that grants the transformation of the physical product into a stock.

Firms now own the physical output 'expulsed' from the negative money, in which it was 'lodged' at the moment of the payment of wages. Yet, the cancellation of firms' monetary debt, due to the instantaneous creation-destruction of money, does not give firms final ownership over their stock of physical goods because their monetary debt is immediately replaced by a financial debt.

Firms owe banks the sum of income received as a loan. Physical goods obtained as a stock are matched by firms' financial debt, so that the 'benefit' they derive directly from the payment of wages and from the transformation of income into capital-time is nil. Concomitantly, wage-earners replace their monetary credit with a financial one. They 'earn a claim on the bank in the operation that transforms their income into capital' (Schmitt 2021: 90), and their gain is net for the economy as a whole.

Capital is formed through saving. Workers are the agents whose income is transformed into capital: they lose their income to recover it instantaneously in the form of capital.

What distinguishes an ordinary loan from a loan entailing the formation of a capital is, respectively, the absence or the presence of a stock of real goods. B spends the income saved by A and annuls it in the final purchase of current output. When the loan falls due, B will have to reimburse it, which they will do by transferring to B an amount of newly created income. A's present income is thus lent to B in exchange for an amount of B's future income. Under these conditions, no net capital is formed. Things change when, instead of being definitively cancelled in the final purchase of output, the income saved is invested by firms in the formation of a stock. This time, income-earners become the owners of a financial capital and firms are the depositaries of its real counterpart.

The presence of a real capital (the stock of firms), that is, of real savings matching monetary savings, 'builds' a bridge between the income saved today and the same income spent tomorrow. Since today's income is transformed by being invested in funding a stock, tomorrow it will be recreated and used to purchase that stock. 'As savers withdraw the funds constituted in the transformation of quantum credits into ordinary credits, firms sell their stocks: savers therefore do not draw on the new income; they simply activate the previous income, frozen in the stocks' (ibid.: 91)

Who owns the stock of goods built up by firms in the period of continuous time separating production from consumption? The answer is less straightforward than one might expect. Saved and lent by its initial owners from the moment it is formed, income is the object of a financial transaction that entails the purchase of financial claims by wage-earners and their sale by firms. From the moment wages are paid, wage-earners own claims on bank deposits and firms witness the transformation of their initial monetary debit into a financial one.

Since the stock of real goods that firms obtain is the very object of their financial debt and of workers' financial claims, it is correct to say that, from an income viewpoint, the stock is owned by workers. However, one must not forget that workers' income is immediately destroyed and replaced by an equivalent amount of capital. This implies the fact that *what firms borrow is not the same object that they will have to pay back when their loan falls due.* They borrow an amount of income, and they return their stock of real goods: 'firms borrow an object and "give back" another; they borrow the product-in-the-money, and they finally give up the product in its physical form' (Schmitt 1996d: 20, m.t.).

The distinction between the object borrowed and that given back by firms implies that the loan, which firms receive from banks, gives them the ownership over the stock formed via their initial investment. Firms are not the *final* owners of produced output because their stock of physical goods is the object of their financial debt to banks and, through them, to workers. Yet, the loan firms receive from banks, which implies the transformation of income into capital, means that firms are the *initial* owners of the real stock which they can sell at their conditions in the market for products.

> After income has been transformed into capital, firms owe bank deposits and households hold claims on bank deposits. As a counterpart to their debt, firms have ownership over the new product, which is the object of the financial claims (the bank deposits) they owe: it is an investment. Households own the corresponding savings.
>
> (ibid.: 21, m.t.)

By selling their stock to households, firms will be able to cancel their financial debt to banks. This final sale will imply the cancellation of capital, the re-creation of income, and its final expenditure on consumption.

Finally, income itself will be annulled and the product appropriated by households in its physical form of use-value. Formed in the possession of wage-earners as a sum of income, produced output is therefore first appropriated by them in the form of financial claims and then, at the moment of its final sale, in its physical form. 'The net formation of capital (or of savings) is the appropriation of the product in the form of financial claims, whereas consumption is the appropriation of the product in itself' (Schmitt 2021: 326).

## From income to capital-time

The saving of income by wage-earners is immediate and does not depend on their behaviour: independently of their decisions, income is formed as a bank deposit, and bank deposits define an amount of saved-up income. In the same automatic way, saved-up income is lent by banks to firms and thus transformed into *capital-time*. As previously said, income does not survive its creation and it is instantaneously destroyed. Yet, its destruction goes through its being saved and corresponds to its transformation into capital. Being reversible, this transformation does not entail the final expenditure of income: households are free to spend their income any time in the future, a transaction that will entail the reverse transformation of capital into income.

As Keynes (1936/1946) claimed, capital-time is what creates a bridge between present and future. Income formed at $t_0$ is immediately transformed into capital in order to be recreated as income at $t_1$, when it will be definitively spent in the final purchase of the product. In other words, capital is what enables today's income to be spent at a later instant in continuous time without stopping its instantaneous destruction. 'Saving destroys today's income. If income is preserved nevertheless, this is because saving is a double action, a negative or destructive one today and a positive or creative one tomorrow: the same action that destroys today's income recreates it tomorrow' (Schmitt 2021: 319).

### *Capital as a flow*

According to common belief, capital is a stock, and income is a flow resulting from putting part of capital-stock into circulation. Referring metaphorically to a tank full of a liquid gradually released into a network of hydraulic pipes, economists maintain that, while capital is a stock whose value can be known at each instant of time, income is a movement in time whose value varies either continuously or discontinuously.

Schmitt's quantum macroeconomic analysis shows, on the contrary, that the reverse is true: 'income is not a flow in the continuum, whereas capital is' (ibid.: 321). The reason for this radical conceptual change is that income is destroyed as soon as it is created and is immediately replaced by capital. Resulting from the emission of money and real output, income defines a quantum of time, but it is not inscribed as a flow in continuous time. Neither money nor real output survives its creation. The issuing bank immediately recovers and destroys money, while real output is at once 'expelled' from its money-form and subsists only as a use-value. Income follows necessarily the same destiny, which is why it cannot be defined as a flow in time.

Unlike income, capital is inscribed in time, where it subsists until it is changed back into income and spent accordingly. In Schmitt's own words, '[c]apital is the income deposited on a "point" of the continuum; since the flowing of this point defines continuous time, capital is itself a continuous movement' (ibid.: 321). Schmitt compares capital to velocity. In the same way as the velocity of a moving body is itself a movement in time even though its measure is instantaneous, capital is a movement or a flow in time. Nevertheless, the concept of capital as a stock can still be retained on the condition that one specifies that it is 'a *quantum stock* and not an integer. Income is transformed into a stock insofar as it is destroyed today to rise again tomorrow' (ibid.: 321).

It is in this precise sense that the idea of capital being a bridge between present and future must be understood. Neither income, which is immediately destroyed as such, 'nor capital take this bridge; capital cannot be both the bridge and the magnitude that travels over it [...]; the bridge is therefore made of *nothingness*: the bridge is itself the definition of the travel' (ibid.: 321–2). Capital enables income to be spent at a later moment. At every instant after its initial creation, income exists in the form of capital and at each instant it can recover its form of income and finance the final purchase of the stock of real goods defining the real component of capital-time.

### *Saving and investment*

An interesting application of Schmitt's analysis of capital-time is the proof of the identity of saving and investment. Keynes (1936/1946) had already claimed the unquestionable consequence of transforming current income into capital-time. The identity $S \equiv I$ is not the tautological consequence of the way investment and savings are defined but the result of an instantaneous process whereby income is saved by wage-earners, lent to firms, and invested by them in the formation of current output as a stock of real goods.

The mere flow of time is not enough to verify the transformation of income into capital. Likewise, the mere loan of saved-up income is not enough for the existence of net savings. If the sum saved by A is lent to B, the negative savings of B match the positive savings of A, and the amount of net savings is zero. For savings to be net, they must derive from 'an operation that defines real savings simultaneously' (ibid.: 320). In other words, to be net, savings must define a transaction in which income holders are lenders, and firms are borrowers.

When wage-earners earn their income in the form of bank deposits, they lend it to banks in exchange for a promise to get it back in the future. Hence, wage-earners give up their income of today and obtain in return the possibility to have it recreated in the future. At the same time, firms invest the income saved by wage-earners and transform it into capital. The stock thus formed is the real aspect of capital, the physical counterpart of the sum saved up by income holders. Saving is net precisely because it results from a transaction defining simultaneously a monetary and a real saving. The identity of saving and investment derives directly from the simultaneous formation of monetary and real saving, that is, from the transformation of income into capital.

At first, the identity $S \equiv I$ seems to derive straight from the fact that wage-earners invest immediately their income in the purchase of claims on bank deposits. '[I]ncome holders purchase financial securities, claims on deposits sold by the bank where their income is deposited; this unique transaction defines at the same time the saving of income and its *investment* in claims on deposits' (Schmitt 1993–94a, 1 février 1994: 9, m.t.). Yet, the deposit of income holders is more a placement than an investment. To establish the identity of *S* and *I*, definitively, it is therefore necessary to pursue the analysis up to the point when the income saved by income holders is lent to firms.

The instant income is deposited in exchange for equivalent claims on bank deposits, physical output is divested of its monetary form and is deposited with firms as a stock. As a consequence of the transformation of income into capital, physical output is owned concurrently by income holders, as the object of their financial claims on banks, and by firms, as the object of their stock. Finally, it is because 'the same product, taken out of money, is owned simultaneously by households (macroeconomic saving) and by firms (macroeconomic investment)' (ibid.: 12, m.t.), that *S* and *I* are always necessarily equal.

### *No capital would exist without banks*

Production does not require the presence of banks and bank money. Commodity-money would be enough to guarantee the emission of the product but not to transform the product into a stock and income into capital. This is so because the payment of wages in physical money would be a bipolar transaction, and 'every bipolar operation of payment is rigorously symmetric: purchase for an agent and sale for their economic counterpart' (Schmitt 1993–94a, 8 février 1994: 4, m.t.). In the presence of physical money, the purchase of financial claims by a given economic agent entails necessarily the formation of a positive financial capital for this agent and of an equivalent negative financial capital for the seller of financial claims. The two capitals neutralize each other, and no net capital can be formed.

Things are radically different when payments are carried out in bank money, at which point transactions become tri-polar, and banks mediate the transformation of bank deposits into net capital.

Through banks' financial intermediation, income is lent *by income holders to income holders through firms*, a loan that might seem circular and meaningless, if it were not for the fact that it implies the passage from income to capital. The emission of bank money enables income-earners to change their real output into a sum of money. Workers obtain their own product in the form of money. It is through an *absolute* exchange that physical output is changed into money. Carried out through the monetary intermediation of banks, this absolute exchange is accompanied by a financial transaction by which wage-earners lend to firms the very income required to finance their investment.

Insofar as it defines a loan by wage-earners to firms, the financial intermediation of banks concerns an ordinary loan and does not lead to the formation of any net or macroeconomic capital. However, *the ordinary loan is accompanied by a quantum loan, and it is the latter that defines the formation of a positive, macroeconomic capital.* In this case emphasis is on the loan granted by wage-earners to themselves. This particular loan takes the form of an absolute exchange through which wage-earners give up the product-in-the-money and replace it with financial claims on bank deposits.

By saving their income in the form of bank deposits, wage-earners lend to themselves their physical output, that is, they give themselves the possibility to spend their present income in the future, which is precisely the object of any loan.

> Absolute loans do not get anyone into debt because, lending his income to himself, the holder destroys it in order to find it again intact later, at the term of the loan that will see the reproduction of the, instantly destroyed, income.
>
> (Schmitt 2021: 324)

Absolute exchanges and quantum loans are possible only if monetary payments are tri-polar transactions, a condition that can be fulfilled only by the presence of banks and using bank money.

Through the monetary and financial intermediation of banks, capital is formed simultaneously as a positive financial capital of wage-earners, a negative capital of firms, and an additional positive capital in the form of a stock of real goods. Financial capital on the one hand and stocked product on the other are the two joint aspects – monetary and real – of capital, and they are both possible only in a world characterized by the presence of banks. '[I]f the economy were not endowed with bank money, no capital, either financial or real, would be formed within itself. *Money makes the product; bank money makes the capital*' (ibid.: 324).

## The formation of fixed capital

A correct analysis of capitalism must explain the formation of capital in its two joint aspects: the monetary one and the real one. If the formation of capital-time were restricted to its monetary or financial aspect, no net capital could see the light because the negative financial capital of the borrower would neutralize the positive financial capital of the lender. As for fixed capital, the formation of a material stock of instrumental goods is, and has been, possible even in the absence of banks and bank money. Yet, the lack of a financial counterpart prevents the transformation of these instrumental goods into real capital.

A purely physical stock is a collection of use-values and not a capital. On the other hand, the loan by A to B being a zero-sum transaction, the mere presence of a financial market is not enough for the formation of a net capital. Consequently, *no fixed capital can be formed in an economy without banks*. 'In spite of the introduction of the financial market, the economy is functioning without any net capital, even if an instrumental "capital", which might be assumed to be of an advanced technology, is available' (ibid.: 85). Obtained through the immediate transformation of income, capital is initially '*a patrimonial value formed to the benefit of income holders*' (ibid.: 100), a transformation of their wages.

Thus, capital-time is, logically and chronologically, at the origin of fixed capital. Saving is their common source. In the case of capital-time, saving is reversible: income holders can recover their initial income at any time and spend it as they wish. The case of fixed capital is different: saved income is fixed forever in the production of the instrumental, real component of fixed capital.

Whether reversible or irreversible, saving is the necessary condition for the existence of capital, and so is investment. Yet, the investment forming the initial stock of wage-goods is substantially different from that forming a stock of instrumental or fixed capital-goods. The analysis of fixed capital must explain the passage from reversible to irreversible saving as well as from a stock of wage-goods to a stock of fixed capital- or investment-goods. Let us accompany

Schmitt as he tries to show that fixed capital is but 'a transformation or an "avatar" of a pure capital-time' (ibid.: 94).

### *From capital-time to fixed capital*

The switch from capital-time to fixed capital requires 'the conversion of a stock of wage-goods into a "stock" of capital-goods or instrumental capital' (ibid.: 94). In turn, this conversion requires the investment of the company profit in the production of instrumental or fixed capital-goods.

In the case of capital-time, firms invest the income lent to them by wage-earners, and this leads to the formation of a stock of wage-goods. In the case of fixed capital, firms must invest their own income: profit. It is true that firms can derive a positive income also from the sale of financial claims, yet the income thus earned will be part of their own income only if they succeed in paying back the lenders. In this case, firms would benefit from an advance of profit, which they will be able to pay back when their expected profit is eventually formed. Whether secured or advanced, profits are the income firms can invest in the production of fixed capital-goods.

Since profit is derived from wages, and since wages are immediately transformed into capital-time, profit itself initially takes the form of capital-time. Indeed, part of the income formed to the benefit of wage-earners is transferred free of cost to firms, which become the owners of the bank deposits corresponding to the wage-goods stocked with them. At the moment of its formation, profit is saved by firms, which are credited with an equivalent amount of bank deposits. Initially, firms' capital-goods have the form of the wage-goods previously owned, financially, by wage-earners. 'Thus, at birth, fixed capital, which takes the form of saved wage-goods, is purely a *capital-time*' (ibid.: 94).

If profits are redistributed to households as dividends and/or interest, capital-time disappears, and households can again spend their income on the purchase of dividend-goods and/or interest-goods. It is important to bear in mind here that, profit formed in the market for products, is necessarily spent in the labour market. This is also the case for redistributed profit. Indeed, it is precisely because profit is spent on financing the production of dividend- and interest-goods that these two categories of goods can be defined. If profit were spent in the market for products, national production would consist of wage-goods only. The existence of other categories of goods confirms the fact that profit is spent in the labour market even when it is redistributed.

Once more it is quantum logic that must be applied, for the distribution of profit as dividends and interest is compatible with its expenditure in the labour market. Production of dividend- and interest-goods (financed by profit) generates the income that, redistributed to households, enables their final purchase. Finally, once profit is redistributed and income spent, capital-time no longer exists, nor can it turn into fixed capital.

### *The investment of profit in capitalism*

Schmitt's main concern in the analysis of capital during the time of his crucial insights is to provide an explanation of the way fixed capital is formed in our capitalist economies. His object of inquiry is capitalism in its present form, and his objective is a theory capable of explaining, clearly and consistently, the pathological formation of fixed capital within capitalism.

In Schmitt's 1984 analysis, firms' expenditure of their profit to their own benefit is possible if the profit formed in any given period is invested in the production of instrumental goods *of a subsequent period*. 'It is essential to understand the necessity of the distinction of two periods: one, $p_1$, when the monetary profit is formed and the other, $p_2$, when it is spent and converted into investment-goods' (ibid.: 95).

Let us suppose that in $p_1$ firms produce wage-goods only, and that they pay 100 wage-units to their workers. Assume, then, that firms fix the selling price at 125 money units, and that workers spend their entire income in the market for products. At the end of $p_1$ firms own bank deposits of 20 wage-units, their profit, which they automatically invest in the provisory purchase of the wage-goods still unsold. Remember that this initial investment is the unavoidable consequence of double-entry bookkeeping and of the emission (creation-destruction) of money, as well as of the monetary and financial intermediation of banks. Whether firms are aware of it or not, their profits are invested the moment they are 'formed', an operation that leads to the transformation of the wage-goods still physically deposited with them into an equivalent stock of real goods (Figure 5.1).

As depicted in Figure 5.1, arrow *a* represents the payment of wages, arrow *b* the expenditure of wages, and arrow *c* the amount of wage-goods (in value terms) obtained by workers through their expenditure of wages. Since the firms' selling price of wage-goods is set to 125 money units, workers can obtain only part of their production by spending their income, 100 wage-units, in full, namely 80 out of 100 wage-units. At the end of $p_1$, firms own a monetary

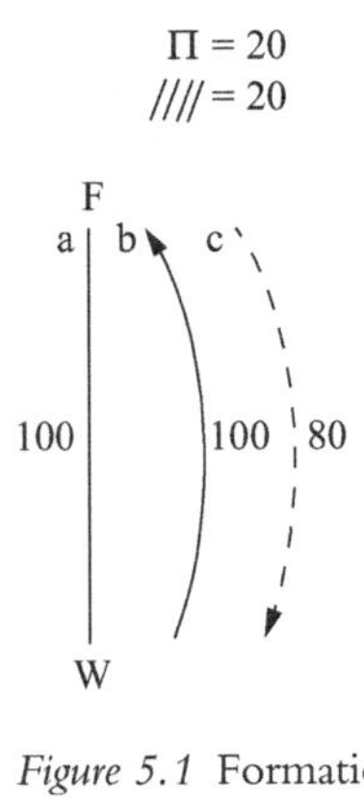


*Figure 5.1* Formation of profit in period $p_1$.

profit of 20 wage-units in the form of financial claims (on bank deposits), and have at their disposal a stock of wage-goods of the same amount, while running a financial debt to banks also equal in value to 20 wage-units.

The following step is the explicit investment of the profit formed in $p_1$ into the production of new capital-goods in $p_2$ (Figure 5.2).

As shown in Figure 5.2, $p_2$ firms' production is still equal to 100 wage-units, but 80 of these 100 units are paid to workers producing wage-goods, while the remaining 20 units, which correspond to firms' profit, are paid to workers producing new investment- or fixed capital-goods. As in $p_1$, production of wage-goods does not entail the expenditure of any positive income, whereas the production of investment-goods is financed by the profit formed in $p_1$ (Figure 5.3).

In Figure 5.3, it appears that workers producing fixed capital-goods in $p_2$ lose them to firms and obtain, in exchange, a right over the wage-goods produced in $p_1$ which are still present in the form of stock. 'The production of the new period, which engenders capital-goods, dislodges wage-goods and replaces them at once, in the unchanged "stock", by instrumental capital' (ibid.: 101).

At the end of the two periods, and assuming that no further profit is formed in $p_2$ (an assumption that is in no way binding and removable at will), the bulk

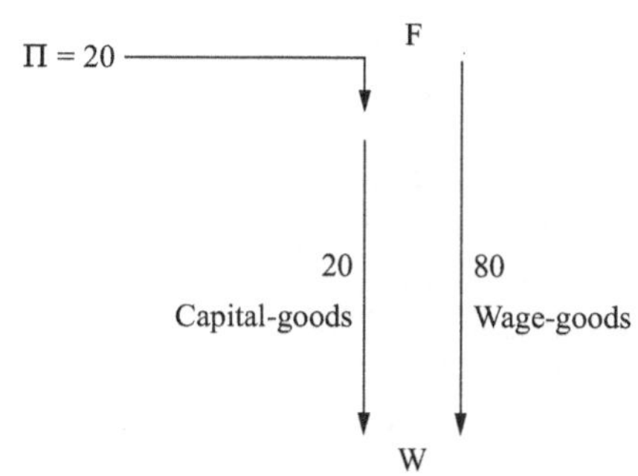


*Figure 5.2* New production of capital-goods in period $p_2$.

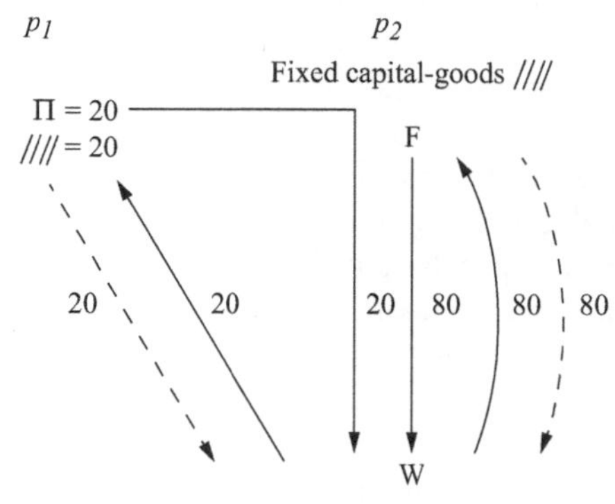


*Figure 5.3* Conversion of wage-goods produced in $p_1$ into fixed capital-goods produced in $p_2$.

of goods produced in $p_1$ and $p_2$ has been purchased – wage-goods in the market for products and fixed capital-goods in the labour market. Wage-goods have been replaced by capital-goods in the stock of goods owned by firms, which proves that investment-goods are the final form of the wage-goods initially stocked by firms in $p_1$ when their profit is formed. '*Capital-goods are all obtained by the transformation of an equivalent quantity of wage-goods*' (ibid.: 329). Whereas the stock of wage-goods corresponding to capital-time consists in goods waiting to be sold, the stock of fixed capital-goods is made up of instrumental goods that will never be sold in the market for products. '[C]apital-goods are stocks by nature: they are so in themselves' (ibid.: 329).

### *The identity I≡S confirmed*

Macroeconomic investment is the expenditure of firms' profit, which takes place in the labour market and finances the production of instrumental goods. Given that profit is that part of wage-earners' income that is transferred to firms, it defines a saved-up income that can be either redistributed to households or invested by firms. In the former case, profit is transformed into dividends, interest or rent and spent in the market for products. Profit is thereby cancelled, and so are savings. In the latter case, profit and investment are the two terms of an identity, and the saved-up income collected by firms is fixed once and for all into the capital-goods obtained through its investment, hence the identity of macroeconomic saving and investment.

A related argument leads to the same conclusion. Consider the impact of the investment of profit on the formation of income. When profit is invested in the production of capital-goods, its expenditure in the labour market (at $p_2$) yields an amount of new wages immediately available as bank deposits. These bank deposits define a sum of macroeconomic savings, that is, savings that are net for the whole economy, because they correspond to an income that will never be spent on purchasing the goods that specify its real content.

The truth is that firms already purchase investment-goods at the very moment of their production. Emptied of their real content, wages paid to workers producing investment-goods are necessarily saved, which establishes a perfect match between investment and saving.

> We thus verify that the income [profit] is destroyed since its expenditure releases the new product, instrumental goods, and destroyed savings are at once replaced: being unable to go to the purchase of instrumental goods (already purchased in the expenditure of capital-time), the wages created in the production of those goods are *definitively saved*.
>
> (ibid.: 329)

Profit is saved-up income transferred to firms, and its investment in the production of capital-goods transforms it, irreversibly, into fixed capital. This means that, to the extent that it is so invested, the income saved as profit is spent for good in the labour market and will never be consumed by income holders. It is true that, when it is paid out to workers producing investment-goods, profit is reproduced in the form of bank deposits. However, these bank deposits result from a payment of wages corresponding to a new production; they do not merely reproduce the same income initially saved in the form of capital-time.

It is a new additional income, generated by the investment of profit and deprived of its real content, which defines the macroeconomic savings induced by the formation of fixed capital. The investment of profit, therefore, is the source of both fixed capital and equivalent macroeconomic savings: $I \equiv S$.

## The pathology of fixed capital formation

Firms' investment occurs through the expenditure of profit (formed in $p_1$) in the production of capital-goods (taking place at $p_2$). Firms purchase instrumental goods in the labour market because wages are paid out of a positive income: their profit. Firms appropriate fixed capital-goods from the very moment of production: the income formed in their production is deprived of its real content. We are confronted with an anomalous operation: instead of receiving their own product in the form of money, workers producing capital-goods are credited with a sum of what Schmitt calls *empty money* (1984a/2021). The remuneration of workers producing fixed capital-goods entails the immediate and final purchase of these goods by firms.

### *The investment of profit as the cause of empty emissions*

Schmitt (1984a/2021) calls the investment of profit a *nested expenditure* because it is made up of a final expenditure of income (profit) taking place within a payment of wages.

Let us represent this with an empty arrow, the payment of wages as it occurs, in period $p_1$ and in any other period, when it does not imply the expenditure of a positive income (Figure 5.4).

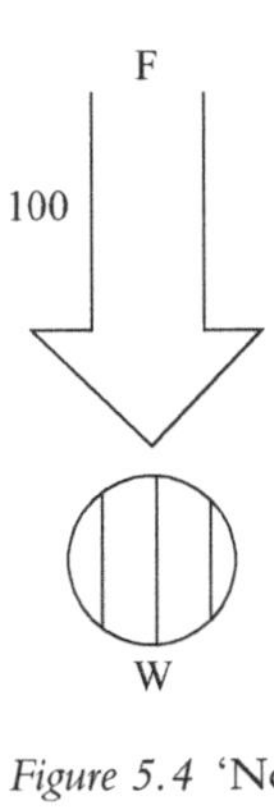


*Figure 5.4* 'Normal' payment of wages.

Paid by banks through an emission of money, wages provide workers with the financial ownership of produced output. As shown in Figure 5.4, workers are credited with a sum of income or *full money*, defined as the-product-in-the-money. This payment of wages is not a nested expenditure, and there is nothing wrong with it.

By contrast, the payment of wages depicted in Figure 5.5 is not as 'simple' as the one in Figure 5.4, but 'composite': it includes the expenditure of a positive income.

The expenditure of profit included in the payment of wages is nothing more than the investment carried out by firms in $p_2$ and defines the final purchase by firms of the capital-goods produced in the second period. Consequently, investment-goods are divested of their monetary form and appropriated by firms as a stock of fixed capital-goods, which transforms the sum paid out to workers into an amount of empty money.

> The emission of wages is *full* when the formation of wages does not coincide with the expenditure of profit. The emission of wages, on the contrary, is *empty* as far as it identifies itself with the expenditure of profit, a condition that is fulfilled in the investment of profit.
>
> (ibid.: 123)

Apparently, the empty emission is not a true anomaly because, in exchange for their product (investment-goods), workers obtain a claim on the wage-goods previously stocked by firms as real content of their capital-time. Wages paid in $p_2$ for the production of investment-goods take the form of claims on bank deposits, but their 'natural' object, the stock of investment-goods, is replaced by the stock of wage-goods of $p_1$ still unsold. Yet, this transaction is far from unproblematic. Over the two periods and for two different productions – of wage- and capital-goods – the set of workers are paid with the same financial claims.

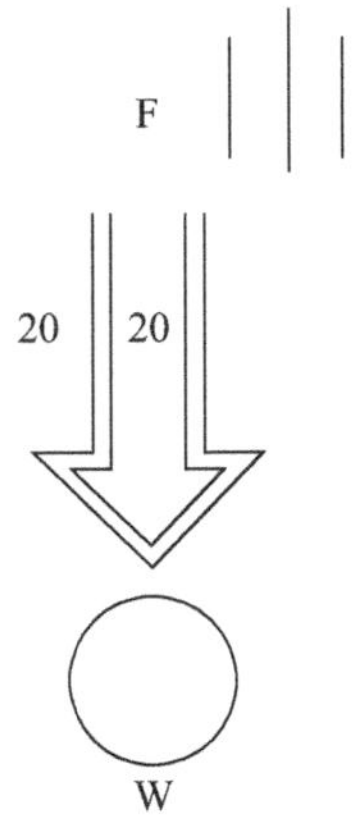


*Figure 5.5* Pathological payment of wages.

Even though the workers in our numerical example produce capital-goods in $p_2$ and also an equivalent sum of wage-goods in $p_1$, for a total product of 40 money units they obtain only 20 money units of wage-goods. The real content of their wages of $p_2$ is that of their wages of $p_1$, which is just another way of saying that their real output of $p_2$ is appropriated cost-free by firms. By paying wages out of their profit, firms give to workers, for the second time, part of the real wages they had already obtained in $p_1$ to produce wage-goods. In so doing, firms take possession of the capital-goods produced in $p_2$, which become forever part of their fixed capital. Thus, the anomaly is clearly identified with the expropriation of households to the benefit of capital.

We reach the same conclusion by observing that, when the payment of wages is financed by a positive income, it involves the purchase of labour pathologically transformed into a commodity. It is in this theoretical framework that Adam Smith's concept of 'labour commanded' comes into its own. When profit is invested in the production of capital-goods, firms exert their purchasing power on labour itself, 'equal to the quantity of labour that it enables [firms] to purchase or command' (Smith 1776/1991: 26). Through the expenditure of the profit formed in $p_{1,}$ firms purchase part of the labour of $p_2$ and, since '[*t*]*he purchase of labour is identically the purchase of the product of labour*' (Schmitt 2021: 122), they acquire the final ownership over the capital-goods produced in $p_2$.

As already clearly established by Marx (1867/1976), labour is at the origin of commodities and of their value, which means that labour itself cannot be a commodity. It is only as a pathological effect of profit spent within the payment of wages of $p_2$ that labour is purchased as if it were a commodity. The cause of the pathology is not the fact that profit is spent in the labour market: this is always and necessarily the case. When profit is redistributed, this expenditure concerns the production of the same period and defines neither an expenditure of firms for their own benefit, nor the transformation of labour into a commodity.

The entire output is owned by households, either directly, through its final purchase in the market for products, or indirectly, through the intermediation of firms acting on behalf of households. Then, when the profit formed in a period is invested in the production of another period its expenditure in the labour market becomes a pathological transaction, the emission of empty money. Firms spend their profit to their own benefit, and households are thus deprived for good of part of current output.

### *The appropriation of fixed capital-goods by depersonalized firms*

The fact that firms get hold of capital-goods from the very moment they are formed leads to an additional purchase in the market for products: 'an investment of profit is an *additional* purchase in the products market' (ibid.: 122). Indeed, the payment of wages out of a previously formed profit is a purchase of labour and, by the same token, of its product. Even though it occurs within the payment of wages, this purchase defines an expenditure of wage-units in the market for products. In our example, the emission of 100 wage-units in $p_2$ is empty for 20 wage-units because one-fifth of the production 'has already been bought in the emission of wages itself' (ibid.: 122). The additional purchase is '*the payment of wages out of profits*' (ibid.: 122).

In the absence of an empty emission, there would be no excess demand and households (income holders) would financially own the entire output. The pathological investment of profit characterizing capitalism defines an additional expenditure that transforms the initial loss of wage-earners occurring in $p_1$ into a definitive loss (taking place in $p_2$).

If the profit formed in $p_1$ were redistributed to households as dividends, interest or rent, income holders would recover their initial loss. When profit is invested, the loss becomes irreversible and households are forever dispossessed of part of their production.

> The activity of period [$p_2$] produces a measure of 100 new goods, of which workers only receive 80 units in their wages of 100 money units. Capital-goods are deposited neither in the money wages, nor in time; they are, on the contrary, directly appropriated by firms.
>
> (ibid.: 123)

It is essential that one understands the pathological nature of the appropriation of capital-goods operated by firms. In this context, it is useful to distinguish between 'personalized' and 'depersonalized' or 'disembodied' firms.

As the words clearly indicate, personalized firms are firms owned by households at large (mainly shareholders), whereas depersonalized or disembodied firms are a non-person. In an orderly system, only personalized firms would exist, and the investment of profit would be carried out to the benefit of households. Present systems are characterized by the pathological investment of profit, and this leads to the appropriation of fixed capital by depersonalized firms. 'The product collected from within money is withdrawn from households *to be definitively appropriated by a "non-person", the disembodied set of the country's firms*' (ibid.: 124).

As clearly stated by Schmitt, the existence of this non-person is entirely due to a pathology, to the presence of an empty emission entailing the appropriation of instrumental goods by disembodied firms. 'The category of "*non-persons*" is introduced by a *pathology*, net investment being a false emission. The notion of an expropriation of income holders or, identically, of the private appropriation of the means of production, thus takes its true, *economic*, meaning' (ibid.:126).

The reader should not draw wrong conclusions. Depersonalized firms are nowhere to be found in the real world. They do not exist as legal persons or companies and have no physical seat, headquarters, or other. Yet, a logical inquiry into the nature of capital establishes their existence beyond doubt. The pathological process of capital accumulation leads to a non-person appropriating part of current production.

As we shall see in the next chapter, both inflation and involuntary unemployment have their source in the capital forever lost to households to the benefit of disembodied firms. The existence of the former establishes therefore that of the latter.

### *The investment of profit and the duplication of monetary capital*

It is worth observing here that in the synopsis of his 1984 book, Schmitt claims that in the present pathological systems, banks lend not only the wages formed as bank deposits, but also the profit invested by firms in the production of capital-goods. Instead of being destroyed, the income (profit) spent by firms in the payment of workers producing capital-goods is reproduced in the form of wages. The financial capital formed in $p_1$ corresponding to company profit is absorbed in the production of instrumental goods and replaced by a sum of empty wages. Deposited with banks, these wages are still available in the financial market and can be lent even though the income spent in their formation has been definitively absorbed by fixed capital.

Schmitt calls the loan financed by the deposit resulting from the investment of profit *redundant* and identifies it with the very 'essence of capitalism' (Schmitt 1993/94a, 8 février 1994: 11, m.t.). What happens is that, even though instrumental capital has absorbed the monetary capital invested by firms, the payment of wages corresponding to the investment of profit recreates it.

Schmitt speaks of the *duplication of monetary capital induced by the investment of profit*.

> Being absorbed into instrumental capital, monetary capital should be cancelled; this is a requirement of logic. However, in our concrete economies, the investment of profit has the effect of making monetary capital rise again: it is integrally found again in the set of income holders.
>
> (Schmitt 2021: 342)

The reason for the duplication of monetary capital resides in the double aspect of the investment of profit, a transaction that is at the same time expenditure of income and formation of a new income. An income, i.e. profit, is spent on the purchase of fixed capital-goods, and another one is created to pay wages to the workers producing them. As the new income is deprived of its real content, definitively appropriated by (disembodied) firms, its nature is altered: reduced to a sum of empty money, it defines a monetary capital corresponding to the stock of wage-goods of $p_1$. This is confirmed by the fact that the wages that workers receive by producing investment-goods in period $p_2$ are a financial claim on the wage-goods produced in $p_1$.

It is precisely because these workers are paid twice the same wages that the second payment reproduces the first and gives rise once again to the same monetary capital.

> Already absorbed into instrumental capital, monetary capital is available a *second time*: it is present in the set of firms (within instrumental capital) and *in addition* in the set of income holders (under the form of claims to the wage-goods in stock).
>
> (ibid.: 342)

The re-creation of profit in the form of (empty) wages increases the amount of bank deposits and, by the same token, the amount of loans granted by banks to households.

## Classical, neoclassical, and Keynesian analyses of capital: a brief comparison with quantum analysis

### *The Classics*

The Classics are the first authors to have explicitly associated capital with time and to have distinguished between circulating and fixed capital. Adam Smith's emphasis is on the role played by each of these two capitals. In particular, circulating capital is identified with a stock of goods to be invested in the production of fixed capital. 'As soon as stock has accumulated in the hands of particular persons, some of them will naturally employ it in setting to work industrious people, whom they will supply with materials and subsistence' (Smith 1776/1991: 42).

Smith is thus very close to identifying the concept of circulating capital with a real wage-fund, a stock of wage-goods used by firms to 'command' the labour of workers who produce instrumental goods. When he maintains that '[e]very fixed capital is both originally derived from, and requires to be continually supported by a circulating capital' (ibid.: 248), Smith is clearly referring to the production and amortization of fixed capital, two operations made possible by an initial sacrifice (saving) enabling firms to 'invest' a real wage-fund.

Ricardo defines circulating capital as the capital employed 'in the support of labour' (Ricardo 1817/1951: 32) and fixed capital as that 'invested in machinery, implements, buildings, &c.' (ibid.: 32). The idea of circulating capital supporting labour is also very close to that of a real wage-fund and to the thesis that fixed capital results from the investment, by firms, of a profit formed as a capital-time and whose real object is a stock of wage-goods. Neither Smith, nor Ricardo provides a thorough analysis of the relationship between capital and time and of that between monetary and real capital, but their distinction of circulating and fixed capital is rich in fruitful insights and shows the *fil rouge* linking Classical to quantum macroeconomic analysis.

Marx's contribution differs from that of his predecessors. His aim is to show that firms obtain profit as a surplus-value, as the result of a direct appropriation of workers' labour-time. He therefore distinguishes constant from variable capital: the latter is invested in the purchase of labour power and is the only one capable to increase its value.

Unfortunately, Marx's analysis runs into two major difficulties, which seriously undermine it, namely

1) The logical impossibility to account for the monetary creation of surplus-value, and
2) The transformation of values into prices, necessary to explain the fact that profit is distributed proportionally to the total capital invested.

Despite some deep insights and promising intuitions, the Classics' theory of capital suffers from an inadequate analysis of money and of its relationship with production. The origin of capital remains elusive, particularly in its monetary aspect, and no satisfactory explanation is provided regarding its pathological formation.

***The neoclassics***

Consistent with his general equilibrium approach, Walras maintains that the equilibrium price of capital-goods is determined by the market through their exchange 'against the excess of income over consumption' (Walras 1874/1984: 269), and that their price depends on the equality of their value and that of this excess, as well as on the equality of their selling price and their cost of production.

In his attempt to derive the price of capital from that of its services, Walras conceives the rate of interest as a relative price and assumes that quantities of capital-goods are given as initial endowments of the system. This assumption is necessary if we want to avoid having to assume as many interest rates as there are different kinds of capital-goods. Unfortunately, Walras's system ends up being viciously circular: his system of equations admits a solution only if the given quantities are those defining equilibrium, which must be determined.

Böhm-Bawerk is rightly considered as one of the greatest specialists of the theory of capital. His roundabout methods of production are a clear indication of the close relation he assumes to exist between capital and time. Böhm-Bawerk's idea is that capital can be evaluated by referring to the average period of production, that is, the average period of time separating investment from its final yield. In his attempt to measure capital, Böhm-Bawerk clearly rejects the neoclassical assumption that capital is a direct source of value and maintains that '[c]apital does not independently deliver an impulse, it merely transmits an impulse delivered by originary productive forces' (Böhm-Bawerk 1889/1959: 95).

If the value produced by a roundabout method is greater than that of another roundabout method, it is not because of the value of the capital employed by each of them, respectively, but because their average periods of production differ. Unfortunately, at this point in his analysis, Böhm-Bawerk switches the focus onto the impact of the roundabout methods of production on utility.

He assumes that, because of individual preferences, future goods tend to be undervalued, and that this is the origin of a 'premium or agio which present goods enjoy in comparison with future goods' (ibid.: 288). The impact of capital on value, mediated by the roundabout methods of production, would thus depend more on a psychological principle than on the objective relationship between capital and time.

After the failure to reconcile Böhm-Bawerk's analysis of capital with traditional neoclassical theory, Wicksell focuses his own investigation on the concept of marginal productivity. Yet, he forgets that the marginal productivity of capital cannot be used to determine its remuneration because marginal productivity must be applied to a measure of capital that depends on this very remuneration.

Despite failing to provide a theory of capital consistent with his choice of general equilibrium analysis, Wicksell's insights bring him close to those of quantum analysis. Let me mention, here, his idea that if the means of subsistence 'are still (directly or indirectly through money) in the possession of the capitalist, then they are undoubtedly means of production *because they serve for the purchase of labour*' (Wicksell 1893/1954: 102–3). In this passage, Wicksell argues that the stock of wage-goods owned by firms in the form of capital-time are means of production because they are invested in the purchase of labour. In a single sentence we find the key concepts of the modern theory of capital: profit, capital-time, real stock, purchase of labour, and (implicitly) fixed capital.

### *Keynes*

Keynes relates capital to investment, '[w]e shall mean by the rate of investment the net increment during a period of time of the capital of the community' (Keynes 1930/1971: 114) and makes it clear that investment comes out of savings, so that capital growth requires an initial sacrifice imposed to households. 'A supply of *new* capital [...] can only come into existence insofar as those who have claims on the community's flow of income are willing to *defer* their claims, i.e. out of "savings"' (Keynes 1973: 19). In our advanced economies, investment is financed out of profit, that is, out of forced savings appropriated by firms at zero cost. Whether present or advanced, profit is a part of current income that is saved up by households that firms can redistribute or invest. Keynes is therefore right to point out that (fixed) capital is the result of the investment of savings.

In *The General Theory of Employment, Interest and Money*, Keynes stresses the relevance of individual's expectations and of the '*prospective yield*' (Keynes 1936/1946: 212) of capital over its current yield. Instead of investigating the origin and nature of capital further, Keynes endeavours to show that capital's marginal efficiency is the way to determine the equilibrium value of capital and that '[i]t is important to understand the dependence of the marginal efficiency of a given stock of capital on changes in expectation' (ibid.: 143). The relevance of Keynes's *General Theory* analysis concerns the dynamic of the process of capital accumulation more than the mechanism leading to its pathological formation, and we will reconsider it in the following chapter.

### *Post-Keynesians*

More recent controversies on the theory of capital have been centred on its measurement rather than on its conceptual definition and on its formation. The debate has mainly concerned the possibility of determining a unit of measure whose value is independent of distribution and prices or of the rate of interest and wages. As such, the problem is ill-defined. Value is not a physical dimension of goods; this undermines the search for a dimensional standard, whose value can be taken as constant. Controversies about the measure of capital are meaningless unless we first establish how physically heterogeneous goods can be made homogeneous – an impossible task unless value is identified with a numerical form.

Heterodox economists are right in pointing out that general equilibrium analysis is viciously circular, and that production functions are of no avail because they take for granted what (the homogeneity of goods) must be established in the first place. However, their analysis lacks clarity with regard to the nature of economic value and its unit of measure. Their analysis of capital suffers from this shortcoming and calls for a new approach, capable of making the most of the intuitions of the past while providing a theoretical framework to include these insights into a richer synthesis, the final phase of a dialectical process that began with the work of the Physiocrats.

# 6 Schmitt's 1984 explanation of inflation and unemployment and the principles of his 1984 reform

During the first two decades of his research, Schmitt developed his analysis mainly in terms of value, relegating prices to a subsidiary, redistributive role. The necessary equality between macroeconomic values and prices is a good enough reason to concentrate on values and explain profit and capital on the basis of production being identified with the payment of wages. This is the approach that I will follow in this chapter in order to show how Schmitt reconciles logical identities with numerical inequalities and explains the latter as the unavoidable result of a pathological process of capital accumulation.

The explanation of inflation and unemployment requires bearing in mind the entire process that accounts for the formation, maintenance, and growth of fixed capital through production, profit investment, and amortization. I shall therefore outline Schmitt's analysis of this entire process, which is affected by a serious, structural anomaly totally unrelated to economic agents' behaviours. By blaming this anomaly for both inflation and involuntary unemployment, Schmitt can explain their co-emergence and search for a solution that addresses both.

The aim of Schmitt's 1984 book *Inflation, chômage et malformations du capital* is to introduce the reader to quantum macroeconomics and to provide both a diagnosis of the pathologies affecting capitalism and the principles of a reform ensuring the switching from monetary disorder to order. In this chapter, I shall refer mainly to the English edition of this book, integrating this fundamental text with references to Schmitt's *Théorie unitaire de la monnaie, nationale et internationale* (1975) and also to a small number of published and unpublished manuscripts he devoted to inflation and unemployment.

## Inflation

### *Identities and numerical inequalities*

Based on his works on the theory of the circular flow of money, Schmitt observes that pathological disequilibria can be defined because logical laws exist. For example, if the necessary equality between the sales and purchases of each single element of the monetary circuit were not established on logical grounds,

DOI: 10.4324/9781351271325-9

it would be impossible to determine which kind of discrepancy the numerical difference between them defines. Hence, if sales of any given element were equal to 10 money units and its purchases amounted to 11 money units, we could not say, in the absence of any specific law, whether this numerical difference defines an excess-demand or a negative excess-supply. '[O]nly the invulnerability of Say's law allows us to define money's equilibrium. Without this positive law, no monetary order could be established because monetary disorder could not even be defined' (Schmitt 1972c: 69, m.t.).

Say's law is a logical pre-requisite for the existence of money's circular flow: every element of the monetary circuit must equalize its sales and its simultaneous purchases. This does not mean that each economic agent's behaviour must conform to this law but that the law applies regardless of the decision made by any economic agent.

Say's law is not a behavioural or an experimental law. Its raison d'être is logical and derives from the necessary condition for the existence of money's circular flow.

> Every formal law is valid under the necessary and sufficient condition that the reasoning that founds it does not suffer from any internal flaw [...]. Say's identity is a law, because it is subject to the criterion of truth, and it is a logical law, because it results from reasoning and not from mere observation.
>
> (ibid.: 70, m.t.)

Nevertheless, this does not prevent sales from being numerically different from purchases. The identity establishes that the *value* of sales and the *value* of purchases of any element (simple or composite) of the monetary circuit be necessarily equal, yet leaves room for a (pathological) numerical difference between its two terms.

In an unpublished manuscript, which I have dated 1972 and entitled *Circuit*, Schmitt distinguishes between *constant* and *current* money units, where the former are units of money in which value is expressed and the latter the units of money currently available and on which value is distributed. 'Constant money is the value of output [...]. Current money is the sum of money units available' (Schmitt 1972d: 37, m.t.). Let us make use of this distinction (which is also to be found in Schmitt's *Génération de la monnaie des monnaies européennes*, 1975) and apply it to Keynes's concepts of global supply ($Y$) and global demand ($C+I$). Say's law is substantially the same as the law derived from Keynes's fundamental equations, i.e. the law establishing the necessary equality or identity between $Y$ and $C+I$.

To claim that firms' sales are identical to firms' purchases is tantamount to claiming that production creates its own demand, i.e. that firms' global supply is necessarily equal to income holders' (firms included) global demand.

$$Y \equiv C + I \qquad (6.1)$$

Equation (6.1) is an identity verified for whatever level of actual production and is numerically expressed in units of constant money. If no inflation or deflation ensued, identity (6.1) would always take the form of a numerical equality. If these two pathologies are present, identity (6.1) still holds true, albeit admitting a numerical imbalance between the value of current production, expressed in constant money units, and the numerical expression, in current money units, of global demand.

In the case of inflation, economists unanimously agree that an excess-demand appears, which, by increasing global demand and leaving global supply unaltered, leads to the disequilibrium

$$Y < C + I \tag{6.2}$$

If both (6.1) and (6.2) were expressed solely in constant money units, they would inevitably contradict each other, and we would have to abandon any hope to ever explain inflation. But this would mean forgetting that (6.1) is a logical law, an identity that can never be broken, which entails that $Y$ is always and necessarily equal *to* $C+I$, whatever the numerical expression of these two terms. Suppose $Y$ to be equal to 100 in constant money units. Expressed in constant money units, $C+I$ is also equal to 100.

Suppose that, for reasons that we will have to determine, global demand increases nominally to 110 units, the identity between $Y$ and $C+I$ would still stand and would take the form of Equation (6.3).

$$Y(100) \equiv C + I(110) \tag{6.3}$$

The meaning of the numerical discrepancy between the two identical terms of Equation (6.3) is unambiguous: the value of global demand, 100 units of constant money, is distributed over 110 units of current money. It is because a global demand worth 100 money units is spread over 110 money units that inflation can be properly defined as the loss of purchasing power suffered by each single monetary unit. As the same production ($Y=100$) is 'vehiculated' by an increased number of money units, it is easy to infer that the 'load' of each money unit decreases proportionally.

The value of output is determined by production through the payment of wages and is expressed in constant money units. The value of global demand is also determined by production. Yet, if a number of nominal money units is added to that resulting from the association between money and product, the numerical increase in global demand expressed in current money units will unmistakably denote an inflationary disequilibrium.

We find the following identity:

110 units of current money = 100 units of constant money.

> In other words, the 110 units of income have a purchasing power equal to 100 wage-units only. Hence, 1.1 units of current money "weight" as a unit of constant money.
>
> (ibid.: 37–8, m.t.)

Following Schmitt (1975a, 1984a, and 2021), we start by providing a few cases of relatively 'benign' inflation of a nominal origin.

## *Four simple cases of relatively benign inflation*

### *Case one*

The first and most straightforward case concerns the possibility for a banking system to finance the purchase of real goods, currencies, or financial assets through money creation. 'The gratuitous money that can be created as a counterpart of net "purchases" of gold and foreign currencies by banks and notably by central banks, can inflate the final demand addressed to firms' (Schmitt 1975a: 64, m.t.). Thus, if a central bank were allowed to finance public spending simply by issuing money, the amount of income generated by current production would be artificially increased by the addition of empty money, which would reduce the purchasing power of each single money unit initially coupled with current output. This pathological over-emission may be considered 'benign', not because its effects would not be serious, but because it is so blatantly illogical that most countries tend to avoid it as much as possible (for example by guaranteeing the independence of central banks and by asking them to transform their 'purchases' into advances).

### *Case two*

The second case concerns the use of firms' private revolving funds. If these funds are used for the payment of wages, they are regularly reconstituted through the sale of produced output, and then no problem arises. Yet, if they are partly used to finance the purchase of other firms' output, global demand increases pathologically. The part of the revolving fund so spent by some firms is recovered by others in the form of an inflationary profit, whose subsequent expenditure generates new inflationary profits in an endless chain, defined by Keynes (1930; 1971) as a *widow's cruse*. This case is relatively benign due to the fact that each firm using its revolving fund has to reconstitute it, so that the inflationary process generated by firms' additional purchases is not cumulative over time.

### *Case three*

A more interesting case is that of banks' over-lending. It provides a clear and simple example of the way inflation can be generated by a mechanism not perfectly in line with the logical laws that our monetary systems *should* comply with.

Let us consider the case of a commercial bank, B, monetizing the production of a firm, F, through the emission of $x$ money units and the payment of wages to workers, W. The amount of income formed as a bank deposit is of $x$ wage-units. *B*'s loans should therefore not exceed that sum. Yet, today, banks' lending capacity is determined by the amount of their deposits, and no structural distinction exists that honours the logical distinction between their monetary and financial intermediations. This makes it possible for B to lend a total sum of $y$ money units, where $y > x$.

Suppose B's clients, C, to obtain a loan of $y$ in order to finance their purchases from F (Table 6.1).

By lending $y > x$, bank B does not incur any disequilibrium: its loans, entered on the assets side of its balance sheet, are perfectly matched by equivalent deposits, entered on the liabilities side (entry (2)). It is clear, however, that B's loans exceed by $x - y$ money units the amount of income generated by production, and define an inflationary gap reducing the purchasing power of each money unit. What is wrong is the fact that part of the bank's loans, $y - x$, is financed by money creation. Because of the lack of distinction between B's monetary and financial intermediations, the latter can be replaced by the former, a mistaken conflation whereby the number of money units 'conveying' current income increases in an inflationary way.

'It is precisely because the same deposit bank is a point of emission and a financial intermediary' (Schmitt 2021: 116) that a monetary creation can feed a financial intermediation. '[T]he operations of creation and intermediation coexist, so much so that the bank never knows the amount of deposits it has at its disposal to feed its loans in the financial market' (ibid.: 116).

As Schmitt argues, inflation generated by banks' over-emissions can be considered benign, because

1) Banks try hard to avoid getting indebted to one another, almost certainly the consequence of over-lending, and because
2) The beneficiaries of their excess-loans must reimburse them when they fall due.

'Any operation of ordinary credit is a zero-sum operation through time. [...] empty emissions due to the activity of banks *are not cumulative over time*' (ibid.:

*Table 6.1* Banks' over-lending

| *Bank* | | | |
|---|---|---|---|
| *Assets* | | *Liabilities* | |
| (1) Firm | m.u. x | Workers | m.u. x |
| (2) Clients | m.u. y | Firm | m.u. y |

117). Even as the source of a relatively benign inflation, this case is relevant, because it shows the link between inflation and the present faulty implementation of double-entry bookkeeping. It lies at the heart of Schmitt's monetary reform, to which we will come toward the end of this chapter. For the time being, let us consider the fourth and most important case of benign inflation.

### *Case four: inflation and the investment of profit*

In Chapter 5 we saw that when the profit formed in $p_1$ is invested in $p_2$ in the production of capital-goods, an empty emission occurs following the appropriation of investment-goods by firms. By paying wages to workers producing investment-goods out of profit, firms spend a positive income, an expenditure that defines an additional purchase in the market for products taking place in the labour market. '[T]he investment of profit is an *additional* purchase in the products market' (ibid.: 122). If profit formed in $p_1$ is of 20 money units and if wages paid out in $p_2$ are of 100 money units, $p_2$'s total production – global supply – is worth 100 wage-units, while $p_2$'s total expenditures – global demand – amount to 120 money units. The additional purchase of firms boosts global demand but leaves global supply unaltered.

The investment of profit defines an empty emission because it is an additional purchase. And it is because it is an additional purchase that national income is identified with the sum of consumption and investment: $Y = C + I$. 'Investment is *additive*; R = C + I = 100 + 20' (ibid.: 124).

If firms did not appropriate investment-goods, their production would not increase global demand (D) with respect to global supply (S). Investment-goods would be economically owned by the undifferentiated set of households and would pertain to the broad category of consumption-goods: $Y = C$. As it occurs today, the investment of profit defines the pathological purchase of investment-goods by firms and generates a numerical disequilibrium between D (120 money units) and S (100 money units). '[I]nflation results from the expenditure, within the emission of wages, of wages emitted previously' (ibid.: 337) and therefore is caused by the pathological formation of fixed capital.

Inflation formed in $p_2$ is defined as 'benign' by Schmitt because, despite obtaining only empty money as remuneration, workers producing capital-goods are entitled to purchase the stock of wage-goods formed in $p_1$ following the formation of firms' profit. Workers are deprived of the economic ownership over investment-goods, but this loss is compensated by the wage-goods saved as stocks in $p_1$. This allows Schmitt to maintain that, in itself, the pathology 'due to net investment is not severe, since income holders obtain in capital what is denied to them in monetary income' (ibid.: 342–3).

Yet, the economic process does not stop here. Instrumental goods formed as fixed capital are used by firms and must be replaced because of wear and tear. Benign in itself, the inflation caused by the empty emission characterizing the pathological formation of fixed capital is the source of serious disorders as soon as the economy takes advantage of the instrumental goods produced in $p_2$.

## Fixed capital amortization and inflation

### *Amortization*

Produced in $p_2$ and definitively appropriated by disembodied firms, fixed capital-goods are used as instrumental goods in period $p_3$. Wear, tear, and obsolescence call for their amortization, that is, for their on-going maintenance and their eventual replacement. Wear, tear, and obsolescence are the root causes of amortization. It is because fixed capital is subject to them, and thus loses part of its value that amortization is necessary. Capital-goods must be restored to their previous value, and this is done through amortization.

One point must be clarified right away: the value lost by instrumental goods cannot be *transmitted* or *transferred* to final output. Schmitt stresses that the idea that a value might migrate from one product to another is metaphysical. It is absurd to maintain that part of the value of instrumental capital passes on to final output and then again from final output to instrumental goods in order for the initial value of fixed capital to be restored.

> The idea according to which the value of a knitting machine used to produce shirts can be "transferred" to the produced shirts is exceedingly naïve. Value units are pure units of measure; how could the measure of a good transforms itself to become the measure of another good?
>
> (Schmitt 1998a: 110, m.t.)

Wear, tear, and obsolescence define a loss that fixed capital cannot recover unless a new capital is produced, which replaces the one lost in the production of consumption- and investment-goods.

Yet, from a microeconomic viewpoint, amortization is financed by firms out of their gross profit and does not define a net income. One must therefore reconcile the need to add the production of amortization-goods to that of wage- and investment-goods with the fact that amortization is a reproduction.

The production of amortization-goods is at the same time a *production* of new capital-goods and the *reproduction* of fixed capital. If no new production of capital-goods occurred, fixed capital would lose part of its value and would not be amortized. Suppose fixed capital to have a total value of X money units and amortization to be equal to $x$ for any given period. If the production of amortization-goods were null, wear, tear, and obsolescence would reduce the value of fixed capital from X to X $-$ $x$. It is only through a new and net production of replacement goods that capital can be restored to its previous initial value. 'It is certain that capital can recover its total value of X only if $x$ units of value newly produced are *added* to it' (ibid.: 110, m.t.).

The first question asked by Schmitt concerns the macroeconomic definition of amortization and may be articulated as follows: is amortization a net production increasing national income or not? His answer is affirmative, derived from the observation that, if amortization were no net production, national income would always and necessarily be equal to $C+I$, and there would be no pathological inflation (or unemployment). The unquestionable existence of inflation and unemployment indicates that the microeconomic definition of amortization is insufficient to deal with the reality of a pathological economy and calls for a new macroeconomic approach.

Schmitt's second question follows on the heels of the first: is it possible to maintain that amortization is at the same time a new production and a reproduction of the old? Once more, the answer is yes: the apparent contradiction can be avoided by switching from binary to quantum logic, where the principle of the excluded middle does not apply. Schmitt's quantum macroeconomic analysis shows indeed that amortization is *both a reproduction and a net production that adds up to that of consumption- and investment-goods.*

Capitalism is thus characterized as an economic system in which national income is determined by the sum of the income formed in the production of consumption-, investment-, and amortization-goods: $Y = C + I + A$, where $A$ stands for amortization or amortization-goods.

The analysis of fixed capital amortization is much less straightforward than it might appear at first. While, indisputably from a microeconomic viewpoint, the costs of amortization are included in the total costs of output and considered part of firms' gross profit, equally certainly, in macroeconomic terms, amortization is a net production.

By sticking to the microeconomic definition of amortization, mainstream economics deprives itself of the conceptual means to account for the presence of inflation and, as we shall soon see, for involuntary unemployment. Schmitt's analysis rests on the macroeconomic definition of amortization and shows that replacement goods are final goods and not mere intermediary goods. Starting from the fact that without a new production of instrumental goods, capital would lose its value and gradually reduce to zero, Schmitt sets to work to analyze what happens in a capitalist economy when current production consists of consumption-, investment-, and amortization-goods.

As previously seen, the addition of investment-goods to wage-goods is the first sign of inflation. In $p_2$, firms appropriate instrumental goods from the very moment they are produced. The expenditure of profit formed in $p_1$ within the payment of wages of $p_2$ defines an additional expenditure and leads to an emission of empty money. In a way, investment-goods produced in $p_2$ 'are therefore paid *twice*: a first time in the expenditure of wages [...] and a second time in the transfer of their ownership from income holders to firms' (Schmitt 2021: 344).

The first payment occurs when workers transfer part of their income to firms as profit. By doing so, they finance the production of investment-goods, which amounts to saying that they should be the economic owners of capital-goods. If this were indeed the case, investment-goods would belong into the category of consumption, and national income would be equal to $C$ only. In reality, in a capitalist economy, firms appropriate instrumental goods produced in $p_2$ through the expenditure of profit in the labour market. This second expenditure of the same wages is inflationary and leads to the production and 'the private appropriation of instrumental capital' (ibid.: 344), which adds up to C in the definition of national income: $Y = C + I$.

### *Dual production*

Benign, the inflation formed in $p_2$ is the cause of the anomaly of fixed capital amortization. Indeed, as fixed capital formed in $p_2$ is appropriated by depersonalized firms, the production of amortization-goods taking place in $p_3$ is also appropriated by firms. '[E]ven though income holders "pay the price" for the amortization of fixed capital, it would be illogical to conclude that this payment that they have to bear makes them (directly) the owners of amortization-goods' (ibid.: 345). Replacement goods newly produced in $p_3$ are annexed by fixed capital, which recovers the value lost in the new production of consumption- and investment-goods. This implies that the income formed in the production of amortization-goods cannot be spent on their purchase.

It is only in an orderly, post-capitalist system that income holders would own fixed capital and that they would purchase amortization-goods (through the mediation of firms). In the present, disorderly system, income holders can purchase them – that is, cover their costs of production – only indirectly, at the cost of what Schmitt calls a '*dual production*' (ibid.: 135).

Let us reflect on a numerical example and suppose, as we did in Chapter 5, that fixed capital formed in $p_2$ is equal to 20 money units. Suppose also that in period $p_3$ wear and tear reduces to zero the value of this capital and that the new production is in part devoted to replacing it. If total production is equal to 100 wage-units, and if we distinguish the firms producing amortization-goods, $F_1$, from those producing consumption- and investment-goods, $F_2$, the situation in $p_3$ would present itself as in Figure 6.1.

Since wages earned by workers producing replacements goods cannot be spent on their direct purchase, $F_2$'s output, whose costs of production are equal to 80 wage-units, is subject to a total demand of $80 + 20 = 100$ money units. This leads to the formation of a net profit of 20 money units for $F_2$ and to the subdivision of the product into wage-goods (60 money units) and profit-goods

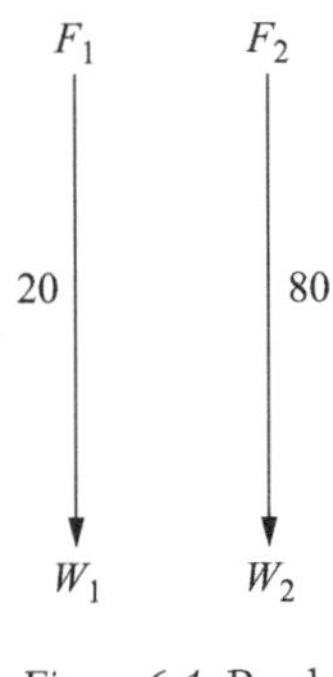


*Figure 6.1* Production of period $p_3$.

(20 money units). 'The whole theory of profit tells us that profits *a* made in the sale of [$F_2$'s] product *a'* cause the partition of this product' (ibid.: 131).

In other words, the formation of a net profit of 20 money units forces us to infer that part of $F_2$'s wages are paid out of this profit, which entails the appropriation by firms $F_2$ of part of their workers' output. This is so, since profit is necessarily spent in the labour market, where it finances the purchase by firms of produced output. As a result, we observe that the production of amortization-goods is the direct cause of an equivalent production of new profit-goods. Such 'dual production' is due to the fact that the same wages are emitted twice, and is the mark of the present pathological nature of fixed capital amortization (Figure 6.2).

As Figure 6.2 shows, amortization is an indirect process entailing a new, equivalent production of capital-goods and causing at the same time the reproduction of fixed capital and its growth. If we suppose that, at the beginning of $p_3$, fixed capital is equal to X, the production of amortization-goods, equal to 20 money units, compensates for the loss of value due to wear, tear, and obsolescence: $X - 20 + 20 = X$. However, dual production adds a value of 20 money units, which brings fixed capital's total value to $X + 20$. 'The conclusion is that the amortization of fixed capital is not a simple reproduction of capital, as it would be in the absence of any pathology, but generates a surplus equal to amortization, profit-goods being added on to capital, X + [20]' (ibid.: 136).

Apparently, the total loss suffered by income holders is equal to 40 money units, 20 because amortization-goods are incorporated into fixed capital, and 20 because of the new capital-goods appropriated by $F_2$. Yet, this would not account for the fact that amortization is eventually paid for by income holders. This means that the loss incurred by income holders is partly compensated by the gain derived from the increase in physical productivity due to the maintenance of fixed capital. Income holders pay for amortization and thus obtain amortization-goods as the object of a financial claim.

When firms $F_2$ pay their workers ($W_2$), they spend a profit of 20 money units and purchase the real product, which, in an orderly system, would have filled $W_2$'s nominal wages. Workers are dispossessed of the real content of

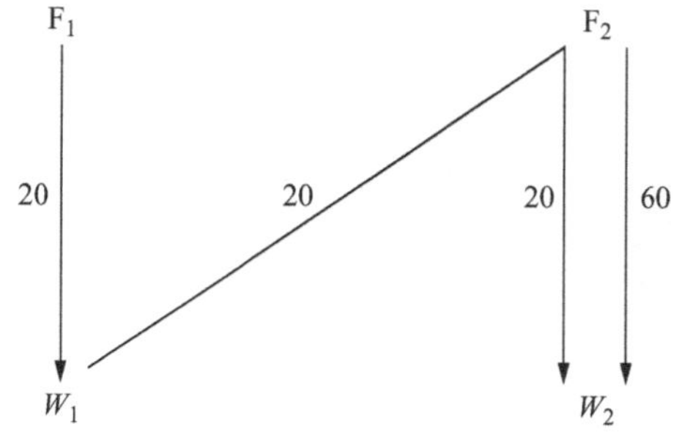


*Figure 6.2* Dual production.

their wages and obtain instead a sum of *empty* money. As in period $p_2$, firms appropriate fixed capital-goods, and households obtain financial claims instead of being credited with a sum of income. Yet, while in $p_2$ the object of these financial claims is the stock of wage-goods formed in $p_1$, in $p_3$ the object can only consist of the amortization-goods households have to pay for. '[A]mortization goods being dislodged, to join the assets of households, by the profit-goods added on to capital' (ibid.: 136).

The final representation of the operations taking place in $p_3$ is in Figure 6.3.

Figure 6.3 is analogous to that in Schmitt's 1984 book (2021 edition, page 135) and shows the 'exchange' between firms, which obtain the profit-goods produced by $W_2$, and households, who 'obtain' the amortization-goods as object of their financial claims. 'Included in the initial emission [of wages], the second emission of [20 money units] brings to income holders the monetary capital corresponding to the real capital constituted by the amortization goods' (ibid.: 349).

It is only at the cost of a duplicate production that households 'obtain' the replacement goods produced in $p_3$, and they obtain them only indirectly, through the payment of their costs of production.

Dual production of new capital-goods deprives wages of their real content and gives workers a monetary capital whose real counterpart consist of amortization-goods. Hence, 'the true funding of amortization-goods is provided by the expenditure of the monetary capital generated by dual production' (ibid.: 347).

'Duplication' of the production of amortization-goods, which induces an equivalent production of capital-goods, explains the fact that, contrary to what happens in the first two periods, the profit formed in $p_3$ because of amortization is spent in this same period. If profit in $p_3$ were formed through the sale of wage-goods, to turn it to their advantage firms would have to spend it at a later period.

Analysis changes when we deal with the profit due to dual production. This time, profit does not define a monetary capital corresponding to a real stock of

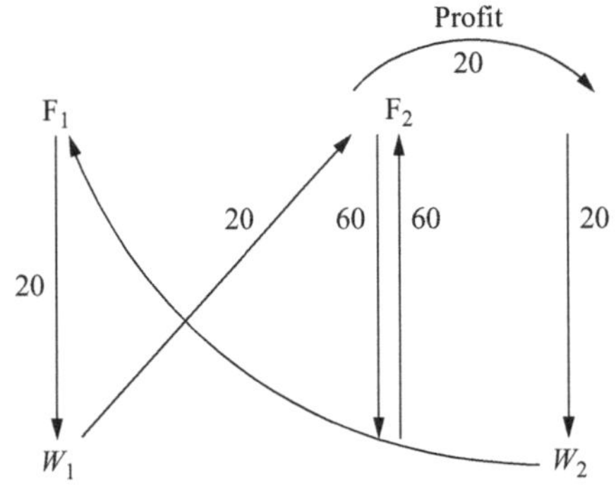


*Figure 6.3* Complete representation of amortization and its impact. Source: elaboration from Schmitt 2021: 135

wage-goods stored by firms but a sum of money whose real content (amortization-goods) is beyond the reach of income holders. The expenditure of this profit in $p_3$ cannot reduce it to zero. On the contrary, it grants firms ownership of an equivalent amount of new capital-goods, while giving households, *but only as a consequence of the firms' new investment*, 'the monetary capital corresponding to the real capital constituted by amortization-goods' (ibid.: 349).

### *Amortization, dual production, and inflation*

The impact of amortization on inflation is due to dual production and to the fact that the wages emitted in the production of profit-goods are 'empty both as an income *and as a capital*' (ibid.: 347). Profit-goods are immediately appropriated by firms and are not replaced by any other real good. Contrary to what happens in $p_2$, households suffer a loss that cannot be compensated, and the empty money formed in $p_3$ causes a malign inflation.

It is true that households obtain the amortization-goods as the real object of their monetary capital, yet it is also certain that they can spend their monetary capital only to enable firms to cover the costs of production of these amortization-goods. The existence of dual production derives from the differentiation between two sectors: the sector producing consumption- or wage-goods, and the sector producing capital-goods. Income formed in the first sector is both nominal and real, whereas income formed in the second sector is only nominal, as capital-goods are appropriated by firms. 'The difference between nominal income and real income is the definition of the inflationary gap' (ibid.: 351).

'As perceived by David Ricardo, inflation is a malady of money: instead of only covering the available product, nominal income exceeds the product to the whole extent of the production of the second sector' (ibid.: 356). Empty money emitted in dual production increases the number of money units available for the purchase of consumption-goods produced in the first sector and causes a reduction in the purchasing power of each money unit.

Since firms purchase profit-goods in the labour market, the macroeconomic selling price of profit-goods is necessarily equal to their production costs. It thus follows that 'in the reality of concrete economies, inflation is defined *only on wage-goods*. [...] The price can be (nominally) superior to the value only for wage-goods, the only goods that are bought *in the products market*' (ibid.: 357). The empty money formed in the second sector is spent on the purchase of wage-goods produced in the first sector, and leads to the formation of an *inflationary profit*, which is nothing other than the profit spent in the production of $p_3$'s new capital-goods. Because wages paid in the second sector are purely nominal (empty) we can infer that, in their remuneration of workers, *firms spend an inflationary profit*.

Is malign or pathological inflation derived from dual production cumulative in time or not? Schmitt's answers to this question seem contradictory at first glance, because he claims both that, '[c]aused by the amortization of fixed capital, empty emissions are cumulative over time' (ibid.: 140) and that 'inflation is not cumulative over time' (ibid.: 358). In reality, these two answers are complementary.

When Schmitt maintains that inflation is cumulative in time, he means that the empty emission resulting from dual production will never be compensated. No future event will ever cancel the inflation formed in any period '$p_3$'. '[M]alignant empty emissions define an excess demand that is not matched by any excess supply, present or future' (ibid.: 140). Schmitt claims that in this precise sense 'cumulative in time' does not mean that the empty emission of any given period repeats itself in time: 'only a new amortization will induce a new empty emission' (ibid.: 140). Toward the end of his 1984 book, when he defines inflation as an event that is not cumulative in time, Schmitt refers to this aspect of inflation. 'If inflation persists over the periods, it is because in each of them it is renewed *ab initio*' (ibid.: 358).

### *In each period a new production of amortization-goods generates a new dual production and an entirely new inflation*

As long as fixed capital grows, amortization increases and inflation with it. Schmitt shows that this increase in inflation has a limit, and that '[*i*]*n no period can inflation (or the production of the second sector) exceed a third of total industrial production*' (ibid.: 359). Indeed, the production of amortization-goods is the source of *two duplications*.

The first results from dual production, which is engendered by amortization and is financed by the profit deriving from the expenditure of the income earned by workers in the production of replacement goods.

The second duplication refers to the purchase of wage-goods through which the profit spent in the second sector is generated.

It is the purchase of wage-goods that forms the profit whose expenditure is at the origin of inflation. Amortization therefore consists of a production of both profit-goods and wage-goods. As time goes by, fixed capital grows faster, because an *over-accumulation* due to dual production adds to the investment of 'ordinary' (as opposed to inflationary) profit. This capital growth is accompanied by an increase in amortization and a consequent and equivalent increase in second-sector production. Therefore, the part of wage-goods purchased by the producers of amortization-goods increases too, until total production is made up equally of amortization-, profit-, and wage-goods. 'There is indeed a *triplication* of the production of amortization goods, which is repeated a first time in the production of wage-goods and a second time in the production of profit-goods' (ibid.: 139).

When the limit is reached, workers are equally employed in each of the three productions (Figure 6.4).

Inflation can reach a third of national income and from then on it will no longer increase. This means that, in each successive period, the process will start all over again and a new inflation would appear, equal to a third of the nominal wages of the whole economy. Or would it? In reality, the process of

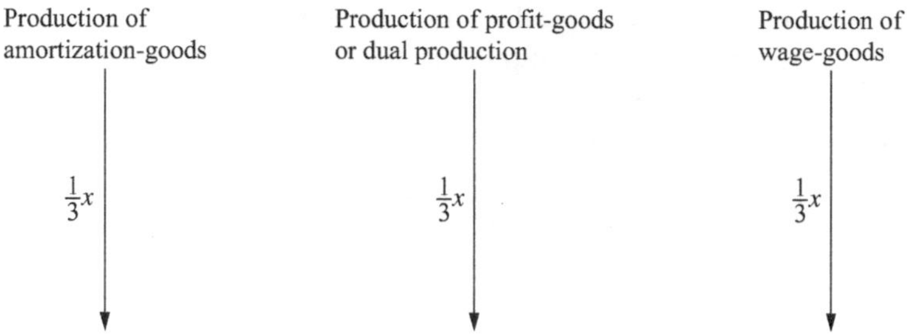


*Figure 6.4* Tripartition of national production.

capital growth (accumulation and over-accumulation) has itself a limit, which explains that the same disorder, namely dual production, is the cause of two distinct pathologies: inflation and unemployment.

## Involuntary unemployment

Let us move on in our analysis of Schmitt (1984a; 2021) and observe that, although it has repercussions in continuous time, inflation is an event occurring in *quantum time.* Because of the empty emission of the second sector, inflation is at the same time a positive excess-demand and an excess-demand equal to zero. 'Once again, we have to reject the principle of the excluded middle. It is not true that the non-negative gap between Demand and Supply is either positive or zero: excess demand is both a positive gap and a zero gap' (ibid.: 146). Positive excess-demand derives from the fact that the expenditure of profit in the second sector is added to the expenditure of wages.

In our numerical example, in $p_3$ total demand is equal to that defined by the sum of wages, 100 money units, plus that exercised by firms $F_2$ in the labour market, 20 money units. Yet, it would be mistaken to define this excess-demand as a useless surplus 'because it is the only demand that can face profit-goods. [...] In its only acceptable logical sense, excess demand is simply the demand sufficient to clear profit-goods' (ibid.: 146). Once this fact is taken into consideration it becomes evident that profit-goods, whose value is 20 money units, are purchased in the labour market through the expenditure of 20 money units and that the rest of current output, 80 money units, is purchased in the market for products through an expenditure of 80 money units. Positive excess-demand appears when the result of the empty emission is added to wages and disappears when it is absorbed in the purchase of dual production.

### *Unemployment and the remuneration of capital*

Unemployment is closely related to deflation, a situation where global supply is greater than global demand. Yet, as in the case of excess-demand, excess-supply is compatible with the identity of D and S. Moreover, monetary macroeconomics shows that every production creates the income necessary and sufficient for the purchase of its output and that no income can logically be hoarded. How it is then possible for D, measured by the amount of available income, to fall short of S? To answer this question, it is necessary to consider the whole process of fixed capital accumulation and over-accumulation including the fact that capital must be remunerated.

It is through the payment of dividends and interest that capital is remunerated, and it is out of profit that this payment occurs. Given that profit derives from wages, it follows that fixed capital finds its remuneration in the sector producing wage-goods. Hence, 'firms are left to find in the sale of wage-goods a profit in an increasing proportion of the income available in the economy' (ibid.: 368).

According to Schmitt 1984's distinction between the sector producing wage-goods at large and the sector producing profit-goods, the burden of capital remuneration rests on the first sector. Dividends are derived from the sale of goods produced in the first sector, and their production, carried out in this same sector, determines their amount. As capital accumulates, dividends must increase. Yet, dividends cannot increase beyond a certain limit. The production of the first sector can at most be equally divided between wage- and dividend-goods. 'Indeed, if workers produce only wage-goods on even days, they provide themselves with the "wage-fund" enabling them to produce only dividend-goods on odd days' (ibid.: 147).

Distributed profits derive from wages, and the part of undistributed wages cannot be reduced further once it reaches half of the total wages distributed in sector one. 'One must be aware of the fact that transferred income (of which dividends are part) cannot extend to more than half of the income earned in the production of wage-goods' (ibid.: 368). Wages of the first sector are at the origin of non-wage income (redistributed profits), which means that redistributed profits cannot be greater than wages. When the limit is reached, dividend-goods are, at most, equal to wage-goods, and the equality of the two productions of sector one has only one meaning: the production of dividends in sector one can at most be equal to that of wage-goods.

The limit imposed to redistributed profits provides the definitive proof of a law first formulated by Marx: the tendency of the rate of profit to fall. Because profit cannot increase more than wages, the ratio between profit and accumulated capital (over-accumulation included) is bound to decrease over time. After a number of periods, the numerator (profit) no longer increases, while the denominator (total capital) can still grow. 'Referred to an ever-growing capital, profit cannot increase indefinitely, nor can it ensure the remuneration of (accumulated and over-accumulated) capital at a sufficient rate, not even, when capitalism is even more advanced, at a rate still positive' (ibid. 369). When the economy is no longer capable of guaranteeing the remuneration of capital, fixed capital accumulation and over-accumulation have to be reduced. Involuntary unemployment is the unavoidable consequence of this reduction.

Schmitt provides two main arguments for the increase in unemployment.

The first is the direct reduction of fixed capital growth. Confronted with the impossibility of remunerating their entire capital, firms might decide to reduce its production. In this case, only part of the profit formed in the second sector is invested by firms in the production of new capital-goods, while the remaining part is lent in the financial market. As soon as production of fixed capital goes down unemployment goes up, while households, granted new loans, become more and more indebted. 'It is particularly interesting to note that the repeated expenditure, in the financial market and to the benefit of income holders, of a fraction of the inflationist profit creates an increasing indebtedness of households' (ibid.: 148).

Schmitt's second argument provides the explanation for the appearance of deflation.

### *Deflation*

Instead of lending part of their inflationary profit, firms could decide to invest it in the production of consumption-goods (wage-goods). Employment would not decrease, but the additional production of consumption-goods would be the cause of a serious problem because it would increase the supply in the market for products without increasing the amount of available income. To the extent that 'inflationist profits are spent for the production of wage-goods, those goods are cast onto the market in front of a *zero* purchasing power' (ibid.: 148). The fact is that the goods produced in the second sector are financed through the expenditure of profit and are, therefore, purchased by firms from the moment they are produced. They are profit-goods that take the form of wage-goods and that 'are produced and acquired *to be sold*' (ibid.: 370).

Now, quantum monetary economics establishes that 'any created income is spent *once*' (ibid.: 369), and no more than once, because its final expenditure destroys it. Since the profit-goods produced in the form of wage-goods are bound for sale in the market for products even though they have already been sold in the labour market, they have to be purchased *twice*. The income available in the economy is not enough to finance this double purchase. This causes D to fall short of S, because the latter is nominally or numerically increased by the amount of profit-goods offered in the market for products in the form of wage-goods.

Deflation is precisely defined as the positive numerical difference between supply, pathologically increased by part of the goods produced in the second sector, and demand, measured by the income formed in the two sectors. Available purchasing power being insufficient to guarantee the purchase of the increased amount of goods offered in the market for products, firms will be forced to reduce production and unemployment will set in as the inescapable result of deflation.

Deflation results from the additional supply of wage-goods of the second sector, and its provenance is the same as that of inflation. Both pathologies are caused by the capitalist process of capital formation and accumulation. Inflation and deflation can coexist precisely because they derive from the same cause. Here is where *stagflation* finds its explanation: inflation is due to empty emissions and deflation does not reduce them in the least, which shows that inflation and deflation are mutually compatible.

## Schmitt's 1984 reform: principles and practical implications

In his 1984 book, Schmitt advocates a reform of banking that, if implemented, would avoid the formation of inflation and unemployment by carrying out payments in accordance with the logical distinction between money, income, and capital.

### *The distinction between monetary and financial departments*

As a first measure, Schmitt urges the introduction of an operational distinction between what he calls the department of emissions or first department and the saving department or second department. The objective of such a distinction is to avoid the conflation of money creation and financial intermediation, namely the financing of banks' loans by money creation. In each period, production creates an income that is necessarily spent on the purchase of current output. This implies that the banking system must make sure that the income formed in each period is not spent on purchasing the product of another period. Individuals are obviously free to spend their income as they wish.

The problem does not concern economic agents' behaviour, but the monetary system as such. Schmitt claims that '[*t*]*he distinction between the two departments is necessary because the economy is equipped with a financial market*' (ibid.: 196). Banks' financial intermediation ensures the loan of saved-up income but must avoid loans being financed out of nominal money. To avoid excess-demand and the consequent inflation, banks must have at their disposal the means to know the exact amount they can lend at each moment in time. The institution of two departments can grant this.

Let us briefly describe how the two departments function in practice, starting from the payment of wages carried out by banks on behalf of firms, F, and to the benefit of workers, W.

If wages are equal to *x* wage-units, the payment is entered in the two departments as represented in Table 6.2.

The department of emissions (Department I) is concerned with the payment of wages, for the twofold reason that this payment is an emission and that it is carried out in nominal money. Yet, the payment extends immediately to the saving department (Department II), because its instantaneous result is the creation of a positive income to the benefit of workers, entered at once on the liabilities side of the second department. 'It follows that the final beneficiary of any emission, the "payee", obtains a money that is at once savings' (ibid.: 197).

*Table 6.2* Payment of wages as entered in the two departments

| *Assets* | | *Liabilities* | |
|---|---|---|---|
| Department of emissions (I) | | | |
| Firms | m.u. x | Department II | m.u. x |
| Saving department (II) | | | |
| Department I | m.u. x | Workers | m.u. x |

*Table 6.3* Reduction of income that banks can lend

| *Assets* | | *Liabilities* | |
|---|---|---|---|
| Department of emissions (I) | | | |
| Firms | m.u. x | Department II | m.u. x |
| Department II | m.u. y | Firms | m.u. y |
| Firms | m.u. x-y | Department II | m.u. x-y |
| Saving department (II) | | | |
| Department I | m.u. x | Workers | m.u. x |
| Workers | m.u. y | Department I | m.u. y |
| Department I | m.u. x-y | Workers | m.u. x-y |

The payment of wages is entered on both departments, I and II, and the amount of the indebtedness of the first to the second defines the amount of income that banks can lend within the period taken as reference. 'At any instant, *the sum of claims of the second department on the first* precisely defines "loanable" savings' (ibid.: 198). For example, immediately after the payment of $x$ wage-units, the debit of Department I is of $x$ money units, and this is what banks can lend to their clients.

Assuming, for example, that wages are paid monthly, before a new payment of wages occurs, the amount of the debit between the two departments decreases each time the initial income is spent on the final purchase of current output, Table 6.3.

Whether income is spent by workers themselves or by any other economic agent, its available amount decreases, and the amount banks can lend drops from $x$ to $x - y$ money units.

If at the end of the month part of the initial income, say $z$ money units, has not been spent, Schmitt's reform requires that it be lent to firms and be spent (implicitly) by them in the purchase of the current output still unsold and stocked with them, Table 6.4.

Firms' debt switches from the first to the second department and is transformed from a monetary to a financial debt. The object lent to firms at the end of the period is an income, and firms are entered on the assets side of banks' saving department, precisely because they benefit from the loan of saved-up income and become sellers of net financial claims. Thanks to this measure, the

*Table 6.4* Loan to firms at the end of the period

| *Assets* | | *Liabilities* | |
|---|---|---|---|
| Department of emissions (I) | | | |
| Firms | m.u. z | Department II | m.u. z |
| Department II | m.u. z | Firms | m.u. z |
| Saving department (II) | | | |
| Department I | m.u. z | Workers | m.u. z |
| Firms | m.u. z | Department I | m.u. z |
| Firms | m.u. z | Workers | m.u. z |

entire income formed over the period is spent on the purchase of the product of this same period. Every risk that the income of a given period may be spent on the purchase of the output of another period is thus definitively prevented, together with the risk of lending more than the amount of available income. Individuals are still free to purchase the product they prefer, but this will simply be an application of generalized exchange, since no overlapping of income generated in different periods is possible any longer at the macroeconomic level.

### *The department of fixed capital*

The second change advocated by Schmitt is the introduction of a third department or fixed capital department.

Quantum macroeconomic analysis teaches us that fixed capital derives from the investment of profit, and that the transformation of income into capital does not permit it to be lent in the financial market. If invested profits were entered in the second department, they would define '*savings still available*' (ibid.: 206), which would be illegitimate, 'because profits result from a final expenditure already *carried out*' (ibid.: 206) when wages are spent in the formation of profits. As Schmitt claims, 'if wages transformed into profits are not withdrawn from the financial market (represented by the second department), they constitute a loanable fund that will feed *a second tier of final expenditures*' (ibid.: 206). Lent by banks, this loanable fund made up of invested profits finances the 'second expenditure of the (same) income [...,] an *empty emission* [that is at] the root of the disorder, inflation, and unemployment' (ibid.: 206). The objective of the third department is to stop this happening by absorbing the net profits of firms as soon as they are formed in the saving department.

Since, at the moment of their formation, profits are made up of both redistributed and invested profits, and since the amount of each category might well not be known, all profits must be transferred to the fixed capital department, Table 6.5.

As represented in Table 6.5, profit entered in banks' saving department is at once transferred to the third department, so that it can never feed any payment of wages. Saved up in the third department, firms' profits remain unaltered because they do not finance any payment of wages. 'And it is essential that it should be impossible, because any net expenditure of profit in the emission of wages defines an *empty emission*' (ibid.: 207).

Redistributed profits, as well as profits spent by firms on the purchase of real products or financial assets (momentarily transferred to Department III) regain their income form when they are redistributed to households or spent by firms. They flow back to the saving department, where they are entered as claims on bank deposits held by households (sellers of financial claims to firms included) or cancelled out in a final purchase. Only invested profits irreversibly transformed into fixed capital will remain deposited in the third department. '*A double and permanent recording on the assets side of the second department and on the liabilities side of the third discloses invested profits*' (ibid.: 207).

The aim of Schmitt's reform is to promote the transition from capitalism to post-capitalism, from a disorderly system characterized by the presence of inflation and unemployment to an orderly one, where the whole production is owned, directly or indirectly, by households. When wages transferred as profits to firms are spent in the payment of wages to workers producing investment-goods, households are dispossessed of their product to the benefit of depersonalized firms.

The same wages 'face two real capitals: the wage-goods "lost" by households when the monetary profits currently invested were formed and the investment goods newly produced' (ibid.: 212). As stressed by Schmitt, '[t]his duplication of real capital is the profound definition of capitalism' (ibid.: 212).

Thanks to the third department, profits will no longer cover the payment of wages and 'the set of undifferentiated households [will be] the unique holder of the monetary savings fixated in the third department and, thus, [...] the sole owner of fixed capital' (ibid.: 212). At the same time, thanks to the distinction between the first two departments, banks will know at each moment the amount of income they can lend, thus avoiding any risk of financing their loans through money creation. No empty emission will be possible, and dual production will become just a bad memory.

*Table 6.5* Transfer of profit to the third department

| *Assets* | | *Liabilities* | |
|---|---|---|---|
| Saving department (II) | | | |
| Product | m.u. x | Firms | m.u. x |
| Firms | m.u. x | Department III | m.u. x |
| Fixed capital department (III) | | | |
| Department II | m.u x | Firms | m.u. x |

## Traditional and quantum analyses of inflation and unemployment: a brief appraisal

Let me finish with a succinct presentation of the main differences between traditional analyses and Schmitt's analysis. The first and most evident one is that the former are essentially microeconomic, whereas the second is macroeconomic.

Whether regrouped under the categories of demand-pull, cost-push, or built-in inflation, Keynesian analyses locate the causes of inflation in the decisions taken by some economic agents or institutions: firms, government, oil producers, insurance companies, and so on. At the other extreme, monetarists identify the main cause of inflation within the excessive growth of the money supply and point the finger at central banks and their monetary policies. Advocates of the rational expectations approach have a similar view, but recognize the relevance of individuals' expectations, which radically limit the impact of central banks' monetary policies. Despite their substantial differences, all three schools of thought share the same approach: they keep looking for a behavioural explanation of inflation. Moreover, they all refer to price indices and identify inflation with a generalized increase in microeconomic prices of consumer goods, retail-goods, tangible assets, financial assets, commodities, etc., according to the chosen price index.

Schmitt's quantum macroeconomic analysis shows, on the contrary, that inflation results from a pathology affecting the structure of capitalist economies and is not influenced by economic agents' decisions. The ingenuous and superficial identification of inflation with a generalized increase in prices is replaced by a definition in which the coupling of money and products is perceived as the effect of an emission, with the logical identity between D and S at its backbone.

Inflation does not alter this identity – nobody and nothing can – but it introduces a numerical difference between its two terms. Inflation is a pathology that affects the purchasing power of money, whereas a rise in prices might well be due to causes that do not alter money's purchasing power in the least. This is the case, for example, of every increase in prices leading to a redistribution of income between economic agents. On the other hand, inflation may hide behind stability or even behind a decrease in microeconomic prices. This is what happens when the price index remains stable despite a constant increase in productivity due to technological progress.

Schmitt's analysis establishes once and for all that the object of economic investigation is the monetary theory of production or, as Schmitt liked to put it, the production theory of money. The emission of wages is the key operation: inflation must be explained within this theoretical framework. Recalling the logical distinction between operations and their result, Schmitt shows that 'the dysfunction in the economy is created by *operations*; once the result is there, it is too late, the damage is already done' (ibid.: 171). Once more, this is to say that individual as well as institutional behaviour is not the cause of inflation, because behaviour has to do with the outcome of operations and not with the operations themselves: '[a]gents can only act on magnitudes the existence of which is positive, therefore on magnitudes *already created* and not yet destroyed' (ibid.: 171).

It is through the expenditure of profit in the payment of wages that empty emissions are formed, and it is dual production that brings about the inflationary increase in money. Inflation exists because the malfunctioning of the system creates empty money, not because this excess money is spent. Income is always totally spent, whether it is derived from production or not. The origin of the pathology resides in the fact that 'fake' income adds itself to income defining current output; this is explained through the mechanism enabling empty emissions to occur.

Involuntary unemployment is traditionally blamed on economic agents' behaviour, notably on their decision to increase their savings, which is said to have a deflationary impact on global demand. This is symptomatic of a specific definition of money, which views savings as reducing available income, and stands in stark contrast with the reality of bank money. The idea that income can be hoarded is not just obsolete, but entirely wrong.

From its very formation, income is deposited with banks and immediately lent by them. By imposing the necessary matching of credits and debits, double-entry bookkeeping defines a mechanism whereby bank deposits are always balanced by bank loans. In other words, banks immediately and automatically lend to other clients, firms included, the income saved by clients and deposited with them. Saving 'is a *positive action* not just an abstention. Saving is by definition an automatic or voluntary purchase of financial claims, [...], hoarding exists for households and the sum of them, but *it does not exist for the set of households*' (ibid.: 180).

Since globally hoarding is necessarily equal to zero, it cannot deflate global demand, whose total amount is precisely defined by the available income, savings included. Deflation is much more difficult to explain than mainstream economics assumes.

Excess global supply cannot be justified by the simplistic reduction in global demand that would result from the behaviour of income holders. Even the hypothetic decision of firms to reduce investment cannot be a conceivable cause of involuntary unemployment, unless it is seen as a logical necessity *imposed* by the process of capital accumulation.

The identity between $D$ and $S$ is verified for every level of production. Whether high or low, any production creates the income needed for the final purchase of its output. Barring any anomaly, no difference of any sort would ever appear between $D$ and $S$, and *involuntary* unemployment would not exist.

> We see therefore that the contraction of domestic employment is due to the reduction in investment only insofar as the mode of production admits of two anomalies:

- the formation of inflationary profits, and
- the expenditure of those profits in the financial market.

(ibid.: 184–5)

Finally, what about expectations? Can they, as mainstream economists assume, be the cause of deflation and unemployment? Certainly not: since the identity of D and S holds for any single production, the income created in any one of them is necessarily spent on the purchase of its own output. Individuals and firms are free to purchase the goods and/or financial assets they want; yet, once generalized exchange is taken into consideration, it appears that their income is spent on purchasing the goods whose production leads to this same income.

Things happen as if workers and firms purchased their own products and then exchanged them against the products of the others. Under such conditions, even if expectations prove wrong, no discrepancy can emerge between demand as measured by available income, and supply as defined by current output. If the production of wage-goods is higher than the demand exerted by consumers, firms purchase the goods produced in excess; they form a stock that will be sold to households at a later stage. In the meantime, the wage-goods stocked with firms and whose costs of production are covered by firms with either actual or advanced profits, are investment-goods *in fieri*. Subsequently, firms will adjust their production and devote a greater part of it to producing investment-goods that will indeed replace the wage-goods previously stocked.

The case where firms' profits are lower than expected is similar. The investment-goods produced in excess are inevitably purchased by firms, which cover their costs of production by borrowing the income saved up by workers. Despite their material form, investment-goods produced in excess are wage-goods waiting to be exchanged for an equivalent sum of consumption-goods at a later stage. In both cases, no pathological increase or decrease in macroeconomic supply occurs, and involuntary unemployment remains unexplained.

In conclusion, orthodox analysis and Schmitt's analysis of inflation and unemployment are mutually incompatible: the acceptance of one implies necessarily the rejection of the other. Yet, the choice between these two alternative theoretical frameworks is not an *ad hoc* issue. The prospect of providing a satisfactory explanation of the two disorders is a further argument for the need to replace mainstream economics with quantum monetary economics.

# B

# From national to international money

# 7 International payments as a cause of monetary disorders

Schmitt's interest in international economics goes back to the early 1970s, and his analysis is an extension of his investigation on the nature of national money and its association to national output. Usually neglected and often superficially analyzed by mainstream economists, international payments are a very challenging topic, only apparently easier than the one concerning the functioning of a national economy of production. The absence of international production should not mislead us: the circulation of goods (commercial and financial) between countries and their payments are far from a self-evident fact. The lack of an international monetary circuit is the cause of serious monetary disorders whose origin is still a mystery for the great majority of economists. The aim of this initial chapter on international economics is to show the originality of Schmitt's analysis and to provide the key elements of his investigation on the nature of international economics and on the monetary disorders that ensue when this nature is ignored.

The first part of the chapter is devoted to Schmitt's analysis of what distinguishes national from international payments and rests on his contributions from 1971 to 1990. More precisely, I will refer to his books *Théorie unitaire de la monnaie, nationale et internationale* (1975), *La monnaie européenne* (1977), and *L'or, le dollar et la monnaie supranationale* (1977) as well as an unpublished paper dated 1971 that I have entitled 'La monnaie internationale' and to an unpublished typescript dated 1990 that I have entitled *Le vice caché des paiements extérieurs.*

The second part of the chapter deals with the inflationary consequences of the present non-system of international payments, and draws from *L'or, le dollar et la monnaie supranationale* (1977), the unpublished paper 'Le vice caché du régime actuel des paiements internationaux' (1983), and *Les pays au régime du FMI* (1984).

## The nature of international payments

### *Countries are distinct from the sum of their residents*

One of the first observations concerning international transactions and their payments is that they take place between national economies and are expressed

DOI: 10.4324/9781351271325-11

in national currencies. In the absence of an international system of clearing like the one existing within countries (the prevailing situation today, 2021), national currencies are bound to remain heterogeneous. 'In fact, different national currencies are at most convertible; never are they subject to a planetary regime of clearing: they are therefore heterogeneous compared to one another' (Schmitt 1990b: 8, m.t.). Schmitt makes clear that *convertibility* is not enough to guarantee *homogeneity*, because conversion amounts to the permutation of the two currencies involved; whereas in the case of clearing or compensation, one currency '*disappears* to leave room for another currency' (ibid.: 10, m.t.),

At present, nations exist (and will continue to do for many years to come) as separate economic entities; their monetary sovereignty makes them so. The economy of a given country is a national economy insofar as it is characterized by a currency issued by a national banking system that is distinct from that of any other country. A planetary clearing system would require the different national currencies to be transformed into a single currency and convert present-day national economies into regional economies of a sole monetary area. In the meantime, nations continue to exist and to be involved in the external transactions of their residents.

In this respect, a distinction must be introduced between the *sum* or the *aggregation* of a country's residents and their *set*. When a resident of a given country, call it A, imports from abroad, their expenditure is net for the sum of A's residents. Does this payment involve also country A defined as the set of its residents? Schmitt's answer is yes, because the payment is carried out in a national currency and implies its conversion into another national currency. The conversion, for example, of money A, $M_A$, into $M_R$, the currency of the rest-of-the-world, 'is an operation of sets [A] and [R]' (ibid.: 13, m.t.).

In the specification of a country's economy, we distinguish a sum from a set essentially because an international economy is solely an economy of exchange presupposing the presence of national economies of production. Both kinds of economies are involved into international transactions. Hence, for example, imports pertain both to an economy of production – and involve the sum of countries' residents – and to an economy of exchange – and involve countries as sets of their residents. 'International payments are exchanges defined both in an economy of production (concerning the SUM of countries' residents) and in an economy of exchange (where countries themselves, i.e. the SETS of their residents, are situated)' (ibid.: 15, m.t.).

Schmitt shows that the payment of imports is a complete transaction as far as the sum of residents is concerned and only a 'half-transaction' for the set of the country's residents. Indeed, importers of A are credited-debited by their banks and end up exchanging a sum of imported goods for an equivalent sum of claims on bank deposits. On the other hand, whether it is carried out in money A or in money R, the external payment of A's residents entails a net demand of foreign currency by country A considered as a whole (set).

Nations will exist as long as their national currencies exist, and they will therefore be involved in any foreign payment of their residents. Thus, the

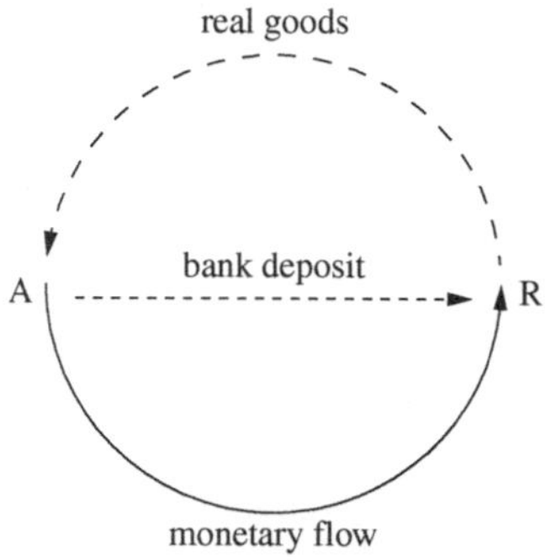


*Figure 7.1* Payment of country A's imports.

imports of country A's residents imply necessarily an external payment of their country entailing the net debit of country A and the net credit of country R (Figure 7.1).

As Figure 7.1 shows, the payment of country A's imports gives country R a bank deposit equivalent to the net monetary debit of A. As Schmitt observes, 'this fact is enough to establish the separation of imports and exports in the international field' (ibid.: 17, m.t.).

Let us state it once more: the payment carried out by importers, residents of A, is both positive and negative, because their imports are sales–purchases: A's residents finance their purchases of foreign goods through a sale of claims on their bank deposits. On the other hand, countries as such cannot exchange bank deposits, because 'nobody (countries being no exception) can become the creditor of oneself' (ibid.: 20, m.t.). Today, country A's imports are not immediately balanced by equivalents exports; they are net imports and not imports-exports.

The net debit concerns country A as a whole, and not the sum of its residents. Imports are carried out by A's residents and importers pay for their total foreign purchases; yet, their country is involved in their transactions and has to convey their payments to R. The payment of country A as a whole is monetary, and it implies the conversion of its national currency or, in other words, the selling to the rest-of-the-world of a sum of money (deposits in money A or in money R).

### National currencies cannot be used to settle international transactions

Money is a numerical means of payment whose circular flow is instantaneous and implies the identity of each economic agent's sales and purchases. Money's power to fully discharge payments rests simultaneously on the spontaneous acknowledgement of debt issued by banks and on production, which is the starting point of money's circular flow. This means that

1) In each country, the purchasing power of money is formed through national production, and that
2) No country can pay international debts using a national currency.

From 1) it follows that '[M]oney issued by the banking system of country A can exercise its purchasing power only over country's A product: *its purchasing power over the products of other countries is formally nil*' (1977b: 12, m.t.). The logical impossibility to spend a national purchasing power in the purchase of foreign output is of a macroeconomic nature and a direct consequence of the real emission that establishes the unity production-consumption (see Chapter 4). The fact that any resident of any given country can spend their income to purchase foreign products is not an exception to this logical law and has to be accommodated within it.

National firms are at the origin of national income, and they absorb it entirely, so that no national purchasing power can be spent in the sphere of international transactions. National income is defined by the relationship between national money and national output, and its destruction can result only from an expenditure implying the destruction of this relationship. It is through the payment of wages that income is formed; it is through their final expenditure that it is destroyed. Any macroeconomic income – resulting from the association of money with a specific product – can be destroyed only through the purchase of this specific product. This clearly means that not even a modicum of a country's national income can ever be destroyed in the payment of its imports. '*The transnational expenditure of a national currency leaves unaltered the sum of purchasing powers available within the importing country*' (ibid.: 109, m.t.).

There is a corollary to the fact that the purchasing power formed within any given national economy can be spent only for the purchase of the produced output of the self-same economy: exports do *not* provide an additional source for the sale of a country's output. Each (national) production creates the income necessary and sufficient for the final purchase of its output; final consumption destroys it. Hence, 'the purchasing power formed in national currency is never insufficient for the sale of the sum total of national product' (Schmitt 1977a: 78, m.t.), nor does it exceed the amount required for the financing of this sale.

This leads Schmitt to conclude that international transactions and their payments cannot be seen as equilibrating factors capable of 'modifying the interaction between Supply and Demand' (ibid.: 78, m.t.). This conclusion, which is perfectly consistent with Keynes's identity of global supply and global demand, further clarifies the specific nature of international payments while helping to set the framework within which the impact of international payments on national economies can be analyzed correctly.

Therefore, any international payment carried out in a national currency comes down to paying by offering a mere acknowledgement of debt. One of the monetary laws Schmitt advocates in his analysis of money's circular flow establishes that a 'distance' must separate the issuer of money (banks) from the set of purchasers. As claimed in 2), the principle that nobody pays by getting indebted is general and applies to countries as well. When a resident of a given country pays another resident using the debt issued by a bank, the payment extinguishes the debt of the payer. If the same resident were to pay by issuing their own acknowledgement of debt, their debt would subsist, and the payment would not even take place.

Applied to countries, this principle means that no country can pay its external purchases by means of its own IOU. Schmitt summarizes the argument as follows.

> Every external purchase of a member (or a resident) of country A is a purchase of country A. On the other side, money A is an emission of the country. Country A is therefore, at the same time, the purchaser and the issuer. Hence, since logic does not allow for any purchaser to pay with its own debt, no purchase of country A is truly paid when it is paid in money A.
>
> (Schmitt 1977b: 61, m.t.)

Within any given country, the principle of the necessary separation between purchaser and issuer applies to each element of the set of purchasers. No element of this set can pay for its purchases by using its own IOU *or* the IOU of any other element of the set. Between countries, the same principle establishes the logical impossibility for any country to pay by using either its own currency or any other national currency. 'Country A would have the logical capacity to pay by means of money $M_q$, issued by any other country, only if country Q had itself the formal power to pay its own imports in its own currency' (ibid: 62, m.t.). The general conclusion is that no national currency can ever play the role of international money, which means that to date no proper system of international payments has ever existed.

## Nominal and real international money

Nationally, money is issued as a nominal amount of zero value and is transformed into an equivalent sum of real money through production. Internationally, no supranational bank exists yet, likely to issue an international nominal money. Hence, the question concerns the possibility for national currencies to be used as international real money, namely international money endowed with a purchasing power over the world's production. Schmitt observes that 'for real money to exist, it is necessary that its purchasing power be net. In other words, the purchasing power of the currency considered must not be deducted from the purchasing power of another currency' (Schmitt 1971c: 4, m.t.).

It is commonly believed that, in practice, countries can pay their net imports either by using their own national currency, by drawing upon their official reserves (made up of foreign currencies, gold, and special drawing rights, SDRs), or by borrowing from abroad. Schmitt shows that in none of these cases what is used as 'international liquidity' has any redeeming purchasing power. He does so by showing that in each case country A pays for its net purchases by offering a mere promise to pay instead of giving up an international income obtained through its foreign sales. 'In each case, the deficit country purchases from the rest of the world an amount of goods and services and pays for it by the expenditure of an international income equal to *zero*' (ibid.: 9, m.t.).

On the one hand, neither foreign currencies, nor gold, nor SDRs are real monies: their purchasing power is borrowed from national currencies. On the other hand, if country A pays its net imports in its own national currency, it gives R its own IOU, because, outside its national borders, money A represents merely the acknowledgement of debt of A's banking system. In other words, A's payment is entirely void: in exchange for a sum of real goods and services, country A gives country R a mere promise that A would not even feel obliged to fulfil, being convinced that its currency is as good an object of payment as any other financial asset.

### *The use of a national currency*

One of the most serious mistakes economists can commit is identifying money with a net asset. The confusion between nominal and real money is widespread both in a national and in an international context. In the latter, this gives rise to the belief that some key-currencies, like the US dollar, are perfectly acceptable *objects* of payment, even though they are issued at zero cost by their respective national banking systems. The payment carried out by a country using its own key-currency is considered valid, because it is financed by a sum of income and not by simple nominal money. However, this is correct only if limited to the payment of the country's importers. We must not forget, in fact, that countries themselves, sets of their residents, are involved in the foreign payments of their residents. Their involvement is monetary; it concerns the need to convey abroad the payment of their importers.

Residents lose part of their national income in this process, and countries must take on the task of conveying this payment to the rest-of-the-world. If country A is a key-currency country, its payment is carried out in $M_A$ while country R is credited with a sum of money that, being issued by A's banking system, defines the acknowledgement of debt of country A itself. Banks in R become the owners of part of A's bank deposits: this is the payment carried out by A's residents. Banks in country R are also credited with a sum of money A: this is the payment of country A as a whole. Schmitt's analysis points out the existence of this macroeconomic payment and shows that, in today's non-system of international payments, it results in the external indebtedness of the country carrying it out. In the example we are examining, country A as a whole 'pays' by giving its own IOU to country R, that is, by incurring a debt any time it pays its net imports in its own currency.

### *The use of international reserves*

Another case concerns the payment of a country's net imports by resorting to its international reserves. As in the previous example, Schmitt's conclusion is that A, the net importing country, gives R a mere promise to pay in real terms at a future date. This is so, because 'the expenditure of a reserve cannot be assimilated to the expenditure of an income' (ibid.: 12, m.t.).

Once again, the problem relates to the macroeconomic payment of countries' net imports. The payment between residents and non-residents is not a cause of disorder. If R's residents were to obtain part of the private reserves of A's residents there would be no imbalance, in country A or in country R, between global supply and global demand. A's private reserves would add to R's private reserves, yet, at the same time, the income of country R's residents would decrease by the same amount, because it would be spent in the purchase of R's private reserves. 'Individuals who purchase 2 units of A's private reserves in order to increase their private reserves, sacrifice two units of their current income' (ibid.: 14, m.t.).

Things are different when part of country A's official reserves are transferred to country R as payment of A's net imports. In this case, A's official reserves are not purchased by any resident of country R and their inflow into R's economy is a cause of inflation. 'Income holders maintain their purchasing power over [R's] current production. It follows that the demand of A exerted on [R] is an additional one' (ibid.: 16, m.t.). The official reserves obtained by country R add up to the national money units associated with R's real production, either directly or through their conversion into a sum of national money.

### *The borrowing of a foreign currency*

A final possibility is that country A pays for its net imports by borrowing a foreign currency from country R either directly or through the mediation of the IMF. In both cases country A's net imports are paid by means of a foreign loan, through international credit. What matters here is the fact that 'the primary source of credit is always set in one or more particular countries' (ibid.: 8, m.t.).

In our example, it is the economy of country R that finances country A's net purchases. It is thus confirmed that the purchasing power exercised by what is used today as international currency is either borrowed or derived from that of one or more national currencies. Under no circumstances 'are A's excess purchases paid by a monetary income earned by country A in its international transactions' (ibid.: 10, m.t.). By paying its net imports through a credit obtained from R, country A is purchasing on credit, that is, by incurring a debt. This clearly means that the payment is still due and that it will (maybe) be made in the future, if A succeeds in obtaining a surplus at least equal to its present deficit.

By showing that the absence of international nominal money is accompanied by the impossibility of treating any international means of payment as real money, Schmitt makes it clear that the conditions for the existence of an authentic and proper system of international payments are not yet met. This conclusion is further corroborated by his detailed analysis of the circuit of international money.

### *International monetary flows: are there any?*

The absence of a true system of international payments is due to the logical impossibility of determining an international, circular monetary flow either directly or by extrapolating from national monetary circuits. Schmitt deals with this issue in *Théorie unitaire*. His first argument aims to show that 'it is impossible to launch an international monetary circular flow directly' (Schmitt 1975a: 83, m.t.), or, in other words, that an international monetary circuit must necessarily be founded on national monetary circuits. This implies that no direct relationship can be established between goods and money starting from international exchange.

As the indeterminacy of relative prices confirms, no monetary circular flow can have its source in the market for products. What is the case nationally is also true at the international level: monetary prices cannot be determined through exchange. Consider an economy in which two countries, A and B, produce goods *a* and *b*, and whose currencies are respectively money A, $M_A$, and money B, $M_B$. By assumption, the prices of *a* and *b* are unknown, and what needs verifying is whether they can emerge from the international exchange between A and B.

As Schmitt observes, there are three variables: the monetary price of *a*, the monetary price of *b*, and the exchange rate between $M_A$ and $M_B$. Yet, these three variables are supposed to be determined by four independent equations, namely

$$\text{Demand for } a = \text{Supply of } a \tag{7.1}$$

$$\text{Demand for } b = \text{Supply of } b \tag{7.2}$$

$$\text{Sales of A} = \text{Purchases of A} \tag{7.3}$$

$$\text{Sales of B} = \text{Purchases of B} \tag{7.4}$$

Equations (7.3) and (7.4) represent nothing more than the first law any monetary circular flow must comply with: the necessary identity of each element's sales and purchases (see Chapter 2). This hypothetical system immediately appears to be over-determined. Indeed, before international exchange takes place, the number of independent equations is greater than the number of variables. This result does not come as a surprise, for the whole theory of the monetary circuit as well as that of monetary emissions clearly show that the determination of prices requires the 'integration' of money and real goods through production. '[T]he monetary circuit presupposes an "exchange-of-production", that is, a purchase in the market for productive services' (ibid.: 86, m.t.).

Having demonstrated that 'the international monetary circuit must be founded on national currencies integrated into economies of production' (ibid.: 91, m.t.), Schmitt argues that this necessary condition is not sufficient. This is to say that an international circular flow of money cannot be derived directly from national currencies.

Let us reason with Schmitt on a practical example and suppose that three countries, A, B, and C carry out their international payments in $M_A$, $M_B$, and $M_C$, respectively. The question we must answer is the following: is it possible to determine an international monetary circuit starting from a system of equations relating the supply of each currency to its demand? The answer is no, since the equality of the supply of and demand for each currency is not enough to guarantee the equality of each country's sales and purchases. The constraint, which compels each country to recover at once the amount of national currency it spends on its foreign purchases, is logical and derives from the circular nature of money. In order for a monetary flow to exist, money must flow in a circle, from and back to its point of injection.

In the example, A's, B's, and C's balances of international transactions must always be equal to zero – a requirement that cannot be met because the equality between the supply of and demand for each currency does not guarantee the equality of A's, B's, and C's monetary gain and losses. '[T]he identity of the circuit creates an insurmountable difficulty, because the equalization between the supply of and demand for each currency gives no assurance about the equality of each country's simultaneous expenditures and receipts' (ibid.: 91, m.t.) What is verified for the three countries applies equally to any number of countries, so the conclusion has general validity: even though national monetary circular flows are a necessary condition, they are not sufficient to generate alone a true international circular flow of money.

It is through the circular flow of money that payments are carried out in a national economy, and it would be a mistake to claim that, as a simple *means* of payment, money can become also the *object* of the payment. The flow nature of money is not a matter of assumption; it derives from the logical impossibility for money to be created as a net asset. The purchasing power of money derives from production and is exercised over the purchase of produced output; it is not created *ex nihilo* by banks. In each payment within a national economy, money is a numerical vehicle, a means of making a real payment for any purchase through a simultaneous sale.

The identity of each single agent's sales and purchases is a fundamental macroeconomic law perfectly consistent with the circular flow of money. In an analogous way, international payments should be carried out through the circular flow of an international currency, in which case net sales and net purchases would never be possible. This is not what happens in today's regime. The purchases of any given country, A, are not balanced by equivalent sales, and a national currency is used as an object of payment. Logic requires each single country's sales to be always, and necessarily, matched by its purchases, so that what a country earns through its foreign transactions would never be a mere sum of (nominal) money. Country A's trade balance can be positive, but this ought to correspond to an equivalent purchase of financial claims, the net sale of goods and services being matched by a net purchase of financial assets.

In the present non-system, country A's net imports, for example, are paid in a national currency, which is transferred from the debtor to the creditor country instead of being used in a circular flow.

> Every purchase, or import of country A is a one-way operation because it makes the country a *net* debtor while its partner becomes a *net* creditor. This is proof that the transaction is not correctly "monetized"; if it were, country A would become a debtor *and a creditor* in the same move.
>
> (Schmitt 1987c: 231, m.t.)

When international transactions are paid in a national currency, payments are void, because they are carried out using a nominal money transferred to the exporting countries as if it were a real asset. Every national production is always and necessarily purchased by the national income that defines it. This means that, despite appearances to the contrary, '[t]he payment of imports logically rests on exporting countries, [which are the] only possible source of the purchasing power' (ibid.: 239, m.t.) needed for the payment of their national products, exports included.

If country A's sales of goods and services exceed its commercial imports, the payment of its net commercial exports requires the expenditure of part of A's national income. This is perfectly in line with the law of sales–purchases: A pays for its net commercial exports on behalf of the importing country, R, and obtains in exchange an equivalent amount of R's financial assets. When external payments have a national currency as their object, the law of money's circular flow is violated, and it is the net importing country that must pay for its net imports. It does so by crediting the exporting country with a sum of national currency that, outside its national boundaries, is purely nominal, and thus void of real content. The payment itself is thus void, because what is transmitted to the exporting country is a mere promise, an acknowledgement of debt whose redeeming power is zero.

As we shall see in the second part of this chapter, the nature of international payments in the present non-system is such that they inevitably become the source of inflation in the countries whose exports are paid in a national currency. Hence, even today net exports are eventually paid by exporting countries, but through inflation. The law of the monetary circuit is logical and, as such, cannot be ignored. If it were explicitly complied with, international payments would take place through the circular flow of an international money and exports would be paid by exporting countries without creating any disorder. If it is not – that is, if national currencies are treated, wrongly, as real assets – the law triumphs anyway, but this time at the cost of a monetary disorder, namely inflation, which affects the exporting countries.

## The inflationary nature of international payments

In the first part of the chapter, reference was made to the inflationary consequences of international payments, when a country's net imports are paid by resorting to its official reserves. In this part we will see how Schmitt generalizes the analysis and shows how international payments lead to an inflationary decrease in the purchasing power of money, whether a country' exports are net or equal to its imports.

### *An introductory example: the case of gold*

Schmitt's first proof (1977b) addresses the inflationary nature of international payments when carried out in gold. He considers the example of two countries A and R whose national production is of 6 and 5 money units, respectively. Figure 7.2 shows national money units (in milliards) represented by circles and national productions by crosses X and X'.

If, the value of A's exports being equal to that of R's exports, country A exports 1X and country R 1X', and both countries pay their imports in gold, the situation is as in Figure 7.3.

The number of goods available in each country is reduced, because of their respective exports, while the units of income expressed in national currencies are not, because exports are paid in gold. The reduction in real goods is the mark of inflation: in country A and in country R, each national money unit has now a lesser real content, to wit, less purchasing power.

This result is confirmed by another argument. This time, Schmitt analyzes the situation in A and R when goods X and X' are simultaneously purchased in the internal and in the international markets, imports being paid in gold. He compares the amount of goods available in each country before exports

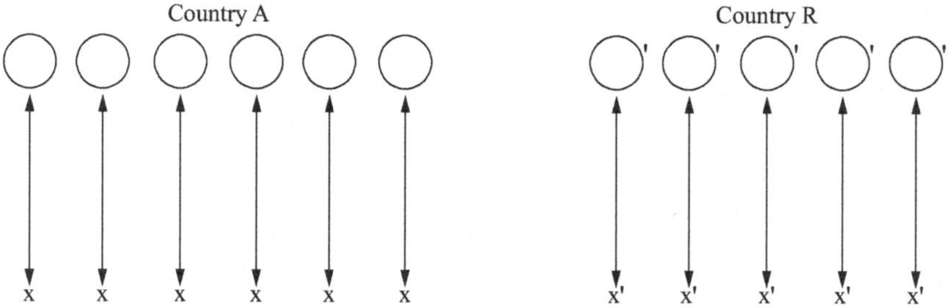


*Figure 7.2* Situation before international payments. Source: elaboration from Schmitt 1977b: 82

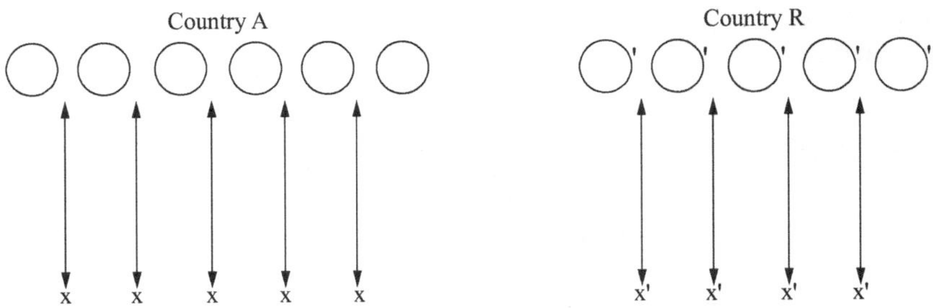


*Figure 7.3* Situation after international payments. Source: elaboration from Schmitt 1977b: 83

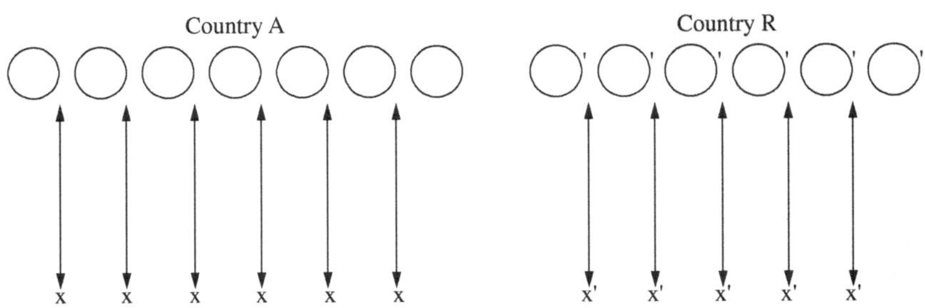


*Figure 7.4* Situation when national and international purchases take place simultaneously. Source: elaboration from Schmitt 1977b: 85

with the amount of national income plus the gold obtained from payments for international transactions. The presence of gold increases the nominal amount of money units present in each country, as depicted in Figure 7.4.

In country A and country R, the number of available money units is boosted by the presence of gold, but neither in A nor in R is this increase accompanied by an equivalent increase in national output. The addition of gold is that of a nominal money whose purchasing power is derived from that of the money units associated with national output. 'Hence, the number of circles increases but not the number of the corresponding crosses. It follows that gold obtains its purchasing power by proxy, because it decreases the purchasing power of the national credit currencies' (Schmitt 1977b: 86, m.t.).

Admittedly, gold is itself a real asset, so that, apparently, it just replaces the exported goods without causing any harm. However, the problem is not identifying gold with a real good but using it as money. As the value of any other currency, the value of money-gold can only derive from production. In the absence of a production monetized by gold, money-gold is bound to remain nominal money: its addition to the number of money units available in any given economy causes inflation. It follows that, carried out in gold, the payment of a country's exports entails a second payment executed within the exporting country. 'Gold [...] does not define the true payment of net sales, because these sales must logically be paid a second time – the "*definitive*" time – by the holders of money A [the net exporting country]' (ibid.: 93, m.t.).

### *The use of US dollars as international currency*

Schmitt then tackles the problem of internationally generated inflation when payments are carried out in US dollars. He first points out that, as claimed by the French economist Jacques Rueff, the US benefits from the exorbitant privilege of paying for its imports using its own national currency, that is, by giving a mere acknowledgement of debt in exchange for any sort of real goods, commercial and financial, of the rest-of-the-world. The US dollars are nothing else than credit money issued by the American banking system: outside their national boundaries they define the debt of the American nation as a whole.

One of the relevant aspects of the external payments in dollars is that they are void of any real content. They give rise to a phenomenon defined as *duplication* by Rueff. As a matter of fact, the dollars paid by US importers are not lost to the US banking system: they remain deposited with the American banks and are immediately lent within the American economy. '[E]ach dollar that exists at a given moment in any place of the globe is by definition deposited in an American bank' (ibid.: 182, m.t.). Since not even a cent can logically abandon the US banking system, the dollars paid to the exporting countries can only be a *duplicate* of those deposited in the United States.

A simple bookkeeping representation shows the duplication very clearly (see Table 7.1).

The US dollars paid by American importers are still entered on the liabilities side of the US banking system; they define a deposit of America's national income that banks lend to the US economy. Yet, the same amount of dollars is entered on the assets side of R's banking system. The $x$ dollars now available abroad are not part of those created by the US banks and associated to the American production; they are just *euro-dollars*: a copy or duplicate generated by the pseudo payment of US imports. '[W]hen it is credited outside the US national border, the creditor obtains only a "double", a duplicate, a kind of mirror image, the true dollars being all fixed in America' (ibid.: 182, m.t.).

It is worth observing that euro-dollars are formed each time America pays for its imports, and not only its *net* imports, in its own national currency. It

*Table 7.1* Duplication of US dollars

| *Assets* | | *Liabilities* | |
|---|---|---|---|
| US banking system | | | |
| Importers | \$ x | R's banking system | \$ x |
| R's banking system | | | |
| US banking system | \$ x | Exporters | $M_R$ y |

is true that, to the extent that American imports are equal to exports, the US pays for its imports *in real terms*, that is, by transferring to R part of its national resources. However, the problem of the existence of euro-dollars accumulating in the world is a monetary one. Even though the US pays the part of its imports equal to its export by giving up part of its national assets, this *real* payment must be conveyed by a monetary payment in which money plays a vehicular role. What happens instead is that the US dollars are used as if they were financial assets. Instead of being matched by equivalent exports, American imports are matched by a sum of dollars.

The lack of a proper means of payment, in the absence of a system of international payments, enables the US to exchange its own IOUs against foreign real goods, a transaction that inescapably duplicates its currency.

Schmitt observes, in addition, that America itself may well be a victim of this process of duplication. Once accumulated abroad, the euro-dollars can be spent everywhere in the world. When they are spent in the US for the purchase of what is produced by the American economy, they add up to the 'true' dollars defining US national output while creating a monetary disorder within the American economy. 'The US itself suffers from the inflationary pressure exercised by its currency in its international functions' (ibid.: 183, m.t.). If they flow back to the US, the euro-dollars do not change their nature; they remain a false currency whose presence reduces the purchasing power of the dollars associated with American production.

The fact of the matter is that no true compensation occurs between the payments of US imports and exports. Compensation can indeed occur only when the same agent is at the same time the importer and the exporter. In general, this is not the case, and it would be illogical to compensate the purchases of some agents with the sales of some other agents. In the absence of a true supranational currency, compensation is not an option, the deep reason being that 'international money should be incapable of gaining entry into national economies' (ibid.: 190, m.t.). If this logical requirement is not satisfied, international monetary payments are false payments that increase pathologically the money units available in the creditor countries, irrespective of what national currency is used as international money and in which country it is spent. Hence, when R spends euro-dollars to purchase American products in the US, the euro-dollars are at the origin of the same disorder caused by the payment in US dollars of American imports.

Let us stress once more the fact that the anomaly is not a microeconomic one. US importers pay their imports entirely: they lose the income they spend in the purchase of foreign products. The problem arises because of the need for America to convey to the creditor countries the payment of its importers. It is at the macroeconomic level that we have to look for the origin of monetary pathologies.

When America pays for the imports of its residents, it does so by using its own national currency. As soon as the American banks credit the rest-of-the-world with a sum of US dollars, duplication is inevitable, and duplications increase in an inflationary manner the sum of money available in R's economy. Dollars and euro-dollars are not the same currency and their exchange rates are parallel yet distinct. The difference between these two currencies is that the US dollars emitted and circulating in the US are a debt of the American banks defined as issuing banks, whereas the euro-dollars are a debt of the American banks as financial intermediaries. Euro-dollars are not linked to US production; they are created as objects of the payment US banks are required to issue to R on behalf of American importers.

When acting as financial intermediaries, American banks issue a debt that, once transferred to R, defines the acknowledgement of debt of 'The House America'. When requested to credit R's banks with a sum of dollars, the American banking system enters on the assets side of its balance sheet a sum of national income and on the liabilities side a sum of newly issued US dollars, which it transfers to country R's banking system. What R's banks obtain is therefore nothing else than a duplicate of the US dollars still being deposited with the American banking system. 'The deposits due to import expenditures are not *borrowed* by the American banking system, which finds them *automatically* only because the dollar, a national currency, is thrown into national purchases' (ibid.: 186, m.t.).

American banks pay the imports of US residents; by doing so American financial institutions are credited with the deposits in US dollars spent by the importers without incurring any debt. On the basis of such 'free deposits', the American banks, acting as financial intermediaries, 'issue vehicular currencies of their own devising, namely euro-dollars' (ibid.: 188, m.t.). In conclusion, euro-dollars are a pseudo American currency that circulates within countries, US included, as a parallel currency. 'Finally, euro-dollars define unpaid claims of American financial institutions, claims that generate automatically from the expenditure of dollars in [the payment of] American imports' (ibid.: 188, m.t.).

### *A general analysis of the inflationary character of international payments*

In an unpublished manuscript dated 1983, Schmitt analyzes the case of two countries, A and B, exchanging real goods of the same value and paying for their foreign purchases in a national currency. For didactical reasons, he assumes that A and B exchange their entire national output valued $1M_A$ and $1M_B$ respectively, and that $1M_A = 1M_B$. Country A can pay its imports in $M_A$ or in $M_B$, and so can country B. For the sake of didactical clarity, Schmitt assumes that each country pays its imports in its own currency. The aim of the exercise is to show that in each country false international payments reduce the purchasing power of income holders by half.

Country A's importers spend all A's national income in the purchase of country B's output, while B's importers, purchasers of A's output, spend B's national income entirely. As we already know, $M_A$ does not abandon A's banking system, nor does $M_B$ abandon B's banking system. What country A obtains

*Table 7.2* Inflationary gap caused by payment of country A's exports in money B

| *Banking system of country A* | | | |
|---|---|---|---|
| *Assets* | | *Liabilities* | |
| Firms | $M_A$ 1 | Income holders | $M_A$ 1 |
| Banking system of country B | $M_B$ 1 | Firms | $M_A$ 1 |

is a duplicate of money B that is immediately and automatically at the origin of an equivalent creation of money A (Table 7.2).

Banks in A *monetize* the foreign currency they are credited with by B's banks. By doing so, they *de facto* monetize a second time the national output financially deposited with them at the moment of the payment of wages. A product initially monetized and valued $1M_A$ is now confronted with $2M_A$, one of which is newly created as a nominal counterpart of $1M_B$, with which A's banks are credited because of the payment of B's imports in money B. Hence, '*two* units of money A are created concerning *the same product*, whose total price in money passes from one to two units of $M_A$; given that income holders obtain one unit of money – and not two, they have the power to purchase half of the national product, nothing more: they lose the other half of the product in the inflationary gap, which profits firms' (Schmitt 1983: 3, m.t.). What explains the formation of the inflationary gap in country A is '*the basic rule of the present regime of international payments*: payments of external origin give rise to a monetary creation in the exporting country' (ibid.: 4, m.t.).

What is true for country A applies also to country B, whose exports are paid in money A. Banks in B create a sum of national money on the basis of the money A credited to them by A's banking system. Country B's national output is thus monetized twice: a first time at the moment of its production, and a second time when its sale abroad triggers a new creation of money B. The analysis must account for both payments, of country A to country B and of country B to country A. At which point one is bound to wonder: given that the two countries' exports and imports are simultaneous and of the same amount, do their payments balance out? If they did, no additional monetary creation would occur. Unfortunately, this is not the case, because, in the present non-system of international payments, both in country A and in country B 'the payment of imports and the payment of exports are two *distinct* flows' (ibid.: 5, m.t.). Compensation occurs, yes, but only *after both* payments have been made.

Let us follow the payments that occur in country A, those in country B being simply their reciprocal. The additional monetary creation by A's banks is the conversion in money A to the benefit of A's firms of the payment in money B by B's importers. Two alternative analyses are possible, which lead to the same result.

On the one hand we can say, with Schmitt, that even though income holders of each country purchase the national product of the other country, things happen as if they purchased their own national output and then exchanged it against that of the other country. It is through the mediation of B's income holders and of country A's and country B's banks that the income holders of country A pay country A's firms, while the income holders of country B pay the firms of B through the mediation of the income holders of country A and of A's and B's banks. Finally, the product of country A is purchased through the expenditure of $1M_A$ by country A's income holders and of an additional unit of money A created on the basis of the payment in money B. The second payment is pathological; it is by nature macroeconomic and concerns the country as a whole. When all the payments have taken place, compensation occurs between the money B entered in banks A's balance sheets and the money A entered in banks B's balance sheets. Yet, it is too late: in both countries the additional monetary creation is the cause of an inflationary gap between Supply and Demand that will inevitably form again each time international transactions are paid in a national currency.

The alternative analysis proposed by Schmitt (1983) rests on backward reasoning, which starts from the inflationary nature of reciprocal international payments. On the basis of his analysis, we find the claim that '[t]he creation of national currency against payment (of exports) in foreign currencies amounts to the advance of an equal monetary profit to firms' (ibid.: 7, m.t.). The 'backward proof' consists in showing that the profit advanced by banks to firms in country A is indeed reimbursed by firms thanks to the second monetization of A's national output that accompanies the payment in money B of A's exports.

The two monetizations taking place in country A can be represented as in Figure 7.5.

Flow (1) represents the creation of income corresponding to production as it occurs through the payment of wage-earners, WE. Flow (2) is the advance to firms of an inflationary profit. If the analysis confirms the advance, then we will obtain more evidence of the inflationary nature of international payments in the case of trade balance's equilibrium.

Let us consider flow (1) first. The sum of income issued by the banks of country A in the payment of wages is re-distributed among income holders and then spent on the purchase of the goods imported from country B. Since we have assumed that country A's and country B's outputs have the same value and that each country exports its national output in full, the income created

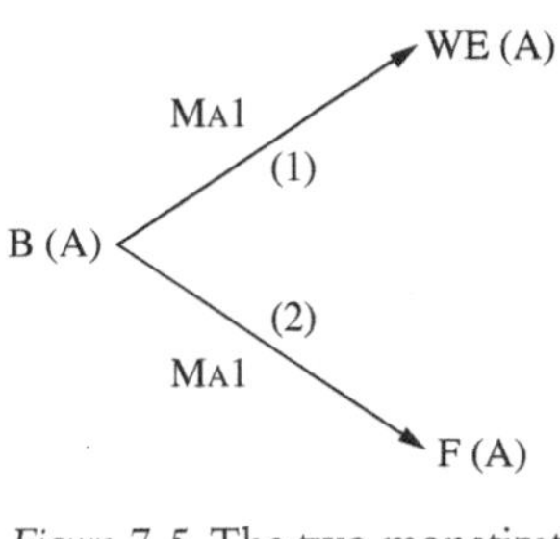


*Figure 7.5* The two monetizations taking place in country A. Source: Schmitt 1983: 8

in country A (B) is entirely spent to the benefit of the banks of country B (A), which act on behalf of B's (A's) firms (see Figure 7.6).

The banks of A are credited with $1M_A$ and the banks of B are credited with $1M_B$, which means that, given that the rate of exchange between money A and money B is of one $M_A$ for one $M_B$, country A's and country B's reciprocal debts counterbalance (Figure 7.7).

After reciprocal compensation, the banks of country A (B) recover the sum issued in flow (1).

It remains to verify if outflow (2), the advance of inflationary profit, is also matched by an equivalent inflow. In other words, we have to verify whether or not the payment of reciprocal imports enables firms to reimburse the advance of profit initially granted by their banks. The answer is that it does because firms in country A (B) benefit from a monetary creation of national currency effected by their banks when they enter an equivalent sum of foreign currency in their ledgers.

Credited with a sum of money B (A), the banks of A (B) create an equivalent sum of money A (B) in favour of their firms, which can thus reimburse the initial advance of profit (Figure 7.8).

The reimbursement of the advance of profit by the firms of country A (B) implies a single flow to the banks of country A (B) because the sum that firms give back is obtained by them through a monetary creation. The sum advanced as profit is therefore matched by an equivalent inflow, which confirms, once and for all, the formation of an inflationary profit.

All the money units issued by country A's banks flow back to their point of injection and are destroyed. The destruction of the money income generated

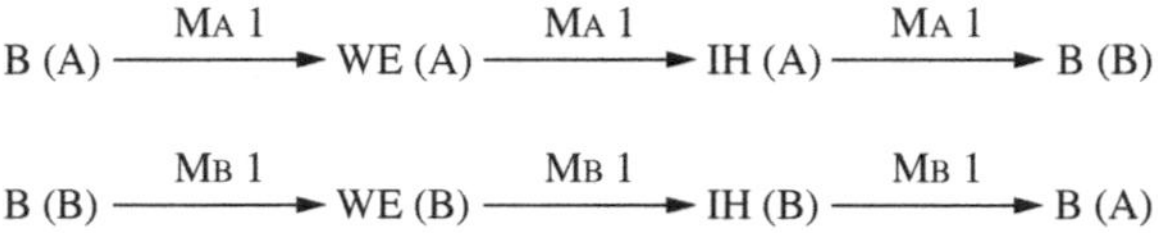


*Figure 7.6* The flows of payment of countries A's and B's reciprocal imports.

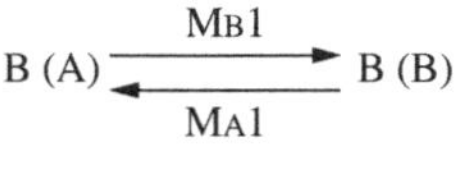


*Figure 7.7* The compensation between the banks of country A and country B.

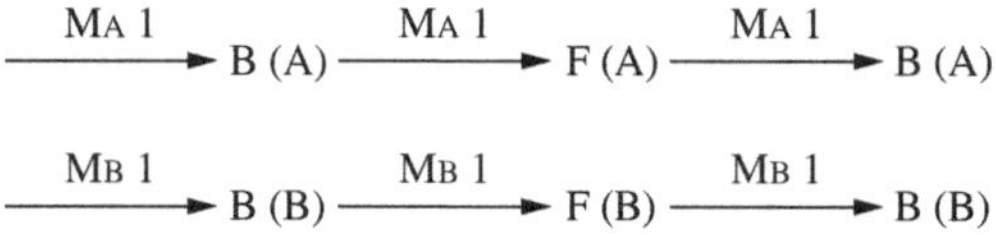


*Figure 7.8* The reimbursement of the advance of profit in country A and country B.

by production takes place through the final sale of output, while the destruction of the money created as counterpart of the foreign currency paid by the importing country results from the compensation between the banks of A and B. In both countries, national products are sold out and banks recover their monetary advances. Yet, in each country, national output is purchased through the expenditure of a sum of money twice as high as that paid to wage-earners.

As Schmitt argues, what matters *is not the stock of money resulting from the payment of the two countries' reciprocal imports-export, but the flows of payments.* In country A and country B 'the flows of payments include the monetary creation for the payment of exports' (ibid.: 8, m.t.), so that, both in country A and country B the payment of exports generates an inflationary emission of nominal money that halves the purchasing power of each money unit.

### *Again, on the inflationary implications of international payments*

Schmitt comes back to the inflationary payments of imports-exports in a small, yet seminal book entitled *Les pays au régime du FMI* (1984). Here, he analyzes again the example of two countries exchanging all their national products. His arguments are similar to the one he used in his unpublished manuscript distributed one year earlier to his students at the Universities of Fribourg and Dijon. Schmitt stresses the fact that, even though they are the same amount, the expenditure of the firms of country A, F(A), to the benefit of the firms of country B, F(B), and the expenditure of F(B) to the benefit of F(A) of their advanced profits do not cancel out. The reason is that they are two distinct payments: 'firms B *do not give F(A) the money A spent by F(A), but the currency B, payment of country A's exports*' (Schmitt 1984c: 20, m.t.).

It is because the flow of F(A)'s payment is unconnected to the flow of F(B)'s payment that the profit advanced to firms is confirmed and, with it, the inflationary nature of country A's and country B's external payments.

What is wrong within the current non-system of international payments is that exports are paid in the exporting country through an additional creation of nominal money. This is so, because '[t]he (national) currency used to pay imports and the (foreign) currency earned through exports *cross each other*, when the two flows, debtor and creditor payments, should logically form a single identical movement' (ibid.: 31, m.t.). Schmitt's diagnosis is clear: 'since import and exports are the terms of a single transaction [...] they should not be paid separately' (ibid.: 31, m.t.).

It is true that international exchanges are carried out through the mediation of money. But this means that monetary payments should not separate the exchange between exports and imports into two distinct exchanges in which money acts as if it were a real good. If money were a simple *means* of exchange, the payment of country A's exports and the payment of country B's exports would not be carried out as two separate transactions. Today this is not yet the case; consequently, the two payments 'are two distinct operations, *one adding to the other*' (ibid.: 32, m.t.).

In his 1984 small book, Schmitt also considers the case of the payment of net commercial exports. Let us follow his numerical example and investigate what happens when a given country A, whose national output is equal to $6M_A$, is a net commercial exporter for $1M_A$.

A figure helps clarify the situation after A's net exports are paid by the rest of the world in a foreign currency, as shown in Figure 7.9.

Circles represent units of $M_A$, while crosses represent country A's real output. A's exports reduce the number of crosses and leave an empty circle; whereas the payment of country A's exports brings one unit of foreign currency into country A's bank accounts. Country A being a net exporter, the foreign currency defines the net external income of the country as a whole entered into A's banking system to the benefit of the State. As a counterpart of the foreign currency entered on its assets side, A's banking system creates an equivalent amount of $M_A$ that is paid out to country A's exporters. In Figure 7.9 the additional unit created by country A's banks is not represented precisely because, being paid out to A's exporters, it covers the costs of production of exported goods, which entails its final destruction.

Following Schmitt, let us represent the situation after the final expenditure of country A's domestic income by A's income holders as in Figure 7.10.

After their final expenditure, income holders own 5 units of real income in the form of five crosses. On the other hand, firms own financial capital in the form of $1M_A$, and the State owns a unit of foreign currencies defining the gain obtained by country A thanks to its net commercial exports. What is wrong is that '[F]inancial capital increases *twice* in the creditor country, that is, both as national money and as foreign currencies' (ibid.: 43, m.t.). An increase of 1 unit is justified, because country A's net commercial exports are indeed equal to $1M_A$, but an increase of 2 units is one too many. The fictitious gain is that of the foreign currencies entered on the assets side of A's banking system. They are a duplicate of the original national currencies deposited in their issuing countries, an amount of nominal money that defines their countries' acknowledgement of debt.

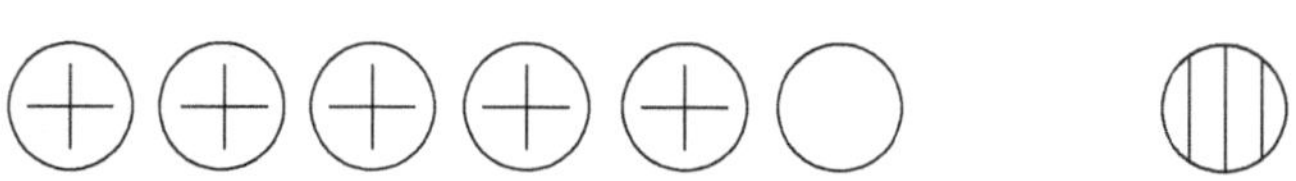

*Figure 7.9* Situation in country A after payment of A's net exports. Source: Schmitt 1984c: 41

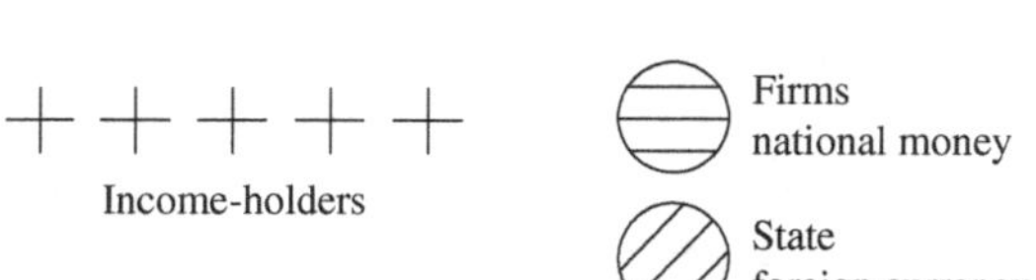


*Figure 7.10* Situation in country A after the final expenditure of A's income holders. Source: elaboration from Schmitt 1984c: 43

The case of country A's net exports differs from that of trade equilibrium in that it requires the payment in money of country A's net commercial exports. The increase in country A's official reserves by a sum of foreign currencies is anomalous: made up of duplicates, it is no true gain for the country. Country A's net commercial exports justify its gain, but the present non-system of international payments prevents its lawful formation. This time, the emission of an additional sum of national currency by country A's banking system is not the source of inflation, because it is logically needed to monetize A's foreign (mercantilist) gain. Inflation arises, because country A's net commercial exports are not compensated by any real import (of financial assets).

The decrease in the amount of goods (crosses) available in country A and the monetization of the foreign currencies obtained as payment from the rest-of-the-world creates an inflationary gap that increases, in an inflationary way, the profit of country A's firms. The disorder looks like an additional financial capital of A's firms at the same time as a fictitious gain for the country.

## Schmitt's analysis of international payments as compared to that of his contemporaries

The contributions of Schmitt's contemporaries to the analysis of international payments may be subdivided into two broad categories: those who are against and those in favour of the gold-exchange standard in one of its variants.

Triffin and Rueff's investigations pertain to the first category. They are both highly critical of a system where international payments are carried out using a key-currency and concentrate their attention on the case of the US dollar.

Triffin (1961) denounces the fragility of a system based on the use of the US dollar convertible into gold as international currency. He points out that, in such a system, America is bound to accept a persistent trade deficit to provide the world with the transnational liquidity necessary to carry out international payments, and that its gold reserves will soon be too small to guarantee the convertibility criteria agreed upon at Bretton Woods. Triffin warns that this situation would soon become unsustainable even if convertibility was abandoned and fixed exchange rates were replaced by floating exchange rates. The continuous growth of the US trade deficit is seen by Triffin as the mark of the increasing incapacity of the US to guarantee the real payment of its net commercial imports, which tends 'to bring about a collapse of the system itself through the gradual weakening of foreigners' confidence in the key currencies [here the US dollar]' (Triffin 1961: 67).

Rueff shares Triffin's critical assessment of the gold-exchange standard and provides a strong argument against the use of any national money as international means of payment. Considering the payment of any key-currency country's net imports, Rueff shows that 'everything happens as if these currencies had never been exported in the first place. Entering the credit system of the creditor country but remaining in the debtor country, the claims representing the deficit are thus doubled' (Rueff 1963: 324).

In his analysis, Rueff goes as far as arguing that the gold-exchange standard grants key-currency countries the exorbitant privilege to 'give without taking, to lend without borrowing, and to get without paying' (ibid.: 322). Indeed, when a key-currency country like the US pays its net commercial imports in dollars, it gets parts of the real output of the rest-of-the-world in exchange for a sum of IOUs, a promise to pay that can be postponed *sine die*.

Rueff's other deep insight refers to the monetization by the receiving banking system of the foreign currency credited to net exporting countries. 'The claims transferred for the settlement of the deficit are bought, against the creation of money, by the banking system of the creditor country' (ibid.: 323). Rueff could not be clearer: *net exporting countries obtain as payment a sum of nominal money, a mere duplicate of zero value, and their banking systems 'purchase' it through money creation.*

Rueff does not seem to be aware that key-currency countries themselves suffer from the present non-system. In the case of euro-dollars, for example, 'no rule of logic opposes the infiltration of dollar duplicates in the United States' (Schmitt 1977b: 184, m.t.). Rueff also seems to ignore that duplication is not confined to the payment of key-countries' trade deficit but concerns the entire amount of their imports. Be it as it may, it must be recognized that Rueff was the first author to explain duplication and link it to monetary creation. His analysis provides the key elements that will later be taken over and further developed by Schmitt in his 1977 book, *L'or, le dollar et la monnaie supranationale*.

Mainstream economics has dealt with the problem of international payments mainly by adopting the monetarist approach to the balance of payments. The fundamental idea on which this approach rests is the substantial homogeneity of national currencies. The basic concepts are supply of and demand for money; their interaction is supposed to restore the equilibrium of the balance of payments whenever it is disturbed by a variation in a country's imports or exports.

Advocates of the quantity theory of money claim that demand for money plays a decisive role in this process. A difference between the domestic demand for, and supply of, money entails a variation in the country's exports accompanied by an increase or a decrease in foreign exchange reserves.

> Since the demand for money is a demand for a stock and not a flow, variation of the supply of money relative to the demand for it associated with deficit or surplus must work towards an equilibrium between money demand and money supply with a corresponding equilibration of the balance of payments.
>
> (Johnson 1974: 153)

According to the quantity theory of money approach, international transactions have a direct impact on countries' national income, which expands or contracts according to whether exports exceed import or the other way around. National currencies being treated as homogeneous, international payments are not considered fundamentally different from regional payments, so that the total amount of income available in any given country is obtained by adding the difference between exports and imports to the sum of national income.

$$\text{Total income} = \text{national income} + (\text{exports} - \text{imports})$$

No distinction is made between money and income, and any foreign currencies earned through net exports are too easily added to the national money supply. The analysis differs when applied to key-currency or non-key-currency countries, yet the central assumption and the mechanism of re-equilibrium remain the same.

These key critical observations are enough to show how different Schmitt's monetary analysis is from that of the Monetarists. The axiomatic assumption of currency homogeneity is totally groundless and alien to facts. Money is erroneously identified with a financial asset, and the theory is trapped between two mutually exclusive alternatives: accept the homogeneity postulate and consider money as a veil or consider money as a positive asset and reject the homogeneity postulate.

The 'quantity theory of money' approach to international payments lacks clarity because of its concept of money in general and of bank money in particular. The simplistic mechanism of adjustment hypothesized by the Monetarists is a figment of their imagination. National currencies are heterogeneous, and their use as international means of payment inescapably leads to serious monetary disorders. By assuming the existence of a homogeneity that can emerge only from the implementation of a reform still to come, the advocates of the monetarist approach have long given up on understanding the nature of today's pathologies that plague the international economy.

# 8 Schmitt's first proposals for a world monetary reform

Schmitt's analysis of the pathological nature of the system of international payments, which is based on the key-currencies standard as the latest evolution of the gold-exchange standard adopted at Bretton Woods, motivated him to elaborate a proposal for world monetary reform already in the early 1970s. Keynes's plan for the establishment of an International Clearing Union (ICU) inspired Schmitt to work on a reform capable of providing the world with a true international currency acting as both a unit of account and a means of payment, albeit not simultaneously. An apposite account of Schmitt's proposals requires understanding his analysis of international money and re-visiting Keynes's plan. That is why this chapter deals initially with the problem of the heterogeneity of national currencies and its solution. Then it turns to a critical review of Keynes's 1942 plan for reform to arrive at the principles of Schmitt's reform and concludes with a few remarks concerning the path that, from Ricardo's monetary writings onwards, leads to the plan for the establishment of a supranational bank and its two departments: monetary and financial.

To trace Schmitt's thought, I have relied on his published books, *New Proposals for World Monetary Reform* (1973), *Théorie unitaire de la monnaie nationale et internationale* (1975), *L'or, le dollar et la monnaie supranationale* (1977), *L'ECU et les souverainetés nationales en Europe* (1988), *La France souveraine de sa monnaie* (1984), and on two published papers, 'Un nouvel ordre monétaire international: le plan Keynes' (1985) and 'Le plan Keynes: vers la monnaie internationale purement véhiculaire' (1987). Also, useful insights are provided by three unpublished manuscripts: 'Plans to obviate the creation of an international fiat money' (1972), 'The theory of international money' (1972), and 'Manuscrit sur la monnaie nationale et internationale' (1985).

## From relative to absolute exchange rates

Chapter 7 has shown that in the absence of a bank of central banks there is no common 'form' that would make national currencies homogeneous. This is confirmed by the logical impossibility of determining currency exchange rates through the interaction of supply and demand. In the previous chapter, we

DOI: 10.4324/9781351271325-12

briefly introduced Schmitt's proof of the indeterminacy of a system of relative prices, where two goods are exchanged between two countries using two different national currencies. Here we refer to two complementary demonstrations, which show that relative exchange rates cannot be determined unless they are derived from *absolute* exchange rates.

### *Is a system of relative exchange rates adequate and coherent?*

Consider the case where three countries, A, B, and C, whose national currencies are respectively $M_A$, $M_B$, and $M_C$, exchange their products and pay their purchases using their national currencies. The problem is to establish whether or not a system of equations derived from exchange can determine 'adequate' and 'coherent' exchange rates through which national currencies would become homogeneous.

Exchange rates are *adequate* if they are equilibrium rates leading to the equality of each country's balance of payments; they are *coherent*, if one of the rates is derivable from the other. Can a system of relative exchange rates satisfy this double constraint?

In his 1972 paper, Schmitt distinguishes the case of bilateral payments from that of multilateral payments. In the former, the equilibrium exchange rate of any two countries, say A and B, is determined *independently* of that of the third. 'When A and B have each found their equilibrium with B and C, the volume of trade between C and A is still unknown' (Schmitt 1972e: I.2). Since each country must determine two rates of exchange, because each country is active in the process of determination, the three countries 'determine six rates of exchange instead of three' (ibid.: I.3). However, 'only three exchange rates are independently determined by the three countries' (ibid.: I.3). Finally, there are three independent equations, each matching the supply of one national currency to the demand for that same currency.

$$\text{Supply of } M_A = \text{Demand for } M_A \tag{8.1}$$

$$\text{Supply of } M_B = \text{Demand for } M_B \tag{8.2}$$

$$\text{Supply of } M_C = \text{Demand for } M_C \tag{8.3}$$

Can the number of independent equations be reduced from three to two? Schmitt's answer is no, because no adjustment factor is available to reduce them: all the adjustment factors are used up to guarantee the equality of each country's bilateral payments.

The case of multilateral payments differs from the preceding one because one can now reduce the number of independent equations and of variables: only two exchange rates are interdependently determined by the three countries.

> The correct conclusion simply is that the three equilibria are independently determined. All three currencies freely fluctuate in the exchange markets until equilibrium is reached in all three balances of payments. But logically this simultaneous determination means that anyone of the three unknowns is implicit in the other two.
>
> (ibid.: I.5)

The exchange rate between any two currencies is fully determined as soon as the two other exchange rates are known. Since reducing the number of independent equations by one also means reducing the unknowns by one, two adjustment factors seem enough to determine the solution in the case of multilateral payments.

However, at this point Schmitt observes that 'there is no basic difference between the two cases [bilateral and multilateral] in hand. When all available adjustment factors have been fully used, all *n* balances must have been brought to perfect equilibrium' (ibid.: I.6). The equilibrium of the balance of payments for each of the three countries, A, B, and C, is achieved when each of them equalizes its sales and its purchases. The exchange rates conducive to equilibrium are *adequate*. The problem is that exchange rates also need to be *coherent*, a condition that can be satisfied only through *arbitrage*. Yet, arbitrage makes exchange rates coherent only at a price, that is, by making them diverge from equilibrium rates. Finally, coherent exchange rates are not adequate, while adequate exchange rates are not coherent. '*When adequate, rates are not coherent, it then follows that coherent rates are no longer adequate*' (ibid.: I.6).

Since arbitrage is a necessary condition for the determination of relative exchange rates, the conclusion is unavoidable: in the case of both bilateral and multilateral payments, the system of equations for determining relative exchange rates must include the equation of arbitrage. In the example of multilateral payments between three countries, a third independent equation is called for, which makes the system over-determined. 'With respect to the requirement of balanced accounts in international payments, freely flexible exchange rates are *over-determined*, for we have *n* independent equations to determine $n - 1$ unknown variables' (ibid.: I. 7, m.t.).

The attempt to determine currency exchange rates directly through exchange is doomed to failure and needs to be replaced by a mechanism whereby relative exchange rates can be derived from absolute exchange rates. Before showing that this is indeed the case, let us clarify further the logical indeterminacy denounced by Schmitt. Any attempt to determine relative exchange rates is based on the belief that

1) They are not substantially different from relative *prices*, and that
2) National currencies are a particular kind of real goods.

The mistake is obvious: money is a flow, a vehicular instrument of no intrinsic value necessary to convey real payments and to express the price of goods numerically. To claim that money itself has a price is deeply wrong, and so is to believe that national currencies can be supplied and demanded for their own sake. In the present non-system of international payments, national currencies are purchased as if they were goods, every demand for a currency in terms of another being a net or excess demand. Yet, 'it is entirely illogical that currencies can purchase one another; by nature, currencies purchase products and not currencies' (Schmitt 1985d: 154, m.t.). Nationally, currencies are numerical vehicles, a means of making real payments; internationally, bank monies are transformed into final goods, they become the objects of monetary transactions.

As national bank monies are considered as positive assets there is demand for them both because of the (national) real goods they are associated with and for their own sake. If they were considered only as intermediaries there would be no problem. Unfortunately, they are also seen as final objects of monetary purchases, which means that demand for any national currency has two components: demand for a means of exchange and demand for a final asset. It is because of these two components that an equation of arbitrage has to be added to the equations of supply and demand in the system of relative exchange rates determination.

In the example of three national currencies, the equation of arbitrage refers to the supply of and demand for currencies as such, which is why it is not included in the equations equalizing the supply of and demand for each currency. The first three equations concern the supply of and demand for $M_A$, $M_B$, and $M_C$ as representatives of countries A, B, and C's national productions. The fourth equation is required to make relative exchange rates coherent given the fact that currencies are also the object of monetary transactions irrespective of their link to national outputs. Once the equation of arbitrage is added to the others, the system becomes over-determined, that is, incapable of determining relative exchange rates.

In our example, exchange rates are coherent when 'one of the rates is equal to the ratio of the two others' (Schmitt 1975a: 89, m.t.). Arbitrage is the equation that brings about this equalization. However, if arbitrage intervenes, exchange rates are no longer consistent with those guaranteeing the equality of countries A, B, and C's exports and imports. It is thus confirmed that exchange rates cannot be simultaneously adequate and coherent.

### *Relative exchange rates and the international circular flow of money*

As we saw in Chapter 7, Schmitt provides another proof of the logical indeterminacy of relative exchange rates by referring to the concept of international circular monetary flow. In particular, he shows that 'it is logically impossible to establish the international circuit of money through the adjustment between imports and exports of the different countries involved in world trade' (ibid.: 89, m.t.). This time the French economist does not distinguish transactions for the exchange of real products from transactions of currencies.

Going back to the case of three currencies, the three equations equalizing the supply of and demand for $M_A$, $M_B$, and $M_C$ now include the equation of arbitrage. However, the identity of the circuit, that is, the necessary equality of each country's expenditures and receipts of national currency is the fourth equation that makes the system over-determined. One of the laws of the international circular monetary flow is the identity between sales and purchases of every country. 'Each country must be "purchaser-seller" of foreign currency, and not a net purchaser or a net seller' (ibid.: 90, m.t.). The role of the additional fourth equation is that of guaranteeing the existence of the international circular monetary flow because 'the reciprocal supply of and demand for [national] currencies are not submitted to the constraint of the identity for each country of its simultaneous receipts and expenditures' (ibid.: 91, m.t.). The 'equation of the circuit' is additional, because the system of the first three equations, (8.1), (8.2), and (8.3), can equilibrate the purchases and sales of $M_A$, $M_B$, and $M_C$ but cannot guarantee the necessary equality of countries A, B, and C's sales and purchases of their own national currencies. The over-determination of the system follows as a necessary consequence.

### *Relative exchange rates and currency heterogeneity*

The question of whether exchange rates can make national currencies homogeneous can also be formulated by asking whether through exchange rates national currencies become 'interchangeable, *undifferentiated*' (Schmitt 1984b: 89, m.t.).

Schmitt considers the example of two currencies, $M_A$ and $M_B$, and claims that 'currencies $M_A$ and $M_B$ are homogeneous elements of the same set on condition that the exchange of $x$ $M_A$ against $y$ $M_B$ defines *the equivalence or the identity of its terms*' (ibid.: 89, m.t.). The relative exchange of money A and money B is not adequate, because it simply defines the spatial substitution of a currency for the other as in Figure 8.1.

Money A takes the place of money B and vice versa in a transaction of barter that leaves them as heterogeneous as before. Since up to now 'the exchange of every currency [has been] *relative*, the operation ending up with *another currency*, exchange rates are "barter prices" and not equivalences' (ibid.: 91, m.t.). It is only if the exchange takes place between a given currency and itself by way of another currency that a true equivalence can be established, say between $x$ $M_A$ and $y$ $M_B$: $x\ M_A = y\ M_B$.

The transaction representing this *absolute* exchange is as in Figure 8.2.

The equivalence of $x$ $M_A$ and $y$ $M_B$ results from that between money A and itself; it is obtained by instantaneously changing $x$ $M_A$ into $y$ $M_B$ and *at the same time* changing $y$ $M_B$ back into $x$ $M_A$.

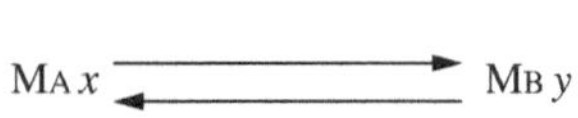


*Figure 8.1* The spatial substitution of $M_A$ and $M_B$.

$$M_A x \rightleftarrows M_B y \rightleftarrows M_A x$$

*Figure 8.2* The absolute exchange of $M_A$ through $M_B$.

No absolute exchange exists in the international field as yet. Today, the purchase of money B by money A is a transaction that does not automatically imply the equivalent purchase of $M_A$ by $M_B$: exchanges between currencies are relative and exchange rates undetermined. 'In world trade, purchase and sale do not merge at each pole of the same transaction: on the contrary, purchase and sale are two distinct realities' (ibid.: 140, m.t.). This is so because currencies are sought after as final objects and not as mere intermediaries in a transaction where real goods are the object of supply and demand.

### *The role of a supranational currency*

In practice, the transition from relative to absolute exchange rates is possible only if the supply of any given currency is recognized as defining simultaneously the demand for this same currency *by the same country*. This is to say that absolute exchange rates require the presence of a supranational currency acting as a catalyst for national currencies.

The role of the supranational currency is that of a common numerical standard of national currencies. Consistent with the nature of bank money, the supranational currency has no intrinsic value or purchasing power of its own. It is a numerical form that lends its homogeneity to the national currencies it is associated with through a system of absolute exchange rates. Relative exchange rates can then easily be derived from absolute exchange rates without having to worry about their coherence, as this would automatically result from the absence of monetary transactions involving currencies. 'Relative exchange rates are now given by the ratio between absolute rates. The coherence problem therefore loses all meaning. When exchange rates are determined by the constraint of balanced international payments, these rates can never come into collision or conflict with each other' (Schmitt 1972d: I.9).

As in the case of bank money within a national economy, supranational money is a numerical common denominator: nationally, bank money makes real goods homogeneous by assigning them a numerical form; internationally, the supranational currency makes national currencies homogeneous. Nationally, bank money is a mere intermediary and purchases are financed through simultaneous sales. Internationally, the supranational currency is also a mere intermediary: a country's sales are financed by its simultaneous purchases.

Each country's exports must be immediately offset by equivalent imports; that is the implication of the law of sales-purchases applied to countries. According to the law of monetary circuits applied to the instantaneous circular flow of international money, each country must simultaneously obtain and spend the same sum of money, thus being prevented from carrying out any transaction on money itself. The exclusion of any monetary equation makes it possible to determine exchange rates that are at the same time adequate and coherent, that is, to respect 'the exigency that all the operations entering the determination of exchange rates be supply of and demand for real economic goods' (Schmitt 1975a: 112, m.t.).

Schmitt distinguishes the monetary from the financial balance of payments and shows that the law of international money circular flow implies the necessary equilibrium of the former. Each country taking part in international trade must comply with this requirement and equalize its monetary outflows and inflows. The equilibrium of the monetary balance of payments is a logical necessity that is automatically respected when countries' purchases are financed by simultaneous and equivalent sales. What induces the distinction between monetary and financial balance is that between nominal and real money. Nominal money is a flow; as such, it can never be held or sold or purchased. Its circular use is consistent with the law of sales-purchases and, if complied with, it guarantees its neutrality. The monetary balance corresponds to the flow of nominal money. Internationally, thanks to the implementation of a system of absolute exchange rates made possible by the introduction of a supranational currency, the monetary balance of each country would always be in equilibrium.

## Keynes's plan for an international clearing union revisited

In 1944, at the conference held at Bretton Woods, Keynes advocated a plan for the establishment of an International Clearing Union (ICU) intended to provide the world with a new system of international payments founded on the principles of banking.

> The idea underlying my proposals for a Currency Union is simple, namely, to generalize the essential principle of banking, as it is exhibited within any closed system, through the establishment of an International Clearing Bank. This principle is the necessary equality of credits and debits, of assets and liabilities.
>
> (Keynes 1980b: 44)

This idea is present in all the subsequent drafts of Keynes's proposals, from September 1941 to April 1943. Its role is central: from the outset, Keynes advocates the establishment of a supranational bank, the ICU, charged with the emission of an international currency, the *bancor*, and operating as a monetary and financial intermediary between nations. Following Schmitt, let us distinguish the bancor as a unit of account from the bancor as a unit of payment.

### *The bancor as a nominal money*

According to Keynes's proposals, the ICU would issue the bancor in the same way as domestic banks issue national currencies, namely by crediting-debiting the beneficiary of the emission. In the case of the bancor, countries are credited by the ICU, which enters them on the liabilities side of its balance sheet, and simultaneously debited by the same ICU, which enters on its balance sheet a claim on the same countries. Being lent to the countries benefiting from its emissions, the bancor must be paid back to the ICU.

The aim of this operation is to provide countries implementing Keynes's plan

(1) With a common numerical form allowing to solve the problem of national currency heterogeneity, and
(2) With a numerical vehicle conveying the real payments of their international transactions.

As a unit of account of national currencies and a means of payment between countries, the bancor would circulate in the international monetary space only, each country maintaining its own national currency and thus preserving its monetary sovereignty.

> We need an instrument of international currency having general acceptability between nations [...], an instrument of currency used by each nation in its transactions with other nations, operating through whatever national organ, such as a Treasury or a central bank, is most appropriate, private individuals, businesses and banks other than central banks each continuing to use their own national currency as heretofore.
>
> (ibid.: 168)

The task of the bancor is to *monetize* countries' transactions. As is the case with national currencies, the bancor does not pertain to the category of real goods, nor is it a financial asset. Best defined as an asset-liability, it is purely nominal. According to Keynes, the ICU's pivotal task is that of acting as a monetary intermediary, providing the world with a unit of account enabling countries to evaluate their transactions and balance them through clearing.

> We call the plan a clearing union because the purpose is to set off transactions against one another so far as you can clear and then to deal with the resulting credit and debit balances as still offsetting one another in the same way they do in internal banking.
>
> (ibid.: 210)

In a letter to Ashton-Gwatkin dated 25 April 1941, Keynes had already expressed his intention to work on a reform based on the principle of multilateral clearing.

> Finally, I return to the point that this means "trading goods against goods" [...]. It does not mean that there would be direct barter of goods against

> goods, but that the one trading transaction must necessarily find its counterpart in another trading transaction.
>
> (ibid.: 18)

In Schmitt's words '[t]he international currency has the task to pay each country's imports *to the extent that they are equalized by the exports of the same period*' (Schmitt 1985c: 205, m.t.). The bancor would monetize each country's imports and exports, thus boosting the expansion of international trade.

> Now this universal currency is essential to the healthy trade of any country, and not least to our own, for it is characteristic of our trade that the best markets for our goods are often different from our best sources of supply. We cannot hope to balance our trading account if the surpluses we earn in one country cannot be applied to meet our requirements in another country.
>
> (Keynes 1980b: 270)

It thus appears that Keynes conceives the bancor as a numerical, international means used to convey reciprocal payments. Yet, the bancor is also a unit of payment, and Keynes's plan must also account for the payment of countries' net commercial imports.

### *The bancor as real money*

Issued as a spontaneous acknowledgement of debt of the ICU, the bancor has no positive purchasing power of its own. Its circular flow conveys the reciprocal payments between countries and complies with the law of sales-purchases: as any national currency within a domestic economy, the bancor is a *means*, not an *object* of payment. This implies that the bancor can in no case finance any net payment. Even though in Keynes's plan international transactions are paid using bancor, the new international currency flows instantaneously back to its point of departure, where it is immediately destroyed. This is why Keynes states that

> [i]f no credits can be removed outside the clearing system, but only transferred within it, the Union can never be in any difficulty as regards the honouring of cheques drawn upon it. It can make what advances it wishes to any of its members with the assurance that the proceeds can only be transferred to the clearing account of another member.
>
> (ibid.: 171)

How can we reconcile the instantaneous creation-destruction of nominal bancor with the possibility for the ICU to provide financial intermediation granting the payment of net commercial imports? Schmitt answers this question by observing that, according to Keynes's insights, the net sum of bancor obtained by the net exporting countries, B, is necessarily and immediately deposited with the ICU, which lends it at once to the net importing countries, A. Hence, the ICU acts as a financial intermediary; it borrows from B and lends to A the real bancor required for the payment of country A's net commercial imports. 'The *financial bancor* is lent by the net exporting countries and borrowed by deficit countries' (Schmitt 1985c: 208, m.t.).

Two arguments confirm this reading of Keynes's plan:

1) His repeated claims that the bancor paid in excess by a deficit country is necessarily 'transferred to the bank account of another customer' (Keynes 1980b: 44);
2) His assertion that what is hoarded by an individual or a country is necessarily lent, by commercial banks or by the ICU, to other individuals or to other countries. 'If an individual hoards his income [...] by keeping a bank deposit, this bank deposit is not withdrawn from circulation but provides his banker with the means of making loans to those who need them' (ibid.: 273).

The ICU's financial intermediation entails the sale of financial claims by the deficit countries that borrow from the ICU and the purchase of financial claims by the surplus countries that lend to the ICU. Once the financial market is taken into account it appears that real payments take place in compliance with the law of sales-purchases, the net commercial purchases of A being financed through an equivalent net sale of financial claims. '*The creditor countries obtain the real equivalent of their own exported product, under the form of a claim issued by the importing countries*' (Schmitt 1988a: 120, m.t.).

Finally, net exporting countries finance their net commercial exports through the loan they automatically grant, via the ICU's financial intermediation, to net importing countries. The ICU's financial role is precisely that of lending at once the sum of bancor earned by countries from their international trade. In so doing, the ICU guarantees both the real payment of all international transactions, and the vehicular use of the bancor, whose neutrality is thus granted by the necessary equilibrium of countries' monetary balances of payments.

### *The shortcomings of Keynes's plan*

As observed by Schmitt, despite its deep insights and its revolutionary implications, Keynes's plan fails to make a clear distinction between national and international monetary flows as well as between nominal and real bancor. Let us start with the former.

#### *National and international monetary circuits*

Keynes claims that the new international currency would not circulate within countries but would convey the payments between central banks, the ICU acting as the central bank of central banks. While it is perfectly correct to limit the circulation of the bancor to the international level, it is not acceptable to conceive the ICU as the bank of banks unless one is prepared to transform national countries into regions of a sole, planetary nation.

> [T]he institution of the international Bank would amount to the redefinition of the pyramidal vertex of member banking systems: indeed, the central bank of adhering countries would be to the international Bank what commercial banks are to their central bank. It follows that in the monetary zone capped by the supranational Bank a sole, unified currency would circulate, national bank currencies being reduced to *regional or local* denominations of the new central currency issued by the supranational institution.
>
> (Schmitt 1987a: 196, m.t.)

What Keynes misses is the distinction between a country considered as the sum of its residents and the same country considered as the set of its residents. It is only if the ICU operates as the bank of countries each considered as a whole or as set of residents that nations maintain their monetary sovereignty. To reach this objective, it is necessary to explain with great clarity that the flow of bancor must be separate and autonomous with respect to the flows of national currencies.

National and international circuits must not intersect: 'external payments and internal payments belong to rigorously disjoint circuits' (ibid.: 197, m.t.). Keynes's plan aims at preserving national monetary sovereignties; it also establishes that the ICU would deal exclusively with Treasuries or central banks. There is nothing wrong with that. What Keynes should have added is that in each country the central bank would have to be entrusted with creating a Bureau representative of the country as such. If he did not feel the need to do so it is because his analysis of monetary flows was still incomplete, as is confirmed by the lack of a clear definition of the nature and role of the real or financial bancor.

### *Nominal and real bancor*

In Keynes's proposals, the bancor is essentially conceived as a nominal currency designed to convey the payment of imports–exports. 'The principal object can be explained in a single sentence: to provide that money earned by selling goods to one country can be spent on purchasing the products of any other country' (Keynes 1980b: 270). This is confirmed by Keynes's choice to favour the monetary intermediation of the ICU over its financial intermediation. 'We have not adopted another possible feature of banking by which you have capital, subscribed capital, which you can lend out. That is an alternative way of approach which our plan does not adopt' (ibid.: 210). While it is absolutely correct to introduce the bancor as a nominal currency within the equality of each country's exports and imports, it is also necessary to explain how the bancor can become a unit of payment. In other words, the bancor must be explained both as a unit of account and as a unit of payment. In this second aspect, the bancor is a capital.

It is true that the bancor can become capital or a real currency only if it is first nominal money issued by the ICU as an asset-liability. It is also true that the bancor can finance only the sales-purchases, its own purchasing power being necessarily equal to zero. However, it is also certain that Keynes's plan must enable countries to run commercial deficits and that net commercial imports must be paid in real or financial bancor.

Even though Keynes claims that what is earned by a country is necessarily deposited and lent to other countries, he does not provide a satisfactory distinction between nominal and real (financial) bancor, between bancor as a unit of money and bancor as a unit of capital. The two bancor are closely related, but not identical. In the case of a net payment, the nominal bancor is transformed into capital and defines the external gain of net exporting countries as saved and lent to deficit countries. 'The financial bancor is the net asset formed by the saving of part of surplus countries' national product, savings deposited with the Union, available for the financing of deficit countries' net purchases' (Schmitt 1985d: 209, m.t.). Keynes did not fully master the distinction between money and capital, which is why his analysis of bancor as a unit of payment is insufficient and only partly explains how his plan works in the presence of net commercial deficits and surpluses.

## Schmitt's 1970s proposals for a world monetary reform

In the early 1970s, Schmitt works out his first proposals for a world monetary reform based on the creation of a supranational institution, which he calls the extended international monetary fund (XIMF), charged with the task of issuing a new international currency called the international dollar, or $i, and acting as a monetary and financial intermediary for any country adopting the new system of international payments.

Schmitt makes clear from the outset that, according to the nature of bank money, $i are to be issued as assets-liabilities, whereas XIMF's financial intermediation can concern only the positive deposits earned by countries in their international transactions. $i cannot be created by financial intermediation, and financial intermediation cannot be 'fed' out of money creation. XIMF's monetary and financial intermediations must therefore be kept rigorously separated, a condition obtained by the institution of two distinct and autonomous departments: 'the Issue Department (ID) and the Financial Department (FD)' (Schmitt 1973a: 6). As Schmitt clearly states in an unpublished paper dated 1972, '[t]he Issue Department exemplifies the rule according to which "loans make deposits"' (Schmitt 1972f: 2), while the FD follows the rule according to which 'deposits make loans'.

### *The Monetary or Issue Department and the Financial Department*

The Issue Department of the XIMF has no financial resources of its own so that its loans 'are necessarily taken out of non-existent deposits, that is "ex-nihilo"' (Schmitt 1973a: 7). In this respect, the XIMF's Issue Department acts on behalf of countries in the same way as commercial banks act on behalf of their clients. Nominal \$i are IOUs of the Issue Department; claims against the ID are balanced by its reciprocal claims against the country benefiting from its monetary creation. No financial reserve is created by the XIMF acting as a monetary intermediary. A nominal \$i has no purchasing power and its role is only that of conveying countries' sales-purchases. Every time a country has to pay for its imports, it borrows an amount of \$i from the XIMF's Issue Department, which instantaneously credits the exporting countries.

Let us represent in Table 8.1 the opening of a line of credit by the ID of the XIMF in favour of country A, entry (1), and the payment of A's imports from country B carried out by the XIMF on behalf of country A, entry (2).

Following Schmitt's suggestion, let us assume that countries adopting the new system ask their central banks to create a National Fund (later to be called Bureau) keeping 'the account of all transactions with both Departments of the XIMF' (Schmitt 1972f: 3). When the XIMF pays country B on behalf of country A, the Issue Department credits the National Fund of country B and debits that of A. Obviously, since the \$i issued by the XIMF have no value, this is only the beginning of the payment for A's imports, which cannot be *financed* by the XIMF's ID. Indeed, the nominal \$i issued by the ID 'finances' only *reciprocal* transactions. Since money defines a circular flow, the \$i must flow back to the Issue Department: '[b]y legal obligation, each National Fund must repay in the short run every international dollar which it has borrowed from the Issue Department' (ibid.: 2). Theoretically, the \$i are bound to flow instantaneously back to the Issue Department; in practice, it is enough to implement a mechanism whereby '[a]t the end of the day *every* country is able to give back to the monetary Department all the money that the Fund creates to finance the country's purchases during the day' (Schmitt 1977b: 129, m.t.).

How can the XIMF recover the claims created against itself by the Issue Department and lent to country A? To answer this question, we need to involve the intermediation of the XIMF's Financial Department. What is earned by country B through its net commercial sales is immediately and automatically

*Table 8.1* Emission of \$i by the XIMF's Issue Department and payment of country A's imports

| *Issue or Monetary Department of the XIMF* | | | |
|---|---|---|---|
| *Assets* | | *Liabilities* | |
| (1) Country A | \$i $x$ | Country A | \$i $x$ |
| (2) Country A | \$i $x$ | Country B | \$i $x$ |

transferred to the Financial Department, which invests it in country A. Country B's gain derived from its net sales is entered on the liabilities side of the FD, where it defines a deposit of *real* \$i. If during the day country B's residents are net purchasers of country A's financial assets, say up to y \$i, country B's deposits of \$i with the Financial Department are reduced accordingly and the remaining \$i entered on the FD's liabilities side are invested by the XIMF in the purchase of country A's financial claims (Table 8.2).

In our numerical example, through the sale of financial assets, country A recovers part of the $x$ \$i obtained from the Issue Department and spent on purchasing country B's domestic output. The remaining sum of \$i necessary to guarantee the perfect daily equilibrium of its monetary balance of payments comes from the investment of $x - y$ \$i carried out by the XIMF's Financial Department. As depicted in Figure 8.3, the entire amount of \$i issued by the first Department of the XIMF flows back to its point of injection at the end of the day.

### *Nominal and real \$i and the redundancy problem*

Carried out through the intermediation of the XIMF's two departments, the payment of international transactions takes place in compliance with the law of sales-purchases applied to countries. As for any other economic agent, the use of bank money imposes on countries, too, the necessary equality of their sales and purchases. It is because \$i define a monetary circular flow and because

*Table 8.2* Investment by the Financial Department of country B's net gain

| *Financial Department of the XIMF* | | | |
|---|---|---|---|
| *Assets* | | *Liabilities* | |
| (1) Reserves | \$i $x$ | Country B | \$i $x$ |
| (2) Country B | \$i $y$ | Reserves | \$i $y$ |
| (3) Investments | \$i $x-y$ | Country A | \$i $x-y$ |

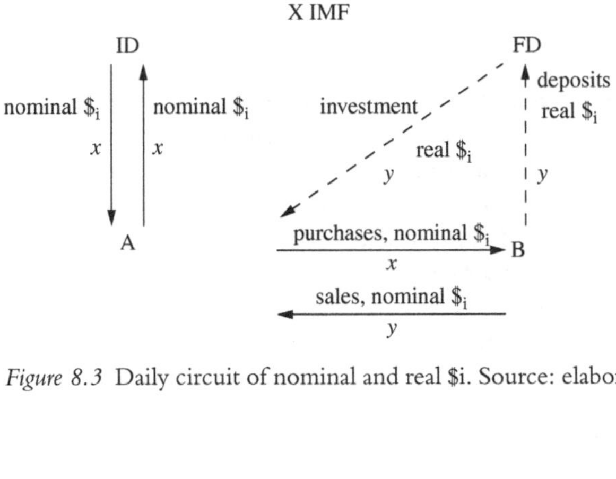


*Figure 8.3* Daily circuit of nominal and real \$i. Source: elaboration from Schmitt 1975b: 38

their own purchasing power is strictly equal to zero that countries' purchases must be financed by their simultaneous and equivalent sales. If this were not the case, international purchases would not be paid for at all. 'Only the equality of each country's sales and purchases in every period guarantees that surplus countries be effectively paid by deficit countries' (ibid.: 154, m.t.). Schmitt's plan complies with the law of sales-purchases: net commercial sales being necessarily matched by equivalent net financial purchases.

Initially, the payment of A's net commercial purchases produces an emission of *nominal* \$i by the XIMF's Monetary or Issue Department but is immediately taken over by the Financial Department, which credits the net exporting country, B, with a sum of *real* \$i. What marks the switch from nominal to real \$i is the formation of a gain derived from international trade. Through its net commercial sales, country B gains a positive income and not a mere sum of nominal money: 'the financial surplus, which was originally received in the form of currency [nominal \$i], is converted into quasi-money, that is, into an official claim to a specified sum of real \$i' (Schmitt 1972f: 22).

It is essential to understand that without the emission of nominal \$i the formation of an income in real \$i would be impossible. The XIMF cannot be at the origin of a positive income, which can derive solely from countries' exchanges. Yet, if the XIMF did not issue the \$i as nominal money, exchanges could not be numerically expressed. 'International dollars allow the world economy to progress from the age of barter to the full condition of unrestricted multilateral trade' (ibid.: 12).

As Schmitt observes, the nominal \$i is a vehicular means of payment whose circular flow prevents its consumption, whereas the real \$i is lent to net importing countries and spent by them. Real \$i are *fungible*: borrowing countries spend and destroy them and will have to pay back the FD with a new, future income.

> Real international dollars cannot be repaid, since they are entirely made away with and destroyed when the borrowers use and consume them. Nominal international dollars cannot be consumed, but rather they flow in a complete circle and ultimately remount to the Issue Department, their original source.
>
> (ibid.: 30)

At the end of each day, real \$i are spent and destroyed while nominal \$i flow back to the Issue Department; '[n]ot a single \$i, nominal or real, can survive from period to period' (Schmitt 1973a: 10).

Countries' external income is identifiable as the difference between each country's total sales and purchases of commercial goods and financial assets. In our example, country B earns an external income of $x - y$ \$i deposited with the XIMF's Financial Department. It is this net deposit of country B that is invested in country A, which means that what is obtained by A is B's external income and not a hypothetical income of the XIMF, which acts only as an intermediary. Yet, the investment of the Financial Department to the benefit of country A can take two different forms: it can identify in the purchase of financial claims denominated in $M_A$ and sold by A's residents or in the purchase of financial claims denominated in $i issued by country A itself, its National Fund or Bureau.

In the first case, no deficit of country A corresponds to the surplus of country B, whereas in the second case the so-called *redundancy* applies: the surplus of country B is the deficit of country A. Schmitt's new plan breaks the redundancy and introduces the possibility for the world financial balance to be positive: '(rich) countries can constitute positive reserves without imposing the slightest deficit to their (developing) partners' (Schmitt 1977b: 136, m.t.). Thanks to the reform advocated by Schmitt, the interests of rich and poor countries will no longer be opposed. The new system of international payments works in such a way that the net income earned by net exporting countries is automatically invested in the net importing countries, whose net imports are therefore paid by the former. Since the investment carried out through the intermediation of the XIMF's Financial Department can end up in the purchase of financial claims issued by the deficit countries' domestic economies, no external debt will result from it.

Poor countries would thus benefit from the possibility to import more without becoming indebted, and rich countries from the opportunity to invest more. 'If it is certain that advanced capitalism finds it profitable to invest abroad part of its financial capital as it is formed; less industrialized countries have interest in accepting this offer in order to develop and consolidate their production economies' (ibid.: 154–5, m.t.).

### *Countries' monetary and financial balance of payments*

The circular flows of nominal and real $i have different implications. In particular they call for a conceptual and practical distinction between countries' monetary and financial balances of payments, where the first refer to nominal money's flows and the second to the flows of real $i. As Schmitt points out, '[e] ach country must be careful to maintain continuous equilibrium in its *nominal* or monetary balance of payments. [...Whereas] there is no logic in the imposition of a permanent equilibrium in the *real* or financial balances of payments' (Schmitt 1973a: 14). The permanent equilibrium of countries' monetary balances is guaranteed by the rule that each country's national Bureau must on a daily basis refund the XIMF's Issue Department the exact amount of nominal $i it is credited with during the day. The rationale for this rule is the logical necessity to comply with the circular flow nature of bank money, of which the $i is the international manifestation.

As represented in Figure 8.3, the nominal $i issued by the Monetary or Issue Department flow back to it, also thanks to the intermediation of the

XIMF's Financial Department, which invests in country A the real $i earned by country B through its net commercial sales. This clearly shows that the monetary equilibrium of B's balance of payments is perfectly consistent with the disequilibrium of its financial balance of payments. Indeed, country B's financial balance is positive, because B is a net creditor of the XIMF's Financial Department, while its monetary balance is in equilibrium, because its loan to the FD defines a purchase of financial claims.

> When country [B] buys a fraction of the world's future incomes, its financial balance is positive insofar as country [B] becomes a positive creditor, but its nominal balance is nonetheless kept at perfect equipoise, since it has to pay for all its acquisitions including all its net purchases of future incomes.
>
> (Schmitt 1972f: 21)

On the other hand, since A's net commercial purchases are matched by equivalent net sales of financial claims, country A's monetary balance is in equilibrium while its financial balance can be either in equilibrium, if the FD invests B's deposits in securities sold by country A's domestic economy, or negative if the FD lends B's deposits to country A's national Bureau.

★

Let us observe here that in Schmitt's first versions of his plan the pathological nature of countries' external debt is not yet fully investigated. Therefore, his solution may induce the reader to wrongly believe that, despite its implementation, it is still possible for countries, as sets of their residents, to run into external debt. It is only in his later analysis of countries' sovereign debt that Schmitt fully clarifies this point and shows that countries can be definitively protected against the formation of an external debt burdening them; see Chapters 18 and 19.

★

### *The $i and national currencies' exchange rates*

The identity of each country's sales and purchases, as well as the distinction of nominal and real $i, confirm the fact that the new international currency issued by the XIMF is first of all a numerical standard whose function is to act as a common denominator for national currencies and as a vehicle for real payments among countries. 'The power to buy real commodities produced in the world belongs to the various *national* currencies. The international dollar simply *borrows* its purchasing power from all national currencies to which it is related by conventional exchange parities' (Schmitt 1973a: 8).

International payments are carried out *in primis* by residents to the benefit of non-residents. The former pay in their national currency and the latter are paid in their domestic currency. The $i is an intermediary whereby national currencies can be spent abroad; in other words, it conveys abroad the purchasing power required for the payment of countries' imports. Yet, this can only take place in compliance with the principle of *reciprocal* transactions, which means that, through the $i, an amount of purchasing power in money A can be spent in country B only to the extent that an equivalent amount of purchasing power in money B is simultaneously spent in country A.

In our example, everything happens as if country A purchased its own financial assets on behalf of B and country B purchased its own domestic output on behalf of A. The international dollar is 'the international form of national currencies' (Schmitt 1977b: 162, m.t.), to which it is related through a system of *absolute* exchanges. This means that in Schmitt's plan national currencies are no longer exchanged for one another; their relative exchange rates can only be derived from the absolute exchange rates they, individually, have with the $i. As a direct consequence, national currencies stop being identified with real goods. Likewise, exchange rates stop being considered as the relative prices of currencies and acquire stability that has nothing to do with the intervention of any monetary Authority but follows naturally from the withdrawal of national currencies from speculation. '[N]o gap will form between market and official exchange rates, because national currencies will no longer be exchanged among themselves, which will avert the actual, enormous speculations' (ibid.: 169, m.t.).

## The precursors of Schmitt's solution to international monetary disorder

In this last section we will trace some of the key elements for a new system of international payments as they were advocated by some great economists of the past. Our aim is to show that Schmitt's proposals are the culmination of an analysis started by the Classics and further developed by Keynes. Schumacher's contribution will also be mentioned, because his reform plan is highly original and complements Keynes's. Finally, a few remarks will be devoted to Davidson's viewpoint, which I take to be representative of the heterodox understanding of the problem of international payments in the years following the publication of Schmitt's first plan of reform. My choice of authors is very limited, and I am perfectly aware that several other plans of international monetary reform would deserve mention, for example, Triffin's (1961) and Machlup's (1963, 1964). However, those we discuss here are the most significant and are enough to give a hint of the process that led to Schmitt's new proposals.

### *Ricardo's insight*

In his 1823 manuscript *Plan for the Establishment of a National Bank* published posthumously in 1824, Ricardo tackles the problem of the Bank of England's privilege to issue banknotes and builds his analysis on the fact that

> [t]he Bank of England performs two operations of banking, which are quite distinct, and have no necessary connection with each other: it issues a paper currency as a substitute for a metallic one; and it advances money in the way of loan, to merchants and others.
>
> (Ricardo 1824/1951: 276)

Ricardo's aim is to show that the emission of bank money by the Bank of England shall never exceed the capacity of financial intermediation of this institution. More generally, his argument shows that money's neutrality requires a clear understanding of the logical distinction between nominal and real bank money as well as of the close interconnection between the banks' monetary and financial intermediations. Even though banks issue it, nominal money is effectively emitted by the economy, which transforms it into a sum of real money through its association with production. Banks are thus acting as both monetary and financial intermediaries.

In their first function, they provide the economy with the nominal money required to give physical products a homogeneous numerical form. In their second function, they transfer to economic agents the deposits resulting from the transformation of nominal into real money. The two functions are logically distinct and, as Ricardo suggests, should be carried out by two distinct bank departments. Although his argument refers explicitly to the Bank of England, his analysis applies to banks in general, because, as Schmitt observes, 'money is issued through an operation of credit; it has its origin in the banking system and not exclusively in the Bank (of England)' (Schmitt 1985a: 81, m.t.).

Monetary disequilibrium is avoided if these two functions are kept separate, if financial intermediation is never financed out of monetary creation. Ricardo is very clear: in no circumstances must payments be financed by printing money; nobody, Government included, must have direct access to money creation.

> If Government wanted money, it should be obliged to raise it in the legitimate way; by taxing the people; by the issue and sale of exchequer bills, by funded loans, or by borrowing from any of the numerous banks which might exist in the country; but in no case should it be allowed to borrow from those who have the power of creating money.
>
> (Ricardo 1824/1951: 283)

What is true of the Bank of England also applies to commercial banks and to the supranational bank envisaged by Keynes's and Schmitt's plans for an international monetary system. In this sense, Smith's distinction between nominal and real money (between money and money's value) and Ricardo's distinction between monetary and financial bank departments are both milestones on the road to the reforms so badly needed nationally and internationally.

### *Schumacher's multilateral clearing*

When Keynes was still working at his plan and before White's plan was accepted at Bretton Woods, the German economist Friedrich Schumacher published in

*Economica* what 'may be considered as the most comprehensive and penetrating plan for placing the world's money on a multiple-currency standard' (Schmitt 1972e: I.37).

Briefly summarized, Schumacher's idea is to internalize international payments through a system of National Clearing Funds, each of which is paid by the country's importers and pays country's exporters in national currency. When countries' exports and imports are perfectly balanced, the internalization of international payments is accomplished: in each country importers pay exporters in national money.

> Importers (of goods and services) make all payments in their own national currency into their own National Clearing Fund. As soon as the Fund has received payment, it informs the National Clearing Fund of the exporter that payment has been received, whereupon the National Clearing fund in the exporter's country makes payment to the exporter. Each National Clearing Fund thus receives and disburses only national currency: it receives such currency from the home importers and disburses it to the home exporters.
>
> (Schumacher 1943: 151)

In the case of trade equilibrium, purchasing power is entirely derived from national currencies proportionally to their exchange rates so that 'one might say, every national currency is made up into a world currency' (ibid.: 154).

Another important characteristic of the system advocated by Schumacher is that it is headed by an International Clearing Office, ICO, which 'requires no finance of its own' (ibid.: 153). The ICO is 'the central accounting office for the different National Clearing Funds' (ibid.: 154). It acts as an intermediary settling international transactions through multilateral clearing. As Schmitt observes, such a system is essentially analogous to the one based on the vehicular use of a \$i, at least to the extent that in both systems: balanced international payments are internalized, that neither the ICO nor the XIMF have the power to finance international transactions on their own, and that each country's commercial purchases are matched by equivalent commercial sales. 'The ultimate reason why the two plans virtually coincide when international trade is perfectly balanced in the short run lies in the fact that all nominal \$i flows are then fully compensated in the absence of any financial transfer' (Schmitt 1972e: I.41).

Things change radically when we move from trade equilibrium to trade surplus (deficit). Schumacher claims that net exporting countries are paid by acquiring a share in the Pool Clearing. In other words, their National Clearing Funds, NCFs, are credited with the net cash balances accumulated by the NCFs of net importing countries. The inflow of national currency due to the payment of importers being greater than the outflow corresponding to the payment of exporters, results in net importing countries' National Clearing Funds gaining a net amount of national currency, which they invest in the purchase of Treasury bills. Through the mediation of the International Clearing Office, these Treasury bills enter the Pool Clearing, and surplus countries acquire shares of the Pool up to the amount of their respective surpluses.

Unfortunately, Schumacher's plan fails to deal with trade surpluses (deficits), because their effective payment requires the expenditure of an income formed through international transactions. To show it, Schmitt resorts to a simple example. Suppose country A exports the totality of its current production to R, the rest-of-the-world. The income generated in A by domestic production enables the purchase of total output and nothing more, regardless of whether it is spent by households or firms. In Schumacher's system, if country A's total output is exported, A cannot import more than the equivalent of its domestic income. In so doing, country A balances its exports with an equal amount of commercial imports: nothing is left to finance its hypothetical net imports. 'When imports exceed exports, the extra quantity of purchasing power which is needed cannot be derived from income currently produced in the importing country' (ibid.: I.43).

What Schumacher's plan is missing is a financial intermediation creating a link between present external income of surplus countries and future external incomes of deficit countries. Payments in his scheme are effective insofar as 'international trade is constantly subjected to the constraint of a strict balance between the values of every country's exports and imports' (ibid.: I.44). His requirement that

> every country must ultimately pay for what it buys, which means, in the long run, that it must achieve a position in which it can supply as much in goods and services to the rest of the world as it receives.
>
> (Schumacher 1943: 155)

is far too restrictive. The equality of each country's sales and purchases is, correctly, a must, but it refers to commercial *and* financial goods. Net commercial imports are paid through equivalent net financial exports, a mechanism that requires the intervention of the XIMF, as a financial intermediary, and of the \$i, both as a nominal and as a real international currency.

### *Keynes's contribution*

Having already considered the main aspects of Keynes's plan for the establishment of an International Clearing Union, it suffices here to recall the pivotal role played by the emission of an international currency based on the essential principle of banking: 'the necessary equality of credits and debits, of assets and liabilities' (Keynes 1980: 44). Keynes conceives of the bancor as a nominal currency used to convey *balanced* payments between countries. Consistent with the teachings of Ricardo, the ICU is subdivided into two departments, monetary and financial. Yet, priority is given to the Monetary or Issue Department. The ICU's financial intermediation occurs within the circular flow of nominal bancor, in compliance with the neutrality of the new international currency. Through the mechanism of multilateral clearing, every country balances its commercial and financial sales with equivalent purchases.

Schumacher's intuition that purchases can be financed only through sales, since real goods must always be exchanged with real goods, finds here its confirmation and is taken to completion: the equivalence is obtained through the intermediation of an international currency and includes the sales and purchases of financial assets. Keynes's great merit is to have advocated the creation of international bank money as well as its circular use within a system of multilateral clearing.

### *Davidson as a representative of the heterodox viewpoint*

Regrettable as it may be, Schmitt's reform proposals have so far largely failed to attract the endorsement of the scientific community. Their impact on the work of heterodox economists, sadly, did not fare any better. Davidson's attempt at reformulating Keynes's plan, for example, misses its target because, while apparently close to Keynes's notion of international currency, it confuses the emission of a nominal, vehicular money with that of a positive real money.

> What is required is a closed double-entry bookkeeping clearing institution to keep the payments 'score' among the various trading nations plus some mutually agreed upon rules to create and reflux international liquidity while maintaining the purchasing power of the created international currency of the international clearing union.
>
> (Davidson 2008: 15)

Davidson's understanding of the nature of international money is as limited and mistaken as his understanding of the nature of national money. He defines money as

> that thing that by delivery discharges contractual obligations [...;] as a temporary abode of general purchasing power [whose acceptance] involves no risks (only uncertainties), since the State will enforce enactment of all future offer contracts which may be entered into, in terms of the unit of account.
>
> (Davidson 1972: 107)

No trace is left of Keynes's principle of banking or of Ricardo's distinction between banks' monetary and financial intermediations.

Davidson's own proposal for changing the international payments system suffers from his limited conception of money. While he rightly points out that the currency issued by the ICU is 'not available to be held by the public' (Davison 2008: 16) and that 'private international transactions clear between central banks' accounts in the book of the international clearing institution' (ibid.: 16), he advocates a series of measures that have nothing to do with a mechanism of monetary multilateral clearing capable of guaranteeing the neutrality of the new international currency. In particular, Davidson calls for a system able

> (1) to prevent a lack of global effective demand [...] (2) to provide an automatic mechanism for placing a major burden of correcting international payments imbalances on the surplus nations, (3) to provide each nation with the ability to monitor and, if desired, to control international movements of funds [..., and] (4) to expand the quantity of the liquid assets used in settling international contracts.
>
> (ibid.: 15)

None of these objectives concern the establishment of a new macroeconomic structure of international payments. The set of rules proposed by Davidson to reach these objectives is nothing more than a series of microeconomic measures whose implementation is supposed to have a positive impact on economic agents' behaviour. To this extent, his proposals do not substantially differ from those supported by orthodox, mainstream economics. Despite his effort to revive Keynes's plan, Davidson fails to apprehend its originality, which essentially consists of the attempt to provide the world with a system of international payments totally independent of any set of rules concerning monetary and economic policies.

Davidson is on the right track when he takes over Keynes's suggestion that the payment of trade deficits must involve surplus countries, not only deficit countries. Yet, he misses the fact that it is through the circular flow of the bancor and through multilateral clearing that the earnings of trade surplus countries are automatically lent to trade deficit countries. As revisited by Schmitt, the ICU's financial intermediation makes sure that net commercial imports of deficit countries are always matched by their equivalent net exports of financial assets. Davidson's suggestion that, if surplus countries do not spend their credits 'the clearing agency would confiscate [...] the portion of credit deemed excessive' (ibid.: 19–20), is symptomatic of his essentially microeconomic approach. If Schmitt's plan were to stand on such premises, it would deserve to be immediately rejected. The implementation of a system consistent with the principle of sales-purchases has nothing to do with Davidson's set of rules. It is only if the reform can enable the effective payment of net commercial purchases while enhancing the interests of both importing and exporting countries that it will be implemented eventually.

> Only the equality of purchases and sales of every country in each period guarantees that surplus countries are effectively paid by deficit countries. The supranational currency thus establishes the solidarity of countries, by making their opposed needs to converge on the financial market.
>
> (Schmitt 1977b: 154, m.t.)

# 9 Schmitt's contribution to the debate on European monetary unification

1975–1988

The aim of this chapter is to analyze two plans of reform of the system of external payments in European countries. Proposed by Schmitt in the 1970–1980s, one applied to the eurozone, and the other was limited to a single country. The first part of the chapter deals with the former: while stressing the main shortcomings of the European project of monetary unification, Schmitt's reform still enables European countries to maintain their monetary sovereignty. The writings referenced in this context are Schmitt's books *Génération de la monnaie des monnaies européennes* (1975) and *L'ECU et les souverainetés nationales en Europe* (1988), as well as the unpublished manuscript *Devenir de l'ECU, avenir de l'Europe* (1986). The second part of the chapter is devoted to the first version of Schmitt's plan to enable any single country to protect itself against the errors of the present non-system of international payments and its structural fragility. In his attempt to find a viable solution, which a country could adopt without causing harm to its trading partners, Schmitt considers the case of his own country, France; hence I will make reference to his book *La France souveraine de sa monnaie* (1984).

## Schmitt's alternative to the present European Monetary System

Before considering Schmitt's plan for the creation of a European Monetary System (EMS) of external payments, let us comment on his critical assessment of the present EMS.

### *The pros and cons of monetary unification*

Let us assume for a moment that European countries were successful in transforming their national currencies into a new, single currency called euro, issued in exactly the same way by each bank operating in the eurozone and entering a catalytic process of clearing managed by the European Central Bank (ECB) with the assistance of the different national central banks of the eurozone.

The advantage of replacing the original national currencies with a singular currency and the national monetary systems with a single European monetary system is that they would put a stop to any *erratic fluctuations of exchange*

DOI: 10.4324/9781351271325-13

*rates*. Acting as the central bank of the EMS, the ECB would issue the euro as the common form of all the currencies issued by every bank, commercial or central, operating in the eurozone. Replaced by the euro, domestic currencies would simply disappear, together with the problem of their reciprocal exchange. As we have already seen (Chapter 8), exchange rates tend to fluctuate erratically because nominal currencies are pathologically transformed into objects of exchange. In the foreign exchange market, national currencies are traded 'as if money were a consumption-good, or a production-good, a share or a security' (Schmitt 1986b: 112, m.t.). It is clear that if European domestic currencies were replaced by the euro, they would no longer be the object of reciprocal exchange. Within the eurozone, exchange rates would become a thing of the past since the disappearance of national currencies implies the disappearance of their exchange rates. One of the main objectives of the European project, namely exchange rate stability, would therefore be achieved by suppressing the very cause of its fluctuation: the exchange of European domestic currencies between themselves.

Now, reality does not correspond to this scenario. The premise for the existence of a single currency clash with the mechanism adopted by the EMS is to convey payments among residents of the different member countries. Today, the real-time gross settlement system (RTGS) operated by the euro system (TARGET 2) is not an RTGS applied to every transnational payment carried out by residents of the eurozone. In the absence of a generalized clearing system, euros issued by national banking systems are bound to remain heterogeneous, as the introduction of a singular currency remains an unfinished project with a highly uncertain future. In its current form, the EMS is incomplete and ill-equipped to carry through monetary unification. The lack of a generalized mechanism of clearing, which would be run by the ECB and would concern all payments carried out between residents of the eurozone, prevents the ECB from attributing a common monetary form to the currencies issued by the banks, commercial and central, operating in the eurozone. As a result, the euros issued within each member country do not pertain to the same monetary zone; they remain as heterogeneous as the national currencies they have replaced. The entries into the accounts of TARGET 2, proof of the existence of substantial debts of some countries and of the equivalent credits of others, are a mark of this state of affairs.

If the euro worked as the single currency it was intended, domestic currencies would no longer exist, and euro-member countries would be transformed into regions of the same monetary area. In such a framework, *the very concept of external debt affecting member countries would lose its meaning*; it would become impossible for a member country to run into debt, directly or indirectly, with another member country. This is far from being the case today, where there are as many different euros as there are member countries of the eurozone. Currently, countries within the eurozone have relinquished their monetary sovereignty and impaired their ability to promote their domestic economies. Indeed, European monetary unification not only clashes with the desire for political sovereignty but it also makes economic convergence (another important objective set by the advocates of the EU) all the harder to attain. Economic discrepancies between euro-member countries have increased since the adoption of the euro because the loss of monetary sovereignty has deprived euro-member countries of the possibility of adopting monetary and fiscal policies better suited to further their economic development. Moreover, by giving up their national currencies, euro countries have partly dismantled the 'protective barrier' of their national monetary systems, which impeded the flight of capital from the poorer to the richer countries. European countries are living in the worst of all possible worlds: lacking the benefit of a unifying currency along with the loss of monetary sovereignty.

Two alternatives are still open to euro-member countries:

1) Modifying the EMS to transform the national euros into a truly singular currency and the eurozone into the United States of Europe.
2) Adopting a reform to enable member countries to recover their monetary sovereignty while providing a mechanism of external payments that guarantees the stability of exchange rates.

The first alternative is unlikely because of a lack of political will but could become feasible in the future; the second alternative is what Schmitt's monetary reform proposes.

### *Schmitt's plan for the creation of a European system of payments*

In Schmitt's view, any plan aimed at adopting a European currency by abolishing monetary sovereignties and creating the United States of Europe is utopian. He proposes, instead, a plan to provide European member countries with a common monetary system for their external payments. The problem he addresses and focuses on is a macroeconomic one: it treats countries as the sets of their residents and addresses the need to convey abroad the international payments carried out by their residents in domestic currencies. In economics, a nation or country is defined by a given geopolitical space if the currencies issued by the banks operating within this space share a common form, namely, that of the currency issued by the central bank to convey inter-banking payments. National central banks act as 'catalysts' and provide a common form to the IOUs issued by domestic commercial banks; this is the necessary condition for the existence of a common monetary space within a single country. Nations will exist as macroeconomic entities as long as countries remain monetarily sovereign, that is, as long as their banks are part of one sole national system. 'Every commercial bank whose emissions engage a given central bank forms a system – or a unity – with it' (Schmitt 1986b: 96, m.t.).

In the same way as payments between national banks require a central bank, payments between countries require the intervention of an international central bank to provide the common form of their national currencies. The crucial step of Schmitt's plan was therefore to call for the European Central Bank to play the role of a central bank of national central banks and to issue thereby the common, numerical denominator of member countries' domestic currencies. Within any national banking system, commercial banks' IOUs are freely exchangeable for one another, because inter-banking payments enter a mechanism of clearing, which renders them homogeneous; 'because it makes them homogeneous to central currency' (ibid.: 99, m.t.). What the European member countries need is an analogously functioning mechanism, which establishes the homogeneity of their national currencies, so that each of them can 'identify itself, by substitution, to the currency of another member country' (ibid.: 99, m.t.).

The task of the new European Central Bank would be, first, to issue the euro as nominal money, a currency that enables the monetization of member countries' external transactions. Since it would be issued by the ECB as nominal or vehicular money intended to convey countries' external payments, the euro would not replace the domestic currencies of member countries.

> National bank currencies will maintain the monopoly of the "monetization" *of every transaction on the internal markets* of member countries; the [euro], a multinational bank money, will have the monopoly of the "monetization" *of every external transaction* of member countries.
>
> (Schmitt 1988a: 49, m.t.)

The monetization of countries' domestic output is already made possible by the existence of national currencies. At the European level, the problem is how to monetize member countries' external transactions by applying a common numerical standard. To this effect, the ECB would issue the euro as its spontaneous acknowledgement of debt and lend it to the importing member country, which would use it as a vehicle to pay exporting countries. The principle is once again that of banking: the identity between assets and liabilities. As an ECB liability, the euro is at the same time an asset, because it is due to the ECB by the importing country that benefits from its emission. Since banks – be they commercial, central, or international – cannot create positive purchasing power, their IOU can define only an asset-liability. Like any other bank money, the euro is issued as a purely numerical form and not as an amount of money-income. Since productions occur within countries, the euro can be associated with them only *indirectly*, through its temporary substitution for national currencies. Instead of being the common denominator of produced output, the euro would therefore be the common numerical standard of national currencies. Each paying member country would carry out its foreign payment through the monetary intermediation of the new ECB.

### *The monetary intermediation of the ECB*

While Schmitt's early versions of his plan for a new European Monetary System follow closely his 1970s proposals for a world monetary reform (see Chapter

8), in his writings of the late 1980s he emphasizes the monetary aspect of the ECB's mediation, hardly mentioning the possible intervention of the ECB as a financial intermediary. His explicit aim is to show the logical priority of monetary intermediation. The emission of the euro as nominal money comes first, logically, because it is thanks to this emission that international transactions and payments can be measured. The euro is first of all the numerical unit necessary to express national currencies in a common, numerical standard. *It is through the determination of absolute exchange rates that national currencies will become homogeneous, that is, through the instantaneous circular exchange of any of them with the euro.*

Suppose that European countries implement Schmitt's reform; if so, let us analyze what happens when two countries, A and B, carry out their reciprocal payments in a situation in which their global imports, commercial and financial, are equal to their global exports. When country A pays country B, it does so by borrowing from the new ECB the necessary amount of nominal euros to pay B on its behalf. Like any other bank money, the euro is defined by its instantaneous circular flow, which means that it must immediately flow back to its issuing bank.

In our example, country A must pay back the ECB as soon as the ECB pays country B, which is indeed possible because, by assumption, A's purchases are equal to its sales (B's purchases). The perfect reciprocity between country A's and country B's purchases (sales) is in line with the circular flow of the euros issued for the payment of A and B. Now, it is essential to note that the equality of country A's and country B's sales and purchases is not just one among many possibilities. In reality, the equality between each country's sales and purchases is the logical identity the system of external payments has to comply with. In practice, this means that the EMS must provide the mechanism for the circular use of the euro so that each member country's purchases are always financed by equivalent sales. The new ECB's main role is to act as a monetary intermediary; as such, it can only provide euro-member countries with nominal money used to convey reciprocal payments. The ECB can never issue a positive *income*, that is, a money capable of *financing* net payments: 'bank money accomplishes simultaneously *two functions of opposite sign*, because it pays at the same time the purchases *and sales* of each commercial partner' (ibid.: 131, m.t.).

If we consider the euro's circular flow in the payment of country A's purchases and sales, we see that the exchange of a sum of money A, $x\ M_A$, paid by A's importers, for a sum of euros, $y$ €, is immediately offset by the reciprocal exchange of $y$ € for $x\ M_A$ paid to country A's exporters. The same operation defines the exchange of $M_A$ against $M_A$ through the euro. Analogously, country B's domestic currency enters an absolute exchange with the euro as represented in Figure 9.1.

As a matter of fact, the emission of the euro defines from the outset an absolute exchange because

> [e]very emission is *strictu sensu* a *conversion* [...and] every conversion is an objective mutation, the final object, the result of the operation, being

> distinct from the initial object, which has undergone the 'metamorphosis'. Such conversion is hence an 'absolute' exchange, a *change strictu sensu*: the converted object is *changed* into another object, which means that it is *destroyed in its original form.*
>
> (ibid.: 67, m.t.)

Through the emission of the euro, the domestic currency conveying the importers' payment, $x$ $M_A$, is changed into a sum of euros and vice versa. This first absolute exchange is necessarily matched by another absolute exchange of opposite sign, where the euro is changed back into $x$ $M_A$. This is so because of the vehicular nature of nominal money: the emission of the euro implies both its creation and its instantaneous destruction. Like any other currency, the euro must be issued in a circular flow, in a wavelike movement that defines its transformation into a sum of national currency and its immediate conversion back to its initial form.

What is true for the euro is also true for the national currencies of member countries: they also enter an absolute exchange with the euro that makes it impossible for any of them to become an object that can be sold and purchased as if it were a real good. Vehicular currencies cannot be final objects of purchase, they are neither consumption- or investment-goods, nor shares or securities, and a mechanism guaranteeing their absolute exchange is the only one respectful of their very nature.

> [I]t is necessary and sufficient that every currency thrown into external payments flows back fully and through an ineluctable mechanism to the importing country itself, which will thus be debited *and* credited in the same movement, which confirms the validity of the payment because it will be wave-like.
>
> (Schmitt 1986b: 113, m.t.)

The aim of Schmitt's plan is to provide European member countries with a common currency, a uniform, numerical means of payment, which enables the *conveyance* of payments between member countries, not their financing. In accordance with the circular flow of the euro, the terms of inter-European exchanges will be actual; purchases of real goods, services, and financial assets will be financed by equivalent real sales.

What is needed is a system of European payments where countries' imports are coupled with their exports. To have a real content, monetary payments

$M_A$ x ⟶ Euro y ⟶ $M_A$ x

$M_B$ z ⟶ Euro y ⟶ $M_B$ x

*Figure 9.1* The absolute exchange of $M_A$ and $M_B$.

must be reciprocal. This calls for the implementation of a mechanism guaranteeing the equilibrium of each country's global balance of payments, that is, the necessary equality of total imports and exports. In compliance with monetary circular flow analysis, credit payments must be immediately balanced by debit payments, so that they merge into a single flow of debit-credit or credit-debit.

Schmitt observes that the logical requirement of the vehicular use of the currency chosen as a means of payment between countries is more stringent than the contingent equality of imports and exports. Even if, in a given period, a country's exports happen to be equal to its imports, this is not enough to avoid 'fake' payments and their pathological consequences. What is needed is an integration: a coupling of each country's exports and imports, rather than mere coexistence: 'co-existence does not mean *fusion: even for the balanced part of its external accounts the country receives and carries out payments that are entirely false, because they infringe the rule of monetary flows' validity*' (Schmitt 1984b: 85, m.t.).

### *Two possible ways to implement Schmitt's plan for a new European Monetary System*

As previously observed, Schmitt provides two complementary analyses of the reform he advocates: one retracing his proposals for a world monetary reform and one, chronologically later, leaving out the financial intermediation of the new European Central Bank. Let us start with the second.

#### *The case where the ECB does not act as a financial intermediary*

The initial step consists in creating an institution within each member country. We shall call it the National Bureau, and it will represent the country considered as a whole, as the set of its residents. The National Bureau, or simply the Bureau, has two faces: one of them, the Internal Department, is oriented towards the country's domestic economy, the other, the External Department, faces the ECB. Every external payment of a country's residents must first be made to the Bureau, which is credited in national currency. As soon as its Internal Department is credited by the commercial banks acting on behalf of the country's importers, the Bureau's External Department asks the new ECB to pay the exporting country. At this point, the ECB must apply the principle of the necessary equality of the country's sales and purchases. It does so by implementing a mechanism like the one adopted by national central banks when acting as clearing houses: the real-time gross settlement system, RTGS. The payment in euros of country B, the exporting country, will in practice take place only if country A, the importing country, is simultaneously credited for its exports to other countries. If the eurozone were reduced to two countries, A and B, country A's commercial and financial purchases would have to be matched by equivalent sales of commercial and/or financial assets to country B.

Acting exclusively as a monetary intermediary, the ECB in its new role makes sure that country A's purchases are financed by equivalent sales and conveys the reciprocal payments by issuing the same amount of nominal euros for country A and for country B.

> If A did not have the *funds* necessary for the payment of its purchases, it would not be backed by the Bank of Europe, which would instruct A as follows: find first on the market of your choice (commercial or financial) the totality of the necessary financing of your imports; when you have all the necessary funds at your disposal I will [...] give them the form of my own currency allowing you to pay in [euros] your importers.
>
> (Schmitt 1988a: 142, m.t.)

In our bilateral example, country A has to find the funds required for the new ECB to convey the payment of A's importers through its commercial and financial sales to country B. As represented in Table 9.1, the amount of money A paid to the Internal Department of A's Bureau by country A's importers is used by the latter to pay country A's exporters; the same *internalization* takes place in country B, where B's importers pay B's exporters.

In the new regime, European member countries' balances of payments concern only the flows of euro, and the system provides a mechanism guaranteeing their automatic equilibrium. Consistent with the vehicular nature of nominal money, euros are issued in a circular movement defining the credit-debit of each country involved. In our example, the inflow of euros benefiting country

*Table 9.1* A bilateral example of the implementation of the RTGS system between European member countries

| *Assets* | | *Liabilities* | |
|---|---|---|---|
| Bureau of A (internal department) | | | |
| Importers | $M_A$ $x$ | (Bureau of A) External department | $M_A$ $x$ |
| (Bureau of A) External department | $M_A$ $x$ | Exporters | $M_A$ $x$ |
| Bureau of A (external department) | | | |
| (Bureau of A) Internal department | $M_A$ $x$ | ECB | Euro $y$ |
| ECB | Euro $y$ | (Bureau of A) Internal department | $M_A$ $x$ |
| ECB | | | |
| Bureau of A (external department) | Euro $y$ | Bureau of B (external department) | Euro $y$ |
| Bureau of B (external department) | Euro $y$ | Bureau of A (external department) | Euro $y$ |
| Bureau of B (external department) | | | |
| ECB | Euro $y$ | (Bureau of B) Internal department | $M_B$ $z$ |
| (Bureau of B) Internal department | $M_B$ $z$ | ECB | Euro $y$ |
| Bureau of B (internal department) | | | |
| (Bureau of B) External department | $M_B$ $z$ | Exporters | $M_B$ $z$ |
| Importers | $M_B$ $z$ | (Bureau of B) External department | $M_B$ $z$ |

RTGS, real-time gross settlement; ECB, European Central Bank.

A is immediately matched by an equivalent outflow, as is the inflow of euros issued by the ECB in order to vehiculate or convey country B's purchases. Finally, both the payment of countries A's and B's purchases are financed by equivalent sales of these same countries. Real goods, commercial and financial, are exchanged against real goods of the same value thanks to the intermediation of the euro, which makes it possible to compare the (numerical) value of the goods traded and to internalize their payment. The mechanism implemented to grant the circular use of the euro is enough to make sure that each country's monetary balance of payments is always perfectly in equilibrium, as no external payment is ever *financed* by the nominal money issued by the new European Central Bank.

### *The solution integrating the financial intermediation of the European Central Bank*

A related solution advocated by Schmitt includes the possibility that the new ECB may act as a financial intermediary as well. This time, payments between euro-member countries do not imply only the use of nominal money but also lead to the emission of real money. As in the previous case, the euro is issued as a nominal currency, yet this time its circular flow includes its transformation into real money deposited in the Financial Department of the ECB. We must clarify from the outset that, if European countries' external transactions were not monetized and paid through the emission of *nominal* euros, no *real* euros could ever form. The logical priority rests with the emission of a vehicular currency; real euros are linked to the payment of negative nominal balances, whose very existence requires the previous emission of nominal euros.

> Financial balances are paid in real money. Now, it is certain that the real euro can only exist on the basis of the nominal euro. [...] Negative nominal balances must be paid in real euros. It is therefore necessary that *all payments* be made in nominal euros.
>
> (Schmitt 1975b: 29, m.t.)

The analysis proposed by Schmitt in his 1975 book on the euro as the currency of European currencies develops along the same lines as his proposals for a world currency, which we investigated in Chapter 8. The proposal introduces a distinction between the Monetary and the Financial Departments of the new ECB and suggests implementing a mechanism that grants the coexistence of the circular flow of nominal euros and the formation of positive deposits of real euros. Thanks to the financial intermediation of the European Central Bank, the real euros earned by a country through its net global sales and deposited with the ECB's Financial Department, FD, are immediately lent to or invested in the net importing country, whose monetary balance of payments is thus always in equilibrium. For example, if country B is a net exporter, its gain is in the form of real euros and defines its external savings, which, being deposited in the ECB's Financial Department, are necessarily lent. 'Real euros define

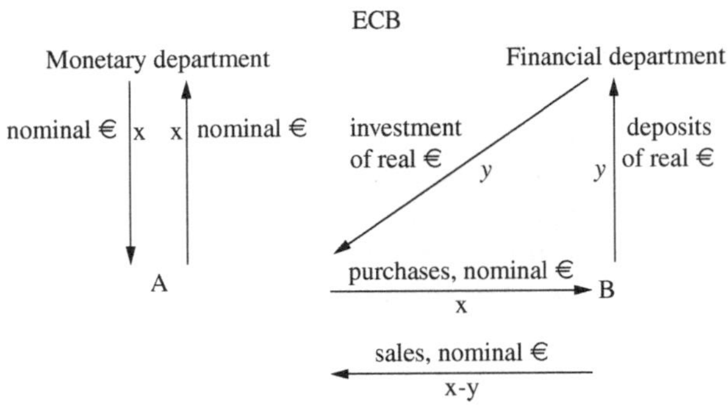


*Figure 9.2* ECB's monetary and financial intermediations. Source: elaboration from Schmitt 1975b: 38

at the same time the net international income and the saving of this income, because, if the international income were spent instead of saved, it would no longer be net' (ibid.: 34, m.t.). The presence of real euros does not break the circular flow of nominal euros because the sum saved by net importing countries is immediately transformed into an investment. In the example of two countries, A and B, used so far, the mechanism involving the monetary and Financial Departments of the ECB is reproduced in Figure 9.2.

The real euros deposited with the ECB's Financial Department, which is the difference between a country's total sales and purchases, define the official reserves gained by the net exporting country and are made up of financial claims. Performing its role of financial intermediary, the new European Central Bank invests the real euros deposited with its Financial Department in the purchase of claims of the net importing countries denominated either in their national currencies or in euros. In both cases, net importing countries benefit from an investment that finances their net imports, which follows from the fact that net exports are paid by net exporting countries (on behalf of their deficit partners). Finally, every country that adopts the reform balances its purchases with equivalent sales. In particular, the circular flow of the nominal euros enforces the necessary equality between commercial and financial imbalances: 'the necessary and sufficient condition of financial capitals' net export is the net export of goods and services. [...] This equivalence is imposed by the equality of nominal euros' flux and reflux' (ibid.: 44, m.t.).

## The advantages of Schmitt's plan

### *Exchange rate stability*

Creating the euro as the nominal means of payment used by European member countries for external transactions would mark *the switch from relative to absolute exchange rates*, thus guaranteeing exchange rate stability while enabling countries to recover their monetary sovereignty. There is no need to insist on the benefit European countries would derive from the re-establishment of their monetary sovereignty. Economic divergences are still too important to deny countries the possibility of adopting monetary and fiscal policies better suited to their specific needs. Thanks to Schmitt's plan, European countries would be able to recover their autonomy without relapsing into a disorderly system characterized by erratic fluctuations in exchange rates, because the circular emission of the euro would introduce the regime of absolute exchange rates. National or international currencies would be withdrawn permanently from the money market. Since each country would necessarily be credited-debited or debited-credited in euros, no external payment would ever be financed through money creation, and currencies would no longer be traded, sold and purchased, as if they were real goods.

> In fact, every demand for currency [B] exerted through the [euro] takes place in a wavelike operation launched by the [new ECB]: in the same flux-reflux the importing country purchases *x* [euros] to sell them immediately, because *it gets them only to pay country* [*B*], which deposits them at once with the [ECB].
>
> (Schmitt 1986b: 135, m.t.)

***Monetary stability and increase in cross-border transactions***

Another benefit of Schmitt's plan is *the increase in monetary stability*, which European countries would gain from the introduction of the vehicular use of the euro. Indeed, external transactions would no longer have an inflationary or a deflationary impact on trading countries. Being issued as an asset-liability, the euro is necessarily created and destroyed so that it can never be a source of inflation (which would result from a net creation) or deflation (which would derive from net destruction). '[E]very purchasing power spent in euro is gained in euro, and every purchasing power gained in euro is spent in euro. Therefore, the new currency cannot introduce any disequilibrium, either inflation or deflation, in the country's economy' (Schmitt 1975b: 57, m.t.).

Both versions of Schmitt's plan would increase European member countries' external transactions, yet the version that incorporates the financial intermediation of the new ECB would have the greater impact. Net exporting countries would indeed benefit from the formation of persistent surpluses, which would enable them to increase their official reserves with the ECB. Invested by the European Central Bank in the net importing countries, these official reserves would take the form of euro-bonds and be the source of interest. 'Precisely, the placements in euro-bonds, which constitute the final form of every official reserve, benefit from the exchange rate's guarantee specific to the euro. On the other hand, these placements generate an interest' (ibid.: 49, m.t.). As for net importing countries, the ECB's investment of the gain made by exporting countries would finance their net purchases and enable them to pay for their net imports through the sale of financial claims. Less developed countries would benefit from this increase in their imports, and more developed countries would be able to invest their financial capitals at a profit.

### *The net gain of countries' national bureaux*

As is often the case with Schmitt's works, his 1986 manuscript devotes a few pages to introduce a far-reaching idea – only to pick it up and develop it more fully later. His insight is difficult to understand at this point because it goes against the grain of traditional thinking. While analyzing the advantages of moving from a disorderly to an orderly system of European payments that remains respectful of the monetary sovereignty of its member countries, Schmitt claims that, in his system, the National Bureau of each country, net importing or net exporting, makes net profits equal to the difference in its global external transactions.

#### *The gain of net importing countries*

Let us consider first what happens on the side of net importing countries.

By collecting the payments made by the country's importers and paying the country's exporters in national currency, the Bureau of every net importing country benefits from the numerical difference between inflows and outflows. What might come as a surprise is the fact that this gain in national currency is *net*, that is, it is not compensated by the increase in the country's external debt. Even though the Bureau might have to sell financial claims to the ECB to finance the country's net foreign purchases, this would have no repercussions on the debt of the country considered as a whole. The entire amount of real euros transferred from the ECB's Financial Department to the Bureau of deficit countries defines an *investment*. In exchange for this investment, net exporting countries obtain part of the deficit countries' internal resources, which makes up for the real payment of their net purchases. Having paid in full for their total imports, deficit countries do not incur any external debt: compliance with the law of sales-purchases is enough to avoid it.

The gain of the country's Bureau 'is *net and irreversible* because the regime of the emitted [euro] does not impose the smallest (external), *additional* debt to deficit countries' (Schmitt 1986b: 123, m.t.). As Schmitt observes, there is nothing original in the fact that macroeconomic savings, equal to the difference between the amount of domestic currency paid by importers and that paid to exporters, are made in the net importing countries. Macroeconomic savings always accrue, whatever the system of external payments. What differentiates the present non-system from an orderly system is that, in today's disorderly regime of external payments, macroeconomic savings are lost to the benefit of the financial bubble. In Schmitt's plan, the sum is gained by the Bureau: 'savings formed in net imports will be *invested* (in its country of origin) instead of being sterilized in the mass of euro-currencies [xeno-currencies], denatured capitals, purely *financial*' (ibid.: 124, m.t.).

Schmitt's analysis of the gain obtained by the Bureau of net importing countries, developed in his 1984 book *La France souveraine de sa monnaie*, is noticeably slightly different from the one advocated in his 1986 manuscript on the ECU. While in the latter he defines the gain as net and irreversible, in the former he distinguishes between what happens in the presence of a generalized regime of absolute exchange rates from what happens when a country is alone in adopting this regime and is confronted with the rest-of-the-world. In the first case, necessarily the gain is used by the Bureau to purchase domestic financial claims. Within a European regime of absolute exchange rates, for example, net imports define an equivalent purchase of euro-bonds by net exporting countries. Resulting from the deposits with the new European Central Bank, the purchase of these euro-bonds is accompanied by the investment of the gain of the Bureau in the domestic financial market. When a country, alone in adopting the new regime, pays for its net imports, the gain of the Bureau is net because it is the Bureau that collects, in the form of domestic currency, the investment of what is earned by net exporting countries through their net commercial sales.

Even though the differences between these two analyses are not trivial, they do not alter the fact that, whether adopted by numerous countries or by a single one, Schmitt's plan makes for a positive gain for the Bureau. Moreover, in both cases this gain is invested in the domestic economy of net importing countries and contributes to their development and to the consequent reduction in their future deficits. What matters most is that in both cases countries adopting Schmitt's reform benefit 'from the totality of their domestic product' (Schmitt 1984b: 251, m.t.): none of them would lose to the financial bubble the slightest part of their domestic resources.

### *The gain of net exporting countries*

As for net exporting countries, initially their Bureau's net gain takes the form of euro-claims with the ECB's Financial Department. Then, the Bureau can sell these claims to its domestic economy in exchange for a sum of national currency and use it, for example, to reduce the country's public deficit. Through the sale of the euro-claims obtained via the deposit of its gain (in real euros) with the ECB, the Bureau transforms the net external gains into net internal gains: 'in each period it acquires the full amount of the net exports of its residents' (ibid.: 128, m.t.).

Here, too, the difference between order and disorder lies in the fact that today 'the exogenous savings formed in the surplus country is fully "expatriated": being purely financial, it is addressed to "euro-banks", where foreign currencies are deposited by their official holders (central bank) or by private agents (commercial banks, firms, individuals)' (ibid.: 129, m.t.). It is true that the Bureau must pay more to exporters than it receives from importers; yet the difference is covered by an initial emission of domestic currency, which is totally justified since it corresponds to the monetization of an external gain perfectly consistent with the existence of trading among nations. Moreover, such a creation takes place only once; a revolving fund is then formed to be automatically activated after every successive period; a new emission is required only if successive net exports are greater than the initial ones and only for an amount equal to their increment.

*The gains of the European Central Bank*

As the bank of the European community, the ECB also benefits from Schmitt's plan. On the one hand, it gains the difference between the interest obtained from net importing countries and that paid to net exporting countries. On the other hand, it can request that member countries transfer part of their Bureaus' net gains to it, which it can invest in European projects as chosen by the European community.

*The extra-European stability of exchange rates*

To conclude, let us note that Schmitt's plan also applies to the payments between euro-member countries and the rest-of-the-world. Among its advantages, we must therefore also include a greater stability of the exchange rate between the euro – and, through it, of the European domestic currencies – and the US dollar, the yen, etc. The euro issued by the new ECB 'is the vehicular money of every foreign currency earned and spent by European member countries, the US dollar included' (Schmitt 1988a: 160, m.t.). This means that, in the new system of European payments, the euro is 'the numerical standard of the dollar in the same way as it is the numerical standard of member currencies' (ibid.: 160, m.t.). In other words, the value of the euro vis-à-vis dollars is determined by the ECB and will remain stable at the level chosen by the European member countries thanks to the regime of absolute exchange rates of Schmitt's plan. The euro 'will behave towards the dollar as it does towards each member currency: vehicular in all its interventions, the European currency can never be the object of a *net* demand or supply in terms of any national currency whatsoever, even extra-European' (ibid.: 161, m.t.).

## Schmitt's first proposals for a single-country reform

In analyzing the present non-system of external payments, Schmitt does not only provide a plan of reform for a group of countries or the entire world but also considers a single-country solution to the problems caused by the international monetary disorder. A country on its own cannot create an international system of payments; even so, it can still protect itself against the present non-system. Schmitt works out a detailed plan using the case of France as an example that, if implemented, would enable his home country to avoid the anomalies of today's disorderly system while paying all its external purchases in full. In this chapter, I confine my exposition to what I consider the most relevant aspects of that analysis; the interested reader is invited to refer directly to Schmitt's 1984 book *La France souveraine de sa monnaie.*

### *Objective and means*

As with a European or a world reform, the main objective of the single-country reform is to implement a system in which international payments are carried out through the circular flow of a nominal currency. Once more, this objective can be reached by internalizing foreign payments, by switching to a regime of absolute exchange rates, and complying with the sales-purchases identity. Internalization is necessary if we want to avoid external payments being the source of inflationary emissions due to intersecting national and international monetary circuits. International payments become internalized when France is able to create '*within its boundaries its own circuit of international payments*' (Schmitt 1984b: 136, m.t.). This is achieved by the institution of France's Bureau, which collects all international payments by French importers and carries out, in France's domestic currency, all the payments addressed to French exporters.

> France's external payments are thus integrated in the flux-reflux or monetary circuit of internal payments. Instead of paying its foreign correspondents, France pays its own exporters; [...] the sale of exporting goods will exert, on the contrary, a withdrawal of importers' income.
>
> (ibid.: 137, m.t.)

The switch from relative to absolute exchange rates implies the implementation of a system where France's domestic currency, the franc, is simultaneously supplied and demanded by the rest-of-the-world in every external payment concerning France's imports and exports. It is France's Bureau that implements this switch by asserting the 'monopoly of setting the national currency's absolute exchange' (ibid.: 141, m.t.). This means that commercial banks will no longer be able to purchase or sell francs against foreign currencies, a result in line with the circular flow of the franc granted by the internalization of France's payments. It is through the coupling of imports and exports that the Bureau avoids the transformation of its domestic currency into an object of exchange and, by the same move, guarantees the implementation of a regime of absolute exchange rates.

Respecting the identity between sales and purchases is indeed the other prerequisite of Schmitt's plan. Since money is vehicular in nature, payments are conveyed through its circular flow, which implies that France must finance its imports by its exports and match net commercial imports by net exports of financial claims. Schmitt's plan proposes a mechanism of clearing to make

France conform to the logical identity of its sales and purchases. '[N]ot a fraction of the purchases of the country considered as a whole will ever be paid in money, the counterpart of net purchases being *fully* obtained through *simultaneous sales*' (ibid.: 149, m.t.). Every purchase of commercial and financial goods will remain coupled with an equivalent sale of commercial and financial goods, so that France's overall balance of payments will always be in equilibrium.

### *A practical implementation of Schmitt's single-country solution*

Since no true international currency is available in the present non-system and since France alone cannot issue any such currency, France must carry out its external payments in a manner that produces the same effects as an orderly system of international payments would. Schmitt advocates the introduction of a nominal currency, called the *grand Franc* (or simply Franc, with a capital letter F), which functions as the official currency of France vis-à-vis the rest-of-the-world and is functionally related to the emission of F-bonds, financial claims on France's economy denominated in Francs and fully convertible to foreign currencies, say the US dollar.

Let me phrase it in the present tense, as if France had already implemented the new system. France's Bureau pays for the country's purchases by sending an equivalent amount of F-bonds to foreign exporting countries. On the other hand, foreign importing countries must purchase F-bonds on the foreign exchange market in order to pay France for its exports. As Schmitt claims, in the absence of production 'the emission of Francs is logically a *directly financial* operation' (ibid.: 205, m.t.). Issued by the Bureau and sold and purchased on the foreign exchange market, F-bonds are convertible securities guaranteed by France; their object is part of France's domestic resources and their *raison d'être* in Schmitt's plan is essentially didactic. Introducing them facilitates the understanding of a system, founded on the principles of absolute exchange rates and multilateral clearing, which could work only through the vehicular use of any currency. Given the present status of national currencies, the introduction of F-bonds makes it easier to avoid misunderstandings deriving from the wrong conception of the nature of money.

What matters most is the fact that France's external payments are carried out in conformity with the immediate clearing of its sales and purchases. Francs exist only for France; foreign countries pay and are paid in F-bonds, that is, in the foreign currencies in which these claims are convertible. Since F-bonds define part of France's domestic resources, it is clear that the payment of France's net imports in F-bonds immediately restores the equilibrium of its balance of overall payments. In particular, it appears that France's purchases of real goods – products and financial assets – are perfectly offset by its sales of real goods (whether in the form of products or financial assets).

The Franc is the currency used by France in a circular flow to convey its real payments. Every payment is, by definition, carried out in money. France's external payments are no exception. Yet, the circular flow of the Franc is determined by its creation-destruction, which results from the transformation '*in each period [of] the payment of France's exports and imports into a full transaction of purchase and sale of Franc-bonds on the international financial market*' (ibid.: 155, m.t.). Thus, the sale of F-bonds defines at the same time the gain in Francs, resulting from the sale of securities and their expenditure in the payment of France's imports, whereas the purchase of F-bonds 'is the expenditure in the international financial market of the Franc gained through net exports' (ibid.: 160, m.t.).

At the same time, the internalization of France's external payments is obtained through the Bureau's intermediation. Paid by French importers in francs (small letter) and paying French exporters with the same domestic currency, the Bureau equalizes its inflows and outflows thanks to the internal financial market: '[e]ach franc spent by importers is immediately placed by the Bureau; and each franc paid to exporters is symmetrically obtained by the Bureau in the market of loanable funds available in France' (ibid.: 212, m.t.).

The role of the Bureau is that of a financial intermediary between importers and exporters as well as between R (the rest-of-the-world) and R. Every inflow of francs is immediately balanced by an equivalent outflow: the francs paid by French importers are paid to French exporters, while the possible difference between imports and exports gives rise either to a purchase of domestic financial assets or to their sale. Likewise, the Francs spent on paying France's imports flow back at once to be replaced by F-bonds, while the Francs earned through the payment of France's exports are immediately spent and converted into F-bonds. Crucially, thanks to the Bureau's monetary and financial intermediations, no net demand or supply of francs, or even of Francs, can ever occur. This is the result of the mechanism through which France monetizes its foreign transactions. Schmitt's 1984 plan for a one-country solution is well thought-out. A couple of years before his death, he reformulated it to give it a more generic form. It is striking to note the similarity between the 1984 and the 2014 versions of Schmitt's solution. Even more so is the close relationship between Schmitt's 1984 thoughts on the consequences of his plan on countries' external debts and his 2014 analysis of sovereign debt. It is therefore worth delving further into what makes Schmitt's 1984 analysis so original and foreshadows his 2014 insights concerning the genesis of sovereign debt.

## Settling a country's net imports under Schmitt's single-country reform

### *No external debt is incurred by net importing countries*

It is currently believed that the payment of a country's net imports necessarily entails the formation of a positive external debt, either in monetary terms, when the country benefits from the privilege to pay with its own acknowledgement of debt, or in financial terms, in all other cases. Schmitt argues that this is true only in the absence of an orderly system of international payments. Let us consider the example of a non-reserve currency country. In the absence of a system that provides, free of cost, the vehicular money required for the monetary transmission of a country's real payments, the deficit (net importing) country is forced to purchase or borrow a foreign currency to pay the surplus (net exporting) countries. Based on the extent of its net imports, the deficit country incurs a foreign debt, because it borrows a foreign currency on behalf of its residents. As a result, savings are formed within the country because a foreign purchasing power finances part of the residents' purchases. In other words, importers spend an amount of domestic income greater than that paid to exporters. These savings are lost to the international financial bubble as the unavoidable consequence of the increase in the country's external debt. 'Within the present regime, dollar-standard, savings released by net imports are lost to the international financial capital, without any benefit for France' (ibid.: 299, m.t.).

By imposing the necessary equality for France's total imports and exports, Schmitt's 1984 plan avoids the formation of an external debt for the country: 'every external flow will be welded to its opposite, every credit (debit) being simultaneously a debit (credit) of the same amount' (ibid.: 249, m.t.). It is because France balances its net imports with the transfer of F-bonds that its purchases are matched by its sales. And it is because F-bonds are claims on France's domestic economy that the country pays for its total imports in full. Freed from the need to borrow abroad, France, defined as the set of its residents, does not incur any external debt. In Schmitt's plan, the Bureau transfers a sum of F-bonds to R. This means that the payment of France's net imports is made possible by the investment of R. Through the intermediation of F-bonds, France's net purchases are financed by the investment of what R earns through its net exports. 'In conclusion, the net sale of F-bonds entails the rigorously *nil* indebtedness of France, because the foreign savings thus drawn are, directly or indirectly, invested in the modernization of the country's production apparatus' (ibid.: 247, m.t.).

### *Net gain in domestic currency*

As for the difference between the payments carried out by French importers in domestic currency and the sum paid to French exporters, also in domestic currency, in the new system it is no longer lost, because it is appropriated by the Bureau on behalf of the set of the country's residents. In the present non-system, the sum of domestic income corresponding to the payment of France's net imports is lost to the country, which can recover it only through a foreign loan. In Schmitt's new system, the Bureau gets hold of every franc spent by French importers. The amount remaining after the payment of French exporters defines the net gain of France's Bureau and corresponds to the sum of national income saved because of France's net imports. 'France's new regime of external payments keeps automatically within the country *all the currency spent by importers*, whatever the balance of payments' situation' (ibid.: 240, m.t.).

Anticipating an argument he will develop in his 2014 paper on countries' sovereign debt, Schmitt claims that what characterizes the present key reserve-currencies-driven non-system is that net imports are paid for twice: once by importers, and once by their country. 'The illogicality of the key-currencies standard is that the payment of deficits is double, because, in this regime, it lies with the residents and additionally with the country itself' (ibid.: 309, m.t.). On the one hand, the sum of national income spent by importers is credited neither to other residents nor to the country itself (as represented by the central bank, the Treasury, or the Budget). On the other hand, the country must pay R in foreign currencies, which it can do either by reducing its official reserves or by borrowing abroad. In both cases, the external debt of the country increases (a decrease in assets corresponds to an increase in liabilities), and the country suffers from both a loss of national income and a rise in debt. No wonder that the implementation of a mechanism preventing the loss of payments made by the country's residents produces a net gain for the Bureau, namely the income spent to pay for residents' net imports.

Bearing in mind that France's net imports are paid by a transfer of F-bonds it will be easy to grasp that, in balancing its total purchases with equivalent sales, France no longer incurs any external debt. It is true that F-bonds are claims on France's economy; yet they do not indebt the country itself. On the contrary, the purchase of F-bonds gives R the ownership of part of France's domestic resources and thus 're-establishes at once the balance of France's commercial payments' (ibid.: 242, m.t.). Finally, the emission of F-bonds to the benefit of R has no impact on France's external debt, for two reasons:

1) It guarantees the equality of France's overall sales and purchases, and
2) It defines an investment of the net exporting countries – if they add the F-bonds to their official reserves – or of the international financial capital – if F-bonds are sold on the foreign exchange market – in France's national economy.

### *The servicing of France's pre-existing external debt*

Another important insight in terms of countries' external debt and the advantages derived from implementing Schmitt's 1984 plan concerns the servicing of France's pre-existing external debt. Schmitt considers the case where France is able to export more than it imports and uses part of its gain of foreign currencies to service its external debt. Today, this payment is double, because it is carried out by France's indebted residents in national income terms as well as by France as a whole in foreign currency terms. Hence, France sacrifices part of its domestic income as well as part of its net exports to the servicing of its foreign debt. '*In the present regime* (dollar-standard), the "payer" has a *double identity*; more precisely, two people pay: residents pay A [a sum of their income, defining part of France's current output] and the set France pays Ex [part of its net exports]' (ibid.: 261, m.t.). This is so, because the indebted country, France in our case, has to obtain at a price – i.e. a part of its exports – the amount of foreign currency required to convey the payments of its residents. If France were in a position to benefit from the circular flow of an international currency issued by a supranational bank, no monetary payment would be added to its real payment: reduced to a single payment, the service of France's external debt would no longer entail the loss of the domestic income spent by France's residents.

Schmitt's plan enables France, or any country adopting it, to move from a regime of relative exchange rates to one of absolute exchange rates, that is, to a system providing cost-free the vehicular means for making the payment of its external transactions. As in the case of France's net imports, the intervention of the Bureau acting as a monetary and financial intermediary prevents the loss of the domestic income spent by France's indebted residents to service their external debt. The Bureau pays foreign creditors in foreign currencies (through the mediation of F-bonds), while France's indebted residents pay the Bureau in francs. The real payment of foreign creditors consists in part of France's net exports and the Bureau obtains as a gain the income spent by France's indebted residents. '*[I]n the new regime of France's external payments the gains of the* [Bureau] *will be net in every period in which the income earned through net exports will be allocated to the payment of the country's external debt*' (ibid.: 260, m.t.).

To conclude, we observe that Schmitt's one-country solution brings with it all the advantages that France would derive from the implementation of a world, or a European, reform. Notably, it enables France to freely determine its interest rate in a way more suitable to the growth of its domestic economy. Today, national interest rates are influenced by the deployment of national currencies, notably the US dollar, in the settlement of international payments. In the future, France will recover its monetary sovereignty and, with it, its financial sovereignty. The franc will no longer be traded on the exchange market: 'in the regime of payments carried out by means of F-bonds, every export or import of financial capitals is automatically converted *into a flow of commercial imports or exports*' (ibid.: 285, m.t.). Flows of international financial capitals will not affect France's national currency so that 'domestic financial markets will, freely and autonomously, find the level of interest rates adequate for the development and growth of [its] national industry' (ibid.: 285, m.t.). Supported by the franc's stable exchange rate and having switched to a regime of absolute exchange rates, France will be greatly helped by Schmitt's reform to recover its monetary and financial sovereignty while paying, but only once, its dues to its foreign partners. In the new regime

> France carries *only once* the burden of its net imports. Nobody can complain: even the rest-of-the-world is satisfied, because its net exports to France are paid: they are paid once, and this is enough. Exporters get all the dollars (or the foreign currencies they prefer) obtained through the sale of F-bonds, up to the exact value of France's net imports.
>
> (ibid.: 299, m.t.)

# Part II

# 1987–1998: The years of further in-depth analysis

The period of Schmitt's activity considered in this Part spans the years 1987 to 1998 and is characterized by his effort to pursue a more thorough analysis of national economics as well as criticism of general equilibrium analysis. Those years were very prolific in terms of manuscripts, most of which have remained unpublished. Part II rests on the analysis developed by Schmitt in these manuscripts.

The main topics covered in the five chapters of Part II refer to national economics and range from the analysis of capital and interest to that of unemployment. In a complementary yet substantially different approach to the pathologies characterizing our national economies, Schmitt switches from the analysis of unemployment in terms of values (Part I) to one in terms of prices. This enables him to complete the investigation he had embarked on in the early 1960s and to outline the question of the passage from capitalism to post-capitalism. While engrossed in his further in-depth analysis, Schmitt's interest in general equilibrium analysis did not wane. His criticism of neo-classical analysis became as sharp as ever, which explains why an entire chapter of Part II is devoted to this subject.

DOI: 10.4324/9781351271325-14

# 10 1987–1995: Schmitt's first extended analysis of countries' external debt

From 1987 to 1995 Schmitt devoted a substantial part of his work to a problem that had only superficially been addressed by mainstream economists and which was to prove one of the most challenging to the discipline: external debt servicing. Through rigorous macroeconomic analysis, Schmitt was able to show that external debt servicing charges the debtor country twice: one charge is borne by the indebted residents and an *additional* one by their country taken as a whole. Schmitt's discovery of the dysfunction affecting the payment of principal and interests on countries' external debts rests on macroeconomic considerations that have never been investigated before. It provides an explanation for the huge discrepancies affecting countries' global balances of payments and introduces guidelines for a reform that puts a stop to any duplication of the charge imposed on indebted countries. In this chapter, reference is made to six unpublished manuscripts distributed by Schmitt to his students in Fribourg and Dijon, one of which is partly reproduced in a book he co-authored with me: *External debt servicing. A Vicious Circle* (1991). Faced with the large number of pages Schmitt devoted to the analysis of this fascinating problem and the great variety of arguments he used to corroborate his thesis I have had to be selective. In particular, I have left out some contributions that, however relevant, would make the understanding of the debt problem less straightforward. I beg the readers' pardon for this drastic cut in Schmitt's theoretical contributions, hoping that they will find my presentation clear enough to convey the richness and depth of Schmitt's thought.

## International payments affect countries and their residents

The fact that a country is involved in the external payments of its residents is universally recognized. Yet, most economists hold the view that the involvement of the country is merely the reflection of the foreign payments carried out by its residents. According to this viewpoint, a country is coextensive with the sum of its residents and never acquires the logical status of a separate entity. Schmitt shows that, in reality, a country is a *set* whose existence is separable from that of its residents, and, as such, it cannot be reduced to the sum of its elements. The existence of a nation-state is of a piece with that of its

DOI: 10.4324/9781351271325-15

national currency. 'The distinction between nations is due to the *heterogeneity* of national currencies. Each monetary nation is a discrete entity when facing other nations' (Schmitt 1990b: 8, m.t.). National currencies are heterogeneous and pertain to distinct monetary systems. Reciprocal exchange of national currencies does not render them homogeneous; it merely leads to their permutation while each currency remains anchored in its national banking system.

In the absence of a system of international clearing, national currencies are bound to remain heterogeneous, so that international payments between residents and non-residents necessarily imply the direct involvement of their reciprocal countries. 'Since two heterogeneous currencies are linked in the payment of a nation's imports, this payment implies not only the *sum*, but also the *set* of its residents' (ibid.: 11, m.t.). To the extent that they refer to countries' imports and exports of real goods, commercial and financial, international payments concern the sum of countries' residents, but insofar as they involve two or more national currencies, they involve the country as a whole.

The payment made by residents implies an expenditure of domestic income and pertains to an economy of production; the payment involving countries implies the expenditure of an *external* income and pertains to an economy of exchange. It thus follows that '[i]nternational payments are exchanges defined both in an economy of production (concerning the *sum* of countries' residents) and in an economy of exchange (where countries themselves, as the sets of their residents, are situated)' (ibid.: 15, m.t.).

The implication of treating countries as sets is particularly clear in the case of external debts. As everybody knows, a country's external debt arises because of its net commercial imports. Although it is true that the country's commercial imports and exports are carried out by its residents, it is likewise clear that net exports or imports cannot be imputed to any specific resident, to any of its exporters or importers. 'The commercial deficit [or surplus] of country A does not concern any of its residents, but the country itself, the *set of its residents*' (Schmitt 1994–95, 17.1.95: 25, m.t.).

It is in the balance of payments that net imports or exports are entered, and the balance of payments concerns the country as a whole, as a nation. 'It is the balance of payments of a whole economy, of a whole country, or nation, confronted with the rest-of-the-world, which is, according to the period, in deficit, in surplus, or in equilibrium' (ibid.: 26, m.t.). Let us consider the case of country A's net commercial imports. Plainly, net imports are carried out by A's residents, who thereby incur a debt to the exporters of the rest-of-the-world. However, the *difference* between A's imports and exports entails also an external debt for country A as a whole. This is so because part of the debt of its residents is not balanced by a credit of some other residents. Since the credit is owned by a non-resident, country A carries a net debt, that is, the debt generated by A's net imports as entered in its balance of payments.

It is important to note that countries' external debt is macroeconomic in nature. Countries exist as macroeconomic entities as well as cultural, linguistic, sociological and political ones. The existence of national currencies proves that countries are distinct macroeconomic entities. This is why net gains derived from net commercial exports define an increase in a country's official reserves. It is true that official reserves are administered by the central bank, but it is also a fact that, in doing so, the central bank acts on behalf of the country as a whole. The owner of official reserves is the nation-state; no particular resident owns them.

### *The double payment of a country's net imports*

Suppose country A's commercial imports from the rest-of-the-world (country R) to be greater than its exports to R. The problem addressed by Schmitt is whether the external payments carried out by country A and that of its residents form a single payment or whether they are logically distinct. For the sake of his argument, payment *a* is the payment between residents and non-residents, and payment *alpha* the payment between countries, and *a* and *alpha* are two distinct flows, because they are defined in two separate and distinct 'spaces' (Figure 10.1).

'[E]ven though they are equivalent, payments *a* and *alpha* are separate and distinct flows because flow *a* is defined in the space of residents, whereas flow *alpha* is defined in the space of countries' (Schmitt 1994–95, 21.2.95c: 6, m.t.). Schmitt corroborates his conclusion by showing that payment *a* consists in the expenditure of an *internal* income by the country's residents, while payment *alpha* is the expenditure of an *external* income. Since a country's external income derives from its net commercial exports, and is not owned by any of its residents, it immediately becomes obvious that payments *a* and *alpha* imply two separate expenditures. In our example, country A's importers pay country R's exporters through an outlay of part of their domestic income, whereas country R is credited with an amount of foreign currency that defines the external income gained through its net commercial exports. Since 'a country's external income cannot be reduced to an income of its domestic economy, payments *alpha* cannot be reduced to the corresponding payment *a*' (ibid.: 9, m.t.).

As Schmitt points out, the two payments, albeit separate and distinct, are closely related: no payment *alpha* is possible in the absence of a payment *a*. In today's system, any international payment *a* entails an equivalent payment

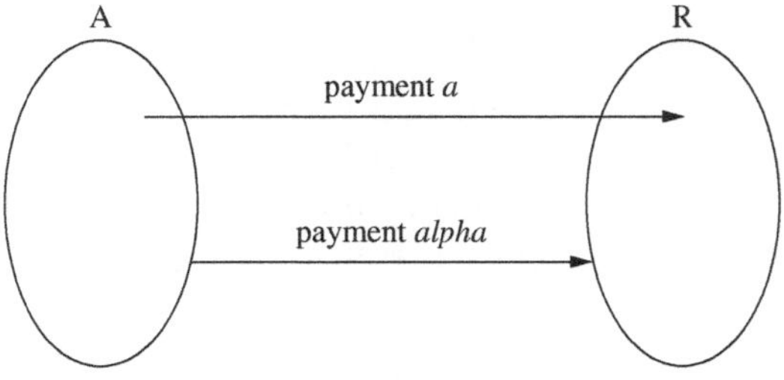


*Figure 10.1* External payments of country R and of its residents.

*alpha*. The payment carried out by A's importers implies at the same time a payment carried out by their country to the benefit of the exporting country. 'It is a single *double* flow or a single *double* payment that takes place between country [A] and country [R]; it is therefore certain that payment *a* is projected into payment *alpha*' (ibid.: 9, m.t.).

One way of explaining the double payment carried out by country A and by its residents, is to consider the necessity of conveying abroad the payment of A's importers. As clearly established by monetary macroeconomics, payments, both national and international, must be 'carried' through the circular flow of money. Between countries, payments must be carried in international 'space'. Given the absence of a system providing, cost free, a supranational currency capable of conveying payments across the international space, countries themselves must purchase the foreign currency needed to vehiculate their payments. '[A] country can carry only in *foreign currencies*, in international space, the domestic income that its residents pay to their foreign correspondents' (ibid.: 31, m.t.).

There is further proof of the fact that the two payments are simultaneous and inseparable, namely the impact of net payments carried out by country A's importers on the exchange rate of A's national currency. Indeed, this payment defines an excess demand for money R, $M_R$, in terms of money A, $M_A$. To counterbalance this excess demand, country A must exert an equivalent excess demand for $M_A$ in terms of $M_R$, which is precisely the payment *alpha* carried out by country A. In other words, the task of country A is to change the payment made by its importers in money A into a payment in money R, that is, to change a payment in domestic income into a payment in external income. '[T]he payment *alpha* accompanying a payment *a* is nothing else than the conversion from a domestic income of the net importing country's economy into a domestic income of the net exporting country' (ibid.: 29, m.t.). It is country A as a whole that must take over the transformation of an income formed in money A into an equivalent income in money R. This transformation is costly, and its cost is charged to country A.

Finally, Schmitt's introductory analysis leads him to formulate what he calls the *theorem* of international payments, which states that '*Each payment of x units of value carried out by a country's resident to a non-resident is duplicated by a payment of x units of value made by the country or the nation of the payer in favour of the nation or the country of the payee*' (ibid.: 32, m.t.).

### *No formal error affects international reciprocal payments*

The first and clearest example of reciprocal international payments is represented by the equality between two countries' commercial transactions. When country A's and country R's trade balances are in equilibrium, their external payments, payments *alpha*, are equal and reciprocal, which means that they mutually compensate. Indeed, in this case,

> each country obtains and spends exactly the same value in the payment *alpha* that is addressed to it and in the payment *alpha* that it carries out.

> In these conditions we observe that the two payments *alpha*, equal and of opposite sign, compensate for one another.
>
> (ibid.: 35, m.t.)

Country A must pay country R the same amount of foreign currency that country R must pay to country A or, alternatively, country A must change the same amount of domestic income into a domestic income of country R and vice versa. The two transformations cancel each other out, so that, finally, the external payments of country A and country R are fully internalized: A's exporters are paid by A's importers, and R's exporters by R's importers. 'The cancellation of the two payments *alpha* has a univocal meaning: the importers of each country pay the exporters of their own country' (ibid.: 37, m.t.). This is so because country A no longer needs to transform the domestic income spent by its residents into a domestic income of country R; at the same time country R is freed from the obligation to transform its domestic income into an equivalent domestic income of country A. '[A] country's trade equilibrium gives the certainty of the *cost-free* transformation of a fraction of its internal product into an equivalent external product' (Schmitt 1992a: 83, m.t.).

The equivalent and reciprocal exchange between country A and country R also guarantees the perfect neutrality of their payments in the exchange market. Any demand for money A in terms of money R is balanced by the simultaneous and equivalent demand for $M_R$ in terms of $M_A$, resulting in a stable exchange rate. '[T]he foreign exchanges *induced* by the mutual imports of commercial [...] goods are *reciprocal*, and, therefore, *neutral*, so that they rigorously preserve the external value of both currencies' (Cencini and Schmitt 1991: 125). Exchanges are monetized and imply the reciprocal exchange of payments between country A and country R. This means that the foreign currency purchased by country A, $M_R$, and that purchased by country R, $M_A$, balance each other out.

By exchanging part of their national product against an equivalent part of the other country's national output, A and R make a circular and vehicular use of their currencies. Whatever currency is used, money A, money R, or a hypothetical supranational currency, it is nothing more than a means of reciprocal payments: 'money is not part of exchanged goods. We express this fact by saying that countries do not carry out any net purchase of foreign currencies' (Schmitt 1987d: 161, m.t.). When countries' commercial balances are in equilibrium, their reciprocal exchanges are monetized, but money is used as a circular means of payment; its vehicular use has no impact on exchange rates and is perfectly consistent with its flow nature.

Countries have to carry the external payments of their residents abroad. The duplication of a country's foreign purchases is inescapable, yet it is balanced by the same duplication affecting the other country when the two countries' trade balances are in equilibrium: country A and country R 'suffer *equally* the rigour of the *paradoxical situation*; the two effects, equal and of opposite sign, balance each other perfectly: the aberration is neutralized on both sides' (Schmitt

1992a: 41, m.t.). Does this conclusion also apply in the case of a country's commercial deficit or surplus?

### *Reciprocity holds true even in the case of countries' commercial deficits or surpluses*

As surprising as this might appear at first sight, the answer to the latest question is 'yes'. Indeed, international transactions define reciprocal exchanges even when a country, say A, is a net commercial importer (exporter). The reason for this is that every country is faced with the obligation to pay for the totality of its purchases. Hence, if country A does not find in its commercial exports the total amount of foreign currency required to pay for its total trade deficit, it has to find the complement in the financial market. Whether it does so by reducing its official reserves or by borrowing abroad, the operation amounts to a sale of financial claims so that '*in each period each country exports financial claims in order to cover the deficit of its trade balance*' (Schmitt 1987d: 131, m.t.).

In our example, country A must – through the sale of financial claims – obtain the foreign currency that it fails to obtain through its commercial exports. A's net imports of commercial goods are thus balanced by net exports of financial assets. Country A's purchases of commercial goods being equal to its sales of commercial and financial goods, the macroeconomic payment, i.e., payment *alpha*, it must carry out in favour of country R is compensated by the payment *alpha* which R must carry out to its (A's) benefit. 'We observe that, in each period, all payments between the two countries are equal on both sides, *whether they balance their commercial exports or not*' (ibid.: 133, m.t.). Both country A and country R balance their earnings and their monetary expenditures, which guarantees the circular or vehicular use of the currencies used as means of payment.

Since A's trade deficit is balanced by an equivalent financial surplus, the net demand for money R in terms of money A exerted by country A is compensated by an equivalent net demand for money A in terms of money R exerted by country R. It thus follows that 'no (international) trade imbalance can be translated into an asymmetrical pressure on the exchange market' (Schmitt 1988e: 4). The neutrality of international payments with regard to exchange rates is a direct consequence of their reciprocity. The equilibrium of a country's overall balance of payments is proof of the fact that its external transactions are reciprocal exchanges, which leaves unaltered its national currency's exchange rate. Given that '[w]henever a country, say [A], sells a commercial commodity, the transaction is at the same time *financial*, [it is thus definitively established that] trade imbalances have no disturbing effect on the equilibria of exchange markets' (ibid.: 16).

Once it is understood that financial claims are, for all intents and purposes, *real goods*, it appears that the case of trade imbalances also defines the reciprocal exchange of real goods: 'each country offers and demands real goods for the same amount' (Cencini and Schmitt 1991: 128). The equivalence of the real goods, commercial and financial, exchanged by country A and country R can only be established in monetary terms, and monetary payments between the two countries require the mediation of their currencies. Yet, when real payments are reciprocal and equivalent, money intervenes as a mere vehicle, as the means to convey commercial and financial goods internationally. The neutrality of exchange rates is thus the direct consequence of the neutrality of money itself when it is used in a circular flow.

### *The formation of external debts*

The compensation between payments *alpha* does not preclude the formation of countries' external debts. In fact, the principle according to which any individual agent must incur a debt to pay for its net purchases applies to countries too. Since trade deficit cannot be imputed to any one importer or exporter, it is the country as a whole that will have to find the external income necessary for the payment of its residents' net commercial imports. 'What is the identity of the person that must incur a debt in order to pay for its net imports? It can only be country A itself, because it is country A that, in period *p*, imports a net amount of commercial goods' (Schmitt 1994–95, 21.2.95a: 8, m.t.). Whether A borrows abroad the sum of foreign currency required to pay for its net commercial imports or uses part of its official reserves, the outcome is the same: an external debt forms equal to country A's net expenditures. Given that a country's official reserves define a credit of the country itself vis-à-vis the rest-of-the-world, their decrease means an increase in the country's external debt. It is thus confirmed that 'it is country A as a whole, the nation-state A, which carries the external debt originating from its trade balance deficit' (ibid.: 9, m.t.).

What must be stressed here is that countries' external debts are not the mirror image of the external debts incurred by their residents – States included. It is true that residents can borrow abroad and incur an external debt; thus, for example the Brazilian State can finance part of its public deficit by selling financial bonds abroad. However, the

> foreign currencies borrowed by the State of Brazil – as any other sum of foreign currencies borrowed by any resident of this country – cannot define a (new) net debt of Brazil toward the rest-of-the-world *unless they are spent on paying for Brazil's net commercial imports.*
>
> (Schmitt 1992a: 11, m.t.)

The set of residents of country A (i.e. 'nation-state A') incurs an external debt only when the sum borrowed by the individual residents feeds the payment of its net commercial imports. '

Once formed, a country's external debt can increase because of the interest foreign creditors are entitled to. This is why the problem addressed by Schmitt in his 1987–1995 texts concerns the servicing of countries' external debt: it includes the payment of both principal and interest.

## The asymmetry characterizing the servicing of countries' external debts

As we have seen, countries are always involved in the external payments of their residents. It is the country as a whole that will foot the bill for converting the domestic income spent by its residents into an external income. The double charge of external payments affects all countries, so that payments *alpha* balance each other out whenever they are reciprocal. The symmetry of payments *alpha* seems therefore to be the desired state-of-affairs, since it ends up cancelling the duplication caused by the need to convey payments in the international space (space *alpha*). Schmitt's insightful analysis shows, however, that this reassuring conclusion falters in one particular yet significant case: the *servicing* of countries' external debts.

### *External debt servicing has an adverse effect in the exchange market*

Formed in period $p_0$, when country A's trade surplus is paid through a sale of equivalent financial claims, A's external debt will need to be amortized and interests to be paid. Let us suppose that country A pays, in part or in full, for its external debt servicing in period $p_1$. It is immediately apparent that the payment of country A's external debt can only take place if A earns a positive amount of external income through its trade surplus of $p_1$. 'It is correct to say that country A cannot obtain a *net* decrease in its external debt (principal and interests) unless it spends a trade surplus for this purpose' (Schmitt 1992b: 5, m.t.). Two conditions must be satisfied for the servicing of A's external debt:

1) A's indebted residents, IR, must be able to tap into a sufficient amount of domestic income, either earned or borrowed;
2) Country A must earn an equivalent external income through net commercial exports.

'[T]he debt could not be paid if country A did not generate a surplus in its balance of trade, nor could it be paid if the residents carrying A's external debt had no positive income at their disposal' (ibid.: 7, m.t.).

Let us represent the two payments in a neutral way, one carried out by A's residents and the other by country A itself (Figure 10.2).

At first sight, as represented in Figure 10.2, payments seem to be symmetrical. Apparently, the payment carried out in a foreign currency, $M_R$, by country A replaces the payment carried out in $M_A$ by A's indebted residents, no room being left for a vicious duplication. However, a rigorous analysis of the effects of these payments on $M_A$'s exchange rate leads to a surprising conclusion: the servicing of country A's external debt implies a depreciation of its domestic currency, which doubles the charge of its payment. Let us consider the effect of payments (1) and (2) depicted in Figure 10.2 on the exchange rate of money A and money R.

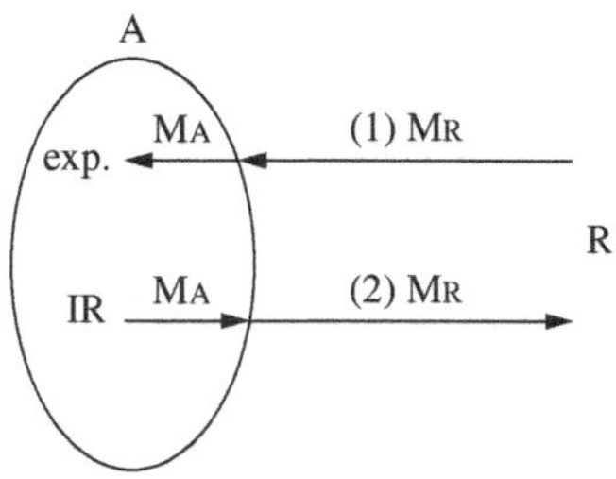


*Figure 10.2* Country A's trade surplus and its external debt servicing.

Payment (1) is carried out in $M_R$ to the benefit of country A, represented by its central bank, which converts it into an equivalent sum of $M_A$ paid to A's exporters. Does this transaction influence money A's exchange rate? Schmitt's answer is clear: 'there is no reason why A's central bank should derive an amount of its currency from the exchange market; instead, A's central bank *creates* or issues $M_A$ at the moment it receives [$M_R$]' (Schmitt 1988e: 9). In so doing, A's central bank *monetizes* in $M_A$ the sum of foreign currency it adds up to the country's official reserves. Therefore, the payment by country R of country A's net commercial exports, payment (1), does not define a net demand for money A in terms of money R. In other words, as the amount of money A paid to A's exporters is created by A's central bank, the supply of $M_A$ is infinitely elastic. Hence, the conversion of $M_R$ into $M_A$ leaves the exchange rate between the two currencies unaltered.

As for payment (2,) this time the sum of money A paid by IR, country A's indebted residents, must be converted into an equivalent amount of money R. In this case, too, the conversion is carried out by A's central bank, which gives up the $M_R$ obtained as payment for A's commercial exports in exchange for the amount of $M_A$ paid by IR. The foreign currency needed to convey the payment of country A's external debt being already available in country A's central bank, 'it would seem that [… $M_R$] is not an object which it should be necessary for A to purchase in the exchange market' (ibid.: 10). Yet, this is to forget that 'A's central bank is not a "charity"; its true function is not to give its foreign reserves away: it *sells* them' (ibid.: 10). Since A's central bank cannot create or issue money R and does not give up its official reserves for free, payment (2) entails an excess demand for money R in terms of money A. It thus appears that country A's external debt servicing has an adverse effect on the external value of $M_A$. The excess demand for money R leads to the devaluation of money A.

Even though both country A and country R equilibrate their global balances of payments, external debt servicing entails a net loss for the debtor country, whose domestic currency devaluates with respect to the creditor country's national currency.

> In period p country [A] sacrifices, for the servicing of its external creditors, the exact sum, in money [R], it earns in its net commercial exports; in p [A's] overall balance of payments is thus in equilibrium; despite this, money [R] is subjected to a devaluation whose proportion is the ratio between the value of the current servicing, in interests and amortization, of country [A's] foreign creditors and the value of its commercial imports.
>
> (Cencini and Schmitt 1991: 175)

Overall, country A pays its external debt twice, once in MR and once through the devaluation of its national currency.

### *External debt servicing implies a unilateral transfer of money*

International transactions pertain to the category of exchanges, and exchanges imply reciprocal payments between partners. The symmetry of external payments is verified in every case except one: external debt servicing. When A's external debt is formed, in period $p_0$, country A's net commercial purchases are balanced by net financial sales. Likewise, in period $p_1$, when country A's commercial exports are greater than its imports, its net commercial sales are balanced by a net purchase of claims on country R's bank deposits. However, when country A services its external debt 'its payment is *truncated* because it defines a *net debit*' (Schmitt 1990b: 83, m.t.).

To service its external debt, country A must transfer to R the claims on R's bank deposits obtained in $p_1$ as *real payment* for its trade surplus; this transfer is unilateral, since it does not imply any real transfer from R to A. '[E]very remittance between nations of an interest or an amortization is a *unilateral* payment, whereas only *exchanges* are achieved and neutral payments' (ibid.: 37, m.t.).

Let us represent in Figure 10.3 the transfer of real goods between country A and country R.

a) when A obtains, through its net commercial sales, the amount of money R – in the form of claims on R's bank deposits – it needs to service its external debt, and
b) when A services its external debt.

Given that *bank deposits are real goods* (financial assets), transaction (1) is an exchange of equivalent real goods between country A and country R in which A is credited-debited and R debited-credited. On the other hand, transaction

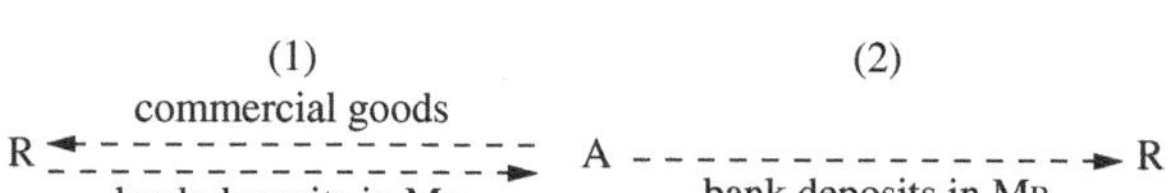


*Figure 10.3* Unilateral transfer defining A's external debt servicing.

(2) defines a net debit for country A: the unilateral transfer of bank deposits in money R from A to R. Indeed, by servicing its external debt, country A does recover, partly or in full, the financial claims it sold to country R in $p_0$; however, this cannot be considered as the counterpart of the claims on bank deposits in money R transferred to country R. The simple reason is that, once they have been redeemed, financial bonds lose their value; they are simply cancelled and cannot represent any real counterpart to country A's real payment. 'What is the value of *overdue* bonds at the instant they are paid? It is strictly zero. Only claims on future payments, not yet carried out, are positive values' (Schmitt 1992a: 49–50, m.t.).

If we now complete Figure 10.3 by introducing the monetary flows that convey the payments between country A and country R in (1) and (2), we obtain Figure 10.4.

The symmetry of payments (1) implies the circular flow of the currency used as a means of payment, here money R. In (1), both country A and country R are at the same time sellers and purchasers, which is why their monetary payments are reciprocal and money R is used as a mere vehicle. Payment (2), on the contrary, is a unilateral transfer in which country A has 'to undergo the sheer loss of the bank deposits in money [R] initially earned through its net commercial exports' (Cencini and Schmitt 1991: 134).

In the case of reciprocal payments, money is used in conformity with its nature as a circular flow conveying equivalent real goods from A to R and vice versa. In the case of A's external debt servicing, country A must purchase the vehicular money necessary to convey its unilateral real payment: if 'it services its external debt, the indebted country [A] is the object of a *net* debit in vehicular money' (ibid.: 138). Insofar as real payments are reciprocal, money defines a neutral circular flow; on the contrary, if a payment does not bring any real good to the country that makes it, the latter is subject to a net debt whose object is a sum of foreign currency. 'It is logically impossible to transfer a bank deposit – a sum of *real* money – if not by debiting its present holder [A] and

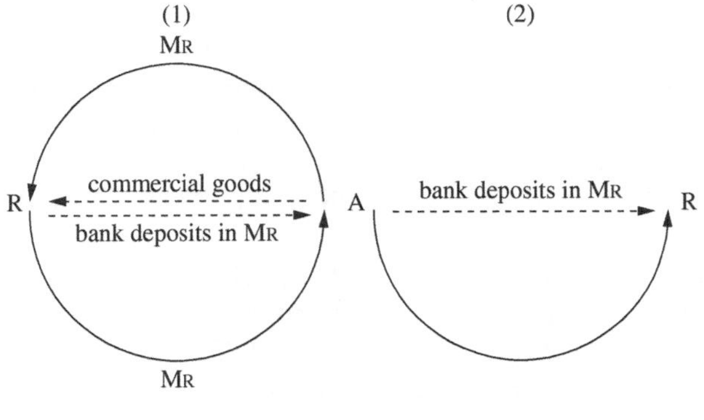


*Figure 10.4* Reciprocal versus unilateral monetary payments. Source: elaboration from Cencini and Schmitt 1991: 148

crediting its new owner [R], which defines a flow of *vehicular* money' (ibid.: 140). To be precise, the lack of reciprocity between country A and country R transforms the vehicular money into the object of a net debt accruing to A on top of the debt defining the loss of the bank deposits transferred to R. '*Diagnosis of the "vice" inherent in international payment*: the indebted country has to buy the vector of the transfer it addresses to its creditors' (ibid.: 154).

### *The payment of countries' external debt adds up to that of their indebted residents*

Undoubtedly, country A's external debt is incurred by A's residents and not by the country itself. Hence, country A's external debt servicing implies first an expenditure of domestic income by A's indebted residents, IR. As the beneficiaries of this payment are non-residents and A's and R's currencies are heterogeneous, the intervention of country A becomes necessary to convey the payment from A to R, that is, to convert the payment in money A into a payment in money R.

> *[T]wo distinct conditions must be met for the extinction of an external debt*, whatever its amount. The indebted residents must succeed in repaying their debt using an income formed in their *national* economy, but *it is also necessary* that the country itself, considered as a whole and of which they are an element, can spend an *external* income to this end.
>
> (Schmitt 1992a: 12, m.t.)

What is crucially important here is that the two payments are *cumulative*, that the expenditure of country A's external income adds up with that of its residents' internal income. The first point made by Schmitt is straightforward: the two payments add up together because the loss of A's external income is not compensated by an equivalent gain in $M_A$. If country A were the beneficiary of the payment carried out by IR, its expenditure of $M_R$ would simply replace it, and the charge of external debt servicing would not be multiplied by two.

> *The charge of external debts is* simple *if and only if the internal income that residents pay to their foreign creditors are obtained in full ownership by their own countries, which give up, in return, an equivalent amount of their external gains generated by their net commercial exports.*
>
> (Schmitt 1992b: 20, m.t.)

Now, it is an undisputable fact that 'nowhere in the world is the internal income spent to the benefit of foreign creditors captured, for their profit, by the indebted countries themselves' (Schmitt 1994–95, 21.2.95b: 38, m.t.). It then follows that, paid by A's residents and, additionally, by their country, the service of A's external debt entails a double loss; one justified by the external debt incurred by IR and one, completely unjustified, due to the lack of a true system of international payments. The present non-system is failing to provide free of cost the vehicular money needed to convey the payment of A's indebted residents in the international space. The cost of purchasing it rests entirely on country A itself, whose sacrifice of its external income is not compensated by a gain in domestic currency.

## *A further proof of the double charge of external debt servicing*

Schmitt provides a complementary argument for the double charge of external debt servicing by showing that the payment made by the indebted residents has a positive and distinct cost, which is added to that of the payment carried out, in foreign currency, by their country.

Let us suppose country A's domestic output to be worth 100 money units (m.u.), the amount of income formed by its production and available in A's domestic economy before part of it is exported to country R. Suppose also that A's external debt servicing is equal to $M_A$ 10, the amount of country A's net commercial exports to country R. A's trade surplus reduces to m.u. 90 the amount of country A's internal product and, by the same token, decreases the purchasing power of A's income holders. '[T]he "exports without imports" of country [A] *are bound to decrease the purchasing power of its income holders for the same amount*' Schmitt 1990b: 40, m.t.). Indeed, the 100 units of money A still available within the country have now a purchasing power of 90 units. A's domestic output being the object of a net demand from R, its macroeconomic price increases from m.u.100 to 110, so that m.u. 100 are now just enough for the purchase of 90 units of A's product.

Country A's exporters are paid through the monetization of the foreign currency, $M_R$, entered on the assets side of A's banking system: country A's net commercial exports are paid within country A through a creation of money A. Yet this increase in country A's monetary income does not accrue to A's income holders; it is paid to exporters and is at once channelled into covering the costs of production of the goods exported in surplus. After the payment of country A's trade surplus, the situation is unchanged: income holders still own $M_A$ 100 whose purchasing power is of 90 units of product. The effect of the payment of country A's indebted residents to the benefit of non-residents is clearly to reduce by $M_A$ 10 the amount of income available in country A, from $M_A$ 100 to $M_A$ 90.

Since country A's external debt is serviced by country A itself through a transfer of its external income, the amount of domestic income paid by A's indebted residents should be transferred to their country. Unfortunately, this is not what happens in today's non-system: the amount of monetary income spent by IR, $M_A$ 10, is lost to the benefit of country R and can be recovered only through a foreign loan.

> [F]inally, when [A's] residents spend [ $M_A$ 10] in amortization and interests in favour of their foreign creditors, the total monetary income of country

> [A] is reduced to [ $M_A$ 90] [...], a sum that must be supplied by a new loan of [ $M_A$ 10] merely in order to maintain the purchasing power of internal income at the level of the available product.
>
> (ibid.: 40–41, m.t.)

The loss of part of country A's domestic output corresponding to its net commercial exports is perfectly legitimate; it takes place when A gives up its gain of foreign currency to the benefit of country R. What is illegitimate is the loss of domestic income incurred when country A's indebted residents pay their debt in money A.

Another way of putting it is to say that the conversion of country A's domestic income into an equivalent amount of external income, a net purchase of money R in terms of money A, is costly; it defines a loss of $M_A$'s purchasing power that is added to that of country A's external income. Country A's indebted residents spend a fraction of their domestic income to *purchase* the foreign currency given up by their country's central bank. It is this purchase of foreign currency that triggers the second, illegitimate charge of external debt servicing. The ensuing loss of domestic income and the need to counter it through additional net commercial exports, or through a new foreign loan, characterize what Schmitt, in his 1990 unpublished manuscript, calls the *disorder theorem*.

> To borrow foreign currencies to import goods is a justified operation; to borrow foreign currencies [or to sacrifice those earned through a new trade surplus] with the sole aim of fulfilling the domestic income (which should have remained intact) is a serious aberration, because the foreign currencies borrowed [or earned] have no other use but in the internal sale of domestic product.
>
> (ibid.: 53, m.t.)

### *The pathology of external debt servicing as a consequence of the fact that international transactions form an economy of exchange*

In his search for the fundamental cause of what he calls the *paradoxical vice* characterizing the present mechanism of external debt servicing, Schmitt does not hesitate in investigating the problem from different angles and developing arguments apparently in contrast with his previous analyses.

What follows is an example of his 'dialectical' approach: his explanation of the paradoxical vice is based here on the logical impossibility for countries to earn a positive external income. Indebted countries are thus caught between two opposed realities:

1) they have to transfer abroad, in foreign currencies, the payment of their indebted residents, and
2) they cannot obtain the external income required to fulfil their task.

Schmitt shows that the reconciliation of 1) and 2) leads to the pathological duplication of the charge of external debt servicing; he thus provides a proof that is 'dialectically complementary' with the previous one, based on the hypothetical formation of countries' external income.

Schmitt's analysis starts from the observation that trade surpluses are always paid by net exporting countries' domestic income: '*whenever they occur, net exports are paid through the equivalent expenditure of a real income formed* within *the surplus country*' (Schmitt 1992a: 89, m.t.). It is true that R pays its net commercial imports in $M_R$, yet the money R paid to country A flows immediately back to country R's banking system, and A obtains in exchange an equivalent sum of claims on R's bank deposits. This means that country A lends immediately to country R the money R obtained from external payment of its trade surplus. The payment of country R is thus postponed in time, while the actual payment of country A's net exports is taken over by A's domestic economy; 'as a consequence, A's residents in their totality pay their country's net exports *in the period these exports take place*' (ibid.: 89, m.t.). It follows that, despite appearances to the contrary, no country can ever benefit from an external income. When country A's external debt is formed, in period $p_0$, in exchange for its net commercial exports to A, country R obtains a sum of financial claims issued by A's economy and not a sum of external income. Likewise, in period $p_1$, when A services its external debt, country A obtains a sum of claims on country R's bank deposits and not a sum of money R in exchange for its trade surplus. This is so because 'international transactions pertain to an *economy of exchange*' (ibid.: 90, m.t.).

The fact that countries' external income is always and necessarily equal to zero is no obstacle for the servicing of A's external debt. Logically, country A's net commercial imports of $p_0$ are perfectly balanced by its net commercial exports of $p_1$, which guarantees the compensation of the postponed payments of both country A (in $p_0$) and country R (in $p_1$). 'The conclusion is that the logical non-existence of countries' external income is no obstacle to the final payment of their external debts' (ibid.: 91, m.t.). It is because international transactions form an economy of exchange that country A faces the need to convert the payment of its indebted residents and with the formal impossibility to benefit from an external income. The paradoxical vice arises from the necessity to reconcile the former with the latter.

Since the indebted country cannot provide the external income required for IR to service its external debt, it has to 'transform or convert the object of its external debt [...] into an *internal* income, a conversion that can succeed only when *a first net commercial export*' is achieved (ibid.: 94, m.t.). This, however, is not enough for the country as a whole to get rid of the external debt it carries on top of that carried by its residents. Once 'the object of external debts is transformed into an *internal* income, the country concerned gets rid of it through *a second net commercial export*' (ibid.: 94, m.t.). Overall, *two* additional trade surpluses are required to settle a single external debt, which confirms the pathological duplication of the charge in external debt servicing.

## The impact of external debt servicing on debt servicing countries

### *The impact on the payment of A's net commercial exports*

Properly speaking, no country can realize a gain in foreign or external income, because the sum of foreign currency obtained in exchange for net commercial exports flows immediately back to its original banking system and the claims on bank deposits obtained in its stead define a loan granted to the net importing country. However, it is beyond doubt that, in the present non-system of international payments, net exporting countries are credited in foreign currencies, which increase their official reserves. In this sense it is legitimate to speak of countries' external gains and their expenditure in the payment of their external debts. Let us therefore go back to Schmitt's distinction between payments *a*, carried out by a country's indebted residents in their domestic currency, and payments *alpha*, carried out by the country itself in foreign currencies. Let us also resume our previous example and analyze the implications of the payment *alpha* carried out by country A. In $p_1$ two payments *alpha* face each other: that of country A and that of country R, which must convert the payment of its residents' net commercial imports (Figure 10.5).

Being equivalent and reciprocal, flow (1) and flow (2) cancel each other: country A's payment *alpha* reduces to zero the payment *alpha* of country R. The same result is obtained if we consider the *real* payments between A and R that take place in $p_1$. Country R pays for its trade deficit by transferring to country A an equivalent amount of claims on bank deposits, while country A services its external debt by transferring back these same bank deposits to country R. The two real payments imply the reflux to R's banking system of the bank deposits given up by R in exchange for an equivalent amount of A's domestic output. This means that country A's gain of foreign currency is reduced to zero by its external debt servicing. Country A is thus 'seriously injured because, from the moment it gives up the foreign currencies initially gained in its exports, it witnesses, by the retroactive effect of this transfer, the cancellation of the payment of these exports' (Schmitt 1990b: 83, m.t.).

The compensation between the two payments *alpha* would not have retroactively any effect on the *formation* of country A's external gain if it entailed the positive and final servicing of its external debt. Formed because of country A's net commercial imports of period $p_0$, A's external debt would be honoured through country A's net commercial exports of period $p_1$, so that the payment of $p_1$ would merely reduce to zero the external gain formed in $p_1$.

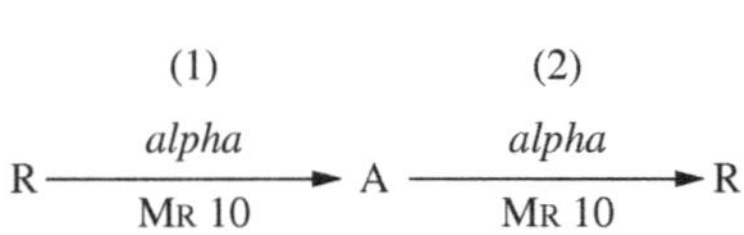


*Figure 10.5* The compensation between the payments *alpha* carried out by R and A.

Unfortunately, as we know, the payment that country A and its residents have to make is twice the amount of A's net exports. The servicing of country A's external debt implies the unilateral transfer of the bank deposits defining its external gain of $p_1$, a transfer that can take place only if A purchases the vehicular money required to convey the payment between country A and country R (see Figure 10.4). It thus follows that country R recovers the bank deposits it transfers to country A as payment of its trade deficit, and country A is forced to purchase the foreign currency needed to transfer to country R, unilaterally, these same bank deposits.

> *The anomaly consists entirely in the fact that the indebted country must purchase as a final good the y units of foreign currency to pay its foreign creditors while the Rest of the World, R, is exonerated from the payment of its excess commercial purchases.*
> (Schmitt 1987d: 159, m.t.)

As Schmitt points out, the payment *alpha* made by country A does not only reduce the amount of A's external gain due to its trade surplus of $p_1$, but it also undoes the very *formation* of this gain, which is thus equal to zero from the very beginning. The expenditure of country A's external income formed in $p_1$ is perfectly logical; in order to service its external debt, country A must give up the external income obtained in exchange for part of its domestic output. What is completely illogical, or pathological, is that this payment has a negative repercussion on the formation of the external income itself. This is precisely what happens today: 'the instant the indebted country sacrifices part of its external gains (invariably due to its trade surplus) to service its foreign creditors, its decision affects retroactively the formation of these gains, which are *purely and simply cancelled out*' (Cencini and Schmitt 1991: 147). As shown in Figure 10.4, the external income formed in (1), due to A's trade surplus, is lost by country A in (2). But this payment is not the only one country A has to carry out. If we consider the monetary aspect of A's external debt servicing, we observe, in fact, that country A must transfer to country R an amount of vehicular money, $M_R$, equivalent to A's real payment (in bank deposits). This payment is not balanced by any inflow of foreign currency: 'the withdrawal takes place at the level of [A's] external income *formation* and not only [...] at the level of its income *formed* in the international market' (ibid.: 149).

Since flows (2) define a unilateral transfer, country A does not obtain, in a circular flow, the foreign currency it needs to convey its real payment and must purchase it, either through a new trade surplus or by getting indebted. It is because of this purchase that the servicing of country A's external debt reduces the formation of its external gain. Country A must obtain the foreign currency, which is required for the *monetary* servicing of its external debt, at a cost. In other words, it has to sacrifice its external gain on top of the domestic goods already exported to country R. Let us say it once more. It is perfectly logical for country A to lose the external income earned in the form of bank deposits through its trade surplus, whereas it is pathological that country A must purchase and spend an equivalent, *additional* amount of foreign currency in order to vehiculate this payment. The first expenditure is incurred on A's *formed* external gain; the second affects the *formation* of this gain.

Finally, since A's external gain is cancelled at the moment it should form, country A must still nourish its external debt servicing; it does so by exporting an additional portion of its domestic output or through a sale of financial claims. In both cases, country A's external debt servicing calls for a double payment, half of which is due to a pathological mechanism that forces country A to purchase what it has already gained through its trade surplus.

> [S]ince its external trade brings a gain invalidated at source, country [A] has no net external income at its disposal which could nourish the current servicing of its external debt; if it can none the less pay its creditors up to [$M_R$] $x$ this is because it finds this sum in the financial [or in the trade] market.
>
> (ibid.: 147)

### *External debt – eternal debt*

The retroactive impact of external debt servicing on the formation of country A's external income is confirmed by the perverse effect it has on the exchange rate of money A. Defining an excess demand of money R in terms of money A, country A's payment *alpha* entails the depreciation of A's domestic currency, whose loss of external value is equivalent to the amount of foreign currency earned through its trade surplus. This loss has therefore a retroactive effect on the formation itself of country A's external income, which is consequently reduced to zero. Country A 'suffers from a deterioration in the terms of international exchange which swallows up and cancels, in the exchange market, the reality of [its] net commercial gain' (ibid.: 176). Country A can avoid the devaluation of its national currency only if it finds, through trade or in the financial market, an equivalent sum of foreign currency. It is only in this case, indeed, that A can exert an excess demand for $M_A$ in terms of $M_R$ that neutralizes the impact of A's external debt servicing on the exchange rate of $M_A$.

When country A exerts a re-equilibrating demand for money A in terms of money R, it spends in the exchange market the foreign currency obtained from country R. If the additional sum of $M_R$ thus lost by country A is that obtained by exporting an additional amount of A's current output, the reabsorption of the excess demand of money A implicit in country A's external debt servicing entails an equivalent reduction in A's official reserves. Since a decrease in credit is tantamount to an increase in debt, and since country A's official reserves are necessarily lent abroad and define therefore a credit of A on the rest-of-the-world, this method of restoring equilibrium on the exchange market has substantially the same effect on country A as the solution of borrowing abroad. In both cases, country A incurs an external debt that cancels out the decrease in debt that should have been enjoyed by the country as a result of its external debt servicing. The devastating conclusion is that country A's external debt is bound to rise again from its ashes. '*Theorem of the disorder of payments between nations: each service (in interests or amortization) of nations' external debt brings it viciously back to its previous level*' (Schmitt 1990b: 30, m.t.). It is this vicious circle that justifies Schmitt's claim that countries' external debt is bound to become an eternal debt.

A further proof that the indebted country has to find an additional amount of foreign currency to compensate for the loss of the external income made from trade surplus is provided by the analysis showing that payments *a* and *alpha* add up to one another/are cumulative. If we consider the payment made by country A's indebted residents, payment *a*, we observe that the servicing of A's external debt defines the unilateral transfer of part of country A's domestic income: the creditor country does not transfer the slightest part of its domestic income to A. Country A must therefore incur a new debt or sacrifice part of its domestic output in order to cover for its loss of internal income: instead of enabling country A to increase its commercial imports, the additional sum of foreign currency obtained from R must be spent 'to cover for the deficit in *domestic* income vis-à-vis the *internal* product on sale *within* the indebted economy' (ibid.: 74, m.t.).

The different analytical steps can be summarized as follows.

1) The payment of A's indebted residents reduces the amount of the domestic income available within A's economy.
2) Country A must sacrifice the external income due to its trade surplus to recover the income lost in 1).
3) The retroactive effect of 2) on 1) is to reduce to zero the formation of A's external gain.
4) Country A must find another amount of foreign currency to service its external debt.

Once again, the charge of country A's external debt servicing is double, because its initial foreign income of $p_1$ is cancelled at the moment of its formation.

## The principles of Schmitt's solution

### *The institution of a national bureau*

Positive analysis calls for normative analysis, that is, for specifying the principles of a reform that enables us to get rid of the paradoxical vice affecting countries' external debt servicing. Let us apply normative analysis to the case of country A's servicing of the external debt initially incurred by its residents. Since A's external payments rest on country A itself, a set of its residents, the first step of the reform consists in explicitly acknowledging the existence of the nation-state A, which will be represented by a Bureau instituted by the central bank, itself charged to act as the bank of country A. 'Given that country A is now an entity whose existence is explicit, its central Bank can act on behalf of this entity' (Schmitt 1994–95, 21.2.95b: 51, m.t.). Concretely, the Bureau will be given a bookkeeping function and will be subdivided into an internal and an external department: the former managing the payments between A's residents and their country, the latter those between the country itself and the rest-of-the-world. Acting on behalf of the nation-state A, its central bank will enter, on the external department of A's Bureau, all the payments made in foreign currency by country R to the benefit of country A, as well as all the payments addressed by country A to country R in foreign currency. In particular, it is in the external department that the payment of A's exports by R will be entered, together with the payment, in money R, of country A's external debt servicing.

Schmitt introduces here an important clarification, namely that the external income sacrificed by any indebted country when servicing its external debt defines an export-without-import independently of whether or not the sum of the indebted country's commercial exports is greater than the sum of its commercial imports. In other words, for country A to be able to service its external debt, it is enough that 'it devotes a positive part of its gains due to its commercial exports' (Schmitt 1990b: 66, m.t.) and none of its *net* external gains. Today, this is not the case: economists believe that country A can positively service its debt only by addressing to country R an amount of its net external income. In so doing, they are unaware of the fact that

> the truncated definition of $E_s$ [A's exports-without-imports] plunges the indebted countries into a vicious circle: the very *formation* of their external income is reduced to zero by the full absorption of their net commercial gains in the current service of their external debts.
>
> (ibid.: 66, m.t.)

The reform will let the payment of A's debt take place without any need for country A to realize a net gain in foreign currency, because A will no longer be forced to purchase the vehicular currency needed to convey its external payment.

As the reader will recall, nowadays a sum of country A's domestic income must be spent in the purchase of a sum of foreign currency, which has a detrimental effect on A's external debt servicing, whose total charge is thus doubled. By instituting A's national Bureau, the reform will no longer impose the purchase of money R: the Bureau will spend in favour of country R the exact amount of $M_R$ it obtains from R. '[E]very inflow (asset) of *foreign currency* will correspond to an outflow (liability) strictly defined in *foreign currency*, and reciprocally, no transaction implying a purchase or a sale of foreign currency against a sum of national currency' (ibid.: 54, m.t.). Since the domestic income paid by A's indebted residents will no longer be spent and lost in the purchase of foreign currency, the solution advocated by Schmitt consists '*in the safeguard to the benefit of the indebted nation, of the internal income that its residents devote to the servicing of external debts*' (ibid.: 56, m.t.).

Let us represent as in Figure 10.6 the payment of country R's imports to the benefit of the external department of A's Bureau, flow (1), and the servicing of country A's external debt, carried out by this same external department in favour of A's foreign creditors, flow (2).

It is immediately clear that the payment of A's foreign creditors, FC, is *internalized*; FC, residents of R, are finally paid by R's importers. Now, it must be kept in mind that it is not country A as such that incurs an external debt in the first place. Indeed, country A as a whole carries the external debt incurred by its residents; it is therefore logical that, taking over the external payment of its indebted residents, country A is entitled to a compensation. Its outflow of foreign currency must be balanced by an equivalent inflow of domestic currency; paying FC in money R on behalf of IR, nation-state A must collect the payment in money A carried out by its indebted residents (Figure 10.7).

> It is not country A itself that had incurred a debt *on its own*; on the contrary, A carries the external debts of its *residents*: because A thus reduces *somebody else's* debt, it is entitled to a compensation: this is obtained from the moment A captures (on behalf of its State) the internal income given up by the true bearer of its external debt.
>
> (Schmitt 1992b: 43, m.t.)

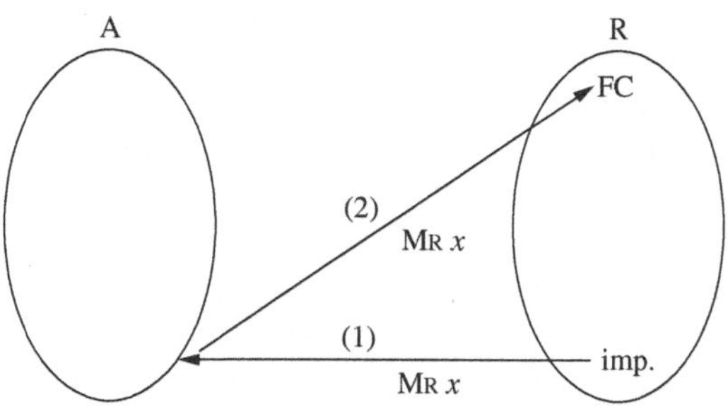


*Figure 10.6* The internalization in country R of the payment of A's external debt.

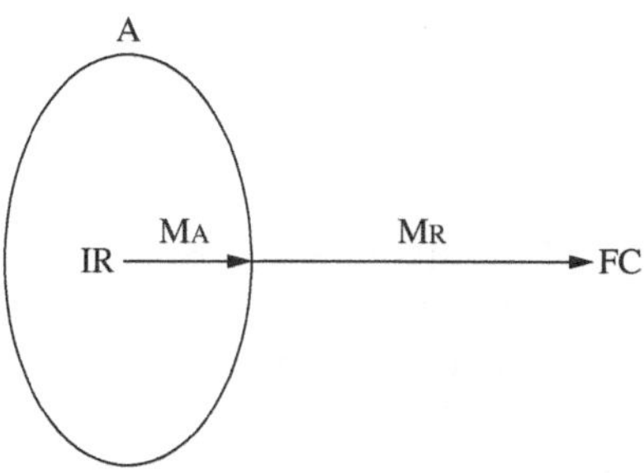


*Figure 10.7* Internalization of payment of external debt incurred by IR.

### *The 'internalization' of the external debt incurred by deficit countries*

When country A's indebted residents, IR, carry an external debt on top of that of their own country, the charge of external debt servicing is pathologically doubled. To avoid this hopeless conclusion, *IR's external debt must be internalized*, that is, 'it is enough to transform the external debt of [IR] into an *internal* debt' (Schmitt 1994–95, 21.2.95a: 14, m.t.). Schmitt's explanation is very clear: being taken over by its country, IR's external debt should no longer exist as such, IR owing to A, in $M_A$, what country A owes to R, in $M_R$, on IR's behalf. '[G]iven that [IR's] *external* debt is finally taken over by its country, the nation-State A, [IR] must imperatively stop carrying its own *external* debt' (ibid.: 17, m.t.). In practical terms, the payment of A's indebted residents will be addressed to the *internal* department of A's national Bureau as compensation for the payment addressed to the foreign creditors of R by the Bureau's external department. Thanks to this simple mechanism, country A will no longer lose its external gain of period $p_1$. Indeed, even though country A's external department pays the foreign creditors with a sum of money R equivalent to the one it obtains through its trade surplus of $p_1$, its external gain is unaffected: the loss of $M_R$ is replaced by the decrease in country A's external debt. The new form of country A's external gain is given by the decrease of its debt, which, as is well known, defines the equivalent increase of its credit: 'country A gains an asset with respect to the rest of the world, which value is exactly equal to the value of the external debt [...] it has got rid of' (Schmitt 1994–95, 21.2.95b: 16, m.t.).

What we must clearly understand is that the reform will not transform today's loss of country A's external income into a double gain, an external one, defined by the decrease in country A's external debt, and an internal one, consisting in the amount of money A paid to A's Bureau by IR. In reality, what A's Bureau gains in money A is nothing more than the conversion of its external gain. The money A gained by the Bureau, and that it will transfer to the State, is the bookkeeping counterpart of the decrease in country A's external debt; the two are the complementary faces of a singular gain resulting from the reduction of today's double charge of external debt servicing to a single charge. Country A's internal gain 'is entirely legitimate, because it is nothing else than the final form (in money A) of country A's external gain' (ibid.: 52, m.t.).

### *A bookkeeping example*

The bookkeeping entries in the internal and in the external departments of country A's national Bureau are represented in Table 10.1, where we assume that the exchange rate of money A is of $M_A$ 1for $M_R$ 1.

Entry (1) refers to period $p_0$, when country A's external debt, of $X$ money units, is formed as a consequence of A's trade deficit. Entries (2) represent the payment, in money R and in period $p_1$, of A's trade surplus, equal to $y$ money units. Following this payment, the external department credits the internal

*Table 10.1* Bookkeeping representation of the reform

| *Assets* | | *Liabilities* | |
|---|---|---|---|
| Bureau's internal department | | | |
| (2) External department | $M_A\ y$ | Exporters | $M_A\ y$ |
| (3) A's indebted residents | $M_A\ y$ | State or government | $M_A\ y$ |
| Bureau's external department | | | |
| (1) Trade deficit | $M_R\ X$ | Exporters | $M_R\ X$ |
| (2) Foreign currency | $M_R\ y$ | Internal department | $M_R\ y$ |
| (3) External debt | $M_R\ y$ | Foreign currency | $M_R\ y$ |
| Trade deficit | $M_R\ X$ | External debt | $M_R\ X - y$ |
| | | Internal department | $M_R\ y$ |

department, which pays country A's exporters, on its behalf, by monetizing in money A the external department's gain in money R. External debt servicing is represented in entries (3); country A's indebted residents credit the internal department with $M_A\ y$, while the external department credits R with $M_R\ y$ and enters a reduction of A's external debt as the counterpart of this payment. Finally, to the net gain, in money A, of the internal department is transferred to the benefit of the State or the government of country A.

### *Capital flight*

Let us conclude this chapter by mentioning Schmitt's considerations about the controversial discussion around *capital flight*. In one of his manuscripts of 1990 (1990b), Schmitt claims first that capital flight is logically impossible in a true system of international payments, because the net flows of financial capitals are necessarily balanced by equivalent net flows of commercial goods. This means that if capital flight is nonetheless a dismal reality, it is because 'the bookkeeping order is not complied with by the present regime of payments between nations' (Schmitt 1990b: 75, m.t.). The reform advocated by Schmitt will establish order and make it impossible for capitals to fly from their country of origin. Net financial flows will always be matched by net commercial flows, so that capitals transferred abroad will finance equivalent commercial purchases of the rest-of-the-world. If this were not the case, if country A's trade balance showed no surplus, the capitals lent abroad would immediately be borrowed back: A's domestic capitals would never be lost by country A. '[E]ach loan that is not based on a commercial surplus is a "loan-borrowing" [which means that an equivalent sum is at the same time lent and borrowed] and not a net loan' (ibid.: 76, m.t.). In practice, country A's domestic capitals invested abroad will be 'captured' by the internal department of A's national Bureau, which will incur a debt to the Bureau's external department, which, in its turn, will incur a debt to the rest-of-the-world (Table 10.2).

*Table 10.2* Neutralization of capital flight

| *Assets* | | *Liabilities* | |
|---|---|---|---|
| Bureau's internal department | | | |
| Capital invested abroad | $M_A\ x$ | Debt towards the external department | $M_A\ x$ |
| Bureau's external department | | | |
| Credit vis-à-vis the internal department | $M_R\ x$ | Debt towards R | $M_R\ x$ |

The residents of country A who invest their capital abroad will lose it in the form of bank deposits expressed in money A and acquire financial assets denominated in money R and deposited in R's banking system. But, contrary to what happens today, their capital will not be lost to their country: transferred to the Bureau's internal department, it will remain available within A's domestic economy. The foreign investment of country A's residents defines a loan to country R that is immediately matched by an equivalent loan of country R to country A's external department. The perfect balance between the two reciprocal loans will prevent any capital flight, which confirms once more Schmitt's positive and normative analyses of countries' external debt servicing.

# 11 The analysis of capital and interest based on Schmitt's unpublished manuscripts of 1993–1996

The problem of capital and interest in income terms was first analyzed by Schmitt in his 1984 book on inflation, unemployment, and capital malformations (see Chapter 6). From 1993 to 1998 Schmitt went back to this subject in a series of lectures delivered at the Universities of Fribourg and Dijon and collected in the form of mimeo manuscripts. They contain several highly relevant observations concerning the nature of interest and its relationship to national income as well as to capital. Presenting them in this volume is justified on their own merit, as they prepare the way to a new analysis of (involuntary) unemployment, which Schmitt developed in his 1998 unpublished manuscript *Le chômage et son éradication* (and which will be the focus of Chapter 12). Is interest a macroeconomic income? Is it additional to wages? What is the rationale for the existence of positive interest? These are some of the questions dealt with in Chapter 11 and answered by Schmitt in his all-important manuscripts.

## Schmitt's first explanation of non-wage income

As explained in Part I of this volume, Schmitt's macroeconomic analysis rests on the well-established fact that human labour is the sole macroeconomic factor of production, because it is through remunerated labour that physically heterogeneous goods are given a homogeneous numerical form. 'The only and unique "factor" that transforms products into money [...is] the work of man' (Schmitt 1993/1994a, 11.1.94: 4, m.t.). It is through the payment of wages that this transformation occurs, and money acquires a positive purchasing power whose origin lies precisely in the fact that wages become the very expression of the product.

Money as such is purely nominal; as soon as it is associated with production it disappears and is replaced by a positive income, by the product-in-the-money. Schmitt's analysis makes it clear that *wages define the product, not its monetary counterpart.* The purchasing power of wages derives from their identity with the product – and not from a chimerical intrinsic value that money would obtain from a supernatural power of banks or from social consensus. The concept of economic value itself must be reformulated accordingly. Far from defining an imaginary dimension that products are supposedly endowed with, economic

DOI: 10.4324/9781351271325-16

value is a numerical relationship between produced output and the monetary form it is associated with. 'Value is the relationship between a *purely numerical* sum of money and the *purely physical* product it contains' (ibid.: 3, m.t.). Wage-units are the unit of measure of economic value, so that the total amount paid out in wages (direct and indirect) defines at the same time the total amount of value and the total amount of income created by production.

The identity established by production between wages and physical output generates identity between wages and national income. 'Workers' wages nationwide [...] are indeed a product, namely national product, and not a part or the whole of the price of this product' (Schmitt 1993; 1994a, 23.11.93: 8, m.t.). Since total wages define the two combined results of national production, i.e. national product and national income, how do we explain the existence of non-wage income and non-wage-goods? This question concerns the formation of profit and its subsequent redistribution in the form of interest, dividend, and rent. In his unpublished manuscripts of the 93–96 period, Schmitt concentrates his attention on interest aiming to show that, while human labour remains the sole factor of production, the presence of capital guarantees the formation of additional income, notably interest.

### *A short summary of Schmitt's analysis of profit*

Schmitt's starting point is the fact that, as shown in his early writings, profit derives from wages. The crucial distinction here is that between production and redistribution, between flows and stocks. Production is a flow: the payment of wages. As such, it gives rise to an undifferentiated income. 'With regard to *flows*, in each period net income is wages; in other words, the formation of a macroeconomic income is without exception, the formation of wages' (Schmitt 1996d: 56, m.t.). Redistribution, on the other hand, applies to stocks; 'it is the operation through which part of wages are withdrawn in favour of profits' (ibid.: 56, m.t.).

It is through the sale of produced output that part of wages is transferred to firms as profit. Yet, the analysis would be incomplete if it stopped here. Formed in the product market, profits would end up defining a sum of wage-goods, if they were spent in the self-same market. The correct analysis requires the expenditure of profit in the labour market, that is, the possibility for the payment of wages to include an expenditure of profit. By arguing for such inclusion, Schmitt's analysis of profit stands out from that advocated by mainstream economists. With the partial exception of Adam Smith's notion of labour commanded, Schmitt's theory is the only one defining capitalism on the basis of this dual expenditure. '[I]n the advanced state of society, firms spend a positive income in the market of productive factors (workers) to the extent of the formation of non-wage income' (Schmitt 1993; 1994a, 11.1.94: 5, m.t.).

Thanks to Schmitt's concept of quantum time, value and price may be seen to overlap. Though distinct in chronological time, production and consumption are simultaneous events in quantum time, because both are complementary parts of a single emission of the identical period of quantized time. It thus appears that the purchase occurring in the market for products retroactively modifies the payment taking place in the labour market. By including expenditure of profits within the payment of wages and formation of profits within the expenditure of wages, we can explain profit in a manner consistent with the necessary equality of values and prices. The difference between price and value of the wage-goods sold to households in the market for products disappears once the expenditure of profit is accounted for. Indeed, the price of wages-goods includes the cost of profit-goods to the same extent that the value of wage-goods – as determined by the payment of wages –includes that of profit-goods. After compensation, it appears that both wage- and profit-goods are purchased through the final expenditure of an income corresponding to their costs of production.

As any other real good, initially profit-goods take the form of wage-goods; in other words, they are monetized through the payment of wages.

> Through the payment of the new wages of a given period, the new product of this period is deposited in the numerical form of money. The new product is thus deposited with banks issuing numerical money in the form of wages: it is the product-in-the-money, i.e. the product-in-the-money-wages that is the only correct definition of every income.
>
> (Schmitt 1995; 1996: 79, m.t.)

If a profit is formed when wages are spent in the product market, we can ascertain retroactively that the initial production of wage-goods consisted partly in a production of profit-goods. Yet, this does not alter the fact that profit-goods are monetized through the payment of wages. The difference between consumption-goods and profit-goods does not concern their monetization but the way they are purchased: the former is purchased in the market for products, the latter in the labour market. It is thus confirmed that profit-goods take initially the form of wage-goods and are measured in wage-units.

## *Schmitt's logical proofs that profit-goods are purchased through an expenditure taking place within the payment of wages*

In his 1996 unpublished *Cours de théorie monétaire*, Schmitt provides what he calls a didactic and analytical proof that any time a profit is formed in the market for products the payment of wages in the labour market includes an expenditure of income defining a purchase of profit-goods.

### *The didactic proof*

Let us start with the didactic proof and assume that a positive profit is formed in period $p_1$ and spent in period $p_2$. Schmitt uses a numerical example where the production of $p_1$ has a value of 100 money units (m.u.), the total amount of wage payments, and is sold at a price of 200 m.u. Can the difference between value and selling price be dealt with by distinguishing between production-price and redistribution-price? In other words, is it possible to maintain that value and price are indeed equal because value (determined by production) must be confronted with production-price rather than with redistribution-price?

Schmitt's answer is unambiguous: the identity between price and value can be proved only by reducing the redistribution-price to the production-price. If wage-earners spend all their income, in $p_1$, firms realize a profit of 50 wage-units. Firms then spend their profit in $p_2$ by investing it in the production of profit-goods of any kind. If in $p_2$ wages paid to income-earners are again equal to 100 m.u., firms acquire half of what is produced in the period by spending their profit. 'Through their own expenditures, conversions of monetary into real profits, firms purchase a production and acquire, therefore, the result of this productive activity' (Schmitt 1996d: 59, m.t.). Despite the fact that in $p_2$ half of the production is lost by workers to the profit of firms, the totality of what is produced in $p_1 + p_2$ is equal to 200 units of value, because in $p_1$ as well as in $p_2$ the amount of wages paid is equal to 100 wage-units. The total value of what is produced in the two periods is 200, even though wage-earners obtain only three-quarters of it.

The inclusion of an expenditure of profit within the payment of wages does not reduce the latter; wage-earners are paid 100 wage-units even in $p_2$, yet half of the product monetized through the payment of wages is appropriated by firms. Given that half of the wage-goods produced in $p_1$ are still unsold, in $p_2$ wage-earners obtain a financial claim on that stock in exchange for the profit-goods appropriated by firms. It thus appears that, when we consider the two periods together, the difference between the redistribution-price of $p_1$ and the value of wage-goods produced in $p_1$ is absorbed by the inclusion of the expenditure of profit formed in $p_1$ within the payment of wages of $p_2$ and by the purchase of the goods stocked in $p_1$ by wage-earners producing profit-goods in $p_2$.

The value of the production of $p_1$ and $p_2$ is of 200 wage-units and the price at which it is finally purchased is equal to 100 + 100 = 200 wage-units. Indeed, wage-goods produced in $p_1$, equal to 100 units of value, are purchased through the final expenditure of 50 wage-units formed in $p_1$ and 50 wage-units of $p_2$, while the goods produced in $p_2$, equal to 100 units of value, are purchased through the expenditure of 50 wage-units in the labour market and of 50 wage-units in the market for products. It is true that in $p_1$ wage-goods of value 50 wage-units are sold at a price of 100 m.u., yet one need only observe that this price is inclusive of the price of the profit-goods produced in $p_2$ to realize that, ultimately, there is no difference between the value of the goods produced in $p_1$ and $p_2$ and their price. *In chronological time prices can be different from values, but this difference is necessarily reabsorbed in quantum time, so that it is correct to conclude that prices are always necessarily equal to values.* The careful reader will have recognized the analysis already proposed by Schmitt in 1984 and based on the refusal of the principle of the excluded middle: values and prices can differ (in chronological time) even though they are the two terms of an identity (in quantum time).

*The analytical proof*

In 1996, Schmitt does not reject his 1984 analysis but considers it a didactic alternative to a more general analysis, where one no longer needs to distinguish between two successive periods. This is the mark of an important switch from an analysis in terms of values (where prices are reduced to values) to one developed in terms of prices (where values are made equal to prices). The two analyses are not opposed but complementary. They lead to the same explanation of inflation and unemployment, while providing a complete picture of how non-wage income is formed and what its nature is. Let us proceed gradually and consider, first, Schmitt's second (analytical) proof of the way profit is formed and spent (invested) in the respect of the identity of values and prices.

This time, everything happens in a single period, $p_1$. The profit formed through the sale of wage-goods at a mark-up is spent or invested in the purchase of part of $p_1$' s current output. Suppose that total production is equal to 100 wage-goods and that firms sell it at a redistribution-price of 125 m.u. By spending their total income, wage-earners obtain wage-goods of a value equal to 80 wage-units, while firms realize a profit of 20 wage-units. In 1936 and 1946, Keynes had already pointed out that what happens in the products market has an impact on what happens in the market for labour. The formation of profit in the market for products transforms the initial emission in the labour market: 'workers' final expenditure in the commodity market modifies retroactively the emission of wages' (Schmitt and Cencini 1982: 143).

The formation of a profit of 20 wage-units modifies the initial payment of 100 wage-units, which now includes a final expenditure of profit. This means that from the very beginning workers produce wage-goods for 80 units of value and profit-goods for 20 units of value. The final purchase included in the emission of wages is the retroactive sanction of the formation of profit: the transfer of income to the benefit of firms defines the simultaneous expenditure of profit within the payment of wages. *The necessary equality of values and prices results from the organic unity of the two markets*; the inclusion of the expenditure of profit within the payment of wages taking place in the labour market perfectly matches the distribution of income between wages and profit in the products market.

> Hereafter, price and value are inevitably identical: value (i.e. the amount of wages) is 100, and 100 is also the amount of income spent for the final purchase of the whole product (80 in the commodity market and 20 in the factor markets).
>
> (ibid.: 144)

To understand better what happens in $p_1$ one can assume that firms ask banks to advance their expected profit in anticipation of the result they expect to obtain in the market for products and use the advance to finance the production of profit-goods. In our numerical example, firms invest 20 units of advanced profit and pay workers to produce profit-goods. Spent in advance, profit would have to be realized later in the market for products and returned to banks.

What must be made clear is that the advance holds no guarantee that an equal profit will form in the products market. If the advance were enough to explain the formation of profit, the explanation would be viciously circular and inconsistent with the fact that households are free to spend their income as they wish on products *and* in the financial market. 'Households are always entirely free to spend part of their income on purchasing financial claims; there exists no mechanism likely to force them to spend their entire income in the market for products' (Schmitt 1996d: 64, m.t.). Expectations may be wrong, in which case part of the production of profit-goods would not be backed financially: in order to pay back their advances, firms would be forced to borrow what households have saved. It is thus confirmed that it is only if 'the purchases of households give rise to a monetary profit for firms [that] the emission of wages of the period [...] means necessarily a purchase by firms of workers' productive activity' (ibid.: 65, m.t.).

#### *The necessary expenditure by any single firm of the profit it obtains in the market for products*

The analytical proof gives Schmitt the opportunity to reiterate his claim that what is true for the set of firms holds true also for every single one of them, which is to say that the profit obtained by each single firm is necessarily spent (invested) on the production of this same firm. Expenditures across firms are possible, of course, but they belong to the category of *inter-industrial* expenditures, and their sum is necessarily nil for the set of firms. 'Profit can be subject to a macroeconomic expenditure – positive expenditure of the set of firms – only if it enables the firm owning it to purchase to its own benefit part of the production that workers carry out for it' (ibid.: 63, m.t.).

Schmitt had already established this apparently astonishing result in 1977 in his analysis of the *horizontal circuit*. In a book co-authored with me and devoted to the critical analysis of Marx's theory of surplus-value, he showed that the profit earned by each firm in a given period is always and necessarily equal to the profit spent by that firm in the same period. Like wages, profit is an income that is both formed and spent. The pair formed by profit-formation and profit-expenditure is crucial. Monetary and real aspects of profit form a unity and, since the real form of profit 'is the conversion of its monetary form' (Cencini and Schmitt 1977: 122, m.t.), it follows that there can be no difference between the profit formed and the profit invested. To show how this equality holds for each single firm, it helps to consider the case of expected profits advanced by banks.

Let us suppose that two firms, $F_1$ and $F_2$ obtain a profit equal to $y$ and $z$ wage-units, respectively. Can profit formed in $F_1$ be spent in $F_2$ and vice versa?

Obviously, the question does not concern the free choice of $F_1$ and $F_2$ to spend their respective profit as and where they wish. The problem is macroeconomic, and its solution cannot be influenced by microeconomic considerations. Firms' reciprocal expenditures are not subject to restrictions; they follow the principle of generalized exchange and have no impact on whether the macroeconomic expenditure of profit can logically take place between firms.

As previously observed, inter-industrial expenditures are zero-sum transactions for the set of firms, which is enough to dismiss them from consideration as an expression of firms' expenditure of net profit. In the latest example, the same conclusion is reached through an alternative argument resting on the need for $F_1$ and $F_2$ to give back to their banks the exact amount of profit advanced to them. It is clear, in fact, that if the amount spent by $F_1$ on purchasing $y$ money units from $F_2$ is different from the amount, $z$ money units, spent by $F_2$ in purchasing from $F_1$, part of the profit advanced to one of the two firms will not be compensated by that firm's receipts. 'If $z \neq y$, after their expenditure, the profits advanced by $F_1$ and $F_2$ are not re-constituted to compensate the advances' (ibid.: 124, m.t.). The existence of a horizontal circuit of profit provides a satisfactory solution. '*The profit earned by $F_1$ ($F_2$) is the profit spent by $F_1$ ($F_2$) and not the profit spent by $F_2$ ($F_1$)*' (ibid.: 124, m.t.). Since each firm invests its profit in its own production, the formation-expenditure of profit defines a perfectly circular flow on each of them, leading to the reconstitution of advances (Figure 11.1).

The validity of this result does not depend on the accuracy of firms' expectations, and it does not prevent firms from investing their profit as they choose. If expectations proved wrong, it would be necessary to re-define the initial investment in accordance with the amount of profit effectively formed. The horizontal circuit is verified for every amount of profit, whatever the amount of advances and whether expectations are exact or not. Likewise, the decisions of firms to invest their profit in the production of instrumental goods or in any category of goods produced on behalf of the beneficiaries of redistributed profits (capitalists, shareholders, property owners), have no impact on the horizontal circuit. Generalized exchange enables firms and the other beneficiaries

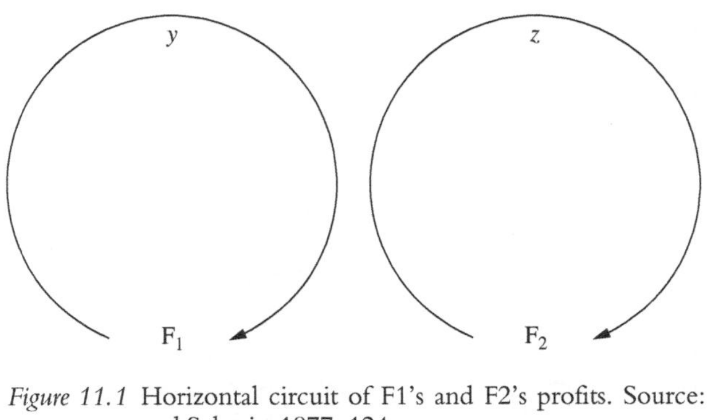


*Figure 11.1* Horizontal circuit of F1's and F2's profits. Source: elaboration from Cencini and Schmitt 1977: 124

of redistributed profits to purchase what they like; it provides the degree of freedom necessary to reconcile the existence of positive macroeconomic profits with economic agents' behaviour. Horizontal circuits are a logical necessity imposed by the very existence of macroeconomic profits. Schmitt's 1996 analysis reiterates the same conclusion: '[e]very profit that is the object of a final expenditure is invested in the same firm in which it is formed' (Schmitt 1996d: 63, m.t.).

## Towards a new explanation of interest

In his analysis of non-wage income developed in his 1994–96 unpublished manuscripts, Schmitt reserves a particular place for the study of interest. The terms of the problem are well-known: how can one reconcile the fact that interest is a macroeconomic income with the fact that capital cannot logically be considered a macroeconomic factor of production? How can interest be positive, if wages define the totality of national income? We already know that the answer rests on the observation that

1) Profit, whether redistributed or not, is derived from wages, and
2) The expenditure of profit (interest included) takes place in the labour market and finances a production of profit-goods.

Yet, Schmitt now pushes his analysis in another direction by investigating the role played by capital in the formation of interest.

### *Interest and capital*

Since human labour is the single macroeconomic factor of production, wages define the totality of the macroeconomic cost of production. It necessarily follows that 'the interest earned from the investment of savings in a new production [...] is not a *macroeconomic* cost of production' (ibid.: 45, m.t.). Interest is undoubtedly a positive *microeconomic* cost of production for firms, but not for the economy as a whole; wages are the only income whose formation does not derive from the expenditure of another income. Even though it does not define a positive macroeconomic cost of production, interest is a *macroeconomic income*, because national income is the sum of wages and non-wage income. It is true that wages define the totality of produced output and income. Yet, the formation and expenditure of profit brings forth a redistribution of wages to the benefit of firms and the financing of a production of profit-goods, interest-goods included. '[I]nterest is an "income of production" [and as such it] must be a sum of wage-units' (ibid.: 40, m.t.) even though human labour remains the unique macroeconomic source of wage-units.

The challenge facing any economist in the analysis of interest is how to reconcile these two apparently contradictory requirements. Starting from the fact that the presence of capital is crucial for the existence of interest, 'we need to explain how capital, like human labour, can produce wage-units' (ibid.: 40, m.t.).

Since capital is not a factor of production, it cannot be the direct source of the wage-units defining interest. To understand better the indirect way through which capital produces wage-units, one needs to investigate the close relationship between capital and interest.

*A brief reminder of Schmitt's analysis of capital*

Initially, capital takes the form of capital-time and results from saving. Income does not turn into capital merely through the flow of time; a transaction must take place, which leads to the destruction of the income formed by production and to its instantaneous substitution with an equivalent amount of capital. Saving is not a mere abstention from spending, but a positive expenditure occurring in the financial market. Wage-earners spend their income immediately in the purchase of financial claims issued by the bank where their income is deposited. While wage-earners purchase claims on bank deposits, their bank lends their savings at once to firms, which invest the sum in the purchase of the stock of wage-goods produced by these same wage-earners.

The result of this instantaneous process is the formation of a positive amount of net or macroeconomic capital. However, this transformation of current income into capital-time is not irreversible; at any time, income holders may decide to spend their savings, thus giving rise to the reverse transformation of capital-time into income. If this happens, the claims on bank deposits are cancelled and wage-earners are credited with a positive amount of income, which they spend on purchasing the stock of wage-goods. In the interval of time that separates the formation of capital-time from the final expenditure of income by households, firms are indebted to their bank and wage-earners own their income in the form of claims on bank deposits. Firms pay interest on their debt, while wage-earners are paid interest. Yet, nothing explains where these interests come from. To find a satisfactory solution, it is necessary to refer to the transformation of capital-time into fixed capital.

The formation of fixed capital requires investment in the production of instrumental goods of the capital-time obtained by firms as profit. By investing their profit in the production of fixed capital-goods, firms irreversibly transform an income into a fixed capital. As we know, profit is an income derived from wages and, as such, it defines saved-up income transferred from households to firms. Once invested in a new production, profit defines a macroeconomic saving that corresponds to the income that the economy sacrifices to accumulate fixed capital.

If the totality of income created by the production of wage-goods were spent on consumption, no fixed capital would ever form. The income transferred to firms as profit is, by definition, an income that is not spent on consumption, i.e., which is saved. Invested in a new production, profit is definitively withdrawn from consumption: its irreversible transformation into fixed capital marks the appearance of macroeconomic saving and establishes the identity, already postulated by Keynes (1936/1946), between saving and investment. Interest has its origin in this macroeconomic saving, in the sum of income transformed into fixed capital. The loss of income fixed into capital calls for the remuneration of income holders, 'capitalists', who have to be compensated for their sacrifice. As Schmitt puts it: 'the income transformed into macroeconomic capital defines the final loss of an income, which is destroyed. This loss calls for compensation and this compensation is nothing other than interest' (ibid.: 38, m.t.).

### *Interest and value*

What remains to be explained is how capital can add a positive value, measured by interest, to the value corresponding to the payment of wages. Two facts are relevant here:

1) Fixed capital increases the physical productivity of labour;
2) Interest is an 'income of production': a positive interest defines a positive production of interest-goods.

From these two facts Schmitt infers that capital is at the origin of a positive value insofar as the increase in labour's physical productivity gives rise to an increase in the value created by human labour. By working with the support of instrumental goods, human labour creates more value than it would have created without their aid.

Let us work through Schmitt's numerical example and assume that the use of capital-goods increases the production of shirts per hour from 1 to 10, that hourly wages are of 10 wage-units, and that interest is equal to 10%. According to these assumptions, every hour, 9 shirts are produced for the wage-earners and 1 shirt for the beneficiaries of interest. What is the value of the 10 shirts given that labour remains the sole source of macroeconomic value? If the answer were 10 wage-units, the totality of output would define the real content of the remuneration of wage-earners, and interest would not be an income of production. Since Schmitt showed that interest is an income of production and the production of interest-goods corresponds to an investment of profit, a final expenditure included in the payment of wages, one must dismiss that possibility.

The formation of a real interest of 1 shirt is possible only if the firm producing shirts pays 1 of the 10 wage-units distributed to its workers out of a profit. In this case, the firm purchases 1 shirt, on behalf of interest-earners, the moment it pays its workers 10 wage-units. To realize a profit of 1 wage-unit out of the 10 wage-units spent by its workers, the firm must sell the 10 shirts at a price of 11.1. This is also the value of the 10 shirts, the increase from 10 to 11.1 wage-units being due to the presence of fixed capital. The expenditure of 10 wage-units in the market for products enables wage-earners to purchase 9 shirts, while the expenditure of 1 wage-units in the labour market defines the purchase of 1 shirt on behalf of interest-earners.

In his unpublished 1996 manuscript, Schmitt does not go so far as to claim that the value increases from 10 to 11,1 wage-unit. Instead, he explains the whole process by saying that 'banks do not create (or emit) only the wages of workers, but also the counter-value of interest and amortization' (ibid.: 43, m.t.). In our example, banks create both the nominal income paid to workers, 10 wage-units, and the nominal income distributed to interest-earners, 1.1 money units. Here, Schmitt applies his distinction between nominal and real income and shows that, through the expenditure of their nominal income, workers obtain a real income consisting in 9 shirts, whose value is 9 wage-units, while, by spending a nominal income of 1.1 money units, interest-earners can purchase 1 shirt of value 1 wage-unit.

If we bear in mind that 'interest of 1.1 money units is spent in the labour market as part of the payment of 1 wage-unit, wages are exactly equal to 1 (and not to 1.1) unit of money' (ibid.: 47, m.t.), it appears that no difference subsists between values and prices. By creating a nominal income of 11,1 money units, banks enable interest-earners to purchase 1 shirt (of value 1 wage-unit) and wage-earners to purchase 9 shirts (of value 9 wage-units). The profit that the firm derives from the expenditure of wage-earners is exactly equal to 1 wage-unit, which is also the exact amount of its expenditure in the labour market for the purchase of interest-goods, 1 shirt. The subsequent sale of this shirt to interest-earners at a price of 1.1 pertains to the field of microeconomics and does not alter the fact that interest-goods are purchased in the labour market at a price equal to their value. As for wage-goods, one need only remember that their selling price is inclusive of the cost of interest-goods to verify that they also finally sell at a price (9 wage-units) equal to their value.

## In the present system of payments, non-wage income is formed pathologically

Schmitt had already established the pathological character of non-wage income in his 1984 book on capital malformations. By distinguishing the period when profit is formed (period $p_1$) from the period in which it is invested in the production of profit- or investment-goods (period $p_2$), he was able to show that instrumental goods are appropriated by de-personalized firms from the moment of their production. This appropriation is the source of empty money that unavoidably defines an inflationary gap as soon as fixed capital is amortized (period $p_3$). During 1993–1996, Schmitt creates the basis for a new, complementary explanation of the anomaly leading to inflation and (involuntary) unemployment. This time everything happens in one single period. In particular, the investment of profit takes place in the period of its formation in the market for products. The crucial points of Schmitt's argument are:

1) The formation of non-wage income calls for the expenditure of profit in the labour market.
2) Banks create the totality of nominal income, non-wage income included.

### *The monetization of profit*

The monetization of profit is a logical necessity. 'If, unlike wages, profits were not monetized, one could think that the national economy did not have enough income for the final purchase of the totality of goods, profit-goods included' (ibid.: 66, m.t.). This risk is avoided because banks lend to the set of households the amount of income necessary for the purchase of wage- and non-wage-goods. If profits are monetized, it is because they are included in wages: indeed 'profits are part of wages in the double sense that the formation of profits is an expenditure of wages and that the expenditure of profits is a formation of wages' (ibid.: 65, m.t.). Since wages are monetized, it necessarily follows that profits are monetized too.

Schmitt provides another proof of the monetization of profit. When firms purchase part of the productive activity of their workers, the emission of wages includes the expenditure of a profit. The purchase of non-wage-goods by firms takes place through an expenditure of profit included in the payment of wages, which means that the expenditure of profit is at the same time a payment of wages. '[T]he monetization of profits simply means the payment in money of the wages to workers whose activity is purchased by firms' (ibid.: 66, m.t.). Here, Schmitt introduces the idea that the economy is subdivided into (at least) two sectors, one producing wage- or consumption-goods and the other producing investment-goods.

In both sectors, wages are paid in money. In the first, the payment of wages to the producers of consumption-goods is 'simple' because it defines a straightforward transaction. In the second sector, the payment of wages is a 'complex' transaction, because it includes an expenditure of profit. The fact remains that, in both sectors, production calls for a payment of wages: investment- or profit-goods are monetized in the same way as wage-goods. 'From the moment wages are paid in money in the two sectors of the economy, producing for consumption and investment, it is certain that profits are monetized' (ibid.: 66, m.t.). It is thus confirmed that banks create, '*on top* of the monetary form of wage-goods, the monetary form or the nominal income of interest-goods, dividend-goods, and rent-goods' (ibid: 11, m.t.) as well as the monetary form or nominal income of investment-goods. In short, banks create the monetary form of profits, whether redistributed or invested.

### *The perpetuity of the bank deposits formed by profit and by its expenditure*

Schmitt's next step consists in showing that profit is a bank deposit that does not disappear after its expenditure. Let us be very clear from the outset: once spent, profit does not reappear as profit. What reappears is a bank deposit of the same amount. When wage-earners or households spend their income on the final purchase of wage-goods, their bank deposits are definitively destroyed 'as the effect of a compensation of bank entries' (ibid.: 67, m.t.). This is not what happens with profit: 'the deposits of profit survive although profits disappear after their expenditure' (ibid.: 67, m.t.).

As he had done previously to prove the existence of macroeconomic profit, Schmitt distinguishes a didactic from an analytical proof to demonstrate that bank deposits corresponding to profit continue to exist after their expenditure.

### *Schmitt's didactic proof*

The didactic proof refers again to two different periods. Suppose that profit equal to 50 wage-units is formed in $p_1$ and spent in $p_2$ to finance the production of profit-goods. Wages paid in $p_2$ are equal to those paid in $p_1$: 100 money units. Final expenditures in $p_2$ are equal to 100 (the expenditure of wages) + 50 (the expenditure of profit included within the payment of wages) = 150 wage-units. The value of goods available in the market for products is equal to 50 (the new wage-goods produced in $p_2$) + 50 (the wage-goods stocked in $p_1$) = 100 units of value. Final expenditures in $p_1$ are 50 wage-units, corresponding to the value of wage-goods purchased by households, the remaining 50 units being transferred to firms as profit. It follows that the difference between the final expenditures of $p_1 + p_2$, 200 wage-units, and the value of the goods purchased in the market for products in the two periods, 150 wage-units, is the measure of the bank deposits still available at the end of $p_2$.

### ***Schmitt's analytical proof***

In the analytical proof, everything happens in the same period. In $p_1$ firms spend, within the payment of wages, the profit they obtain in $p_1$. Wages paid in $p_1$ are equal to 100 wage-units, the value of all the goods produced in $p_1$. When wages are paid, firms purchase half of the product, which is equal to the profit-goods.

> [T]he other half, 50 units of value, is purchased by households who spend their income of 100 wage-units to this end; the expenditure of their income of 100 money units, therefore, means the destruction of deposits of 50 money units only, while the complement of deposits, 50 money units, is preserved.
>
> (ibid.: 67–8, m.t.)

It is immediately clear that the deposits corresponding to the profits do not vanish when profits are spent.

### *A simpler proof*

Schmitt adds a third and simpler proof of the permanent availability of the deposits of profit, in which he separates the set of firms into two sub-sets,

$F_1$ and $F_2$. If $F_1$ obtains a profit of $x$ money units from selling its product to the workers employed by $F_1$ and $F_2$, we must conclude that $F_2$ cannot sell all its product until $F_1$ invests its profit in the production of profit-goods. '[T] he product of $x$ units of value that firm 2 cannot immediately sell will be purchased after firm 1 has converted its profit into wages' (ibid.: 68, m.t.). The profit-goods produced by $F_1$ are purchased by the same firm itself in the labour market through the expenditure of profit that takes place within the payment of wages. This expenditure gives rise to a new deposit, in the form of wages, of the same value as the profit invested by $F_1$. Even though the expenditure of profit does not perpetuate the profit itself, it generates a new deposit that can be spent by wage-earners for the purchase of the wage-goods still available in $F_2$.

Schmitt explains the difference between the expenditure of wages in the products market and the expenditure of profit in the labour market.

> Wages are the effect of the payment of productions costs; therefore, the expenditure of wages defines the covering of costs; and to cover a monetary cost is to delete an equivalent monetary deposit.
>
> Profits are defined beyond production costs; [macroeconomically,] profits are not spent to cover any costs; hence spent profits, which are no longer profits, continue to exist as deposits: in the present example, the deposits of profits become or become again deposits of wages.
>
> (ibid.: 68, m.t.)

### *Profit and banks' loan in capitalism*

The process of capital accumulation in a capitalist regime suffers from a pathology. Its causes are to be found in the permanence of the deposits of profits that firms spend on paying out interests to beneficiaries, on dividends, on rents or on producing investment-goods for themselves. In an orderly system, 'every expenditure of firms to the benefit of households is exclusively a creation of income [...] [and] every expenditure of the set of households to the benefit of the set of firms is exclusively a destruction of income' (ibid.: 68, m.t.). It is only in today's disorderly system that the existence of positive profits leads to an additional creation of monetary income: 'in capitalism, global demand is increased by the amount of monetary profit of each period' (ibid.: 70, m.t.).

The fact is that the expenditure of profit by firms generates a bank deposit that, as any other deposit, is lent by banks. More precisely, from the moment of its formation, profit defines bank deposits of identical value, which banks lend to households. The loan of the deposits of profit increases global demand. If in a given period wage-earners are paid 100 wage-units and firms realize a profit equal to 50 wage-units, the loan to households of the corresponding deposits increases their demand from 100 to 150 money units. Thus, a difference of 50 money units appears between global demand and global supply as defined by the macroeconomic cost of production. This difference is of an inflationary nature and exposes the fact that pathological capital has appropriated the production of investment-goods.

Schmitt observes that, in a disorderly system, de-personalized firms appropriate profit-goods, which should logically remain the economic property of households. National income should be equal to consumption only, $Y = C$, and not to the sum of consumption and investment, $Y = C + I$. The problem is economic, not juridical. It is not a question of determining the juridical ownership of investment- or capital-goods; what matters here is to determine whether the set of households is dispossessed of part of produced output to the benefit of a non-person, namely the set of de-personalized firms. If households' (economic) entitlements were not violated, interest-, dividend-, rent-, and investment-goods would all pertain to the category of consumption-goods. Today, the

> loan of profit has the fundamental consequence of separating households from the ownership of profit-goods or fixed capital. [...] In a perfect regime, the only category of national income would be consumption, with investment being itself a consumption, called "productive consumption". The present economic world is imperfect because investment *adds* to consumption.
>
> (ibid.: 12–13, m.t.)

It is worth noting that, in his 1984 book on capital malformations, Schmitt had already mentioned the fact that, in today's disorderly system, investment-goods add to consumption. His explanation rested on the presence of empty emissions resulting from the investment of profit. 'Investment is additional to consumption for the only reason that empty emissions are additive to full emissions' (Schmitt 2021: 127). The reader may recall that, in his 1984 main volume, Schmitt explained the pathology of capital formation by distinguishing between the period in which profit is formed and the successive period in which it is invested in the production of capital-goods. What he calls the didactic proof in his 1966 lectures at the University of Fribourg, rests on the observation that when profit is spent within the payment of wages of a later period, investment cannot be considered as a 'nested category' (*catégorie gigogne*) of consumption.

As established by Schmitt's quantum macroeconomic analysis, profit is a nested category of wages, it is included in wages, and wages define the totality of national income. In the same way, investment should be included under consumption. Today this is not the case; investment is a purely nominal addition that increases global demand with respect to global supply. Through the investment of profit, de-personalized firms become the final owners of fixed capital. Excess demand is the consequence of the expenditure of profit included in the payment of wages. '[E]xcess demand only [means] eventually the already-known additional movement: the absorption by Capital of the invested profits' (ibid.: 128).

Schmitt's 1994–96 analysis represents the prolegomenon to a new explanation of the process of capital accumulation, which leads to inflation and involuntary unemployment. It introduces the idea than an increase in labour's physical productivity (induced by the presence of instrumental capital) produces an increase in value. It replaces the chronological distinction between successive periods (1984a; 2021) with the distinction between sectors. It also suggests that the theory may be developed in terms of prices, that is, by pushing up values to the level of prices instead of reducing prices to the level of values.

Yet, Schmitt's 1994–96 analysis considers the problem of fixed capital amortization only marginally. Its aim, in fact, is to establish that non-wage income in general and interest in particular increase the value of produced output even though they are necessarily derived from wages. Emphasis is put on the fact that capitalism as it exists at present is a regime in which firms can only spend their monetary profits on purchasing profit-goods in the labour market. Let us observe once more that what is wrong is not the fact that profit is spent within the payment of wages, but that this expenditure benefits de-personalized firms. If firms purchased profit-goods on behalf of households, things would be fine; the problem is that the deposits of profit are lent by banks to households, a loan that increases global demand nominally and prevents households in general from exercising economic ownership over all produced output. Thus, Schmitt considers the macroeconomic loan of the deposits of profit granted by banks to households as the crucial anomaly affecting today's capitalism.

## A critical assessment of Böhm-Bawerk's and Keynes's analyses of capital and interest

### *Böhm-Bawerk's analysis*

Böhm-Bawerk's analysis of interest and capital is undoubtedly one of the greatest ever. The Austrian author rejects the notion of capital as a macroeconomic factor of production and advocates 'a definition of capital independent of whether the economic regime is socialist or capitalist' (Schmitt 1993/94a, 25.1.94: 2, m.t.). According to Böhm-Bawerk, capital furthers an increase in labour's physical productivity through what he calls the roundabout methods of production. The presence of instrumental goods has an impact on the period of production; to produce with the support of fixed capital means switching to indirect methods of production, that is, to production processes that must include the period of production and utilization of instrumental capital. In other words, the period of production of capital-goods is part of the indirect methods of production leading to final output.

Capital itself is not a factor of production: '[c]apital does not independently deliver an impulse; it merely transmits an impulse delivered by originary productive forces' (Böhm-Bawerk 1889/1959: 95). However, capital increases the physical productivity of the 'originary productive forces' and to this extent it is 'indirectly productive because it makes possible the adoption of new and fruitful roundabout methods of production' (ibid.: 101). Through his concept of the roundabout methods of production, Böhm-Bawerk introduces time in the analysis of capital. He shows that the increase in the roundaboutness of the methods of production required to produce final output measures the increase in value due to the need to account for the role of time.

Ricardo had already claimed that the value created by labour can be increased by the flow of time, namely, the period required to bring produced output to the market. Böhm-Bawerk goes deeper into the analysis of capital and endeavours to show that the increase in physical productivity due to the roundabout methods of production gives rise to an increase in the value of final goods. The presence of fixed capital-goods increases the efficiency of human labour. More final goods can be produced if part of labour is devoted to the production of instrumental goods, that is, if production proceeds in roundabout ways.

As Schmitt observes, the crucial point Böhm-Bawerk's theory is confronted with consists 'precisely in the explanation of the transformation [...] leading from the physical productivity of the roundabout methods of production to its productivity in value terms' (Schmitt 1993/94a, 25.1.94: 5, m.t.). According to Böhm-Bawerk, capital is the source of a net return that increases the value of produced output. On the one hand, capital is subject to wear and tear, and it is through amortization that it reproduces its value. On the other hand, capital is at the origin of a surplus-value equal to the amount of interest. 'It makes sense to claim that the value invested or cast in the production instruments reproduces itself before turning into a source of positive interests, category of national income. Of no other value can the same claim be made' (ibid.: 6, m.t.).

To the extent that it endeavours to show that fixed capital is the source of a net return, Böhm-Bawerk's theory of capital closely relates to his theory of interest. According to him, the existence of interest rests on the positive difference between the subjective value possessed by present and future goods of the same quantity and kind. This is so, Böhm-Bawerk says,

1) Because present goods can be consumed immediately, whereas the consumption of future goods can only take place in the future;
2) Because individuals tend to underestimate their need for future goods;
3) Because instrumental capital, through the roundabout methods of production it involves, increases the number of goods that will be available in the future.

While the first two reasons justify the existence of interest as an agio (a premium paid to individuals accepting to postpone their consumption), the third refers to the possibility of transforming the physical yield of capital into a yield of value. Böhm-Bawerk tells us that a capital can be formed only if a wage-fund is available to remunerate workers producing instrumental goods. Invested in the production of capital-goods, the fund increases the roundaboutness of the process leading to the production of final output. More goods are finally produced whose value is perceived to be the lesser the longer the roundabout methods of production made possible by the investment of the wage-fund. In Böhm-Bawerk's theory, the increase in physical productivity increases the subjective value of present goods against that of future goods: the use of instrumental capital and the flow of time lead to an increase in the value of present goods relative to that of future goods. Interest derives from this difference. The roundabout methods of production together with individuals' underestimation of future goods determine a premium on present goods that explain the origin of interest.

In his 1993–94 unpublished manuscript, Schmitt criticizes Böhm-Bawerk's theories of capital and interest. His critique of the roundabout methods of production rests on the fact that the optimum length of the indirect period of production cannot be determined. In fact, Böhm-Bawerk's attempt to reconcile his claim that future goods are worth less than present goods, and that the quantity of future goods is greater than that of present goods, is doomed to fail. The optimum level of the roundabout methods of production is hopelessly undetermined because any period considered as ideal for the productive investment of the wage-fund would lead to a never-ending chain of successive investments. For example, if the period were one year, at the end of the year firms would reinvest their wage-fund for one more year, which would mean that the optimum period would now be two years. As Schmitt claims: 'one has to reason by recurrence, and so the roundabout methods of production can never reach their optimum value' (ibid.: 10, m.t.).

As for Böhm-Bawerk's theory of interest, Schmitt observes that 'it could be correct only if supply of and demand for financial claims were the objects of an adjustment capable of determining two distinct magnitudes, namely the value of these claims and, moreover, the interest paid on loans. Now, a single adjustment can determine only one variable, the price of the financial claims – and therefore the value of financial capital – so that interest remains undetermined' (ibid.: 12, m.t.). If financial transactions took place only between individuals, they would define zero-sum transactions, and there could be no positive interest for the economy as a whole.

From an individual or microeconomic viewpoint, each loan implies a borrowing and each borrowing a loan, so that interest is at the same time positive, for the lender, and negative, for the borrower. Böhm-Bawerk rightly considered interest as a macroeconomic income, but was unable to explain its formation. His theory focuses on subjective behaviour and misses the fact that 'capitalism is an order of things – and not of individuals. [...] In other words, capitalism is the regime in which a part of savings is demanded by the production process itself, and not by economic agents' (ibid.: 12, m.t.). Subjective transactions in the financial market determine the price of financial claims, whereas 'the production process absorbs savings that are lent without being borrowed by anybody. It is this excess of demanded savings over supplied savings that is the cause of interest' (ibid. 12, m.t.). Böhm-Bawerk correctly distinguishes the interest generated by macroeconomic capital (*Urzins*) from the interest paid on individual loans (*Leihzins*) but leaves the formation of the *Urzins* totally unexplained.

### *Keynes's analysis*

Keynes's theory of interest closely relates to the concept of the marginal productivity of capital, and it is here that Schmitt's critical appraisal starts. Schmitt criticizes Keynes's concept of the marginal productivity of capital, defined as 'the relation between the prospective yield of one more unit of capital [...] and the cost of producing this unit' (Keynes 1936/1946: 135), for the following three reasons.

1) Keynes claims that the prospective yield of capital is expressed in value terms and not in physical units, yet he does not provide the slightest explanation of how capital's physical productivity can be transformed into a productivity of value. 'But in fact, nothing is said about the operation capable of transforming the physical productivity of capital into a productivity of value units' (Schmitt 1993/94a, 18.94: 3, m.t.).
2) In Keynes's theory, only the net yield of capital is considered, when, 'before worrying about capital's net yield, the theoretician must explain how the value absorbed by this capital is reproduced' (ibid.: 4, m.t.). Keynes does not explain amortization, and the determination of capital's *net* yield remains a mystery.
3) Keynes claims that interest must be kept distinct from the marginal efficiency of capital, but he misses the fact that capital cannot produce, at the same time, a yield and interest. '[I]f capital produces a yield distinct from interest, the production process can no longer produce any interest – because, evidently, interest is not produced twice' (ibid.: 4, m.t.).

Then, Schmitt turns his attention to Keynes's different theories of interest and shows that they are mutually incompatible.

According to Keynes's first theory, interest is the supply price of savings. In particular, he claims that '[t]he schedule of the marginal efficiency of capital may be said to govern the terms on which loanable funds are demanded for the purpose of new investment; whilst the rate of interest governs the terms on which funds are being currently supplied' (Keynes 1936/1946: 165). Schmitt observes that Keynes argues as if the increases in real capital were merely demanded, while the funds necessary to finance new investments are merely supplied. In fact, real capitals are also supplied, and financial capital is demanded. Keynes's analysis turns out to be a stratagem to corroborate his distinction between marginal efficiency of capital and interest – and nothing more.

> One need only remember the pair Supply and Demand of financial and real capitals to realize the fact that the rate of the marginal efficiency of

> capital and the rate of interest form the rate of one and the same reality. Indeed, the rate of capital efficiency is but a different name for the rate of interest.
>
> (Schmitt 1993/94a, 18.1.94: 6, m.t.)

Keynes's second theory introduces the concept of 'liquidity preference' and the idea that interest is the price or 'the reward for parting with liquidity' (Keynes 1936/1946: 167). Keynes identifies liquidity preference with money: the rate of interest 'is a measure of the unwillingness of those who possess money to part with their liquid control over it' (ibid.: 167). As Schmitt observes, this concept of liquidity of a sum of money comes from Keynes being unaware that money 'has only an instantaneous existence' (Schmitt 1993/94a, 18.1.94: 7, m.t.). Having stated that 'the rate of interest governs the terms on which funds are currently supplied' (Keynes 1936/1946: 165), the author of *The General Theory* should have concluded that interest is the price paid to savers, because savers are those who supply the funds that finance investment. Interest relates to savings, not to money. Liquidity plays no role, because money disappears, instantaneously, as soon as its circular flow is accomplished, and because the income resulting from production is immediately transformed into capital. This transformation occurs independently of the agents' willingness to retain their savings in one form or another.

In the third theory, Keynes maintains that the rate of interest is the price that 'equilibrates the desire to hold wealth in the form of cash with the available quantity of cash' (ibid.: 167). Keynes claims that it is through the liquidity preference that 'the quantity of money enters into the economic scheme' (ibid.: 168). Individual liquidity preference depends on the rate of interest and 'fixes the quantity of money which the public will hold when the rate of interest is given' (ibid.: 168). Yet, this is to forget that 'whatever the variations of interest rates, economic agents are totally incapable of modifying the quantity of money available in their national economy' (Schmitt 1993/94a, 18.1.94: 11, m.t.).

Overall, Keynes's analysis of interest is confused, partially inconsistent, and increasingly eclectic. In his attempt to explain interest as the variable of adjustment between desired and available quantity of money, Keynes discards his own previous claim that savings are not a mere sum of money, but an income subtracted from consumption, and he goes back to 'a rough notion of undifferentiated money that is money *strictu sensu*, income and capital at the same time' (ibid.: 9, m.t.). What Keynes did not see is that the formation of interest requires the definitive saving of part of current income. It is through its transformation into fixed capital that a portion of current income is forever removed from consumption. What is relevant here is not individual savings, but the macroeconomic saving resulting from the investment of profit in the production of instrumental goods. The macroeconomic transformation of savings into fixed capital goes to explain the existence of interest as a macroeconomic income, which is due to the set of households to compensate for their initial sacrifice. '[I]nterest is therefore a macroeconomic income that the process of production must form in each period to replace the fund initially invested and finally cast into instrumental-goods through yearly instalments' (ibid.: 12, m.t.).

# 12 Schmitt's new analysis of unemployment

## His 1998 contribution

Schmitt wrote *La formation du pouvoir d'achat* before 1960. By then, he had already hinted at the need to take into account the sectors corresponding to the production of wage-goods (first sector), interest-goods and investment-goods (second sector), and amortization-goods (third sector). The same differentiation can be found in his unpublished manuscript of 1987–88, *Résumé du cours de macro-économie*, as well as in several other, published and unpublished texts. However, it is only between 1996 and 1998 that he developed fully this alternative approach and applied it to the analysis of involuntary unemployment. In this chapter, I shall refer to the most completely developed version of Schmitt's contribution to the study of unemployment as presented in his 1998 unpublished manuscript *Le chômage et son éradication*.

In this text, Schmitt proposes an explanation of involuntary unemployment in which values are increased by the increase in the physical productivity of labour driven by fixed capital. Unlike his 1984 analysis, which takes prices to the level of values and runs through an explanation involving three successive periods, the new analysis takes values to the level of prices, and periods are replaced by sectors. Fundamentally, the two analyses are complementary; they provide different arguments that converge towards the same result and call for the same remedy. Both are difficult and require a deep understanding of the nature of money and production.

One of the main difficulties lies in explaining how unemployment can set in even though every production creates the income necessary and sufficient for the final purchase of its output. How can one explain unemployment while complying with the logical identity of global supply and global demand? To answer we must try to explain the existence of a pathology, and do so logically – that is, without turning reality into a figment of our imagination. In this chapter I follow the analytical steps proposed by Schmitt in his 1998 text, showing, first, that unemployment cannot arise in an economy where production is made up of wage- and profit-goods, and second, that amortization, although not a direct cause, paves the way for unemployment when the rate of profit no longer exceeds the market rate of interest.

DOI: 10.4324/9781351271325-17

## Unemployment is impossible in an economy where income is made up of wages and redistributed profits

### *The case where national income is determined by the production of wage-goods only*

There can be no unemployment in an economy where wages are the only income. This is due to the fact that wage-goods are sold (and therefore demanded) the moment they are produced. This result derives from the nature of money and from its relationship with production. Let us summarize the aspects of this investigation relevant to the present analysis, even though this topic has already been tackled in previous chapters.

#### *Money is purely a means of payment, not an object of exchange*

Monetary wages are not the counterpart of workers' output. Indeed, money is not a good distinct from money's real content; it is *identical* to it. Therefore, there cannot exist a single transaction in which money is a term of a relative exchange. This is self-evident when one considers national output as a whole: the only possible exchange is an *absolute exchange* of the national output with itself: 'considered as a whole (in each period), the product can be exchanged only for itself' (Schmitt 1998a: 19, m.t.). It is through money that this absolute exchange takes place, and it is through this absolute exchange with money that national output acquires a *numerical* dimension. The payment of wages is the transaction through which national output is measured.

Banks pay wages, on behalf of firms, through the emission of a nominal money, a pure numerical form deprived of any intrinsic value. Yet, wage-earners do not obtain a mere sum of empty money units, but the product of their work, the real content of their monetary wages. '*The object of the monetary wages deposited with the bank is nothing other than the set of wage-goods*' (ibid.: 28, m.t.). When wages are paid to them, workers exchange their physical product with this same product; they literally 'change it "into" this same product, which they obtain in the form of bank deposits' (ibid.: 28, m.t.). In other words, wage-earners spend the sum of money banks pay to them immediately and purchase their own output, the real object of their bank deposits. Since money is a flow and not an object of exchange, wage-earners spend it, necessarily, at the very moment banks credit them.

#### *Money wages and real wages are the terms of an identity*

The identity of monetary and real wages results from the fact that the exchange between production and money creation is an absolute exchange and not a relative exchange between real goods on one side and money units on the other. At the very instant of their payment, money wages are deposited within the bank carrying out the payment, and the object of the deposit are the real goods produced by wage-earners. An absolute exchange thus takes place between the physical product and the money paid to workers, so that real wages and money wages define the two faces of one and the same reality. 'Monetary wages are indistinguishable from real wages; monetary wages *are* real wages' (ibid.: 30, m.t.). The sum of monetary wages is a stock of money, but the object of this stock is workers' real wages, the real goods that define money's content. In the payment of wages, workers give up the physical product (stocked in firms' warehouses) and get it instantaneously back under the form of money: they own it as the object of their bank deposits. This means that wage-earners are the first owners of the real product, which they obtain as real content of their money wages.

> [T]he payment of wages is a circular operation, absolute, by which workers give up their product to recover it at once in an exchange of identical terms, the only difference is that the product is thus introduced or injected in the numerical form of money.
>
> (ibid.: 31, m.t.)

*Wage-earners exert a demand on real goods at the very instant these are deposited in the bank as the real object of their monetary wages*

According to traditional thinking, produced goods and services can be demanded only through the *expenditure* of income. The *formation* of income would therefore not define a demand on products. However, as Schmitt points out, there is something wrong in this dichotomous approach. The nature of money is such that workers spend their wages as soon as they are paid, in an absolute exchange where they purchase their real output and deposit it immediately with their bank as a real object of their credit. It thus follows that 'the *demand* for wage-goods is an action completed within the very formation of monetary wages and, consequently, without any need to wait for the expenditure of this income' (ibid.: 32, m.t.). Wage-goods are demanded twice: first in the labour market, when wages are paid and the product obtained as real content of bank deposits; and the second time when wages are spent in the market for products and wage-goods are appropriated in their physical form, as values-in-use.

The immediate transformation of wages into bank deposits defines the first demand for wage-goods, which occurs in the labour market and is implicit in the formation of wages. The whole output, made up of wage-goods only, is therefore demanded from the moment wages are paid. The result of the payment of wages

> is real goods and not a sum of money, every money stocked in banks having the new product as content: in purchasing the deposit of their wages, that is, in forming these deposits, workers purchase the product that is the real content of these monetary deposits.
>
> (ibid.: 47, m.t.)

Thus, supply of and demand for wage-goods appear to be identical from the moment these goods are produced.

At this point it seems legitimate to ask if this result may be jeopardized by the existence of savings and/or the loan of wages.

### *Neither savings nor the loan of savings can alter the identity between supply of, and demand for, wage-goods*

The hypothetical impact of savings on the demand for wage-goods concerns the expenditure of the income created by production and deposited with the banking system. We already know that wage-goods are subject to a first demand when wage income is formed. What we are investigating now is whether savings can reduce the second demand for wage-goods, that is, the demand exerted by income holders in the market for products.

First, we ask whether saving can be identified with hoarding or not, that is, whether the income deposited with the bank by savers can be once and for all lost to consumption and, therefore, to demand. If the income saved is lent by savers to consumers (for example through the purchase of financial securities), hoarding is avoided, but what happens if savers leave their income deposited with their bank? Even in this case there can be no doubt. Double-entry bookkeeping mandates the immediate loan of bank deposits; the necessary balance of liabilities (deposits) and assets (loans) leaves no room for hoarding.

Workers are paid in money units, and it is through the expenditure of these money units that they become the owners of an income deposited with their banks. This income is the object of the *financial intermediation* of banks. Deposits are fungible goods. Banks are free to lend them and to reimburse the owners of the deposits with other equivalent deposits. 'Since the bank lends all the wage income not withdrawn, or withdrawn only later, by its holders, macroeconomic savings are reduced immediately to zero: today borrowers are spending the income that depositors will only spend at a future date' (ibid.: 37, m.t.).

But what if nobody were to borrow what is saved by wage-earners? The answer is determined by the fact that banks' financial intermediation is not hampered by the willingness of households to borrow wage-earners' savings. The sum deposited on the liabilities side of banks is necessarily matched by an equal sum entered on their assets side, which is to say that the totality of what is deposited is lent. If savings are not lent to consumers, they are lent to firms, which invest them in the purchase of a stock of wage-goods, that is, by covering the costs of production of the goods not yet sold in the market for products. Whether purchased by wage-earners, by consumers borrowing the income saved by wage-earners, or by firms wage-goods are demanded in full and no difference can form between global supply and demand as long as production consists in wage-goods only.

The necessary equality of supply and demand arises from the nature of money, a flow that implies the debit-credit or the credit-debit of the economic agents taking part in the payments, particularly in the payment of wages. The inference that unemployment, i.e. a gap between global supply and global demand, cannot arise when production is made up of wage-goods only, is a corollary of the law of sales-purchases: wage-earners sell the physical output and purchase it in the form of money, while firms purchase it (in its physical form) and sell it under its monetary form. Firms act as pure intermediaries between wage-earners and themselves: workers are their own employers, for the simple reason that workers and workers alone are at the origin of wage income. It is through the purchase of bank deposits by wage-earners that this income is formed and is entered on the liabilities side of banks.

Given that workers give up their wage-goods in their physical form and get them back in a monetary form, they pay themselves through the intermediation of firms and banks.

> [T]he formation of wages in an operation of credit-debit of the factors of production defines an intermediation carried out by firms, which therefore do not employ anybody. Producers are employed by the person who pays the wages. Now, workers pay themselves, by their activity. The factors of production, and nobody else, form wage income; this income is produced by the purchase of bank deposits; the purchasers of deposits are the workers and not the firms.
>
> (ibid.: 39, m.t.)

The entire amount of wage-goods is therefore simultaneously supplied and demanded, which pre-empts the formation of a deflationary disequilibrium, in an economy where only wage-goods are produced.

> The necessary equality of Demand and Supply derives from the nature of money, of which every flow or movement is necessarily a double credit and a double debit. Credit money, another name for bank money, cannot but be spent. The income of wage-earners would not exist if it were not spent in the market of productive services. It is spent in advance, within the very formation of wages; and it is finally spent in the market for products, because every depositor is a lender and the work of banks, in their role of financial intermediators, is to lend the income that is lent to them.
>
> (ibid.: 47–8, m.t.)

### *The case where redistributed profits are added to wages*

Let us use the term 'interest' to designate all the non-wage income of households: interest *strictu sensu*, dividends, rents. The aim of this section is to show that unemployment is formally impossible in an economy where produced output is made up of consumption-goods only (wage-goods and interest-goods).

As we know from Chapter 11:

1. The existence of macroeconomic interest derives from the fact that the formation of fixed capital implies that of macroeconomic savings;
2. Interest is a compensation for the initial sacrifice of income holders, who forever give up spending part of their current income;
3. Paid out of profit, interest is derived from wages;
4. The production of interest-goods (category of production) accompanies the formation of interest (category of distribution).
5. Interest-goods, as is the case for wage-goods, are produced by labour, and their production generates a wage income. Part of this income is transferred, in the form of interest, to the holders of non-wage income. The whole process takes place through the intermediation of firms, which guarantees the payment of wages and the redistribution of profit as interest.

What remains to be explained now, following Schmitt, is that:

6. The presence of positive interest has a multiplying effect on the value of production;
7. In the present economic systems, the production of interest-goods implies the subdivision of the economy into two sectors;
8. Non-wage-goods are based on a macroeconomic loan granted by banks to households.

*Interest increases the value produced by labour*

The increase in physical productivity driven by instrumental capital leads to a substantial increase in the production of values-in-use, hence a proportional increase in the purchasing power of wages. But what about value? Does it increase too? If so, to what extent? Schmitt shows that the increase in physical productivity entails an increase in the production of value by the amount of interest, so that the value labour produces with the help of instrumental capital is 'multiplied' by a coefficient between 1 and 2. Labour remains the sole factor of production, but the value it produces is greater, the more its physical productivity fuelled by fixed capital.

Consider the following example proposed by Schmitt. Suppose national income to be equal to 1,000 money units and sufficient instrumental capital to increase the physical product from 100 shirts to 600 shirts. Interest-goods are like wage-goods in that they are both produced by human labour (helped by fixed capital). Labour is the only factor capable of assigning a numerical form to products; it follows that the totality of produced goods are necessarily wage-goods and that interest-goods must be integrated in the wage-goods. We are thus confronted with another reality, where the principle of the excluded middle does not apply: interest-goods are and are not wage-goods. The explanation lies in the fact that interests are redistributed wages and that their presence implies a multiplication of wages. We are thus faced with 'a duplication of wage-goods that are henceforth present simultaneously in the two categories, as wage-goods and in the form of interest-goods' (ibid.: 70, m.t.).

Interest is paid out of profit. Profit is derived from wages in the market for products and is spent, within the payment of wages, in the labour market. This means that interest, too, is derived from wages: in this sense interest-goods are wage-goods. At the same time, part of the production of workers is appropriated by firms and takes the form of interest-goods. These interest-goods are an additional production, which would not have occurred if the presence of physical capital had not promoted an increase in labour physical productivity. Interest measures the compensation 'capitalists' are entitled to because of the macroeconomic savings invested in the formation of fixed capital and also measures the value added to the production of wage-goods. Total production is the sum of wages and interest, where interests imply a multiplication of wages.

Let us suppose that the production of interest-goods has reached its upper limit and is equal to that of wage-goods, namely 300 shirts. In the example we are considering, physical production is multiplied by 6 thanks to the contribution of fixed capital, while the production of value is multiplied by 2. The value of national production is therefore of 2,000 money units, comprising 1,000 wage-goods (equal to 300 shirts) and 1,000 interest-goods (also equal 300 shirts).

### *In the present economic systems, the production of interest-goods implies the subdivision of the economy into sectors*

Financial interest (distributed by firms as a remuneration for the loans they obtained from income holders) is a category of redistribution and must be fed by a category of production. 'If national production did not include a positive amount of interest-goods, borrowers would not pay positive interests to lenders' (ibid.: 71, m.t.). Once interest-goods are produced, positive interest can be paid out. The value of 300 shirts can be assigned to interest only because capital enables the production of 600 shirts instead of 100; of these 600 shirts, 300 correspond to the production of interest-goods. It follows that the presence of interest involves the subdivision of the economy into two sectors: one in which wages-goods are produced and one in which the production is made up of interest-goods.

In our numerical example, assuming that the production of interest-goods has reached its maximum, workers of the first sector receive a salary of 500 wage-units, equal to the wages paid to the workers of the second sector. Total wages remain equal to 1,000 money units and enable workers to purchase half of the entire production; its value is multiplied by 2 and is therefore equal to 2,000 money units. Indeed, by spending all their income (1,000 wage-units) wage-earners purchase only half of produced output, whose total price is 2,000 money units. The identity of values and prices is fully maintained.

The problem arising now concerns the total amount of income available for the purchase of the entire production of wage- and interest-goods. Wage-earners have at their disposal an income equal to 1,000 wage-units, whereas the value (and price) of the goods available on the market is of 2,000 wage-units. How can we bridge the gap, and avoid the rise of unemployment? Schmitt's answer is that 'the multiplication of produced values (by 2 in the example) is accompanied by an equal multiplication of available income' (ibid.: 75, m.t.) and rests on a macroeconomic loan granted by banks to the set of income holders or households.

### *Non-wage income is based on a macroeconomic loan of banks to the set of households*

As Schmitt points out, the division of the economy into sectors is the result of a macroeconomic loan granted by banks. In order to understand the nature of this loan, we need to refer back to the analysis of profit and to the insight that, in the current system of national payments, the formation of profit is the basis for a perennial bank deposit. The expenditure of the deposits of profit does not annul the deposits; it reproduces them in an infinite series of expenditures. What persists in time is not profit, but the deposit formed with the formation of profit: 'at no time can the *deposit* of a profit, or of previous wages, be erased or destroyed' (ibid.: 96, m.t.). Today we are confronted with two types of bank deposits, those that disappear once they are spent for the first time and those that are reproduced through their expenditure. The deposit of profit belongs to the second category: the expenditure of profit cancels it, but reproduces the bank deposit that accompanies its formation.

> Within the macroeconomic costs of production, which are all wages, every income is destroyed at the instant it is spent in a final purchase. Yet, insofar as macroeconomic costs of production are outstripped, *deposits* obey the law of "circulation": they endlessly move around within the national economy.
>
> (ibid.: 98, m.t.)

In the case of wages, their final expenditure entails the cancellation of a positive deposit that covers the negative deposit formed in the firm at the moment of production (payment of wages). In the case of profit, on the other hand, profit spent does not entail the cancellation of its deposit, because, given that profit does not define any macroeconomic cost of production, there is no negative deposit to cover. Profit defines

> deposits formed above the line of macroeconomic costs. These deposits exist only in the domain of positive numbers: therefore, they cannot come under negative deposits; each expenditure of such a deposit defines its reconstitution in the hands of a new holder.
>
> (ibid.: 99, m.t.)

What characterizes the present capitalistic system is that banks lend to the set of households the deposits created when profit is formed. This loan is what makes the sale of profit-goods possible – production associated with the formation of profit, and which in our case coincides with the production of interest-goods. If banks did not lend the deposit of profit, the available income would not suffice for the purchase of the entire production, of wage- and interest-goods, and interest would remain unexplained. 'In order to obtain the partitioning of production into two sectors and the repartitioning of the product into wage-goods and interest-goods, it is indispensable to recur to a loan granted to the *set* of households' (ibid.: 76, m.t.). When the second sector reaches its maximum expansion, half of total production takes place in the first sector (wage-goods) and half in the second sector (interest-goods). Non-wage income therefore cannot exceed wage income. This is explained by the fact that profit derives from wages and that the amount of macroeconomic loan is determined by the amount of profit deposits.

> It is a true superposition that we have before our eyes: the 1,000 wage-units borrowed correspond exactly to the 1,000 wage-units emitted. We thus reach a first explanation of the fact that, strictly defined, households' non-wage income cannot exceed wages: the second sector cannot employ more than half of the active population.
>
> (ibid.: 77, m.t.)

*A complete representation of the case under investigation*

Let us go back to our numerical example and consider what happens when the production of interest-goods reaches its maximum level, that is, when the amount of profits is equal to that of wages: 1,000 money units. Since production is for the moment limited to wage- and interest-goods, the economy is subdivided into two sectors, whose payment of wages is equal to 500 wage-units each. The selling price of the product of each sector is of 1,000 money units, as is their respective value. The increase in value of the entire production, wage-goods plus interest-goods, from 1,000 to 2,000 money units comes from the transformation of the increase in the physical productivity of labour into an increase in the production of value. To the multiplication of the value produced by labour by a factor of two corresponds an equal multiplication of the available income, made possible by the deposits of profits lent by banks to households. 'We observe that the wage-goods already present in the money wages emitted by the two sectors are present a *second time* in the units of money that banks lend to the set of households' (ibid.: 76, m.t.).

Following the macroeconomic loan granted by banks, the purchasing power of each wage-unit is divided by two: to each unit of wages emitted there is a unit of wages that is lent. The purchasing power is thus divided equally between wage-earners and interests' holders. In the example, wage-earners and those entitled to the payment of interests share the entire

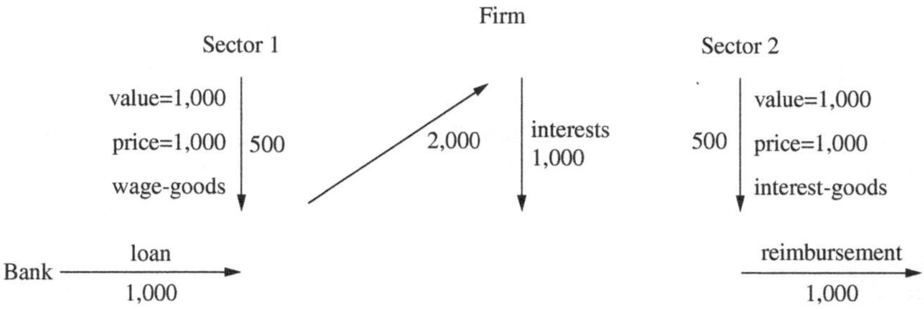


*Figure 12.1* The case where total production consists of wage-goods and interest-goods.

production in equal parts, 300 shirts each. From this time onwards, when production is equally distributed between the two sectors, the situation is as represented in Figure 12.1.

Wages distributed in each sector = 500
Value of wages-goods = 1,000
Value of interest-goods = 1,000
Macroeconomic loan of banks = 1,000

Finally, regarding the macroeconomic loan granted by banks we observe that, logically, global supply cannot exceed global demand, in an economy where produced output is entirely made up of consumption-goods. In fact, global supply, as determined by the value of the entire production, wage-goods plus interest-goods, is always equal to global demand as determined by the sum total of wages and of the macroeconomic loan granted by banks to households.

## Unemployment is impossible in an economy where all final expenditures are either consumption or investment

First, we must explain the formation of profits invested into the production of instrumental goods. As in the example of redistributed profits, firms obtain a profit by selling consumption-goods at a mark-up. Resuming our previous numerical example, we observe that the profit redistributed as interest does not stop firms realizing other profits and investing them in the production of instrumental goods. We thus witness a superposition of the production of interest-goods and investment-goods in the second sector. Redistributed and invested profits, both valued 1,000 money units, are the cumulative effects of the physical productivity of capital transformed into a production of value. '[P] rofits redistributed as interests do not reduce in the least the power of firms to produce investments' (ibid.: 106, m.t.).

***The case where the entirety of profit is invested in the production of investment-goods***

Let us suppose for a moment that the production of interest-goods is equal to zero while the production of investment-goods reaches its highest possible level, equal to the production of wage-goods. The situation is the one represented in Figure 12.2.

Wages distributed in the two sectors = 1,000
Value of wage-goods = 1,000
Value of investment-goods = 1,000
Macroeconomic loan of banks = 1,000

One has to explain how households can reimburse the macroeconomic loan obtained from the banking system. When profit is redistributed, households benefit from the payment of interest, which provides the amount of income needed to cover their debt. When profit is invested no redistribution occurs, and households seem to fall short of the 1,000 wage-units spent by firms to finance the production of investment-goods.

Schmitt repeatedly claims that every loan granted by banks to the set of households is subject to perfect inertia in time and maintains that this inertia also applies to invested profits. The difference between redistributed and invested profits is that, in the first case, the profit realized by firms, equal to 1,000 in value terms, is not spent by them, whereas in the second case it is. In both cases, firms obtain a profit equal to 1,000 wage-units. In the first case the 1,000 units are redistributed to households, thus enabling them to recover the sum borrowed from banks and spent on purchasing the interest-goods stocked with firms. In the second case, firms spend their profit in the purchase of the investment-goods produced by workers. In their sector 2, at the moment of their production, firms purchase the investment-goods produced in this sector. Firms finance their purchase through the expenditure of profit, obtained through the expenditure of households' income (partly earned as wages and partly borrowed from banks). This means that firms appropriate

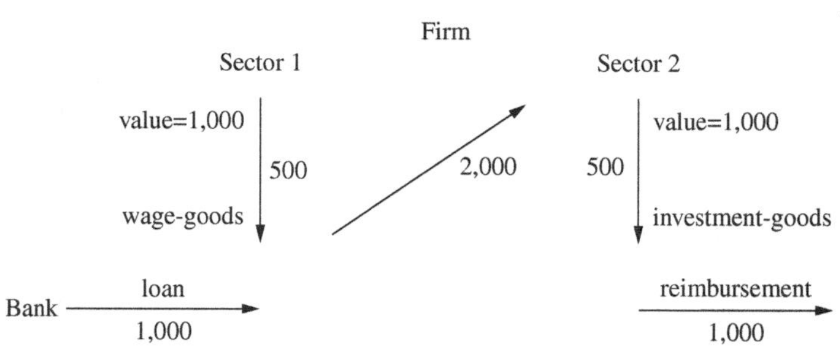


*Figure 12.2* The case where only wage-goods and investment-goods are produced.

investment-goods by spending a sum of money units obtained at zero cost from households. Firms' expenditure of profit grants them final ownership over investment-goods and the sum spent remains available as bank deposit. Hence, households can borrow this sum and pay back to banks the exact amount initially borrowed from them. Ultimately, by subtracting part of the income of households, investment increases their indebtedness to banks, which means that in capitalism wage-earners are deprived of the economic ownership over instrumental goods.

### *The case where profit is invested in the production of both interest- and investment-goods*

If we now reintroduce the production of interest-goods and suppose that production in the two sectors reached maximum expansion, we obtain the situation as represented in Figure 12.3.

Wages distributed in the first and second sectors = 1,000
Value of wage-goods = 1,000
Value of interest-goods = 1,000
Value of investment-goods = 1,000
Macroeconomic loan of banks = 2,000

When the expansion of sector 2 has reached its upper limit, banks lend in each period an amount equal to 2,000 money units, 1,000 corresponding to interests and 1,000 to investment. The production of sector 2 is made up of goods whose total value is equal to 2'000 money units, half of which is transferred in the form of interests. Wages paid out in each of the two sectors are equal to 500 wage-units, while the value of wage-goods is multiplied by 2 and raised to 1,000 wage-units.

As far as unemployment is concerned, neither redistributed nor invested profits can lead to insufficient global demand relative to global supply. The macroeconomic loan of the deposit of profit granted by banks to households

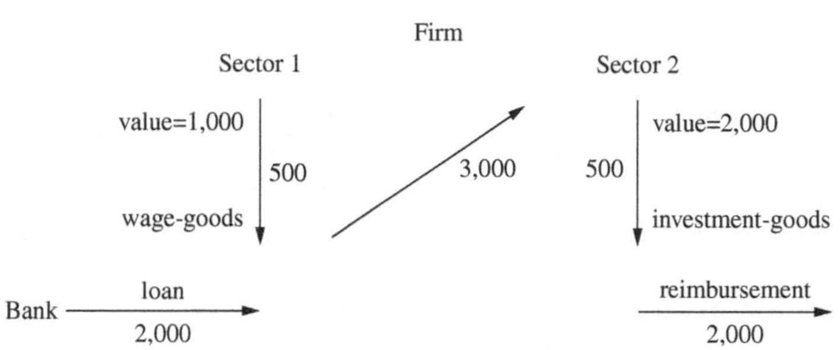


*Figure 12.3* The case where production consists in wage-goods, interest-goods, and investment-goods.

takes the amount of available income to the same level as the price (and value) of produced output, including wage-goods, interest-goods, and investment-goods. It is only 'if the bank did not lend this deposit that the income of households captured by the firm would not be available, in the *regime of capitalism*, for the general purchase of the product [market clearing]' (ibid: 101, m.t.). Moreover, if we observe that profits are always necessarily spent, we immediately realize that the presence of profits invested in the production of fixed capital-goods does not reduce global demand. The increase in global supply, due to the production of investment-goods, cannot be at the origin of unemployment, because it is unavoidably accompanied by an equal increase in global demand, due to the formation of profits and to their expenditure by firms on purchasing investment-goods in the labour market.

## Amortization is not a direct cause of unemployment, but creates the conditions for its rise

### *The twofold nature of amortization*

We need to reconsider now the definition of national product and national income to account for the fact that the value of fixed capital declines through wear and tear and obsolescence. Keynes's definition, adopted by the great majority of economists,

$$R = C + I$$

must therefore be replaced by one imposed by the analysis of amortization,

$$R = C + I + A$$

where $A$ represents the production of amortization-goods. To keep the value of fixed capital intact, the production of amortization-goods must define a new production, which is added to that of consumption-goods (wage-goods plus interest-goods *latu sensu*) and investment-goods. Let us suppose that the value of the fixed capital accumulated during $n$ periods is equal to X and that the loss of value due to wear and tear in period $n$ is equal to $x$. As Schmitt observes, '[i] t is certain that capital can recover its complete value of X units only if $x$ units of newly produced value are *added* to it. The production of amortization-goods is therefore identical to the production of new investment-goods' (ibid.: 110, m.t.). It follows that the definition of national income, too, must be modified, adding the income generated by the production of $A$ to that formed by the production of $C$ and $I$.

In the same way as amortization-goods are a new product, the income corresponding to their production is net. Since amortization-goods are part of the net product, alongside consumption- and investment-goods, the activity of the national economy is subdivided into three sectors. Yet, we must amend this conclusion by observing that amortization is also a reproduction of fixed capital (see Chapter 6). Thus, it appears that, unlike the principle of the excluded middle, amortization is at the same time reproduction and net production. The goods produced in the third sector reproduce the value of fixed capital lost due to wear and tear. In this sense, the third sector involves only the reproduction of capital and not its production, which concerns solely the first two sectors. In spite of this, the reproduction of capital is a net production, because amortization-goods must be produced anew. Amortization-goods

> are at the same time pure reproduction goods and true production goods. Considered in their strict definition of reproduction goods, amortization-goods contribute no net value to the national economy. But considered in their definition, equally exact, of production goods, amortization-goods contribute their full value to the national economy.
>
> (ibid.: 115, m.t.)

It follows that amortization-goods are both a 'gross' value and a 'net' value. 'The division of the economy into sectors – which, far from being a pure theoretical construction, exists in reality – allows us to understand this duplication of the value, gross, and net of amortization' (ibid.: 116, m.t.).

### *Again, on the subdivision of the economy into sectors*

Let us recall that Schmitt's quantum macroeconomics is a theory of *emissions*, so that the payment of wages is best defined as an emission of money through which bank money is given a real content. The subdivision of the economy into sectors closely relates to the nature of money and to its emission. 'The reason why it is *indispensable* to analyze the activity of the economy by distinct sectors is that money, *per se*, independently of its content or its legal definition, is an asset-liability, a strictly nil asset, a pure number' (ibid.: 118, m.t.). Initially, the content of money is always necessarily a sum of wage-goods: 'under no circumstances, either in a formally correct analysis or in the real world, can a unit of money be directly enriched by an investment-good or by an amortization-good' (ibid.: 119, m.t.). This means that the production of profit-goods (investment-goods) and of amortization-goods takes place in two stages.

The first stage is a production of wage-goods, the second stage is the transformation of wage-goods into investment- and amortization-goods. The distinction into sectors is due to this characteristic of money, which cannot directly 'take in' either investment- or amortization-goods. The first content of money is necessarily made up of wage-goods, and it is only through a transformation of part of the wage-goods that profit-goods and/or amortization-goods can be obtained. The first sector can therefore be defined as 'the place where each unit of money is emitted only once, [whereas] the second [and third sectors ... are places] where each money unit is emitted a second time' (ibid.: 119, m.t.).

Let us momentarily put aside the production of interest-goods, because 'it is redundant with respect to profit-goods' (ibid.: 120, m.t.). As Schmitt maintains, sectors can also

> be defined by claiming that in the first sector the money emitted to pay wages has not previously incorporated any real product [whereas in the second and third sectors] each money unit emitted integrates a positive product for the second time.
>
> (ibid.: 119, m.t.)

In sectors 2 and 3, investment- and amortization-goods are integrated into money in place of wage-goods. The second emission of money (which, when first emitted, was associated with wage-goods) gives it a new real content: investment-goods and amortization-goods replace wage-goods. The transformation of wage-goods into profit- and amortization-goods implies that workers of the second and third sector receive products (wage-goods) already emitted within the wages paid to the workers employed in the first sector as real remuneration of their work. 'The factors of production employed in the second [and third] sector obtain, within their wages (real content of nominal wages), products already emitted in favour of workers of the first sector' (ibid.: 121, m.t.).

If we consider the first two sectors alone, we observe that workers obtain wages whose real content has been halved. Firms obtain the other half as profit and use it to finance a production of investment-goods. Now, to finance a production means to emit wages. Firms utilize the wages taken from workers to finance a new payment of wages, corresponding to the production of investment-goods. We thus observe a true 're-emission of wages. [...] workers employed in the second sector obtain as real remuneration the products already obtained by the workers employed in the first sector' (ibid.: 121, m.t.). The employment of workers in the second sector, therefore, comes at no cost to firms: the products of the second sector are not part of the purchasing power of workers employed in the entire economy. The workers of the second sector produce for firms, not for consumers.

If we now add amortization, we observe that national production is subdivided into three sectors. Once maximum expansion is reached in each sector, total activity is distributed in equal parts over the three sectors, each of which employs a third of active workers and pays out wages equal to 333.3 wage-units. Measured on the basis of the wages paid to workers, the value produced in each sector is thus equal to 333.3 units. The production of amortization-goods is net, and workers employed in the third sector receive wages whose real content is necessarily defined in wage-goods. In the third sector, workers produce amortization-goods and obtain wage-goods as real content of their remuneration. In no circumstances can a monetary emission lead to the association of wages with products that are not wage-goods. 'We thus observe the existence of a perfect *dissociation* between the object produced by workers of sector 3 and the object they obtain as a remuneration' (ibid.: 123, m.t.). Firms get hold of amortization-goods, and workers purchase part of the production of wage-goods of the first sector: '*consumption-goods already included in the wages emitted in the first sector are "served up" to the producers employed in the third sector*' (ibid.: 124, m.t.).

In conclusion, in today's capitalism neither investment-goods nor amortization-goods can be a *direct* production: 'their production must first go through the production of wage-goods in the strictest sense' (ibid.: 125, m.t.). Productions of the second and third sectors entail a duplication of the production of the first sector, which is why the subdivision into sectors is essential in a capitalistic regime.

### *The value of wage-goods is increased by the value of amortization-goods*

Let us suppose for a moment that the economy is active only in the first and third sectors. In this case, firms finance the production of amortization-goods through the sale of the goods produced in the first sector. On the one hand, by purchasing wage-goods, consumers purchase at the same time the amortization-goods on behalf of firms. On the other hand, consumers enjoy the benefits of capital being kept at the initial value. Thus, consumers benefit from the preservation of physical productivity and pay for it. By selling wage-goods, firms realize the profit necessary to cover the costs of production of amortization-goods.

> It is within the sale of the first sector that firms find the funds necessary to finance the production of the third sector. It is absolutely normal, because households are the beneficiaries of amortization, the maintenance of capital. If capital went downhill, the production of physical goods would decrease in time, which would lessen households' well-being.
>
> (ibid.: 114, m.t.)

Bear in mind that the presence of fixed capital triggers the transformation of an increase in physical productivity into a rise in value production. This applies also to capital reproduction. Through amortization, the increase in the physical productivity of capital remains unaltered and is also the cause of an increase in value. The value of production in the first sector is thus increased by the value produced in the third sector. '[T]he production of value units of the first sector is increased, *in this same sector*, by all the value produced in the third sector' (ibid.: 124, m.t.). Once sector expansion reaches its maximum level, the production of the third sector doubles the production of the first sector, measured in value units. The totality of wages emitted in sector 1 is newly emitted in sector 3. As a consequence, wage-earners employed in sector 3 obtain the totality of the consumption-goods initially obtained in the wages paid to workers of sector 1. This notwithstanding, wage-earners of the first sector can benefit from the entirety of the real wages formed by the production of consumption-goods, because their value doubles as soon as amortization-goods are produced.

The rise in value of the product of sector 1 due to capital's amortization is determined by the production of amortization-goods in sector 3. It is the value of the production of sector 3 that sets the amount of value added by fixed capital amortization to the production of wage-goods. With Schmitt, we distinguish financial from real amortization: the former takes place in the first sector, the latter in the third sector. From what we have previously seen, real amortization determines financial amortization. Financial amortization cannot exceed the value of what is produced in sector 3; it is determined by it: 'financial and real amortization are one and the same operation, and it is real amortization that prevails, financial amortization being its other face' (ibid.: 127, m.t.).

Taking into account only the first and third sectors, we observe the multiplication of the value produced in sector 1 by a factor of two.

> If we count, according to scientific principles as one ought, produced goods by their value (and not, inversely, which would be wrong, the value of goods by their number), we observe that the number of goods produced in sector 1 is multiplied by 2 because of the production of sector 3.
>
> (ibid.: 124, m.t.)

Wage-goods are sold at a price equal to their value, but higher than their production cost. The profit derived from this sale finances the production of amortization-goods in sector 3.

### *Amortization entails a new macroeconomic loan of the banking system*

As in the case of the production of profit-goods, we know that the banking system intervenes with a loan to households equal to the difference between prices and production costs. In our example, when both sectors have reached their upper limit, the macroeconomic loan corresponding to the production of the third sector is of 1,000 wage-units. The same applies to the production of investment-goods. The production of sector 2 implies also a duplication of sector 1's production, whose value increases to the same extent as the wages paid out in the production of profit-goods. If we now consider sectors 1, 2, and 3, and the situation when the entire production takes place in equal parts in the three sectors, then the value produced in sector 1 increases by twice 333.3 money units; first because of the production of investment-goods and, then again, following the production of amortization-goods. Value increases by 666.6 units in total, raising the value of wage-goods to 1,000 money units.

Overall, if we consider both the production of interest-goods and investment-goods of sector 2, and that of amortization-goods, the value added by the transformation of physical productivity is of 3,000 money units. The macroeconomic loan of banks reaches 3,000 money units and, together with the 1,000 units corresponding to the wages paid out in the three sectors, represents the amount of income required for the purchase of the entire production. Altogether, global production has a value of 4,000 units and can be purchased through the expenditure of the 4,000 money units available to households (1,000 units of wages + 3,000 units of macroeconomic loans), as represented in Figure 12.4

Wages distributed in each sector = 333.3
Value of wage-goods = 1,000
Value of interest-goods = 1,000
Value of investment-goods = 1,000
Value of amortization-goods = 1,000
Macroeconomic loan of banks = 3,000

The value of wage-goods is multiplied by three and passes from 333.3 to 1,000 wage-units, because of the production of goods in sectors 2 and 3. The multiplication of value due to the increase in labour's physical productivity applies also to the other two sectors and takes the value of profit-goods to 1,000 units – both of interest-goods and investment-goods – as well as of amortization-goods. With the sale of wage-goods firms earn 4,000 money units, 1,000 of which are redistributed as interests and finance the purchase of interest-goods produced in sector 2. Of the remaining 2,000 units, 1,000 pay investment-goods and 1,000 pay amortization-goods. The total value of the production of the three sectors is 4,000 units, while the amount of wages is 1,000 units. The macroeconomic loan granted by banks to the set of households provides the remaining 3,000 units necessary for the purchase of the entire production.

To identify the portion of national income obtained by households and the portion obtained by firms, we must compare the value of wage-goods and interest-goods with the value of total production. We should therefore conclude that total production is equally distributed between households and firms: households receive wage- and interest-goods worth 2,000, half of national production, and firms receive the other half in the form of investment- and amortization-goods. However, this proportion does not correspond to that of national accounting. What must be remembered now is that amortization is at the same time a reproduction of fixed capital and a net production. To the extent that it defines a reproduction, amortization is financial and must be situated in the first sector; at the same time the production of amortization-goods

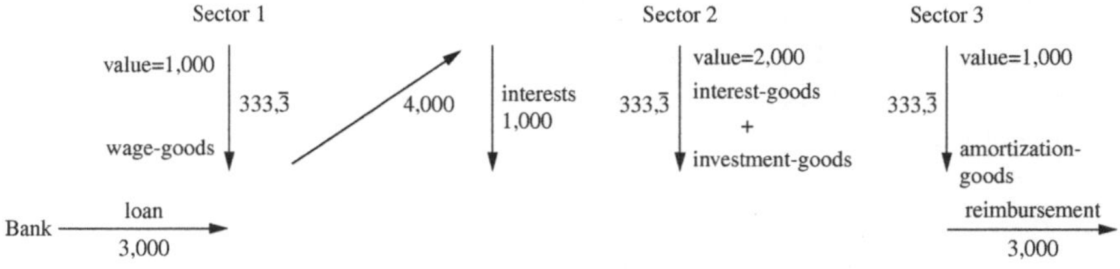


*Figure 12.4* The subdivision of the entire production into three sectors.

taking place in the third sector is a net production and defines a real profit. 'The financial value of goods A is included in the cost of production of the goods of the first sector; the value of the goods actually produced in the third sector is a genuine real profit' (ibid.: 136, m.t.).

If it is true that firms obtain the profit needed to finance the production of amortization-goods through the sale of wage-goods, it is also clear that households benefit from the increase in labour physical productivity derived from the preservation of instrumental capital. As Schmitt claims, consumers do not obtain the amortization-goods, but their value increases that of the goods they purchase. '[T]he value of amortization-goods is obtained by households, who benefit from the "intact" production of amortized capital' (ibid.: 136, m.t.). The total amount of value obtained by households is thus equal to 3,000 units, corresponding to the value of wage-goods, 1,000 units, the value of interest-goods, 1,000 units, and the value of amortization-goods, 1,000 units. If we consider that the production of amortization-goods adds 1,000 units of value to national product because 'it is the value of the net product of the third sector' (ibid.: 136, m.t.), the total value of production comes to 5,000 units. Of these units, households obtain 3,000 and firms 2,000, a proportion in line with that of national accounting.

### *Amortization and unemployment*

In the present capitalist regime, fixed capital is formed and amortized within the payment of wages in the second and third sectors as the expenditure of firms' profit is introduced. Unlike wages emitted for the second time in the second sector, whose content is the wage-goods saved and transformed into stock the moment profits are formed, those emitted in the third sector have no real content. Wages paid for the production of investment-goods and for the production of amortization-goods are *empty*, because they are 'stripped' of the goods purchased by firms in the labour market. Yet, wages paid to the producers of investment-goods define withdrawal rights over that part of wage-goods corresponding to net profits, whereas those paid to producers of amortization-goods are definitively empty. The payment of wages in the third sector defines a final expenditure of income by firms. In this sector, firms get hold of the product and give nothing in exchange to their workers. Thus, firms spend the income owed to workers at the very moment it is formed, and workers receive no real remuneration whatsoever.

> [T]he product of sector 3 is "purchased" by the set of firms – in fact they get it for free – because they give as a "counterpart", a rigorously nil purchasing power; so, firms, rather than households, spend the real income made from their production in the third sector.
>
> (ibid.: 138, m.t.)

In Schmitt's example, total wages paid in the three sectors are equal to 1,000 units, 333.3 units in each sector. Wage-earners lose a third of their purchasing power, because wages emitted in sector 3 are devoid of real content. The loss concerns the set of wage-earners, not only those of the third sector, and reduces the real content of wages from three times 333.3 to twice 333.3 units. As Schmitt states:

> capitalism is a regime where the set of firms manage, within fixed capital amortization, to impose the exchange of a product whose value is three times 333.3 units, supplied by the factors of production, against a product of twice 333.3 units of value, obtained by these factors. The difference is the net profit realized by the set of firms in the third sector
>
> (ibid.: 138, m.t.)

The reason why wages paid out in the third sector are devoid of real content lies in the nature of amortization, which, as we know, is at the same time a reproduction of capital value and a new net production of value. Situated in the third sector, the new production is an additional investment, so 'goods of the third sector may be referred to as an over-accumulation of capital' (ibid.: 136, m.t.).

Nevertheless, the presence of the empty money emitted in sector 3 is not enough to explain unemployment. Indeed, if we consider the fact that 'any income (wages) formed in sector 3 is fully spent' (ibid.: 117, m.t.), it appears that there can be no difference between global supply, S, and global demand, D, even when the production of amortization-goods is added to that of consumption- and profit-goods. In general, the income created by production is all necessarily spent, so that the totality of productions and of final expenditures are inevitably equal. Unemployment, therefore, cannot derive from a discrepancy between S and D, but must be explained by a process that hampers production without altering the equivalence between national output (S) and national income (D).

## Unemployment as the unavoidable consequence of capital over-accumulation

What we have considered so far is the accumulation of new fixed capital due to the production of investment-goods in the second sector and the consequent over-accumulation as a result of the production of amortization-goods in the third sector. Starting from a situation in which national production is uniformly subdivided into the three sectors, amortization would restore the value lost by instrumental capital because of wear and tear in each successive period, while fixed capital would increase by 1,000 units of value because of the production of investment-goods in sector 2. If we now add the production of sector 3, which is a true net production and defines a capital over-accumulation, we should observe an increase in fixed capital equal to 2,000 units of value in each period following that in which the three sectors reach their maximum expansion.

### *The remuneration of fixed capital*

The use of the conditional mode is intentional, as we want to stress the fact that the renewal of the situation that we have described is far from guaranteed. Indeed, up to now we have not considered that fixed capital must be remunerated. The remuneration of capital consists of the interests to be paid to it. What needs determining is whether or not the payment of interests can expand unrestrictedly. Accumulated capital increases with the passage of time, thanks to the production of investment- and amortization-goods. Therefore, interests must grow alongside accumulated capital. However, the production of interests takes place in the second sector and cannot exceed the amount of profits, which, in turn, cannot exceed the amount of wages. '[T]he interests produced in a given period cannot exceed the value brought about, with the aid of capital, by the third of the factors of production employed in the national economy' (ibid.: 129, m.t.).

We witness what Marx (1894/1981) called *the law of the tendential fall in the rate of profit* and Wicksell (1898/1965) identified with the evolution of *the natural rate of interest*. The rate of profit (interest) is the ratio between the profits (interests) paid to capital and produced in a given period and the sum of fixed capitals accumulated during all the previous periods. While fixed capital does not stop accumulating period after period, profits cannot exceed the sum of wages in each single period. Profits paid to capital are none other than the interests produced in the second sector. Therefore, the fall in the rate of profit (interest) marks the evolution of the ratio between total interests and accumulated fixed capital.

> *The limit imposed on the production of interests and its relation to an unlimited increase in capital (which must be remunerated in interests) constitute the terms of the objective or natural law of the dynamic of capital and the falling rate of profit (interest).*
>
> (ibid.: 129, m.t.)

The phenomenon described by Marx, and confirmed by quantum macroeconomics as well as by empirical observation, is not sufficient to explain the existence of a problem that unavoidably leads to involuntary unemployment. One could think that the only consequence of the falling rate of profit (interest) is to make it tend towards zero. Here Wicksell's concept of *monetary or market rate of interest* enters the picture. The monetary rate of interest is the rate of interest as determined in the financial market; it is formed through the bargaining between banks, savers, and investors, which begins at the base rate (benchmark) settled by central banks, i.e. the rate at which private banks can borrow from their central bank. Those who want to spend their future income today and those who prefer to postpone the expenditure of their present income try to come to an agreement through a fluctuation of the market interest rate.

What truly matters now is to compare the level reached by Wicksell's natural rate on interest (Marx's rate of profit) with the money interest rate. If the latter were to fall freely below zero, then the process of capital accumulation could continue endlessly and it would not be possible to explain involuntary unemployment. In reality, however, monetary or financial interest remains positive or, at worst, is equal to zero or just slightly below it. Thus, the economy is confronted, on the one hand, with a steady rise in accumulated fixed capital and, on the other hand, with a limit imposed by the production of interests: this leads inescapably to a situation where the natural rate of interest (profit) falls short of the money interest rate. When this happens, financial investment prevails over productive investment, and we observe a continuing contraction in the production of investment-goods. As Schmitt claims, what we are facing is the gradual transfer of the production of amortization-goods from the third to the second sector and the ensuing drop in the employment level.

> Concretely, this means that firms give up producing investment-goods in the second sector – which only worsens the negative difference between natural and monetary interest rates – and produces amortization-goods instead: *hence, the production of the third sector replaces the production of the second sector.*
>
> (ibid.: 131, m.t.)

When the natural rate falls below the money rate of interest, it becomes more profitable for firms to invest their profits in the financial market rather than in a new production of investment-goods. On the other hand, new production of investment-goods leads to an excessive growth in fixed capital and makes its remuneration impossible. In concrete terms, this means that firms would gradually give up producing new investment-goods in the second sector and switch to producing amortization-goods previously produced in the third sector. To secure full employment, the production of amortization-goods must take place in the third sector. Its transfer from the third to the second sector reduces global production and leads to unemployment, which, in its maximum expansion, affects one-third of the active population.

> When unemployment reaches its upper limit in the industry, amortization-goods are produced instead of the investment-goods of the second sector; it is perfectly natural that, in their quality of final goods, amortization-goods be investment-goods. But value produced by the national economy is then reduced by 1,000 units of value, which corresponds to the wages of a third of the population expected to be active in full employment; unemployment then hits one-third of the population active in the industry.
>
> (ibid.: 132, m.t.)

# 13 The development of Schmitt's criticism of general equilibrium analysis

Alongside the development of his quantum macroeconomic analysis, Schmitt's interest in general equilibrium analysis (GEA) never faded. To Walras and his followers, Schmitt ascribes the great merit of replacing the dimensional notion of economic value advocated by the Classics with a numerical notion of value as a relationship between real goods and numbers. At the same time, he endeavours to show that GEA's attempt to build such a relationship out of direct exchange between real goods is doomed to failure because of the logical indeterminacy of relative prices. An astonishing number of mainly unpublished manuscripts marks the period 1987–2000, where Schmitt goes deeper into the critical analysis of general equilibrium that he had already started in the first decades of his investigation into the nature of value, money, and prices. The quality of these manuscripts and the variety of arguments developed in each of them make it very difficult to choose which to include in an overview of Schmitt's contribution. Reluctantly, I had to put aside some of his proofs of what he calls the *inanity of neoclassical thought*. Including them would have made it too arduous for the reader to follow Schmitt into one of the most difficult, critical analyses in the history of economic thought.

GEA is the foundation of mainstream economics; its criticism must therefore be as accurate and watertight as possible and must be *internal* to GEA itself: it must show that the neoclassical attempt at determining relative prices is self-contradictory, that it suffers from an internal logical incoherence. In this chapter, I refer to seven unpublished manuscripts, some of which I have entitled and dated myself, and to one paper 'A new paradigm for the determination of money prices' published in 1996.

## GEA on the determination of relative and monetary prices

### *The aim of GEA*

What Schmitt makes clear from the outset is that the aim of GEA is to *express goods numerically* through their direct exchange. Prices are the fundamental concept of economics; without prices, goods would remain heterogeneous and could not become the very object of inquiry of our science. Prices are

DOI: 10.4324/9781351271325-18

numerical and are determined by an exchange between physical goods and numbers: this is the essence of the neoclassical revolution. Goods are both physically defined and measured in purely numerical units. Rejecting the Classics' attempts to measure the value of goods through a dimensional standard, neoclassical authors replace the dimensional labour-unit with an a-dimensional unit expressing the numerical price of goods. As Schmitt claims, relative prices are at the same time a relationship between two distinct goods and a *numerical* relationship between goods and numbers.

> In its *first definition*, the price of a commodity is another commodity; this is why prices are relationships between goods. However, in its *second definition*, the price of a commodity is a *pure number* and not – we can never be too emphatic – a number of physical units of another commodity.
>
> (Schmitt 1999a: 2, m.t.)

What is crucial here is that the transformation of real goods into numbers is the first, necessary step required for building an economic theory, and that this transformation takes place through an exchange.

Schmitt observes that the contradiction between the claim that exchanges take place between commodities, and that the two terms of every exchange are a real good and a number, is only apparent.

> Neoclassical economists have thoroughly understood one fact. Though initially abhorrent to common sense, it is not contradictory to claim in one breath that every exchange has a physical good and a pure number as its terms while also being made up of terms that are both goods, *one as well as the other.*
>
> (Schmitt 1997c: 5, m.t.)

Contradiction is avoided if numbers are *interposed* between the two physical terms of an exchange between commodities. For example, if 2 oranges are replaced by the number 10, and the number 10 is immediately replaced by 3 apples, then 2 oranges and 3 apples are the real terms of the exchange, and the number 10 acts as a catalyst. The relative exchange between 2 oranges and 3 apples defines simultaneously an exchange of equilibrium and a price of equilibrium. Like any other exchange, that between 2 oranges and 3 apples implies the equivalence of its two terms. Yet, 'the pertinent equivalences are *strictly numerical*' (Schmitt 1999a: 3, m.t.), which means that 'the same number is the price of both terms of the exchange' (ibid.: 3, m.t.). In our example, the number 10 is interposed in the exchange between 2 oranges and 3 apples in such a way that it gives them the same numerical form and makes them equivalent. '[E]xchange creates an equivalence (only positive, non-metaphysical definition of value in economics) between purely physical goods, devoid of a dimensional value and pure numbers' (Schmitt 1997c: 6, m.t.).

What is at stake is neither the neoclassical conception of prices as numbers, nor the neoclassical claim that it is through exchange that goods and numbers enter a relation of identity. Both assertions are beyond dispute and characterize the main contribution of GEA to the making of economics as a science. What must come under closer scrutiny is the neoclassical identification of the operation whereby real goods are transformed into numbers with the direct exchange between goods apparently available as economic agents' original endowments.

Can relative exchange determine numerical prices? This is the question to be answered. As we know, Schmitt's critical analysis of GEA leads to a definitive, negative answer: the logical indeterminacy of relative prices necessarily makes it logically impossible to determine numerical prices. '[O]ur discipline cannot derive any unit of measure from the transactions in which already given goods are exchanged between themselves' (Schmitt 1993/94a: 2, m.t.). What Schmitt, in his 1993/94 unpublished manuscript, calls the impossibility theorem holds whether we refer to the direct exchange between real goods, or to the exchange occurring through the mediation of a unit of account (the *numéraire*) or money. Let us start with the case in which goods are directly confronted with one another.

### *Direct exchange between goods is not a means for determining relative prices*

Let us consider, as Walras did in his *Elements of Pure Economics*, the simplest example, where two agents, A and B, exchange their respective goods, *a* and *b*. Each agent has an initial endowment of *a* and *b* respectively, say *x* units of *a* and *y* units of *b*, and the aim of the exercise is to allow each agent to maximize its utility through exchange. 'Each agent is a free and autonomous person; each conceives exchange in their imagination, according to their own preferences' (ibid.: 4, m.t.). It is by confronting supply and demand that GEA believes it possible to determine relative prices.

In our example, two equations must simultaneously be satisfied, one establishing the equality between the supply of and demand for *a*, and the other, the equality between the supply of and demand for *b*.

$$S(a) = D(a) \tag{13.1}$$

$$S(b) = D(b) \tag{13.2}$$

Prices being relative, the variable to be determined by these two equations is only one, the price of *a* in terms of *b* or, inversely, the price of *b* in terms of *a*. The system is *determined* and a solution possible only if the number of independent equations drops to one, which is what happens when the supply of *a* (*b*) is defined by the demand for *b* (*a*) (Walras's law).

The role played by Walras's law is crucial, which calls for an in-depth analysis of its logical meaning. Schmitt had already established the tautological character of this law and shown that it cannot apply during the adjustment process leading to equilibrium (see Chapter 3). In 1993, he reiterates this fact by claiming that 'supplies and demands are each the expression of subjective desires that are not yet reciprocally reconciled' (ibid.: 7, m.t.), which is why the equality between the sum of supplies and the sum of demands does not hold outside equilibrium. The arguments presented in Chapter 3 are enough to establish the logical impossibility to reduce the number of independent equations of the system of general equilibrium by resorting to Walras's law. However, the relevance of this law is such that Schmitt investigates it further with the explicit goal of making its logical status as clear as possible and to explain what role, if any, it can effectively play in the determination of relative prices.

### *The logical status of Walras's law*

Returning to the example of two goods and two commodities, the law of Walras states that the demand for $b$ exerted by A is always and necessarily equal to the supply of $a$ made by A, while B's demand for $a$ is likewise identical to B's supply of $b$.

$$\text{Demand for } b = \text{Supply of } a \tag{13.3}$$

$$\text{Demand for } a = \text{Supply of } b \tag{13.4}$$

In a world with two agents and two commodities, each agent can demand the other agent's commodity only by supplying their own commodity. Thus formulated, Walras's law must be regarded as a definition and applies equally well to equilibrium, when $a$ and $b$ are effectively exchanged, and to the period preceding equilibrium. In any circumstance, A and B can demand $b$ ($a$) only by offering $a$ ($b$): 'the demand of each agent *defines* the corresponding supply of this agent' (Schmitt 1997b: 5, m.t.).

The key question now is whether the identities between each agent's demands and supplies are enough to establish the *equivalence between the two commodities a* and $b$. At equilibrium, the answer is clearly yes, because the exchange of $a$ and $b$ brings about the equivalence of its two terms. However, outside equilibrium, during the phase of adjustment that should lead to the reciprocal exchange of $a$ and $b$, the identity of A's supply and demand is logically distinct from the identity of B's supply and demand: 'the two couples supply–demand remain distinct and autonomous from one another (ibid.: 6, m.t.). During the process of adjustment, no imaginary exchange can verify the equivalence of its two terms, so that $a$ and $b$ are bound to remain heterogeneous. '"Imaginary" exchanges, which are all identities between demands and supplies, are in no case equivalences between the quantities demanded and the quantities supplied' (ibid.: 5, m.t.).

According to GEA, it is through exchange that real goods become commensurable and that an equivalence between the terms of the exchange is established. Before an exchange takes place, no equivalence exists; the relative price between *a* and *b* is still unknown so that the identity of A's demand and supply cannot even be quantified. It is true that when A offers *a* this defines a reciprocal demand for *b*, but the amount demanded is entirely undetermined. 'Outside exchange it is impossible to establish the slightest correlation between the demand for one good and the supply of another' (ibid.: 7, m.t.).

As Schmitt claims, the reason why Walras's law is nothing more than a truism is that relative exchanges imply that if the supply of *a* is the demand for *b* it is also immediately true that the demand for *a* is the supply of *b*. Hence, if the demand for *a* defines the supply of *b*, which defines the demand for *a*, it necessarily follows that the demand for *a* is equivalent to itself. Likewise, the supply of *b* defining the demand for *a*, and the demand for *a* defining the supply of *b*, the only equivalence determined by relative exchanges is that between the supply of *b* and itself. In each relative exchange '*demand and supply measure* one another *so that demand cannot measure supply nor can supply measure demand; demand measures itself in the same way as supply measures itself*' (ibid.: 8 m.t.).

Walras's law would provide a true solution to the problem of relative price determination if we could reasonably assume that each supply or each demand of a given commodity is a physical quantity of the same commodity. In this case, for example, the supply of *a*, measured in physical units of *a*, would at the same time define a demand for *b*, measured in physical units of *b*, and establish the equivalence between these two goods. As Schmitt shows, however, this would amount to a 'serious formal mistake' (Schmitt 1998c: 19, m.t.). This is so because the two terms of Walras's identities are necessarily 'measured in physical units of one and the same good' (ibid.: 22, m.t.).

Following Schmitt, let us start from the identity between the demand for *b*, D(*b*), and the supply of *a*, S(*a*). What does this identity tell us? That the measure of D(*b*) is also the measure of S(*a*). And what is the precise meaning of the measures of D(*b*) and S(*a*)? The answer rests on the fact that, according to GEA, supplies and demands are initially measured in physical units of the goods that agents A and B are willing to exchange. Thus, the demand for *b* is measured in physical units of *b*, oranges, while the demand for *a* is measured in physical units of *a*, apples. Does this mean that from the identity between D(oranges) ≡ S(apples) we can derive the equivalence of oranges and apples? Not in the least. Before exchange, oranges and apples are distinct, heterogeneous goods, and no one would ever maintain that oranges are apples and apples oranges.

On these premises, we can only conclude that the demand for *a* measuring the supply of *b*, if D(*a*) is of 3 oranges the measure of S(*b*) is also of 3 oranges. It follows that '[t]he apples that are offered by the demand for 3 oranges are *a measure of apples equal to 3 oranges*' (ibid.: 8, m.t.). If agent B exerts a demand for 3 oranges by offering apples, the measure of his supply derives from its identity with the demand for oranges and is therefore equal to 3 oranges.

The analysis of the identity of D(*a*) and S(*b*) leads to an analogous result. If D(*a*) is of 5 apples, the measure of S(*b*), a supply of oranges, is of 5 apples. 'As the measure of the demand for *a* is the measure of the supply of *b*, and as good *a* is measured in units of apples, the measure of the supply of oranges is a number of apples' (ibid.: 8–9, m.t.). To say that the demand for apples is identical to a supply of oranges only means that both terms of the identity have the same measure, that is, that both the demand for apples and the supply of oranges are measured (in Schmitt's example by 5 apples). Nothing is said or can be inferred as to the relationship between apples and oranges, which cannot be considered as the terms of an equivalence.

> The only thing we know is that, whatever the number of oranges offered to demand 5 apples, this number of oranges is measured by 5 apples [...] *we do not have the slightest piece of information concerning the number of oranges whose measure is 5 apples.*
>
> (ibid.: 9, m.t.)

The total indeterminacy of the number of oranges defining the demand for 5 apples confirms the fact that '*no orange is measured by apples or in apples*' (ibid.: 10, m.t.).

The only acceptable meaning of Walras's law is the following:

Measure of D(apples) = Measure of S(oranges) = 5 apples
Measure of D(oranges) = Measure of S(apples) = 3 oranges

No relationship is established between apples and oranges, which remain two distinct goods that cannot be considered as equivalent.

The only result of Walras's law is that of imposing the measure of the demand for *a* on the measure of the supply of *b*, which is tantamount to imposing the measure of *a* on *b*. No adjustment can therefore be made between demands and supplies, which leaves relative prices entirely undetermined. Walras's identities would contribute to the determination of relative prices only if they provided some positive information about the number of physical units of a given commodity that economic agents are willing to exchange against a given number of physical units of another commodity. That is, 'if the demand for *a* and the supply of *b* were simultaneously measured in physical units of the *two* goods' (ibid.: 17, m.t.). In reality, Walras's law is nothing more than the definition of relative exchanges, where the demand for (supply of) a good is the supply of (demand for) another good, but where *a* and *b* remain two distinct and heterogeneous goods. Schmitt puts it clearly:

> [s]ince the only formally correct measures are carried out in terms of a *unique* good, *a* or *b*, Walras's first identity, demand for *a* = supply of *b*, is the very definition of vacuity, nobody is better off for it. For the same,

peremptory reason, Walras's second identity, demand for $b$ = supply of $a$, is an absolute vacuum.

(ibid.: 17, m.t.)

### *A final critique of Walras's law*

In one of his unpublished manuscripts of 1997, Schmitt (1997b) develops what he calls a *decisive critique of Walras's law*, which deserves our greatest attention. Its central point concerns the logical status of the law advocated by Walras. Let us refer again to the example of two agents and two goods. The following relationships are available for the determination of relative prices:

$$\text{Supply of } a = \text{Demand for } a \tag{13.5}$$

$$\text{Supply of } b = \text{Demand for } b \tag{13.6}$$

$$\text{Supply of } a = \text{Demand for } b \tag{13.7}$$

$$\text{Supply of } b = \text{Demand for } a \tag{13.8}$$

As we know, relationships (13.7) and (13.8) stand for Walras's law and, according to GEA, they are supposed to reduce to one the number of independent equations of the system of relative prices determination.

Schmitt starts his 1997 analysis by asking once more whether (13.7) and (13.8) must be taken as equivalences or conditions of equilibrium. In the first case, the equalities between S($a$) and D($b$) and between S($b$) and D($a$) are *identities* and merely state the fact that 'the supply of $a$ ($b$) is identically the demand for $b$ ($a$), that is identically the supply of $a$ ($b$)' (Schmitt 1997b: 22, m.t.). On these conditions, Walras's law is reduced to a truism whose heuristic value is strictly nil. 'When we develop to its end the logic underlying Walras's law, we see that it is founded on the identity of $a$ and $a$ as well as on the identity of $b$ and $b$. Nice law, entirely void' (ibid.: 23, m.t.). Yet, the law of Walras can also be considered as a condition of equilibrium without contradicting the obvious fact that, in a world of relative exchanges, the demand for $b$ ($a$) is necessarily exerted through a supply of $a$ ($b$). It is indeed possible to maintain the (tautological) definition of relative exchange while asserting that 'the supply of $a$ and the demand for $b$ *have not the same measure*' (ibid.: 23, m.t.).

To supply $a$ is to demand $b$, but the fact that any time agent A demands $b$ he offers $a$ is entirely unrelated to the numerical measure of their demand and supply. It '*does not imply that* A *offers and demands goods of the same numerical value*' (ibid.: 23, m.t.). It is only if the terms of a relative exchange could be determined that, simultaneously accepted by A and B, they would share the same numerical measure. Before exchange occurs, no equality can be established between the two terms of Walras's law, even though it remains true that to supply *a* (*b*) is to demand *b* (*a*). During the process of adjustment, the quantities of *a* that A is willing to supply are different from the quantities of *b* that A wants to demand, because their numerical value is not the same. Likewise, agent B demands *a* by offering *b*, but the numerical values of B's demand and supply differ. The quantities B requests in exchange for good *b*, are different from the quantities A requested in exchange for good *a*.

If Walras's law is considered as an identity establishing the equivalence between the two terms of (13.7) and (13.8), no adjustment is possible, because each exchange proposed either by A or B would immediately define an exchange of equilibrium 'accepted without discussion by their counterpart' (ibid.: 24, m.t.). In this case, the law is useless and must be rejected. If (13.7) and (13.8) are considered as conditions of equilibrium, they are no longer used to reduce the number of independent equations, and the system of relative price determination advocated by GEA is unavoidably over-determined. The four equations we have initially written down can be reduced to three independent equations, because one is included in the others, but three equations are two too many, the number of variables to be determined being equal to one: the price of *a* in terms of *b* or the price of *b* in terms of *a*.

In conclusion, whether we reject Walras's law on the ground that it is nothing more than a truism, of no use in the process of relative prices determination, or we interpret it as a condition of equilibrium, the result is the same: the logical indeterminacy of relative prices. 'Indeed, regardless of whether Walras's law is postulated or discarded, the distinct determinations to which the unique unknown (equilibrium price) is submitted are in any case three in number' (ibid.: 25, m.t.).

### *The auctioneer's intervention plays no part in relative prices determination*

To show once more that relative prices cannot be determined through direct exchange it is useful to introduce the figure of the auctioneer and analyze what happens if an auctioneer intervenes as a mediator between A and B. In terms of the rate of exchange between *a* and *b*, two things may happen: the auctioneer can either *impose* it or *propose* it to our two agents. In the first case, the proportion between *a* and *b*, say 1*a* for 3*b*, is not only cried out by the auctioneer, but it is also perceived as the rate at which any exchange achieved will have to submit. This is not to say that equilibrium is already known, imposed, from the outset. Indeed, A and B have still to determine the quantities of the reciprocal goods they will in fact exchange. The rate of exchange is predetermined, not the coefficient by which it is multiplied at equilibrium. Before equilibrium, the quantities of respective goods A and B are prepared to exchange at the rate of 1*a* for 3*b* are different, so that the equality between the supply of and the demand for *a* (or, alternatively, between S(*b*) and D(*b*)) is yet to be established. As Schmitt observes, in this case 'the equalization of the supply and demand of one of the two goods has the following, univocal meaning: it is *identified* with the equalization between the coefficients *ca* and *cb*' (Schmitt 1997d: 11, m.t.).

It is worth noticing at this stage that to reduce to one the number of independent equations required to determine equilibrium, one cannot just admit that initially the auctioneer imposes the ratio of exchange. One must also assume that the ratio of exchange remains constant during the process of adjustment between D(*a*) and S(*a*) and between D(*b*) and S(*b*).

> [I]f the equalization of supply and demand of a good is to be implied in the equalization of supply and demand of another good, the proportion of the two goods must crucially (a *sine qua non* condition) remain constant throughout the groping process.
>
> (ibid.: 11, m.t.)

This is indeed what would happen in the first case, where the proportion between *a* and *b* is imposed by the auctioneer all along the hypothetical process of adjustment. It should be clear that this assumption, which amounts to claiming that the ratio of exchange is *predetermined*, cannot be made by GEA, whose aim is *to determine* relative prices. If Schmitt introduces it in the analysis, it is to show that, even though GEA never mentions this assumption, the advocates of the neoclassical paradigm reason as if the rate of exchange were constant during the search for equilibrium. This is indeed a consequence of assuming that, thanks to Walras's law, the equalization of D(*a*) and S(a) is implied in the equalization of D(*b*) and S(*b*), and reciprocally.

As soon as we stop assuming that the auctioneer imposes the ratio of exchange, we see that the two equalizations are valid, which confirms that GEA cannot account for the adjustment leading to the proclaimed determination of relative prices.

> *Since the auctioneer does not force the agents to exchange their goods according to a pre-defined proportion, Pr***0***, it is formally wrong to reduce to a unique adjustment the equalization of the demand and supply of the two goods.*
>
> (ibid.: 12, m.t.)

Schmitt suggests another reason why relative prices cannot be determined even when the auctioneer proposes a rate of exchange that both A and B accept as the proportion likely to maximize their satisfaction. Let us reason *ad absurdum* and assume that such a rate of exchange can indeed be found and proposed to our two agents. Apparently, in this case and *assuming*, additionally and again against formal logic, that the rate of exchange remains stable during the process of adjustment, equilibrium can be determined by equalizing either the supply of and demand for *a*, or the supply of and demand for *b*. The acceptance of a single rate of exchange by A and B is enough to establish the necessary equality between the sum of supplies and the sum of demands (Walras's law) and thus reduce to one the adjustments required for the determination of the quantities of *a* and *b* to be exchanged at equilibrium. Apparently, if the rate of exchange is chosen by the auctioneer and accepted by A and B, the only unknown still to be determined is the coefficient of multiplication of this rate of exchange. Thus, for example, if the proportion accepted by the two agents is of 2 apples for 1 orange, what remains to be determined is how many apples A and B agree to exchange. If both A and B agree on a coefficient equal to 10, then the exchange would settle at 20 apples for 10 oranges.

What is wrong with this argument is that it entirely misses the fact that the rate of exchange is sensitive to the variations of the coefficients chosen by the two agents during the phase of adjustment. 'Now, it is logically impossible to adjust the coefficients [chosen by A and B] to one another without calling into question the equality of proportions *Pr*A and *Pr*B [the rates of exchange of A and B]' (ibid.: 8, m.t.). Even if, at the beginning of the experiment, A and B agree on a unique rate of exchange, we cannot claim that A's and B's rates will remain unchanged when the quantities involved vary. If the ratio of 2 apples for 1 orange provided the maximum satisfaction to A when c = 10, a change in the coefficient, say from 10 to 100, would not be irrelevant for A. Agent A could indeed find that, for a coefficient equal to 100, the ratio maximizing its utility is of 1.5 apples for 1 orange or any other proportion different from the initial one. The same reason applies also to B, whose choice of the proportion *Prb* varies with the variation of the coefficient proposed by the auctioneer.

> The proportion *Prx* given at the beginning of the adjustment of the coefficients is therefore modified by each agent when coefficients cA and cB adjust; we can on no account consider that the variation of *Prx* stirred by A and the variation of *Prx* stirred by B are variations of the same proportion.
> (ibid.: 6, m.t.)

The conclusion is thus confirmed that, during the search for equilibrium, the equalization of S(*a*) and D(*a*) is not implied in that of S(*b*) and D(*b*), and vice versa. Walras's law being of no avail, the only system of equations consistent with GEA and logic is made up of three independent equations, the two equalizations above and that between the proportions *Pr*A and *Pr*B. Since the only variable to be determined is the relative price of *a* in terms of *b*, or, which is the same in reverse, the price of *b* in terms of *a*, the logical indeterminacy of relative prices stands out as the only possible result of a rigorous, critical analysis of GEA.

Does the introduction of a numerical unit of account, Walras's *numéraire*, or of money, produce another result? Let us prove, following Schmitt, that this is not the case.

## Introducing the numéraire, or money, will not help GEA to determine numerical prices

### *The introduction of Walras's numéraire*

Let us start from Schmitt's observation that exchanges are an object of inquiry of economics 'at the *sine qua non condition* that their terms can be grasped in their *numerical* expressions' (Schmitt 1993/94, *Notes sur le cours du jeudi 18 novembre*: 8–9, m.t.). According to GEA, relative exchange between real goods makes it possible for physical heterogeneous goods to be introduced 'into a unique and the same space of measure' (ibid.: 9, m.t.). Goods are not numbers, and it would be metaphysical to believe otherwise. Yet, they can be associated to numbers, and neoclassical authors believe that this comes from direct exchange. Following Walras, they choose a good as reference, and assume its price to be equal to a pure number, that is, a number not associated with any dimension: the *numéraire*. Hence, for example, good *a* can be chosen as a *numéraire* and its price arbitrarily set equal to the number 1. Relative prices remain GEA's problem, but they may be determined through the determination of numerical prices. In the example, if the price of *a* is the number *x*, the relative price of *a* in terms of *b* can be immediately derived from the determination of the numerical price of *b*. During the search for equilibrium, the 'forces' at work are those of supply and demand as expressed in terms of the two goods.

Two equations,

$$\text{Supply of } a = \text{Demand for } a \tag{13.9}$$

$$\text{Supply of } b = \text{Demand for } b \tag{13.10}$$

are available to determine the numerical prices of equilibrium of *a* and *b*. By setting the numerical price of a given unit of *a*, assumed equal to 1, and by determining the numerical price of *b*, neoclassical economists make *a* and *b* homogeneous: they introduce them into the homogeneous space of numbers. Both the demand for and supply of *a* and the demand for and supply of *b* 'are numerical flows' (ibid.: 14, m.t.). Thus, it seems possible to determine the two monetary prices of *a* and *b* through Equations (13.9) and (13.10), and to derive from them the relative price of *a* (*b*) in terms of *b* (*a*).

Before assessing the possibility of arriving at the determination of relative prices passing through that of numerical prices, let us observe that, in the case of two goods, the arbitrary choice of number 1 as the numerical price of a given quantity of *a* does not reduce to one the number of numerical prices Equations (13.9) and (13.10) must determine. This is so because, before exchange actually takes place, '*we still know nothing about the physical quantity of the good-*numéraire *that will enter realized exchange*' (ibid.: 17, m.t.). The quantity of *a* that will be exchanged with *b* at equilibrium being still to be determined, the numerical price of equilibrium of *a* and that of *b* are both unknown.

As Schmitt observes, the methodology followed by Walras is peculiar. Even if it is possible to fix arbitrarily the numerical price of a commodity chosen as *numéraire*, this is not enough to abstract from the physical dimensions of the other goods. If *a* is made equal to 1, *b* does not miraculously lose all its physical dimensions and become a pure number. Fundamentally, 'the good-*numéraire* remains, despite everything, an object inseparable from its physical dimension' (ibid.: 16, m.t.), which makes it impossible to transform physically heterogeneous goods into homogeneous numbers by choosing one of them as *numéraire*. GEA's mistake is believing that, despite the initial arbitrariness of the 'construction' of the *numéraire*, exchange can 'transfer to all its other terms the numerical character of the *numéraire*' (ibid.: 17, m.t.). Two arguments prove it beyond dispute.

According to Schmitt's first analytical method, the number of independent equations is greater than the number of unknowns. In the example, two independent equations are available to determine a unique unknown, which entails the over-determination of the system designed to generate relative prices through the formation of numerical prices. The two independent equations are those equalizing the demand for *a* to the supply of *a* and the demand for *b* to the supply of *b*. Now, at least apparently, the unknowns are also two: the numerical price of *a*, and the numerical price of *b*. As we have seen, the price of *a* remains to be determined, even though the price of a unit of *a* is arbitrarily identified with the number 1. However, this is to ignore the fact that, according to GEA, the two terms of any exchange are physical goods; it never happens that real goods exchange against pure, dimensionless numbers. In reality, given that it is only in one relative exchange that *a* and *b* are exchanged for one another, '[*t*]*he ratio of the quantities exchanged of these two goods is the only unknown identifiable within the logic of the neoclassical paradigm*' (ibid.: 18, m.t.).

Since GEA does not contemplate the existence of the *numéraire* as a unit of payment, and prices are axiomatically defined as relationships between commodities, the ratio between *a* (*b*) and *b* (*a*) is the only variable that must be determined. Exchange would have to determine two distinct prices, the monetary price of *a* and the monetary price of *b* only if the *numéraire* were identified with money and goods exchanged through its mediation. However, Walras's *numéraire* has fundamentally no real existence, and goods are directly exchanged for one another: the relative price of *a* in *b*, or of *b* in *a*, is the only conceivable unknown within GEA. Absurdly, therefore, the introduction of the *numéraire* establishes the independence of Equations (13.9) and (13.10) without contrasting the reduction of the number of unknowns to one. If we now add the need to equalize, at equilibrium, the numerical price of *a* and the numerical price of *b* as determined by (13.9) and (13.10), we end up with three independent equations:

$$\text{Supply of } a = \text{Demand for } a \tag{13.11}$$

$$\text{Supply of } b = \text{Demand for } b \tag{13.12}$$

$$\text{Monetary price of } a = \text{Monetary price of } b. \tag{13.13}$$

Finally, in the case of two goods, the system of relative price determination is twice over-determined even when a *numéraire* is introduced as a unit of account, and the price of one good is made equal to any number arbitrarily chosen by the auctioneer or by any other gimmick we could think of.

The second analytical method chosen by Schmitt consists in showing that '*one single equation is responsible for determining two distinct unknowns*' (ibid.: 18, m.t.). This time, it is established from the outset that we are looking for the ratio of the exchanged quantities of *a* and *b*. Since direct exchange defines the equality of the supply of *a* and the demand for *b* as well as that between S(*b*) and D(*a*), the intervention of Walras's law can be formalized only on condition that *a* and *b* are made homogeneous by introducing them into the 'space' of numbers. The comparison between the sum of supplies and the sum of demands is possible only if both can be expressed in numerical terms. The sum of supplies itself, like the sum of demands, can be determined only if the offered (demanded) quantities of *a* can be added up to the offered (demanded) quantities of *b*.

To make the two goods comparable, the introduction of the *numéraire* is required. Yet, 'at the very instant the prices of goods *a* and *b* are expressed in a *numéraire*, the price of good *a* and the price of good *b* are necessarily *two distinct unknowns*' (ibid.: 19, m.t.). As Schmitt observes, 'the neoclassical paradigm is thus caught between two contradictory requirements: the ratio of two physical quantities constitute one single unknown; but it is indispensable to transform the physical quantities into numerical quantities' (ibid.: 19, m.t.), which can only be done through the determination of the numerical prices of *a* and *b* in terms of a *numéraire*. Before equilibrium, these two numerical prices are distinct, and their determination requires two distinct equations: as only one independent equation is available, no solution compatible with GEA can be found.

The advocates of GEA mix up these two analytical methods and analyze the *numéraire* in the same way as they analyze direct exchange. They believe that the choice of the *numéraire* is enough to transform a commodity into a number, and that relative exchange can then transform all the other commodities into numbers. Moreover, they also believe that prices remain essentially determined by the physical quantities exchanged at equilibrium by agents aiming at maximizing their satisfactions. Their attempt at transforming goods into numbers via their direct exchange fails despite the introduction of Walras's *numéraire*. Is the introduction of money more helpful?

### *The introduction of money*

Even though it is only fair to recognize that in GEA money does not play any essential role, it is legitimate to ask whether the use of money as a concrete means of payment can avoid the shortcomings inherent in the use of the *numéraire* as an abstract unit of account. More precisely, we can analyze what would happen in the theoretical framework of GEA if money were introduced 'in a strictly instrumental capacity' (Schmitt 1996b: 114), that is, when it 'serves purely as a *catalyst* distinct from an *object* of exchange' (ibid.: 114). Even as a concrete means of payment, money remains a mere numerical instrument:

real goods remain the terms of any actual exchange even though money conveys them. This is perfectly in line with GEA, according to which 'even in a monetary economy, exchanges occur only *between real* terms' (ibid.: 115). For money to intervene as a numerical means between exchanges whose terms are real goods, in each transaction the amount of money spent by any agent must be exactly equal to the amount of money earned by this same agent. '[A] t general equilibrium, each agent spends the exact sum of money which he simultaneously earns' (ibid.: 114).

In the example of two agents and two goods, the equations accounting for the vehicular use of money at equilibrium are the following.

$$\text{Purchases of A} = \text{Sales of A} \tag{13.14}$$

$$\text{Purchases of B} = \text{Sales of B} \tag{13.15}$$

$$(13.14) = (13.15) \tag{13.16}$$

Equation (13.14) must determine the monetary equilibrium price for A, that is, the price at which A agrees to exchange a given quantity, *x*, of good *a* against another quantity, *y*, of good *b*, money playing only the role of intermediation. Equation (13.15) determines the monetary equilibrium price for which B agrees to exchange *x'* units of *a* against *y'* units of *b*. Equation (13.16) is required to equalize the terms of the exchange agreed by A with those agreed by B.

At equilibrium, it is certain that the purchases of A (B) are identical to the sales of B (A), that is, that the sum of sales is equal to the sum of purchases. Walras's law applies, and the three equations are reduced to one. However, at equilibrium everything is already determined; there is no need for any equation, and Walras's law is a mere tautology, 'not to say a truism' (ibid.: 115). Let us suppose that, before equilibrium, the auctioneer states a monetary price, *p*. For this price, it may happen that A would accept to exchange *x a* against *y b*, whereas B would agree to exchange *x' a* against *y' b*. Nothing allows us to establish a relationship between

(a) $x\,a \,/\, y\,b$ and
(b) $x'\,a \,/\, y'\,b$.

As Schmitt states, equality

(c) $x\,a \,/\, yb = x'\,a \,/\, y'\,b$

'is neither axiomatic nor postulational; it is a *condition of equilibrium*' (ibid.: 116). If Equation (c) were considered as a definition, or if the equality of *x* (*y*) and *x'* (*y'*) were assumed to hold in any circumstance, no adjustment would take place between supplies and demands. Walras's law defines what happens at equilibrium; if it defined also what happens before goods are exchanged, every possible price would be, by definition, an equilibrium price, which clearly means that GEA would be totally unable to explain the process of prices determination. However, if we ignore, as we must, Walras's law during the phase of adjustment, we end up with three independent equations, and the logical indeterminacy (over-determinacy) of neoclassical prices stands out as the only, unavoidable conclusion. Logic forces us to choose the second term of the alternative, because, as recognized by GEA, individuals are free to determine both the monetary prices at which to exchange their goods, and the quantities they are willing to exchange.

> No law can supersede the freedom of agents A and B in determining the monetary price, $p_0$, at which they both decide to exchange positive amounts, *x*, *x'*, *y*, and *y'* of goods *a* and *b*: it is entirely up to them whether at price $p_0$ they positively engage in trade, or otherwise. [...] Furthermore, no law can give us any assurance as to the equality of *x* and *x'*, or of *y* and *y'*. Again, agents are free to decide in what quantities they purchase goods at given prices.
>
> (ibid.: 117)

### *The intervention of banks*

In an unpublished manuscript distributed to his students at the University of Fribourg during the academic year 1993–94, Schmitt shows that the theorem of the logical indeterminacy of relative prices stands even when we introduce in the analysis the hypothetical intervention of a bank acting as a monetary intermediary. Let us slightly simplify his analysis by reducing to two the number of goods whose exchange is supposed to determine their relative price. Under which conditions would the intervention of a bank, injecting money into the system through its purchase of good *a*, enable the determination of the monetary prices of *a* and *b*? Schmitt shows that there are two conditions and that, together with the GEA's assumption of relative prices, both lead to an absurd consequence.

The first condition is that the price paid by the bank for the purchase of *a* be predetermined. The second condition is that this price be constant during the whole process of adjustment. '*Adjustments can have no repercussion either on the unitary price or on the physical quantity of the* numéraire-*good (*a*) thrown into exchanges*' (Schmitt 1993/94, *La fin du paradigme néoclassique*: 22, m.t.). If the bank purchases *x* units of *a* against a sum of 6 money units and if this price cannot vary, then the system is reduced to a single equation; and so is the number of unknowns – the quantity *y* of *b* sold by B against 6 money units – and a solution is possible. Agent A earns 6 money units by selling *a* to the bank and spends 6 money units in purchasing *b* from the bank, while agent B spends the 6 money units obtained from its sale of *b* to the bank to purchase good *a* from it. Finally, through the mediation of money, *x* units of *a* are exchanged against *y* units of *b* and the relative price of *a* (*b*) in terms of *b* (*a*) is fully determined.

To be sure, the price of *a* may vary, but since its quantity is constant, its variation would necessarily entail a variation in the price of *b of the same proportion*. 'It is therefore useless or "trivial" to make the price of *a* vary, which, on the contrary, can be maintained constant throughout all the adjustments' (ibid.: 23, m.t.). This means that, whatever the adjustments between the price of *b* in terms of *a*, the monetary price for *a* initially chosen by the bank is bound to be unaffected. As Schmitt claims, even though prices are all relative, it is the price of *b* 'that adjusts to the price of *a*, the price of *a* being prevented from adjusting to the price of *b*' (ibid.: 24, m.t.).

Thus, the possibility of determining monetary prices seems to rest on such restrictive conditions that the process of adjustment is meaningless and is in open contrast with the fundamental aim of GEA: to determine relative prices through the free and reciprocal interplay of each agent's supplies and demands. The observation that, in the case we are examining, the assumption of relative exchanges implies the necessary equality of each agent's income, reinforces such a dismal conclusion. Indeed, general equilibrium requires A's income to be exactly equal to B's income: the bank purchases *x* units of *a* for the same amount (6 money units) it spends on purchasing *y* units of *b* from B. '*The hypothesis following which prices are relative implies an absurd consequence: an agent's income is necessarily equal to any other agent's income*' (ibid.: 25, m.t.).

It should be superfluous to stress how unrealistic such a condition is. To claim that the budgetary constraint prevents any economic agent to spend more than it earns is certainly correct and perfectly consonant not only with the neoclassical axiom that only real goods are the terms of an exchange but also with the identity of each agent's sales and purchases. On the contrary, by claiming that any economic agent 'spends and earns the exact sum of money that any other agent earns and spends in the same general equilibrium' (ibid.: 27, m.t.), we introduce such an absurd restraint that the neoclassical attempt to determine relative prices via the determination of monetary prices loses any epistemological value. Relative prices can indeed derive from monetary prices, but not via relative exchange.

### *Money and GEA are incompatible*

In GEA, money does not really exist, either as a unit of account or as a unit of payment. In fact, the only conception of money consistent with the neoclassical paradigm is that of a unit of account, a numerical instrument that in no way alters the real terms of exchange. Let us suppose money as a unit of account to be used as an instrument of exchange interposed between the direct exchange of *a* and *b*. Agent A surrenders *x* units of *a* in exchange for *z* units of account and at the same time exchanges z' units of account against *y* units of *b* sold by agent B (Figure 13.1).

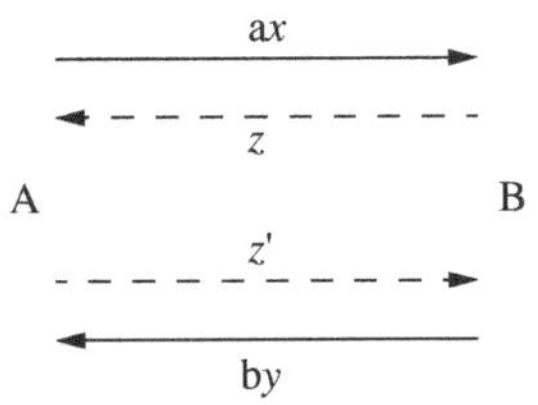


*Figure 13.1* Exchange as mediated by the use of money.

Only if the money earned by A is immediately spent on purchasing *b* (i.e., if $z = z'$) does it play an intermediary role that leaves unaltered the real terms, *x a* and *y b* of the exchange between A and B. Any difference between the sum of money earned by A (B) and spent by A (B) would imply the transformation of money into an *object* of payment, and the analysis would again fall victim to the criticism of direct exchange. The use of money as an intermediary unit of account requires *z* and *z'* to define a unique amount, thus imposing to A and B the monetary terms of the exchanges that are supposed to be determined by the adjustment of their supplies and demands.

Yet, this is not the only problematic implication of the introduction of money into GEA. As Schmitt points out, money being a pure unit of account, 'the reason why agent A accepts mere units of account "as payment"' (Schmitt 1998c: 38, m.t.) remains a mystery, 'a contradiction in terms [because] units of account are no object of payment' (ibid.: 38, m.t.).

Nowhere in neoclassical analysis is it explained how vehicular money, a flow of units of account, could be transformed into a money-income, a stock of units of payment. This leaves entirely unexplained how real goods are associated with money, and how money can become a unit of payment accepted by economic agents without transforming it into an object of payment added to produced goods and services. Furthermore, in the only, hypothetical exchange between real goods and money compatible with GEA, it is impossible to explain how A and B 'could "calculate" the numerical values, in units of account or "tokens", of the goods exchanged' (ibid.: 38, m.t.). At equilibrium, the equality of *z* and *z'* is imposed by the exchange between *x a* and *y b*. However, during the search for equilibrium, neither *z* nor *z'* are known, and no comparison can be made between them. Finally, how can it be assumed that, before groping starts, 'an agent can have at his disposal a sum of units of account?' (ibid.: 39, m.t.). As Schmitt claims, 'it is inconceivable that a person *holds* units of account. Only goods can be held or possessed. Monetary units of account are immaterial objects that cannot be inscribed into a positive interval of time' (ibid.: 39, m.t.).

By assuming that goods are already present as initial endowments, neoclassical authors give up an opportunity to explain their association with money, not to mention to distinguish between money as a unit of account and money as a unit of payment. The only concept of money they can introduce in their analysis is that of a unit of account (the *numéraire*). Yet, it is incomprehensible how a unit of account can intervene in a process of adjustment where economic agents are supposed to plan their exchanges and exert their demands and supplies through the mediation of monetary units that can concretely play their role only if they are units of payment.

Whether we limit our analysis to direct exchange, or we introduce the concept of the *numéraire*, the conclusion is the same: neither relative nor numerical prices can logically be determined within the neoclassical paradigm. Following Schmitt, let us try to point out the crucial mistake ascribable to GEA.

## The crucial mistake of GEA

### *Physical goods and numbers*

The method followed by GEA consists in determining prices through a system of equations equalizing supplies and demands. This method applies to the determination of relative prices as well as to the determination of numerical prices. Given the physical heterogeneity of real goods, economists are faced with the need to make them numerically homogeneous, to transform them into numbers. Neoclassical authors believe in the possibility of determining numerical prices through their method: the choice of a *numéraire*, whose price is settled arbitrarily, reduces by one the number of independent equations of the system and allows for the determination, through exchange, of the remaining $n - 1$ numerical prices. 'We thus become aware of the philosophy on which the neoclassical school rests: exchanges *reveal* (this term is indeed used by the adepts of the school) the numbers that are hidden within goods' (Schmitt 1993/94, *Notes sur le cours de jeudi 18 novembre*: 21, m.t.).

The equations of exchange do not really determine numerical prices; they merely make it easier to express the numbers that are already "contained" in real goods. 'Exchanges have the power to transform goods into precise numbers, because goods are already numbers before exchanges occur' (ibid.: 21, m.t.). As Debreu puts it, the numerical nature of goods is an unquestionable truth, an axiom (Debreu 1959: 28–30). Schmitt was right, then, when he told Debreu, during a lecture the latter held at the University of Bourgogne in 1993, that he assumed the numerical nature of goods to be given by 'an operation of the spirit, not to say the Holy Spirit' (ibid.: 21, m.t.).

However, even if it were possible to accept such a metaphysical concept of goods, GEA would not be able to determine the number of numerical units contained in the quantity of a given good that agents decide to give up in exchange for another good.

> It is obviously impossible – and neoclassical authors do not do so – to decide that physical goods exchange objectively for one another, irrespective

> of agents' free will, according to the proportion of the exact number of numerical units they are supposed to contain.
>
> (ibid.: 22, m.t.)

Two determinations are needed, one revealing the numbers hidden in each good, and one establishing the terms at which exchanges are planned during the process of adjustment and at which they take place at equilibrium. Even if it were possible for a system of equations to reveal the numbers contained in the initial endowment of physical goods, it would be impossible for the same system to determine the numerical prices of equilibrium.

> It is logically forbidden to assign to the same system of mathematical relationships the *double task* of revealing the numbers hidden within physical goods and to organize on top of it the exchanges between these numbers, according to the supplies and demands that agents exert freely on the goods transformed into numbers.
>
> (ibid.: 22–3, m.t.)

According to GEA, economic prices have a double nature: they are both *real*, a relationship between physical goods, and *numerical*. In their first aspect, prices are determined through direct exchange and take the form of relative prices. The transition from relative to numerical prices can happen through the choice of a *numéraire*. Prices are thus defined both as commodities and as numbers. As Schmitt points out and neoclassical authors explicitly claim, from this dual nature of prices follows a dual nature of goods that are, at the same time, physical products or commodities and numbers. Let us go back to the example of two agents and two goods. If relative prices can be determined, the quantity $q$ of $a$ is the price of the quantity $q'$ of $b$. Consequently, if the quantity $q$ of $a$ is a pure number – the numerical price of the *numéraire* – good $a$ pertains simultaneously to the 'space' of commodities and to that of numbers.

> [S]tarting from the double definition of prices, relationships between distinct goods and relationships between a real good and a pure number, one same good, that is, the quantity $q$ of good $a$ is at the same time a commodity and a pure number.
>
> (Schmitt 1999c: 5, m.t.)

'[G]oods are defined by two magnitudes that are the terms of an identity: goods are commodities, but they are also numbers' (ibid.: 6, m.t.); this is the axiom on which GEA rests. In a way, this axiom is the greatest contribution of GEA to economics, because it is 'the discovery of the double nature of goods, commodities, and numbers that enables our discipline to become a true science [...] it is thanks to this "quantum leap" in thought that economics has become the object of an exact science' (ibid.: 7, m.t.). What is wrong with GEA is not the claim that goods are commodities and numbers, but the belief that goods can be *simultaneously* commodities and numbers, i.e. they can simultaneously be present 'in their own space and in the space of numbers' (ibid.: 7, m.t.). The discovery that goods are numbers is crucial, yet its correct implication is that goods are physical products in one of their dual aspects and numbers in the other, complementary aspect.

### *The role of numbers in economics*

To clarify the nature of the relationship between goods and numbers, Schmitt (1999c) investigates the role of numbers in the field of economics. Starting from the work of Husserl, Schmitt analyzes here the definition of numbers according to which they are the result of a transformation of goods, that is, he inquiries into 'the way numbers can exist in the field of economics' (ibid.: 8–9, m.t.).

#### *'Unit' and 'number'*

Before considering the possibility for goods to be transformed into numbers, Schmitt asks the question of whether numbers can exist in the real world without being related to a physical dimension. Husserl (1900/2001) claims that the concept of *number* must be distinguished from the concept of *unit*, and Schmitt observes that '[e]ach unit has an object, a precise object, we can thus speak of a unit of orange to point to one of these fruits; yet an orange is not in any way whatsoever the number 1' (ibid.: 11, m.t.). Units do not exist as such, for they must 'designate an object, seized as a whole' (ibid.: 11, m.t.). We can measure a given quantity of oranges by counting the physical units of this fruit making up, for example, the initial endowment of agent A. This simply means that oranges are counted in physical units and not that they are transformed into numbers. Since physical units of different goods are heterogeneous, economics can have its proper object of inquiry only if it succeeds in switching from units to numbers, that is, if it manages to move from the enumeration of physically heterogeneous units to the purely numerical expression of goods.

The distinction between dimensional and purely numerical measures is not substantially different from that between units and numbers. 'Every measure of a dimension is an indirect measure, in that it is not the object considered that is measured; what is measured is a *dimension* of the object, as its mass, or its length' (ibid.: 14, m.t.). Now, physically heterogeneous objects cannot become homogeneous through the measure of their dimensions, not even through the measure of a common dimension. Indeed, for example, even though a common dimensional standard, the kilo, measures the mass of oranges and that of apples, a kilo of oranges and a kilo of apples are as heterogeneous an object as the oranges and apples themselves.

Goods are physically heterogeneous whether taken as such or expressed dimensionally. It immediately follows that their transformation into homogeneous 'objects' can only result from the possibility of measuring them through a purely numerical standard, in pure (a-dimensional) numbers.

> As goods are disparate objects and as it is not possible to make them uniform through an *objective and uniform* quality, attribute, or predicate, such as a labour-value or a utility-value which they share, in economics the measure can only be founded on an enumeration that does not refer to *any dimension* of goods.
>
> (ibid.: 15, m.t.)

To measure goods through a numerical standard, in numbers, we must first make them homogeneous; what is required is therefore a double operation capable of transforming physically heterogeneous goods into uniform objects and to measure them numerically. Whereas it is possible to count different objects or units, the measure in economics implies the possibility to count objects (goods) that are strictly similar, identical: '*only the counting of objects reciprocally equal gives the measure of these objects and of their sum*' (ibid.: 19, m.t.).

### *Prices as numerical forms*

Schmitt's answer to the question of whether numbers exist in the real world is yes: 'the equality of the objects of arithmetic is a fact and not an assumption' (ibid.: 20, m.t.). In mathematics, numbers are abstract objects 'in that they do not refer to any concrete object' (ibid.: 20, m.t.); yet, their existence is real, objective: 'a number present in a theorem is identical to this same number included in another theorem' (ibid.: 20, m.t.). Economics confirms this, since the existence of numerical prices means that physical goods are *de facto* integrated into the space of numbers. It is correct to say that numbers are immaterial, but that does not mean that they do not exist; the fact is that numbers are *forms* and no one can doubt the existence of forms in the concrete world.

### *The transformation of physical goods into numbers*

Exchange gives real goods a numerical form; it transforms them into numbers, whose real existence is thus established once and for all at the instant exchanges take place. '[E]xchanges are concrete operations; at the instant of exchange, commodities are numbers; it follows that numbers are concrete realities within exchange' (ibid.: 22, m.t.). What must be determined is through what exchange real goods acquire their numerical form. Neoclassical authors believe in their ability to transform units of goods into numbers through direct exchange; if their attempt is doomed to fail, it is because they fail to introduce money as a numerical unit of account. They correctly maintain that real goods enter the space of numbers but miss the fact that the numbers goods are transformed into are monetary units of account, the only concrete units of account available in the real world of economics.

> [M]onetary units, and only they, are units of account whose presence, as catalysts, can be observed in concrete economies. Money units are concrete units of account or "concrete numbers"; in the absence of money, economies do not admit the effective intervention of pure numbers within exchange.
>
> (ibid.: 24, m.t.)

By founding their analysis on *relative* exchange, advocates of Walras's GEA deprive themselves of the possibility of transforming goods into numbers, a process that, when successful, implies that 'the object thus transformed *no longer exists in its primitive definition*' (ibid.: 24, m.t.). If transformed into numbers, real goods abandon the space of commodities to enter that of numbers. In GEA this is not so: real goods never abandon the space of commodities, which makes it logically impossible for them to be transformed into numbers.

Finally, GEA's mistake consists in assuming that numerical prices are an object of inquiry in mathematics from the outset. What neoclassical authors do not seem to be aware of is that, even if it is true that they are numbers, prices are formed through an economic process, production, that has nothing to do with mathematics. As Schmitt observes,

> mathematics and physics investigate magnitudes that existed well before being analysed. Economics, on the contrary, is the study of magnitudes brought about, created we could say, by national production. Mathematics is unable to seize production, because, in production as correctly defined, the result is not included in the premises.
>
> (ibid.: 27)

# 14 From capitalism to post-capitalism

Schmitt's analysis of capitalism shows that up to now the process of capital accumulation has occurred without taking into account the logical nature of money and income. In this sense, capitalism is a (transitional) phase in the development of a well-ordered economy based on the use of capital. Once understood, the reasons behind the pathological working of this system pave the way for a reform leading to a new phase: *post-capitalism*, to use Schmitt's term for it. The transition from one system to the other, from disorder to order, does not require getting rid of capital; it will require changing it from a source of alienation to a support of human labour benefitting households. Schmitt's post-capitalism is not a system without capital, but a system where capital is no longer formed as a pathological, external power to which all, capitalists and non-capitalists, are enslaved. Schmitt's references to post-capitalism are rare. His main interest lies in investigating the pathologies of capitalism and developing the reforms needed to 'cure' them. However, a description of post-capitalism can be deduced from the shortcomings of capitalism, and it offers us the opportunity to go over Schmitt's revolutionary findings once more.

This chapter is based mainly on what can be found in two unpublished manuscripts, *Cours de théorie monétaire* (1996) and *Le chômage et son éradication* (1998) as well as in his 1984 seminal book *Inflation, chômage et malformations du capital*.

## Capitalism

### *Capitalism and banks*

As we saw in Chapter 5, the existence of capital has its origin in the creation of banks. Before that, only physical means or instruments of production were available, the absence of the financial market leaving no room for the presence of monetary capital. Capitalism, therefore, goes back to the discovery of double-entry bookkeeping and to its implementation by banks.

Thanks to banks' monetary and financial intermediation, income is formed as a bank deposit and is immediately saved, lent, and transformed into capital-time (see Chapter 5). It is because the product is emitted as a quantum of time

DOI: 10.4324/9781351271325-19

that capital is identified with time, allowing the transposition of income (the product in its monetary form) from quantum to chronological time. This transposition could not occur before the creation of banks, where production and consumption necessarily coincided in time. Before banks, physical output was appropriated at the moment of its production and did not acquire a monetary form. The presence of banks changes things radically. Production acquires a monetary dimension and identifies itself with a *creation of money*.

From the moment of its monetary emission, a product becomes the object of a bank deposit and its transformation into capital-time makes it possible for consumption to take place later in chronological time. The identity of production and consumption, always given in quantum time, is not contradicted by the distinction of these two events in chronological time, because capital-time is the bridge that unites them. Through its transformation into capital-time, income is inscribed in chronological or continuous time and can survive, in the form of capital, until its final expenditure. 'Income is a magnitude belonging to quantum time. Capital is defined in chronological or continuous time. Capital is therefore literally the *transposition* of a magnitude, from one "space" into another' (Schmitt 2021: 373).

The transformation of income into capital must be ascribed to the possibility, provided by banks, to lend to firms, F, the income earned by workers, W. As soon as wages are paid, they are saved as bank deposits, lent to firms, and invested by them in the formation of a stock of wage-goods. This initial investment transforms workers' income into an equivalent amount of capital-time. Firms' debt to banks and the wage-goods stocked in F are the two joint aspects, monetary and real, of capital-time, which is the originary form of every capital created within a monetary economy: any other kind of capital has its origin necessarily in a sum of capital-time. In particular, fixed capital is an elaborate form of capital-time resulting in the transformation of the initial stock of wage-goods into a stock of instrumental goods. Fixed capital builds up through the investment of profit by firms, and profit is first of all that part of income that is not spent on consumption, that is, *saved*. It is thus confirmed that 'in its first state, a capital-good is constituted of *stocked wage-goods* corresponding to monetary savings. Thus, at birth, fixed capital, in the form of saved wage-goods, is purely a *capital-time*' (ibid.: 94).

### *Capitalism and fixed capital*

The correct understanding of capitalism rests on an accurate analysis of the process leading to the formation of fixed capital within the actual economic system. How does fixed capital take on its real and monetary aspects, and what are the implications of this process for the equilibrium of the entire system?

#### *The role of profit*

Schmitt's analysis of the formation and investment of profit provides an answer to these questions. As the reader will recall, profit can be satisfactorily explained only as an organic unity comprised of its formation *and* its expenditure. Earlier theories of profit offer only a truncated explanation. They either reduce profit to an income derived from circulation, or to an amount of real goods produced at zero cost, thus missing the point that fixed capital is at the same time real and monetary. Formed in the products market through the sale of wage-goods at a mark-up, profit cannot be spent in the same market. If it were, its expenditure would mean *purchasing* the very wage-goods which brought it into being – a logical impossibility. Schmitt's quantum macroeconomic analysis shows that the quantum identity of production and consumption ensures the retroactive expenditure of profit, which takes place through the payment of wages. 'The formation of profit is an expenditure of wages; the expenditure of profit is a formation of wages; thus, the destruction-creation of profit is a movement already included in the creation-destruction of wages' (ibid.: 76).

Capital is formed from saving: in its initial form, capital is a stock of wage-goods. Part of this initial stock is purchased by income holders. Another part defines the real content of firms' profit. Through the investment of profit, the stock of wage-goods corresponding to firms' capital-time is transformed into a stock of instrumental goods corresponding to firms' fixed capital. The income initially saved as capital-time is permanently subtracted from consumption and defines an irreversible, macroeconomic saving. '[W]age-goods converted into fixed capital are *fixed savings*, the dissolving of which is forever postponed, from one day to another' (ibid.: 98).

So far, capitalism does not show any disorder. There is nothing wrong with the fact that profit is formed in the products market and is spent (invested) in the labour market. Likewise, it makes perfect sense for firms to purchase a stock of instrumental goods by giving a stock of wage-goods in exchange. It is true that, by spending a positive purchasing power within the payment of wages, firms purchase the activity of their workers (Adam Smith's 'labour commanded'). Yet, the inclusion of an expenditure of income in the payment that creates this very income is legitimate if it maintains 'the strict equivalence [...] in money units between the expenditures that create and the expenditures that destroy national income' (Schmitt 1996d: 69, m.t.). The inclusion of an expenditure of income in the payment of wages is perfectly justified by the inclusion of a formation of income in the expenditure of wages.

Since every payment is an emission, the payment leading to the formation of profit leads necessarily to a payment of opposite sign defining its destruction. The identity between creations and destructions is a strict consequence of the nature of bank money.

> [W]ithin the logic of bank money that we have developed it is inconceivable that an income is formed without being spent; it is the rule, never to be ignored, of the necessary equality of each agent's debits and credits.
> (ibid.: 57, m.t.)

It follows that, like wages, profit is necessarily spent: 'a non-spent profit is a contradiction in terms' (Schmitt 1998a: 93, m.t.). The formation-expenditure of profit complies with the logical laws of macroeconomics and does not cause monetary disorder.

### *The pathologies of capitalism*

Fixed capital is formed through the investment of profit, and there is nothing wrong with including the expenditure of profit in the payment of wages. How come, then, is capitalism a source of monetary disorder, inflation, and unemployment? Schmitt shows that capitalism rests on lending of income already transformed into fixed capital. Invested profit gives rise to bank deposits, which are still available in the financial market and feed a macroeconomic loan of banks to households. 'It is the loan to households of an income already lent to a firm (or, generally, of an income that had already been formed as a firm's asset) that is the essence of capitalism' (Schmitt 1993–94, 8 février 1994: 11, m.t.).

As shown in Chapter 11, the expenditure of firms' profit (whether realized or advanced) is the source of a chain of bank deposits that are lent and spent again and again instead of being destroyed. The income spent by firms in the labour market reappears in the form of bank deposits and is lent to households to enable the purchase of national output, the value (and price) of which increases because of the use of fixed capital. '[I]f banks did not lend this deposit, the income of households captured by firms [...] would be missing, *in the regime of capitalism*, for the general disposal of the product' (Schmitt 1998a: 101, m.t.).

The direct consequence of the additional macroeconomic lending, owing to the perpetuity of the deposits of profit, is the subdivision of the economy first into two and then into three sectors. Banks lend deposits without reference to their owners. Such a loan is inescapable; it is a necessary implication of the identity between credit and debit imposed by double-entry bookkeeping. First profit, then the deposits resulting from the expenditure of profit, remain financially available, and banks cannot avoid lending them to the set of households. It is this additional *macroeconomic* loan that leads to the appropriation of fixed capital by the set of disembodied firms and introduces the distinction between the sector producing wage-goods and those producing investment- and amortization-goods. Hence, it follows that 'it is only in capitalism [...] that the division of the economic activity into three distinct sectors is imperative' (ibid.: 133, m.t.).

The second and third sectors are financed through the macroeconomic loan granted by banks to households and would not exist in its absence. Profit is appropriated by firms and lost by households in the form of both income and capital because the formation of profit is accompanied by an equivalent formation of debt affecting households. It is therefore clear that '[t]he precise action that separates households from the ownership (either in the form of income or capital) [of profit] is the loan that the banking system grants them out of the deposits formed by profit' (ibid.: 134, m.t.).

The pathology of capitalism can also be located in the mechanism whereby non-wage incomes are added to wages. The production of investment-goods (sector 2) and amortization-goods (sector 3) creates additional monetary incomes as a consequence of the loan of the deposits of profit. This means that non-wage incomes are formed thanks to the pathological duplication of wages already spent in the formation of profit; wages are nonetheless the only macroeconomic income that can logically be formed in accord with the nature of money and production. Schmitt's analysis is clear. The existence of non-wage incomes is not the logical result of the presence of capital as a macroeconomic factor of production. Only human labour can be the source of an emission that gives produced output a monetary form. This means that, logically, non-wage incomes should be derived only from wages, and therefore they should be included in wages. If they are not, i.e. if they are added to wages, it is because when profit is formed and subsequently transformed into fixed capital, no deposit of profit is withdrawn from the financial market. The loan of this deposit increases the amount of income available in the system by adding non-wage incomes to wages and this is pathological. 'In the regime of capitalism, every profit is an outgrowth of wages. Because of the loan of the deposits of profit, interest, dividends, profit latu sensu *are added* to wages' (ibid.: 143, m.t.).

What one must clearly understand is that the addition of non-wage incomes to wages is an option only if it refers to the *distribution* of national income and not to its *formation*. Wages are the only original macroeconomic income resulting from production; in other words, the payment of wages is the only transaction able to explain the formation of national income. Once formed, national income can be, and is, distributed among different economic agents and takes the form of interest, dividends, and rent. In short, *monetary wages define the totality of national income*, whereas real wages are only the part of national income spent on the final purchase of wage-goods. The rest corresponds to what is transferred to firms as profit and is spent on purchasing interest-, dividend-, and fixed capital-goods. The existence of non-wage incomes does not alter the fact that, initially, the entire income is made up of monetary wages only. If capitalism were a well-ordered regime, non-wage incomes would derive from wages, and they would be included in the sum total of all direct and indirect wages paid to workers.

If things work out differently it is only because capitalism is a pathological regime, where additional incomes are formed because invested profit is not removed from the amount of bank deposits available in the financial market. The investment of profit entails the irreversible transformation of part of national income into fixed capital. Nevertheless, if banks lend what amounts to a saving in perpetuity, the loan of the deposits of invested profit increases the available amount of income and the indebtedness of households. Therefore, a capitalist regime is a pathological system in which fixed capital is formed as an external entity, where 'workers do not produce for income holders; they do not produce for persons: *they are enslaved to Capital*' (Schmitt 2021: 137).

## Y = C + I + A

As we have seen, the loan of the deposits of profit gives rise to the anomalous subdivision of the economy into three sectors. The production of consumption-goods, investment-goods, and amortization-goods take place in the first, second, and third sectors, respectively. This is tantamount to saying that the production of these three categories of goods creates three distinct and additional incomes: wages, invested profit, and profit financing amortization. Hence, in capitalism, national income is given by the equation

$$Y = C + I + A, \tag{14.1}$$

where $Y$ stands for national income, $C$ for consumption, $I$ for investment, and $A$ for amortization. Let us consider first the addition of $I$ to $C$.

### *In capitalism investment is not a category of consumption*

A numerical example might be helpful. Suppose the amount total of wages paid for the production of consumption- and investment-goods to be equal to 100 wage-units. If 20 wage-units are paid to workers producing investment-goods and 80 to workers producing consumption-goods, total income should be equal to 100 wage-units. Yet, one must not forget that *investment is financed through profit*. This alone would not alter the amount of income, which would still be equal to the sum of the wages paid for the production of $C$ (80) and I (20). However, in a capitalist regime, the formation of profit and its subsequent expenditure (to finance the production of investment-goods) is accompanied by the formation of bank deposits, and their loan increases (numerically or nominally) the amount of income available in the system. In our numerical example, the loan of 20 units of profit, formed through the sale of consumption-goods at a mark-up, increases the income generated by the production of $C$ and $I$ from 100 to 120 m.u. The additional loan granted by banks to households relegates the production of investment-goods to a sector distinct from that of the production of consumption-goods.

The consequence of this separation is that the production of the second sector is added to that of the first sector, and the value of the latter increases from 80 to 100 money units. On the whole, the production of $C + I$ has a value of 120 money units even though the sum of wages is only 100 wage-units. Nominally, income increases from 100 to 120 money units and the entire production can be purchased. However, the 20 money units added to wages through banks' lending define an inflationary excess demand caused by the appropriation of investment-goods by depersonalized or disembodied firms.

In this 1984 analysis, Schmitt introduces a distinction between periods and uses this to show that invested profit, formed in $p_1$ and spent in $p_2$, is the source of an empty emission that increases the nominal expression of national income. Wages paid to workers producing investment-goods in $p_2$ are emptied of real content, because the payment of wages in $p_1$ encompasses the expenditure of profit (taking place in $p_2$). The presence of empty money is the mark of a pathology, namely the nominal increase in global demand over global supply. If we add the demand for investment-goods exerted by the expenditure of profit (m.u. 20) to that financed by full (m.u. 80) and empty (m.u. 20) wages, we end up with a total demand equal to 120 money units. Total supply being equal to the value, in wage-units, of the product of $p_2$, and total demand being necessarily equal, in value terms, to total supply, it appears that

Nominal demand (120 money units) = real demand (100 wage-units) = real supply (100 wage-units).

The increase in global demand is purely nominal and leads to what Schmitt calls a case of benign inflation (because, here, empty money defines a claim on the stock of wage-goods that is formed in $p_1$). This does not diminish the pathological relevance of $p_2$'s empty emissions, which is symptomatic of the appropriation of instrumental goods by Capital. Finally, the switch from $Y = C$ to $Y = C + I$ is explained in 1984 by the inclusion of an expenditure of income (profit) within the payment of wages of a period subsequent to the one of the formation of profit. Adding $I$ to $C$ is pathological: it can be done only on the basis of empty money, which increases nominally the amount of national income, while this should be determined by wages alone. 'Investment is additive to consumption for the only reason that empty emissions are additive to full emissions' (ibid.: 127).

In the years following the publication of *Inflation, chômage et malformations du capital* (1984), Schmitt elaborates his analysis of capitalism further, and emphasizes the role played by the deposits of profit and by their being used for macroeconomic lending. The addition of $I$ to $C$ is ascribed to the increase in global demand, consequent to the deposits of profit being lent to the set of households. '[W]ithin capitalism as it exists, global demand is increased by the monetary amount of profit that is formed in each period' (Schmitt 1996d: 70, m.t.). If firms did not obtain their profit in a monetary form, this pathological increase would not occur. The purported formation of profit as an amount of investment-goods directly appropriated by firms must be discarded, because it stands in contrast with the necessary monetary realization of profit.

The cause of the disorder does not lie in the monetary formation of profit, but in the additional creation of income made possible by the deposit of profit. The loan of this deposit gives rise to a new income, equal to the amount of invested profit, $I$, which is added to consumption, $C$, defined by the total amount of wages paid for the production of national output. The pathological increase in income is tantamount to a pathological increase in global demand and is the direct source of disorders, like inflation and involuntary unemployment.

> We have just discovered the only formally possible origin of a difference between global demand (increased by the loan of profit) and global supply, defined by the wage cost of production, in terms of money units. This positive difference is the foundation of any valid explanation of inflation and unemployment.
>
> (ibid.: 70, m.t.)

### *The addition of amortization to consumption and investment*

The same mechanism that leads to the subdivision of economic activity into sectors also operates in the production of amortization-goods. Income increases by the amount not only of investment, but also of amortization, so that the measure of national income in capitalism is given by equation (14.1).

The addition of $A$ to $C+I$ rests on the fact that amortization is both a reproduction – in that it restores the initial value of capital diminished by wear, tear, and obsolescence – and a *net production*.

To replenish capital, it is indeed necessary to produce new instrumental goods and services to replace or repair those deteriorated by their use. If a capital of value $X$ loses $x$ because of wear and tear, '[i]t is certain that capital can recover its total value of $X$ units only if $x$ units of value newly produced are *added* to it. The production of amortization-goods is therefore identical to a production of new investment-goods' (Schmitt 1998a: 110, m.t.). The income created by the payment of wages is increased by the amount corresponding to the production of investment-goods, $I$, and of amortization-goods, $A$. This increase is obtained through the loan of the deposits of profit required to finance $I$ and $A$ and marks the subdivision of the economy into three sectors.

With the introduction of amortization, the situation becomes worse: financed through the expenditure of a positive income, the production of amortization-goods defines another empty emission of nominal wages deprived of any real content. Firms operating in the third sector realize a net profit, while workers in sector 3 are paid in empty money, their product being purchased by firms through the expenditure of the profit they derive from the production of this same sector.

> [P]rofit of sector 3 is "purchased" by the set of firms – in reality it is free of cost for them – because they offer, in return, a purchasing power that is strictly equal to zero. Thus, firms, rather than households, spend the real income they derive from their production in the third sector.
>
> (ibid.: 138, m.t.)

Including the expenditure of profit in the payment of wages is not in itself the hallmark of a pathology. It becomes so only when the deposits of profit become the object of loans. In particular, it is with the appearance of the third sector that empty emissions acquire their full significance.

The quotation that follows highlights to what extent the positive expenditure of a profit-income in the market for labour defines the essence of capitalism.

> In sector 1, factors of production obtain wages that are units of "full" money; in sector 2 they obtain units of "empty" wages; however, the units of money wages emitted in the second sector are filled by the real wages formed as capital (forced savings) the moment net profit is formed. Wages emitted in the third sector are therefore the only, entirely empty wages remaining. Thus, the macroeconomic income spent in the third sector stands alone, as the expression of positive expenditures occurring in the market for productive services.
>
> (ibid.: 137, m.t.)

When capitalism reaches full maturity, economic activity is equally distributed across the three sectors and the measure of national income is given by the addition of *C*, *I*, and *A*: $Y = C + I + A$. From this moment on, capital accumulation (sector 2) and over-accumulation (sector 3) create the conditions for involuntary unemployment and its worsening over time. As fixed capital grows, so does the need to find enough profit to guarantee the remuneration of capital (payment of interest). Since, in capitalism, the profit growth is limited by the amount of wages, the rate of profit tends to fall. When the rate of profit drops below the market rate of interest, the process of capital accumulation and over-accumulation must slow down, and this implies that, gradually, the second sector will be overtaken by the third. The production of amortization-goods in sector 3 gradually replaces that of investment-goods in sector 2. This leads to an increase in unemployment equal to reduction in the production of new investment-goods in sector 2: 'firms give up producing new investment-goods in the second sector – which will only worsen the negative difference between natural and monetary rates of interest – and produce amortization-goods instead' (ibid.: 131, m.t.).

To sum up, capitalism is the system in which monetary profit is spent by (disembodied) firms rather than by (personalized) firms on behalf of households. Removing profit from the economic ownership of households is the consequence of a perverse mechanism whereby wages, already spent in the formation of profit and irreversibly transformed into fixed capital through their investment, are still available in the financial markets. The lending of these deposits of profit is the key feature of capitalism and leads to the formation of distinct sectors and to the increase of national income from $Y = C$ (=wages) to $Y = C + I + A$. Hence, capitalism turns out to be a regime where the system of payments implemented by banks does not comply with the principles based on the nature of money and production. In capitalism, profit is added to wages – not included in them, as logic requires. Adding profit to wages is the pathological consequence of a mechanism resting on spending anew an income already spent. The transition from capitalism to post-capitalism calls for replacing this mechanism with one that is consistent with the logical identity $Y \equiv$ nominal wages.

## Y ≡ C

Production, in its proper economic sense, is a creation of money; it is an emission through which physical output is metamorphosed into a sum of money. This process is instantaneous and takes place through an expenditure that transforms the product into the object of a bank deposit, namely, into the real content of money. The only expenditure that enables the emission of the product as a sum of money is the payment of wages; this makes wages the only originary macroeconomic income formed by production. The identity $Y \equiv$ nominal wages is therefore imposed by logic, and economic practice must conform to it. More specifically, the existence of non-wage incomes – such as profit proper, interest, dividends, and rent – must be explained in accordance with this identity.

Reasoning in terms of real and monetary emissions and by leveraging his discovery of quantum time, Schmitt shows that profit, which stands for all non-wage incomes, is derived from wages, in which it is included. A direct consequence of this inclusion is that profit-goods, under their various forms, are avatars of wage-goods. Initially, the totality of produced output must take the form of wage-goods, because it can only be emitted as the real content of a sum of wages. It is only after this that part of produced output takes the form of profit-goods. Thanks to quantum retroactivity, profit-goods are formed at the same time as the goods finally purchased by households, while being first emitted as the real content of wages.

### *Investment as a 'nested' category of consumption*

If we define and measure consumption as the amount of nominal wages, it immediately follows that $Y \equiv C$. Since the production of investment-goods results from the investment of profit and since profit is derived from wages, it also follows that $I$ must be part of $C$. 'Order would require therefore that investment should be a "nested category" of consumption, in the same way that profits are a nested category of wages' (Schmitt 2021: 128). Schmitt's idea here is that investment belongs to the consumption category, because it derives from the productive consumption of profit, which is spent (i.e. consumed) within the payment of wages. 'In a perfect regime, consumption is the only category of national income, investment being itself a consumption, called "productive consumption"' (Schmitt 1996d: 12, m.t.).

#### *The compatibility between* Y ≡ C *and* Y ≡ C + I

If, instead, we adopt the traditional Keynesian definition of $C$ and $I$ as the final expenditures for the purchase of consumption- and investment-goods, respectively, the measure of national income is given by $C+I$. At this point, a legitimate question arises: is it contradictory to define national income both as $C$ and as the sum of $C$ and $I$? The answer is no, both definitions are correct and compatible, since they refer to two distinct aspects of national income. $Y \equiv$

$C$ refers to the measure of production, resulting from the payment of wages. $Y \equiv C+I$ refers to production measured by the final expenditure of wages, profit included. This distinction is just a variation of that between the flow measure of national income, $Y \equiv$ nominal wages, and its measure in real terms, $Y \equiv$ real wages + real profit.

By writing $Y \equiv C$ we emphasize the fact that production is an emission of money that creates wage-goods. By choosing $Y \equiv C+I$, we stress the fact that part of the initial production of wages-goods is *de facto* transformed into a production of investment-goods. Yet, $Y \equiv C$ is the first and more fundamental identity, because it is the one that shows best the essence of an orderly system, that is, a system in which the entire output is held by households.

The definition of national income as the sum of the final expenditures corresponding to the purchase of consumption- and investment-goods is fully legitimate and in line with Keynes's definitions. How, then, can $C+I$ be read as the mark of a pathology in capitalism? This happens when $Y=C+I$ defines the *formation of national income* as the sum of wages and investment, that is, when investment, as the expenditure of profit, is added to the amount of wages.

Our previous numerical example may help us again. Nominal wages being equal to 100 wage-units, if consumption-goods are sold at a distribution price of 125 money units, the equation $Y=C+I=80+20=100$ states that the purchase of consumption- and investment-goods requires the final expenditure of 80 and 20 wage-units, respectively. If, instead of referring to the final purchase of consumption- and investment-goods, the equation were used to represent the sum of the nominal or monetary expressions of the amounts of income spent by households on purchasing consumption-goods (sold at a mark-up) and by firms on purchasing investment-goods (through the expenditure of profit), $C+I$ would be equal to $100+20=120$ money units. It is the increase in national income from 100 to 120 money units, caused by the addition of profit to nominal wages, that distinguishes the present form of capitalism from an orderly capitalist system in which investment is a nested category or component of consumption.

### *The meaning of identity* $Y \equiv C$

Let us go back to $Y \equiv C$. How do we interpret this identity? Essentially, this is what it means:

1) National income is measured by wages only,
2) The totality of production consists of wages-goods only,
3) Economic activity takes place only in sector one.

Point 1), as previously investigated, states that the payment of wages is the sole macroeconomic source of income. Any other income must be derived from wages. This means that, initially, wage-earners – or households – own the entire output as the real content of their bank deposits. If a profit is formed, part of income is transferred from households to firms. Yet, if the economic system works in compliance with the identity $Y \equiv C$, households gain in the form of capital what they lose in income, and remain the sole owners of national output.

> [P]rofit, which remains the property of households, reduces their assets in the form of income (the very definition of invested profit), but makes them richer in capital: each new profit will be represented by new financial claims, shares and securities, *in the hands of households.*
>
> (Schmitt 1998a: 134, m.t.)

With profit being part of wages and no additional income being injected into the economy by banks, the totality of income is spent – directly or indirectly, through the intermediation of personalized firms – by households, profit included: 'wages are the only fund of profit' (ibid.: 139, m.t.).

Point 2) emphasizes the fact that, since the payment of wages is the only expenditure through which physical output acquires a monetary form, the result of any production is a sum of wage-goods. This does not mean that the production of other goods, investment-goods in particular, necessarily shrinks to nought, but that these goods are a *transformation* of wage-goods. Point 2) is but a consequence of point 1), because from the inclusion of profit within wages follows the inclusion of investment-goods within wage-goods.

The formation of output as a sum of wage-goods does not exclude the possibility that part of production consists of investment-goods. For this to be the case the sale of consumption-goods at a mark-up is all we need to enable (personalized) firms to obtain a profit. The retroactive expenditure of this profit in the labour market then transforms part of the initial production of wage-goods into a production of investment-goods.

Only if investment-goods result from a transformation of wage-goods will the undifferentiated set of households maintain ownership of the whole output, instrumental goods included. If profit is considered as an *add-on* to wages, as is the case in present-day capitalism, the production of investment-goods is added to that of wage-goods, and the deposits of profit are lent *again*. This leads to the indebtedness of households, depriving them forever of their legitimate ownership over investment-goods. By respecting the identity, $Y \equiv C$, profit will not be added to wages, nor will investment-goods be treated as a nested category of wage-goods.

Point 3) restricts all economic activity to that of sector 1. As the reader will recall, the subdivision of production into three sectors is part of a mechanism where banks grant loans based on deposits generated by the expenditure of profit. The existence of three distinct sectors 'holds entirely on a thread, which is none other than the loans granted by the banking system to the set of households' (ibid.: 134, m.t.). The road to post-capitalism forces one to abandon such a pathological lending practice. The economic system will be set to work in compliance with its logical laws through a reform that removes invested profit from the financial market from the outset.

Schmitt's reform, which was analyzed in Chapter 6, introduces a new mechanism for monetary payments whereby invested profit is transferred from the saving department to the fixed capital department of banks, thus ensuring it will not be lent on the financial market. 'The structuring of banking activity, to be dealt with by three departments of commercial banks, greatly facilitated by information technology, replaces the division of the economic activity into three sectors' (ibid.: 145, m.t.). After the reform, production will take place only in the first sector, so that profit (redistributed and invested) will be included in wages- and investment-goods derived from wage-goods, in conformity with the identity $Y \equiv C$.

## Post-capitalism

Schmitt's works contain no structured analysis of post-capitalism. I can therefore only refer to the few hints one can find in his 1996 and 1998 manuscripts, in order to sketch an analysis that will have to be expanded further by Schmitt's followers. In particular, I will try to clarify some of the most significant issues concerning the formation and expenditure of profits as well as the evolution of the rate of profit and its relationship to the rate of interest.

### *Profit and capital in post-capitalism*

By reducing economic activity to that of the first sector alone, one might fear that it would no longer be possible for capital to remain positive. Schmitt rejects this prospect straightaway and states that '*[t]he production of sector one, which absorbs the whole activity of the national economy, allows for all the conceivable sharing of domestic income between labour and capital*' (ibid.: 141, m.t.). The fact that, in post-capitalism, the totality of produced output is owned exclusively by households does not prevent the formation of profit followed by that of fixed capital. The difference between capitalism and post-capitalism does not lie in the way profit is formed in the products market and spent in the labour market. The mechanism is the same; what changes is the fact that, in capitalism, profit gives rise to a bank deposit that is *lent* to households, whereas in post-capitalism, profit is transferred to the fixed capital department of banks and no longer goes to feed the financial market.

Now, a question might arise concerning the amount of income available for the purchase of wage-goods and profits-goods sold at a mark-up. In capitalism, this would not be a problem because the loan of profit deposits increases, pathologically, the amount of income households can spend. In the absence of such a loan, how can wages finance the purchase of goods, whose price (and value) increases together with labour physical productivity driven by instrumental goods? Schmitt answers this question by referring to the velocity of circulation measured by the number of times income is spent within a referenced period. Thus, if the payment of wages forms an income of 1,000 wage-units, and if the value of produced output increases from 1,000 to 5,000 wage-units, the entire output can be purchased because the 1,000 units of income are multiplied by a coefficient equal to 5: $V=5$.

Schmitt illustrates this mechanism by referring to a simplified example, where wages and profit are both equal to 1,000 wage-units. In this case, national output is sold at a price of 2,000 money units. If wages are totally spent, firms obtain a profit of 500 wage-units, which they spend in the labour market on the purchase of profit-goods. An income already spent by wage-earners is thus spent a second time by firms. 'We observe that 500 units of money income are spent twice, first by households then by firms' (ibid.: 142, m.t.). Given that profit-goods are also sold between firms at a price twice their cost of production, the entire amount of wages must be spent twice over to enable the purchase of both wage- and profit-goods. 'The totality of national income is thus spent twice to compensate the difference between price (2,000 wage-units) and value (1,000 wage-units) of national output' (ibid.: 142, m.t.). Whether we reason in terms of value, as Schmitt does in 1984, or in terms of prices, as he does in 1998, the result is unchanged: the whole national output can be sold, because wages are multiplied by $V=2$.

Schmitt's example is only didactic, one representative case among a whole set of possible situations. What matters most is that $V=2$ is just one among the possible values of coefficient $V$.

> There are no reasons to assume that $V$ is formally limited; this coefficient can reach any numerical value and can far exceed the number 2. Any distribution of output among households and between households and firms is therefore technically allowed by the variations of coefficient $V$, without limit.
>
> (ibid.: 142, m.t.)

This is to say that, in post-capitalism, profit can greatly exceed wages, even though it analysed continues to derive from wages and to be still owned by the set of households.

### *Profit and wages in post-capitalism*

This last conclusion calls for a clarification. Indeed, one might wonder how a profit, which derives from wages, can be greater than their amount. Let us suppose once again, with Schmitt, that profit and wages are each equal to 1,000 wage-units. What does this situation imply? Certainly not that national income is reduced to profit and that households' purchasing power is 'reduced to zero' (ibid.: 143, m.t.). The relevant point is that, measured in wage-units, employment is equally distributed among the production of wage-goods and profit-goods. Wage-earners work half of their time to produce consumption-goods and the other half to produce investment-goods. In other words, 'households spend wages in the proportion of one unit for themselves and one unit for [personalized] firms' (ibid.: 143, m.t.). If profit were much greater than wages, say ten times greater, this would mean that workers devote 1/11 of their activity to the production of wage-goods *strictu sensu* and 10/11 to the production of profit-goods (*lato sensu*). That is to say that households 'would spend their wages in the proportion of one unit over 11 for themselves and 10 units over 11 for firms' (ibid.: 143, m.t.).

Finally, can we still maintain that profit is embedded in wages given that 10,000 money units cannot obviously be included in 1,000 money units? Schmitt answers this question by observing that 'to claim that profits are included in wages does not at all mean that profit is a monetary income measured *at a given moment* by10,000 money units' (ibid.: 143, m.t.). There is no single moment at which the numerical measure of profit can exceed that of wages, yet this still does not stop profit being greater than wages. For this to happen, we only need a series of profit generating expenditures of wages to take place, the amount of which does not exceed 1,000 money units each time and the sum of which is equal to 10,000 money units.

> [T]he 10,000 units of profit are obtained as a result of a *whole chain of expenditures*, of which only the sum of successive elements is equal to 10,000 m.u. If each time these elements are included in the sum of 1,000 wage-units, the total profit is itself included in wages.
>
> (ibid.: 143, m.t.)

***In post-capitalism, inflation and involuntary unemployment will no longer be possible***

The renewed expenditure of an already spent income is the main source of disorder in present-day capitalism because it is coextensive with a macroeconomic loan additionally granted by banks to households. In post-capitalism, no such loan will be possible. The boundaries to the growth of profits will be set only by entrepreneurs' inventiveness, technical progress, and competition. Moreover, only households, whose ownership of national production will no longer be jeopardized, will benefit from increases in profit and, subsequently, in capital. Nobody will work for Capital (or disembodied firms) any longer; alienation and exploitation to the benefit of Capital will be relegated to the past; and so will inflation and involuntary unemployment.

The existence of unemployment is a consequence of the activity of the third sector being transferred to the second sector. In post-capitalism, this transfer can no longer occur because the division into sectors is suppressed, and all economic activity takes place in sector 1 only. Amortization-goods, together with investment-goods, are incorporated into the first sector; they do not add to the production of wage-goods. Likewise, the income corresponding to the production of amortization-goods is not added to wages, as it happens in capitalism; households do not lose even a fraction of produced output, which they own either in the form of real income or of capital. Amortization is prevented from adding to consumption and investment, while involuntary unemployment loses its *raison d'être* – and so does inflation.

### *Post-capitalism, profit, and interest*

An important aspect of post-capitalism is the relationship between invested profit and interest. As we know (see Chapter 11), the existence of interest is related to the transformation of income into fixed capital. By definition, every capitalized income is saved: it is through saving that income is transformed into capital. This transformation is final and irreversible when it refers to the formation of fixed capital, but reversible in case income is temporarily transformed into capital-time and spent at a later date. The loss of income that is irreversibly saved calls for compensation, which explains the existence of interest as a net income. '[I]nterest is not additive to capital; it is, on the contrary, the compensation obtained by the lender who definitively loses the income fixed into capital' (Schmitt 2021: 374).

For the payment of interest to be positive, a new production must take place resulting in the creation of a new income *that guarantees the (reverse) transposition of capital from chronological time to quantum time.* Fixed capital is forever lost to the set of income holders, who are entitled to a compensation in the form of income, namely the income formed in the production of interest-goods. Even though some individual or institutional savers can recover the income invested into fixed capital, the economy as a whole cannot. This is so because 'any refunding implies necessarily the consolidation or *the amortization* of the initial loan, in the hands of a new creditor' (ibid.: 375).

This conclusion holds both in capitalism and in post-capitalism, the difference being that, in capitalism, interest is added to wages and becomes part of the income produced in the second sector of the economy. Reasoning within post-capitalism, Schmitt gives a further proof of the law according to which interest is never an addition to capital and for the fact that eventually 'dividends and interest form [...] a unique category' (ibid.: 379). He considers what happens when firms 'buy back' their invested savings, that is, when they recover their initial investment. In this case, Schmitt tells us, interest stops being a cost of production; 'instead of being emitted periodically under the form of interest, profit is at once "an actualization of this (quantum) flow": it is a capital' (ibid. 379). At the moment of its transformation into fixed capital, invested profit is an income lost to the economy. At the moment of its reconstitution, when investment is recovered, firms find a monetary capital and stop paying interest to the initial creditors. '[M]onetary capital is no longer lost (or given up), [and] interest is no longer collected by *anyone*' (ibid.: 379). This confirms that interest is never added to capital. *When capital defines an income lost by the economy, interest is positive; when capital is an available income, interest is nil.*

Schmitt's analysis of this case – namely, the reconstitution of the sum of profit initially invested by firms – does not stop here. He immediately observes that as soon as firms add the recovered sum to their capital, that is, as soon as they capitalize it, they transmit this increase in capital to their shareholders in the form of dividends. Interest 'comes to life again, both [as] cost of production and income' (ibid. 379), so that we can legitimately conclude that interest and dividends belong to the same category.

In a manner analogous to profit-goods in general, the production of interest-goods is now included in that of wage-goods, which shows interest as a nested category of wages. This means that interest is at the same time an income of transfer (because it is derived from wages) and a production cost (because it implies the production of interest-goods). Schmitt's analysis of interest provides therefore another example of quantum logic, where the principle of the excluded middle does not apply. 'Interest is indeed an income of transfer; [...]. Nonetheless interest is a cost of production, not just for the set of firms, but even in the eyes of the whole nation' (ibid.: 377). Hence, interest is a macroeconomic cost, both because it defines a new production and because it 'is but the transposition of a capitalized income, which changes space, shifting from continuous to quantum time' (ibid.: 377).

The link between interest and profit is now made clear: interest is a compensation, paid at regular intervals to households, for the loss of (national) income resulting from the investment of profit and the formation of fixed capital. In other words, fixed capital is an income lost to the economy and recovered in the form of interest. It thus follows that *the measure of profit proper (invested profit) is essentially equal to that of interest.* Profit is essentially 'absorbed by interest. Only the "Schumpeterian innovation" can *temporarily* introduce a discrepancy between profit and interest' (ibid.: 378). In post-capitalism, profit tends to coincide with interest or, in Schmitt's words, 'interest [...] is the centre of gravity of profit' (ibid.: 378). At the same time, the distinction between the rate of profit (Wicksell's natural rate of interest) and the market or monetary rate of interest is cancelled, and households are the only beneficiaries of capital and key in determining its amount. '*The two interest rates, natural and monetary, will be reduced to one and the monetary rate will be the one influencing all the options exercised between consumption and saving; households will be the only judges in this respect*' (Schmitt 1998a: 144, m.t.).

### *On the 'natural' rate of interest*

During one of his lectures at the University of Fribourg in the Summer semester of 1996, as he himself reports in the *Cours de théorie monétaire* distributed to his students, Schmitt put forward the idea that the value of the natural rate of interest (that is, of the equilibrium rate of profit) is equal to Euler's number (Schmitt 1996d: 38). The number of Euler, first discovered by the Scottish economist John Napier in 1618, is $e=2{,}7182818284590$. It is an irrational, non-periodic number like $\pi$, and it is at the foundation of natural logarithms. It is represented by the formula

$$\lim_{n\to\infty}\left(1+\frac{1}{n}\right)^{n}$$

and may be found any time a growth phenomenon depends on time. Number *e* can be derived from the study of compound interest, where the formula for the determination of the value of a capital, *C*, increased by compound interest at a period *n* is the following

$$C_n = C_{n-1}e^r$$

where *r* is the rate of interest. Schmitt does not dwell on his intuition, which needs to be substantiated both on theoretical and on practical grounds. Yet, the fact that number *e* is a constant in the formula for the determination of compound interest seems to corroborate Schmitt's intuition. In post-capitalism, profit will grow indefinitely, and so will capital. If, as Schmitt suggests, the natural rate of profit or interest were equal to *e*, this would mean that, with the passing of time, the ratio profit/capital would tend to

$$\lim_{n\to\infty}\left(1+\frac{1}{n}\right)^n$$

where *n* is the number of periods considered. In other words, profit would initially increase faster than capital until the profit/capital ratio reaches the value of *e*, after which profit and capital would increase at the same rate. Be that as it may, Schmitt's intuition has to be investigated further and submitted to empirical verification.

## Post-capitalism: a new phase in the evolution of capitalism or an entirely new regime?

This last section reiterates Schmitt's conception of post-capitalism based on his analysis of capitalism and the possibilities for reform. The changes necessary to the transition from disorder (capitalism) to order (post-capitalism) do not imply abandoning either banks as monetary and financial intermediaries, or firms – also as intermediaries – or money, profit (invested and redistributed), and capital. The revolutionary insight of Schmitt's analysis lies in the identification of a pathological mechanism of capital accumulation and of its consequences for the ownership of produced output. According to Schmitt, the distinguishing marks of capitalism are: the *expropriation* of income holders to the benefit of pathological capital, the formation of inflationary profit, and the rise of, as well as increase in, involuntary unemployment. Schmitt's remedy is not a socio-political revolution to destroy capitalism, but the replacement of a perverse mechanism with a sound one that complies with the logical laws highlighted by the rigorous analysis of money, income, and capital.

***Post-capitalism and money***

The utopia of an economy without money is foreign to Schmitt's analysis, which does not view money as a harmful fetish or the source of alienation and exploitation. As a matter of fact, the money targeted by advocates of a socio-political and economic change is ill-conceived and erroneously confused with income or even with capital by the great majority of economists. The true nature of money is still unknown to those who believe that banks are gifted with the supernatural power to create a positive asset out of nothing. In reality, as Schmitt's quantum macroeconomics shows, banks do not issue money enriched with positive purchasing power. On the contrary, money originates as a mere asset-liability, as a numerical form, whose intrinsic value is strictly zero. As such, bank money is nothing more than a unit of account, an a-dimensional, immaterial, and purely numerical 'envelope', whose task is to give a numerical expression to production.

It is true that money is endowed with a positive purchasing power from the very moment of its creation. However, what most economists have not yet fully understood is that this is not because of the activity of banks, but because of production. It is production that gives money a real object or content, not banks. Those who demonize money entirely miss the distinction between money as such, a flow, and money-income, a stock. As issued by banks, money is a flow, a nominal means or vehicle necessary to convey payments and *not* their object. 'The true object of the credit of individuals on banks, of central as well as of 'secondary' money, is to obtain a flow, not a stock. [...] this flow is a *payment*' (Schmitt 1998a: 4–5, m.t.). If monetary payments can clear a debt, it is because what money conveys is a stock. The object of a payment is not money, but what money conveys in its flow, its real content, that is, a sum of real goods in financial form. Moreover, payments being instantaneous, the flow of money is also instantaneous, and so is the life span of money. '[M]oney exists only at the instant of payments; all money is destroyed the very same instant it is created' (ibid.: 7, m.t.).

How could an instantaneous, immaterial flow of zero intrinsic value be the cause of the evils of capitalism? How can one maintain that order can be obtained only by rejecting the use of money? The answer is that money in itself is but a means necessary to express real goods numerically and thus make them homogeneous, a means without which economics could not claim pride of place in the realm of science. Without money, economics would have no proper, *measurable* object of inquiry and the economy could not be organized into a system. Far from being the source of evil, money is a neutral instrument the presence of which will be necessary for centuries to come; its rejection is an ill-conceived goal that, if attained, would be disastrous. What must be done instead is replace the system of payments characterizing capitalism with an orderly system in which banks' monetary intermediation is no longer mixed up with their financial intermediation; a system in which capital is no longer removed from households' economic ownership by a mechanism that lends in the financial market the deposits of an income (profit) already spent in the labour market and irreversibly transformed into (fixed) capital.

### *Inflation and involuntary unemployment are neither functional nor inescapable consequences of capitalism*

In a way, the aim of Marx's *Kapital* can be viewed as essentially similar to that of Schmitt's macroeconomic analysis. Both authors want to determine how capitalism works. In other words, what are the objective mechanisms that lead to an alienating mode of production and to the expropriation of households by (pathological) capital? They both identify the causes of capitalism's disorder at a structural level, in the processes of capital accumulation and over-accumulation affecting the economic system as a whole. What distinguishes the two authors in their substantive analysis of capitalism is that Marx remains indebted to a dimensional conception of labour value, whereas Schmitt rejects labour-time and advocates a purely numerical measure of real goods in terms of wage-units. Consequently, Marx is unable to provide a full picture of the pathological working of capitalism or of the logical laws that would allow the transition to post-capitalism. This said, it is only fair to recognize that Marx's contribution to economic analysis is, together with Smith's and Ricardo's, a milestone in economic thought, the first step of a dialectical process leading to Schmitt's quantum macroeconomics.

The second step, the phase of antithesis, is Walras's conception of relative economic value. By abandoning the Classics' idea of absolute value as a physical dimension of goods (incorporated labour-time), Walras lays the foundations of modern economics. His concept of *numéraire* is full of fruitful implications with regard to money. Even though Walras does not go that far, his intuition marks an important advancement in the understanding of economics. In this respect, it is interesting to observe that in the neoclassical representation of an ideal economy, based on 'pure and perfect competition', profit comes down to interest, and the rate of profit is equal to the rate of interest. In general equilibrium analysis, this result obtains in a hypothetical and utopian world in which individual behaviour is central. Yet, as sometimes happens in science, the conclusion proves to be correct, even though it has been reached through an incorrect analysis. For GEA, the equality of interest and profit is a condition of equilibrium of capitalism, a system that is believed to be fundamentally sound if based on free competition. In Schmitt's macroeconomic analysis, this same equality is a logical result of another system, post-capitalism, which complies with the laws or identities of monetary macroeconomics.

Schmitt's analysis is closer to that of the Classics than to GEA in many respects. One exception is the need for a reform to guarantee the orderly working of a system freed from the appropriation of part of national output by disembodied firms and its pathological consequences. Neither classical theory nor GEA envisages the need for such a reform. Pushing classical analysis to its extreme consequences, Marx treats exploitation and alienation as structural phenomena functional to the development of capitalism until its final defeat, which makes room for a new society whose economy no one has yet envisaged. Advocates of GEA, on the other hand, believe capitalism to be the best possible economic system on condition that market forces are allowed to adjust without external interference.

Schmitt's analysis differs substantially from both approaches; it provides a new alternative promoting the peaceful transition to an orderly system in which transactions are carried out through a mechanism that makes the structural formation of inflation and unemployment impossible. Post-capitalism is thus seen as a system in which money is fully neutral, as is the process of capital accumulation in all its distinct phases. In such an economic framework, pathological capital can no longer be formed, and any form of enslavement of households to capital is forever removed. Socio-economic inequalities, however, will not automatically disappear, and socio-political changes will be necessary for building a society truly founded on 'liberty, equality, fraternity'. Schmitt's monetary reform is no panacea, but remains the first bold but necessary step towards building such a society.

# Part III

# 1999–2014: The final years of ground-breaking analysis

From the close of the 20th century to the year of his death, Schmitt devoted his main effort to the analysis of international payments and to his critique of general equilibrium analysis (GEA). His interest in these topics goes back to the first decade of his research activity and never faded with the passing of time. On the contrary, Schmitt's endeavour to master the problem of countries' external debt, intensified and he directed all his energies to providing the clearest possible analysis of what he considered one of the most beautiful and difficult subjects of macroeconomics. His lucidity and his uncompromising, rigorous logic never abandoned him. Despite suffering a stroke, which affected him physically but not intellectually, Schmitt worked until a few days before his death to complete his analysis of sovereign debt formation.

Part III deals with Schmitt's last, seminal contributions to economic analysis. It completes his investigation of the pathology affecting the interest payment of countries' external debt as well as his original analysis of the way external debt is formed in the first place. While one chapter is concerned with Schmitt's final criticism of GEA, the other three of this third and final Part are devoted to his discovery of the perverse mechanism underlying the formation and payments of countries' sovereign debt, and to his proposals for reform.

DOI: 10.4324/9781351271325-20

# 15 Towards the 'interest theorem'

## The double cost of interest payments

The problem of interest payments on countries' external debts caught Schmitt's attention at an early stage of his analysis of international payments. As we saw in Chapter 10, he became aware of the existence of a perverse mechanism, which multiplies by two the charge of net interest payment. Schmitt's first arguments are based on his analysis of the flow nature of money. They stress the existence of an asymmetry forcing indebted countries to purchase at additional cost the vehicular currency required to convey the external payment of net interest by their residents. During the 1990s, he refined his conceptual analysis and looked for its factual, statistical confirmation as well as for a reform that would allow countries to avoid the double cost of interest payments. From then on, he made multiple attempts to find the clearest possible proof of what he was to call the *interest theorem* and was able to show that the pathology affects all payments of interest on countries' external debts. His many unpublished manuscripts on the topic (I personally have more than forty of them in my archives) bear witness to his unabated interest for the subject as well as to its inherent difficulty. Out of these, I have selected only 17 papers (5 of which have been published), to which I refer throughout, implicitly or explicitly. I have also restricted the number of proofs of the double charge provided by Schmitt from 1997 to 2012, in an attempt to make it easier for the reader to follow his arguments.

## Presentation of the problem

### *The distinction between countries and residents*

Even though international payments are always carried out by countries' residents, i.e. by the economic agents of the private and public sectors, countries themselves experience the consequences of these payments without being able to attribute them to any resident. A country may thereby acquire a debt or benefit from a credit, even though none of its residents is a foreign debtor or creditor. The clearest example of this is given by the increase in official reserves generated by net commercial exports.

Suppose country A's residents to be net commercial exporters. Clearly, the difference between commercial exports and imports entered in A's balance

DOI: 10.4324/9781351271325-21

of payments concerns the country as a whole; it defines A's trade surplus. No individual exporter or importer can be singled out as the cause of A's surplus, which can only be attributed to the country as a whole, undifferentiated set of its residents. This is confirmed by the fact that, *ceteris paribus*, the net inflow of foreign currency from R's payment of its net imports will eventually increase A's official reserves. Country A's commercial exporters are paid in A's domestic money, which is issued by A's banking system through monetization of the foreign currency entered on the assets side of its balance sheets. Once country A's exporters are paid, they are no longer creditors of R; yet their country is, since the increase in official reserves defines an increase in A's foreign credit.

The gain resulting from the increase in A's official reserves applies to country A as a whole. Official reserves are managed by A's central bank on behalf of the country. As Schmitt observes, *the State itself is a resident*, and thus it is not entitled to any portion of its country's official reserves. It is only as the representative of a country or a nation that the State can handle its official reserves, the ownership of which is essentially economic, not political. '[I]n any country, the payment of trade surplus flows into its banking system account, in particular that of its central bank, on behalf of the surplus country considered as an undivided whole' (Schmitt 1997a: 54, m.t.).

The situation where country A faces a trade deficit is also a clear example of A's involvement in the transactions of its residents. If in $p_0$ A's residents are net commercial importers, the ensuing trade deficit concerns their country as a whole, independently of their own situation. A's importers pay, in domestic income, the totality of their foreign purchases; yet, their country runs an external debt equal to its trade deficit. The trade deficit burden rests on country A. Whether or not residents get indebted to non-residents, *their country* is indebted as a result of its trade deficit.

> [E]very country carries directly or "immediately" its own debt, born out of its trade deficit; [...] the debt is formed directly for the country as a whole; it is necessarily so because, remember, no resident carries a debt defined by the difference in value between all the imports and all the exports of a country.
>
> (Schmitt 1999d: 18, m.t.)

### *The macroeconomic nature of countries' external debt servicing*

The problem is of a macroeconomic nature. Payments carried out by residents, including those carried out by the State, are *microeconomic*, which is why they are entered on the current account and the capital and financial account of the balance of payments. On the other hand, payments concerning the country as a whole are *macroeconomic*; they affect the official reserves account, and 'variations in reserves are macroeconomic flows because they concern the country as a whole' (Schmitt 2004b: 10, m.t.).

Consider the case of a country, A, which, following the debt incurred by its residents in a period $p_0$, must pay a sum of interest to foreign creditors, who are residents of the rest-of-the-world, R. The payment of interest has to be carried out by A's indebted residents, but it also involves country A defined as a whole. This is so because the payment of interest by A's residents is carried out by A's banking system and corresponds to a debit-without-credit assumed by country A on behalf of its residents. Now, Schmitt claims that the macroeconomic and the microeconomic payments of interest are subject to a pathology, which multiplies by two the charge of the interest payment.

In this respect, let us clarify from the outset that the pathology concerns the payment of interest on *a country's external debt* or, alternatively, the payment of *net* interest carried out by the country's residents. If we look at the payment of interest of the country's indebted residents, we have to take into account the fact that residents may also be the beneficiaries of interest payments from the rest-of-the-world. In this case, equivalent reciprocal payments compensate, and only *net* interest payments are subject to a pathological duplication. If, on the other hand, we look at the payment of interest on the external debt incurred by the country (as a whole as a consequence of the payment of its residents' *net imports*), then we are focusing on the whole payment of interest. The two alternatives are equivalent.

In the following pages we shall speak exclusively of the payment of interest, since all the arguments proving the existence of a double cost are the same, whether they refer to the payment of interest on a country's external debt or to the payment of net interest by its residents. '[I]ndebted country (A) suffers *twice* from the charge of interest on its external debt; first as it affects its residents, indebted to non-residents, and secondly as it affects the set of its residents' (Schmitt 1997a: 3, m.t.).

The problem of interest payment must be viewed in the context of countries' spiralling external debt. If, as Schmitt claims, indebted countries are forced to pay twice interest on their foreign debt, then the second payment is bound to increase their foreign borrowings and consequently their external debt. The challenge facing Schmitt was to show that this is indeed the case, that the present non-system of international payments is such that the payment of interest by an indebted country's residents to the benefit of non-residents entails, as a pathological consequence, an additional debt burden for their country.

Given the apparent paradox of this claim and the difficulty of disclosing the problem it introduces, Schmitt has provided many lines of argumentation converging in several, complementary proofs of the duplication engendered by interest payment. While each of these alternative proofs is self-contained, they all contribute to establishing what Schmitt has named 'the *interest theorem*'. Being closely related, they share a common theoretical background and are in part repetitive; however, each of them provides fresh elements and allows us to see the problem from different, yet reciprocally supporting viewpoints. The decision to present at least some of them is justified by the need to give the sceptical reader the choice between alternative lines of reasoning.

## First proofs of the double charge of the payment of interest on countries' external debts

The proofs proposed in this section are not the first ever advocated by Schmitt, but they are the first in a long series of proofs worked out by Schmitt between 1997 and 2012, which is the period in which he devoted most of his time to mastering this thorny issue.

### *A straightforward proof*

Let us consider again the case of a country, A, as it incurs an external debt in period $p_0$. Is A's external debt of $p_0$ the mirror image of the debt incurred in the same period by its residents, or is it formed directly on country A as a whole? We already know the answer to this question: a country's external debt can only derive from its net imports and neither net imports nor net exports can be attributed to any of its residents. Even if A's residents borrow abroad the sum of foreign currency needed to pay for their net imports from non-residents, the difference between imports and exports defines the external situation of the country itself, not that of its importers. Since country A's importers pay for their imports in full, country A's external debt, which results from its trade deficit, cannot reflect the debt incurred by its residents. Hence, it appears that, being formed, like an 'excrescence', directly on the country itself, A's external debt is added to that incurred by its residents, and two distinct payments of interest are associated with this circumstance: one payment must be carried out by the indebted residents and the other by their country.

> From the moment two distinct deficits coexist in $p_0$, namely the deficit of D [the debtor of interest, resident of A] element of A and the deficit of set A, the two payments of interest entailed by these two distinct debts are themselves two distinct payments – joint, certainly, but distinct.
>
> (Schmitt 1999d: 24, m.t.)

The double payment of interest is a direct consequence of the fact that the debt itself is double, the debt of the country and of its residents being cumulative. Simple and straightforward, this proof of the double charge of interest should be enough to establish the pathological character of interest payments at the international level. Yet, its result is so much in contrast with common sense that more arguments are needed to convince the incredulous reader. One way of doing so is to provide a detailed demonstration that countries' external debts are added to the debts incurred by their residents. This is what Schmitt does in his last manuscript (Schmitt 2014), and we shall consider it in Chapter 17. Another way is to dig deeper into the analysis of interest payment to show that its charge is twice as high as it should be and infer from this that the initial debt is *de facto* doubled. Between 1997 and 2012, this is the way Schmitt chose, and we shall follow his argument.

### ***Time-interest and space-interest***

Schmitt distinguishes between *time-interest* and *space-interest*, where time-interest is the interest country A's indebted residents owe to foreign creditors, and space-interest is the interest owed by country A considered as a whole. What must be demonstrated is that the two interests are distinct and cumulative. The term time-interest indicates that, as time goes by, indebted residents of any country (A) must transfer to their foreign creditors part of A's domestic production generated by the investment of the capital borrowed in $p_0$. On the other hand, the term space-interest indicates that country A owes an interest on the debt formed in the international space because of the country's deficit. To determine whether the two interests are distinct, or whether one is the mere repetition of the other it is necessary to investigate them and their consequences separately.

#### *Time-interest*

As Schmitt tells us, if residents paid time-interest in kind, no problem would arise. A's indebted residents would purchase part of A's domestic output through the expenditure of an equivalent part of their income and transfer it to their foreign creditors. Yet this is not what happens because interest payments between countries are carried out in foreign currency. Indebted residents pay their interest debt by spending part of their income, expressed in the money of country A, $M_A$, it is true; yet, foreign creditors are paid in money of country R, $M_R$. It is through the intermediation of banks that the payment in $M_A$ is converted into a payment in $M_R$. The national income spent by A's indebted residents is thus used up in the payment of country A's exporters.

> [T]he domestic income spent by the debtors of interest ends up, through the mediation of banks, with the exporters of their *own* country, a flow that means that the payment of time-interest must be analysed as a payment of exports of the indebted country.
>
> (ibid.: 7, m.t.)

The consequences of the payment of time-interest by A's indebted residents is that part of country R's imports is paid by country A instead of being paid by R. Because of the payment carried out by its residents, part of country A's exports is not paid by R: 'for as long as time-interest servicing lasts, the indebted country considered as a whole obtains no external payment for its exports' (ibid.: 7, m.t.).

Let us suppose, following Schmitt, that in $p_1$ country A has a trade surplus of twice the amount of interest it has to pay to its foreign creditors. The payment of time-interest, the monetary transfer of a part of A's domestic resources equal to the interest, uses up half of country A's trade surplus without compensation. In other words, half of A's net exports to R is given up by country A without obtaining any payment from country R. It is country A itself that pays for a part of its net exports, so that A's trade surplus of twice the interest gives rise to an increase in A's official reserves equal to one time the interest amount only: the payment of time-interest implies an equivalent reduction in the *formation* of country A's international reserves.

A's exporters are fully paid, but an amount equal to *interest-debt* is paid by country A's indebted residents through the expenditure of their domestic income. At the same time, the foreign currency paid by R flows back to that country to pay for A's time-interest. Country R, therefore, obtains for free the amount of foreign currency required to pay for half of its trade deficit. This is another way of saying that the payment of a part of R's net imports, equal to interest, fails to increase A's official reserves. '[E]ven though they are normally paid to the indebted country's exporters, net exports of a value [equal to interest] carry an amount of foreign currency that does not flow into the country's reserves (ibid.: 7, m.t.). The payment of interest by A's residents is the free transfer of part of country A's national output to country R; since this transfer is conveyed through a monetary payment, the sum of foreign currency equal to interest spent by R for its imports is in reality provided by A. If country A's exports were entirely paid by country R, country A's official reserves would increase by twice the amount of interest. Given that a sum of A's exports equal to interest is paid by country A itself, the formation of A's official reserves is reduced by the amount of A's time- interest: country A's reserves increase only by once the amount of interest.

### *Space-interest*

We now must account for the payment of A's space-interest. Since it forms as a consequence of the trade deficit incurred in $p_0$ by nation A, space-interest cannot be assumed to be included in time-interest. It would also be wrong to claim that country A's indebted residents carry A's space-interest, because A's trade deficit affects the country itself and cannot be blamed on any of its residents. As the two interests are carried by two distinct categories of 'agents', we can immediately conclude that they necessarily call for two distinct (and cumulative) payments. Schmitt corroborates this astonishing result by arguing that the two kinds of interest require their homologous modalities of payment. Indeed, whereas the payment of time-interest implies a non-increase in country A's foreign reserves, the payment of space-interest takes place through a reduction in A's reserves. One payment affects the *formation* of reserves, the other the reserves already *formed*; one is 'negative' the other 'positive':

> *time-interest*, which rests on the indebted country's residents, is carried out in a *negative way*, through the *external* non-payment, as far as reserves are concerned, of the corresponding trade surplus; *space-interest* is paid in a *positive way*; it is the country itself [...] that pays this second interest and thus loses the reserves obtained as payment for its second tranche of net exports.
> (ibid.: 8, m.t.)

A consideration based on the well-known distinction between stocks and flows corroborates this result. The two effects, negative and positive, of the payment of interest are distinct and cumulative, because the former is a flow-effect, the latter a stock-effect. The former reduces the inflow of foreign exchange into the indebted country's reserves, the latter reduces the amount of foreign exchange accumulated in the country's reserves, it decreases its stock. 'The payment of time-interest is a depletion of the flow of formation of reserves, which it curtails. The payment of space-interest is a depletion of the stock of effectively formed reserves' (ibid.: 8, m.t.). As Schmitt puts it, '[i]t is clear that reserves that have never been formed (reduction in a flow) cannot be drawn upon (reduction of a stock)' (ibid.: 8, m.t.). Finally, the total cost of the payment of interest for country A is equal to 2 times the amount of interest; half of this cost is due to the payment of time-interest by A's indebted residents, the other half is covered by country A as a whole, which carries the debt generated by A's trade deficit of $p_0$.

### *The payment of interest by country A finances part of the imports of country R*

The second proof is a development of the first. Schmitt drops the didactic assumption of A's realizing a trade surplus of twice the amount of interest in period $p_1$ and only implicitly refers to the distinction between time-interest and space-interest. Emphasis rests on the fact that country A pays the interest on its external debt by transferring the amount of foreign currency R needs to pay for an equal amount of its imports. It is correct to say that country R pays for the totality of its imports, yet country A, by paying for interest, returns to R part of its initial expenditure.

Let us use Schmitt's example and assume that country A pays for its imports and its interest on debt in US dollars, the domestic currency of R. Let us assume, also, that A's domestic production amounts to $M_A$ 100 = \$100.

Figure 15.1 shows that, since country A transfers \$10 to R as payment of interest, country R obtains at zero cost the \$10 required for the payment of an equivalent amount of its imports from A. This means that it is country A that pays for its exports of \$10; R gets them for free. It is true that country R is entitled to the payment of interest in real terms, because country A owes it part of the yields deriving from the investment of the capital borrowed by A in $p_0$. However, country A must carry out the payment in \$, which enables country

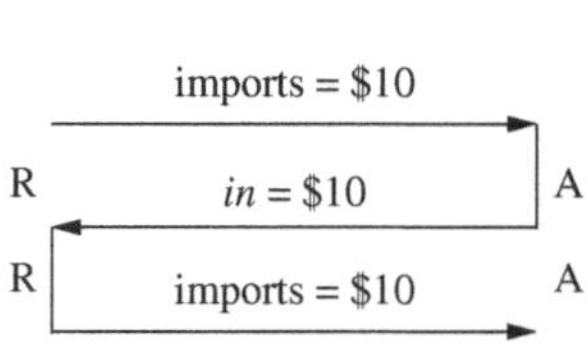


*Figure 15.1* Payment of country R's imports as financed by country A. Source: Elaboration from Schmitt 1997: 15

R to import at zero cost part of A's domestic output. Annoyingly, this reduces to $90 the sum finally obtained by country A in exchange for exports, worth $100. '[A]s the effect of the payment of interest, $10, exports of a total value of $100 [...] are paid only up to $90' (Schmitt 1997a: 15).

It thus appears that the payment of interest engenders a new debt. The payment of interest-debt leaves an equal part of A's exports unpaid, which means that it is the cause of a difference between the value of its total exports, $100 in our example, and what R pays for them, $90. In order to cover this deficit, country A must borrow $10 from R or reduce its official reserves. In both cases it increases its external debt by $10. As absurd as this may seem, we are faced with a pathological situation in which country A incurs a new debt when it pays its interest-debt. If country A did *not* pay the interest due, its foreign debt would increase, because, at maturity, interest would be added to the principal of the debt formed in $p_0$, and nobody would contest this. What happens here is substantially different because country A *does pay* its interest-debt and, precisely because it pays it, it runs a new external debt of the same value.

A's interest-debt means that, because of country A's net borrowing from R in $p_0$, country R is entitled to part of A's production until country A repays the principal of its external debt. A must transfer to R an amount, equal to the interest, of its national output in each period following $p_0$. Conveyed in US dollars, this *unilateral transfer* corresponds to the non-payment by country R of part of country A's commercial exports. In Schmitt's own words, 'to say that nation A serves 10 dollars in net interest to nation R is tantamount to asserting that A pays, in dollars, for an equivalent value of R's commercial imports' (Schmitt 2004d: 25). As a consequence, A's inflow of dollars to pay for its commercial exports drops to $90. Equilibrium is re-established at the level of $100 only through a reduction in reserves or through a new loan from R. On the whole, the total charge of the payment of interest is doubled; while transferring $10 worth of its domestic resources to R, country A incurs at the same time a new debt (a decrease in reserves, financial assets, is an increase in debt) of $10 toward the rest-of-the-world.

## The peculiarity of interest payments

### *The macroeconomic nature of the problem*

As previously observed, the pathological duplication of the payment of interest-debt pertains only to the realm of *macroeconomics*; it concerns the indebted countries, each treated as the *set*, not the sum, of its residents. The payment of interest carried out by country A's indebted residents is a single, not a double, payment; they pay interest-debt only once and their creditors, residents of country R, benefit from a single payment. Insofar as it is carried out between residents and non-residents, the payment of interest-debt is *microeconomic* and does not entail any duplication. Yet, transnational payments involve also the presence of countries as the set of their residents. This would not be the case if nations did not exist as distinct economic entities, if the entire world were made up of a single economic nation where payments were carried out in a single economic currency. This not being the case, payments between residents and non-residents are mediated between distinct nations and 'come within the competence of *macroeconomics*' (Schmitt 2004c: 17).

The duplication of the charge of interest is due to the involvement of countries in transnational payments as they occur in the present non-system of international payments; it is the consequence of indebted countries transferring part of their domestic resources to creditor countries. It is because country A gives up part of its commercial exports that it incurs a new deficit involving a decrease in its international reserves.

Microeconomic payments are entered on the current account (CA) and on the capital and financial account (KFA) of countries' balances of payments; 'these accounts deal with all "*microeconomic*" flows defined between residents and non-residents' (ibid.: 17). *Macroeconomic payments, on the other hand, are entered on the international reserves account.*

> The reserve account provides the funds in foreign exchange needed by the domestic economy (in the two other accounts) when the sum of dollar-outflows exceeds the sum of dollar-inflows; inversely, when inflows exceed outflows, the "net gain" enlarges the pool of *private* reserves (the law permitting) or the stock of *official* reserves.
>
> (ibid.: 17)

While CA and KFA reflect the impact of the microeconomic payments carried out by countries' residents, the reserve account, RA, concerns the impact of the payments as they relate to countries themselves. What happens in the present non-system of international payments is that when A's indebted residents pay interest, their country gets involved in the transaction, and its transfer of domestic resources to R implies an equal decrease in its international reserves.

### *The pathological transformation of money into a real asset*

Whereas the microeconomic payment of interest-debt is in line with the circular flow of money, the macroeconomic payment is an excess expenditure implying a net outflow to the benefit of creditor countries. As soon as the payment of interest is taken over by the indebted country, it defines an outflow of foreign exchange that is not compensated by any inflow.

In reciprocal exchanges, monetary payments are neutral; money is used in an instantaneous circular flow conveying real, commercial and financial, goods between nations. The payment of interest is an exception: the unilateral transfer of real goods from country A to country R is conveyed through a unilateral flow of foreign currency, so that the money paid by A to R is transformed from a numerical means of payment into a real asset. 'The sum of foreign currencies flowing out of [A] for the interest payments are thrown into a state of dysfunction owing to the fact that they *usurp the status of real assets*' (Schmitt 2004a: 46).

The real payment of interest has a positive monetary cost; it forces country A to purchase the monetary vehicle that the present system of international payments is unable to provide free of cost. *In the payment of interest, therefore, money acts both as a means and as a real object of payment.*

If the monetary 'vehicle' conveying transnational payments were provided free of cost by a true and proper system of international payments, monetary flows between A and R would cancel out and the payment of interest would not be double. This is not the case today. The payment of interest implies a net outflow of foreign currency that entails an equal reduction in country A's foreign reserves. It follows that, being reserves-depleting, the payment of interest 'implies the use of foreign currencies as final goods; foreign currency compensating for the deficit created by the net outflow of foreign exchange is *never recovered*: its expenditure is final, definitive' (Schmitt 2008: 8, m.t.).

### *The payment of interest as unrequited transfer*

Interest is owed by any indebted country, A, on a contractual basis. Having benefited from a foreign loan in period $p_0$, A must transfer to R, from period $p_1$ onward, a part of the gain it derives investing the borrowed capital. Country R owns part of country A's current product from $p_1$ onwards. 'The value of A's current output is thus inclusive of the product added thanks to the use of a foreign capital in its domestic process of production' (Schmitt 2012c: 252). In contrast with the financial debt formed in $p_0$, which derives from a foreign loan, the debt of interest is *spontaneous*, and its payment calls for a unidirectional transfer of domestic product from country A to country R. The official term used by IMF experts is '*unrequited transfer*', which means that part of the indebted country's domestic output is given up without any counterpart in the debtor's country. When interest falls due, country R is the legitimate owner of an amount of country A's current output equivalent to what is required by the payment of interest. The transfer takes place through A's commercial exports, a part of which, therefore, remains unpaid by R. In other words, the part of A's commercial exports transferred to R as the real payment of interest stops country A financing any import from country R. Part of A's exports are thus '*unrequited* for the compelling reason that they finance the interest instead of equivalent imports' (Schmitt 2004a: 24).

Being financed by country A's exports, the payment of interest-debt reduces the amount of foreign exchange available to pay for country A's imports and is thus the source of a trade deficit. At term, interest defines a spontaneous debt that is nothing but 'a *trade* deficit. This is so because interest *payments* cut the sum of foreign currency available for imports' (Schmitt 2000b: 15). Trade deficits are part of a country's current account, which means that, contrary to what is commonly believed, interest-debt is not paid by a financial loan, entered on the capital and financial account (KFA), but by an unrequited export entered on the current account (CA). This should not come as a surprise, since, if interest were paid by the KFA, it would be paid by country R, whereas it is certain that it is by giving up part of its national output, and not part of R's national income, that country A pays its interest on debt.

One of the great merits of Schmitt's analysis is to have clearly pointed out that a country's interest-debt cannot be paid by its KFA, even though a foreign loan might be necessary to re-establish the balance between the country's monetary outflows and inflows. Having to resort to a new foreign loan or to a reduction in reserves is the consequence of the payment of interest and not of the way the payment is made. Since part of country A's national output is owned by country R's residents from the moment of its production, the payment of A's interest rests on country A's current account. '[T]he interest paid to the creditor country R brings to it [country R] the product corresponding to the contractual yield of its financial capital lent abroad' (Schmitt 2012c: 255).

The fact that the payment of interest is indeed entered on the current account of the balance of payments is therefore no mere convention; 'on the contrary it is a logical necessity [...] because the payment of interest in real terms is the transfer of a domestic product of the indebted countries and not the transfer of a product first borrowed from the creditor countries' (Schmitt 2006b: 23, m.t.). When interest-debt falls due, country A must transfer to R that part of its domestic output of which country R is already the legal owner, a transfer that takes place through country A's exports. Since country R obtains what it already owns through part of its imports, that part of A's exports is not paid by R. The circular flow of country A's exports-imports is thus reduced by the amount of interest. The payment of interest-debt curtails country A's importing capacity, determined by its exports as paid by country R.

> The real payment of interest, *out of the current account*, reduces the volume of imports by an equivalent amount. We can, therefore, safely conclude that the circular flow of exports and imports is indeed 'ruptured', the gap between exports and imports being equivalent to the interest payments.
>
> (Schmitt 2004a: 24)

The presence of this gap explains the peculiarity of interest payment, and, because the existing non-system of international payments does not take it into account, the total charge of interest-debt is doubled.

Let us analyze this pathological duplication further by following Schmitt in his assessment of what he calls the 'interest theorem'.

## The Interest Theorem

In 2005, Schmitt introduced the phrase *interest theorem* to refer to his discovery of the double charge of interest payment. He offered a price of 1 million US dollars to whomever could prove him wrong. Among the several proofs offered by Schmitt for his theorem, I have chosen those that best complement the ones so far introduced in this chapter.

### *Analytical proof of the interest theorem*

Let us work out the numerical example where A, the indebted country, pays an interest of $10 (in billion) to R, the creditor countries taken as one entity, and suppose that A's and R's imports are equal to $60 (also in billion). The crucial point of Schmitt's proof is that the payment of interest-debt is bound to take place through an *unrequited export* of country A. $10 worth of A's exports ($ex_{in}$) are obtained free of cost by country R in payment for country A's interest.

As we have pointed out in the previous section, country R owns part of country A's domestic output from the moment of its production and acquires it when A fulfils its contractual obligations and pays the interest on its external debt. 'In reality, R obtains $ex_{in}$, which it lawfully owns as the yield of its capital lent to [A], without spending a single penny' (Schmitt 2005: 9, m.t.). As a consequence of this *unrequited transfer*, now R will need to pay merely $50 for imports worth $60. The rest is paid by A. Country A is faced with paying $10 on top of its imports of $60 while having to cover, *additionally*, the difference between its exports, $60 in value, and R's payment of $50. In other words, the payment of interest has the dual effect of increasing country A's monetary outflows, from $50 to $60, *and* reducing country A's monetary inflows, from $60 to $50.

> The payment of interest in favour of R has the double effect of increasing A's expenditures and of reducing its receipts. It increases expenditures because the payment of interest is added to that of IM [A's total imports] and reduces receipts because it is country A itself that pays a part of its exports equal to the interest.
>
> (Schmitt 2010a: 17, m.t.)

The difference between country A's total outflows, $60, and its total inflows, $40, is equal to $20, that is, twice the amount of interest-debt, which confirms Schmitt's interest theorem.

A figure, first used by Schmitt in 2004 (2004a), illustrates the double charge of interest payment (see Figure 15.2).

Since country A pays interest on top of its imports and since country R finances part of its imports out of it, the two effects double the charge of A's interest payment. A further argument settles the question. The two effects are cumulative, because they do not pertain to the same numerical dimension: the reduction in country A's receipts is the reduction in a credit, whereas the increase in country A's expenditures is the increase in a debit. The former concerns the set of *positive numbers*, whereas the latter concerns the set of *negative numbers*, and it is logically impossible for '*one single flow* of value [10] to cover at

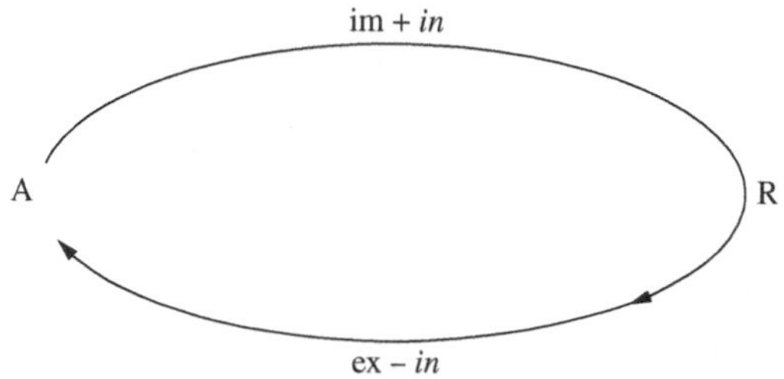


*Figure 15.2* Double effect of payment *in*. Source: Schmitt 2010a: 17

the same time the increase in expenditures [+ 10] and the reduction in receipts [– 10] of the same country' (Schmitt 2005: 13, m.t.).

Schmitt provides the following example to help the reader understand his argument better. Suppose two persons, A and R, face each other across a distance of 100 meters. A crosses the distance separating him from R, takes R on his shoulders, and walks back for 10 meters, then R walks the rest of the distance to reach A's point of departure. What are the distances covered on foot by A and R, respectively? The answer is simple: A walks a distance of 110 meters, while R walks for 90 meters. Thus, a gap 'of twice 10 meters is created by a single movement (or "flow") of 10 meters, namely R being carried on [A]'s back over this distance' (Schmitt 2007a: 11, m.t.). By analogy, the same thing happens when country A pays interest: it takes on a payment of country R equal to $10. As a result, country A's total expenditures amount to $110, while country R's expenditures are only equal to $90. 'As a consequence of the payment of 10 in net interest, [A] spends *20* more than R: it is the faithful transposition of the *interest theorem*' (ibid.: 11, m.t.).

In the numerical example we have analyzed so far, country A's and country R's trade balances are at equilibrium. This means that, in order to cover for the payment of interest = $10, country A must obtain a new foreign loan (a loan disbursement, LD, in the terminology of the World Bank) equal to $10. However, this amount alone cannot make up for the $10 country A needs to pay for the totality of its imports. Since country R pays only $50 for its imports from country A, the latter needs to find $10 to cover the gap between its total imports, $60, and its total exports as paid by R, $50. It is by cutting country A's international reserves that the gap is filled, which brings the total charge of interest-debt to the level of $20.

Now, it would be naïve to think that the double charge applies solely to this particular case, i.e. to the trade equilibrium of the indebted country. As can easily be seen, the mechanism of the payment of interest-debt is always the same, whether A's trade balance is in surplus, in deficit, or in equilibrium. *What changes is not the duplication of interest, but the way the double cost is financed.* Thus, if country A's total exports exceed by at least $20 its imports, the payment of interest-debt can take place without resorting to a new LD. Instead of paying interest by incurring a new debt of $10 and by decreasing its foreign reserves by $10, country A gives up the totality of its foreign gains of $20, which should increase its reserves. All conceivable combinations are possible without altering the conclusion: whatever the state of A's trade balance, the payment of interest-debt has a total cost that is twice the amount of interest.

### *Real and monetary payments of interest accumulate*

The following proof starts from the observation that '[*e*]*ach international payment is both a monetary and a financial flow*' (Schmitt 2004d: 8). To understand this, just bear in mind that money is a *means* of payment, a circular flow through which the object of the payment is conveyed from purchaser to seller. Hence, for example, if country R pays $10 to country A for its exports, at the very instant A is credited with $10 by R's banks, it is debited for $10 by the same banks. The nature of money is such that each payment defines a circular monetary flow from and to the banks of emission. What country A obtains in exchange for its commercial exports is not a sum of money, but a claim on an equal amount of country R's bank deposits. The vehicle of the payment is monetary, while its real object is financial. Whether A spends the $10 received from R to purchase foreign securities or deposits them with R's banks, country A spends the $10 it receives; it is credited-debited for $10, monetarily, and credited financially.

With a single exception, in each payment between nations we observe a strictly *circular* flow of money accompanied by a *one-way* flow of financial assets. Thus, in $p_0$, when country A's external debt is formed, A's trade deficit is financed by a sale of financial assets that flow from country A to country R. It is precisely because A exports financial assets in exchange for its net commercial imports that A is debited-credited in money. As a rule, all the payments referring to countries' exports and imports define a circular monetary flow: 'a country considered as a whole borrows abroad the foreign currency it needs for its imports and lends to the rest of the world the foreign currency earned by its exports' (ibid.: 11). Financial flows, on the other hand, are unidirectional and go from importing to exporting nations.

The only exception is the payment of interest on countries' external debts. This is so because '[*a*]*s a consequence of interest payments, country A is deprived of the* real *payment of equivalent exports*' (ibid.: 11). In order to pay interest-debt, A must export at least an equivalent part of its national output. Through its exports, country A obtains a claim on R's bank deposits of $10, which it gives up paying for interest-debt. This amounts to saying that when country A pays interest-debt it sacrifices the financial inflow to which it would have been entitled because of its exports to country R.

As Figure 15.3 shows, the payment of interest is financed by a commercial export of $10 value and is conveyed through the circular flow of $10 originating in R. Given that $10 out of the $100 country A earns through its commercial exports is spent to pay for interest-debt, A does not obtain any real or

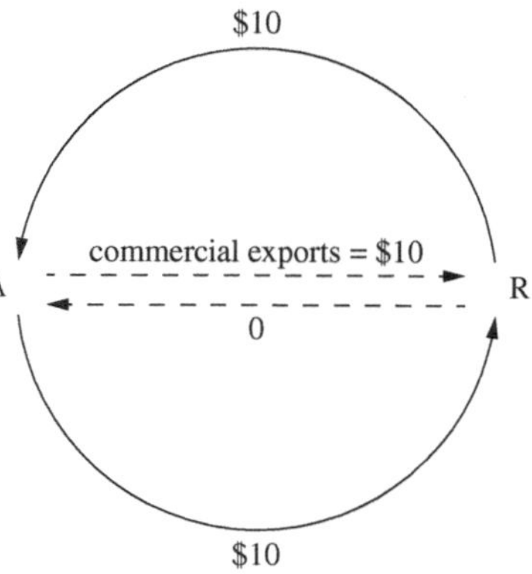


*Figure 15.3* Payment *in* as a unilateral transfer.

financial payment for this part of its commercial exports. To be precise, what country A obtains is the cancellation of its interest-debt, and a financial claim whose object is reduced to zero is a zero financial asset. '*In the present situation the real asset which is flowing into country A is nothing but the repurchase by A of its obligation to pay 10 dollars bill in interest to country R*' (ibid.: 12).

A first tranche of country A's exports, equal to $10, is in fact paid by country R, which allows A to pay interest financially. Yet, the payment of interest-debt allows R to obtain for free a second tranche of country A's exports, also equal to $10. Country R's second payment is only *nominal*. '[T]o the exact extent that they fulfil the international payment of interest, exports elicit a purely *nominal* payment from the importing countries, that is, a *real* payment (in financial claims) which is strictly nil' (ibid.: 17).

*Real and monetary payments of interest-debt*

Schmitt distinguishes between the real payment of interest-debt, denoted as *in*-products, and its monetary payment, denoted as *in*-foreign exchange. The former consists in the unrequited transfer of part of the indebted country's national product to the creditor countries. The latter is the monetary payment the indebted country must make to creditor countries. In the period interest falls due, A's exports and imports are equal to $60 (in billions) and the payment of *interest* is equal to $10 (also in billions). Comparing monetary flows, represented by continuous lines, and real flows, represented by dotted lines, Schmitt (2004a) shows that the payment of interest by country A is the source of two additional gaps.

Figure 15.4 shows the existence of a real gap, gap 1, in country A's real imports, which drop from $60 (in value terms) to $50. This is so because its expenditure of $60 enables country A to obtain only $50 in real imports, the difference being the unrequited export of A's products as real payment

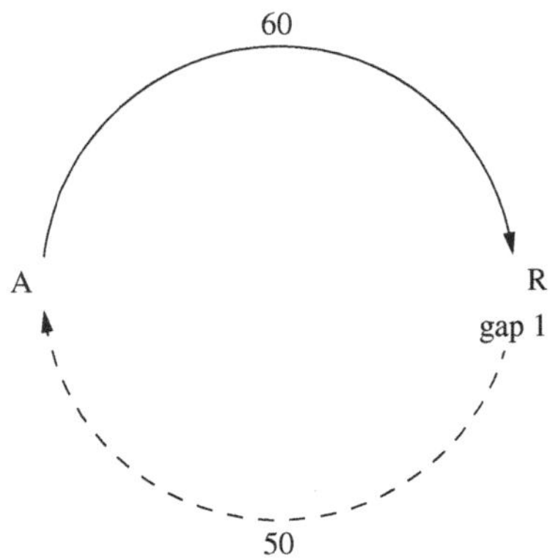


*Figure 15.4* Difference between country A's monetary outflows and its real inflows caused by payment *in*. Source: elaboration from Schmitt 2004a: 2

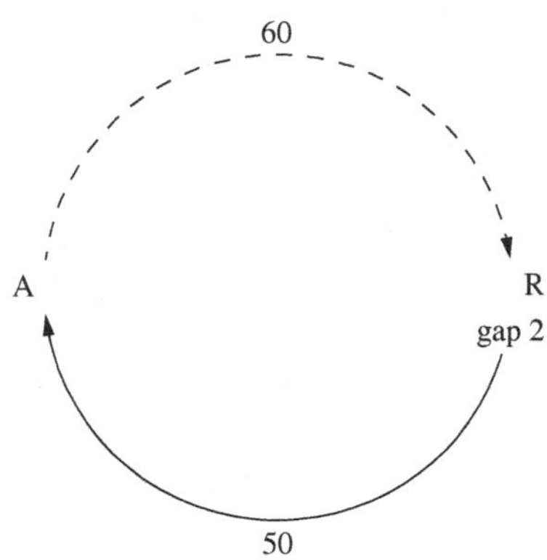


*Figure 15.5* Difference between country A's real outflows and its monetary inflows as determined by payment *in*. Source: elaboration from Schmitt 2004a: 3

of interest to country R. 'The interest payments are equal to [10] precisely because [A] only obtains [50] in imports for its total expenditure equal to 60. Gap 1 = [10] is the exact measure of the interest payments' (Schmitt 2004a: 2).

Gap 2 is a monetary one; it comes from the lack of payment by country R of a part of country A's real exports equal to $10. As Figure 15.5 shows, 'the rest of the world (that is the set of creditor countries) imports goods and services to the value of 60 at a cost of [50]; if the cost were equal to the value, the interest accruing to R would be null' (ibid.: 2).

Gap 1 is covered by a new loan allowing country A to bring back its real imports to the value of $60:

> when the trade account is at equilibrium, the debtor country is mechanically unable to settle the totality of its current bill, *including the interest due*

> *on its foreign debt*, unless it complements its export-receipts by net exports of *financial assets*.
>
> (ibid.: 7)

Yet, once country A's real imports are back at the level of $60 in value, its total expenditures increase from $60 to $70, $10 being the payment on *in*-foreign exchange. If A's monetary outflows were balanced by equal monetary inflows, the real cost of interest-debt would be the single charge country A has to face. However, this is not the case, because the conversion of *in*-foreign exchange by country R, that is, its purchase of part of country A's national output, is *included in the payment of R's imports*. 'The dollars spent by R on the conversion of [*in*-foreign exchange] are lost to [A] for the obvious reason that they are merged or fused into the payment of an equivalent measure of R's imports' (ibid.: 13). This means that country A must find $10 more to fill in gap 2, a requirement that leads to an equivalent decrease in A's international reserves and brings the total cost of interest-debt at a final level of $20, that is, interest times 2.

The real payment of interest, *in*-products, reduces country A's importing power from $60 to $50; it is gap 1. The monetary payment of interest, *in*-foreign exchange, is due to the need to balance country A's net foreign exchange outflows, gap 2. Finally, *in*-products and *in*-foreign exchange being 'two distinct and *separated* costs, their unavoidable addition establishes the *interest theorem*' (Schmitt 2007a: 20, m.t.).

### *Interest theorem and the identity EX≡IM*

Another proof of the interest theorem that Schmitt provides in the first decade of the new millennium is founded on the balance of payments identity between the totality of a country's exports, commercial and financial, EX, and the totality of its imports, commercial and financial, IM. The identity

$$\mathrm{EX} \equiv \mathrm{IM} \tag{15.1}$$

has a different meaning according to whether it refers to payments between residents and non-residents, or to payments between countries as the sets of residents. In the first case, the identity derives from the principle of double-entry and from the circular use of money as guaranteed by national banking systems. 'All payments between residents of the world, of the same country or of distinct countries, obey the rule of credits-debits; no one bank debits its client without crediting them at the same instant and in the same movement or flow' (Schmitt 2006a: 6, m.t.). This is not what happens in the second case where, in the absence of a supranational bank (central bank of central banks), credits and debits are separated: each country considered as a whole 'carries out imports and exports and never imports-exports or exports-imports; each country is credited and not "credited-debited" for its exports' (ibid.: 6, m.t.).

If a true system of international payments existed, payments between countries would imply the vehicular use of an international currency, imports would pay for exports, and the cost of interest-debt would correspond to the transfer of a domestic product, either present (in the case of a trade surplus) or future (through a sale of financial claims). The only cost of interest-debt would be *in*-products; the payment of *in*-foreign exchange would be cost-free because the system would provide free of charge the vehicular currency necessary to convey the real payment of interest.

In the present non-system, however, the 'magnificent logic of "algebraically null" payments does not apply to countries, as sets of their residents' (ibid.: 8, m.t.). It thus follows that the addition of interest to A's expenditures cannot simply be compensated by the additional monetary receipts deriving from a new loan disbursement, $LD_{in}$. The transition from EX = IM to

$$EX + LD_{in} = IM + in, \tag{15.2}$$

which would be guaranteed in a true system of international payments, is logically unacceptable in the present non-system, where the correct relation is

$$EX + LD_{in} < IM + in. \tag{15.3}$$

This is so because payments between countries are not carried out through debits-credits and credits-debits, so that creditor countries are not debited at all for the payment of the unrequited exports, $ex_{in}$, of debtor countries.

The non-payment by R of A's unrequited exports reduces the amount earned by country A through its global exports, a reduction that is compensated by $LD_{in}$, which cannot at the same time compensate the difference between IM + *in* and IM. Inequality (2) is best written as

$$EX - ex_{in} + LD_{in} < IM + in, \tag{15.4}$$

where it is made clear that the real payment of interest, *in*-products, reduces EX by the amount of $ex_{in}$. The difference between the two terms of inequality (3) is equal to interest and corresponds to the cost of the monetary payment of interest, *in*-foreign exchange, of which country A must also take charge. The two charges are separate and cumulative because one affects the formation of country A's monetary assets while the other affects the stock of monetary assets already formed. 'We thus observe a double allocation of interest:

- On the *formation* of LDCs' resources of dollars;
- On LDCs' resources actually *formed* in dollars' (Schmitt 2006b: 22, m.t.).

Fundamentally, it is because country A's inflow of foreign currency is reduced by the value of $ex_{in}$, and its outflow is increased by interest, that, as in Equation

(4), equality between A's total expenditures and its total receipts is re-established only through a new foreign loan, $LD_{in}$, *and* a reduction in reserves, $res_{in}$.

$$IM + in = EX - ex_{in} + LD_{in} + res_{in} \tag{15.5}$$

***Schmitt's last proof of the interest theorem***

Before turning our attention to the consequences of the pathological duplication of the payment of interest, let us mention the last proof of the interest theorem proposed by Schmitt; its simplicity should convince even the most sceptical reader. Let us start from the well-established fact that interest on a country's external debt is paid through its current account through an unrequited export $ex_{in}$. Another undisputed fact is that, starting from a trade balance, the indebted country, A, must borrow abroad the sum of foreign currency needed to cover the totality of its imports. $LD_{in}$ denotes the foreign loan required to pay for $im_{in}$, the part of A's imports that fails to be covered by its exports, because of $ex_{in}$. Then, the need for country A to draw on its reserves is the necessary consequence of another fact: once it has paid for its total imports, country A must still pay its interest-debt.

The interest theorem states that country A suffers both from an increase in debt *and* from a decrease in reserves. Is that correct? A simple thought experiment settles the question. If A's total inflows of foreign exchange compensate for its loss of reserves, the theorem is disproved and must be dismissed; if not, it is definitively established. Just compare country A's total outflows with its total inflows of foreign currency. The former are obviously equal to $IM + in$. Are the latter enough to offset the loss in reserves?

Reduced by $ex_{in}$, the inflows due to the payment of A's total exports by country R are nevertheless equal to X, because $LD_{in}$ compensates $ex_{in}$:

$$EX - ex_{in} + LD_{in} = EX. \tag{15.6}$$

But country A's total monetary inflows are also increased by the foreign currency provided by its reserves, which builds them up to the amount of

$$EX - ex_{in} + LD_{in} + res_{in} = EX + res_{in}. \tag{15.7}$$

It is immediately clear, then, that country A's total inflows are entirely used up to cover for its total outflows, $IM + in$. The conclusion is straightforward: 'the sum of inflows is merely equal to the sum of foreign currency outflows, official reserves do not recover [their] loss, which is added to the increase in A's external debt generated by the new loan obtained from R, $LD_{in}$' (Schmitt 2012c: 260).

## A generalization of the interest theorem and its consequences

At this point of the analysis, it is important to refer to a major conclusion reached by Schmitt in 2010, namely that the duplication of interest *always* entails a loss for the indebted country, *whether it concerns the payment of the country's net interest or not*. Apparently, if country A's payment of interest in favour of country R is matched by an equal payment of interest by R to A, country A's and country R's second payments should cancel out. Yet, Schmitt shows that this is not the case for the simple reason that both A's and R's second payments benefit the *international financial bubble*.

Formed through the duplication of the key currencies used to settled international transactions, the international financial bubble is a pathological, stateless capital, whose presence is the main cause of today's financial crises. By transforming key currencies into objects of exchange, the present non-system of international payments is at the origin of an international financial capital that is purely nominal, deprived of any real content. It is this stateless capital that is concerned with the second, pathological payment of countries' interest.

If country A's payment of interest to country R is equal to R's payment of interest to A, country A's and country R's first payments are reciprocal and compensate one another. However, country A 'would still be forced to carry out a second payment, which avoids compensation because it is not addressed to R, but to the financial bubble' (Schmitt 2010a: 17, m.t.). Schmitt is therefore able to conclude that 'gross interest on debt entails an additional payment, entirely unjustified, which reduces by an equal amount the indebted country's reserves' (ibid.: 18, m.t.).

The interest theorem can therefore be extended to any payment of interest between countries in the present non-system of international payments. In the absence of a mechanism that provides a vehicular means of payment between countries guaranteeing the equality of monetary outflows and inflows, the payment of interest turns into a net outflow of money. 'The payment of interest is an "outflow without inflow" of money; this time money affirms its presence and becomes a kind of "monster" as a pure instrument is transformed into a final good' (Schmitt 2006b: 11, m.t.).

### *The interest theorem and the 'mystery of the missing surplus'*

One of the implications of the double cost of interest payment worth mentioning is related to the so-called 'mystery of the missing surplus', so named by Krugman and Obstfeld (2003). The discrepancy between the world's current account deficits and surpluses had already been investigated by a team of experts gathered by the IMF in 1987. Contrary to what one should expect from the implementation of double-entry bookkeeping, *the current account of all countries taken together is not balanced at all*. 'In principle, the combined surpluses and the combined deficits arising from the current account transactions of all countries (including international organizations) should offset each other, because one country's credits are the debits of another' (IMF 1987: 2).

By definition, the deficit of some countries is necessarily equal to the surplus of other countries, so that, for the sum of all countries, current account deficits and surpluses should cancel out. Yet, this is not what happens. Statistical evidence shows that from 1979 to 2003 a large discrepancy between the world CA deficits and surpluses has seriously affected and hampered the development of international transactions.

Even though it contravenes the logic of double-entry, the huge amount of the 'missing surplus', which since 2004 has become an equally important 'missing deficit', is a matter of fact. If, according to logic, payments were entered simultaneously as credits and as debits, or as debits and credits, no discrepancy could appear. How can we explain logically what seems to defy logic?

Schmitt's interest theorem provides a satisfactory answer to the mystery of the missing surplus. Indeed, the double charge of interest payment weighs on the indebted countries' current accounts, which are debited twice for a payment that is entered only once on the creditor countries' current accounts.

> The payment of interest-debt respects the equality of debits and credits of the sum of current accounts. Yet, covering the deficit created by the flow of interest (*in*) forms a void of payment in the first term of the equivalence EX ≡ IM; reserves filling this "hole" [...] are a zero credit of the current accounts of the rest-of-the-world.
>
> (Schmitt 2007b: 15, m.t.)

As the experts of the IMF Working Party observe, the discrepancy affecting the CA of all the countries taken together can also be expressed by the fact that, 'corresponding to the current account excess of debits for the world as a whole, a large cumulative net credit balance for recorded capital flows has developed' (IMF 1987: 12). Since payments entered on the CA of a paying country give rise to an equivalent inflow into the KFA of paid countries, 'current and capital accounts should be mirror images' (ibid.: 12). In particular, the sum of the payments entered on the CA of indebted countries should be equal to the sum flowing into the KFA of creditor countries.

Considering the payment of interest, which is identified by Krugman and Obstfeld (2003: 322) as the likely cause of the missing surplus, it is clear that there would never be a discrepancy if interest were paid by country A's KFA, that is, if the following equation applied

$$EX + LD_{in} = IM + in. \tag{15.8}$$

In reality, statistical evidence shows that from 1979 to 2003 the sum IM + *interest* was largely greater than the sum $EX + LD_{in}$:

$$EX + LD_{in} < IM + in. \tag{15.9}$$

As experts well know, the fact is that interest is paid by country A's CA through a transfer of domestic output in favour of country R, and Schmitt's interest theorem shows that this transfer, which corresponds to an unrequited export, leaves part of country A's exports unpaid. The discrepancy observed by statisticians is therefore consistent with the imbalance on which Schmitt's analysis of interest-debt focuses. 'Studies carried out both by the experts of the IMF "Report" and by academics have brought to light an interesting correlation: the difference between ($IM + in$) and ($EX + LD_{in}$) is equal to *in*' (Schmitt 2006b: 2, m.t.).

What Schmitt's interest theorem shows is that the 'mystery' of the missing surplus is no mystery at all. Indeed, it would be so only if international payments were carried out according to the principle of double-entry. Only if every payment, interest included, is entered as the simultaneous debit-credit and credit-debit of each country, is a duplication avoided and the missing surplus explained. As things stand, in the absence of a true system of international payments, money cannot remain neutral; so a unilateral payment like that of interest requires the purchase of the monetary 'vehicle' to convey its real object or content. Instead of acting as a pure means of exchange, money is transformed into a positive asset, the purchase of which redoubles the charge of interest payment. What is considered a mystery by Krugman and Obstfeld, is but the effect of this state of affairs: the second payment of interest, *in*-foreign exchange, affects the debtor country's CA without being entered on any other country's account. What is lost by A is not gained by the rest-of-the-world, but accrues to the financial bubble, which is why this loss goes unrecorded and is missing from official statistical data.

It is clear that the payment of interest-debt cannot explain the missing *deficit* that since 2005 has characterized the World Current Account. However, the missing deficit is none other than the balance of payments transposition of the widely held belief that deficit countries do not pay their net imports. This corresponds to the claim, endorsed by the majority of economists and experts of international institutions, that deficit countries live beyond their means, and enjoy 'free lunches'. Trade deficits have increased so much since 2005 that the (hypothetical) fact that deficit countries do not pay their net imports more than offsets the double payment of interest they are subject to. This explains why, despite the persistence of the double charge of interest payments, the world current account is systematically running a substantial surplus. In Chapter 17 we will see how Schmitt deals with this problem and how he proves that, in reality, deficit countries have fully paid their net imports and that their external or sovereign debt is totally unjustified.

### *Schmitt's open challenge*

Let me conclude this chapter by quoting a passage from the open letter addressed by Schmitt to the President of Brazil, Lula da Silva in 2007.

Is it true or false that the real yield of the foreign capital invested in Brazil, domestic product $ex_{in}$, reaches the rest-of-the-world free of cost, through the feedback of the external payment of $ex_{in}$? [...]. I offer an award of 1 million US dollars, in my own name, but also in my capacity as co-director of the RMELab (Research Laboratory in Monetary Economics) of the Centre of Banking Studies, Lugano (Switzerland), to whoever first can prove that the feedback of payment $ex_{in}$ does not exist.

Then you will know, Mr President, whether the pathology I denounce is a reality or an intellectual conceit. If this enormous malfunctioning does not exist, it should be easy to show that the alleged feedback is purely imaginary and that Brazil is safe and unaffected by it; on the other hand, if no attempt is made to invalidate it, the scales will already have tipped in favour of the discovery. Finally, all you need is a team of serious economists, in the government administration or the central bank, to understand the exact functioning of double-entry bookkeeping – *a discipline that does not exist in the space of international payments* – for the feedback of the external payment of $ex_{in}$ to finally swing from suspicion to scientific certainty.

(Schmitt 2007b: 4–5, m.t.)

# 16 The final criticism of general equilibrium analysis

Schmitt's interest in general equilibrium analysis (GEA) never faded. As with the interest theorem, he tirelessly sought the clearest possible way to convey his analysis to the dubious reader. In the case of GEA, his rejection of the neoclassical attempt to determine relative prices through direct exchange rests on the proof that they remain undetermined regardless of the behaviour of purchasers and sellers. Even though he had already clearly established (what we may call) the 'theorem of impossibility' in several published and unpublished texts of the period 1987–2000 (see Chapter 13), Schmitt did not give up scrutinizing GEA until he published what he saw as the final critique of the neoclassical paradigm in 2012. Chapter 16 covers the main arguments presented in this text, and refers to a paper published in 2003, co-authored by Schmitt and Curzio De Gottardi (a former PhD student of Schmitt, research and teaching assistant in econometrics at the University of Fribourg), as well as to an unpublished manuscript distributed to Schmitt's students in Switzerland during the Spring semester 2000.

## The logical indeterminacy of relative and numerical prices in GEA

GEA rests on the concept of relative prices and on the belief that they can be determined by direct exchange. According to the neoclassical paradigm, equilibrium prices can be determined through the simultaneous solution of a system of equations. Yet, a critical investigation shows that the GEA system of equations that is supposed to determine relative prices is over-determined (see Chapter 13).

### *Again, on the logical indeterminacy of relative prices*

In the paper co-authored with De Gottardi, Schmitt continues his previous analysis and further refines his criticism of the neoclassical attempt to determine relative prices through direct exchange. The two authors invoke the widely accepted assumption that economic agents are price-takers. If this assumption is read to imply that exchange rates are imposed on the market,

DOI: 10.4324/9781351271325-22

and that economic agents are only free to adjust the quantities of goods they are prepared to exchange at the set price, it would contradict the principles of GEA. According to the neoclassical paradigm, equilibrium prices depend on the supply and demand freely exerted by economic agents and cannot be imposed on them. However, if the price-taking assumption is rejected altogether, the determination of relative equilibrium prices is hopelessly unsuccessful.

Is there a chance to maintain the price-taking assumption while attenuating its implications and ensuring a degree of freedom for the economic agents? Schmitt and De Gottardi analyze the result of the presence of an auctioneer and answer in the negative: correctly understood, the auctioneer's intervention does not reduce the number of independent equations and leaves relative prices undetermined.

Let us trace Schmitt's and De Gottardi's example and suppose that the auctioneer 'announces the price vector $p=(1,2)$' (Schmitt and De Gottardi 2003: 286), where $p$ defines the rate of exchange between good 1 and good 2. If this (relative) price vector were imposed on the agents, who own good 1 and good 2, respectively, they would play no role in the determination of either the equilibrium numerical price or the equilibrium rate of exchange of their goods. The only logical explanation compatible with the freedom of economic agents is that the price vector indicates a relationship between the two goods that each agent interprets to its advantage. Hence, the price vector $p=(1,2)$ must *not* be read as $p^*$, that is, as the equilibrium relative price between goods 1 and 2. What the auctioneer announces is a price vector that agent 1, owner of goods 1, interprets as $p=(1,2)$, whereas agent 2, owner of goods 2, interprets as $p=(2,1)$. In the words of Schmitt and De Gottardi,

> [w]e will say that this vector is compatible with the freedom of the agents if they *permute* $p^1$ and $p^2$. To permute means that agent 1 interprets the prices announced as $p^1=1$ and $p^2=2$, and agent 2 interprets the prices as $p^2=1$ and $p^1=2$.
>
> (ibid.: 286, my emphasis)

It is immediately clear that, even in the case where prices are suggested by the auctioneer, the adjustment between supply of and demand for each good are distinct. The two agents enter a process of groping around the price vector $p=(1,2)$ that may or may not lead to an agreement as to the quantities supplied and demanded of good 1. If no agreement is reached, another price vector must be proposed and so on, until the equilibrium price is reached. The same happens for good 2, the only substantial difference being that this time the price vector as interpreted by agent 2 is $p=(2,1)$. Hence, an exchange between good 1 and good 2 can take place only if

1) An agreement is reached on the equilibrium numerical price allowing for the supply of good 1 to be equal to the demand for good 1;

2) The two agents agree on the equilibrium numerical price for which supply of good 2 = demand for good 2;
3) The two equilibrium prices are equal.

The system of equations introduced by the advocates of GEA must satisfy these three conditions; this means that three independent equations are supposed to determine the relative price of good 1 in terms of good 2 or of good 2 in terms of good 1. Three independent equations for the determination of a single variable are two equations too many, which leads us once more to conclude that in GEA, relative prices are undetermined.

The proof put forward by Schmitt and De Gottardi is based on the necessary condition that the excess demand function of each good is equal to zero at equilibrium. If the price vector the auctioneer proposes to our two agents is $p$ (1,2), agent 1 expects to be able to exchange one unit of good 1 for two units of good 2: $r_1 = ½$, where $r_1$ stands for the exchange rate as interpreted by agent 1. On the other hand, agent 2 *permutes* the price vector, which he interprets as $p$ ($p^1 = 2$, $p^2 = 1$), and considers it as a proposed exchange rate of two units of good 1 for one unit of good 2: $r_2 = 2/1$. The two exchange rates being distinct and different, the excess demand function for good 1, $z^1 (r_1, r_2)$ and the excess demand function for good 2, $z^2 (r_1, r_2)$ are independent.

> As we have done above, we write down the excess demands for the commodities as a function of the exchange rates $r_1$ and $r_2$. [...] The market clears if $z^1 (r_1, r_2) = 0$ and if $z^2 (r_1, r_2) = 0$. These two equations are independent because $r_1 \neq r_2$. Therefore, it is not true that if $z^1 (r_1, r_2) = 0$ ($z^2 (r_1, r_2) = 0$) then $z^2 (r_1, r_2) = 0$ ($z^1 (r_1, r_2) = 0$). The equations are not consistent.
>
> (ibid.: 286)

The necessary condition for markets to clear is that excess demands be equal to zero. In a two-goods two-agents market, good 1 and good 2 clear if their excess demand functions, $z^1$ and $z^2$, are equal to zero. Since relative prices are not imposed on the market, the different interpretation of each agent of the price vector announced by the auctioneer corresponds to a difference in the exchange rates initially chosen by the two agents: $r_1 \neq r_2$. Two independent equations are therefore needed to represent the two excess demand functions and the necessity for each of them to be equal to zero. However,

> $z^1 (r_1, r_2) = 0$ and $z^2 (r_1, r_2) = 0$ are not a sufficient condition for the realization of exchange. In fact, $z^1 (r_1, r_2) = 0$ and $z^2 (r_1, r_2) = 0$ do not imply that the value of the effective demand (supply) of agent 1 is equal to the value of the effective supply (demand) of agent 2.
>
> (ibid.: 285)

Once more, given $r_1 \neq r_2$ the value of effective demands for agents 1 and 2 have to be equalized. The need for this equalization calls for a third independent equation and makes the system devised by Walras and his followers over-determined.

### *From relative to numerical prices: the role of the numéraire*

In GEA, the switch from relative to numerical prices is ensured by the introduction of Walras's *numéraire*. Essentially, GEA is a mathematical construct designed to explain the existence and determination of numerical prices through relative prices. 'The problem of the determination of relative prices pertains to explaining how numerical equilibrium prices can be established through direct exchange' (Schmitt 2012a: 19).

In his 2012 paper, Schmitt analyzes this problem by presenting the simplified case of exchange between two different goods, pens and razor-blades. His starting point is the fact that if the ultimate goal of GEA is to determine *numerical* prices, the number of independent equations entering the system is equal to three, namely the equation equalizing the supply of and demand for razor-blades; the one equalizing the supply of and demand for pens, and the one equalizing the numerical prices determined by the first two equations.

Supply of razor-blades = Demand for razor-blades (16.1)
Supply of pens = Demand for pens (16.2)
Numerical price of pens = numerical price of razor-blades (16.3)

> The search for a precise number that would be the agreed price of pens and razor-blades to be exchanged between the parties is an equation in its own right, an *additional* determination, leading to a total of three distinct and totally independent equations.
>
> (ibid.: 20)

If this were the end of the story, we would have to conclude that, its system of equations being determined twice over, GEA is logically incapable of accounting for the determination of (relative) prices.

In order for prices to be mathematical magnitudes, they must be *numbers*, and the *numéraire* is apparently up to the task of transforming physical goods into numbers and, by the same token, relative prices into numerical prices. As the word chosen by Walras clearly indicates, the *numéraire* is not an additional good, but a number arbitrarily assigned to one of the goods exchanged in the products market. 'In its most rigorous definition, the *numéraire* is a *price*, a number attached to one physical unit of the commodity chosen to be used as a measuring rod' (ibid.: 22). Either a pen, or a razor-blade can be chosen as the good the price of which is set at a number chosen arbitrarily from the set of positive numbers. What needs investigating is the possibility for reducing the number of independent equations supposed to determine relative prices by attaching a pure number to a physical good.

If the number used as a price unit is external to goods, the determination of the price of pens or razor-blades is beyond our reach, the number of independent equations exceeding that of the unknown variables, namely, the relative price of razor-blades and pens. Do things change radically when the numerical price, say 1, is attached to one of the two goods confronting each other on the market? Schmitt's answer to this question is a clear no: the number of independent equations in not affected by the introduction of the *numéraire*.

> As a function of the numerical price, even when the price units are indissolubly linked to a commodity, the equalization of the supply of and demand for razor-blades is one thing while the equalization of the supply of and demand for pens is quite another thing, distinct and separate, neither equation being solved by the solution of the other.
>
> (ibid.: 23)

Let us pin the number 1 to one pen, the *numéraire* will then be the numerical price of one pen, a pure number and *not* a number of pens. Let us also suppose that economic agents agree to exchange six razor-blades at a price of 3. Can we infer from this that they must agree to exchange three pens at a price of 3? Schmitt claims that, if so, neoclassical authors mistakenly identify numbers with physical goods, 'the pure number 3, and the three pens taken in themselves, as if pens were numbers' (ibid.: 23). While it is possible to maintain that the supply of and demand for razor-blades equalizes when the equilibrium price of six razor-blades is equal to 3, there is no way of working out the equilibrium price of pens. The exchange of six razor-blades at a price of 3 is no guide to the exchange between razor-blades and pens. It is only if we misunderstood Walras's concept of *numéraire*, if we identified it, erroneously, with a physical good, that we could believe otherwise.

Since it must be conceived as a pure number, the *numéraire* can be neither an object of exchange nor an intermediary between pens and razor-blades. In GEA analysis, prices are pure numbers, and pure numbers are logically distinct from physical goods; even when a number is pinned on a physical good, the physical good is not transformed into a number or the number transformed into a commodity. To say that 1 is the numerical price of a pen does not mean that one pen is the number 1. Likewise, it would be absurd to maintain that, since 3 is the numerical price of six razor-blades, one razor-blade must be identical to the number 0.5, or that three pens are identical to the pure number 3. 'Three pens and the number 3 are two distinct "objects" that no operation of the mind, even when grandly adorned in mathematical garb, can fuse together' (ibid.: 23–4).

Since the determination of the equilibrium price of razor-blades leaves the equilibrium price of pens undetermined, three independent equations are needed even when a numerical price is attached to one of the two goods. The ensuing over-determinacy of the system confirms the 'impossibility theorem': relative prices cannot be determined through direct exchange even in the presence of the *numéraire*. Walras's *numéraire* appears for what it really is: a mathematical device without economic implications.

By arbitrarily setting the numerical price of a pen equal to 1 we do not transform pens into numbers, and we do not reduce the number of equilibrium prices that have to be determined by GEA. The determination of prices is first and foremost an economic problem that calls for an economic solution. By over-simplifying it conceptually and formalizing it mathematically, neoclassical economists give up an opportunity to understand the real world and so downgrade economics to an artificial construct where the determination of prices is reduced to a mathematical exercise alien to economic reality.

### *The indeterminacy of neoclassical numerical prices*

Can equilibrium-relative prices be determined through a groping process whereby supply and demand adjust following the variation of numerical prices proposed by an auctioneer? We have already seen that, if the auctioneer proposes a *relative* price vector to the market, equilibrium cannot be determined. What we are wondering, therefore, is whether this negative result may be avoided by switching from proposing rates of exchange to proposing numerical prices.

Since the purpose of GEA is to determine numerical prices *via* the determination of relative prices, it seems legitimate to invert the order of causality, all the more so, as both numerical and relative prices are assumed to be the joint result of the simultaneous solution of one and the same system of equations. Let us suppose, therefore, that an auctioneer announces a *numerical* price vector $p=(1,2)$ to the owners of razor-blades and pens, respectively. If the two economic agents do not agree to exchange their goods for this price vector, an adjustment must take place between the prices of razor-blades and pens.

As Schmitt observes, in this phase, two distinct numerical prices face each other, one for each unit of pens and the other for each unit of razor-blades. 'Throughout the market session, when agents are groping towards an equilibrium, they are apprised (by an auctioneer) of two distinct numerical prices per physical units of each commodity' (ibid.: 27). The system of equations imagined by GEA must then be able to determine:

1) $p_1$, the equilibrium price of pens, that is, the price at which the supply of pens is equal to the demand for pens;
2) $p_2$, the equilibrium price for razor-blades, that is, the price equalizing the supply of and demand for razor-blades; and
3) the equilibrium price of $p_1^*$ and $p_2^*$, that is, the price for which $p_1$ is equal to $p_2$.

To illustrate this point, let us refer to the example proposed by Schmitt and suppose that the owners of pens and razor-blades agree to give up and acquire the same number of pens, namely 3 pens, when the price for one pen is equal to the number 1: $p_1=1$. In other words, we assume that

$$\text{Supply of pens} = \text{Demand for pens} = 3 \text{ pens, for } p_1 = 1 \qquad (16.4)$$

Once this exchange has been agreed, we still do not know whether our two agents will reach an agreement on the price at which their supply of and demand for razor-blades equalizes. Let us suppose they do, their supply of and demand for razor-blades being equal to two razor-blades when the numerical price for one razor-blade is 2.5.

$$\text{Supply of razor-blades} = \text{Demand for razor-blades} = 2 \text{ razor-blades, for } p_2 = 2.5 \quad (16.5)$$

It is immediately clear that the two equations, (16.4) and (16.5), are incapable of determining the relative terms of the exchange that is supposed to define the equilibrium relative price for pens and razor-blades. To this end, a third equation is needed, equalizing (16.4) and (16.5), which makes the system helplessly over-determined. 'So long as the two total prices remain different numbers, no solution is obtained and, what is more, no solution is even possible' (ibid.: 27).

### *Final remarks*

Let us add here a few final remarks concerning the neoclassical failure to determine numerical prices, even in the case where the price of one good is exogenously set by the auctioneer. With Schmitt, we have already observed that Walras's greatest contribution to economic analysis is the acknowledgement that prices are numerical. However, this claim seems at odds with the neoclassical belief that prices are relative, that they are relations between goods and not between goods and numbers.

Can the patent contradiction be avoided by choosing arbitrarily one good as commodity-*numéraire* and assuming that its price is a number, say the number 1? If this attempt succeeded, and relative prices could indeed be determined through direct exchange, we would have to admit that – tough clashing with the reality of monetary economies – neoclassical theory is formally unassailable. In fact, 'the definition of the commodity-*numéraire* and of its price being known, the other goods would find a relation with a number in any exchange, even simply planned, implying the commodity-*numéraire* as one of its terms' (Schmitt 2000c: 30, m.t.).

From a logical viewpoint there is nothing wrong with the choice of a commodity-*numéraire* and with pinning a purely numerical price on it. Any good can be chosen as reference 'for all the others, and it is not at all illogical to ascribe a numerical price to the chosen good' (ibid.: 31, m.t.). It is therefore correct to claim that '*the price of one good is perfectly determined in the neoclassical theory*' (ibid.: 31, m.t.).

The problem arises when we go from the determination of the numerical price of a good, arbitrarily chosen as *numéraire*, to that of the prices of the other goods in terms of the *numéraire*.

> What is the price of an orange given that the price of an apple is the number 1? This time the question cannot be solved through a convention. It

is necessary to activate a process of determination that complies with a law or a rule.

(ibid.: 32, m.t.)

Unfortunately for the advocates of GEA, the price of the orange cannot be determined through the relative exchange of apples and oranges. This is so because 'the exchange between the commodity-*numéraire* and any other good cannot be "formalized", either in mathematics or in pure logic' (ibid.: 32, m.t.).

As Schmitt notes, an exchange defines the equivalence of its two terms, which implies that both goods must be part 'of the same measure space' (ibid.: 32, m.t.), they must be commensurable to compare and adjust the supply of one to the demand for the other. Distinct and heterogeneous goods cannot be compared, nor can their supply and demand. Hence, the relative price of oranges and apples can be determined only if both goods are first transformed into numbers.

The decision to attach the pure number 1 to one orange does not tell us anything about the numerical price of apples, which is why the choice of a *numéraire* is not enough to make it possible to compare the two goods, which remain completely heterogeneous. GEA fails, because relative exchange is unable to transform physical goods into numbers and to compare them to one another in order to equalize their supplies and demands. This twofold result cannot be obtained through the single operation of relative exchange; and determination is possible only if the goods exchanged have already been introduced into the 'space of numbers'.

## The neoclassical theory of relative prices determination is marred by a mathematical error

The last proof provided by Schmitt of the indeterminacy of neoclassical prices goes deep into the concept of relative prices and its implication for the mathematical system adopted by GEA. Its basic idea was already there in the paper he co-authored with De Gottardi in 2003: relative prices are such that, in a two-goods economy, the variation of the price of one good necessarily entails the opposite variation in the price of the other good.

If we start from a numerical price vector $p = (1, 1)$, a situation in which one unit of good 1 would be exchanged with 1 unit of good 2, and if we suppose that the numerical price of one unit of good 2 is multiplied by 2 in the phase of groping, we must acknowledge that the numerical price of a unit of good 1 is at the same time divided by 2 and vice versa. The new rate of exchange between the two goods is now two units of good 1 for one unit of good 2, that is, 'the new "physical" price of 1 unit of commodity 2 is 2 units of commodity 1' (Schmitt and De Gottardi 2003: 278). This can also be expressed as follows: the new physical or relative price of one unit of good 1 is 0.5 units of good 2. In the authors' own words, 'if the "physical" price of 1 unit of commodity

2 *changes*, the "physical" price of 1 unit of commodity 1 *also changes*. The two changes have to be inversely proportional' (ibid.: 278).

### *The neoclassical attempt to determine relative prices mathematically*

The variation in numerical prices has an immediate effect on relative or 'physical' prices, but Schmitt's critique can be better understood if we concentrate our attention on numerical prices and their variations. Let us therefore follow his analysis as developed in his 2012 paper. The example is again that of a two-goods two-agents economy, and the problem is to determine the numerical equilibrium price of pens and razor-blades.

Neoclassical authors rely on mathematics to reach their result. In particular, they believe that the equilibrium price can be determined through a process of groping: the equalization of the supply of and demand for razor-blades (pens) is obtained by letting the numerical price of razor-blades (pens) suggested by the auctioneer vary. As Schmitt observes, in this process of *tâtonnement* 'the mathematician is allowed to scan the whole set of real numbers, to the exclusion of negative numbers, negative prices being devoid of meaning' (Schmitt 2012a: 28). Yet, mathematics is at the service of neoclassical economics, which claims that prices are relative, so that, in a two-goods example, one price is necessarily the inverse of the other. Our mathematician 'feels compelled to reduce the two price-series [for pens and for razor-blades] to a singular one' (ibid.: 28).

The close relationship between the two price-series derives directly from the neoclassical definition of prices. If the two price-series were *independent* of one another, relative prices would be over-determined, and analysis would have to move from the relative definition of prices to their absolute definition, from relative to absolute prices. Therefore, neoclassical authors ask our mathematician to work out a mechanism capable of determining equilibrium prices through the variation of one price-series only. Consistently with GEA, our mathematician must assume that if the price of razor-blades (pens) varies, the price of pens (razor-blades) also varies (inversely): if the price of razor-blades as expressed in terms of pens is multiplied by 2, the price of pens as expressed 'in terms of razor-blades is *ipso facto divided by 2*' (ibid.: 28–9).

Schmitt repeatedly stresses the fact that 'neoclassical economists have no choice but to establish a *link* between the price variations of the two commodities' (ibid.: 29) if they are to avoid the over-determination of relative prices. This link is no other than 'the correspondence between a multiplication and a division' (ibid.: 29). The reduction of the two equations determining the equality between the supply of and demand for razor-blades and between the supply of and demand for pens to a single independent equation is possible only if the price-series of razor-blades and the price-series of pens are the mirror image of each other.

> If we are inclined to grant, at least at the beginning of the analysis, a positive lease of life to the concept of relative prices, we must assume, as a *sine*

> *qua non* condition, that the two series of price variations are so intimately linked together as to be fused into a *single series* of price variations.
>
> (ibid.: 30)

The intervention of the *numéraire* in GEA seems to avoid the illogical assumption that razor-blades are *measured* in pens and pens in razor-blades. The two goods are distinct and heterogeneous objects, and the claim that the measure of the supply of and demand for razor-blades (pens) is a number of pens (razor-blades) is meaningless. However, if the two physical goods are represented by pure numbers, it becomes possible to express one in terms of the other 'or, more accurately, in terms of the "*numéraire*" (a pure number)' (ibid.: 31) pinned on it.

As explicitly claimed by the advocates of GEA, choosing a physical good and making its unit equal to the number 1 is arbitrary. Nothing changes substantially whether razor-blades or pens are chosen as '*numéraire*-commodity', and nothing prevents us from choosing both. 'What is more, there is no need to choose between the two commodities in this respect, for nothing formally prevents them from being, *each, simultaneously*, the one and the other at the same time, a full-fledged "*numéraire*-commodity"' (ibid.: 31). It is therefore possible to represent the process of groping as the adjustment between the variations in the price of pens and in the price of razor-blades where 'the initial price of razor-blades [is] the number 1 attached to one pen and the initial price of pens [is] the number 1 attached to one razor-blade' (ibid.: 31).

Founding his argument on the established fact that within GEA the price-series of razor-blades and that of pens are closely linked together, Schmitt claims that, because of the *inverse* relationship between the two price-series, a variation in the price of razor-blades entails an inverse variation in the price of pens, the consequence of which is that '*an entire range of prices goes missing*. These prices are simply *lost*, irretrievably so' (ibid.: 35, my emphasis). Obviously enough, this does not mean that numbers representing these prices vanish, but that they are no longer available in the process of relative prices determination. The problem is not the existence of numbers, but the existence of prices in the price-series mathematically available to neoclassical economists.

### *A mathematical contradiction affects the neoclassical system of relative prices determination*

Schmitt provides two illustrations of what he calls the *mathematical contradiction* implied in the neoclassical attempt at determining relative prices through a variation in numerical prices defined in terms of a *numéraire*. Let us clarify at once that the mathematical contradiction that Schmitt denounces is not a contradiction in mathematics itself but in its implementation in the field of economics as envisaged by GEA. It is the logic of the neoclassical system of relative prices that manifests itself as mathematical nonsense.

The first illustration rests on the fact that, when the *numéraire* is attached to one razor-blade, one price in two goes missing any time that the price of one of the two goods varies.

'One in two prices is systematically missing in the series of the prices of razor-blades in terms of pens.

One in two prices is systematically missing in the series of the prices of pens in terms of razor-blades' (ibid.: 31).

Let us suppose that the price of razor-blades is multiplied by 2. The price variation of razor-blades being fused with the price variation of pens, the multiplication by 2 of the price of razor-blades is immediately accompanied by the division by 2 of the price of pens. As a consequence, we move instantly from the price of 2 in one price-series to the price of 1/2 in the other price-series: the price of 2 goes missing in the price-series of pens in terms of razor-blades.

> As a conspicuous result, *the price of 2 for one pen is missing*, overstepped as it is by the analysis, which goes straight from the relative price of 1 to 1 [the starting point of the process of groping] to the relative price of 2 to ½.
>
> (ibid.: 31)

The same reasoning applies to the price of razor-blades when it is the price of one pen that varies. If the numerical price of a pen passes from 1 to 1/2, the price of a razor-blade drops from 1 to 2, so that the price of 1/2 for one razor-blade goes missing. Generalizing, it appears that

> [i]f we multiply by any number $x$ the initial price of razor-blades in terms of pens, then we miss out on one price in two of pens in terms of razor-blades. If we multiply by any number $y$ the initial price of pens in terms of razor-blades, then we miss out on one price in two of razor-blades in terms of pens.
>
> (ibid.: 32)

Schmitt's second demonstration is based on an alternative method of showing that the search for the relative equilibrium price of razor-blades and pens cuts off a whole series of prices whose existence is incompatible with the axioms of GEA. This method consists in considering all the prices included in the interval between the initial price of razor-blades in terms of pens and this same price multiplied by 2 (or by any number $x$) rather than considering one by one all the prices that are missing in the two series of prices. 'Instead of counting, one by one, the prices that are *in* versus the prices that are *out*' (ibid.: 32), we refer to the effect that a variation in the price of razor-blades in terms of pens has on an interval of the prices of pens in terms of razor-blades. Schmitt illustrates his argument by imagining two parallel lines, 1 and 2, 'meant to carry the price variations of razor-blades in terms of pens and of pens in terms of razor-blades' (ibid.: 32), respectively. On line 1 the reference point is the one for which the price of one razor-blade is equal to the number 1 attached to one pen. On line

2, the central point is the price of one pen expressed in terms of the number 1 attached to one razor-blade.

The need to measure razor-blades using a pen as a *numéraire* and to measure pens using a razor-blade as a *numéraire* derives from the nature of relative prices and from *the logical impossibility to measure pens in a number attached to a pen.* In the theoretical framework of GEA '[a] given commodity cannot be a price unto itself' (ibid.: 32). Hence, the numerical price of 1 for one razor-blade is the central point of line 1, while the central point of line 2 is the numerical price of one pen as expressed by the number 1 attached to one razor-blade. This implies that 'the number 1 attached to one pen is a mathematically possible price for razor-blades [...and that] the number 1 attached to one razor-blade is a mathematically possible price for pens' (ibid.: 33).

When the process of adjustment that is supposed to determine the equilibrium prices of razor-blades and pens starts, prices are made to vary either on line 1 or on line 2, indifferently, the only important consideration being that 'eventually *all* price variations must be taken into account' (ibid.: 33). Let us start from line 1 and suppose that the price of razor-blades in terms of pens is multiplied by 2. When the price of one razor-blade jumps from 1 to 2, all the prices within this interval are excluded, 'they are subject to what we may refer to as the "principle of exclusion"' (ibid.: 32). Since the theory of relative exchanges maintains that any variation in the price of razor-blades in terms of pens defines the inverse variation of the price of pens in terms of razor-blades, the multiplication by 2 on line 1 is accompanied by a simultaneous division by 2 on line 2. At the same time that the price of a razor-blade jumps from 1 to 2, the price of a pen jumps from 1 to 1/2; as a consequence, all the prices within the interval 1/2–1 are also subject to Schmitt's principle of exclusion: they 'are wiped off the map' (ibid.: 35).

As Schmitt puts it:

> [w]henever, starting from the "central point" or reverting to it, we multiply the price of razor-blades by any number $x$, the corresponding price of pens is divided by $x$, so that all those prices of pens in razor-blades that lie between the closed interval from 1 to $1/x$ are *still-born.*
>
> (ibid.: 32)

What is crucial here is to understand that we must reason 'along line 1 and line 2 simultaneously' (ibid.: 35) because the two series of price variations are fused together 'into a *single series* of price variations' (ibid.: 30). When, in a process of adjustment mediated by the auctioneer, the suggested price of one razor-blade varies from 1 to 2 in the *numéraire* attached to one pen, in line 2 the price of one pen moves simultaneously, in a single 'jump' from 1 to 1/2 in the *numéraire* attached to one razor-blade. 'It immediately follows, in elementary logic, that an entire range of prices goes missing. These prices are simply *lost,* irretrievably so' (ibid.: 35). If, instead of suggesting a new numerical price for razor-blades, the auctioneer suggests a new price for pens, the range of prices that are literally non-existent in the system of relative exchanges is situated on line 1 and concerns razor-blades. Thus, for example, if the price of one pen drops from 1 to 1/2, the prices that are lost are those of razor-blades comprised between 1 and 2.

Neoclassical authors rely on mathematics for the determination of relative prices, and mathematics could indeed provide a solution if

> all possible price variations, in the set of real numbers [were] available for study, as reference points for the simultaneous determinations of the equality between the supply of and the demand for razor-blades and the equality of the demand for and the supply of pens.
>
> (ibid.: 33)

As Schmitt shows, however, a 'mathematical hole' appears both on line 1 and on line 2, because one price in two is lost and therefore inexistent in each of the two series of prices of razor-blades in terms of pens and of pens in terms of razor-blades.

Mathematics is powerless here, the 'hole' being generated by the assumption of GEA that relative prices derive from the direct exchange between physical goods.

> Prices that are mathematically prevented from being born cannot be a researched topic in mathematics. If a positively existing variable or magnitude is an unknown in a given interval, a mathematical method may be able to extrapolate its numerical value at each point included therein. But a variable that is altogether inexistent in a given interval is not amenable to any form of calculation.
>
> (ibid.: 36)

## Prices and money

As economists know well, price determination is the crucial problem of macroeconomics. Prices are necessary to express the economic value of goods, to account for their distribution, to explain the formation of profit, and to define both inflation and unemployment when considered in terms of global demand and global supply. 'The fundamental problem of macroeconomics is the determination of the price of commodities' (Schmitt 2000c: 1, m.t.). Determination of prices is the building block of the entire GEA theory. According to neoclassical authors, prices are relations between goods, their relative exchange being the transaction that ensures their determination. On the other hand, the same authors cannot deny that prices are essentially monetary. Therefore, a question arises spontaneously: how can relative prices be transformed into monetary prices?

### *Relative prices versus monetary prices*

Economists embracing GEA claim that relative prices are determined through direct exchange and that they can be expressed numerically by using one of the goods exchanged on the market as *numéraire*-commodity with the number 1 attached to one goods unit. Properly defined, the *numéraire* is a pure number and not a physical good. As Schmitt observes, this implies that if we told a neoclassical economist that 'money is made of pure units of account, none of which is a good, while every one of them is a pure number, he will not even dream of confuting the claim that [...] all the prices are expressed in money units' (ibid.: 4, m.t.). If the authors advocating GEA do not identify numerical prices with monetary prices, it is only because they identify money with a real good rather than the *numéraire*. From the moment money is considered a net asset, its exchange with produced goods and services can only be object of relative exchanges.

Schmitt notes that the neoclassical doctrine rests on three 'concentric' notions, namely,

- 'Every exchange occurs between distinct agents;
- Every exchange occurs between distinct goods or assets;
- Every exchange is an action-reaction, a good being given up "against" another good' (ibid.: 5, m.t.).

The third concept prevents the correct understanding of money and leads neoclassical economists to assume the existence of a dichotomy between real and monetary magnitudes and to introduce unrealistic and restrictive axioms such as the homogeneity postulate.

### *The role of sales and purchases in the determination of relative prices*

Let us follow Schmitt and set down the two necessary conditions for the determination of prices when two individuals, a purchaser (I) and a seller (II) face each other.

(i) I (II) can be a purchaser only if II (I) is a seller in the same operation and for the same good.
(ii) I (II) can be a purchaser only if I (II) is a seller in the same operation and for the same good.

(ibid.: 2, m.t.)

Condition (i) is fulfilled by GEA; it merely states that, in the presence of two agents, the purchase of one of them is necessarily the sale of the other. The simultaneity of sales and purchases is verified, but it refers to two distinct individuals exchanging two distinct goods. Thus conceived, the necessary equality between sales and purchases is nothing more than a truism: any time that, in a two-agents economy, one agent purchases, the other agent sells.

Walras's law rests on this tautology and provides no information concerning the phase of the search for equilibrium, when supplies and demands are supposed to adjust to one another. Walras tells us that when an exchange actually takes place, the purchaser is debited and the seller is credited, but this is a platitude that tells us nothing about the adjustment of the values attached to supply and demand, which should determine relative prices. This is why relative prices suffer from a logical indeterminacy, the number of independent equations being hopelessly greater than the number of variables. 'The most profound reason why the equilibrium of relative exchanges cannot be reached is that the equivalence of one person's credit and his partner's debit affords no information at all because it is a truism, a tautology' (ibid.: 17, m.t.).

Moreover, as Schmitt observes, the identity between agent I's purchases and agent II's sales does not account for the fact that 'every agent must be a seller before being a purchaser, otherwise he would not have the purchasing power needed to make the available purchase' (ibid.: 6, m.t.). GEA cannot explain how 'all the residents of a given country [can be] sellers without being purchasers' (ibid.: 6, m.t.) while maintaining that money is a real good or an asset. The very concept of relative exchange requires the simultaneous presence of sellers and purchasers, which is why the two conditions, (i) and (ii), cannot be fulfilled simultaneously by GEA. This also explains why money is identified with an asset whereas the *numéraire* is correctly conceived as a pure number.

If condition (i) and condition (ii) are simultaneously satisfied, the equivalence of sales and purchases is verified *on each single agent*. It is interesting to note, with Schmitt, that Walras was close to discovering this logical identity when he referred to the principle of double-entry bookkeeping and to its relevance for business, that is, for the concrete definition of sales and purchases. Unfortunately, the author of the *Elements of Pure Economics* did not develop his intuition further and settled for a definition that merely reflects his tautological claim that the credit of an agent is necessarily the debit of another agent and vice versa. 'This is double entry bookkeeping. Its cardinal principle is never to enter a sum to the debit or credit of an account without simultaneously entering the amount to the credit or debit of some other account' (Walras 1926/1954: 230). As this quotation clearly shows, Walras advocated a simplistic definition of double-entry, where the identity of sales and purchases, of debits and credits, is verified *across two distinct* accounts. This interpretation reduces double-entry to simple entry and prevents us from seeing that every exchange is at the same time a double debit and a double credit, each agent being simultaneously debited-credited or credited-debited.

If Walras had analyzed in detail the monetary intermediation of banks, he would have discovered that 'there is no way […] any economic agent can, at whatever moment, be credited, particularly by a bank, without being debited by exactly the same number of units of account and in the same movement' (Schmitt 2000c: 10, m.t.). Walras gets very close to this discovery when he claims that every exchange is a double purchase and a double sale: 'there is always a double sale and a double purchase in every exchange transaction' (Walras 1926/1954: 88). However, his claim rests on the assumption that every exchange takes place between two distinct goods, so that agent I can purchase (demand) one good only if he sells (supplies) another good and, at the same time, agent II's sale (supply) is also a purchase (demand). 'The only reason one offers anything is that one cannot demand anything without making an offer' (ibid.: 89).

What Walras missed is the fact that the law of the equivalence between sales and purchases takes on its full meaning when related to money. In order to reach this conclusion, however, it would have been necessary for him to identify money with the *numéraire conceived as a pure number* instead of considering money as a commodity. The introduction of money as a pure *numéraire* would have forced Walras to abandon his notion of relative prices in favour of a theory of absolute or monetary prices founded on absolute exchanges. Double double-entry establishes the necessary equality of each economic agent's debits and credits, an identity that makes sense only if referred to payments carried out in bank money.

Every exchange establishes the equivalence of its two terms. Advocates of GEA are thus led to believe that, through direct exchange, two distinct physical goods can turn into each other. The logical indeterminacy of relative prices denounced by Schmitt confirms what should have been clear to Walras and his colleagues: '[t]o change an object into another object of a distinct nature belongs to the realm of miracles, not of science' (Schmitt 2000c: 18, m.t.). What is considered as an exchange by neoclassical economists is in reality a *barter*, a transaction that leaves the two objects swapped totally unchanged. Pens and razor-blades remain two distinct and heterogeneous physical objects; the neoclassical attempt to make them homogeneous fails, because they have been unable to see that barter does not transform razor-blades into pens and pens into razor-blades.

Two distinct physical goods cannot be made reciprocally equivalent by direct exchange (barter), which is why analysis must switch from the neoclassical concept of relative exchange to that of absolute exchange. Only through the absolute exchange of any product against itself in the form of money can physical goods acquire their numerical measure. 'It is double-entry bookkeeping that makes it possible to transform the physical product [...] into a product deposited with banks, integrated within the numerical form of money' (ibid.: 19, m.t.).

### *Relative exchange and bank money*

At this point, it is worth analyzing whether bank money can be consistently integrated in the theory of relative exchange or not. Schmitt observes from the outset that '*[i]f money is useful it is because it intervenes in the phase of the determination of prices*' (ibid.: 19, m.t.). If prices were determined before money intervenes, its introduction would be pointless; bank money would play no role in the determination of relative prices. On the other hand, banks cannot alter the principle of free competition by issuing different amounts of money to the benefit of the economic agents, whose bargaining is supposed to determine the price of their reciprocal goods. Banks must issue the same amount of money for each agent in each period: 'for the market session under consideration, the bank cannot "advance" to agent I a sum of money different from the one advanced to agent II' (ibid.: 20, m.t.).

The equality of the number of units of account advanced to each agent does not preclude the search for equilibrium. What must be determined by the system of relative prices is the equality between the supply of and demand for each good exchanged on the market, and not the equality of the demand exerted by the two agents. The fact that each agent exerts the same demand in money units is not enough for exchange to take place; bargaining must still achieve equality between the quantity of razor-blades supplied and demanded, and equality between the quantity of pens supplied and pens demanded. While assigning the same numerical expression to the demands exerted by agents I and II, the intervention of money does not impose a rate of exchange between razor-blades and pens. Is this enough to conclude that bank money can be integrated into GEA?

To answer this question, Schmitt investigates, first, the impact that the presence of money would have on the amount of income each agent can derive from a system of relative exchanges, in which banks equip each economic agent with the same amount of money. In a two-agents economy, there can be no difference between the income of I and II for the simple reason that each agent's earnings derive necessarily from the other agent's expenditures: 'hence, as the price of its sales [...] each agent derives an income equal to the income of the other agent. It is the perfect equality of incomes expressed in units of account' (ibid.: 22, m.t.).

Not surprisingly, the outcome is the same when exchanges occur among a greater number of economic agents. Indeed, the hypothesis that any one agent could derive a greater income from the expenditure of the other agents clashes with the necessity for each agent to give back the same amount advanced to him. '[E]ach agent is subject to the obligation to pay back to the bank the total sum of units of account he receives as part of the initial creation of money' (ibid.: 23, m.t.). The very principle of general equilibrium, together with that of the neutrality of money, commands the equality of the incomes of each economic agent: this is an absurdity that forces one to reject the attempt to introduce bank money in GEA.

### *Bank money and the transformation of physical goods into numbers*

Schmitt provides us with a further argument to confirm the substantial incompatibility of GEA with the logical requirements of a monetary economy. In a system of relative prices, the mathematical solution of the equations of supply and demand requires a stable numerical relationship between goods and money during the process of groping. If the numerical expression of goods in terms of money varied, economics would lose a stable unit of measure, and the determination of prices, whether relative or absolute, would be forever out of reach.

As Schmitt observes, the only chance to avoid a variable correspondence between physical goods and units of account is to ensure the instantaneous reflux of money to the bank that issues it. '[T]o define a sound, scientifically exact, unit of measure, all that is needed is for the units of account created by the bank, to be returned, *immediately*, without the *slightest* delay, to their source' (ibid.: 25, m.t.). What must be ensured is not the absolute stability of monetary prices, but the possibility to determine them altogether. Physical goods must be integrated into money if the economy is to be monetized and prices expressed numerically. The mere juxtaposition of bank money to real goods is not enough; we need true integration, whereby physical goods are transformed into numbers.

There is no doubt that the rule according to which any economic agent must return at once the sum of money credited to him by his bank is at odds with GEA, where exchanges are defined as relations between distinct goods and are carried out by distinct agents. Credits and debits are the terms of an identity if they refer to the sales-purchases of a single good carried out by a single bank on behalf of a single client. Relative exchanges require, on the contrary, that a simultaneous sale and purchase refers to at least two distinct goods owned by two distinct economic agents. Hence, we are caught between the two horns of a dilemma: either we stick to GEA and give up the possibility to integrate bank money into relative exchanges, or we recognize that our economies are fundamentally monetary and replace general equilibrium with a theory of absolute exchanges based on Schmitt's law of sales-purchases (credits-debits).

What is important to stress here is that, despite their substantial differences, the theories of absolute and relative prices share two fundamental ideas, namely that prices are numbers and that prices are determined through exchange. The two theories differ as to the way numerical prices can be determined, but neither disputes the fact that prices are expressed numerically. The need to incorporate bank money into GEA, therefore, derives from the need to comply with the final goal of GEA as well as from the need to provide a theory consistent with factual reality. Unfortunately, the neoclassical attempt to do so fails because of the incompatibility between the concept of relative exchange and the identity of each agent's credits and debits. Money's neutrality commands the equality of the sum of money created and destroyed by each bank for each economic agent, a condition that GEA cannot fulfil.

### *The role of production for the determination of numerical prices*

Walras starts his analysis of prices by considering the exchange between goods already present as initial endowments of economic agents, but he is well aware of the fact that goods must be produced before being exchanged. If he introduces the analysis of production after that of the exchange between already produced goods, it is because he considers production as an exchange between two distinct goods, namely the productive services and their product. Is he right? Can productive services and product be considered as two distinct magnitudes?

The answer to both questions is unmistakably no, for the simple reason that the product is the result of the productive services. As a matter of fact, the relationship between productive services and product is one of equivalence:

$$\text{Productive services} \equiv \text{Product}$$

'[S]ervices and their *own* product define one and the same good' (ibid.: 34, m.t.). Indeed, a 'productive service is not a good in itself, because it is a good only in its product' (ibid.: 34, m.t.). This is to say that productive services and product are the two aspects of one single reality; and a productive service is a good only to the extent that it is identified with the product it produces. Production is therefore an exchange fundamentally distinct from any relative exchange conceived by the advocates of GEA. 'The "exchange of production" is thus radically distinct from any relative exchange because, once more, it is the exchange of a good as it is grasped in its production and this *same* good grasped as result of this action' (ibid.: 34, m.t.).

Schmitt observes that not only does everyone agree that productive services are paid by firms, but that Walras himself claims that firms are mere intermediaries when they pay wages. This means that the exchange of production is an absolute exchange carried out through the intermediation of banks and firms. Productive services pay themselves, and, in so doing, they transform their product into a sum of money.

Walras never went as far as acknowledging the existence of absolute exchange; nor did he identify the *numéraire* with money, or produced output with wages. For him, relative prices are founded on the hypothetical exchange between distinct goods, and production itself is considered a relative exchange. Yet, despite appearances to the contrary, the equivalence between productive services and their product is not an arbitrary assumption, but a matter of fact. Production can be determined only by its result, the product; production and product define one another, no adjustment of any kind is possible between the two terms of an identity.

Production and relative exchange mutually exclude one another; the analysis of production is alien to that of relative exchange, because the relation of identity between production and product is at odds with the assumption that an adjustment takes place between productive services and production considered as distinct magnitudes.

> [I]f one thinks that prices are determined through a series of adjustments, it is formally impossible to include production into the explanation; literally, production cannot exist, because any production establishes a relation of equality that is foreign to any relation of equality between distinct goods; but if one thinks that the economy is inclusive of production, one must

> abandon the idea of relative exchange and found the relations of equivalence on the relations between each good and itself.
>
> (ibid.: 35, m.t.)

Let us consider the monetization of production. Can it be seen as a relative exchange between an already given product and a sum of money issued by a bank? If this were the case, GEA would be correct, and production would belong to the category of relative exchanges. Schmitt rejects this possibility by observing, first, that the only logically conceivable exchange would be between production and money, not between its result, the product and money. He observes, secondly, that GEA cannot account for an exchange between 'a production, an action that is necessarily inscribed in time, and a payment or a monetary creation that can only take place in an instant' (ibid.: 36, m.t.).

The fact is that, according to GEA, exchanges take place between *stocks*, which makes it impossible to explain the exchange of production, in which at least one term, money, is a flow. However, Schmitt's critique of GEA would be sterile unless Schmitt himself were able to provide a satisfactory explanation of the exchange of production. To claim that production defines an exchange between a stock and a flow would be highly unsatisfactory, because a magnitude with a positive time dimension cannot be equivalent to an instantaneous magnitude.

As we already know from Chapter 4, Schmitt's solution consists in showing that production is an exchange between flows. Both production and the emission of money are instantaneous events, neither being 'fed' by a pre-existing stock. The two flows are the terms of an absolute exchange through which the product acquires a numerical form and becomes the object of a bank deposit. The contrast between the neoclassical paradigm and monetary macroeconomics could not be clearer. According to GEA, exchanges take place between stocks and

> comply with the principle of conservation (of matter and energy), every exchange giving back the entirety of the physical goods involved, which simply change hands. According to quantum analysis, everything is creation in the world of economics.
>
> (ibid.: 49, m.t.)

# 17 The discovery of the pathological nature of countries' sovereign debt (2010–2014)

Until 2010, Schmitt's investigations into the pathologies of the present non-system of international payments concentrated mainly on the problem of external debt servicing, whose peculiarity consists in the unilateral payment that indebted countries must address to their foreign creditors. Since the formation of countries' external debt does not involve a unilateral payment, its pathological nature is more difficult to spot. A new discovery enabled Schmitt to show that the payment of a country's net imports – despite being a reciprocal transaction – entails a duplication of its total cost.

As shown in Chapter 15, Schmitt's analysis of countries' external debt servicing had led him to the conclusion that the total cost of the payment of interest is twice the amount of what is due by the debtor to the creditor countries. The fact that indebted countries pay twice the expected cost indicates that something is wrong also in the formation of the principal of countries' external debt. The double payment of interest on a total debt of X money units is equivalent to the single payment of interest on a total debt of 2X. This is to say that 'it is possible to induce that a country's external debt is twice as high as it should be from the proof that the country pays twice the net interest due to the rest of the world' (Schmitt 2012c: 242). The capitalization of the pathological duplication of interest shows that the origin of the problem lies in the duplication of the external debt itself. It is not surprising, therefore, that Schmitt's last investigation of today's non-system of international payments deals with the formation of countries' sovereign debt.

His interest in the field of international macroeconomics never weakened and came to dominate the last years of his research. He completed his most dense and difficult text just a few days before his death. The second part of the present chapter is based on this long and articulated paper. The first part refers to three unpublished manuscripts written between 2010 and 2012 (one of which was untitled and that I have named *Paiements en monnaie bancaire* and dated 2010) and to his paper 'Sovereign Debt and Interest Payments' published in 2012.

DOI: 10.4324/9781351271325-23

## The problem

Nobody disputes the fact that the increasing rise in countries' external debt is a major cause of today's financial crises. Yet, since the Greek crisis of 2010 economists all over the world have switched emphasis from external to *sovereign* debt and supported the implementation of austerity measures aimed at reducing its increase. It is therefore necessary to clarify from the outset what countries' sovereign debt is and how it is determined.

Let us first observe that sovereign debt shall not be confused with *public* debt, that is, with the debt incurred by the State to domestic and foreign purchasers of government bonds. As Schmitt notes, the definition of sovereign debt as public debt 'is far too narrow because it reduces the country to the State, and too muddled, because it mixes up domestic debt and external debt' (Schmitt 2010a: 13, m.t.). The concept of sovereign debt refers to countries as sets of their residents, and not merely to any one of these residents, as important as they may be. The State is only a resident, among others, and it would be mistaken to identify it with the country as a whole. On the other hand, a country cannot become indebted to its residents. A country's debt is necessarily an external debt, a debt incurred to the rest-of-the-world. It thus follows that, correctly defined, the sovereign debt encompasses 'the totality of the debt, public and private, incurred by a country vis-à-vis the rest-of-the-world' (ibid.: 1, m.t.).

The problem singled out by Schmitt concerns the nature of countries' sovereign debt and stresses the fact that, far from being a simple image of the foreign debt incurred by its residents, a country's sovereign debt is an *additional* debt, which weighs on the country as a whole. Schmitt's discovery concerns the way a country's external debt is formed in the present non-system of international payments. Before dealing with it, it is worth showing that statistical data confirm the existence of a problem and support Schmitt's claim as to the pathological nature of countries' sovereign debt.

### *A statistical example*

Let us consider the increase in the gross external debt of Greece, Italy, Ireland, Portugal and Spain (GIIPS), taken together from 2005 to 2020, and verify whether this increase was economically *justified* (Table 17.1).

Bearing in mind that 'the foreign currencies borrowed abroad, and the loans of international organizations are used to cover the current account deficit and to increase official reserves' (Schmitt 2011: 1, m.t.), we can safely claim that these two entries provide the measure of the justified increase in debt of any deficit country. In the case of the GIIPS, and for the period considered, the sum of their current account deficits and of the increase in their international reserves is equal to $1,106,846,714,630.82. If we compare this amount with

*Table 17.1* Statistical data concerning the external debt of Greece, Italy, Ireland, Portugal and Spain (GIIPS) from 2005 to 2020. All values in USD

| | *CA* | *TR* | *GEDP* |
|---|---|---|---|
| 2004 | | 99,444,589,534.94 | 4,532,444,232,415.88 |
| 2005 | −144,930,380,791.25 | 96,701,625,212.51 | 4,957,359,629,719.49 |
| 2006 | −198,648,663,700.02 | 108,677,874,390.99 | 6,413,919,874,458.36 |
| 2007 | −251,072,296,798.81 | 129,222,750,497.32 | 8,078,703,803,456.90 |
| 2008 | −309,946,996,051.37 | 142,472,579,661.20 | 8,082,402,535,301.78 |
| 2009 | −166,903,899,136.34 | 182,967,021,401.71 | 8,816,884,409,799.72 |
| 2010 | −175,418,321,598.19 | 219,753,163,325.82 | 8,163,964,705,859.82 |
| 2011 | −145,272,965,919.10 | 245,816,723,510.22 | 7,868,960,324,310.60 |
| 2012 | −21,836,561,246.82 | 263,879,582,828.21 | 7,580,756,197,420.00 |
| 2013 | 54,154,099,823.60 | 217,048,249,308.41 | 8,089,210,711,953.00 |
| 2014 | 62,089,171,034.86 | 220,854,751,940.33 | 7,751,484,154,342.21 |
| 2015 | 62,062,408,891.34 | 212,199,659,237.70 | 7,566,805,862,156.45 |
| 2016 | 74,836,816,256.61 | 233,603,564,520.69 | 7,279,065,104,891.03 |
| 2017 | 91,323,106,892.10 | 258,833,578,742.65 | 8,272,232,797,609.87 |
| 2018 | 98,120,591,827.13 | 260,716,647,448.41 | 8,423,243,312,008.13 |
| 2019 | 46,725,614,928.94 | 289,372,238,340.76 | 8,694,201,564,860.14 |
| 2020 | 59,256,041,177.43 | 340,829,069,755.87 | 6,691,560,170,323.33 |
| | **−865,462,234,409.88 (CA sum)** | **241,384,480,220.94 (TR change)** | **2,159,115,937,907.45 (GEDP change)** |

CA, current account; TR, total reserves; GEDP, gross external debt position.
Source: elaborated from data of The World Bank and Ceicdata.com.

that of the actual increase in the GIIPS's external debt from 2005 to 2020, we observe that the latter exceeds the former by $1,052,269,223,276,63. This huge sum is the *unjustified* increase in the GIIPS's external debt in the interval considered. Statistical data point to the existence of an *unjustifiable* debt; macroeconomic analysis shows that it originates from an anomaly characterizing the payment of net global imports through a foreign loan. What applies to the GIIPS case can also be verified for many other deficit countries and is symptomatic of a condition that affects the countries themselves.

The unjustified increase in external debt revealed by statistical investigation cannot be blamed on any resident, whose transactions are already accounted for by the entries in current account and international reserves. External payments carried out by a country's residents are of a *microeconomic* nature and should not involve an additional, *macroeconomic* cost for their country. However, statistical evidence indicates that this is not what happens in the present system of international payments. The amount of the unjustified increase in external debt points to the existence of a debt totally distinct from, and in addition to, that incurred by countries' residents, of the public and private sectors, for the payment of their net foreign purchases. Yet, one needs more than statistical evidence to reach a conclusive diagnosis of the pathology. An analysis is also needed, which studies the problem of countries' external debt from both a real and a monetary viewpoint.

Throughout this chapter we shall refer to two hypothetical countries, country A and the rest-of-the-world, country R. Schmitt defines country A as the deficit country, that is, as the country whose overall foreign purchases, commercial and financial, exceed its global sales. Country R is thus the surplus country: its global exports are greater than its global imports. Country A's domestic currency is denoted $M_A$; its exchange rate with $M_R$, country R's domestic currency, is of $M_A1$ for $M_R1$. R's currency is by assumption the US dollar, but we could easily choose any other key-currency instead. To cover its deficit, country A borrows an equivalent amount of dollars from country R.

## The difference between country A's monetary outflows and inflows is the cause of its sovereign debt

### *A premise*

It is worth recalling here some fundamental principles of monetary economics. First, money is a flow: it has no intrinsic value whatsoever, and its role is to convey payments. What makes it difficult to understand the true nature of money is the fact that bookkeeping entries refer to the *result of payments*, a stock, and not to their flows. Macroeconomic analysis shows that money exists as a circular flow only; it is not a stock put into motion.

Second, double-entry bookkeeping guarantees the circular flow of money: every time an economic agent is credited with a sum of money, they are immediately debited for the same amount. 'When an economic agent is the beneficiary of a bank's payment, he benefits from an inflow of money immediately balanced by an equivalent outflow that defines the instantaneous reflux to the bank of the sum received' (ibid.: 3, m.t.). Since 'banks carry out all their payments, on behalf of their clients, through "instantaneous fluxes-refluxes" of money' (Schmitt 2010b: 1, m.t.), money can never be the object of the payment, that is, nobody can ever hold a sum of money. Although paid in bank money, a seller becomes the holder of a bank deposit and not of the sum of money issued by the bank to convey the payment of the purchaser. The all-important result of this situation is that, as far as money is concerned, '*the payment of the seller is indeed a zero-sum transaction*' (Schmitt 2012c: 240, my emphasis).

In a domestic or national economic system, every payment is indeed a zero-sum transaction with respect to money; the same amount of money is created and destroyed on each economic agent entering a payment in a movement that implies, at the same time, 'the credit-debit of purchasers and the debit-credit of sellers' (Schmitt 2010b: 1, m.t.). Money is neutral, and no economic agent is faced either with a net outflow (debit) or with a net inflow (credit) of money. Do things change when payments are carried out between residents and non-residents? To answer this question, let us analyze the two cases identified by

Schmitt as representative of all the possible transactions financed by country A through a foreign loan granted by country R.

### *Foreign borrowing as the source of countries' sovereign debt*

Between 2010 and 2012, Schmitt's analysis focuses on the monetary aspects of the payment of net foreign purchases. Didactically, Schmitt distinguishes between two cases according to whether country A uses R's loan to increase its international reserves or to pay for its net imports. He then endeavours to show that the

> foreign borrowings, public or private, by the domestic economy from any country are at the origin of a monetary deficit implying the pathological over-indebtedness of the country, regardless of whether the borrowed foreign currencies are deposited into the country's reserves or used to finance additional imports.
>
> (Schmitt 2010a: 2, m.t.)

Let us see how Schmitt deals with these two cases.

#### *The case in which A's foreign borrowing finances an increase in international reserves*

In the pages that follow we bestow a character of intentionality, as Schmitt does, on both country A's domestic economy and country A's foreign reserves. And so, we reason as if their representatives were reflecting on the actions consequent to their decisions. It is the task of theoretical analysis to make explicit what is only implicit and often hidden from the perception of economic agents. Hence, what we shall describe as an explicit request coming from A's domestic economy, $E_A$, is but a didactic expedient to facilitate the understanding of the different analytical steps involved in a transaction. For example, whether the agents representing A's economy do really ask the banks of R to pay country A's reserves, $R_A$, on their behalf, is irrelevant. What really matters is that the different operations interlock as if they did.

Schmitt assumes first that the domestic economy of country A borrows a sum of *x* (billion) dollars from country R to obtain from the banks of A a credit in money A. The sum of dollars initially borrowed by $E_A$ is exchanged for an equivalent amount of bank deposits in money A and A's international reserves replace A's domestic economy as holders of a bank deposit in dollars. 'In the event the foreign currency borrowed abroad ends up in A's reserves, the sale of financial claims by $E_A$ is designed to allow it to re-finance itself by obtaining a bank deposit in national currency' (ibid.: 4, m.t.). Let us analyze the different phases of these transactions, emphasizing their monetary aspect.

The starting point is the sale of financial claims by country A's domestic economy to country R's residents. In exchange for the IOUs exported by economy A, the banks of R, on behalf of their clients, credit $E_A$ in dollars. In compliance with the flow nature of money and with the principle of double-entry book-keeping, the credit of $E_A$ is immediately matched by an equivalent debit. The dollars flow instantaneously back to R's banks and A's economy becomes the holder of bank deposits formed in the banks of country R. In exchange for the IOUs it exports to R, economy A does not obtain a sum of money R (*x* dollars), but a claim on equivalent bank deposits formed in R, that is, part of country R's domestic output. 'The object of the deposit to which $E_A$'s banks are now entitled on behalf of their clients is not a sum of money R, but part of the national product of R' (ibid.: 4, m.t.). It is through a flux-reflux of dollars that R's purchases of economy A's financial claims are paid: country R's purchases are matched by economy A's purchase of an equivalent sum of claims on R's bank deposits.

The second step is the conversion of the deposits in dollars in deposits in money A. Country A's domestic economy gives up its claims on R's banks to the benefit of its country's international reserves and obtains in exchange equivalent claims on deposits formed in A's banking system. Does this mean that $E_A$ transfers a sum of dollars to $R_A$? Certainly not, because A's economy cannot transfer what it does not possess. What $E_A$ can do is ask R's banking system to pay *x* dollars to A's reserves on its behalf. When it does so, economy A's claims on R's bank deposits are cancelled and an equivalent amount of claims is created to the benefit of A's reserves.

Things happen as if $E_A$ told R's banks: 'please destroy my deposit and create an equivalent deposit to the benefit of my country's central bank, which manages "my" country's official reserves' (Schmitt 2012c: 243). Let us consider the flows of (nominal) money that convey this transaction. When economy A gives up its claims on R's bank deposits, it is credited with *x* dollars. Yet, it is also simultaneously debited with *x* dollars, because of the payment country R's banks carry out on its behalf to the benefit of $R_A$. At the same time, A's reserves are credited with *x* dollars and immediately debited with the same amount, a credit-debit in dollars through which $R_A$ becomes the owner of new claims on R's bank deposits of *x* dollars in value.

If in our reasoning we separate A's economy from A's reserves, we observe that for each of them the inflows of dollars are equal to the outflows of dollars. No monetary asymmetry seems to affect the transactions, whose apparent result is simply the exchange of a sum of claims on country A's national output sold by A's economy to R for an equivalent sum of claims on country R's bank deposits sold by R to A's reserves. If this completed the transaction, the debt incurred by A's economy to country R, because of its net borrowing of *x* dollars, would be offset by the increase in A's official reserves, whose investment on the forex increases country A's credit as against the rest-of-the-world. No net debt would form for the country, and no sovereign debt crisis would arise. To spot the asymmetry denounced by Schmitt we need to reason on $E_A$ and on $R_A$ simultaneously. Let us do so and count the outflows and the inflows of dollars for country A considered as a whole.

As far as outflows are concerned, both economy A and A's reserves are debited with *x* dollars, which brings the total value of outflows to 2*x* dollars. Can we legitimately add the debit of $E_A$ to the debit of $R_A$, both equal to *x* dollars and both caused by the purchase of bank deposits formed with R's banks? The answer is yes because the deposit initially purchased by A's economy is not the same as the deposit purchased by A's reserves:

> the deposit of $E_A$ is destroyed when $E_A$ requests R's banks to pay $R_A$, and another deposit is formed when $R_A$ is debited in dollars. The formation of the deposits of $E_A$ and $R_A$ [...] are two distinct operations that require two distinct monetary flows.
>
> (Schmitt 2010a: 6, m.t.)

It would be wrong to reduce the two outflows to a single one, because the debit of A's reserves does not cancel that of A's economy. Both A's economy *and* A's reserves, two distinct subjects, are debited since each of them spends *x* dollars on the purchase of two distinct deposits. '[T]he two debits, one imposed on A's domestic economy and the other on A's central bank, are distinct and separate (they are even separated *in time*)' (Schmitt 2012c: 247).

Let us now consider the inflows of dollars into country A as a whole. Initially country R credits A's economy for the amount of *x* dollars that it pays to purchase the IOUs issued by $E_A$. This first inflow of dollars is accompanied by an equivalent outflow that grants A's economy ownership over part of country R's bank deposits. This ownership gives $E_A$ the right to request R's banks to make a payment on its behalf; a right that A's economy exercises by asking R's banks to credit A's reserves with *x* dollars.

When R's banks comply with A's economy request, $E_A$'s claims on R's bank deposits are cancelled, and $E_A$ is credited-debited with *x* dollars; it is credited because it surrenders its claims, and it is debited because R's banks pay A's reserves on its behalf. The second credit of *x* dollars of which economy A benefits simply repeats the first. Country A's inflows are of *x* dollars, the exact value of the financial claims it sells to country R:

> the destruction by R's banks of the deposit of *x* billion US dollars owned by EA gives rise to an equivalent credit in favour of EA, and this credit is but *the reproduction of the credit initially obtained by EA as payment of its IOUs subscribed abroad*.
>
> (ibid.: 248)

Is the inflow into A's reserves simply a repeat of the initial inflow of *x* dollars into A's domestic economy? Schmitt's answer is, unconditionally, yes:

> [i]t is a factual certitude that the credit by which A's official reserves finally benefit is merely the reproduction of the credit payment initially aimed at A's domestic economy, since the export of IOUs whose value is equal to *x* billion US dollars can only elicit a credit payment equal to *x* billion US dollars.
>
> (ibid.: 248)

Let us represent the monetary flows by solid lines and the real flows by dotted lines as in Figure 17.1.

Flows (1) correspond to the credit-debit of economy A implied by its sale of financial claims or IOUs and by its purchase of claims on country R's bank deposits. Flows (2) are implied in the cancellation of A's economy bank deposits of $x$ dollars and in the payment of $x$ dollars carried out by R's banks in favour of A's reserves on behalf of $E_A$. Flow (3) is the final reflux of $x$ dollars to R's banks, which allows A's reserves to obtain an equivalent sum of *new* claims on R's bank deposits.

The solid lines representing flows (2) are linked to show that the inflow into A's reserves is not distinct and in addition to the inflow into A's domestic economy. It is because A's economy gives up its bank deposits and asks R's banks to credit A's reserves that $R_A$ benefits from a single inflow of $x$ dollars. The inflow into A's reserves matches that into A's economy, and since the second inflow is but the repetition of the first, country A, as a whole, benefits from one inflow of $x$ dollars only. As Schmitt observes, this is perfectly in line with the fact that the sum borrowed abroad by A's domestic economy is of $x$ and not of $2x$ dollars. 'If the credit payment of RA was to be added up to the credit payment of EA, then the same IOUs would be paid by R twice, thus doubling their value, which is absurd' (ibid.: 248).

Whereas both economy A and A's reserves are credited-debited by R's banks with $x$ dollars, their country benefits from a unique inflow of $x$ dollars. Country A sells IOUs of a value of $x$ dollars abroad and benefits from a single inflow of the same amount, regardless of whether it is to the benefit of its domestic economy or of its official reserves.

Country R pays country A only once; whether this payment increases the deposits of A's economy in R's banks or the deposits of A's reserves is irrelevant: in both cases there is only one payment carried out by country R, and only one inflow of dollars into country A.

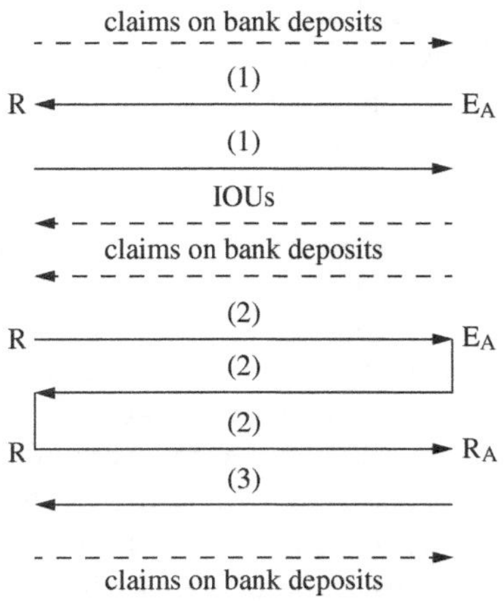


*Figure 17.1* Monetary and real flows of case 1.

> The credit payment of economy A and the successive credit payment of A's reserves are one and the same flow that is first issued in favour of economy A and then ends up in favour of country A's reserves.
>
> (Schmitt 2010a: 6, m.t.)

Two outflows of $x$ dollars each are faced by a single inflow of $x$ dollars. At first, this could seem the mere consequence of the fact that A's economy spends the sum borrowed abroad and that this expenditure is net. This would indeed be the case if the financial debt incurred abroad by A's economy was balanced by an increase in A's reserves: $R_A$ would merely replace $E_A$, and everything would be 'normal'. In reality, this reasoning clashes with the way banks carry out payments and with the principle of double-entry bookkeeping.

The *direct transfer of money* from A's economy to A's reserves would be possible only if money were not a flow, and if economic agents could be credited with a sum of money without being simultaneously debited. However, bank payments are such that 'no one in this world can avoid enacting the rule according to which every credit payment is an equal and simultaneous debit payment, every debit payment being an equivalent and simultaneous credit payment' (Schmitt 2012c: 250). Likewise, the hypothesis of a *direct transfer of bank deposits* from $E_A$ to $R_A$ must be discarded because it is at odds with the way banks carry out their clients' payments. When A's economy asks R's banks to credit A's reserves, its bank deposits are cancelled, and new bank deposits are created to the benefit of $R_A$. *Neither money, nor bank deposits move from one agent to another.*

From the logical impossibility to increase a country's reserves by transferring the bank deposits obtained by its domestic economy as a loan, it follows that a monetary deficit of $x$ dollars is added to the financial debt incurred by A's economy to the rest-of-the-world. The initial loan granted by country R to A's domestic economy places A's economy financially in debt, while the monetary expenditures (outflows of dollars) of $E_A$ and $R_A$ exceed by $x$ dollars their monetary gains or inflows. Hence, A's economy and A's reserves taken together incur a monetary debt on top of their financial debt, which raises the total indebtedness to $2x$ dollars. It is true that A's reserves lend immediately the $x$ dollars obtained from R's banks, but the debt incurred by A's economy is only apparently offset by the credit obtained by A's reserves.

Since country A's total monetary outflows exceed by $x$ dollars its total monetary inflows, the monetary deficit must be covered, and this costs country A an additional amount of $x$ dollars. This means that the increase in A's reserves is immediately reabsorbed into the financing of country A's monetary deficit. In other words, since A's reserves increase their financial assets (claims on R's bank deposits) through an outflow of dollars added to that of A's domestic economy, the increase itself is immediately cancelled by the need to cover the excess outflow of dollars suffered by the country. 'RA's gain is therefore of $\pm x$ billion US dollars as for the payment in foreign currency, and of $\pm x$ billion US dollars as for the bank deposits formed abroad: it is zero on both sides' (Schmitt

2012c: 251). No financial gain of country A's reserves is thus available to match the financial debt incurred by country A's domestic economy abroad. Contrary to what mainstream economists still believe, country A's external debt is not balanced by an increase in reserves and is consequently *net* for the country as a whole even though both $E_A$ and $R_A$ accounts are in equilibrium. '*The increase in A's external debt, equal to x billion US dollars, has no counterpart at all in the borrowing country*' (ibid.: 251).

### *The case when the sum borrowed abroad finances country A's surplus imports*

Since the analysis of the second case proposed by Schmitt is similar to the first, we can reduce it to a few additional considerations. What changes in case 2 is that A's economy uses the sum borrowed to pay for an additional sum of imports. From a stock viewpoint, $E_A$'s sales of IOUs are perfectly balanced by its additional purchases of goods and services from country R. As in the previous case, however, a problem arises that concerns the monetary flows enabling this real exchange.

When A's domestic economy borrows *x* dollars from R, its bank account is simultaneously credited and debited with this sum, an inflow-outflow of dollars that allows $E_A$ to obtain claims on R's bank deposits for a value of *x* dollars. When A's economy asks R's banks to cancel this deposit and to pay R's commercial exporters on its behalf, it is again credited-debited so that, for $E_A$, the equality between monetary inflows and outflows is, once again, maintained. Yet, this is no longer the case when we look at both transactions, the sale of IOUs and the purchase of goods and services, at the same time.

Monetary outflows amount to a total of 2*x* dollars because the purchase of claims on bank deposits and the purchase of goods and services are two distinct transactions. 'The debit of $E_A$ when the deposit is formed and the debit of $E_A$ in the purchase of real goods are two different operations, which doubles the total number of foreign currency outflows' (Schmitt 2010a: 10, m.t.). Monetary inflows, on the other hand, are *x* dollars only, because A's domestic economy is paid by R only once for its sale of financial claims. The second credit of *x* dollars merely repeats the first: '[t]he second inflow of dollars is already fully taken into account by the initial inflow, of which it is but a replica' (ibid.: 10, m.t.).

The difference between monetary outflows and inflows has no repercussions for A's domestic economy; the cost of its net imports does not exceed the sum initially obtained through its net financial exports. Yet, what is true for $E_A$ is not true for country A as a whole. The monetary deficit is a macroeconomic consequence of the way cross-border transactions are conveyed in the present non-system of international payments; it weighs on the deficit country and increases pathologically its external debt. If the equality of monetary outflows and inflows applied also to trading countries, no sovereign debt would be formed, and deficit countries would not be forced to pay it. Unfortunately, the monetary character of the problem has yet to find a satisfactory solution and 'external borrowings are at the origin of a monetary deficit that involves the pathological over-indebtedness of countries' (ibid.: 12, m.t.). Country A's monetary deficit can be covered or financed either through an additional foreign loan or through a reduction in reserves; in either case, country A's external debt increases. In other words, a new sovereign debt is formed even though A's domestic economy has paid its net imports in full.

## The 'sovereign debt theorem'

In this section, we follow Schmitt in his 2014 analysis of countries' sovereign debt. As before, we consider the case of deficit country A versus the rest-of-the-world, and assume that A's global imports, commercial and financial, are equal to 11 billion dollars while its global exports amount to 10 billion dollars. The dollar is the domestic currency of country R, money A is the domestic currency of country A, and $M_A 1 = \$1$ is their rate of exchange.

Schmitt claims that a country's sovereign debt is formed each time the country's net purchases, or imports, are financed through a foreign loan. This is to say that when a country finances its deficit by borrowing abroad – which is always and necessarily the case if the country *pays* for its net imports – it incurs an external debt that is added to that incurred by its domestic economy.

Although the case analyzed is always the same, Schmitt provides several complementary arguments that corroborate his claim of the pathological nature of countries' sovereign debt. As with the double charge of interest payment (Chapter 15), I present his proof in slightly different ways because we need to both

1) Substantiate as much as possible a result that can only sound absurd to the sceptical reader, and
2) Provide a satisfactory rendition of Schmitt's constant search for the deepest implications of his insight.

To avoid excessive repetition, I have incorporated Schmitt's arguments into three strands; each of them is self-contained and sufficient to establish the sovereign debt theorem; taken together, they answer the most important criticism that might be levelled at it.

### *Real and monetary payments of a deficit country borrowing abroad*

The first line of reasoning closely follows Schmitt in his 2010–2012 analyses in that it demonstrates the existence of a monetary deficit incurred by the indebted country as a whole. Schmitt's thesis is that the specific presence of countries' sovereign debt 'is the result of a pathology that affects the formation of external debt of the very countries whose net purchases are financed by foreign loans' (Schmitt 2014: 2).

Schmitt maintains that country A, whose net imports are of 1 billion dollars, must pay 2 billion dollars in order to cover a real and a monetary deficit, each equal to one billion dollars. *Two foreign loans of $1 billion each are required.* To show that they are *separate* and *cumulative* all we need is to prove that they are both necessary. The first part of the proof rests on the fact that the loan enabling country A to equalize its expenditures and its gains has a sum of *money* as its object, whereas the loan equalizing A's real exports and imports 'has a sum of *real goods* as its object' (ibid.: 4). Since each of the two loans has a different object, they are themselves distinct.

The second part of the proof is less straightforward. It seems obvious that only a single foreign loan of 1 dollar (from now on we assume 1 dollar to mean 1 billion US dollars) is required to pay country A's net imports. This would be correct if a single loan of 1 dollar could enable country A to pay its net imports *both* in real and in monetary terms. Two questions arise in this context:

1) Why must country A pay its net imports in real terms?
2) Why does this not imply the cancellation of A's real net imports?

The answer to 1) is that any payment must have a real content to be redeeming. The answer to 2) is that country A does not balance its net imports through an additional export of actual goods, but by exporting an amount of its *future* goods.

In Schmitt's words,

> [e]ven though this direct exchange between real goods is purely imaginary, it already gives a precise indication as to the borrowing of foreign currencies that provides country A with the power to take possession in advance – in the current period – of future goods, equal to 1 dollar, that it exchanges against equivalent goods handed over by the rest of the world. (ibid.: 5)

By borrowing 1 dollar abroad, country A's domestic economy obtains an equivalent value of its own future product, which it gives up immediately in exchange for an equivalent sum of R's actual production. A's economy will reimburse R through its future exports. It is crucial to understand that, although the transfer of economy A's future output will take place only later, the sale of A's future production occurs when country A's domestic economy becomes indebted to country R. This is necessarily the case, because country R becomes the owner of A's future output at this very moment: 'foreign lenders become the owners of 1 [dollar] worth of value that economy A will export in the future' (ibid.: 22). When A's economy borrows 1 dollar from R, it promises R's lenders to reimburse them; this promise, which A's economy will fulfil through its future exports, gives country R immediate ownership over part of $E_A$'s future production. A's economy balances at once its foreign purchases with equivalent sales of actual and future goods, the latter in the form of financial claims.

Two requirements must be met by country A and its residents. It must

1) 'Equalize purchases and sales of produced values' (ibid.: 20), that is, imports and exports of real goods, including financial assets; and
2) Equalize the outflows and inflows of dollars.

Clearly, one single loan of 1 dollar cannot satisfy both these requirements: 'it is obviously inconceivable that the same loan of 1 [dollar] pays, at the same time and for the same period, for an export of 1 [dollar] and an import of the same economy' (ibid.: 22). Since the loan obtained by A's economy finances its future exports, another loan is necessary to finance its present net imports, that is, to fill the gap between its outflows and its inflows of dollars. The second payment of net imports is pathological and rests on country A: 'the country's domestic economy carries out the *real* payment of the deficit, its payment in foreign *money units* being carried out separately, by the country as a whole' (ibid.: 17).

A critical and doubtful reader might object that there is no need for country A's second loan, because the first one compounds country R's payment to a total amount of 11 dollars. A's domestic economy would thus be able to finance its total purchases worth 11 dollars with the dollars obtained from R. Is this correct? No, answers Schmitt, because country R's purchases of country A's current output, that is, its global imports in the period considered, are equal to 10 dollars only. R's residents import and pay only for a part (10 dollars) of economy A's current output. They are not purchasers of $E_A$'s future output, even though their country owns indeed part of economy A's future production, due to be paid by R's importers at a future date. As Schmitt observes, it is important to understand that what matters here is the *macroeconomic* nature of the loan granted to A's economy 'and not the *microeconomic* nature of lenders [...]. It is country R as a whole that becomes the owner of the real goods that will be exported by country A' (ibid.: 38).

The distinction is subtle, but crucial: A's domestic economy sells part of its future output from the moment it borrows 1 dollar from country R, yet the purchases of R's economy are not increased from 10 to 11 dollars. Although country R acquires a right over economy A's future production, it does so through a loan, and not by increasing its residents' purchases of $E_A$'s output. Country R's importers 'are by no means "current buyers"' (ibid.: 23) of economy A's future exports, which are *future sales*. Finally, it is correct to say that country R's initial loan to country A 'is the *advanced* payment of a future export of A's economy. But it is wrong to induce from it that, in the period under consideration, foreign purchasers actually spend 11 [dollars] in order to pay for economy A's exports' (ibid.: 23). Foreign purchasers spend $10 in payment of $E_A$'s actual exports, which is why another loan of $1 is needed to cover the gap between the payments of country R in favour of country A, $10, and those of country A to the benefit of country R, $11.

It is not easy to decide whether or not the loan obtained by A's economy increases its receipts. The correct answer is: it does not. This is so, because 'the loan is not yet net' (ibid.: 27). If the dollar borrowed by A's economy became its property, its receipts in dollars would increase. However, precisely because it is only lent to A's economy, the dollar borrowed remains the property of country R. Foreign lenders become the owners of part of $E_A$'s future production, but they will get hold of it only later. In the meantime, they remain the owners of the sum of dollars lent to A's economy: '*the sum borrowed does not add to the foreign currencies that A's economy acquires in the period under scrutiny*' (ibid.: 27). Until the moment they purchase $E_A$'s future output, foreign lenders maintain their right over the sum lent to A's economy, whose receipts in dollars remain unaltered. It follows that country A's economy cannot pay for its surplus imports through the expenditure of the dollar initially borrowed abroad.

### *The nature of the foreign loans required to pay for a country's net global imports*

Let us call 'microeconomic' the debt incurred by A's domestic economy and 'sovereign' the debt weighing on country A. The initial foreign borrowing of A's economy defines the formation of a microeconomic debt of A's economy to R's lenders. Since country A itself does not carry out any transactions, its own indebtedness should be nil, 'whatever the value, even if it is high, of its entire national economy's surplus imports' (ibid.: 28). How is it, then, that an additional, pathological debt is formed when economy A's foreign borrowing finances country A's net imports? The answer lies in the particular nature of the loan used to pay for country A's deficit.

Schmitt defines as '*ordinary*' the loans that 'result in the equality, for both lenders and borrowers, between purely monetary assets and liabilities' (ibid.: 38). Before being allocated to any specific payment, any loan is 'ordinary' and defines the credit-debit of the borrowers and the debit-credit of the lenders. County A is credited-debited with 1 dollar and becomes the owner of equivalent claims on R's bank deposits, whereas country R is debited-credited for the same sum and obtains in exchange equivalent IOUs issued by A's economy. Yet, the loan obtained by A's economy changes in nature when it is used to finance country A's net imports.

> As soon as the international loan of a currency has the function and effect to increase the revenues of a deficit country, to bring them to the level of its total imports, *it changes its nature: it becomes the payment of a future export of real goods.*
>
> (ibid.: 38)

When the loan is granted, it defines a monetary asset and a monetary liability for country A's economy; as soon as it is allocated to the payment of economy A's net imports, the foreign currency borrowed defines a '*monetary asset* and [a] *real liability*' (ibid.: 37).

Whereas the asset obtained by country A is a sum of dollars, the asset obtained by country R is real, a right over economy A's future production. As the logical outcome of country A, equalizing its total imports of R's current output with its exports of current and future goods, the dollar borrowed by A's economy should increase A's official or private reserves. But this is not the case: the dollar must be spent to cover for the difference between the actual expenditures of A's importers, \$11, and that of R's importers, \$10. Once this gap is bridged, what remains is the foreign debt incurred by A's economy. 'The payment of "imports-without-*actual* exports" leaves only the obligation of country A's residents, who still owe the sum of 1 dollar borrowed abroad' (ibid.: 40).

Finally, the debt of A's domestic economy and the additional loss of A's future production bring to 2 dollars the total cost of country A's net imports worth 1 dollar. '[T]o settle the deficit of 1 dollar formed by an "import-without-export" of equal value, the country concerned has to give up real goods of 1-dollar value of its future exports and suffer, additionally, 1 dollar debt to foreign lenders' (ibid.: 40).

### *The payment of net imports and the principle of international exchanges*

The problem of paying for country A's net imports can also be analyzed by referring to the logical rule of all international transactions, which establishes the equality of country A's global imports (IM) and exports (EX). Despite appearances to the contrary, it is a mistake to claim that, if A is a deficit country, the rest-of-the-world is necessarily a net exporter. Even if it is true that A is a deficit country and R a surplus country, it is not necessarily true that A's imports exceed R's imports. Yet, indisputably, A's imports are R's exports.

We are thus confronted with an apparent contradiction. According to the tautological relationship between A's imports and R's exports, when country A runs a deficit, its imports are greater than country R's imports. On the other hand, the logical identity of each country's imports and exports imposes the equality of A's and R's imports. Can these two irrefutable facts be reconciled? In other words, can we show that country A's imports are at the same time equal and greater than country R's imports? Schmitt's answer is yes, because we must take into account the impact of the foreign loan obtained by A's economy to finance the payment of its net imports.

Through its loan to A's domestic economy, country R acquires ownership over an equivalent sum of $E_A$'s future production, which raises R's purchases to the level of A's imports.

> [T]he object of the sum borrowed is an export of country A since period *p*, therefore an import of country R, which does not need to wait for a successive period ($p^*$) to bring the payment of its purchases to the level of its sales.
>
> (ibid.: 67)

Hence, while we correctly claim that country A's imports of R's *current* output are greater than country R's imports of A's *current* output, it is a fact that the foreign loan obtained by country A makes R's imports of A's output, *current and future*, equal to A's imports.

The specificity of the debt incurred by A's domestic economy to foreign lenders enables Schmitt to show, from a different perspective, the duplication of the payment necessary to finance A's net imports (see Figure 17.2).

As Figure 17.2 shows, A's economy must reimburse the foreign lenders *and* pay R's exporters. This is not enough to conclude that, in period *p*, A's economy must pay 2 dollars for its net imports of 1 dollar: 1 dollar to the foreign lenders and another dollar to R's exporters. Indeed, while the sum borrowed in *p* will have to be reimbursed only at a later stage, the dollar borrowed in *p* is exactly what country A's economy needs in order to pay country R's exporters. Neither in *p*, nor in $p_1$, or in any other period, is A's domestic economy subject to a net debtor payment. In both periods, its monetary outflows are matched by equivalent monetary inflows. This might lead one to think that no pathology arises after all. Since A's economy pays its net imports only once, why should anyone worry about the inadequacy of the present system of international payments?

The law governing international exchanges addresses this question. 'According to this law, any country that pays the totality of its purchases cannot obtain in real goods what it does not immediately give up, equally in real goods' (ibid.: 68). It is certain that indebted countries' residents pay the totality of their imports, no one being allowed to leave its purchases unpaid for an unlimited period of time. It is also certain that country A balances its imports of real goods with equivalent exports of real goods: EX≡IM. From the moment A's domestic economy borrows 1 dollar from R it gives up the ownership over its future production worth 1 dollar. But how does this real payment of A's net imports imply the net indebtedness of the country itself on top of the debt incurred by its economy?

The answer is related to the macroeconomic impact of the transactions carried out by A's residents. If one considers country A's domestic economy alone, one will infer that its situation is perfectly balanced. The debt that country A's economy incurs in period *p* corresponds to an exchange of claims on its future goods against a sum of foreign currency whose expenditure pays for its imports of foreign goods. On the other hand, given that country A pays for its net imports in period *p*, it should incur no net debt when it gives R ownership over its future output. In other words, it should balance its debt with

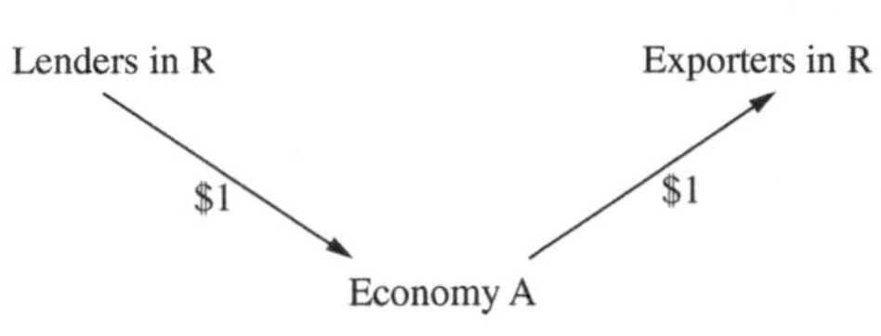


*Figure 17.2* The two flows implied in payment of country A's net imports. Source: Schmitt 2014: 74

an equivalent sum of foreign currency. This means that the dollars borrowed abroad by A's domestic economy are likely to remain available in the country and increase its official or private reserves. Their expenditure by A's domestic economy causes a loss to the country, which suffers from a pathological decrease in reserves, that is, from a pathological increase in its external debt.

The monetary payment of country R's exporters by country A's domestic economy is perfectly justified, but it should be carried out without involving a loss for the country as a whole. This is not what happens today: in the absence of a proper system of international payments, country A suffers from a net monetary outflow that defines the formation (or the increase) of its sovereign debt. The problem does not lie with A's economy, public or private, whose debt is fully justified, but with the macroeconomic implication of the monetary payment of country R's exporters in a system that does not grant the cost-free use of a circular *means* of payment between countries.

### *Two more proofs of the pathological formation of countries' sovereign debt*

Among the numerous proofs presented by Schmitt, two additional ones deserve to be mentioned here. They are simpler than the others and tackle the problem from yet another angle, which should give the reader a further opportunity to appreciate the depth of Schmitt's thought.

#### *The necessary impact of country A's net imports on its exports*

A's economy pays for its net imports by borrowing an amount of 1 dollar from R. This means that the net imports of country A's economy are financed by a sum of income produced by country R's domestic economy. 'Surplus imports [...] are paid by an income formed within the domestic economies of the rest of the world' (ibid.: 8). With this payment, country A enables country R to recover part of the domestic income it spends to pay for its imports from A. This is to say that '[*f*]*or R this payment of 1 dollar in value finances its imports from A*' (ibid.: 8). It is country A itself that finances its own exports worth 1 dollar. Consequently, country's R payment of A's exports is reduced from 10 to 9 dollars, because if 'R pays for A's *surplus* imports, scientific logic requires that R pays *less* and for an equal amount (1 dollar) A's exports' (ibid: 11).

This apparently astonishing result is but the consequence of the principle of action-reaction applied to the payment of a country's net imports through a foreign loan. Indeed, a variation in country A's imports (action) is necessarily accompanied by an inverse variation in country A's exports (reaction). In Schmitt's case, the increase of 1 dollar in the payment of A's imports engenders necessarily an equivalent decrease in the payment of A's exports: imports go from 10 to 11 dollars, while exports pass from 10 to 9 dollars. In other words, 'at the instant country A's "imports-without-exports" are brought from 0 to 1 dollar, country A's "exports-without-imports" are also brought from 0 to 1

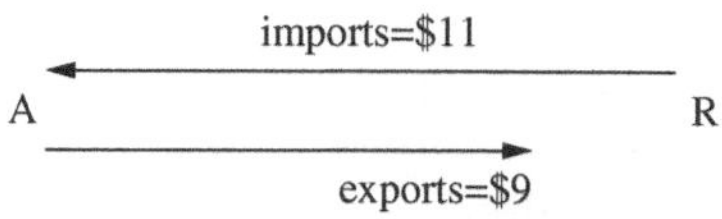


*Figure 17.3* Gap between country A's imports and exports. Source: elaboration from Schmitt 2014:11

dollar' (ibid.: 10). This is to say that 'the rest of the world reduces the payment that it devotes to A's exports by the exact value of the payment it devotes to A's surplus imports' (ibid.: 11).

Because of the impact of the payment of country A's net imports on the payment by country R of A's exports, the gap between the reciprocal payments of the two countries widens from 1 to 2 dollars (see Figure 17.3).

The result is clear: country A is 'forced to borrow abroad *two times 1 dollar* in order to settle the total payment of its imports of 11 dollars value' (ibid.: 12). One of the loans obtained from R is perfectly justified and corresponds to the sale of IOUs carried out by A's domestic economy, which incurs a foreign debt also perfectly justified. The second loan, on the contrary, is not at all justified since the amount of economy A's net imports is equal to 1 dollar only. The resulting debt, which is carried by country A as a whole, is pathological and defines A's sovereign debt.

### *A multi-period analysis*

The aim of this proof is to show that the cost of net imports is multiplied by 2 by analyzing 'the operations that occur *in a number of successive periods*' (ibid.: 85). By assumption, in period $p_0$ and in each period thereafter the foreign purchases of real and financial assets of country A's economy exceed its foreign sales by 1 dollar. What must be determined is whether, starting from period $p_1$, the deficit is covered through an expenditure of 1 or 2 dollars.

In period $p_0$, A's economy borrows 1 dollar from R, which it reimburses in the subsequent period. If it did not reimburse it, net imports would not be paid, and country A's foreign debt would increase. Yet, this is not what happens in the real world, where deficits are in fact paid by the economies of net importing countries. Neither is this what Schmitt wants to prove. Let us assume that each loan incurred in one period is reimbursed in the next period: in each period from $p_1$ onwards, the debt formed by the new loan is equal to the reimbursement of the debt formed in the previous period. The question now is: 'What are the values, before and after the reimbursement of the debt of [1 dollar] formed in the immediately preceding period, of the income brought to economy A by its exports?' (ibid.: 86). Since the total exports of country A's economy are equal to 10 dollars in each period, and since the reimbursement of the previous debt is of 1 dollar, the answer must be 9 dollars.

Schmitt analyzes the situation in $p_1$ first. The revenue in money R derived from country A's exports is equal to 10 dollars; the reimbursement of the loan of 1 dollar obtained in $p_0$ reduces it to 9 dollars. The conclusion is straightforward: '[a] new loan of [1 dollar] is [...] required in $p_1$ in order for the external revenue to be still equal to 10 dollars' (ibid.: 87). Nothing changes when we consider what happens in all the successive periods. Given that country A's net imports are repeatedly equal to 1 dollar in each period, and since A's total exports in each period are worth 10 dollars, the reimbursement made regularly, period after period, reduces to 9 dollars the external revenue still available in country A's economy. However, A's total imports amount to 11 dollars in each period, which brings to a total of 2 dollars the sum A's economy must borrow abroad to finance its net purchases worth 1 dollar.

Two loans of 1 dollar each are required to cover the initial deficit of 1 dollar and the monetary gap deriving from its payment. The first loan cuts to 10 dollars the foreign revenue obtained by A's economy, whereas the second loan increases it to 11 dollars, the sum of foreign currency needed to pay in full economy A's imports.

> The revenue is re-established at the level of 10 dollars thanks to the first loan of [1 dollar] in $p_q$. The country's revenue is thus again of 10 dollars in period $p_q$. Yet it is mandatory that it be increased to [11] dollars to complete the current payment of A's purchases (imports) of a value of [11] dollars.
>
> (ibid.: 87)

Finally, the deficit of 1 dollar of country A, which derives from the net imports of its residents, requires A's economy to obtain two loans, for a total value of 2 dollars, one of which affects country A as a whole and leads to the formation of its sovereign debt.

## Concluding remarks

Let us start by clarifying that the scenario chosen by Schmitt, in which a net importing country finances its deficit through a foreign loan, in no way limits the general validity of the sovereign debt theorem. In fact, this case covers all the possibilities for a deficit country to pay for its net imports in the present non-system of international payments. Resorting to foreign currency reserves does not help, since reserves are not available for residents to pay their foreign creditors. Even if they were, nothing would substantially change, because the reduction in reserves, further to the second payment of A's net imports, would define an increase in country A's external debt. Whether A's sovereign debt derives from a foreign loan, or from a decrease in A's foreign financial asset, it defines a pathology caused by the duplication of the payment of A's net imports.

Let us summarize the main aspects of Schmitt's discovery.

### *The macroeconomic nature of the pathology*

Exports and imports, both commercial and financial, are always carried out by the private and public sectors of a domestic economy, that is, by a country's residents. An external loan is obtained through the sale of IOUs and defines a transaction between residents of two different countries. The reimbursement of a loan as well as the payment of imports are also transactions carried out by residents. If the system of international payments was sound, payments between residents and non-residents would involve their countries only as *intermediaries*, and no macroeconomic payment would ever be added to the microeconomic payments of residents.

What must be clearly understood is that, even though the country as such does not carry out a payment, it can nevertheless carry the charge of a transaction of its residents. This is what happens in the case of country A's net imports. As far as A's residents are concerned, they pay their imports once only. They do so in money R, even if A's importers pay in money A, because R's exporters want to be paid in their own currency. Country A's residents in general must therefore obtain another loan from R in order for the payment of A's importers to be transformed into a payment in money R. It is here that the country itself enters the picture, because the loan obtained by A's residents has an impact on their set: it defines a loss of part of economy A's future production, which reduces to zero the debt of the country as a whole.

Country A's current net imports are balanced by its future net exports, and no other payment should involve the country as such. Unfortunately, this is not the case, because the money R borrowed by A's residents is lost in the payment to country R's exporters. Because of the net debt that it leaves behind, this loss has an impact on country A, whose domestic income is reduced accordingly.

Whereas country A's residents do not incur any net debt, their country does. A's borrowers do not suffer any net loss when money R is paid to R's exporters, because they give it up in exchange for an equivalent amount of money A. Their country, on the other hand, suffers a net loss, because nothing compensates the decrease in foreign currency due to the payment of country R's exporters. Since imported real goods worth 1 dollar cannot be the counterpart of *both* financial exports worth 1 dollar and a monetary payment worth 1 dollar, country A's loss of money R entails the formation of a net external debt of a pathological nature: its sovereign debt.

No one is responsible for this state of affairs, which must be blamed on the absence of a true system of international payments and not to the behaviour of country A's residents. Yet, eventually the burden of country A's sovereign debt falls on their residents, who suffer from the consequences of the impoverishment of their country's economy. No single resident is directly hit by the second payment of A's net imports, but its consequences, which affect the undifferentiated set of country A's residents, will necessarily be distributed among them. For example, the sovereign debt crisis suffered by Greece in 2010 has entailed the adoption of austerity measures that have seriously affected the living standard of the Greek population, in particular its lower and middle classes.

Essentially, what is wrong with these measures is not that they are excessive or unequally distributed (which they undoubtedly are), but that they are *totally unjustified*. In fact, they rest on the erroneous belief that Greece has lived above its means, that it was 'freeloading'. Schmitt shows that this is not at all the case and, on the contrary, Greece has fully paid for its net imports. The payment required from Greece and from other countries hit by the sovereign debt crisis is a *second* payment, the pathological nature of which has been missed by mainstream economists and experts of international institutions. 'If, nevertheless, indebted countries suffer from the intolerable conditions imposed on them, it is precisely because their debt is multiplied by austerity, itself dictated by the logical flaw in the system' (ibid.: 83).

### *The monetary nature of the pathology*

To the extent that a country's imports are balanced by its exports, no monetary payment is added to its real payment. The payment of A's imports and exports are monetary, of course, yet they are carried out through the circular flow of money R without involving any additional cost for country A. The equality of imports and exports guarantees the equality of the inflows and the outflows of money R, which is used merely as vehicular means of payment, whose content is real.

When net imports enter the picture, things change radically, because this time the expenditure of money R required to finance the monetary payment of R's exporters is unilateral. Country A is debited with an amount of money R that it obtains from country R through a loan. Thus, country A must *purchase* the money R required to convey to country R the real payment of its residents' net imports. In other words, the conversion of the payment by A's importers into a payment in money R takes place at a positive cost because money R is not provided for free by a true system of international payments.

> [I]t is a fact that the payment in the importers' domestic currency is not valid when addressed to exporting countries. A conversion is necessary. Yet, the conversion of the domestic deficit in foreign currencies is a cost-free transaction only to the extent that the country balances its imports and its exports.
>
> (ibid.: 44)

Albeit monetary, payments between residents and non-residents should have a real content and no monetary cost. Within any given economy, this is indeed the case, and the sole cost of an agent's net purchases is a sum of income: domestic payments are conveyed by the circular flow of domestic currency provided at no cost by the national banking system. A similar system does not exist between countries yet, so that a net importing country is forced to purchase the foreign currency needed to convey the real payment of its economy's net imports. Money is nothing but an immaterial flow, a numerical means of payment issued at zero cost by banks. By transforming it into an asset, the present non-system of international payments forces deficit countries to purchase it, a transaction that pathologically multiplies the total cost of its net imports by two.

### *The double payment of country A's net imports fuels the international financial bubble*

If academic economists and experts of the international institutions have failed to discover the double payment of countries' net imports so far, it is because it defies common sense and challenges the conviction that net importers pay their external purchases once only and foreign exporters are paid for their external sales once only. The pathology would be blatant, if importers were forced to pay twice or if exporters benefitted from a double payment. The worldly situation is more complex: it is the net importing country as a whole that assumes the cost of the second payment, and it is the international financial bubble formed in the rest-of-the-world that benefits from it.

The debt 'due to the monetary deficit generated by the disorder of the system of international payments is formed toward the stateless financial bubble' (Schmitt 2010a: 14, m.t.). Neither country R's residents, nor their country are the beneficiaries of country A's payment, which increases the purely nominal capital that feeds speculation all over the world. 'It is the international financial capital, an essential cause of the financial crisis that rages today at the international level, which is the over-indebted countries' creditor' (ibid.: 14, m.t.).

By being macroeconomically involved in the payment of net imports carried out by its residents, the deficit country contributes to the formation of its own sovereign debt. The latter is an external debt incurred by the deficit country as a whole to the international financial bubble, which replaces the rest-of-the-world as country A's creditor. Consequently, the financial bubble will also benefit from the payment of interest that the country will have to carry out on top of the payment of its residents. However, the beneficiaries of the second payment are financial lenders no different from those who gain from the first, normal payment of the debt incurred by A's residents and the interest accruing to it.

Residents of country R who lend to country A's borrowers might be, and mostly are, different economic agents, though they are all financial lenders. In this respect, it is vain to try and distinguish them according to whether their loans are financed out of a pathological capital or not. Even if country A as such is indebted to the international financial bubble, all foreign loans are granted to A's residents by foreign lenders, and it is to them that principal repayment and interest payments must be made.

> The beneficiaries of the *second* payment are only financial lenders, exactly in the same way as the lenders of justified monetary funds. It would therefore be illogical to voice criticism in this respect: the *"second"* loans and the "normal" loans have exactly the same origin. *"Second" borrowings* generate flawless loans; they simply *should not exist.*
>
> (Schmitt 2014: 41)

No particular foreign lender can be pinpointed as acting on behalf of the financial bubble. The disorder is macroeconomic and is distributed all over the undifferentiated sets of deficit countries' residents. Likewise, the international financial bubble is not concentrated in the hands of few 'powerful capitalists' but is available to the undifferentiated set of financial lenders. It remains true that surplus countries 'derive no profit from the double payment of their partners' debts. The second payment of external debts does accrue only to, let us repeat it, the famous (and still insufficiently defined) financial bubble' (ibid.: 95).

What explains the formation of the financial bubble is the transformation of key currencies from means into objects of payment. Through duplication, key currencies form a supranational pathological capital, which is purely nominal, deprived of any real content (see Chapter 7), and invested in the international financial market. The purchase by country A's residents of the foreign currency needed to pay their foreign correspondents is a transaction that ends up raising the value of this nominal capital, an impact that is highly detrimental to deficit and surplus countries alike.

# 18 The one-country solution to the sovereign debt problem

Due to the shortcomings of the present non-system of international payment, deficit countries' sovereign debt is a source of disorder crying out for reform. The best solution would require a consensus to modify the system on a world-wide scale. However, a new Bretton Woods-like agreement is not in the cards. Therefore, the countries currently worst affected would have to wait helplessly for their trading partners to realize that they too would be better off if a true system of international payments replaced the present one. To give a single country the chance to protect itself against the double charge of the payment of its net imports, Schmitt devoted the last years of his life to the elaboration of a one-country reform. Chapter 18 deals with this solution as proposed by Schmitt in his 2014 paper.

## The aims and principles of Schmitt's reform

### *The aims of Schmitt's reform*

The aim of Schmitt's reform is to avoid the formation of a country's sovereign debt in the first place. As we saw in Chapter 17, the payment of deficit countries' net imports costs twice the amount due to foreign exporters in the present non-system of international payments. This additional charge triggers the formation of sovereign debt: in order to cover the *monetary* cost of the payment of net imports, which is added to the *real* cost, deficit countries incur a foreign debt that is entirely groundless.

Let us refer again to the example of a deficit country A facing the rest-of-the-world, R, and assume that its total imports, equal to \$14 billion, exceed by \$4 billion its total exports, which are equal to 10 billion US dollars. Country A's domestic currency is money A ($M_A$), and its rate of exchange with the domestic currency of R ($M_R$ or the US dollar) is of $M_A1$ for $M_R1 = \$1$. When A's economy borrows \$4 (billion, we shall no longer spell it out) from R in order to bring its *monetary* inflows up to the level of its monetary outflows, it gives up a sum of IOUs, whose object is an equivalent amount of its *future* production. In so doing, A's domestic economy pays fully, in real terms, for its net imports of R's output. If cross-border transactions occurred within a properly

DOI: 10.4324/9781351271325-24

functioning system of international payments, country A would not have to take on any further payment of its net imports: the system would automatically provide the *vehicular* currency needed to convey A's real payment free of cost. It then logically follows that 'external debts incurred by countries should not even exist' (Schmitt 2014: 95).

Only if net imports were *not* paid by A's residents would the external or sovereign debt of their country be justified. Yet, this is sadly not the case. Importers, residents of country A, pay for all their foreign purchases through an expenditure of their domestic income. It is true that R's exporters must be paid in dollars, but it is equally true that A's importers pay their due in money A terms. 'In observable actual practice, imports, whether compensated or net, are definitely paid in money A by the residents concerned, who do not care about payments in foreign currency' (ibid.: 93).

If no one of A's residents is indebted, why should their country be? The answer is that it should not: '[a]s the country's residents do not incur any external debt, it is necessarily the same for the country itself, the set of its residents' (ibid.: 94). The conversion of the payment in $M_A$ into a payment in $M_R$ should not entail any additional cost for country A. Schmitt's reform, therefore, aims to provide deficit countries with an accounting protocol that guarantees the cost-free conversion of the payment carried out by A's economy (by its private and public sectors) in money A into a payment in money R, say US dollars. In the absence of an international solution, Schmitt's reform offers to protect any single country implementing this protocol against a dysfunctional system that forces deficit countries to *purchase the vehicular means of payment* issued at zero cost by creditor countries' banking system.

Schmitt's reform also provides deficit countries with a mechanism designed to prevent any loss of domestic resources due to the additional payment on their net imports. This will prove highly beneficial for them, as well as help their international partners. It is clear that, by curbing the expansion of the international financial bubble and by increasing the resources of indebted countries, *surplus countries*, too, will benefit from a sounder economic framework, leading to a reduction in the intensity and number of financial crises and the emergence of wealthier foreign partners. The impact would be amplified were more countries to implement Schmitt's reform. To make this possible, we must first review the principles on which this reform rests and reiterate the rationale behind them.

Let us first present the principles of Schmitt's 2014 reform, which are closely related to those he elaborated in *La France souveraine de sa monnaie* (1984) (see Chapter 8).

### *The principles of Schmitt's reform*

Conceptually, one must clearly distinguish the residents of any given country from the country itself, i.e., from the set of residents. The status of countries as being the set of residents must be recognized and affirmed, if we are to avoid *mixing* domestic monetary flows with international monetary flows. Specifically, this means that deficit countries must create a *national* or *sovereign Bureau*, whose mandate is to keep the two flows separate and make sure that no national currency is purchased as if it were a real good.

In our example, country A's Bureau will replace R as the recipient of the payment in money A of A's importers and will be in charge of carrying out the payment, also in money A, of A's exporters.

> The Bureau will address the banks [acting on behalf of exporters and importers] as follows:
>
> - *Addressed to exporters*: your only rights are defined in your national currency and the Bureau is your only debtor.
> - *Addressed to importers*: your only debts are defined in your national currency and the Bureau is your only creditor.
>
> (ibid.: 54)

At the same time, A's Bureau will pay R in dollars for the external purchases of A's economy, and it will be paid by R, also in US dollars, for its external sales. The aim of this measure is twofold:

1) To avoid the loss of domestic income spent to pay for net imports, and
2) To internalize all cross-border payments. To reach this goal, the Bureau will operate *simultaneously* as a resident and as the representative of the country vis-à-vis the rest-of-the-world.

> The safest and simplest method of preventing the domestic economy to suffer the consequences of the second charge of debts it to guarantee that the external payments of the domestic economy are all carried out between residents. To this effect, it is enough that the Bureau transforms every domestic payment addressed abroad [...] into an external payment of which the Bureau is itself personally the only debtor.
>
> (ibid. 53)

However, if the Bureau were a mere *intermediary* between country A's residents and country R's exporters, the reform would prove inadequate, since the Bureau's net gain in domestic currency due to the difference between the sum paid by A's importers, $M_A 14$, and that paid to A's exporters, $M_A 10$, would still be the object of the debt of A's Bureau to R. If the payments in money A were not disconnected from the payments in dollars, which would be the case if A's Bureau was nothing more than an intermediary, the present situation would not change. Schmitt's reform

> is more rigorous, because it no longer allows for a payment in domestic currency to be the object of a foreign loan. No purchaser and no lender abroad can include a sum of money A among their credits in country A.
>
> (ibid.: 54)

In other words, A's Bureau will have to carry out the payment of R's exporters 'as if it was itself the national economy's exporter' (ibid.: 54) so that the conversion in dollars of the payment in money A of its country's residents 'will no longer concern the rest of the world' (ibid.: 54).

Schmitt's first insight is that all external payments in domestic currency will go to the deficit country's Bureau, which will be responsible for paying R's exporter in money R (dollars), while avoiding the conversion of money A into dollars, that is, the purchase of dollars by the banks of A. His second insight concerns a net gain in money A, which the Bureau will obtain as the difference between its inflows and its outflows of MA. As a consequence of avoiding the loss of domestic resources, the value corresponding to the net payment of A's exporters will turn into a *net profit* for country A as a whole.

Schmitt's third insight is to ensure that the Bureau's net gain in money A remains the property of country A itself; to this effect '*it is necessary and sufficient that the Bureau lends abroad, in foreign currency, the whole value of its country's net imports*' (ibid.: 56). If the gain of A's Bureau corresponded to a net loan *of* R, it would not be a net profit and would be appropriated by the rest-of-the-world as the object of its loan. To avoid this, *the loan of R to A must be counterbalanced by an equivalent loan of A to R*. The counter-loan of A's Bureau to R will take place immediately, automatically, but it will be distinct from the loan of R, because 'borrowers and lenders in the economy R are distinct residents' (ibid.: 62), and so are the borrowers and lenders of A's economy.

This third insight is crucial: the implementation of the loan of country A to country R will have the twofold effect of 1) avoiding the loss of domestic income for country A, which A's residents spend to pay for their net imports, and 2) avoiding the formation of country A's external debt. 1) and 2) are not two distinct and additive effects but the two aspects of the same result. It is because the loan of A's Bureau *balances* that of R that country A will not incur a net debt to R, and it is for this reason that A's Bureau will not have to surrender its gain in money A to R.

The Bureau's counter-loan is the device that will ensure the circular flow of dollars needed to convey the cross-border payments of country A and country R. This means that, thanks to this automatic loan, country A will be able to guarantee the real payment of its net imports without having to purchase the foreign currency (dollar) required to convey it.

What Schmitt calls the fourth main idea of his reform, namely that '*surplus imports, paid by the sovereign Bureau, no longer create an external debt for the deficit countries*' (ibid.: 60) is a corollary of his third insight. By adding a reverse loan to the one obtained from R, A's Bureau will establish the 'coexistence of two equal-size financial transactions[...]: the loan of [4 dollars] granted by R to country A is offset by the loan of [4 dollars] granted by A's Bureau to non-residents' (ibid.: 62). *The aim of A's counter-loan is to balance A's and R's foreign transactions and transform A's net purchases into a reciprocal exchange.* Reciprocity guarantees the circular flow of money, which is what country A needs to avoid the additional cost of purchasing country R's domestic currency.

Ensuring the reciprocal real payment of A's and R's external transactions forestalls the formation of country A's sovereign debt. It is clear that if A's residents pay their total imports in full, and if there is no need for country A to pay for the conversion of money A into money R (a redundant requirement of the present non-system of international payments), country A's external debt can only be zero.

The principles of Schmitt's reform are clear and could be implemented easily. The clearest way to promote their implementation is to compare the present situation with the presumable outcome of the reform. Let us do it with the help of a novel presentation of the double payment of countries' net imports, slightly different yet complementary to the analysis in Chapter 17.

## Before and after Schmitt's reform: a useful comparison

### *The cumulative payment of country A's net imports in money A and in money R*

As we have seen in Chapter 17, Schmitt's analysis shows that, today, deficit countries pay for their net imports twice, once in real terms and once in monetary terms, and that the two payments are financed by two distinct loans. One of the loans is *microeconomic* and entails the foreign indebtedness of A's domestic economy; the other is *macroeconomic* and, even though it is incurred by A's economy, defines a sovereign debt that weighs on country A as a whole. We are now going to develop further the idea that the payment of A's net imports entails a double loss: the loss of a *future income* suffered by A's domestic economy and the loss of an equivalent *current income* suffered by country A as a whole.

The object of the loan obtained by A's domestic economy from R is the equivalent of the output that economy A will produce in the future, currently given up *in advance*. This means that the moment it receives the loan, A's economy transfers to R the rights over part of its future income. On the other hand, since R's exporters must be paid in money R and country A does not earn enough through its own real economy's exports, the money R obtained as a foreign loan is necessarily spent to the benefit of R's economy. If it were not so spent, it would balance the debt incurred by economy A and country A's net imports would be paid only once. But today this additional payment deprives country A of the counterpart of its loan-debt. As a result, A's economy ends up with *a net increase in debt*, which corresponds to the loss of an equivalent part of A's current income.

> [C]ountry A's domestic economy gives up a current product whose value is [4 dollars] *since period p*. This is necessarily so, because the external borrowing of [4 dollars] in *p* creates the external debt of A, which hits the domestic product of this country, also *in this period*.
>
> (ibid.: 80)

It is because country A runs a net debt vis-à-vis country R that R acquires ownership of part of the current domestic income previously owned by A's residents. Finally, 'country A loses, to the benefit of R, the property of a domestic product [or income] equivalent to its current deficit' (ibid.: 80) on top of losing a future product (or income) of the same amount. On the whole, the payment of net imports worth \$4 costs A \$8: four units as the loss of a future income suffered by A's residents and four of an actual income suffered by country A as a whole.

> The loss of future products is equivalent to [4 dollars]. The net loss of a current income is also equivalent to [4 dollars]. The total transfer amounts to the equivalent of [8] dollars, that is, to the value of the net import '*multiplied by 2*'.
>
> (ibid.: 81)

Exchanges between countries are always carried out by their domestic economies, and so are international payments. Importers are residents of country A, and it is on them that the burden of the first payment of net imports rests. Country A's payment is, first of all, a payment in money A carried out by A's residents, who spend part of their income to this effect. Yet, foreign exporters, residents of country R, demand to be paid in $M_R$ (dollars). It is here that a second payment is required. The payment in $M_A$ has to be converted into a payment in dollars, which means that the payment in an income of country A must be transformed into a payment in an income of country R.

> The two payments involved are clearly defined: even though it is a question of the payment of non-residents, A's domestic economy carries it out using part of its national income, and therefore in money A, whereas, through its change into money R [dollars], the same imports are settled through the expenditure of a foreign income from the moment they are defined to the debit of country A, considered as a whole.
>
> (ibid.: 58)

Country A must have access to dollars, which is why its domestic economy borrows these from R's economy. Then A's banks must convert the payment in money A of A's importers into a payment in dollars. They do so by debiting A's importers in money A and by crediting R's exporters in dollars. We are thus faced with a purchase of dollars through the expenditure of an equivalent income in money A. A sum of dollars is transformed into an object of exchange; it is purchased as if it were a real asset. As a result, the income in money A spent by A's importers for payment of their net imports is no longer available in A's economy.

The domestic income lost by country A because of the net debt incurred abroad is nothing other than the income in money A spent by its residents toward payment of their net imports. This income is not recovered by anybody in country A, since it has been spent on the final purchase of the dollars needed to pay R's exporters. According to Schmitt, this loss of domestic income reflects a reduction in economy A's domestic production, *which leads to an equivalent increase in unemployment.*

The measure of a country's employment is given by that of its current income. If available income decreases, so does employment. The level of 'the income produced in real goods [...] falls in line with the value of the monetary income available for the purchase of national output' (ibid.: 88). As this value suffers a reduction of 4 dollars, the level of real production decreases accordingly. However, the payment in income A of A's residents is not enough; economy A must also borrow an amount of income R to enable the payment of R's exporters in dollars. 'Even though country A suffers from the decrease of its employment, [...] it must still borrow 4 dollars abroad in order to cover the surplus of its expenditures in dollars' (ibid.: 89). The decrease in employment is accompanied by the loss of economy A's future output, which is the proper object of the loan granted by R's economy and raises the total cost of the payment of net imports worth 4 dollars to 8 dollars.

Whether we identify the cost thus incurred with a loss of current domestic income, hence with an increase in country A's unemployment, or with the formation of country A's sovereign debt, the outcome is the same: the present non-system of international payments multiplies by two the cost of net imports paid through a foreign loan. Country A as a whole must shoulder the second payment, which forces it to either cover the loss worth 4 dollars in its economy's domestic income or to counterbalance the increase in unemployment. Each of these two steps implies the other, and they both are subsumed under the third, which defines the final result: a pathological duplication that affects the payment of net imports. The formation of new external debt is the cost A must face restoring its domestic income, i.e., its employment, to its former level.

### *Once the reform is instituted, country A will no longer suffer from a loss of its national income*

Schmitt aims to provide a mechanism that will *internalize* all the payments carried out by A's importers, while at the same time avoiding the expenditure of a sum of domestic currency on the purchase of foreign currency. The country's sovereign Bureau will receive the payments in money A previously made by A's indebted residents to their foreign creditors. As an institution of country A, the Bureau is a resident, so all payments made to it will be internal to A's domestic economy. At the same time, the money A spent to pay for A's net imports will no longer be lost on purchasing the foreign currency (dollars) needed to credit R's exporters in their own currency. A's Bureau will be tasked with paying R's exporters in dollars, but the Bureau will not allow the conversion of money A into dollars that occurs today. The payment in money A of A's importers will be kept totally distinct and separate from that in dollars, thus avoiding the conversion of country R's domestic currency into an object of exchange.

Country A's net expenditures are determined not only by its current net imports but also by the amounts it has to pay in interest and principal repayments relative to previously incurred debts. A's Bureau will collect all the payments in money A carried out by A's indebted residents, those corresponding to the *new* debt as well as those corresponding to *previous* debts. A's Bureau will gain far more than the amount of economy A's net expenditures needed for balancing its current imports. 'All payments to the external world, even to offset debts, will be carried out by purchasers to the ultimate benefit of the Bureau, which will receive them in place of the foreign countries' (ibid.: 45).

Having pointed out that a country's net global imports must be calculated by considering the totality of the country's expenditures, all new and old outstanding debts, let us work through our numerical example, assuming that they are included in the total amount of $14. The difference between imports and exports of country A's residents corresponds to the Bureau's net gain in money A. 4 units of A's current income worth 4 dollars are not lost in paying for economy A's net imports but are entered into the Bureau's account as net profit of country A.

The difference between the present disorderly system and the system put in place by the reform concerns not only the loss of country A's current income but also that of its future income. By avoiding the payment of R's exporters through a net foreign loan, the reform will avert the loss of part of economy A's future output, which is the real object of the external loan obtained by A's domestic economy.

'Before the reform, the deficit country suffers the formation of an external debt while yielding to the rest of the world the ownership of real goods that it will itself produce in the future' (ibid.: 46). After the reform, the payment of A's net imports will no longer be *financed* by a foreign loan; as a consequence, country A will no longer pay for its current imports with its future exports. Thanks to the reform, both the loss of country A's current income and that of its future income are reduced to zero because the payment of country R will be carried out by A's Bureau, which will no longer permit the formation of external or sovereign debts affecting country A as a whole.

As we already know, the gain in money A of the Bureau will be *net* only if the reform can allow the payment of R in dollars to take place without transforming A's Bureau into a mere intermediary. If the Bureau was simply to replace A's economy as the payer of country A's net imports through a foreign loan, its gain in money A would be appropriated by R and the loss of A's domestic and future income could not be avoided.

> [T]he reform must indeed ensure that the domestic payments, in money A, be disconnected from external payments, defined in money R. The Bureau's intermediation is not enough. Nothing changes if it simply passes

> on the payments it receives. It is necessary and essential that the Bureau first cancels all foreign credits for its domestic economy's imports.
>
> (ibid.: 54)

Let us see how this is achieved by Schmitt's reform.

***No sovereign debt will ever be formed***

To avoid the unfair and dysfunctional result of the present non-system of international payments, the reform makes it impossible for country A to incur an external debt while still benefitting from a foreign loan. Schmitt specifies the mechanism of his reform as an *automatic loan* of A's Bureau to country R of an amount of dollars equal to the one borrowed from R. The loan of A's Bureau will counterbalance that of R and thus avoid the formation of A's external debt. But would it not cancel R's loan, too? Would it have no impact at all on the payment that A would still be expected to make and on the formation of A's external debt this entails? Schmitt's answer is no.

The two loans

> cannot cancel each other out. It is true, of course, that the foreign currency borrowed and lent is a zero-sum; yet the initial borrowing and the lending that follows it are positive transactions even though one is the *inverse* of the other. This is the case simply because the Bureau lends [4 dollars] to residents of R distinct from the initial lenders.
>
> (ibid.: 78)

At any rate, the impact of the loan of A's Bureau to R appears to be jeopardized by the call for the Bureau to borrow another sum of 4 dollars in order to pay country A's net imports. The need for a second loan is beyond dispute: the actual problem concerns its role in the formation of country A's sovereign debt. Schmitt maintains that the second loan will not affect country A's external indebtedness, because it 'is indeed only the reproduction of the first. It is certain therefore that the loan granted by country A compensates both the second and the first loan to country A' (ibid.: 63).

The logical sequence is as follows.

1) First external borrowing of A's Bureau = 4 dollars
2) External loan of A's Bureau to R = 4 dollars
3) Second external borrowing of A's Bureau = 4 dollars
4) 1) + 3) = 4 dollars
5) 1) + 3)−2) = 0 dollars

It appears that

> [c]ountry A's external debt is initially of [(4−4) = 0 dollars] since the Bureau lends also [4 dollars]. Finally, the debt incurred is of [4 dollars]

> because of the second loan. Since the credit that adds to it is of [4 dollars], the "experts" of the Bureau do not have the choice, but to add – [4 dollars] to + [4 dollars], which gives the value of their country's indebtedness at 0 dollars.
>
> (ibid.: 63–4)

Today, two different loans of 4 dollars each are required for the payment of A's net imports worth 4 dollars. The first loan gives economy A ownership over part of R's current output in exchange for the right over an equivalent part of A's future product. The second loan gives country A an amount of dollars in exchange for its acknowledgement of debt. The monetary payment of A's net imports deprives country A of the dollars obtained from R and leaves it with a net foreign debt worth 4 dollars.

According to the new protocol, two loans will still be necessary, but A's sovereign debt will be avoided thanks to the loan of A's Bureau to R. Today, this loan does not exist, which is why country A as a whole suffers from a net foreign debt. After the reform, although the two loans obtained by country A's Bureau will be of 4 dollars each, the ensuing debt will amount to 4 dollars only, and it will be compensated by the loan of A to R. In the present situation, country A borrows twice without lending anything to country R. The consequence is an increase in A's sovereign debt of 4 dollars. In the new system, country A will still borrow twice, but it will also lend 4 dollars to country R. This loan will define a debt of R to A, which will neutralize the debt of A to R from the outset.

Here, it is important to uphold the distinction between the *microeconomic* debt incurred today by A's domestic economy for the real payment of country A's net imports and the *macroeconomic* debt that rests on country A, and which is due to the monetary payment of A's net imports. 'What remains for the external payment of net imports is the second loan only, which is now their *sole cost*' (ibid.: 65). One cost, the microeconomic one, is unassailable; it corresponds to the real payment of country A's net imports. The other cost is uncalled for and will be cancelled by the Bureau's counterbalancing loan. Here, we simply need to observe that the cost of the second (microeconomic) loan is real, i.e., covered by a transfer of real goods to R, to understand that country A cannot incur a net debt to R. In other words, it should be clear that, by allowing country A to pay its excess imports once only and in real terms, Schmitt's reform will avoid the formation of any net debt of country A.

Schmitt distinguishes between the *substance* and the *form* of the payment of A's surplus imports. The substance 'is simply the domestic product handed over to R. The form of this product, in an income A as the entire domestic product, is in money A and not in money R' (ibid.: 64). Therefore, the *raison d'être* of the reform is to make sure that paying for net imports does not mean paying for their substance as well as their form.

> The domestic economy pays its deficit by giving up real funds, in that it provides the rest of the world with the gain and possession of a part, equal

> to the external deficit, of its national product. [...] The function of the sovereign Bureau could not be simpler or clearer: to prevent that the payment in foreign currency be costly.
>
> (ibid.: 64)

At present, the form of the payment entails an additional cost, because the payment in money A must be transformed into a payment in money R. In future, '[i]n order to cancel the cost in foreign currencies, which transform or give another *form* to the payment of the surplus imports, the Bureau [will lend] abroad all the sum of foreign currencies borrowed' (ibid.: 65).

If the dollar is mistakenly purchased as a net asset in its function of means of payment, the payment of 4 dollars has a form that costs \$4 to country A, which must purchase what is not provided for free by the system of payments. In the present non-system, the outflow of dollars is greater than the inflow even though surplus imports are fully paid in real terms, and the difference must be covered by an additional loan, that is, through the purchase of \$4. The reform will equalize inflows and outflows and provide the monetary form of the payment of A's net import for free. 'Through the counterbalancing debt, incurred by R as a result of the loan granted by the Bureau, the sum of gains in foreign currency is equal to the sum of its losses despite the fact that imports exceed exports' (ibid.: 65).

According to the rule of international exchanges, a country's real exports must always be balanced by equivalent real imports and vice versa. The necessary equality of global imports and global exports is always verified, whether in an orderly system or in a disorderly one. At present, the equality of country R's imports and exports, as well as that of country A's exports and imports, is obtained by increasing R's imports from a value of 10 dollars to one of 14 dollars through a loan granted to country A. It is because the object of this loan is worth 4 dollars of A's future production, of which R becomes the owner at once, that R's imports rise from \$10 to \$14. For the same reason, A's exports of current and future output are increased by the same amount as the level of A's global imports. Yet, the loan obtained by country A cannot at the same time increase its exports in real terms and provide A with the amount of foreign currency it needs to cover its monetary deficit.

A single loan cannot have two distinct and equivalent objects. Another loan is needed to cover the difference between country A's monetary outflows and its monetary inflows.

The reform must also conform with the rule of international exchanges, and it can do so by reducing R's exports from \$14 to \$10, thanks to the loan of A's Bureau to R.

> The sovereign Bureau acts in such a way that R's imports in period *p* relate all to the period *p* itself. The value of R's imports is thus equal to 10 dollars and no longer to [14 dollars], as is the case before the reform.
>
> (ibid.: 81)

R's domestic economy will still export goods for a value of $14, but the counter-loan of A's Bureau will bring R's external gains down to $10. By the same token, country A's imports will drop from $14 to $10. A's domestic economy will still import goods worth $14, but country A will no longer have to borrow $8 in order to pay for net imports worth 4 dollars. A's Bureau will pay for a part of A's imports equal to 4 dollars through its loan to R and the remaining $10 through A's exports. Its outflows of dollars will be matched by equal inflows, without any need to resort to a net loan from R.

While at present country A must obtain the $4 required to equalize its outflows and its inflows of dollars through a *net* foreign loan, in future A's Bureau will obtain them for free, through a credit-debit that will inhibit the formation of any net external debt of country A. Today, the payment of A's surplus imports is double: the payment in money A carried out by A's residents is added to the payment in money R whose cost is borne by country A itself (see Figure 18.1).

The reform will reduce the two payments to a single one: country A will give up part of its current domestic product worth $4 through the vehicular use of a foreign currency at no cost to its economy.

A final argument might further clarify this difficult but crucial aspect of Schmitt's reform. As we have observed, two loans will still be necessary after the reform. Yet, one of them will finance a counterbalancing loan that will cancel country A's sovereign debt from the get-go. In the absence of this *counter-loan*, A's Bureau would incur a macroeconomic debt that would reduce to zero its gain in money A obtained as the difference between the sum paid by A's importer and that paid to A's exporters. In this hypothetical case, the reform would be useless.

The intervention of the Bureau is significant only if it *prevents* the formation of A's sovereign debt. The counter-loan has this effect, because it counterbalances the loan of R and enables A's debit to be matched with a simultaneous and equivalent credit. Since the formation of a net sovereign debt will no longer be possible, the gain of the Bureau in money A will not be appropriated by R; it will remain at the disposal of country A and define a net profit. The second loan that A's Bureau will obtain from R will thus be compensated by its gain in money A, which confirms the fact that if a deficit country's economy pays for its net imports in real terms, neither the economy nor its country would end up carrying a net external debt.

Finally, the Bureau's first loan will be balanced by its counter-loan to R, while its second loan will be compensated by its net gain in money A.

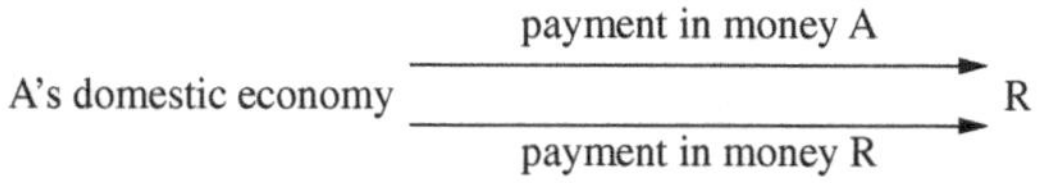


*Figure 18.1* Double payment of country A's net imports before the reform. Source: Schmitt 2014: 65

> The deficit country's external debt, 4 dollars, will thus be entirely compensated by an income formed and acquired in money A. Logic will thus be respected: a country does not carry any debt distinct from the debt of its residents, so that a country whose residents have fully paid their debt does only carry "debts-credits", that is, zero sum debts.
>
> (ibid.: 96)

### *The gain obtained by the Bureau must be invested in a new production*

As we have seen, today the impact of the loss of domestic current income suffered by country A is manifest in the increase in A's unemployment. If we suppose A's domestic production to be equal to 154 units of money A before the payment of A's surplus imports, the payment of a deficit of $4 reduces the amount of income available in A's economy to 150 units of $M_A$. The reduction in the monetary income available in the country implies an equivalent reduction in real production because the value of the real goods produced by A's domestic economy is measured by the monetary income actually available. This means that the second payment of country A's net imports reduces the level of production to a value of $150, a loss in production mirrored in an equivalent increase in unemployment.

> Yet, the income produced in real goods cannot remain at this level; on the contrary it falls in line with the value of the monetary income available for the purchase of national output. As this value is reduced by 4 dollars, the level of real production is reduced accordingly, from the value of 154 to the value of 150 dollars.
>
> (ibid.: 88)

In the present non-system of international payments, country A suffers from an increase in unemployment due to the loss of a part of its domestic income, equal to 4 units of money A, and, at the same time, it must borrow $4 abroad to cover the surplus of its expenditures in dollars. The reform will avoid the loss of A's domestic income, because, instead of being spent on purchasing the $4 borrowed abroad, the net expenditure in money A of A's importers will define a gain of A's Bureau. Schmitt observes, however, that the reform would not succeed in reducing unemployment if the Bureau did not invest its profit in a new production. 'The reform requires that the [Bureau's] profit finances a new production, additional, of economy A' (ibid.: 90).

The fact is that, even if they are obtained by A's Bureau, the 4 units of money A spent by A's residents on purchasing R's output would nevertheless be lost because of the expenditure of $4 by the Bureau.

> If expenditures of income formed in money A were all for purchases of pre-existent goods, the net expenditures of foreign currency (dollars) would compulsorily lead to the reduction of national income, whose value would only be of 150 instead than of 154 dollars.
>
> (ibid.: 91)

Even after the implementation of Schmitt's reform, the deficit country will have to pay its net imports by borrowing abroad a sum of dollars. Unlike what happens today, the payment of A's net imports will no longer be *financed* by a foreign loan, which is why it will not cause a positive sovereign debt. Yet, country A's Bureau will still need to find $4 on top of the $10 obtained through its economy's exports. The expenditure of these $4 would reduce A's domestic production from $154 to $150 in value terms unless the Bureau (acting on behalf of its country's budget or of its government) invested its profit in an additional production. The investment by A's Bureau of its gain worth $4 in a new production re-establishes economy A's production at the level of 154 units of money A, thus avoiding the increase in country A's unemployment.

> In order to maintain the domestic production of its national economy unchanged at the level of a value equal to 154 dollars, it is imperative that its government or its budget obtains more than a mere purchasing power: it must obtain the power to produce and not just to buy.
>
> (ibid.: 91)

As previously argued, the gains of country A's Bureau would not be net if the Bureau acted purely as an intermediary between its domestic economy and the rest-of-the-world. Thanks to the loan of A's Bureau to R, A's macroeconomic debt will no longer build up, and the gain of the Bureau will be *net*. However, A's Bureau will still have to borrow an extra $4 in order to cover the difference between its outflows and its inflows of dollars. Country A will not incur a *net* external debt because of this new loan, because the debt will be fully compensated by the Bureau's net gain in money A.

Now, the problem is that the profit of A's Bureau cannot compensate A's foreign debt while also remaining available to finance the purchase of A's domestic output. The same sum of money A, worth $4, cannot fulfil simultaneously two different tasks, each requiring the availability of a positive entry of $4. This is why, to avoid reducing A's employment from $154 to $150 in value, the net gain of A's Bureau will have to be invested in a new production.

> [T]he value of 4 dollars spent to cover the difference between expenditures and receipts is no longer available for the selling of a domestic product. In order to restore the balance between real and monetary income of economy A it is therefore absolutely necessary that the profit of the Bureau finances an additional production.
>
> (ibid.: 98)

A's production, initially reduced from a value of $154 to one of $150 by the domestic payment of net imports, is finally re-established at the level of $154 by the Bureau's investment of its profit worth $4 in a new production, for example, of structural goods.

It is important to observe that, as shown in Chapter 4, a profit is always spent in the labour market. The net gain of A's Bureau is a kind of profit too, albeit of a very special kind, because it is obtained at zero cost as the difference between the expenditures of A's economy in favour of the Bureau and the expenditures of the latter in favour of the former. This means that the investment of this profit defines its expenditure for the final purchase of the new product from the moment of its production.

> [T]he expenditure of the Bureau's or the government's profit is an expenditure that is active both on the production and on the sale of goods: at the very instant this profit is transformed into new incomes, it is precisely an income already spent for the final purchase of the corresponding output.
> (ibid.: 98)

The Bureau will be able to employ people that A's domestic economy leaves unemployed today, because of the decrease in A's current income due to the double payment of its net imports. But what advantage would R derive from this new situation? The answer is self-evident: a system allowing deficit countries to increase their production enables creditor countries to benefit from the increased opportunities of reciprocally advantageous exchanges. It is obviously more beneficial to trade with a richer than with a poorer partner. As Schmitt puts it, it 'is obviously favourable to countries whose sales exceed their purchases on the international scene that unemployment does not increase in their partners' economies' (ibid.: 89).

### *Country R's exports will be fully paid by country A*

The aim of Schmitt's reform is to avoid the double payment of deficit countries' net imports, not to reduce their payments to zero. What must be eliminated is the emergence of the second payment that causes the formation of A's sovereign debt, not the legitimate payment country R is entitled to. What today causes the double payment of country A's net imports is the fact that a *monetary payment must be added to its real payment*. Tomorrow, thanks to the intervention of A's Bureau, the monetary cost of country A's payment will be reduced to zero, and the real cost will be covered by part of A's *current* product. Country R will be fully paid for its net imports with an equivalent amount of A's domestic output.

Let us repeat here that the necessary equality between A's (and R's) global imports and exports is but the law of international transactions, which is already fully complied with today. The reform will merely conform to it more closely, that is, without forcing country A to give away part of its *future* production. At the same time, the reform will suppress the need for country A to finance its net imports through a net foreign loan.

The key measure of Schmitt's reform is the counter-loan of A's Bureau to R. It is thanks to this loan that country A's external debt does not arise.

Likewise, it is because A's Bureau lends $4 to R that R benefits from the real payment of country A's net imports. This is so because, through its loan to R, country A pays an equivalent part of R's imports. In the same way as the loan of $4 granted by country R to country A amounts to the payment by country R of country A's net imports, the counterbalancing loan of country A to country R amounts to the payment by country A of country R's imports worth $4. The credit obtained by R 'brings to this country the payment of an import of equal value. This means that R's imports of [4 dollars] value are paid by country A and not by country R' (ibid.: 61).

Of the real goods worth 10 dollars imported by country R, a part equal to 4 dollars is paid by A's Bureau, 'which lends an income of this value to country R' (ibid.: 61). In the same way as country A obtains, in dollars and through R's loan, part of country R's domestic production, through the loan of A's Bureau country R obtains part of A's domestic production. As Schmitt claims,

> 1. Country A imports real assets equivalent to [14] dollars, but it pays them 10 dollars, the additional value being provided by country R's economy.
> 2. Country R imports real assets equivalent to 10 dollars, but it pays them only to the extent of [6] dollars, the difference being settled by economy A, of whom a product equal to [4] dollars is lent by Bureau A to non-residents.
>
> (ibid.: 61)

Since the loan of R to A is counterbalanced by an equivalent loan of A to R, the two countries' reciprocal debts cancel each other out, while each one pays an equal part of the other's imports. In Schmitt's words, 'R owes A exactly what A owes R. As a consequence, if country R does not get indebted to country A, it is logical and perfectly correct and just that country A does not get indebted to country R' (ibid.: 61).

The payment of country R's exports takes on its full meaning with reference to the production of country A, increased by the production financed by the Bureau's net profit in money A. Thanks to the loan granted by A's Bureau to R, a part of country A's domestic production worth $4 will be owned by country R. At present, R obtains part of A's future production and, on top of this loss, country A also loses an equivalent part of its current income. After the reform, country A will no longer lose part of its future output, and R will be paid for its net exports by obtaining at zero cost an equivalent part of A's current domestic production. R will not obtain the production financed by A's Bureau, purchased from the outset by the Bureau itself, in the labour market, but an equivalent part, worth $4, of the production of A's domestic economy. In other words, country R will benefit, in real payment for its net exports, from a production equivalent to the additional production of A's Bureau.

In the numerical example followed so far, country A's production will be equal to $150+4=154$ units of money A, where 150 units will be produced by A's domestic economy and 4 units by A's Bureau. Country R will obtain 4 of the 150 units of value produced by A's economy, while the Bureau will be the final purchaser of the output of the 4 units of value whose production will be financed by the investment of its net gain or profit. '[C]ountry R becomes the owner not of the "personal" product of A's government [Bureau], but of the equivalent of this product in any of the goods worth $150 produced by economy A in addition to its government [Bureau]' (ibid.: 91).

The payment of country R's net exports must have real content in order to be redeeming. In exchange for that part of its real production that R exports in excess, country A must give up an equivalent part of its own real production. This is not to say that country A must increase its exports from a value of $10 to one of $14. The aim of Schmitt's reform is not to impose a perfect balance of trade between countries. Countries will be totally free to import and export what and how much they wish and can. Their only constraint will be to avoid paying twice for their net imports. His protocol affords deficit countries the ability to pay for their net imports only once. Hence, country A will pay for its net imports in real terms without increasing its exports from $10 to $14. Country R will nevertheless be paid fully, because a part of its imports will be paid by A. Country A will still import more goods than it exports, and its net imports will still be paid by country R. Yet, R will be fully satisfied, because an equivalent part of its own imports will be paid by country A.

> Country R is not in the least harmed, because on one side it gives up real goods out of its own real product, while on the other side it cancels this expenditure, because it obtains the equivalent of the additional goods produced by the government [Bureau] of country A.
>
> (ibid.: 92)

The exchange between the goods imported in excess by country A from country R and the goods, of the same value, given for free by country A to country R will take place without any need for A to purchase the $4 that fills the gap between its imports and its exports. The elimination of the monetary cost of A's payment of its surplus imports will be achieved by the new 'method by which country R's expenditures become immediately equal to the expenditures of country A. The equality is necessary, but it is permissible and remains possible to give it an entirely different form' (ibid.: 72). The new method consists in equalizing the payment of country A to country R with those of country R to country A, that is, A's imports with R's imports, without taking into account the production of any future period.

> The sovereign Bureau acts in such a way that R's imports in period *p* relate all to the period *p* itself. The value of R's imports is thus equal to 10 dollars and no longer to [14 dollars], as in the case before the reform.
>
> (ibid.: 81)

By reducing the payments between A and R to a reciprocal exchange, the reform will enable country A to benefit from a circular flow of foreign currency without the need to purchase any.

> Through the counter-balancing debt, incurred by R as a result of the loan granted by the Bureau, the sum of gains in foreign currency is equal to the sum of its losses despite the fact that imports exceed exports. The equality between losses and gains means that the foreign currency that provides the final form to the payment of net imports is for *free* for the reformed country, as is the foreign currency used for the payment of offset imports.
> (ibid.: 65)

## The practical workings of Schmitt's reform

In this final section we shall consider two slightly different ways in which Schmitt's reform can be implemented in practice. I have drawn the former from Schmitt's own account of such implementation in his 2014 paper and the second from a description of the situation where A's Bureau has access to the country's foreign reserves.

### *Alternative number 1*

Let us think through the same numerical example we have followed so far and see what would happen in the first two periods after the implementation of the reform. For the sake of clarity, we assume that in the two periods considered, of one month each, country A runs a net deficit of $4, and it reimburses in the second period the sum borrowed from R in the first. We denote as $p_0$ the initial period and as $p_1$ the period that immediately follows it.

In $p_0$, A's sovereign Bureau borrows $4 from country R in order to pay country A's net imports (Figure 18.2).

In the same period, A's Bureau borrows another sum of $4, which it immediately lends to country R (Figure 18.3).

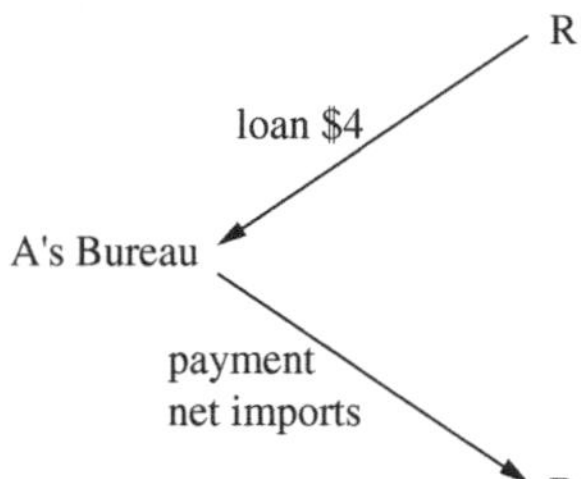


*Figure 18.2* Payment of country A's net imports by A's Bureau.

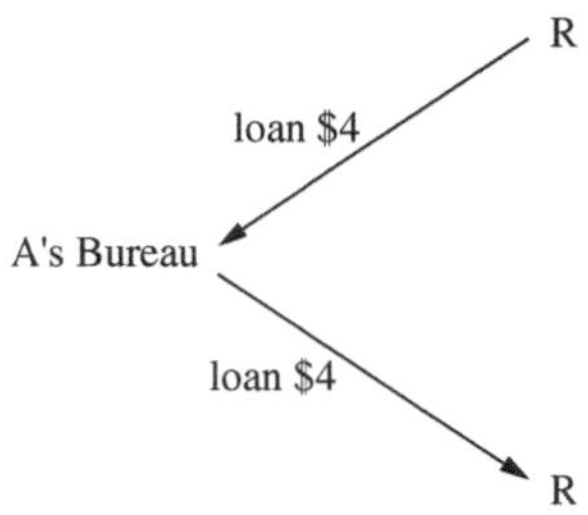


*Figure 18.3* Counterbalancing loan of country A's Bureau.

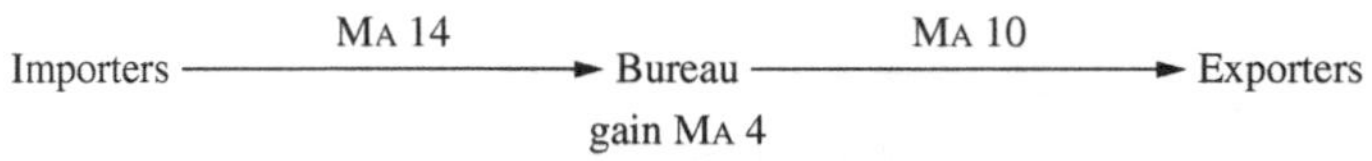


*Figure 18.4* Net gain of country A's Bureau.

We know the aim of the Bureau's counter-loan: to avoid the formation of country A's sovereign debt. As for the ordinary debt deriving from the first loan obtained by A's Bureau, it is compensated by the net gain, worth $4, which the Bureau realizes as the difference between the amount of domestic income paid by A's importers and the amount paid to A's exporters, as in Figure 18.4.

At the end of period $p_0$, we observe that country A has paid for its net imports in full, because its net purchases of R's products, paid by country R, are perfectly balanced by an equivalent sale of A's products financed by country A. The counter-loan granted by country A to country R allows country R to obtain a part of economy A's current production in exchange for an equivalent part of its own current production. Neither A nor R is required to add a monetary payment to their real exchanges, which explains why country A as such does not incur any net external debt despite the fact that its imports exceed its exports.

In $p_1$, A's Bureau has to reimburse the first loan obtained in $p_0$, which it does by borrowing a new amount of foreign currency, $4, from country R, as in Figure 18.5.

All the other transactions are the same as those carried out in $p_0$. Figure 18.6 shows all the payments carried out in $p_1$ by A's Bureau as well as all the payments that R makes to it in the same period.

As in $p_0$, country R is paid for its net exports in full, while the net gain in money A of A's Bureau compensates the ordinary debt incurred in paying for country A's net imports of $p_1$. The only difference with $p_0$ is that at the end of $p_1$ A's Bureau is still indebted to R, because of the loan that enables it to reimburse the ordinary loan obtained in $p_0$. However, suffice it to consider what happens over a long succession of periods (during which country A goes on importing more than it exports) to realize that this $4 debt will merely renew

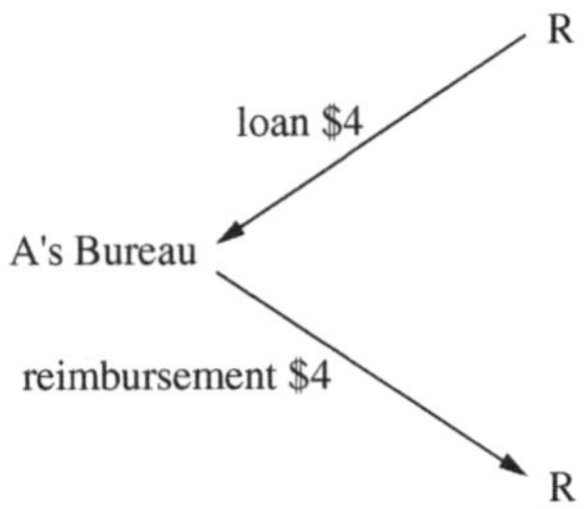


*Figure 18.5* Reimbursement of loan obtained in period $P_0$.

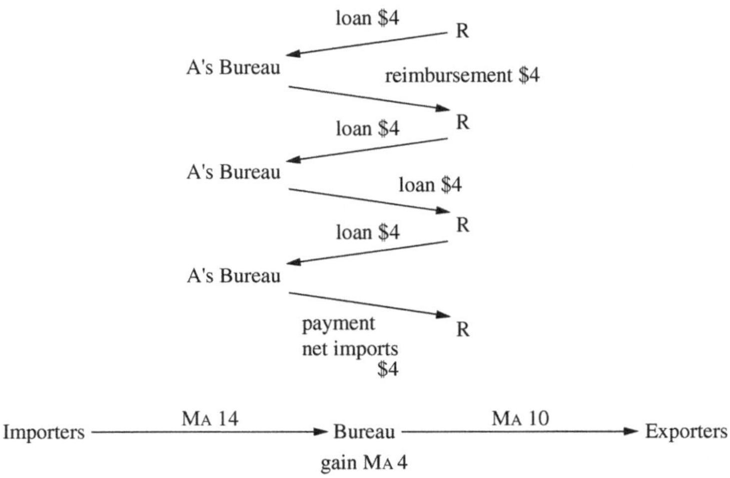


*Figure 18.6* Transactions of period $P_1$.

itself unchanged period after period. Hence, in period $p_2$ all the payments will be the same as those of $p_1$, and at the end of the period A's Bureau will still have a debt of $4. As long as country A runs a deficit of $4, the situation at the end of each period will remain unchanged so that, over a long series of periods country A's debt goes asymptotically to zero.

Finally, the practical implementation will confirm what has been shown analytically, namely that a country, which pays its deficit fully in real terms, should not incur any external debt. Thanks to Schmitt's reform, countries, considered as sets of their residents, will be able to mutually offset their debts.

### *Alternative number 2*

In this scenario, which is fully compatible with Schmitt's analysis even though it is nowhere explicitly mentioned by him, the protocol allows country A's

Bureau to obtain one or more loans in foreign currency from country A's official reserves. This assumption, which should not be surprising since both Bureau and official reserves act on behalf of country A considered as a whole, does not modify the terms of the problem, and of its solution, on condition that A's Bureau is compelled to reimburse A's official reserves in the period following the one in which it borrows from them.

In $p_0$, A's Bureau still borrows 4 dollars from country R in order to finance its counter-loan of 4 dollars to R, as in Figure 18.3. However, this time A's Bureau borrows from country A's official reserves the 4 dollars it needs to pay country A's net imports, as in Figure 18.7.

The net gain of A's Bureau in money A remains the one depicted in Figure 18.4 and compensates for the decrease in country A's official reserves. At the end of $p_0$, the financial situation of country A is perfectly balanced, and country R has been fully paid for its net exports.

In $p_1$ the loan and the counter-loan of A's Bureau are the same (Figure 18.3), and so are the payments of country A's net imports as financed by a loan of country A's reserves (Figure 18.7) and the gain in money A (Figure 18.4) that compensates the decrease in reserves. What A's Bureau must do in $p_1$ is, first, to reimburse the loan of A's official reserves obtained in $p_0$. In order to do that, A's Bureau borrows a new sum of $4 from country R, Figure 18.8.

Reintegrated at their previous level, country A's reserves can provide, as done in $p_0$, the foreign currency necessary to cover the difference between country A's imports and exports.

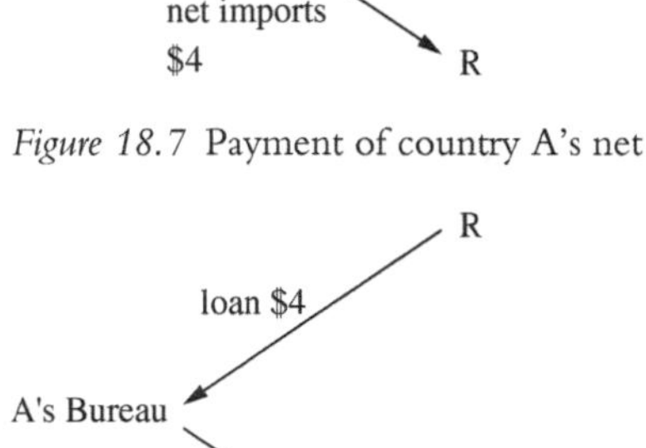


*Figure 18.7* Payment of country A's net imports as financed by A's international reserves.

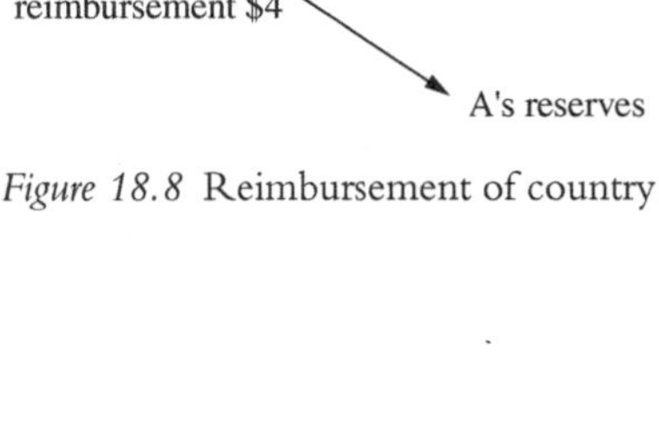


*Figure 18.8* Reimbursement of country A's official reserves.

At the end of $p_1$ the situation is the same as the one in the first alternative, except for the fact that this time the elimination of every net debt of country A can be verified at once, without resorting to the asymptotic cancellation of a debt constantly renewed at its previous level. The loan of country R that enables A's Bureau to reimburse A's official reserves is indeed balanced by the loan that accompanies the restoration of country A's reserves. As economists know well, foreign currencies are not kept idle in countries' international reserves but are immediately lent on the international financial market. Thus invested, foreign currencies define a credit of the country's official reserves and, therefore, of the country itself. It immediately follows that the debt incurred by country A's Bureau to country R is balanced by the credit of country A's reserves: for country A as a whole debit and credit, both of \$4, cancel each other out. Finally, in each period the reform guarantees the full payment of country A's net imports without subjecting it to today's second and pathological payment and to the iniquitous austerity measures whose devastating consequences have so dreadfully affected and affect deficit countries all around the world.

# Conclusion

Schmitt's scientific investigation is the final step (synthesis) of a dialectical process started by the Physiocrats and the Classics (thesis) and developed further by the Neoclassics (antithesis). Together with the innovative insights of Keynes, it provides the (macroeconomic) foundations of a macroeconomic analysis whose building blocks are monetary. Both thesis and antithesis have played a crucial role, and some of their main findings are confirmed in Schmitt's synthesis. Yet, the phase initiated by Keynes marks a relevant, not to say revolutionary, progress in mainstream economic thinking. Walras's concept of *numéraire* and his claim about the immaterial nature of value are incorporated into Schmitt's analysis, but equilibrium, relative exchange, economic agents' behaviour, modelling, etc. are uncompromisingly rejected.

Wrongly considered as an applied field of mathematics, economics has for too long played the role of a socio-mathematical science of a lesser scientific value than 'hard' science. The conceptual difficulty of mainstream economics is indeed very low, and the complexity of its mathematical apparatus is only a small fraction of one of physics. The well-known law of supply and demand is a good illustration of the logical depth reached by conceptual thinking in the great majority of today's economic theories.

Schmitt's analysis is richer. His laws are not equilibrium conditions of intrinsically unbalanced situations resulting from opposing forces exerted by individuals. They are logical identities whose conditional validity derives from the very nature of eminently economic concepts, such as money, income, prices, production, expenditure, and capital. The point of Schmitt's quantum theoretical approach is not to construct yet another description of economic events as influenced by economic agents' behaviours, but to provide a correct understanding of the laws governing any economic system, to which economic agents are necessarily subject, whatever their behaviour.

If economics aims to become a true science, it must provide a consistent and rigorous explanation of the logical principles on which our economic system rests. Schmitt's quantum macroeconomics investigates the nature of capitalism, which he identifies as a system where economic disorder, inflation, and unemployment are caused by a process of capital malformation. The pathology characterizing the present system of capital accumulation is caused by the

DOI: 10.4324/9781351271325-25

lack of compliance in the way transactions are entered in banks' ledgers with the logical distinctions between money, income, and capital. Hence, Schmitt's analysis shows that the pathologies affecting capitalism result from our ignorance of the laws on which an economic system rests, from our very patchy understanding of its nature.

All the great economists of the past have endeavoured to get to the root of the economic system. Schmitt shares the same goal, and his analysis goes a step further in the identification of the laws governing the process of capital accumulation. His theory of emissions, which he applies to money and production, is what best characterizes his macroeconomic approach to macroeconomics quantum. It shows that the study of economics requires the use of a modern form of logic that goes beyond the traditional and obsolete form of binary logic.

Quantum logic opens the way to a new analysis set to transform economics into a science as rigorous as physics. Even though totally independent from it, economics is not less 'exact' and compelling than the sciences closely connected to mathematics. Logic is the mother of all sciences and, when used in such a rigorous way as Schmitt's, it is not easier or less compelling than mathematics. It is even plausible to predict that quantum logic will prove useful in other fields than economics and will allow for new discoveries in many of them, mathematics included.

The 21st Century has already seen the emergence of new and revolutionary lines of inquiry into many scientific fields. This might be a sign that soon times will be ready to accept Schmitt's analysis as the new paradigm in economics. Old-fashioned and 'metaphysical' concepts such as those of the multiplier or of the quantity of money will then finally be rejected and recognized for what they are: kindergarten representations of a misconceived reality.

For the time being, Schmitt's analysis still requires a great effort from the reader unaccustomed to quantum logic and to a conceptual rigour alien to the great majority of economic theories. Disoriented by the microeconomic approach to macroeconomics that still reigns supreme today, many economists will find it difficult to adjust to the quantum realm of macroeconomics. Logical laws or identities are alien to microeconomics, whose principles are much easier to understand, being much closer to everyday perception of economic activity. Yet, to discover the very nature of our economic system, there is no need to go beyond the flimsy screen of appearances. This is what Schmitt asks us to do. It is a demanding task, but there is no easy way to discovery in science that is engaged in the quest for reality beyond appearance.

Schmitt takes us to the core of capitalism with a view to identifying its inner laws and the mechanism that generate its pathologies. His goal is twofold.

1) To determine the logical laws of any economic system based on the process of capital accumulation.
2) To specify the principles of the reforms required to transform the present, pathological system (capitalism), nationally and internationally, into a new and orderly system (post-capitalism).

Since the death of Keynes in 1946, economics has gradually lost its capacity to delve into the true causes of economic disorders and to provide a remedy against financial and economic crises. Instead of investigating the nature of capitalism further, economists have concentrated their efforts on the search for more and more sophisticated mathematical models designed to mimic the real world. Their approach is empirical. Starting from statistical data and from the choice of a model based on a series of axioms derived from general equilibrium analysis (Walrasian and non-Walrasian) and from Keynesian and new-Keynesian analysis, they attempt to reproduce on paper economic events as they occur and as they might occur in the future. If they have failed to forecast the major crises that have beset the development of capitalism so far, it is because economic reality is beyond the reach of mathematical modelling. On the one hand, behaviour is too complex and unforeseeable to be the object of mathematical modelling; on the other hand, the nature of economic and financial crises is structural and cannot be investigated by using models whose theoretical basis is microeconomic.

Whereas mainstream economics has proved incapable to develop a positive and a normative analysis of capitalism, Schmitt's quantum macroeconomics succeeds in developing both. The theory of monetary and real emissions provides the analytical framework required to understand the logic of capitalism and its actual, pathological working. It enables us to pinpoint the principles of the reforms needed to move from disorder to order in the national and international domains.

The mechanisms of Schmitt's reforms are relatively easy to grasp. It is less easy to understand why these mechanisms are necessary and why they will be enough to guarantee the non-pathological working of our future economic systems. Yet, if we are prepared to set aside preconceived ideas and start the analysis afresh, guided by Schmitt's quantum macroeconomics, we will find all the arguments we need to overcome all difficulties.

Young and less young economists dissatisfied with the present level of theoretical economics will find Schmitt's analysis stimulating in many respects. They will agree that his quantum approach provides the key to a new and decisive critique of mainstream economics, while opening the way to a quantum macroeconomic analysis in which bank money plays a central role, together with the concepts of creation, destruction, instantaneous circular flows, and monetary and financial intermediation. With Schmitt, economic analysis leaves adolescence behind and advances in great strides towards adulthood; it progresses from a pre-scientific to a scientific state and is well-equipped to make change happen, a change that our socioeconomic systems are badly in need of. It is up to the new generations of economists to take over Schmitt's analysis, to develop it further, and implement the reforms he advocates.

The transition from capitalism to post-capitalism is a necessity; Schmitt shows us the way; let me hope that our younger generations will follow boldly in his footsteps, complete his journey, and so help build a better society.

# Bibliography


Bailly, J.-L., Cencini, A., and Rossi, S. (eds) (2017) *Quantum Macroeconomics: The Legacy of Bernard Schmitt*, London and New York: Routledge.

Baranzini, M. (ed.) (1982) *Advances in Economic Theory*, Oxford: Basil Blackwell.

Baranzini, M. and Cencini, A. (eds) (1987) *Contributi di analisi economica*, Bellinzona, CH: Casagrande.

Baranzini, M. and Scazzieri, R (eds) (1986) *Foundations of Economics: Structures of Inquiry and Economic Theory*, Oxford: Basil Blackwell.

Böhm-Bawerk, E. (1889/1959) *Capital and Interest, Vol. II Positive Theory of Capital*, South Holland: Libertarian Press.

Bradford, W. and Harcourt, G.C. (1997) 'Units and definitions', in G.C. Harcourt and P.A. Riach (eds), *A 'Second Edition' of the General Theory*, London and New York: Routledge, Vol. I, pp. 107–131.

Cencini, A. and Schmitt, B. (1976) *La pensée de Karl Marx: critique et synthèse, Vol. I La valeur*, Albeuve: Castella.

Cencini, A. and Schmitt, B. (1977) *La pensée de Karl Marx: critique et synthèse, Vol. II La plus-value*, Albeuve: Castella.

Cencini, A. and Schmitt, B. (1991) *External Debt Servicing: A Vicious Circle*, London and New York: Pinter Publishers.

Cencini, A. and Schmitt, B. (1992) 'Per la creazione di uno spazio monetario europeo garante della sovranità di ogni singolo paese', in R. Chopard (ed.), *Europa '93! E la piazza finanziaria svizzera?* Lugano: Centro di Studi Bancari and Meta Edizioni, pp. 99–136.

Cencini, A., Corti, M., Crivelli, R., and Schmitt, B. (1987) 'Dossier economia ed epistemologia', *Bloc Notes*, 15–16, pp. 45–130.

Cencini, A., Gnos, C., and Rossi, S. (2016) 'Quantum macroeconomics: A tribute to Bernard Schmitt', *Cuadernos de economia*, 39 (110), pp. 65–75.

Davidson, P. (1972) 'Money and the real world', *The Economic Journal*, 82 (325), pp. 101–115.

Davidson, P. (2008) 'Reforming the world's international money', paper presented at the *Conference Financial Crisis, the US Economy, and International Security in the New Administration*, November 14, New York: The New School, pp. 1–25.

Debreu, G. (1959) *Theory of Value: An Axiomatic Analysis of Economic Equilibrium*, New Haven, CT: Yale University Press.

Devillebichot, G. (1969) 'Note sur les travaux de Bernard Schmitt', *Revue d'économie politique*, 79 (3), pp. 693–702.

Devillebichot, G. (1979) 'Pour sortir enfin d'un régime inepte de « paiements » internationaux: le plan Bernard Schmitt', *Revue d'économie politique*, 89 (5), pp. 623–636.

Fisher, I. (1925) *Mathematical Investigations in the Theory of Value and Prices*, Yale: Yale University Press, and London: Humphrey Milford.

Gnos, C. and Rossi, S. (eds) (2012) *Modern Monetary Macroeconomics*, Cheltenham, UK and Northampton, USA: Edward Elgar.

Gnos, C. and Schmitt, B. (1989) 'Le circuit, les profits et la crise', in *AAVV Les théories contemporaines du circuit*, Bordeux: University of Bordeux, mimeo, pp. 143–156.

Gnos, C. and Schmitt, B. (1990) 'Le circuit: réalité exhaustive', *Economies et sociétés*, 24 (2), pp. 63–74.

Graziani, A. (1988) 'Il circuito monetario', in A. Graziani and M. Messori (ed.), *Moneta e produzione*, Torino: Einaudi, pp. XI–XLIII.

Grubel, H.G. (ed.) (1963) *World Monetary Reform*. Stanford, CA: Stanford University Press.

Guitton, H. (2021) 'Foreword' to B. Schmitt *Inflation, Unemployment and Capital Malformations*, London and New York: Routledge.

Harcourt, G.C. and Riach, P.A. (eds) (1997) *A 'Second Edition' of the General Theory*, London and New York: Routledge.

Husserl, E. (1900/2001) *Logical Investigations*, London and New York: Routledge.

International Monetary Fund. (1987) *Report on the World Current Account Discrepancy*, Washington, DC: International Monetary Fund.

International Monetary Fund. (2009) *Balance of Payments and International Investment Position Manual – Sixth Edition (BPM6)*, Washington, DC: International Monetary Fund.

International Monetary Fund. (2021) *Balance of Payments Statistics. Part 1: Country Tables.* Yearbook *2021*, Washington, DC: International Monetary Fund.

Johnson, H.G. (1974) 'Towards a general theory of the balance of payments', in J.A. Frenkel and H.G. Johnson (eds), *The Monetary Approach to the Balance of Payments*, London: Allen & Unwin, pp. 46–63.

Keynes, J.M. (1929) 'The German transfer problem', *Economic Journal*, 39 (153), pp. 1–7.

Keynes, J.M. (1930/1971) *A Treatise on Money, Vol. I: The Pure Theory of Money*, London and Basingstoke: Macmillan.

Keynes, J.M. (1936/1946) *The General Theory of Employment, Interest and Money*, London: Macmillan.

Keynes, J.M. (1973) *The Collected Writings of John Maynard Keynes, Vol. XIII, The General Theory and After: Part I, Preparation*, ed. by D.E. Moggridge, London and New York: Macmillan and Cambridge University Press.

Keynes, J.M. (1980) *The Collected Writings of John Maynard Keynes, Vol. XXV, Activities 1940–1944. Shaping the Post-War World: The Clearing Union*, ed. by D.E. Moggridge, London and New York: Macmillan and Cambridge University Press.

Krugman, P.R. and Obstfeld, M. (2003) *International Economics: Theory and Policy*, Reading, MA: Addison-Wesley.

Lab, M. (2015) *L'Alsace en héritage: Histoire d'une famille*, Paris: L'Harmattan.

Machlup, F. (1963) 'Reform of the international monetary system', in H.G. Grubel (ed.), *World Monetary Reform: Plans and Issues*, Stanford, CA and London: Stanford University Press and Oxford University Press, pp. 253–260.

Machlup, F. (1964) 'Plans for reform of the international monetary system', in *Special Papers in International Economics*, 3, Princeton, NJ: Princeton University Press, pp. 40–41.

Marx, K. (1867/1976) *Capital, Vol. I, The Pelican Marx Library*, Harmondsworth: Penguin Books.

Marx, K. (1885/1978) *Capital, Vol. II, The Pelican Marx Library*, Harmondsworth: Penguin Books.

Marx, K. (1894/1981) *Capital, Vol. III, The Pelican Marx Library*, Harmondsworth: Penguin Books.

Pasinetti, L. (1975) *Lezioni di teoria della produzione*, Bologna: Il Mulino.

Pasinetti, L. (1993) *Structural Economic Dynamics*, Cambridge: Cambridge University Press.

Patinkin, D. (1965) *Money, Interest and Prices: An Integration of Monetary and Value Theory*, second edition. New York: Harper & Row.

Ricardo, D. (1816/1951) 'Proposals for an economical and secure currency', in P. Sraffa and M.H. Dobb (eds), *The Works and Correspondence of David Ricardo, Vol. IV: Pamphlets and Papers 1815–1823*, Cambridge: Cambridge University Press, pp. 43–141.

Ricardo, D. (1817/1951) 'On the principles of political economy and taxation', in P. Sraffa and M.H. Dobb (eds), *The Works and Correspondence of David Ricardo, Vol. I*, Cambridge: Cambridge University Press.

Ricardo, D. (1823/1951) 'Absolute value and exchangeable value', in P. Sraffa and M.H. Dobb (eds), *The Works and Correspondence of David Ricardo, Vol. IV: Pamphlets and Papers 1815–1823*, Cambridge: Cambridge University Press, pp. 357–412.

Ricardo, D. (1824/1951) 'Plan for the establishment of a national bank', in P. Sraffa and M.H. Dobb (eds), *The Works and Correspondence of David Ricardo, Vol. IV: Pamphlets and Papers 1815–1823*, Cambridge: Cambridge University Press, pp. 276–300.

Ricardo, D. (1985) *Scritti monetari*, Rome: Istituto della Enciclopedia Italiana.

Rueff, J. (1963) 'Gold exchange standard a danger to the West', in H.G. Grubel (ed.), *World Monetary Reform: Plans and Issues*, Stanford, CA and London: Stanford University Press and Oxford University Press, pp. 320–328, reprinted from *The Times*, June 27–29, 1961.

Samuelson, P. (1966) 'Paradoxes in capital theory: A symposium. A summing up', *Quarterly Journal of Economics*, 80 (4), pp. 568–583.

Say, J.-B. (1803/2001) *A Treatise on Political Economy*, London and New York: Routledge.

Say, J.-B. (2009) *Oeuvres complètes*, Paris: Economica.

Schmitt, B. (1959) 'L'équilibre de la monnaie', *Revue d'économie politique*, 69 (6), pp. 921–950.

Schmitt, B. (1960) *La formation du pouvoir d'achat*, Paris: Sirey.

Schmitt, B. (1966a) *Monnaie, salaires et profits*, Paris: Presses Universitaires de France.

Schmitt, B. (1966b) 'La monnaie au centre de la répartition', *Revue d'économie politique*, 76 (1), pp. 92–114.

Schmitt, B. (1971a) *L'analyse macroéconomique des revenus*, Paris: Dalloz.

Schmitt, B. (1971b) 'Le problème de l'intégration de la monnaie', *Revue suisse d'économie politique et de statistique*, 107 (1), pp. 203–222.

Schmitt, B. (1971c) 'La monnaie internationale', University of Fribourg, mimeo.

Schmitt, B. (1972a) *Macroeconomic Theory: A Fundamental Revision*, Albeuve: Castella.

Schmitt, B. (1972b) 'Vers une nouvelle théorie macro-économique', *Revue d'économie politique*, 82 (1), pp. 139–152.

Schmitt, B. (1972c) *Théorie du circuit*, Fribourg: University of Fribourg, mimeo.

Schmitt, B. (1972d) *Circuit*, Fribourg: University of Fribourg, mimeo.

Schmitt, B. (1972e) *Plans to Obviate the Creation of an International Fiat Money*, Fribourg: University of Fribourg, mimeo.

Schmitt, B. (1972f) *The Theory of International Money*, Fribourg: University of Fribourg, mimeo.

Schmitt, B. (1973a) *New Proposals for World Monetary Reform*, Albeuve: Castella.

Schmitt, B. (1973b) *Monnaie matérielle et monnaie bancaire; flux monétaires et stocks de monnaie*, Fribourg: University of Fribourg, mimeo.

Schmitt, B. (1975a) *Théorie unitaire de la monnaie, nationale et internationale*, Albeuve: Castella.

Schmitt, B. (1975b) *Génération de la monnaie des monnaies européennes*, Albeuve: Castella.

Schmitt, B. (1977a) *La monnaie européenne*, Paris: Presses Universitaires de France.

Schmitt, B. (1977b) *L'or, le dollar et la monnaie supranationale*, Paris: Calmann-Lévy.

Schmitt, B. (1978a) *Teoria unitária da moeda*, São Paulo: Editora da Universidade de São Paulo.

Schmitt, B. (1978b) *Die Theorie des Kreditgeldes*, Stuttgart: Gustav Fisher.

Schmitt, B. (1979) *Le temps quantique*, University of Fribourg, mimeo.

Schmitt, B. (1982) 'Time as quantum', in M. Baranzini (ed.), *Advances in Economic Theory*, Oxford and New York: Basil Blackwell and St. Martin's Press, pp. 115–125.

Schmitt, B. (1983) *Le vice caché du régime actuel des paiements internationaux*, University of Fribourg, mimeo.

Schmitt, B. (1984a) *Inflation, chômage et malformations du capital: macroéconomie quantique*, Paris and Albeuve: Economica and Castella.

Schmitt, B. (1984b) *La France souveraine de sa monnaie*, Paris and Albeuve: Economica and Castella.

Schmitt, B. (1984c) *Les pays au régime du FMI. Le vice caché du système actuel des paiements internationaux*, Albeuve: Castella.

Schmitt, B. (1985a) 'Introduzione agli scritti monetari di David Ricardo', in D. Ricardo (ed.), *Scritti monetari*, Rome: Istituto della Enciclopedia Italiana, pp. 3–85.

Schmitt, B. (1985b) 'L'identité de l'offre et de la demande globales dans le temps', in A. Barrère (ed.), *Keynes aujourd'hui: théories et politiques*, Paris: Economica, pp. 171–194.

Schmitt, B. (1985c) 'Un nouvel ordre monétaire international: le plan Keynes', in F. Poulon (ed.), *Les écrits de Keynes*, Paris: Dunod, pp. 195–209.

Schmitt, B. (1985d) *Manuscrit sur la monnaie nationale et internationale*, Fribourg: University of Fribourg, mimeo.

Schmitt, B. (1985e) *Esquisse d'une histoire de l'analyse économique*, Fribourg: University of Fribourg, mimeo.

Schmitt, B. (1986a) 'The process of formation of economics in relation to other sciences', in M. Baranzini and R. Scazzieri (eds), *Foundations of Economics: Structures of Inquiry and Economic Theory*, Oxford and New York: Basil Blackwell and St. Martin's Press, pp. 103–132.

Schmitt, B. (1986b) *Devenir de l'ECU avenir de l'Europe*, Fribourg: University of Fribourg, mimeo.

Schmitt, B. (1986c) *Cours de théorie monétaire*, Fribourg: University of Fribourg, mimeo.

Schmitt, B. (1986–7) 'La théorie de l'équilibre général et la transformation des biens en nombres sans dimension', paper presented at the 'Grand séminaire', University of Bourgogne, mimeo, pp. 1–13.

Schmitt, B. (1987a) 'Le plan Keynes: vers la monnaie internationale purement véhiculaire', in M. Zerbato (ed.), *Keynésianisme et sortie de crise*, Paris: Dunod, pp. 192–211.

Schmitt, B. (1987b) 'Lo sviluppo interrotto o la crisi del capitalismo', *Fondamenti*, 8, pp. 75–105.

Schmitt, B. (1987c) 'Comparaison du système et du non-système des paiements internationaux dans le cas du commerce extérieur équilibré', in M. Baranzini and A. Cencini (eds), *Contributi di analisi economica*, Bellinzona: Casagrande, pp. 231–249.

Schmitt, B. (1987d) 'Endettement des pays: produit de l'étalon change-or', in R. Barre, A. Dunkel, G. Gaudard, A. Lamfalussy, J. L'Huillier, H. Mercillon, B. Schmitt, and R. Triffin (eds), *Les déséquilibres monétaires et financiers internationaux*, Fribourg: Editions Universitaires, pp. 107–174.

Schmitt, B. (1987e) 'Per un'analisi epistemologica comparativa della scienza economica', *Bloc Notes*, 15–16, pp. 115–130.

Schmitt, B. (1987f) 'Prix relatifs', University of Fribourg, mimeo.

Schmitt, B. (1987–88) *Résumé du cours de macro-économie*, Fribourg: University of Fribourg, mimeo.

Schmitt, B. (1988a) *L'ECU et les souverainetés nationales en Europe*, Paris: Dunod.

Schmitt, B. (1988b) 'Nature de la monnaie: une approche théorique', in AAVV *Droit et monnaie. Etats et espace monétaire transnational*, Paris: Latec, pp. 63–99.

Schmitt, B. (1988c) 'The identity of aggregate supply and demand in time', in A. Barrère (ed.), *The Foundation of Keynesian Analysis*, London: Macmillan, pp. 169–193.

Schmitt, B. (1988d) 'Circuito monetario e moneta bancaria', in A. Graziani and M. Messori (eds), *Moneta e produzione*, Torino: Einaudi, pp. 5–43.

Schmitt, B. (1988e) 'External debt: eternal debt', paper presented at the conference on "The Future of the International Monetary System" at Glendon College, Toronto: York University, March, unpublished.

Schmitt, B. (1989a) 'La France appauvrie par le service da sa dette extérieure', *Economies et sociétés*, 23 (8), pp. 91–100.

Schmitt, B. (1989b) 'A monetary reform', paper presented at the Gerzensee Swiss National Bank Seminar, 3 March, unpublished.

Schmitt, B. (1990a) *El ECU y las soberanías monetarias en Europa*, Madrid: Editorial Paraninfo.

Schmitt, B. (1990b) *Le vice caché des paiements extérieurs*, Fribourg: University of Fribourg, mimeo.

Schmitt, B. (1992a) *Vers un nouvel ordre mondial des relations Nord-Sud*, Fribourg: University of Fribourg, mimeo.

Schmitt, B. (1992b) *Cœur de la démonstration du vice des paiements extérieurs*, University of Fribourg, mimeo.

Schmitt, B. (1993) *Teoria unitaria della moneta, nazionale e internazionale*, Napoli: Liguori.

Schmitt, B. (1993–94a) *Théorie macroéconomique*, Fribourg: University of Fribourg, mimeo.

Schmitt, B. (1993–94b) *Notes sur la théorie de l'intérêt*, Fribourg: University of Fribourg, mimeo.

Schmitt, B. (1994–95) *Projet de manuscrit sur la dette extérieure*, Fribourg: University of Fribourg, mimeo.

Schmitt, B. (1995–96) *Cours de théorie monétaire*, Fribourg: University of Fribourg, mimeo.

Schmitt, B. (1996a) 'Unemployment: Is there a principal cause?', in A. Cencini and M. Baranzini (eds), *Inflation and Unemployment: Contributions to a New Macroeconomic Approach*, London and New York: Routledge, pp. 75–105.

Schmitt, B. (1996b) 'A new paradigm for the determination of money prices', in G. Deleplace and E.J. Nell (eds), *Money in Motion: The Post Keynesian and Circulation Approaches*, Basingstoke and New York: Macmillan and St. Martin's Press, pp. 104–138.

Schmitt, B. (1996c) 'Monnaie et création monétaire', in *Encyclopaedia Universalis*, Paris: Encyclopaedia Universalis, pp. 693–699.

Schmitt, B. (1996d) *Cours de théorie monétaire*, Fribourg: University of Fribourg, mimeo.

Schmitt, B. (1997a) *Note à l'attention des étudiants*, Fribourg: University of Fribourg, mimeo.

Schmitt, B. (1997b) *Les prix relatifs n'existent pas: preuve préliminaire mais certaine*, Fribourg: University of Fribourg, mimeo.

Schmitt, B. (1997c) *Prix relatifs et prix monétaires*, Fribourg: University of Fribourg, mimeo.

Schmitt, B. (1997d) *Prix relatifs et prix monétaires: suite*, Fribourg: University of Fribourg, mimeo.

Schmitt, B. (1998a) *Le chômage est son éradication*, Fribourg: University of Fribourg, mimeo.

Schmitt, B. (1998b) *Annexe au cours écrit*, Fribourg: University of Fribourg, mimeo.

Schmitt, B. (1998c) *Introduction à une critique des prix relatifs*, Fribourg: University of Fribourg, mimeo.
Schmitt, B. (1998d) *Pour une critique des prix relatifs*, Fribourg: University of Fribourg, mimeo.
Schmitt, B. (1998e) 'A critical appraisal of Pasinetti's analysis', paper presented at the Conference Wealth of Nations in Economic Theory, held in Monte Verità, Ascona, Switzerland, pp. 1–17.
Schmitt, B. (1999a) *Critique fondamentale de la pensée néoclassique*, Fribourg: University of Fribourg, mimeo.
Schmitt, B. (1999b) *Preuve analytique de l'inanité de la pensée néoclassique*, Fribourg: University of Fribourg, mimeo.
Schmitt, B. (1999c) *En marge du cours: quelques considérations sur les nombres en économie, dans la pensée néoclassique et au-delà*, Fribourg: University of Fribourg, mimeo.
Schmitt, B. (1999d) *Les intérêts nets de leurs dette extérieures sont dus deux fois par les pays concernés*, Fribourg: University of Fribourg, mimeo.
Schmitt, B. (1999e) *L'intérêt étant excepté, toutes les dépenses effectuées entre un pays et le reste du monde sont égales de part et d'autre*, Fribourg: University of Fribourg, mimeo.
Schmitt, B. (1999f) *Les intérêts dus par les résidents des pays en voie de développement à des résidents des pays riches sont payés deux fois, à savoir une première fois par les résidents concernés et une deuxième fois par une ponction dans les réserves officielles des PVD*, Fribourg: University of Fribourg, mimeo.
Schmitt, B. (2000a) 'The double charge of external debt servicing', *Research* Laboratory *in* Monetary Economics *Working Paper*, No. 1.
Schmitt, B. (2000b) 'Why the net interest on external debt weighs double on LDCs', *Research* Laboratory *in* Monetary Economics *Working Paper*, No. 3.
Schmitt, B. (2000c) *Monnaie et prix: les « achats-ventes »*, Fribourg: University of Fribourg, mimeo.
Schmitt, B. (2003a) *Le paiement des intérêts par les PVD est double; les statistiques de la Banque mondiale ainsi que l'analyse le prouvent*, Lugano: University of Lugano, mimeo.
Schmitt, B. (2003b) 'LDCs pay twice the interest due to creditor countries', *Research* Laboratory *in* Monetary Economics *Working Paper*, No. 11.
Schmitt, B. (2004a) 'Between nations, the interest multiplier is equal to 2', *Research* Laboratory *in* Monetary Economics *Working Paper*, No. 12.
Schmitt, B. (2004b) *Les deux coûts de l'intérêt*, Lugano: University of Lugano, mimeo.
Schmitt, B. (2004c) *An Open Letter to President Lula*, Lugano: University of Lugano, mimeo.
Schmitt, B. (2004d) *A Major Discovery in Macroeconomics*, Lugano: University of Lugano, mimeo.
Schmitt, B. (2005) *Théorème de l'intérêt: le double poids des intérêts afférents aux dettes extérieures*, Lugano: Reaearch Laboratory in Monetary Economics, mimeo.
Schmitt, B. (2006a) *Lugano papers, mars 2006*, Lugano: University of Lugano, mimeo.
Schmitt, B. (2006b) *Le paiement des intérêts nets et la discrepancy découverte par les experts du FMI*, Lugano: University of Lugano, mimeo.
Schmitt, B. (2007a) *Le thèorème de l'intérêt*, Lugano: Research Laboratory in Monetary Economics.
Schmitt, B. (2007b) *Texte pour le Brésil*, Lugano: University of Lugano, mimeo.
Schmitt, B. (2008) *Brésil en 2008*, Lugano: University of Lugano, mimeo.
Schmitt, B. (2010a) *Les emprunts extérieurs comme cause du surendettement des pays et de l'expansion de la bulle financière*, Lugano: University of Lugano, mimeo.
Schmitt, B. (2010b) *Paiements en monnaie bancaire*, Lugano: University of Lugano, mimeo.

Schmitt, B. (2011) *Les emprunts extérieurs sont une cause du surendettement des pays et de la crise financière*, Lugano: University of Lugano, mimeo.

Schmitt, B. (2012a) 'Relative prices are undetermined by a mathematical error', in C. Gnos and S. Rossi (eds), *Modern Monetary Macroeconomics: A New Paradigm for Economic Policy*, Cheltenham, UK and Northampton, MA: Edward Elgar, pp. 19–38.

Schmitt, B. (2012b) 'Money, effective demand, and profits', in C. Gnos and S. Rossi (eds), *Modern Monetary Macroeconomics: A New Paradigm for Economic Policy*, Cheltenham, UK and Northampton, MA: Edward Elgar, pp. 71–99.

Schmitt, B. (2012c) 'Sovereign debt and interest payments', in C. Gnos and S. Rossi (eds), *Modern Monetary Macroeconomics: A New Paradigm for Economic Policy*, Cheltenham, UK and Northampton, MA: Edward Elgar, pp. 239–260.

Schmitt, B. (2014) 'The formation of sovereign debt: Diagnosis and remedy', available at http://papers.ssrn.com/sol3/papers.cfm?abstract_id=2513679.

Schmitt, B. (2021) *Inflation, Unemployment, and Capital Malformations*, London and New York: Routledge.

Schmitt, B. and A. Cencini (1982) 'Wages and profits in a theory of emissions', in M. Baranzini (ed.), *Advances in Economic Theory*, Oxford and New York: Basil Blackwell and St. Martin's Press, pp. 137–146.

Schmitt, B. and C. De Gottardi (2003) 'An internal critique of general equilibrium theory', in L.-P. Rochon and S. Rossi (eds), *Modern Theories of Money: The Nature and Role of Money in Capitalist Economies*, Cheltenham, UK and Northampton, MA: Edward Elgar, pp. 265–294.

Schmitt, B. and S. Greppi (1996) 'The national economy studied as a whole: Aspects of circular flow analysis in the German language', in G. Deleplace and E.J. Nell (eds), *Money in Motion: The Post Keynesian and Circulation Approaches*, Basingstoke and New York: Macmillan and St. Martin's Press, pp. 341–364.

Schumacher, E.F. (1943) 'Multilateral clearing', *Economica*, 10 (38), pp. 150–165.

Smith, A. (1776/1970) *An Inquiry into the Nature and Causes of the Wealth of Nations*, New York and Toronto: Everyman's Library Knopf.

Sraffa, P. (1960) *Production of Commodities by Means of Commodities*, Cambridge: Cambridge University Press.

Triffin, R. (1961) *Gold and the Dollar Crisis*, New Haven: Yale University Press.

Walras, L. (1874/1954) 'Éléments d'économie politique pure', translated by W. Jaffé (ed.), *Elements of Pure Economics*, London: George Allen & Unwin.

Wicksell, K. (1893/1954) *Value, Capital and Rent*, London: Allen & Unwin.

Wicksell, K. (1898/1965) *Interest and Prices*, New York: Augustus M. Kelley.

Williamson, J. (1977) *The Failure of World Monetary Reform, 1971–74*, New York: New York University Press.

World Bank. (2021a) 'External debt stocks, total (DOD, current US$)', available at http://data.worldbank.org/indicator/DT.DOD.DECT.CD.

World Bank. (2021b) 'Gross external debt position', available at http://data.worldbank.org/data-catalog/quarterly-external-debt-statistics-ssds.

World Bank. (2021c) 'Interest payments on external debt, total (INT, current US$)', available at http://data.worldbank.org/indicator/DT.INT.DECT.CD.

World Bank. (2021d) 'Total reserves (includes gold, current US$)', available at http://data.worldbank.org/indicator/FI.RES.TOTL.CD.

# Name index

# Subject index